STREE ATLAS

Buckinghamshire

and Milton Keynes

C000154717

First published in 1990 by

Philip's, a division of
Octopus Publishing Group Ltd
2-4 Heron Quays, London E14 4JP

Third colour edition 2005
First impression 2005

ISBN-10   0-540-08669-X (hardback)
ISBN-13   978-0-540-08669-6 (hardback)
ISBN-10   0-540-08670-3 (spiral)
ISBN-13   978-0-540-08670-2 (spiral)

© Philip's 2005

Ordnance Survey®

This product includes mapping data licensed
from Ordnance Survey® with the permission of
the Controller of Her Majesty's Stationery Office.
© Crown copyright 2005. All rights reserved.
Licence number 100011710.

Printed and bound in Spain by
Cayfosa-Quebecor

Contents

III **Key to map symbols**

IV **Key to map pages**

VI **Route planning**

VIII **Administrative and Postcode boundaries**

1 **Street maps** at 3½ inches to 1 mile

214 **Index** of towns and villages

217 **Index** of streets, hospitals, industrial estates, railway
stations, schools, shopping centres, universities
and places of interest

Digital Data

The exceptionally high-quality mapping found in this atlas is available as digital data in TIFF
format, which is easily convertible to other bitmapped (raster) image formats.

The index is also available in digital form as a standard database table. It contains all the details
found in the printed index together with the National Grid reference for the map square in which
each entry is named.

For further information and to discuss your requirements, please contact Philip's on
020 7644 6932 or james.mann@philips-maps.co.uk

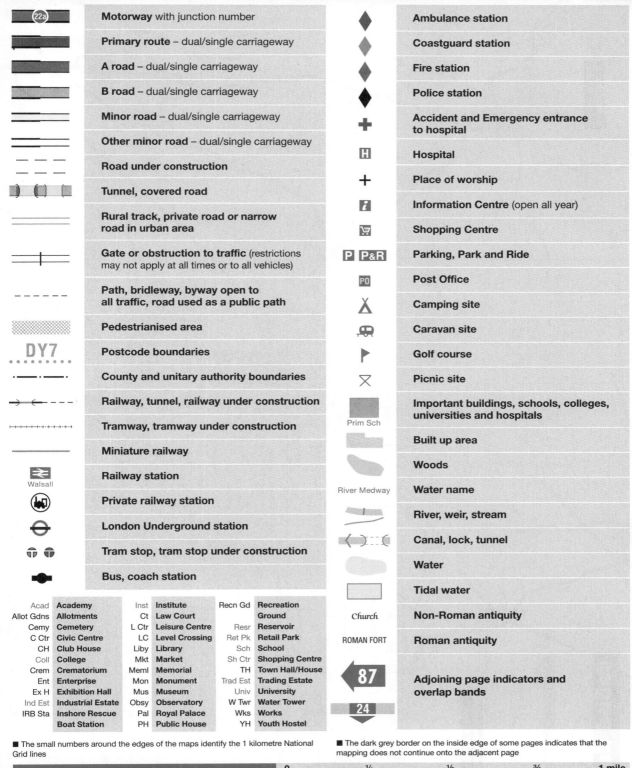

Motorway with junction number (22a)	
Primary route – dual/single carriageway	
A road – dual/single carriageway	
B road – dual/single carriageway	
Minor road – dual/single carriageway	
Other minor road – dual/single carriageway	
Road under construction	
Tunnel, covered road	
Rural track, private road or narrow road in urban area	
Gate or obstruction to traffic (restrictions may not apply at all times or to all vehicles)	
Path, bridleway, byway open to all traffic, road used as a public path	
Pedestrianised area	
DY7 **Postcode boundaries**	
County and unitary authority boundaries	
Railway, tunnel, railway under construction	
Tramway, tramway under construction	
Miniature railway	
Walsall **Railway station**	
Private railway station	
London Underground station	
Tram stop, tram stop under construction	
Bus, coach station	

◆	**Ambulance station**
◆	**Coastguard station**
◆	**Fire station**
◆	**Police station**
✚	**Accident and Emergency entrance to hospital**
H	**Hospital**
+	**Place of worship**
i	**Information Centre** (open all year)
🛒	**Shopping Centre**
P P&R	**Parking, Park and Ride**
PO	**Post Office**
Å	**Camping site**
🚐	**Caravan site**
▶	**Golf course**
✕	**Picnic site**
Prim Sch	**Important buildings, schools, colleges, universities and hospitals**
	Built up area
	Woods
River Medway	**Water name**
	River, weir, stream
	Canal, lock, tunnel
	Water
	Tidal water
Church	**Non-Roman antiquity**
ROMAN FORT	**Roman antiquity**
87 24	**Adjoining page indicators and overlap bands**

Acad	**Academy**	Inst	**Institute**	Recn Gd	**Recreation Ground**
Allot Gdns	**Allotments**	Ct	**Law Court**		
Cemy	**Cemetery**	L Ctr	**Leisure Centre**	Resr	**Reservoir**
C Ctr	**Civic Centre**	LC	**Level Crossing**	Ret Pk	**Retail Park**
CH	**Club House**	Liby	**Library**	Sch	**School**
Coll	**College**	Mkt	**Market**	Sh Ctr	**Shopping Centre**
Crem	**Crematorium**	Meml	**Memorial**	TH	**Town Hall/House**
Ent	**Enterprise**	Mon	**Monument**	Trad Est	**Trading Estate**
Ex H	**Exhibition Hall**	Mus	**Museum**	Univ	**University**
Ind Est	**Industrial Estate**	Obsy	**Observatory**	W Twr	**Water Tower**
IRB Sta	**Inshore Rescue Boat Station**	Pal	**Royal Palace**	Wks	**Works**
		PH	**Public House**	YH	**Youth Hostel**

■ The small numbers around the edges of the maps identify the 1 kilometre National Grid lines

■ The dark grey border on the inside edge of some pages indicates that the mapping does not continue onto the adjacent page

The scale of the maps on the pages numbered in blue is 5.52 cm to 1 km • 3½ inches to 1 mile • 1: 18103

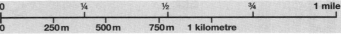

0 ¼ ½ ¾ 1 mile
0 250m 500m 750m 1 kilometre

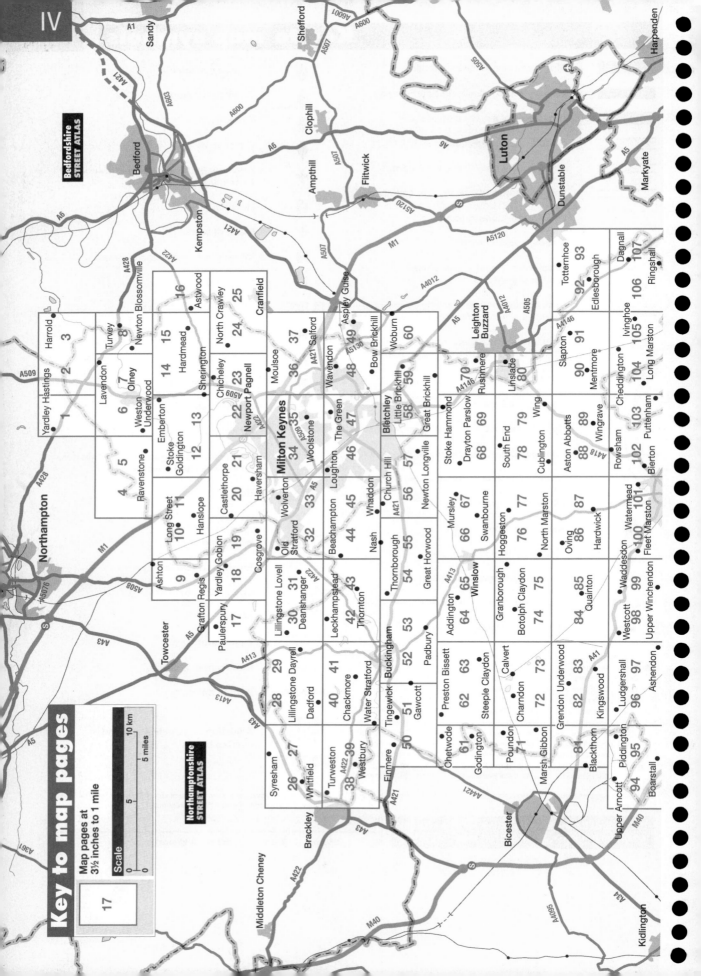

Hertfordshire STREET ATLAS

London STREET ATLAS

Surrey STREET ATLAS

Oxfordshire STREET ATLAS

Berkshire STREET ATLAS

St Albans

Hemel Hempstead

Watford

Harrow

Ruislip

Southall

Hayes

Hounslow

Feltham

Ashford

Staines

Egham

Bracknell

Binfield

Wokingham

Reading

Sonning Common

Goring

Wallingford

Didot

Abingdon

Oxford

Radlett

Bushey

Rickmansworth

Redbourn

Kings Langley

Brentford

Ealing

Harmondsworth

Stanwell

Colnbrook

Old Windsor

Clewer Green

Twyford

Maidenhead

Slough

Windsor

Datchet

Iver

Upton

West Drayton

Yiewsley

Cowley

Uxbridge

Higher Denham

Iver Heath

Wexham Street

Eton Wick

Bray

Taplow

Burnham

Cookham

Cookham Rise

Bisham

Marlow

Little Marlow

Wooburn Common

Hedgerley

Farnham Common

Gerrards Cross

Chalfont St Peter

Seer Green

Chalfont St Giles

Maple Cross

South Harefield

Felden

Bovingdon

Flaunden

Chenies

Chorleywood

Chesham

Latimer

Amersham

Amersham Old Town

Winchmore Hill

Beaconsfield

Loudwater

Flackwell Heath

Wooburn

Lower Woodend

Marlow Bottom

Hambleden

Hurley

Mill End

Henley-on-Thames

Lower Assendon

Fawley

Maidensgrove

Turville

Frieth

Lane End

Booker

High Wycombe

West Wycombe

Naphill

Cryers Hill

Hazelmere

Little Missenden

Great Missenden

Prestwood

Speen

Little Hampden

Lee Common

Chartridge

St Leonards

Cholesbury

Wigginton

Tring

Wilstone Green

Aldbury

Little Gaddesden

Northchurch

Berkhamsted

Hastoe

Ashley Green

Botley

Wendover

Wendover Dean

Ellesborough

Weston Turville

Aston Clinton

Aylesbury

Stone

Bishopstone

Ford

Little Kimble

Longwick

Princes Risborough

Lacey Green

Rout's Green

Bledlow Ridge

Stokenchurch

Crowell

Chinnor

Henton

Haddenham

Kingsey

Cuddington

Westlington

Thame

Shabbington

Tiddington

Milton Common

Long Crendon

Chilton

Upper Pollicott

Brill

Oakley

Horton-cum-Studley

Worminghall

Ickford

Wheatley

Christmas Common

Lewknor

108 109 110 111 112 113 114 115 116 117 118 119 120 121

122 123 124 125 126 127 128 129 130 131 132 133 134 135

136 137 138 139 140 141 142 143 144 145 146

147 148 149 150 151 152 153 154 155 156

157 158 159 160 161 162 163 164 165 166 167

168 169 170 171 172 173 174 175 176 177 178

179 180 181 182 183 184 185 186 187 188 189 190

191 192 193 194 195 196 197 198 199 200 201

202 203 204 205 206 207 208

209 210 211 212 213

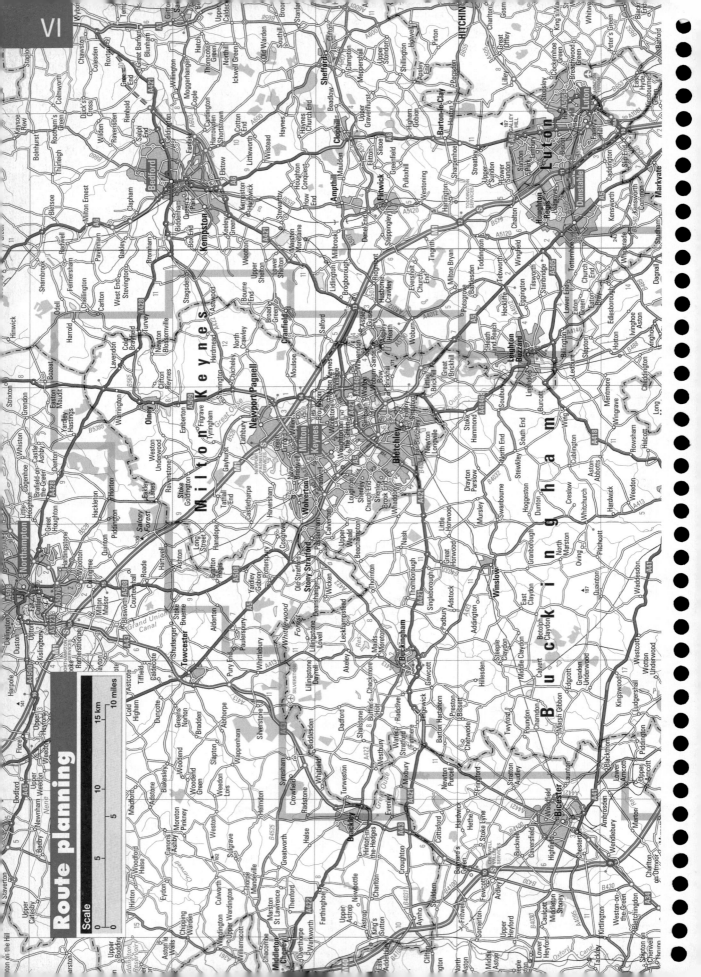

Route planning

Scale

0   5   10 miles

0   5   10   15 km

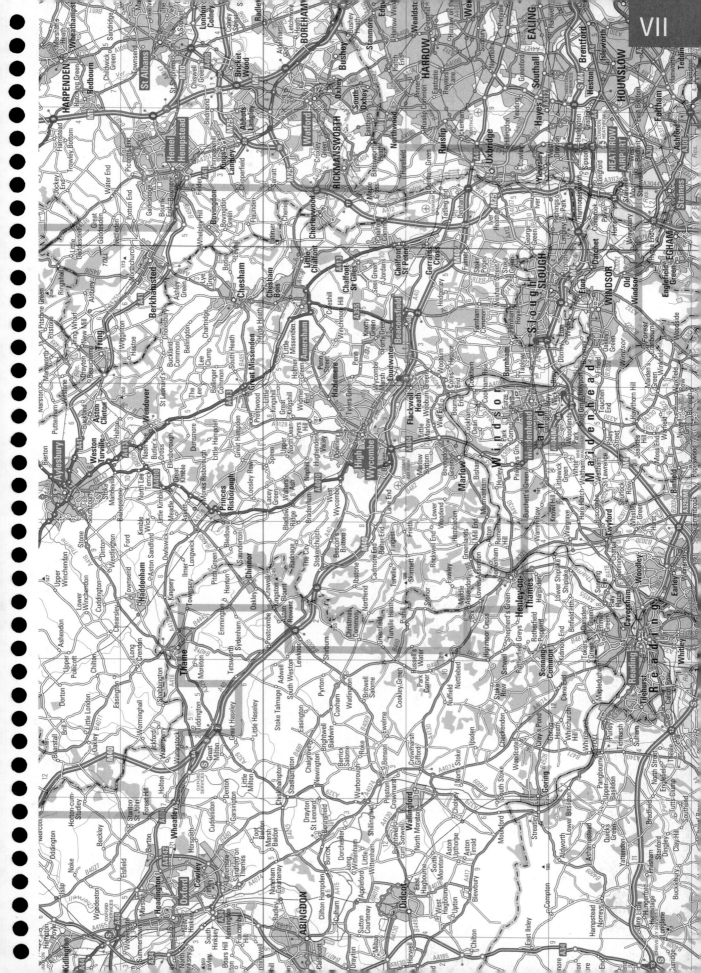

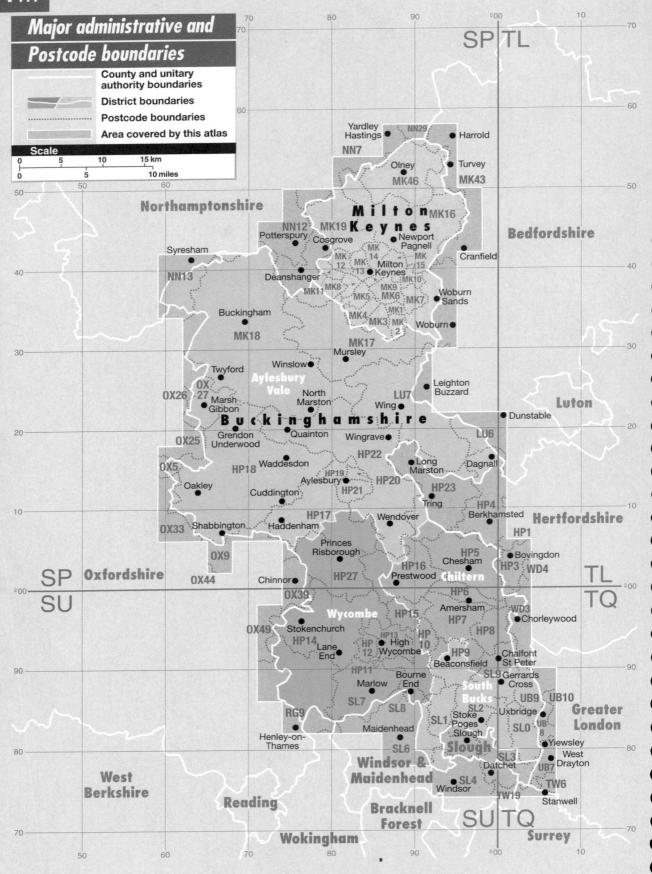

Major administrative and Postcode boundaries

	County and unitary authority boundaries
	District boundaries
	Postcode boundaries
	Area covered by this atlas

Scale

0 — 5 — 10 — 15 km
0 — 5 — 10 miles

SP TL

Northamptonshire

Bedfordshire

Yardley Hastings
NN29
Harrold
NN7
Olney
Turvey
MK46
MK43
Cranfield

Milton Keynes
MK16

NN12
Potterspury
MK19
Cosgrove
Newport Pagnell

Syresham

NN13
Deanshanger
MK12
MK14
Milton Keynes
MK13
MK15
MK10
MK8
MK9
MK11
MK5
MK6
MK7
Woburn Sands
MK4
MK1
MK3
MK2
Woburn
Buckingham
MK18
MK17
Mursley

Twyford
Winslow
OX27
OX26
Marsh Gibbon
North Marston
Leighton Buzzard
LU7

Aylesbury Vale
Wing
Dunstable
Luton

OX25
Grendon Underwood
Quainton
Wingrave
LU6

Buckinghamshire

HP22
OX5
Waddesdon
HP18
HP19
Long Marston
Dagnall
Oakley
Aylesbury
HP20
HP23
Cuddington
HP21
Tring
HP4
Berkhamsted
Hertfordshire

OX33
Shabbington
HP17
Haddenham
Wendover
HP1
OX9
HP5
Bovingdon
Princes Risborough
Chesham
HP3
WD4

SP
Oxfordshire
OX44
HP27
Prestwood
Chiltern
SU
Chinnor
HP16
TL
TQ

OX39
HP6
WD3
Wycombe
HP15
Amersham
Chorleywood
OX49
HP7
HP8
Stokenchurch
HP13
HP10
HP14
Lane End
HP12
High Wycombe
HP9
Chalfont St Peter
Beaconsfield
HP11
SL9
Gerrards Cross
Bourne End
South Bucks
UB9
UB10
Marlow
SL7
SL2
Uxbridge
SL8
SL1
Stoke Poges
UB8
SL0
RG9
Maidenhead
Slough
Yiewsley
SL6
West Drayton
Henley-on-Thames
SL3
UB7
Datchet
TW6
Windsor & Maidenhead
SL4
Windsor
TW19
Stanwell

West Berkshire

Reading
Bracknell Forest
SU TQ
Surrey

Wokingham

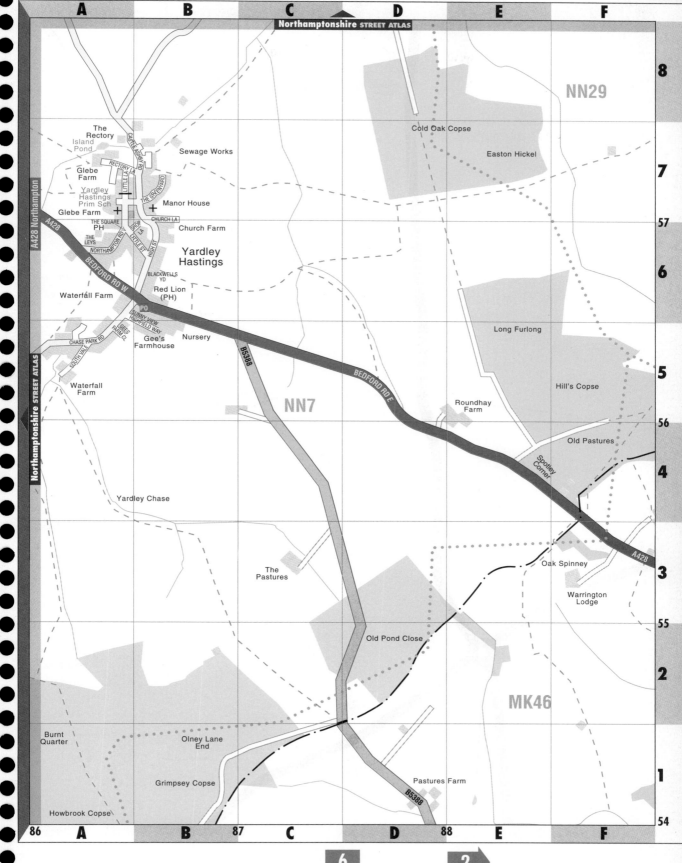

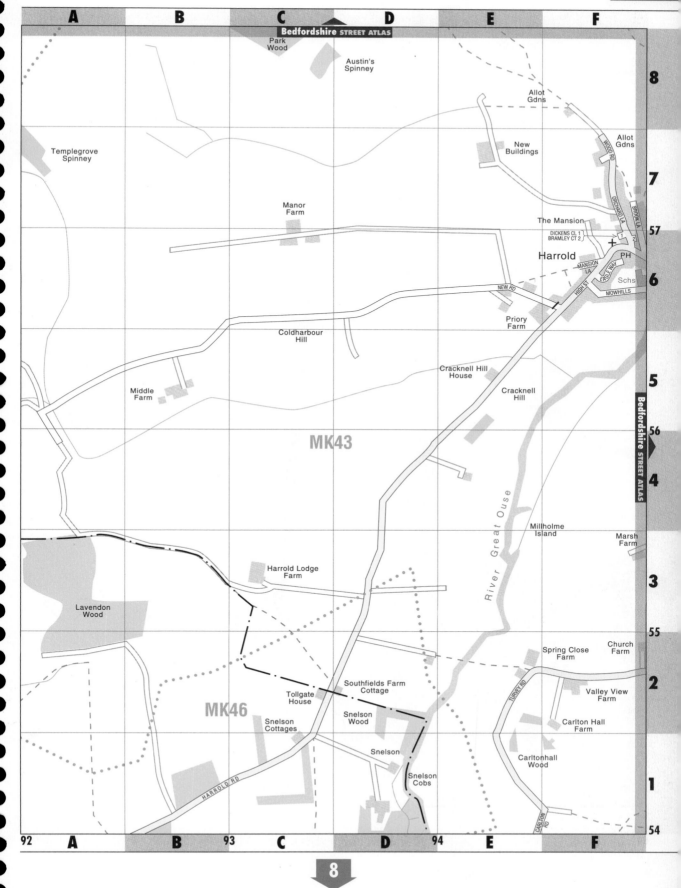

Bedfordshire STREET ATLAS

Park Wood

Austin's Spinney

Allot Gdns

Templegrove Spinney

New Buildings

WOOD RD

Allot Gdns

Manor Farm

The Mansion

ORCHARD LA

BROOK LA

57

DICKENS CL 1
BRAMLEY CT 2

Harrold

MANSION LA

CABLE WAY

PH

NEW RD

HIGH ST

Schs

6

Coldharbour Hill

Priory Farm

MOWHILLS

Cracknell Hill House

Middle Farm

Cracknell Hill

5

56

MK43

River Great Ouse

4

Millholme Island

Marsh Farm

Harrold Lodge Farm

3

Lavendon Wood

55

Spring Close Farm

Church Farm

TURVEY RD

Southfields Farm Cottage

2

Tollgate House

MK46

Snelson Wood

Valley View Farm

Carlton Hall Farm

Snelson Cottages

Snelson

Carltonhall Wood

HARROLD RD

Snelson Cobs

1

CARLTON RD

54

Bedfordshire STREET ATLAS

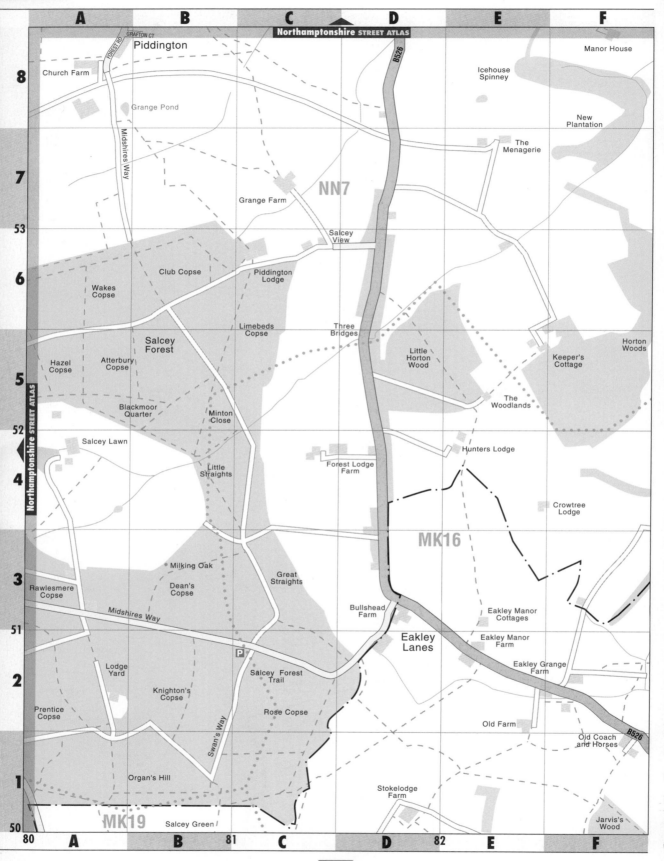

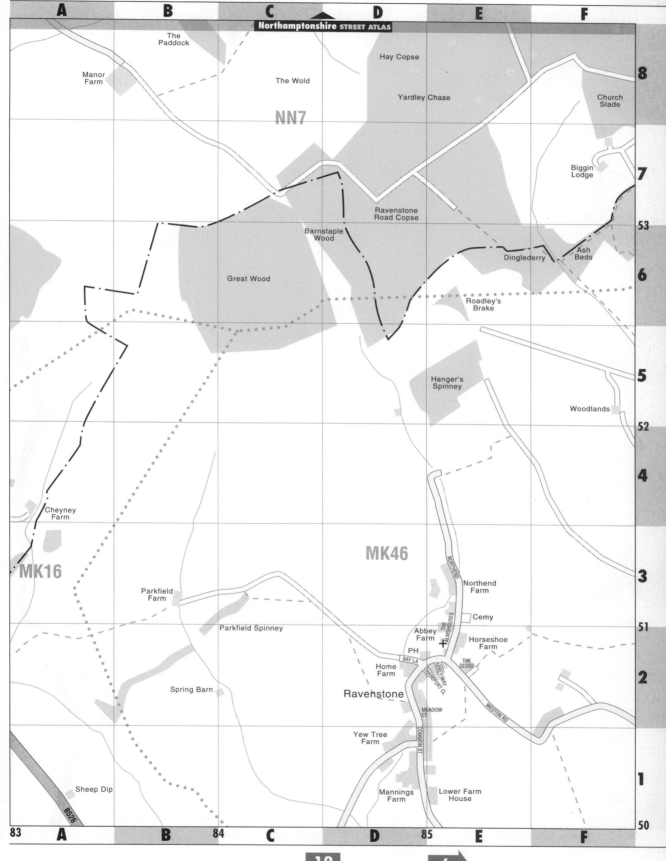

6

Northamptonshire STREET ATLAS

The Paddock

Hay Copse

8

Manor Farm

The Wold

Yardley Chase

Church Slade

NN7

Biggin Lodge

7

53

Ravenstone Road Copse

Barnstaple Wood

Ash Beds

6

Great Wood

Dinglederry

Roadley's Brake

Hanger's Spinney

5

Woodlands

52

4

Cheyney Farm

MK46

Northend Farm

3

MK16

Cemy

51

Parkfield Farm

Abbey Farm

Horseshoe Farm

Parkfield Spinney

PH

THE CLOSE

2

BAY LA

Home Farm

Spring Barn

Ravenstone

MEADOW CT

Yew Tree Farm

1

Sheep Dip

Mannings Farm

Lower Farm House

50

A B C D E F

8
7
53
6
5
52
4
3
51
2
1
50

86 A B 87 C D 88 E F

Howbrook Copse
Grimpsey Copse
Yardley Chase
Church Slade
NN7
Kilwick Wood
Olney Park Farm
Olney Park Cottages
B5388
Olney Hyde
Smith's Farm
Court Farm
Yardley Rd
Sewage Works
Ind Est
Warrington Road Farm
A509
Dickens Spinney
SHORT MASSEY 1
CRAB TREE CL 2
Olney Mid Sch
Olney
MK46
Resr
Pheasants Nest
Olney Fst Sch
Dinglederry
Liby
The Old Mews
ORCHARD RISE
Mus
The Alcove
Weston Park
Flamingo Gardens Zoo Park
Overbrook Spinney
Weston Rd
FOUNTAIN CT 1
BERRELL'S CT 2
ROSE CT 3
MARKET PL
OSBORN'S CT 5
CHURCH ST 6
PEMBROKE HO 7
Goosey Bridge
Sluice
Otter Pool
The Wilderness
Laundry Cottage
Manor House
PH
Church Farm
Wood La
Cross La
High St
Cowpers Orch
Pevers La
The Close
PO
Weston Underwood
Heron Water
River Great Ouse
Emberton Country Park
Grebe Lake
Visitor Ctr
Snipe Pool
The Willows
HARVEY DR
A509
Bridge St
High St

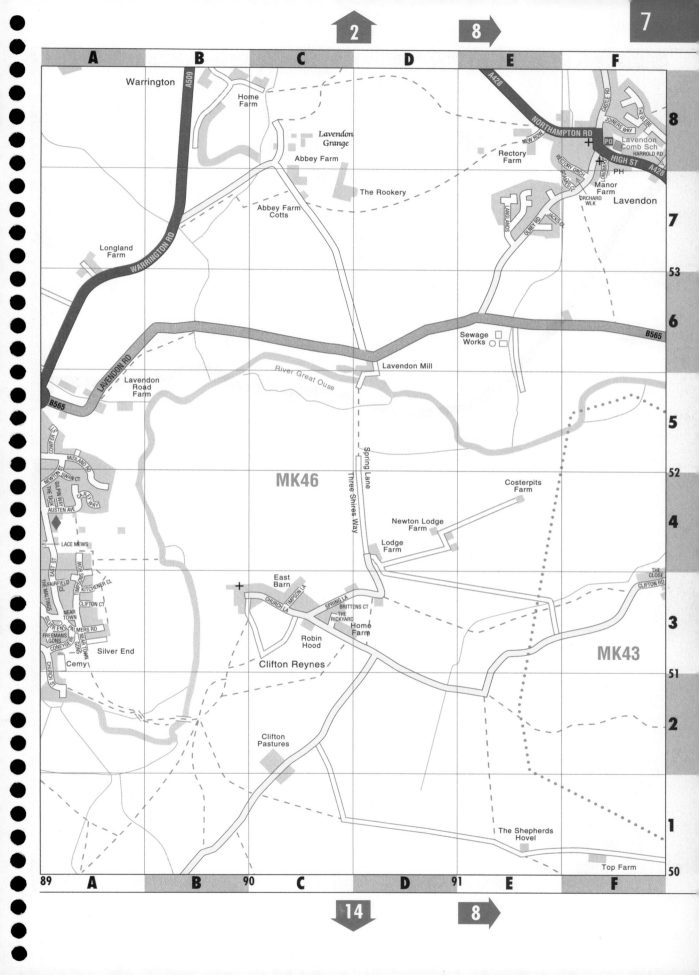

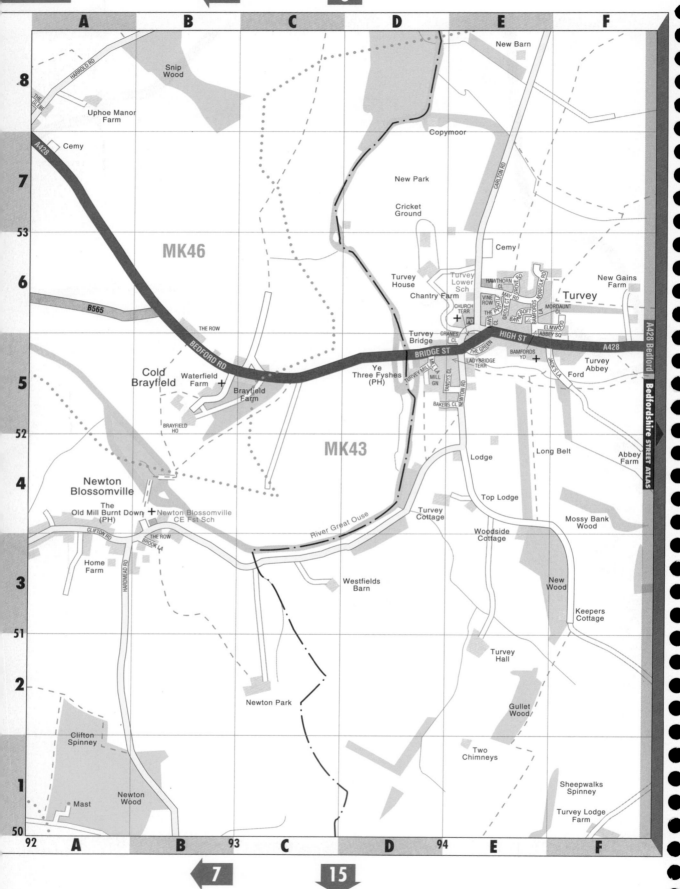

A **B** **C** **D** **E** **F**

8

HARROLD RD

Snip
Wood

THE GLEBE

Uphoe Manor
Farm

New Barn

A428

Cemy

Copymoor

CARLTON RD

7

New Park

53

MK46

Cricket
Ground

Cemy

6

B565

Turvey
House

Turvey
Lower
Sch

HAWTHORN
CL

GROVE RD

NORFOLK RD

New Gains
Farm

Turvey

Chantry Farm

VINE
ROW

MAY RD

THE PYGHTLE

Turvey

THE ROW

CHURCH
TERR

GROVE CT

CROFTS RD

BAMFORDS
LA

MORDAUNT
CL

BEDFORD RD

Turvey
Bridge

CRANES
CL

HIGH ST

ELMWD

ABBEY SQ

A428
Bedford

5

Cold
Brayfield

Waterfield
Farm

Brayfield
Farm

BRIDGE ST

Ye
Three Fyshes
(PH)

TURVEY MILL LA

MILL
GN

THE GREEN

LADYBRIDGE
TERR

NEWTON RD

BAMFORDS
YD

JACK'S LA

A428

Turvey
Abbey

Turvey
Abbey

Ford

Abbey
Farm

Bedfordshire STREET ATLAS

52

BRAYFIELD
HO

MK43

BAKERS CL

FANDYS CL

Lodge

Long Belt

4

Newton
Blossomville

The
Old Mill Burnt Down
(PH)

Newton Blossomville
CE Fst Sch

River Great Ouse

Turvey
Cottage

Top Lodge

Woodside
Cottage

Mossy Bank
Wood

CLIFTON RD

THE ROW

BROOK LA

HARDMEAD RD

Home
Farm

3

New
Wood

51

Westfields
Barn

Turvey
Hall

Keepers
Cottage

2

Clifton
Spinney

Newton Park

Gullet
Wood

Two
Chimneys

Sheepwalks
Spinney

1

Mast

Newton
Wood

Turvey Lodge
Farm

50

92 **A**   **B** 93 **C**   **D** 94 **E**   **F**

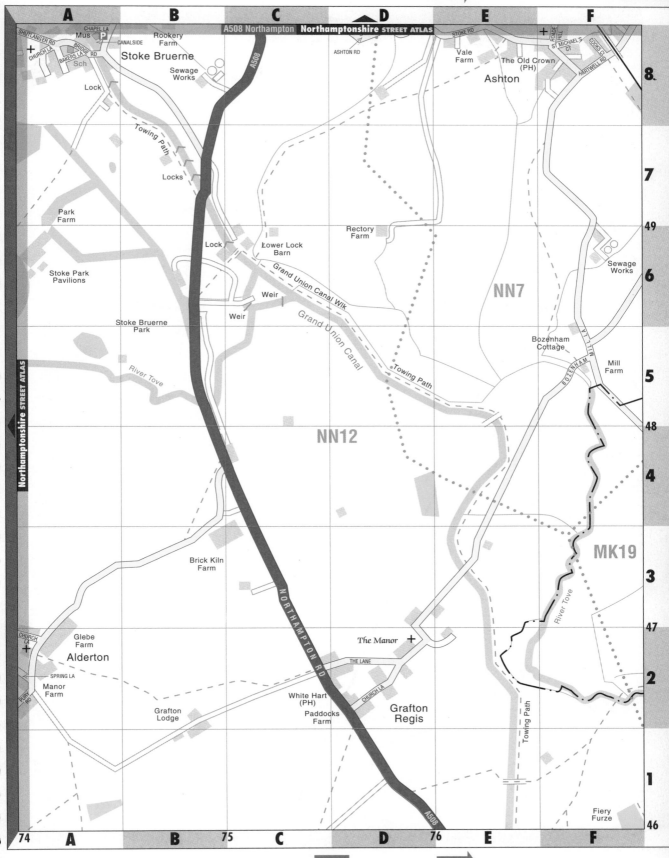

Map labels (reading order):

A B C D E F

SHUTLANGER RD
CHAPEL LA
Mus P
CHURCH LA
BRIDGE RD
BAKERS LA
Sch
Stoke Bruerne
CANALSIDE
Rookery Farm
A508 Northampton   **Northamptonshire** STREET ATLAS
ASHTON RD
STOKE RD
Vale Farm
The Old Crown (PH)
St MICHAEL'S CT
ROADE HILL
COOKS CL
HARTWELL RD
Ashton

8

Lock
Sewage Works

Towing Path

Locks

7

Park Farm

49

Stoke Park Pavilions

Lock
Lower Lock Barn
Rectory Farm

Sewage Works

6

Grand Union Canal Wlk

NN7

Weir
Weir
Grand Union Canal

Stoke Bruerne Park

Bozenham Cottage
Mill Farm

River Tove

Towing Path

5

BOZENHAM LA

48

NN12

4

MK19

Brick Kiln Farm

River Tove

3

47

Glebe Farm
CHURCH LA
Alderton

The Manor
THE LANE
CHURCH LA

47

SPRING LA
Manor Farm

NORTHAMPTON RD

2

PURY RD
Grafton Lodge
White Hart (PH)
Paddocks Farm
Grafton Regis

Towing Path

1

A508
Fiery Furze

46

74   A   B   75   C   D   76   E   F

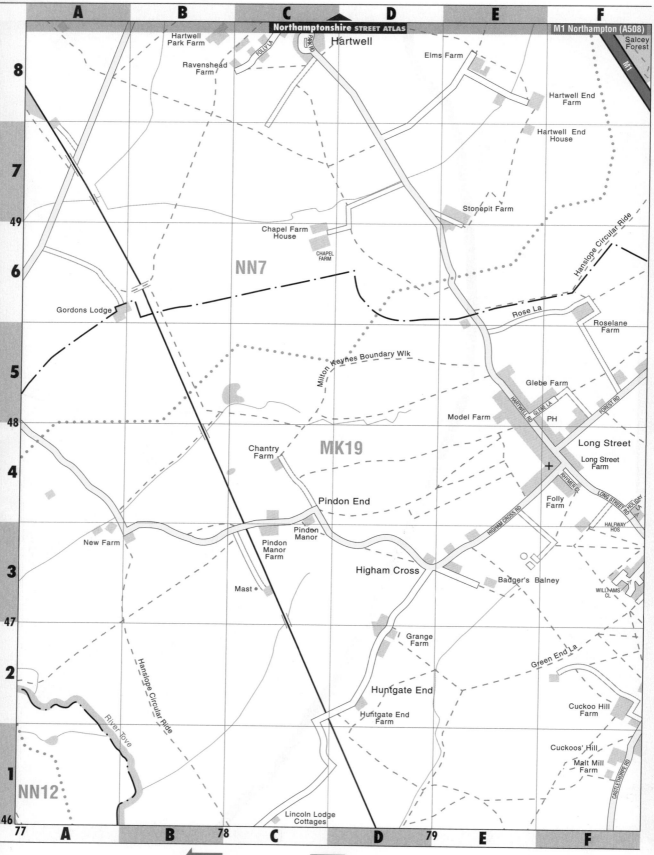

Northamptonshire STREET ATLAS

M1 Northampton (A508)

Salcey Forest

M1

Hartwell Park Farm

Hartwell

FOLLY LA

PARK RD

Ravenshead Farm

Elms Farm

Hartwell End Farm

Hartwell End House

Stonepit Farm

Hanslope Circular Ride

Chapel Farm House

CHAPEL FARM

NN7

Rose La

Roselane Farm

Gordons Lodge

Milton Keynes Boundary Wlk

Glebe Farm

GLEBE LA

HARTWELL RD

Model Farm

PH

MK19

Long Street

Chantry Farm

Long Street Farm

RHYMER CL

Pindon End

Folly Farm

LONG STREET RD

HOLIDAY LA

New Farm

Pindon Manor

HALFWAY HOS

Pindon Manor Farm

HIGHAM CROSS RD

Higham Cross

Badger's Balney

WILLIAMS CL

Mast

Grange Farm

Green End La

Huntgate End

Cuckoo Hill Farm

Huntgate End Farm

Hanslope Circular Ride

River Tove

Cuckoos' Hill

Malt Mill Farm

CASTLETHORPE RD

NN12

Lincoln Lodge Cottages

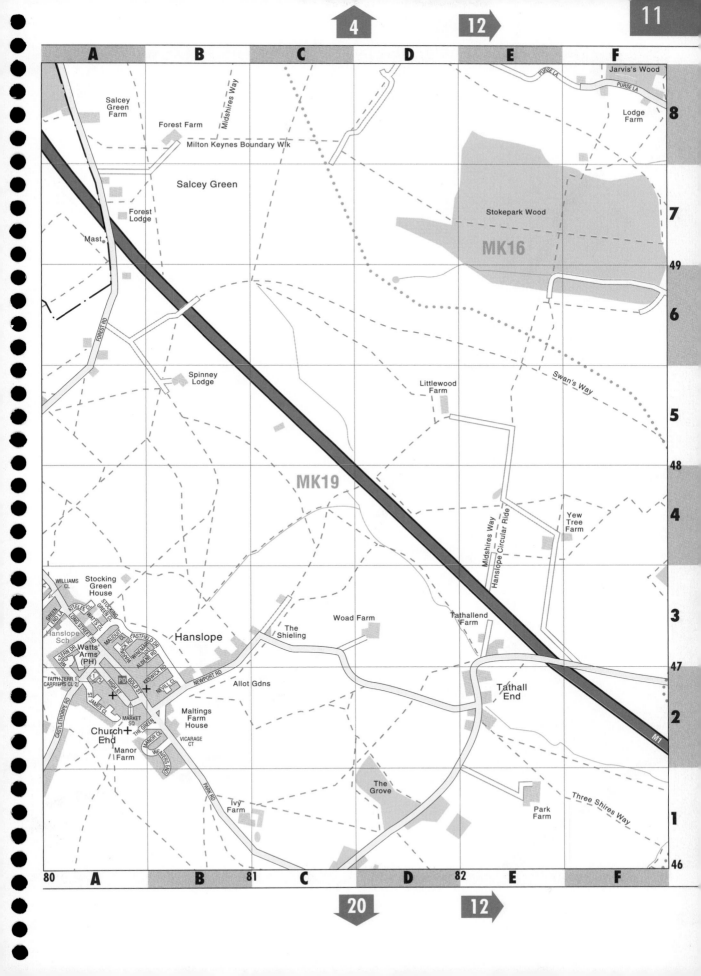

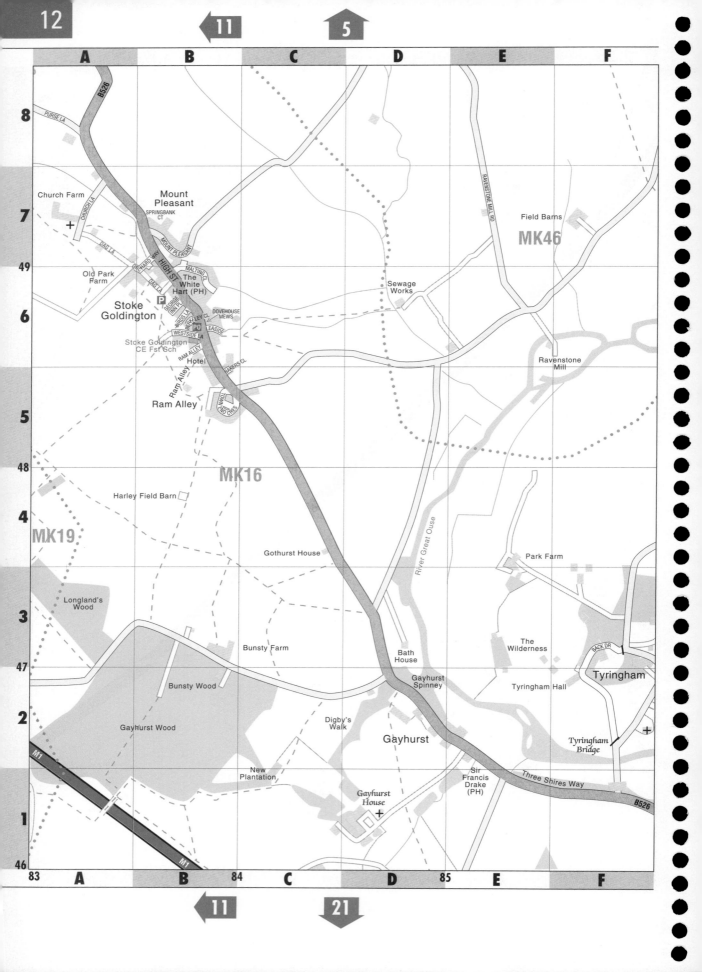

11
5

A   B   C   D   E   F

8   PURSE LA

Church Farm

Mount
Pleasant

SPRINGBANK
CT

7   MK46

Field Barns

CHURCH LA

DAG LA

49   ORCHARD WAY

Old Park
Farm

MOUNT PLEASANT

HIGH ST

DAG LA

MALTING CL

The White
Hart (PH)

Sewage
Works

6   P

Stoke
Goldington

GEORGE
(INN) PL

ROSS LA

WESTSIDE LA

PO

BERKELEY CL

DOVEHOUSE
MEWS

LEASIDE

Ravenstone
Mill

RAVENSTONE MILL RD

Stoke Goldington
CE Fst Sch

RAM ALLEY

Hotel

BAKERS CL

Ram Alley

TOWN
END CRES

5

48

Harley Field Barn

MK16

4

MK19

River Great Ouse

Park Farm

Longland's
Wood

Gothurst House

3   Longland's
Wood

47

Bunsty Farm

Bath
House

The
Wilderness

BACK DR

Tyringham

Bunsty Wood

Gayhurst
Spinney

Tyringham Hall

2

Gayhurst Wood

Digby's
Walk

Gayhurst

Tyringham
Bridge

New
Plantation

Sir
Francis
Drake
(PH)

Three Shires Way

B526

1

M1

Gayhurst
House

46

11
21

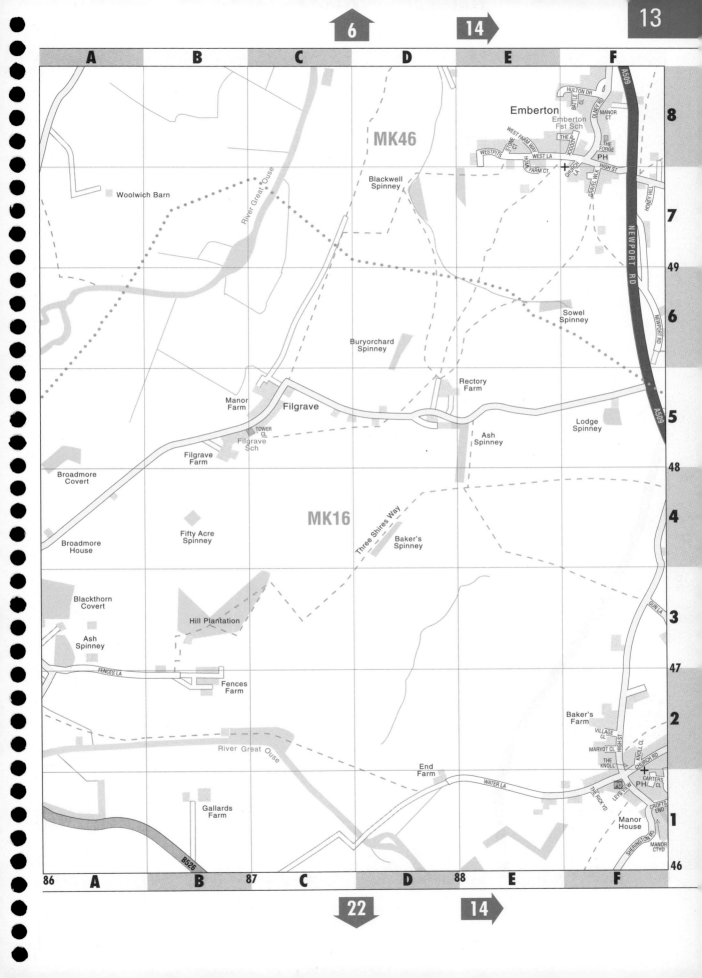

A B C D E F

8

Three Shires Way

Rectory Farm

Petsoe Manor Farm

Petsoe Manor

7

Petsoe End

Hill Farm

Clay Farm

Grange Farm

49

MK46

6

Hollington Wood

Wood Farm

Mulducks

Parrages Wood

Seven Acre Covert

Short Wood

5

48

A 509

4

MK16

3

Gowle's Farm

Thickthorn Wood

47

GUN LA

FIELD CL

CHURCH END

PARK RD

2

CHURCH RD

SCHOOL LA

BURYS END

Sherington

Sherington CE Fst Sch

Grange Farm

Brickyard Cottage

A 422

CARTERS CL

HILLVIEW

CROFTS END

BEDFORD RD

Chicheley Brook

NEWPORT RD

1

Crofts End

Bedlam

BEDLAM WLK

BEDLAM LA

Brandon's Wood

46

A 509

Bedlam Spinney

A 422

89 A B 90 C D 91 E F

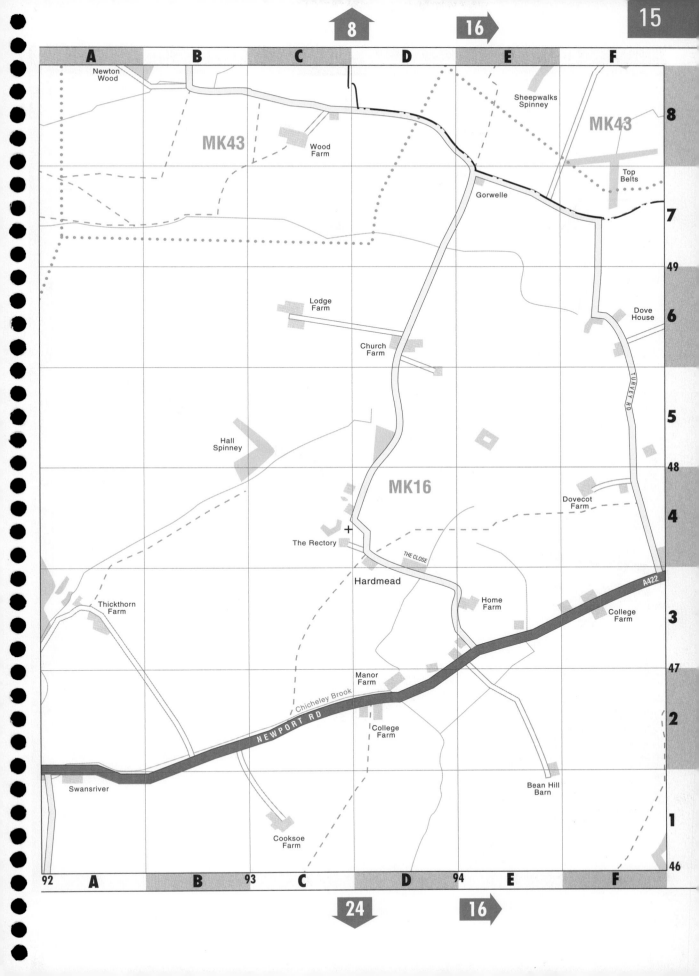

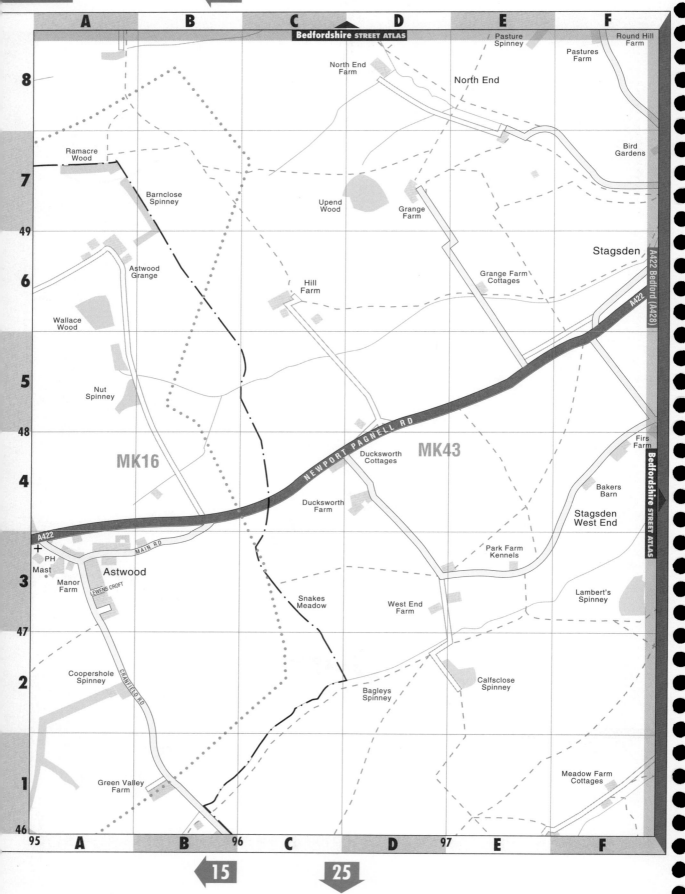

15

Bedfordshire STREET ATLAS

A B C D E F

8

North End Farm

Pasture Spinney

Round Hill Farm

Pastures Farm

North End

Bird Gardens

7

Ramacre Wood

Barnclose Spinney

Upend Wood

Grange Farm

49

Astwood Grange

Stagsden

A422 Bedford (A428)

6

Wallace Wood

Hill Farm

Grange Farm Cottages

A422

5

Nut Spinney

48

NEWPORT PAGNELL RD

Ducksworth Cottages

MK43

Firs Farm

MK16

4

Ducksworth Farm

Bakers Barn

Stagsden West End

Bedfordshire STREET ATLAS

A422

MAIN RD

+ PH Mast

Astwood

Park Farm Kennels

3

Manor Farm

LEWENS CROFT

Snakes Meadow

West End Farm

Lambert's Spinney

47

Coopershole Spinney

CRANFIELD RD

Bagleys Spinney

Calfsclose Spinney

2

1

Green Valley Farm

Meadow Farm Cottages

46

95 A B 96 C D 97 E F

15

25

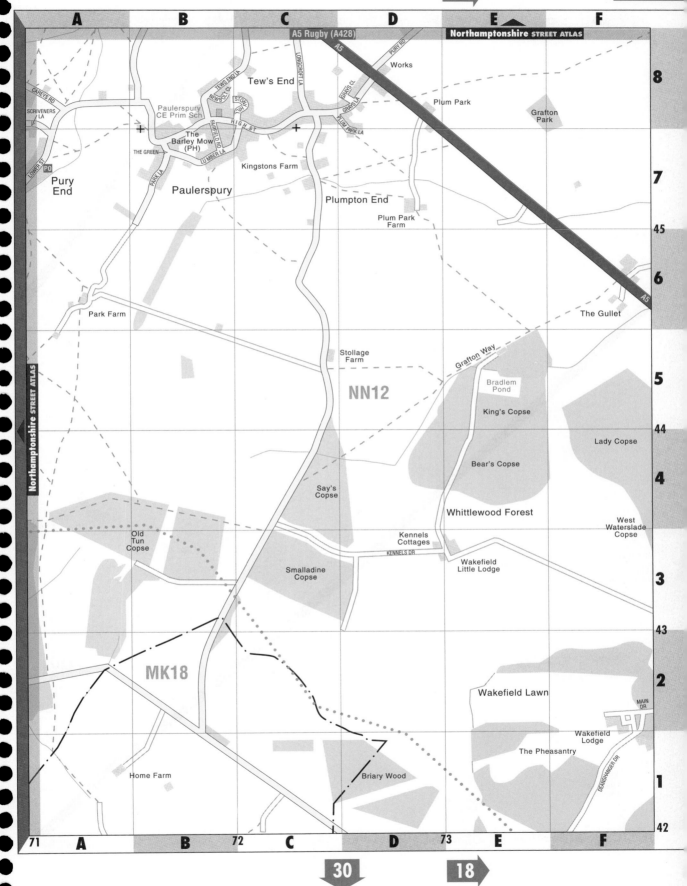

Northamptonshire STREET ATLAS

Northamptonshire STREET ATLAS

A5 Rugby (A428)

Works

Plum Park

Grafton Park

Tew's End

Paulerspury CE Prim Sch

The Barley Mow (PH)

THE GREEN

Pury End

Paulerspury

Kingstons Farm

Plumpton End

Plum Park Farm

45

6

The Gullet

A5

Park Farm

Stollage Farm

Grafton Way

Bradlem Pond

NN12

5

King's Copse

44

Lady Copse

Bear's Copse

4

Say's Copse

Whittlewood Forest

West Waterslade Copse

Old Tun Copse

Kennels Cottages

KENNELS DR

Wakefield Little Lodge

3

Smalladine Copse

43

MK18

2

Wakefield Lawn

MAIN DR

Wakefield Lodge

The Pheasantry

DEANSHANGER DR

Home Farm

Briary Wood

1

42

71   A   B   72   C   D   73   E   F

CAREYS RD

SCRIVENERS LA

LOWER ST

PO

TEWS END LA

NEWB OTT CL

STONE WK

HIGH ST

FAIRFIELD RD

PARK LA

LUMBER LA

LONGCROFT LA

PURY RD

A5

GRAYS CL

GRAYS LA

PLUM PARK LA

17 9

A B C D E F

8

Grafton Cottage Farm

Grafton Fields

Grand Union Canal Wlk

Grand Union Canal

NORTHAMPTON RD

A508

Yardley Wharf

Old Wharfe Farm

7

45

Queens Oak Farm

Wr Twr GRAYS

Mount Pleasant Farm

MOOREND RD

GRAFTON RD

Potterspury Lodge Sch

White Rose Farm

HIGHCROFT CL

VICARAGE CL

WOODY CL

CRESH

DRUCE END

PO

MOUNT PLEASANT

PROSPECT CT

HIGH ST

Manor Farm

6

LIME RD

MANOR WAY

SCHOOL LA

BROWNSFIELD

HESKETH RD

WARREN RD

ORCHARD CL

CHESTNUT RD

A508

Brookfields Farm

Moor End

Yardley Gobion CE Prim Sch

GREEN RD

HORTONSFIELD RD

PH

Castle Barn

Yardley Gobion

MALBOROUGH WAY

BUDGE RD

EASTFIELD

Manor Farm

5

Oakley Spinney

A5

44

NN12

4

East Waterslade Copse

YARDLEY RD

BEECH HOUSE DR

Beech House Farm

Sunnyside Farm PH

Assart Farm

TOWCESTER DR

BLACKWELL END

THE ORCHARD

WATLING ST

SANDE PS LA

MEADOW VIEW

CHURCH END

3

Wakefield Gdns

Nursery

Greystone Lodge

HIGH ST

PO

WOODS LA

COACH YD

CHURCH LA

KENNELLS DR

Wakefield Farm

ELMFIELD CL

Potterspury

DUCHESS GDNS

Sch

HOMESTEAD CL

HIRSCH

WAY

FURTHO LA

GRAFTON CL

MK19

Dairy Quarter

Main Drive Cottages

MAIN DR

MAYS WAY

BROWNSWOOD RD

QUEETLE PL

POUNDFIELD RD

Potterspury House

2

Redmoor Copse

Puxley Farm

Dairy Farm

1

Cherrytree Lodge

A5

42

74 A B 75 C D 76 E F

17 31

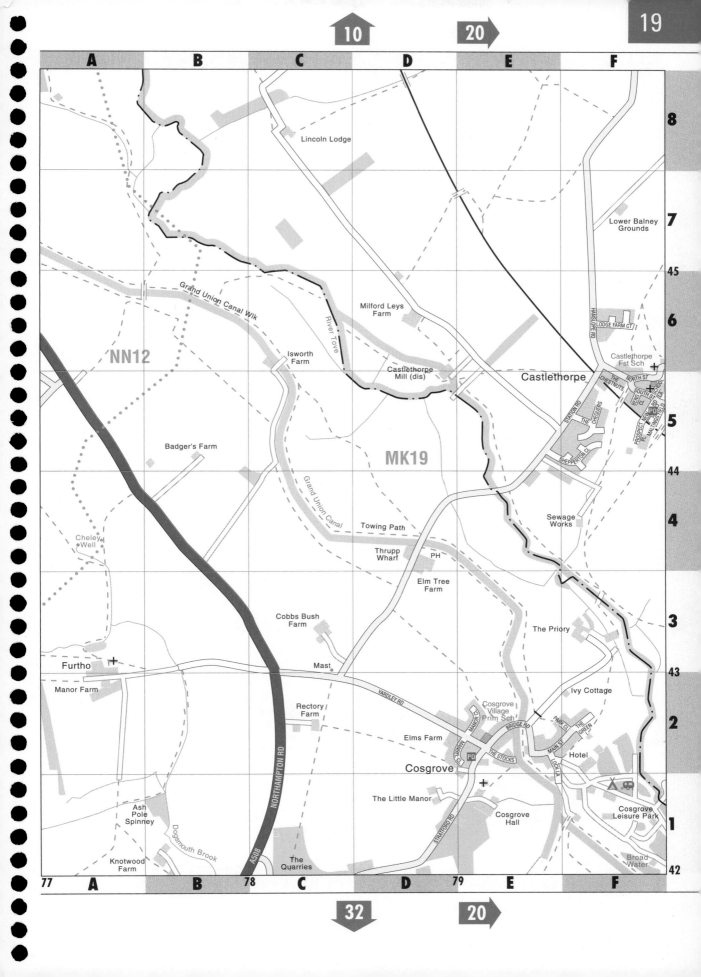

A | B | C | D | E | F

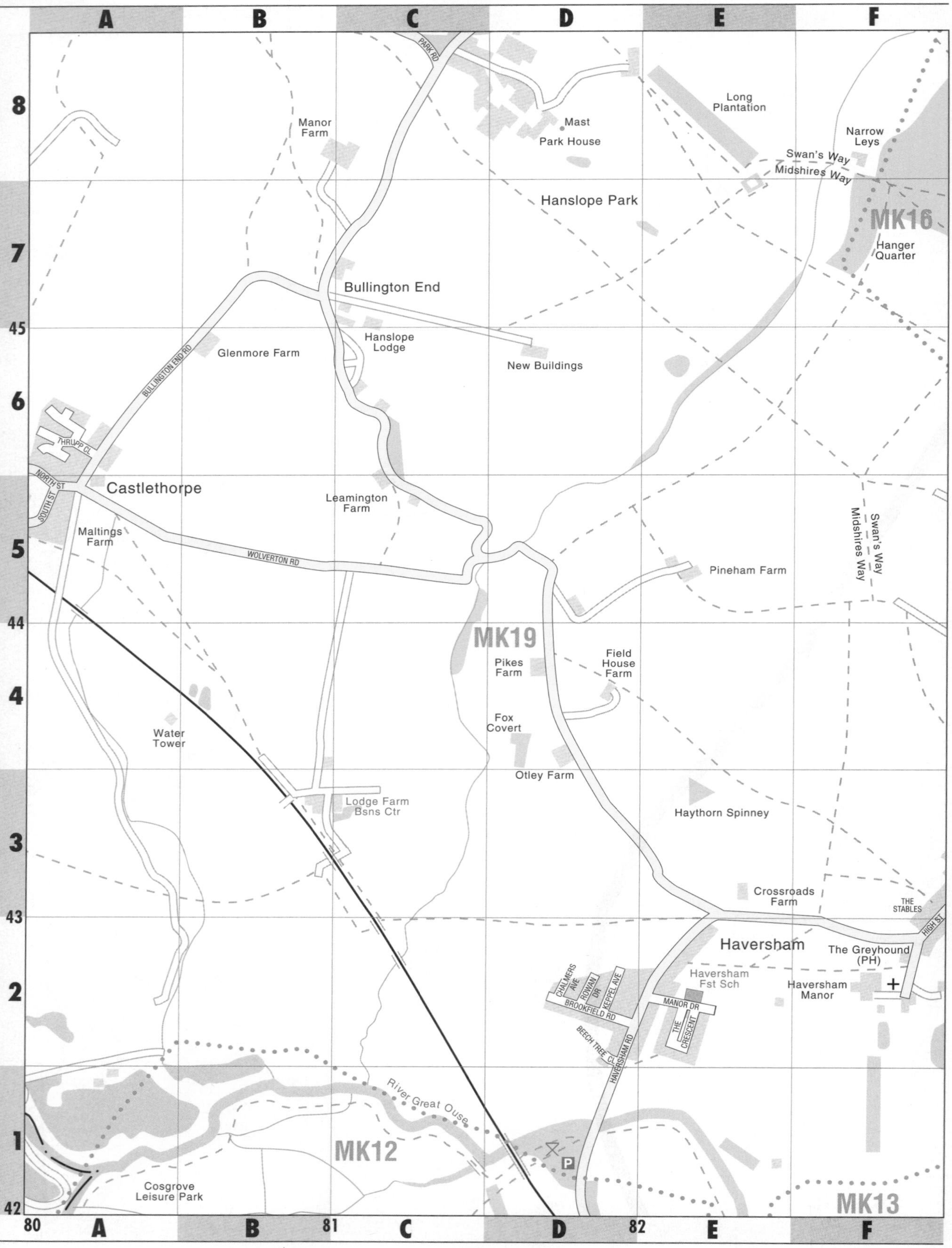

8

Manor Farm

Mast
Park House

Long Plantation

Narrow Leys

Swan's Way
Midshires Way

MK16

Hanslope Park

Hanger Quarter

7

Bullington End

45

Hanslope Lodge

Glenmore Farm

BULLINGTON END RD

New Buildings

6

THRUPP CL

Castlethorpe

NORTH ST

SOUTH ST

Leamington Farm

Swan's Way
Midshires Way

Maltings Farm

WOLVERTON RD

5

Pineham Farm

44

MK19

Pikes Farm

Field House Farm

4

Water Tower

Fox Covert

Otley Farm

Lodge Farm Bsns Ctr

Haythorn Spinney

3

43

Crossroads Farm

THE STABLES

Haversham

The Greyhound (PH)

HIGH ST

2

CHALMERS AVE
ROWAN DR
KEPPEL AVE
BROOKFIELD RD

Haversham Fst Sch

Haversham Manor

MANOR DR

THE CRESCENT

BEECH TREE CL

HAVERSHAM RD

+

River Great Ouse

1

MK12

P

MK13

42

Cosgrove Leisure Park

80 A | B 81 | C | D 82 | E | F

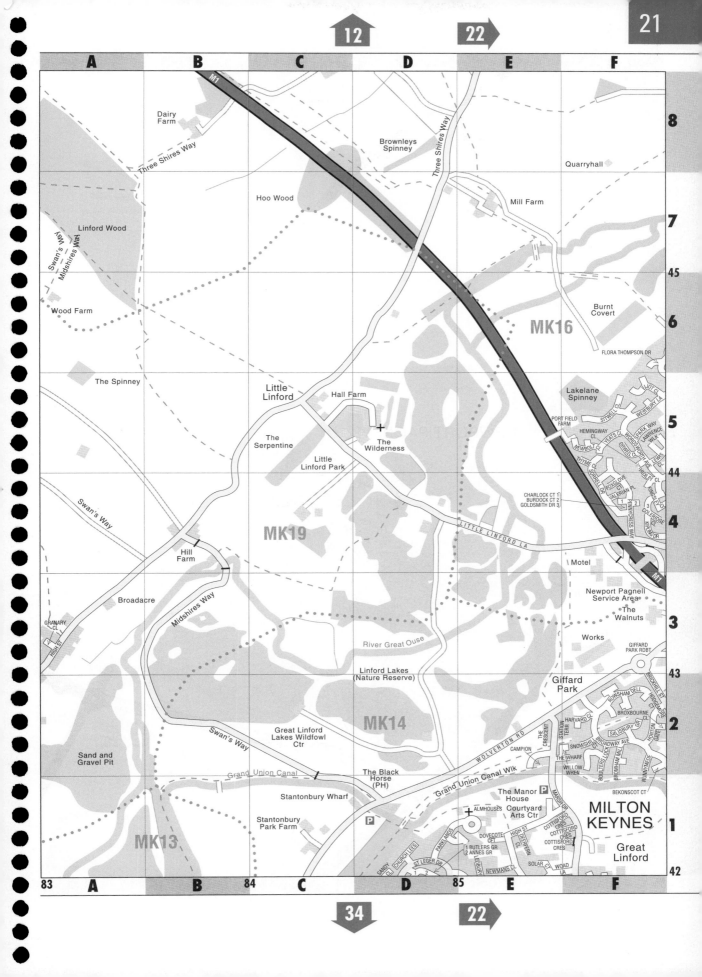

12
22

A B C D E F

8
7
45
6
5
44
4
3
43
2
1
42

M1

Dairy Farm

Three Shires Way

Brownleys Spinney

Three Shires Way

Quarryhall

Hoo Wood

Mill Farm

Linford Wood

Swan's Way

Midshires Way

Wood Farm

Burnt Covert

MK16

FLORA THOMPSON DR

The Spinney

Little Linford

Hall Farm

Lakelane Spinney

PORT FIELD FARM

SITWELL CL
WESTBURY LA
ELIOT CL

The Serpentine

The Wilderness

HEMINGWAY CL
YEATS CL
NEWBY CL
THYME CL
SORREL DR
ORMEL CL
WOODSWORTH CL
FOXGLOVE CL
ARKWAY
LAWRENCE WLK
HUXLEY CL
LEWIS CL
KINGS CL
VALERIAN PL

Little Linford Park

CHARLOCK CT 1
BURDOCK CT 2
GOLDSMITH DR 3

COLERIDGE CL
KIPLING CR

MK19

Swan's Way

LITTLE LINFORD LA

PENNYCRESS WAY

Hill Farm

Motel

M1

Broadacre

Midshires Way

Newport Pagnell Service Area

The Walnuts

GRANARY CL
HIGH ST

River Great Ouse

Works

GIFFARD PARK RDBT

Linford Lakes (Nature Reserve)

Giffard Park

43

MK14

BRICKHILL ST
BOWSHAM DELL
HODGE LEACE
BROXBOURNE CL
HORTON GATE

Sand and Gravel Pit

Swan's Way

Great Linford Lakes Wildfowl Ctr

Grand Union Canal

The Black Horse (PH)

Grand Union Canal Wlk

WOLVERTON RD

CAMPION

THE CRESCENT

STATION TERR
HARVARD CL
SALISBURY GR
SNOWSHILL
BROADWAY AVE
THE WHARF
RUNNYMEDE
BROMHAM MILL
BOULTERS LOCK
WILLOW WREN

Stantonbury Wharf

The Manor House

BEKONSCOT CT

MILTON KEYNES

Stantonbury Park Farm

ALMHOUSES

Courtyard Arts Ctr

Great Linford

MK13

SANDY CL
CHURCH LEES
ST LEGER DR
PARKLANDS
1 BUTLERS GR
2 ANNES GR
DOVECOTE CL
LEDBURY
NEWMANS CL
HIGH ST
DEFFERN CL
SOLAR CT
WOAD LA
COTTISFORD CRES

34
22

21
13

A B C D E F

8

Quarryhall Farm

B526

Ash Spinney

7

Inn Farm

Lathbury

Bridge House
Sherington Bridge

Chicheley Hill

Sherington Rd

45

THE CLOSE

Lathbury Park

CHURCH LA

INN FARM CT

New Woad Farm

Works

6

Kickles Farm

NORTHAMPTON RD

River Great Ouse

Bury Field

Woad Farm

5

Flora Thompson Dr
Thomas Dr

Larkin Cl
Heaney Cl
Alder
Holtsman
Wordehouse Cl

Lakes Lane Farm

Shakespeare Cl
Carroll Cl
Herriot Cl
Scott Dr
Swift Cl

NEWPORT PAGNELL

MK16

North Sq

Mill St

Tickford Abbey

Cemy

1 Pollys Yd
2 Ousebank St

44

Lewis Cl
Christie
Portfields Sch
Shaw
Westbury
Longfield Dr
Cowper
Kingsley
Marlow
Burns Cl
Browning Dr

Charles Way
Queens Ave
Windsor Ave
Doycote

Lakes La

Coopers Ct
High St

St John St
Liby

Church View
Works

Castle St
Priory St

Lagonda
Milton
Keynes Cl
Carlton Rd

Tickford End

4

Morris Wlk
Collins Wlk
Lamb
Carlyle Cl
Kipling Dr
Chaucer Cl
Byron Dr
Keats Cl
Masefield
Tennyson
Shelley Cl
Ash Hill Rd
Foxgate
Westbury
Park Ave
The Lodge Vw

Courthouse Mews
The Green

Bury St
Lovat St
Sch
Caldecote St

St Pauls Yd
1 Station Rd
2 Beaconsfield Pl

Tickford St
Chicheley St
Ribble Cl
Dove Cl
Derwent

Margarets Cl
Hartwell
Severn Dr
Stour Cl

L Ctr
Cemy

North Crawley Rd
Leary Cres
Vantage Ct

3

M1
Wolverton Rd
Greenlands
Walnut Cl
Hornbeam
Cypress
Carrington Rd
Sandringham Ct
Balmoral Ct
Ousedale Sch

Buckingham
Almond Cl
Lime
Broad St
Cherry Rd
Annesley Rd
The Grove
Whaddon Way
Kennington
Holland Way
Norwood La

Barnsbury Gdns
The Green
Fr80erica Cotts
Mainstend Rd
Willen Rd

Teign Cl
Nene Cl
Dart
Medway Cl
Deben Cl
Thames
Thurne Cl
Riverside Fst Sch
Lovat Mid Sch

River Ouzel or Lovat

B526 London Rd
Plover Rd
Howard Cl
Ind Est

Samuel Cl

43

Tanners Dr
Ind Est

The Kingfisher Ctr

Stanmore Gdns
Greenwich Gdns
Elthorne Way
Waterlow Way
Ruskin St
Avery Ct
Alexandra Rd
Ranelagh

Green Park Dr
Mountsfield Cl
Petersham
Glasscott Way
Ostrich La

Sewage Works

A422

Caldecote La

Newport Stables

2

MK14

Giffard Park Comb Sch
Huntsman Gr
Hargraves
Metcalfe Gr
Nook
Smeaton Cl

Burgess Gdns
Dilworth Ct
Sloan Gdns
Tabard Gdns
Tongwell La

Caldecote Mill

Caldecotemill Weirs Bridge

A509

1

Grand Union Canal
Broadway Ave
Bracknell Cl
Minton Ct
Hainault Ave
Teviold
Wedgwood

Giffard Park

Blakelands

Tongwell Lake

TA Ctr
Knebworth Gate
Ind Est

Monks Way

Delaware Dr

Vermont Pl
Michigan Dr
Ind Est

Caldecote

Caldecote Farm

42

Harle Stone Ct
Oversley Ct
Whichford
Yeomans Dr

A422

MK15

M1

21
35

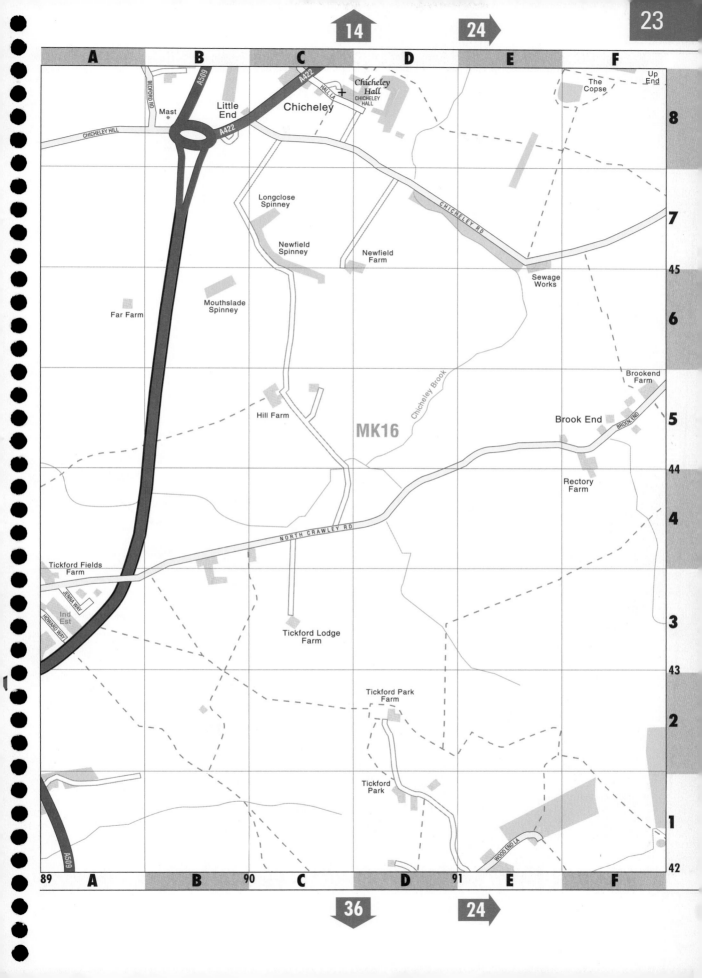

A   B   C   D   E   F

8

Up End

Chicheley Brook

Dollars Grove Farm

7

Little Crawley Farm

Horncastle Farm

Gumbrills Farm

Dollars Grove

East End Farm

Old Moat Farm

45

CHICHELEY RD

ORCHARD WAY

HACKETT PL.

KILPIN GV.

POUND LA.

Quaker's Farm

North Crawley

BRYANT

LYLE'S

Crawley Grange

Rookery Farm

Manor Farm

East End

6

BROOK END

HIGH ST

PH

CHEQUERS LA.

CHURCH WLK

Church Farm

Broadmead

Ford

North Crawley CE Fst Sch

5

MK16

Lodge Farm

Ringtail Farm

44

FOLLY LA.

SHIRE LA.

Ring Croft Farm

4

Murtland's Farm

Rings Wharley Farm

Hurstend Farm

3

Hurst End

Sewage Works

Wharley Farm

43

FEDDEN HO

WEST RD

ROYCE RD

EAST RD

MITCHEL RD

HENSON CL

REYNOLDS CL

HANDLEY

PAGE CL

DUNCAN RD

Con Ctr

MERCHANT LA.

2

THE DRIVE

PRINCE PHILIP AVE.

THE GREEN

STRINGFELLOW CL

COLLEGE RD

THE CRESCENT

LANCHESTER RD

PO

Cranfield Univ

CENTRAL AVE.

Moulsoe Old Wood

Chapelclose Spinney

The Cottage

Wharley End

Liby

MK43

Cranfield Airfield

1

Wharley End Farm

UNIVERSITY WAY

42

92   A   93   B   C   93   D   94   E   F

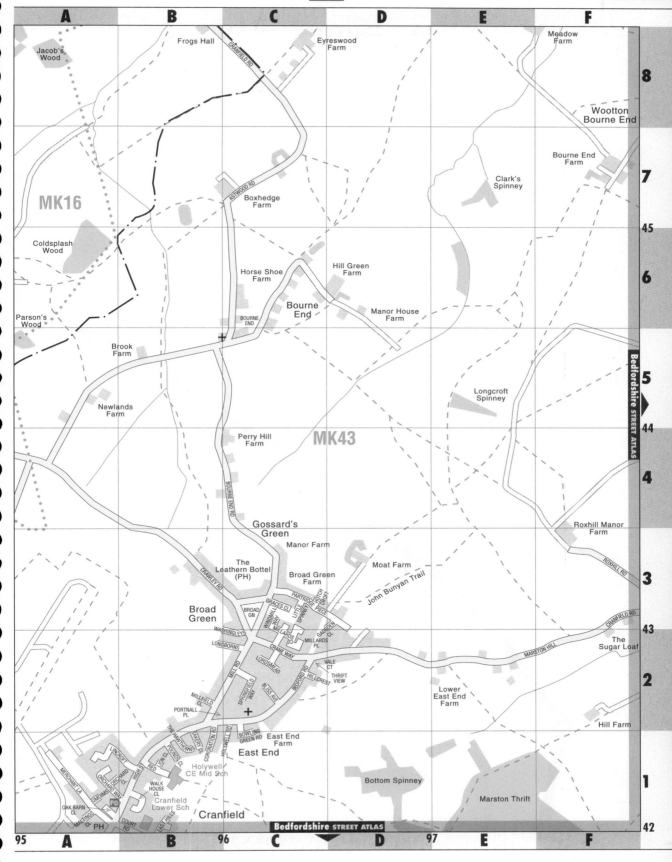

A   B   C   D   E   F

Jacob's Wood
Frogs Hall
CRANFIELD RD
Eyreswood Farm
Meadow Farm

8

Wootton Bourne End

MK16
ASTWOOD RD
Boxhedge Farm
Bourne End Farm

7

Clark's Spinney

45

Coldsplash Wood
Horse Shoe Farm
Hill Green Farm

6

Parson's Wood
BOURNE END
Bourne End
Manor House Farm

Brook Farm
Longcroft Spinney

5

Newlands Farm
MK43

44

Perry Hill Farm

4

BOURNE END RD
Gossard's Green
Roxhill Manor Farm

Manor Farm
Moat Farm
ROXHILL RD

The Leathern Bottel (PH)
Broad Green Farm
John Bunyan Trail
CRANFIELD RD

3

CRAWLEY RD
PARTRIDGE PIECE
LITTLE SPINNEY
HATCH CRAFT

Broad Green
BROAD GN
GRACES CL
MARSTON HILL
The Sugar Loaf

43

WASHINGLEYS
WINDMILL WAY
MILLARDS CL
GAMBYN CL
MILLARDS PL

LONGBORNS
CRANE WAY
VALE CT

MILL RD
LORDSMEAD
HILLCREST
THRIFT VIEW

2

BEDFORD RD
BLISS AVE

MILLFIELD CL
SPRINGFIELD WAY
Lower East End Farm

PORTNALL PL
BOWLING GREEN RD
East End Farm
Hill Farm

THE HAWTHORNS
BAKERS CL
CORONATION RD
MAXWELL RD
East End

MERCHANT LA
LINCROFT
HIGH ST
TON CL
POUNDS CL
Holywell CE Mid Sch
Bottom Spinney

1

ORCHARD CL
ORCHARD CL
SIMDIMS WAY
WALK HOUSE CL
Cranfield Lower Sch
Marston Thrift

OAK BARN CL
PO
EAST HILLS
Cranfield

MALTINGS CL
PH
COURT RD

95   A   B   96   C   D   97   E   F

42

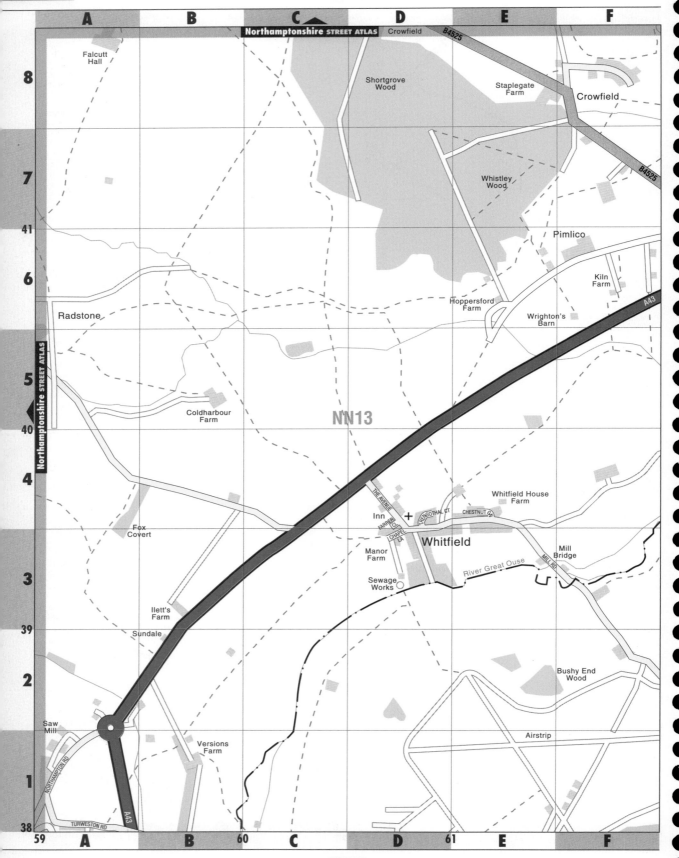

Crowfield

B4525

Falcutt Hall

Shortgrove Wood

Staplegate Farm

Crowfield

8

Whistley Wood

7

B4525

41

Pimlico

6

Kiln Farm

Hoppersford Farm

Radstone

Wrighton's Barn

A43

5

Coldharbour Farm

NN13

40

4

Whitfield House Farm

The Avenue

Fox Covert

Inn

Trengothal Ct

Chestnut Cl

Farren Cl

Chapel La

Whitfield

Manor Farm

Mill Bridge

Mill Rd

Ilett's Farm

Sewage Works

River Great Ouse

3

Sundale

39

Bushy End Wood

2

Saw Mill

Versions Farm

Airstrip

Northampton Rd

1

A43

38

Turweston Rd

28

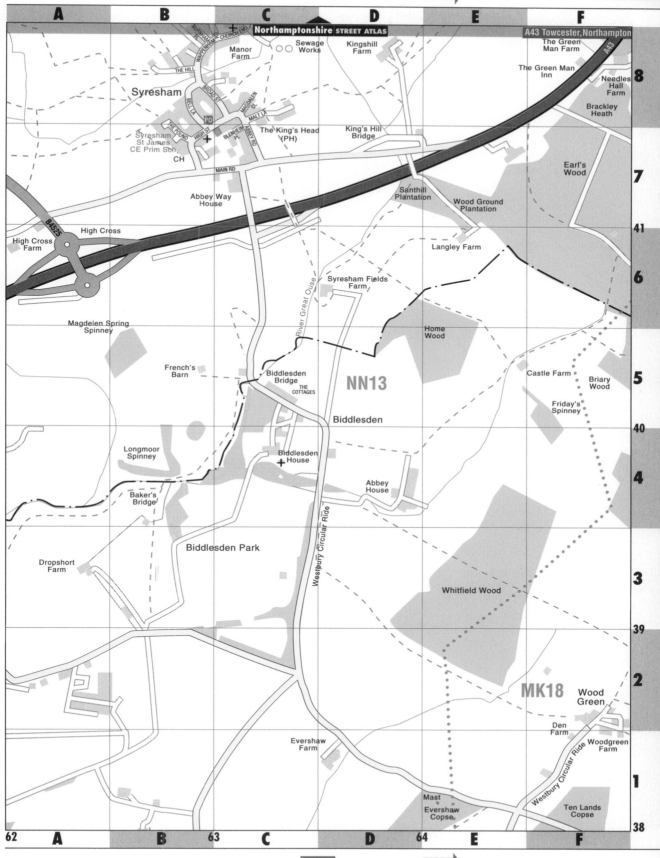

Northamptonshire STREET ATLAS

A43 Towcester, Northampton

8
The Green
Man Farm
The Green Man
Inn
Needles
Hall
Farm
Brackley
Heath

7
Earl's
Wood

41

6

Syresham

Manor
Farm
Sewage
Works
Kingshill
Farm

THE HILL

BURHAM PL
WAPPENHAM RD
CHURCH END

BROAD ST
BELL LA
MAGDALEN
CL
MALT LA

HIGH ST
THE POUND
PO
BLENHEIM
PL
ABBEY RD

The King's Head
(PH)

King's Hill
Bridge

Santhill
Plantation

Wood Ground
Plantation

Langley Farm

Syresham
St James
CE Prim Sch
CH

Abbey Way
House

MAIN RD

B4525

High Cross

High Cross
Farm

Magdelen Spring
Spinney

French's
Barn

Biddlesden
Bridge
THE
COTTAGES

River Great Ouse

Syresham Fields
Farm

Home
Wood

NN13

Biddlesden

Castle Farm

Friday's
Spinney

Briary
Wood

5

40

Longmoor
Spinney

Biddlesden
House

Abbey
House

4

Baker's
Bridge

Biddlesden Park

Westbury Circular Ride

Whitfield Wood

3

39

Dropshort
Farm

MK18

Wood
Green

2

Den
Farm

Woodgreen
Farm

Evershaw
Farm

Westbury Circular Ride

1

Mast
Evershaw
Copse

Ten Lands
Copse

38

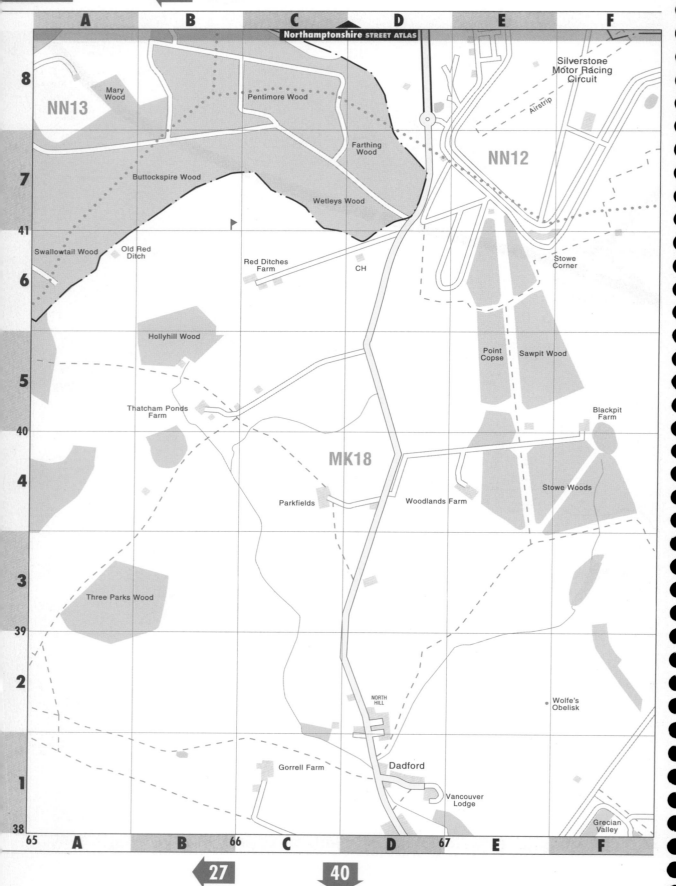

Northamptonshire STREET ATLAS

NN13

NN12

Silverstone Motor Racing Circuit

Airstrip

Mary Wood

Pentimore Wood

Farthing Wood

Buttockspire Wood

Wetleys Wood

Stowe Corner

Swallowtail Wood

Old Red Ditch

Red Ditches Farm

CH

Hollyhill Wood

Point Copse

Sawpit Wood

Blackpit Farm

Thatcham Ponds Farm

MK18

Stowe Woods

Parkfields

Woodlands Farm

Three Parks Wood

NORTH HILL

Wolfe's Obelisk

Gorrell Farm

Dadford

Vancouver Lodge

Grecian Valley

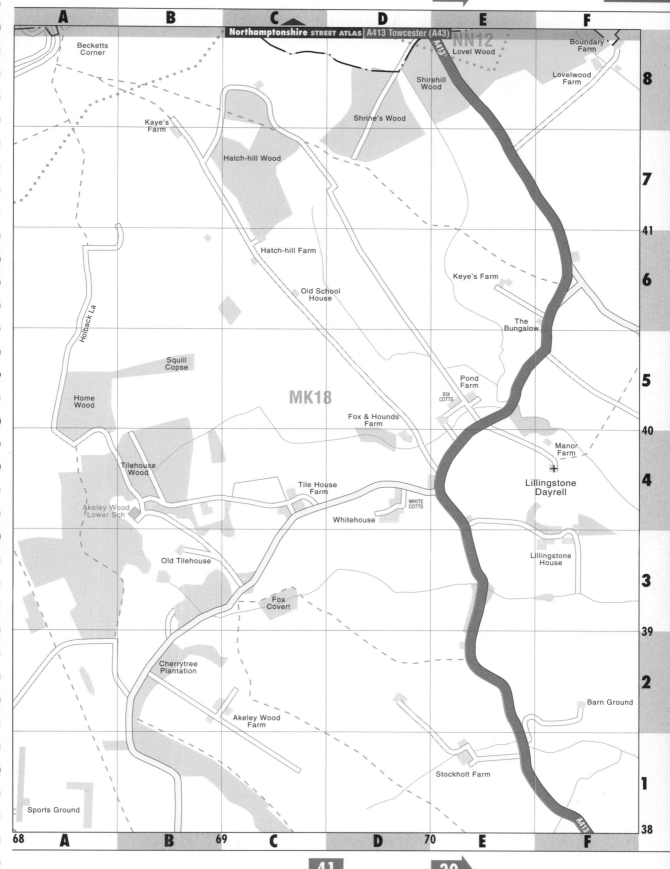

NN12

Boundary Farm

Lovel Wood

Shirehill Wood

Lovelwood Farm

8

Becketts Corner

Kaye's Farm

Shrine's Wood

Hatch-hill Wood

7

41

Hatch-hill Farm

Keye's Farm

6

Old School House

The Bungalow

Holback La

Squill Copse

Pond Farm

5

Home Wood

SIX COTTS

40

Manor Farm

Fox & Hounds Farm

Tilehouse Wood

Lillingstone Dayrell

4

Tile House Farm

WHITE COTTS

Akeley Wood Lower Sch

Whitehouse

Old Tilehouse

Lillingstone House

MK18

3

Fox Covert

39

Cherrytree Plantation

2

Barn Ground

Akeley Wood Farm

Stockholt Farm

1

Sports Ground

A413

38

29
17

A   B   C   D   E   F

8

Hill Copse

NN12

West Ashalls Copse

Manor Cotts

Manor House

Briary Wood Farm

East Ashalls Copse

DEANSHANGER DR

7

The Spinney

Briary Lodge

Long Copse

41

Manor Lodge

Forest Farm

6

Bradley Fields Farm

Valley Farm

PO

Church Farm

CHURCH LA

BROOKSIDE

Wicken Wood

Lillingstone Lovell

Notamore Copse

5

Glebe Farm

Leckhampstead Wood

Lilby Wood

MK19

40

Hall Farm

MK18

4

Hill Farm

3

39

2

1

Brook House (Ruin)

Lodge Farm

Wicken Road Farm

WICKEN RD

The Shaw

Park Copse

Pottery Farm

CHAPEL LA

Leckhampstead House

Limes End

LONG ROW

38

71   A   B   72   C   D   73   E   F

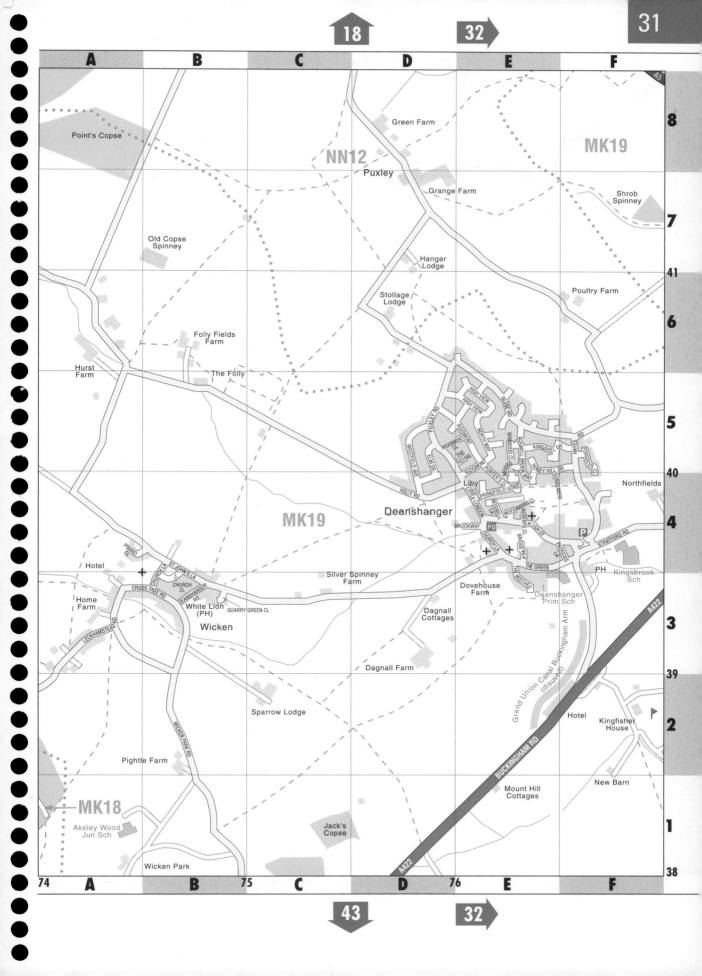

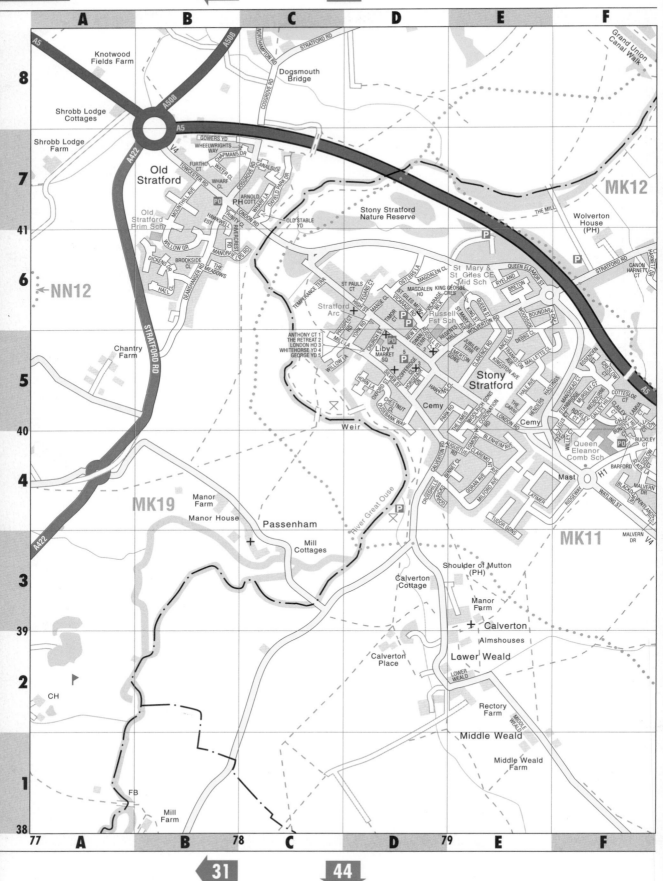

Knotwood
Fields Farm

Shrobb Lodge
Cottages

Shrobb Lodge
Farm

Old
Stratford

NN12

Chantry
Farm

MK19

Manor
Farm

Manor House

Passenham

Mill
Cottages

CH

FB

Mill
Farm

Dogsmouth
Bridge

Stony Stratford
Nature Reserve

Stratford
Arc

ANTHONY CT 1
THE RETREAT 2
LONDON HO 3
WHITEHORSE YD 4
GEORGE YD 5

Liby
MARKET SQ

Weir

River Great Ouse

St Mary &
St Giles CE
Mid Sch

Russell
Fst Sch

Stony
Stratford

Cemy

Cemy

Shoulder of Mutton
(PH)

Calverton
Cottage

Calverton

Manor
Farm

Almshouses

Lower Weald

Calverton
Place

Rectory
Farm

Middle Weald

Middle Weald
Farm

MK12

Wolverton
House
(PH)

Queen
Eleanor
Comb Sch

Mast

MK11

Grand Union
Canal Walk

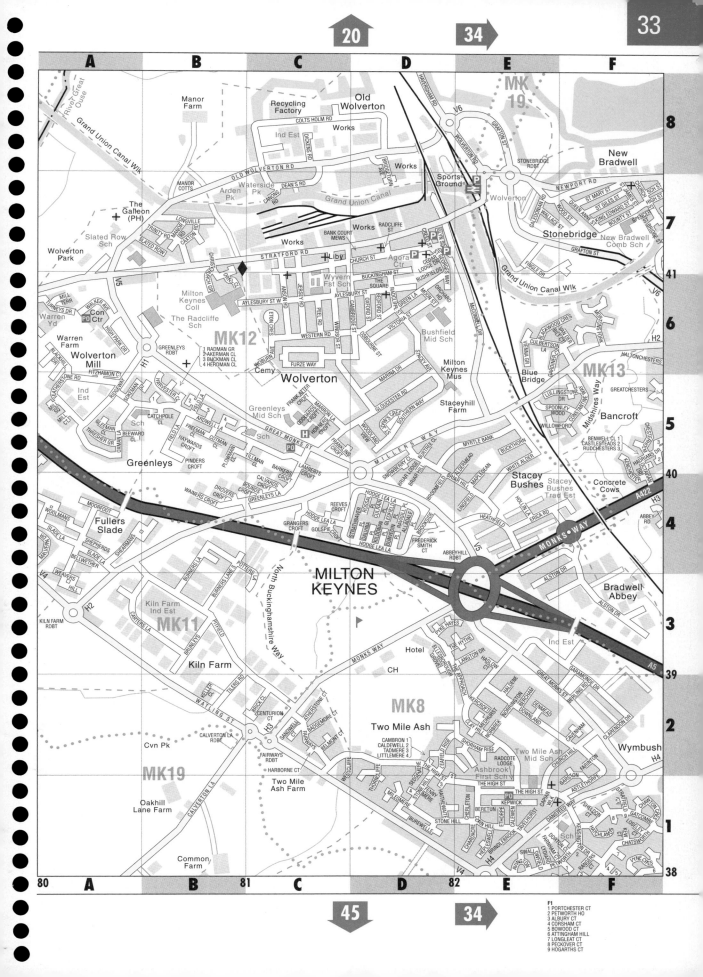

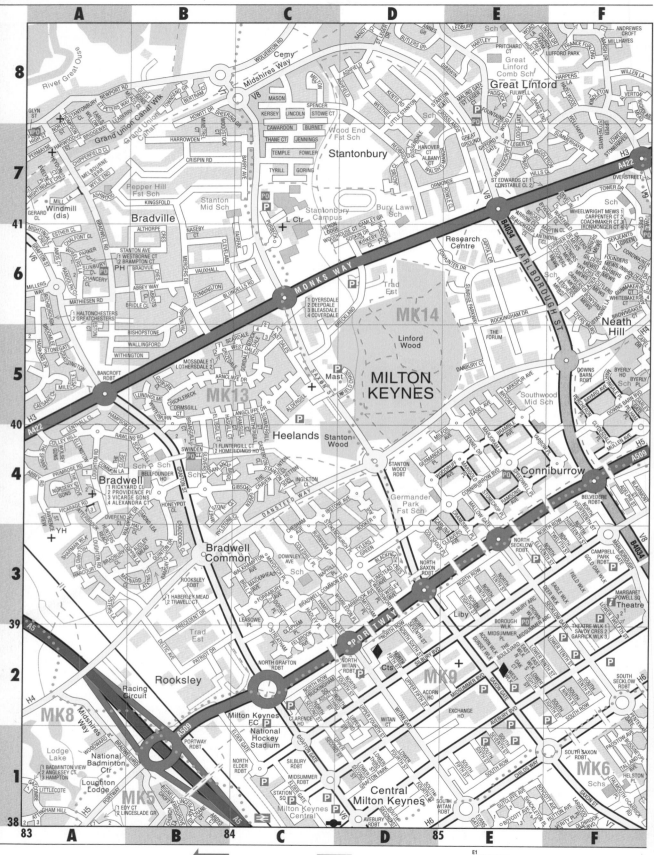

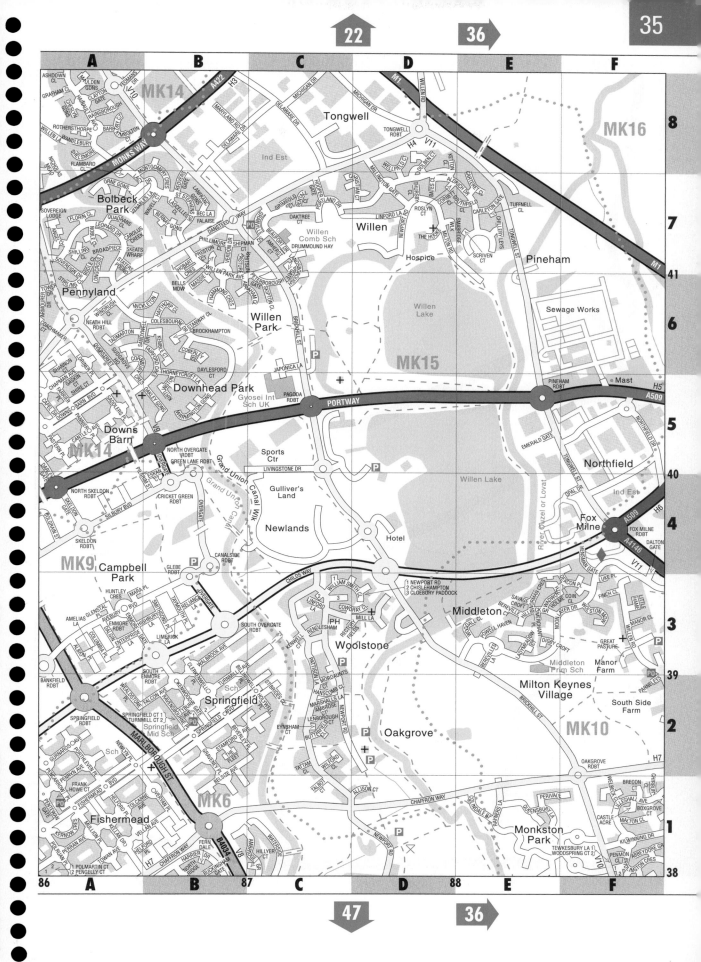

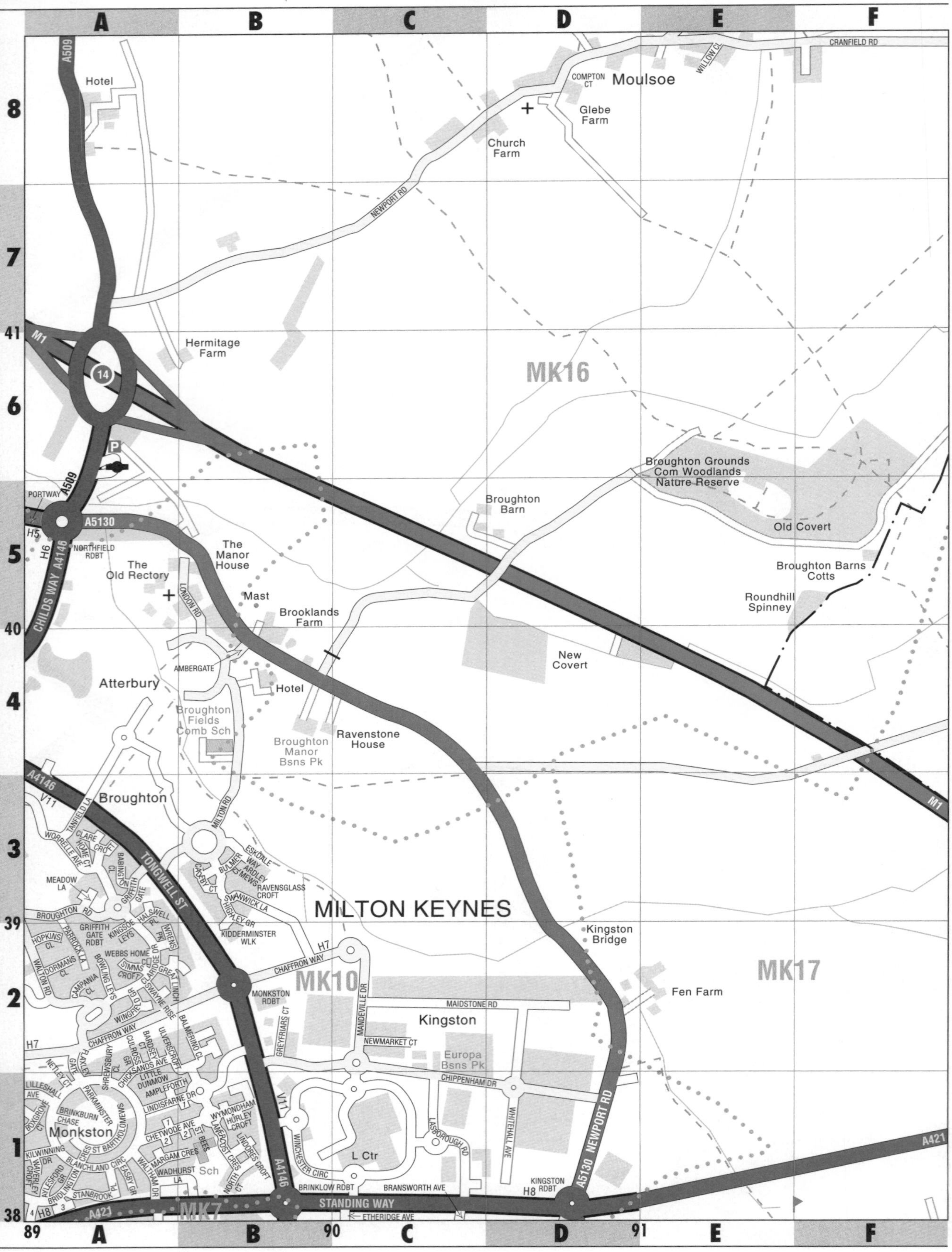

A1
1 PERSHORE CROFT
2 STAVORDALE
3 TYNEMOUTH RISE
4 LEOMINSTER GATE

B1
1 LAUNDE
2 ST BOTOLPHS

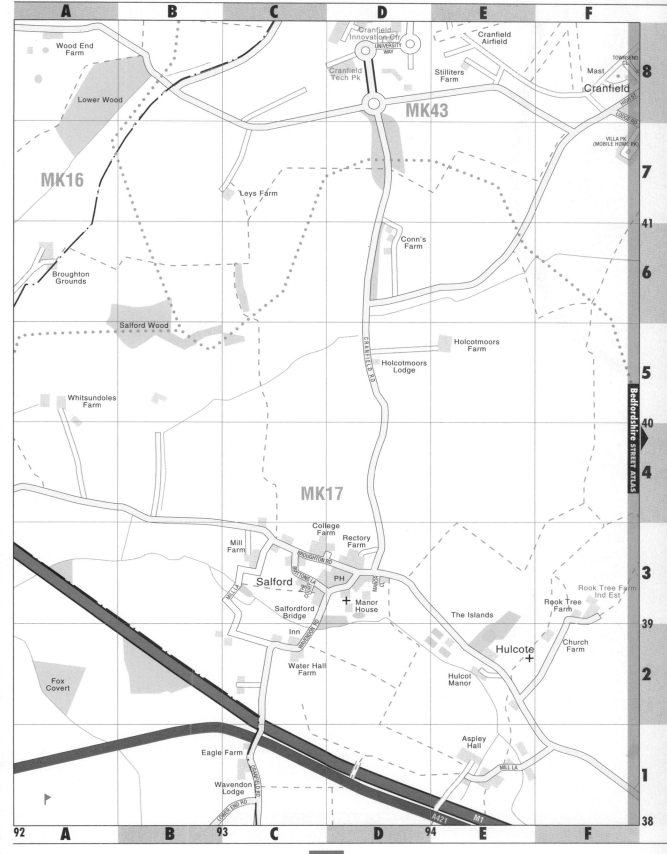

| A | B | C | D | E | F |

8

Wood End Farm

Cranfield Innovation Ctr

UNIVERSITY WAY

Cranfield Tech Pk

Cranfield Airfield

Stilliters Farm

Cranfield

Mast

TOWNSEND CL

Lower Wood

MK43

HIGH ST

LODGE RD

VILLA PK (MOBILE HOME PK)

7

MK16

Leys Farm

41

Conn's Farm

6

Broughton Grounds

Salford Wood

Cranfield Rd

Holcotmoors Farm

5

Whitsundoles Farm

Holcotmoors Lodge

40

4

MK17

College Farm

Rectory Farm

Mill Farm

BROUGHTON RD

BOTTOMS LA

THE COURT

Salford

PH

MANOR CL

Rook Tree Farm Ind Est

Rook Tree Farm

3

MILL LA

Salfordford Bridge

Inn

WAVENDON RD

Manor House

The Islands

Hulcote

Church Farm

39

Water Hall Farm

Hulcot Manor

2

Fox Covert

Eagle Farm

CRANFIELD RD

Aspley Hall

MILL LA

1

Wavendon Lodge

LOWER END RD

A421

M1

38

| 92 | A | B | 93 | C | D | 94 | E | F |

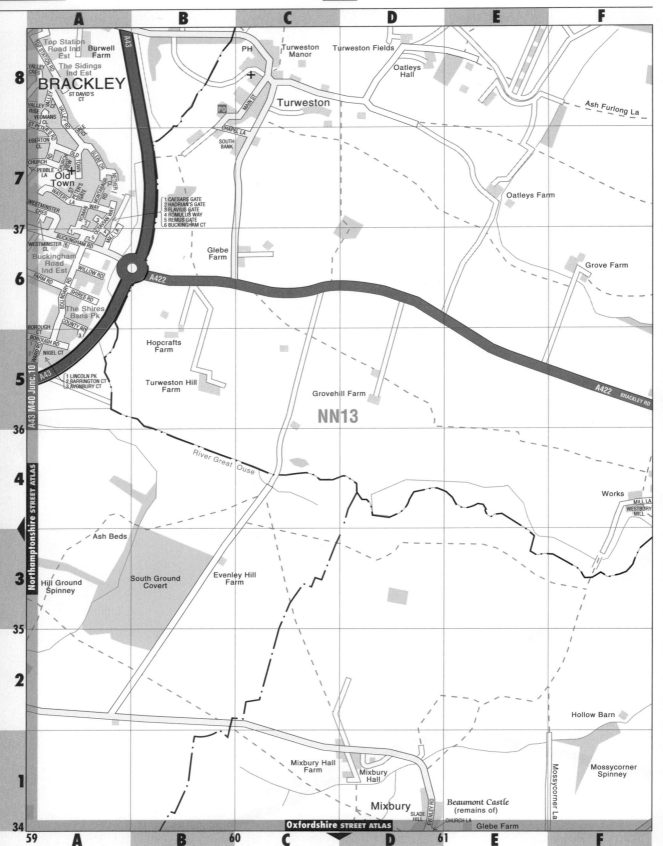

Oxfordshire STREET ATLAS

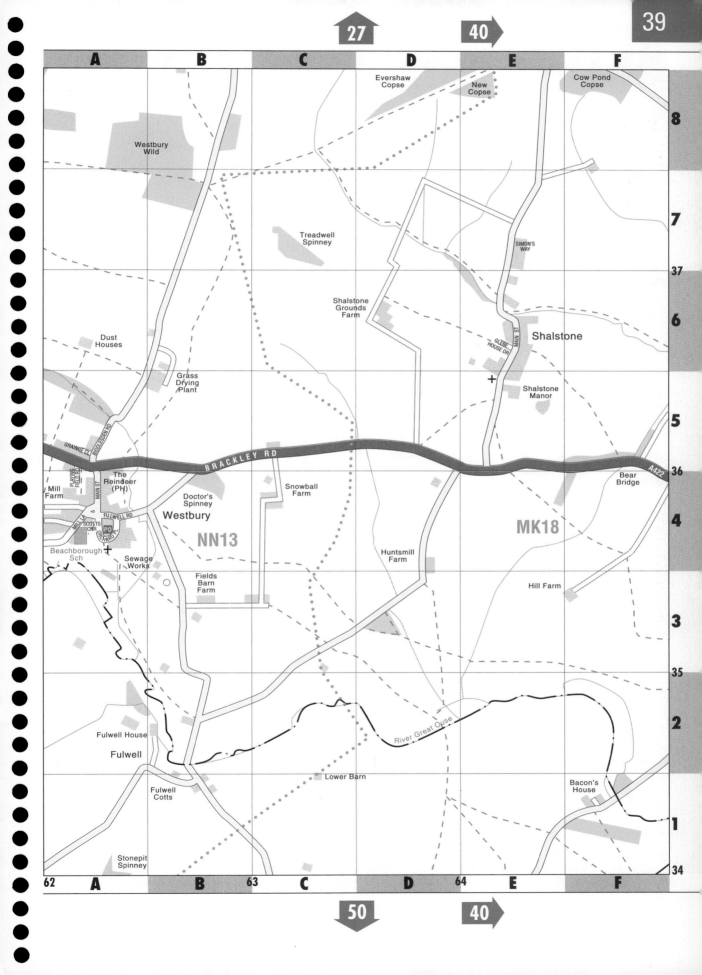

39
28

A B C D E F

8

Hill Gate
Spinney

Boycott Manor
Farm

Home Farm

Grecian Valley

Mon

Temple

Kiln Spinney

7

Boycott Manor

Stowe
Sch

Stowe
Landscape
Gardens

Shell Bridge

Stowe Park

37

CH

The Lake

6

Welsh Lane
Farm

Boycott Manor
Lodge

Weir

Temple

Oxford
Water

Ashmore Farm

5

Water
Stratford
Wood

MK18

Boycott Farm

Park Farm

36

A422

WELSH LA

Guernsey Hill
Spinney

4

Grounds Farm

Stonepit Hill
Spinney

Ford

3

Spinney Hill
Farm

The Robin Hood
(PH)

Buffler's Holt

35

Manor Farm

2

Manor Farm
Buildings

A422

Town
Farm

Water
Stratford

WATER STRATFORD RD

1

Rectory Farm

Tingewick Mill

Radclive Grange

34

65 A B 66 C D 67 E F

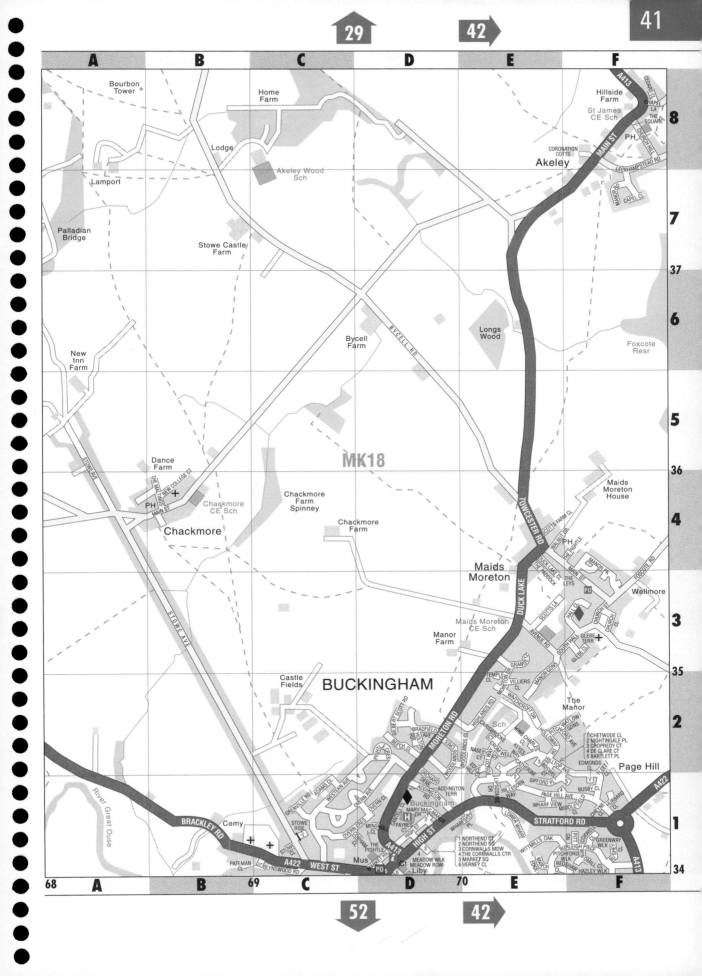

41
30

A B C D E F

8

CHAPEL LA

Duck End

Akeley

Manor Farm

THE CLOSE

LECKHAMPSTEAD RD

Willow Farm

Oak Tree Farm

Manor Farm

CHURCH END

Manor House

Middle End

Valley Farm

Limes End Bridge

WICKEN RD

The Limes

P Leckhampstead

Weatherhead Farm

Barretts End

7

Foxcote Wood

37

Home Farm

South End

Lower Farm

Limes End Farm

6

Foxcote Resr

Grove Spinney

Foxcott Wood Farm

MK18

A422

5

Ash Close Spinney

36

Foscote Manor

Foscote

Leckhampstead Wharf House

4

FOSCOTE COTTS

Hydelane Farm

Thornborough Mill

3

Home Farm

STRATFORD RD

Buckingham Canal Nature Reserve

Reservoir

35

College Farm

River Great Ouse

2

A422

Old Mill House

1

34

Sewage Works

Thornborough Grounds

71 A B 72 C D 73 E F

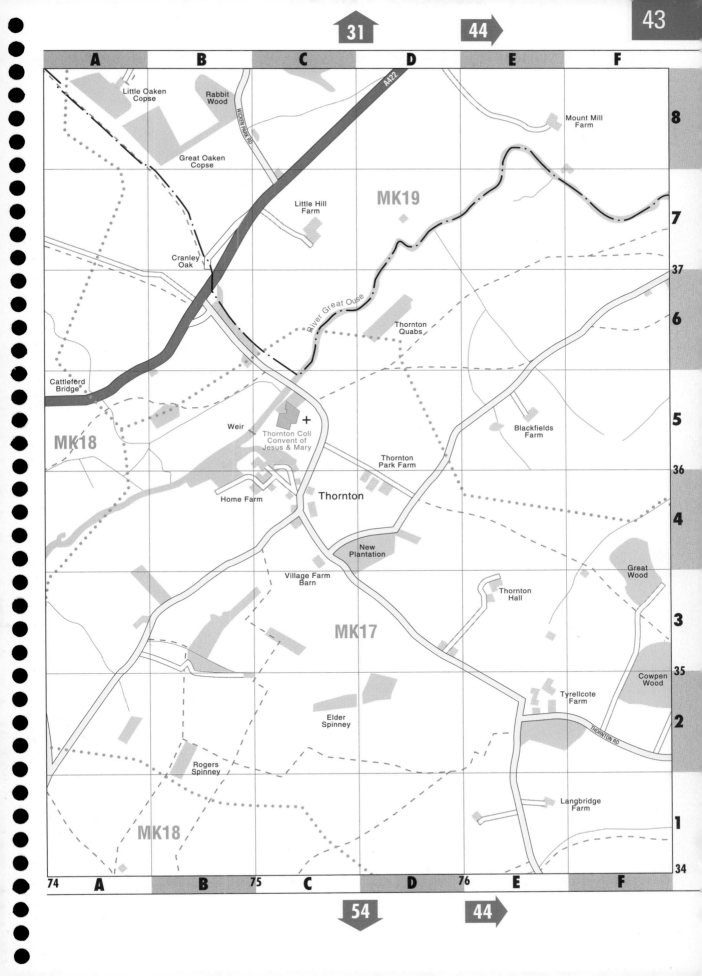

43
32

| | A | B | C | D | E | F |

8

River Great Ouse

Blacon Spinney

Upper Weald

7

Beachampton Hall

Manor Farm

Hill Farm

37

Beachampton

The Bell (PH)

MK19

6

Home Farm

WATERY LA

Red House Farm

ELMERS CL

MAIN ST

Beachampton Grove

Grange Farm

Grove Farm

5

36

School Furze

The Oaks

4

Beachampton Bsns Pk

Potash Farm

3

Furzenfield Farm

35

Elm Farm

2

MK17

Basshill Farm

Yew Tree Farm

WHADDON RD

THORNTON RD

Town's End

North Buckinghamshire Way

1

Holywell Farm

Holywell Cottages

PANTERS CL

The Hill

STRATFORD RD

Nash

HIGH ST

THORNBOROUGH RD

OLD ENGLISH CL

WINSLOW RD

Barnhill Farm

34

| 77 | A | | B | 78 | C | | D | 79 | E | | F |

43
55

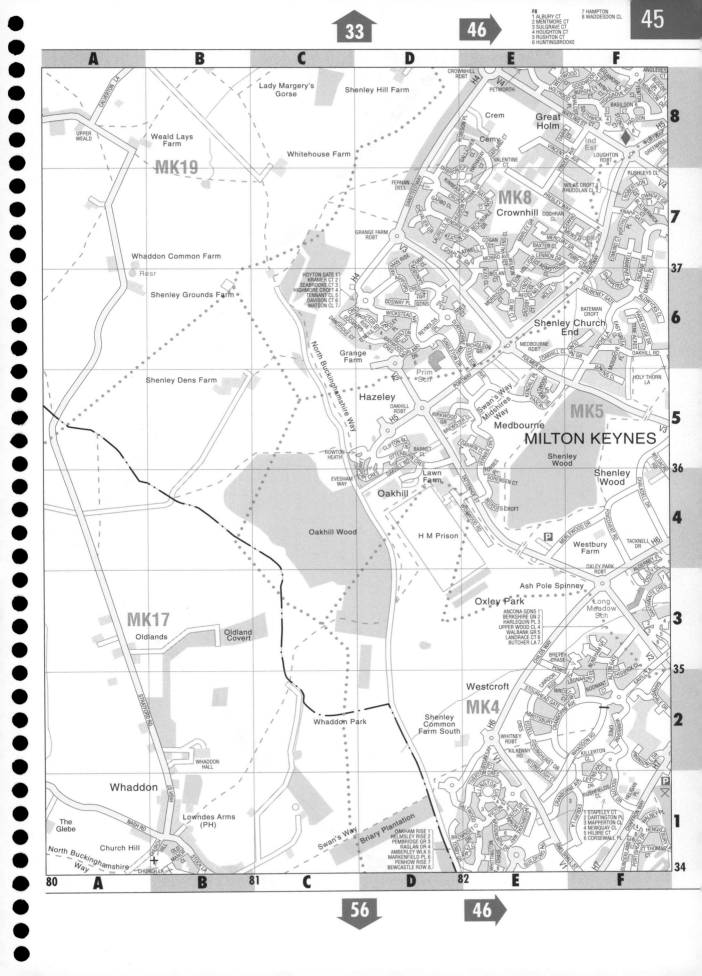

45
34

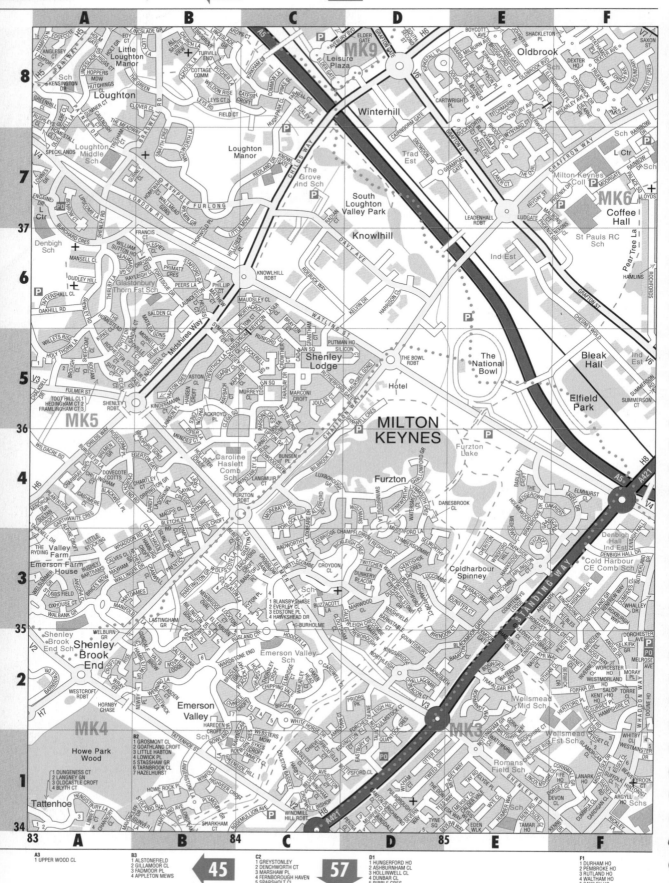

45
57

A3
1 UPPER WOOD CL

B3
1 ALSTONEFIELD
2 GILLAMOOR CL
3 FADMOOR PL
4 APPLETON MEWS

C2
1 GREYSTONLEY
2 DENCHWORTH CT
3 MARSHAW PL
4 FERNBOROUGH HAVEN
5 SPARSHOLT CL

D1
1 HUNGERFORD HO
2 ASHBURNHAM CL
3 HOLLINWELL CL
4 DUNBAR CL
5 RIBBLE CRES

F1
1 DURHAM HO
2 PEMBROKE HO
3 RUTLAND HO
4 WALTHAM HO
5 SAWLEY HO
6 NORFOLK HO
7 FLINT HO

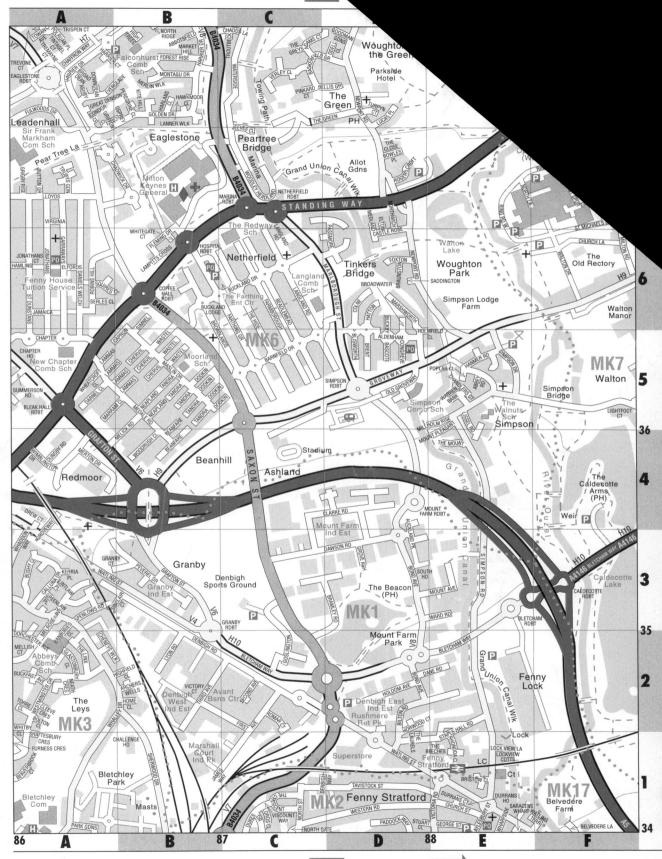

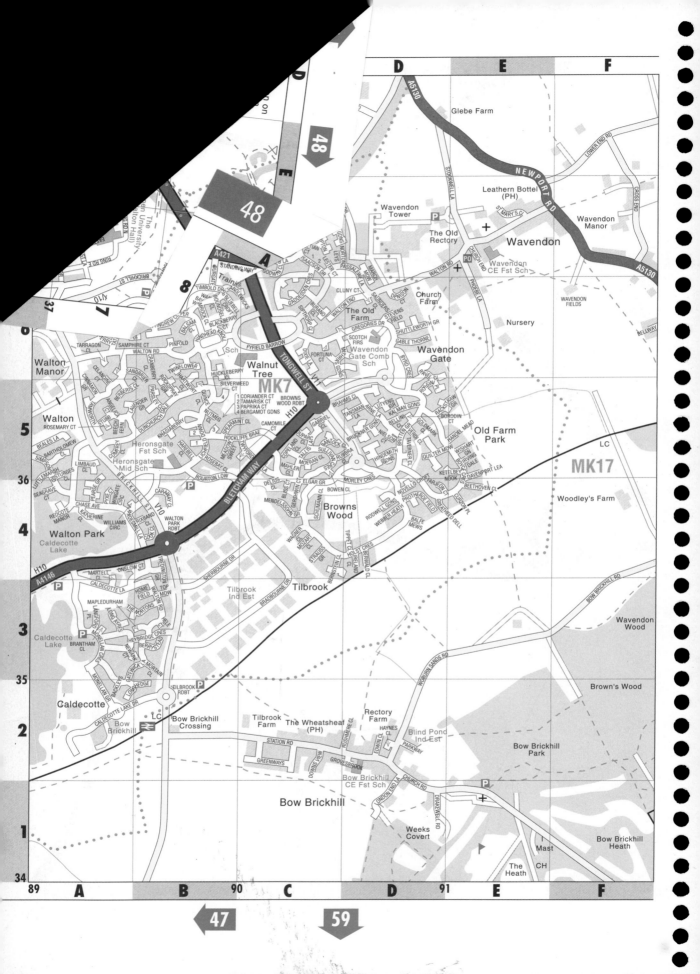

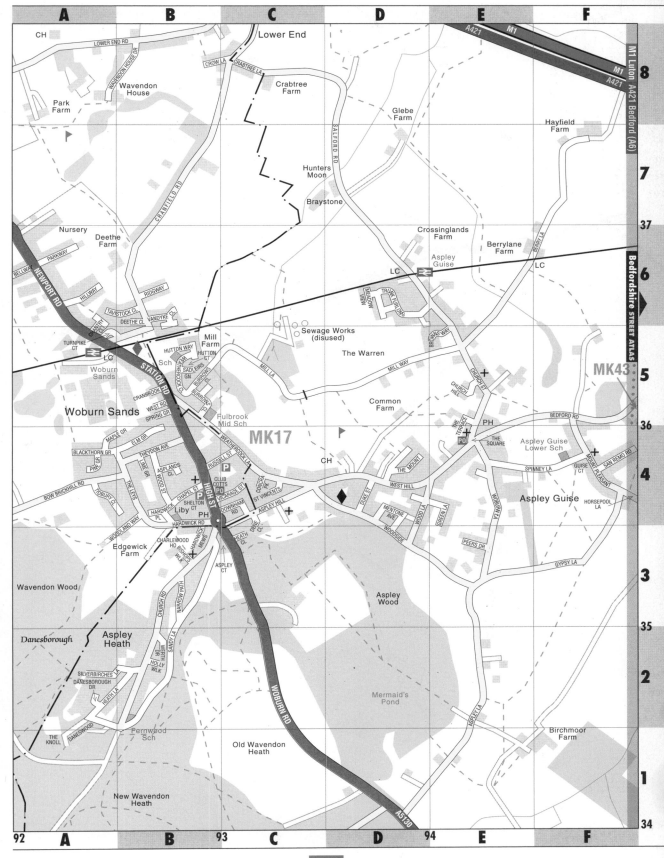

M1 Luton A421 Bedford (A6)

Bedfordshire STREET ATLAS

MK43

MK17

MK36

A **B** **C** **D** **E** **F**

92 93 94

8 7 37 6 5 36 4 3 35 2 1 34

Lower End

CH
Park Farm
Wavendon House
Crabtree Farm
Crabtree La
Crow La
Lower End Rd
Wavendon House Dr

Glebe Farm
Salford Rd
Hunters Moon
Braystone
Hayfield Farm

Nursery
Deethe Farm
Cranfield Rd
Crossinglands Farm
Berrylane Farm
Berry La

Newport Rd
Bellway
Parkway
Hillway
Ridgway
Deethe Cl
Vandyke
Tavistock Cl
LC
Aspley Guise
LC

Turnpike Ct
LC
Woburn Sands
Station Rd
Mill Farm
Sch
Hutton Way
Hutton Ct
Sadleirs
GN
Burrows
Burrons
Sewage Works (disused)
The Warren
Mill La
Meadow View
Trunk Furlong
Brogmag Way
Church Hill
Church St
PH
The Terrace
PO
The Square

Cranbrook
West Rd
Spring Gr
Fulbrook Mid Sch
MK17
Common Farm
Mill Way
The Mount
The Square
Aspley Guise Lower Sch

Maple Gr
Elm Gr
Blackthorn Gr
Pink Gr
Theydon Ave
Line Gr
Asplands Cl
Wood St
Russell St
Club Cotts
PO
Concra Pk
St Vincents
CH
West Hill
West Hill
Wood La
Green La
Spinney La
Woburn La
Aspley Guise
San Remo Rd
Guise Ct
Mount Pleasant
Horsepool La

Bow Brickhill Rd
Tubury Cl
The Leys
High St
Shelton
P
Chapel St
Vicarage St
Downham Rd
Aspley Hill
Duke St
Mentone Ave
Woodside
Peers Dr
Gypsy La

Hardwick Pl
Liby
Ct
PH
Hardwick Rd
Drive Cl
Heath Cl
Aspley Ct

Woodland Way
Edgewick Farm
Charlewood Ho
Narrow Path
Church Rd
Aspley Heath
Danesborough

Wavendon Wood
Silverbirches
Danesborough Dr
Heath Lk
Holly Wlk
Sandy La
Werth Dr

Aspley Wood
Woburn Rd
Mermaid's Pond
Aspley La
Birchmoor Farm

The Knoll
Daneswood
Fernwood Sch
Old Wavendon Heath
New Wavendon Heath
A5130

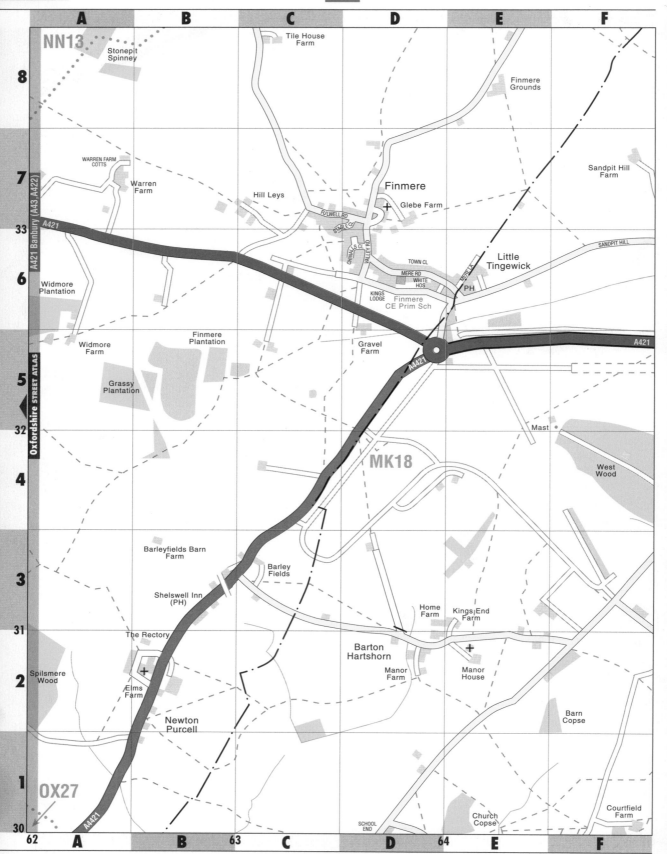

NN13

Stonepit Spinney

Tile House Farm

Finmere Grounds

WARREN FARM COTTS

Warren Farm

Hill Leys

Sandpit Hill Farm

Finmere

FULWELL RD

Glebe Farm

A421 Banbury (A43, A422)

A421

33

STABLE CL

Little Tingewick

SANDPIT HILL

Widmore Plantation

CHINALLS CL

VALLEY RD

TOWN CL

6

MERE RD

MERE LA

WHITE HOS

PH

KINGS LODGE

Finmere CE Prim Sch

Widmore Farm

Finmere Plantation

Gravel Farm

A421

Grassy Plantation

A4421

Mast

32

West Wood

Oxfordshire STREET ATLAS

5

MK18

4

Barleyfields Barn Farm

Barley Fields

Home Farm

Kings End Farm

Shelswell Inn (PH)

31

The Rectory

Barton Hartshorn

Manor House

Spilsmere Wood

Manor Farm

Barn Copse

Elms Farm

2

Newton Purcell

OX27

A4421

SCHOOL END

Church Copse

Courtfield Farm

30

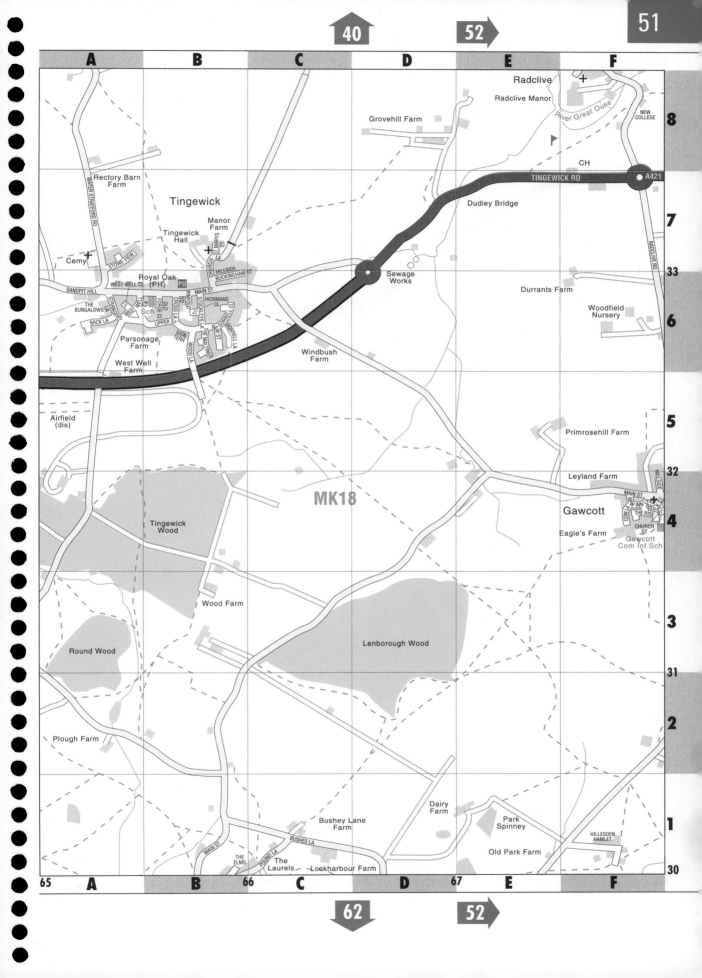

A   B   C   D   E   F

Radclive

Radclive Manor

River Great Ouse

NEW COLLEGE

8

Grovehill Farm

CH

TINGEWICK RD   A421

Rectory Barn Farm

WATER STRATFORD RD

Tingewick

7

Dudley Bridge

Manor Farm

Tingewick Hall

CHURCH ST   ST MARYS CT

33

Cemy

STOWE VIEW

Durrants Farm

HILLSIDE   BUCKINGHAM ST

Royal Oak (PH)   PO

RADCLIVE RD

Woodfield Nursery

SANDPIT HILL   WEST WELL CL

6

MAIN ST

HICKMANS CL

THE BUNGALOWS

STRANGERS LA

WEST WELL LA

Sch

OLD FORGE CL   CROSS LA   NEW ST   GORRELL LA

BACK LA

PINFOLD

UPPER ST

Parsonage Farm

SION TERR

WOOD LA   THE MALTINGS   STOCKLEYS LA

Windbush Farm

Sewage Works

West Well Farm

5

Airfield (dis)

Primrosehill Farm

32

Leyland Farm

MAIN ST   HILLSIDE

MK18

NEW INN   BACK ST   THE RISE

Gawcott

COW LA

Tingewick Wood

4

Eagle's Farm

CHURCH ST

Gawcott Com Inf Sch

Wood Farm

3

Lenborough Wood

Round Wood

31

Plough Farm

2

Dairy Farm

Park Spinney

1

HILLESDEN HAMLET

Bushey Lane Farm

BUSHES LA

MAIN ST   POUND LA

THE ELMS

The Laurels   Lockharbour Farm

Old Park Farm

30

65   A   B   66   C   D   67   E   F

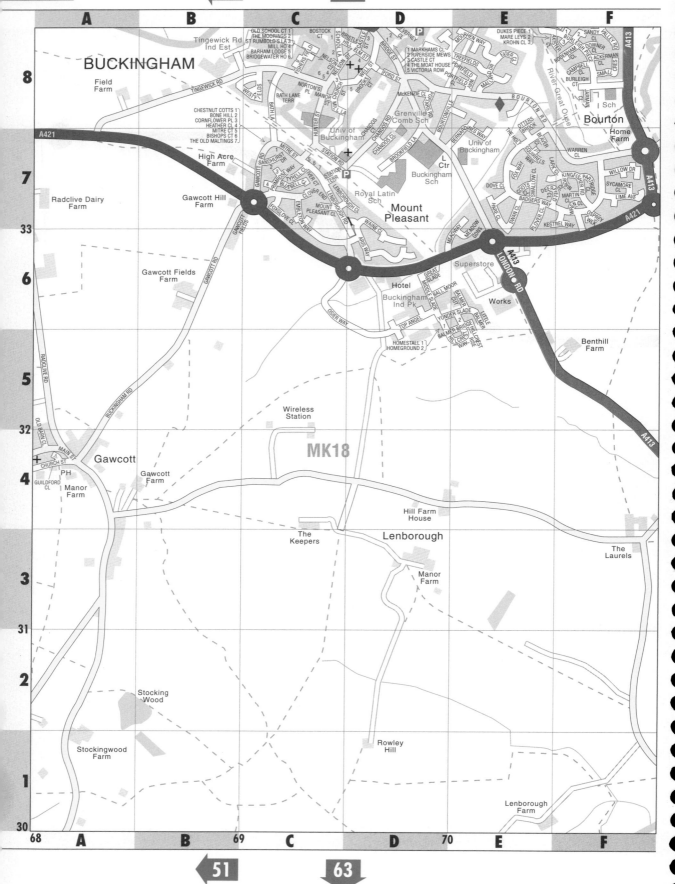

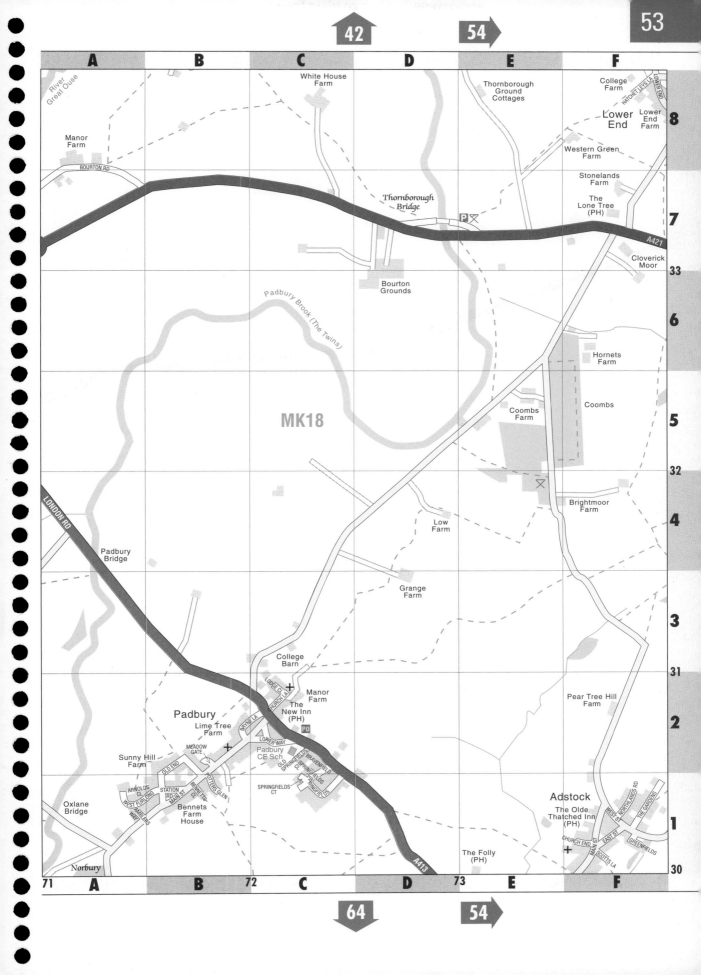

A | B | C | D | E | F

8

Ford

Home Farm

Thornborough Inf Sch

BACK ST

LOWER END

HIGH ST

CHAPEL LA

THE GREEN

PALMERS MOOR

Thornborough

The Two Brewers (PH)

THORNHILL

NASH RD

BRIDGE ST

SPROUT LA

Coates Farm

Bungalow Farm

Willow Farm

Brakes Farm

THORNBOROUGH RD

Dancer's Grave

Nansley's Brake

Nash End Farm

Middle Shelspit Farm

7

MK18

33

The Folly

Priory Farm

A421

Lower Shelspit

Upper Shelspit Farm

6

Maywynn Farm

Mangland Farm

A421

Poultry Farm

Singleborough

5

Dean Farm

Laurel Farm

32

Pilch Farm

MK17

PILCH LA

Great Furze House

Sch

4

SCHOOL END 1

SINGLEBOROUGH LA 2

3

Home Farm

B4033

31

Adstockfields House

Adstockfields Farm

Wigwell Farm

2

Midshires Way

North Buckinghamshire Way

WINSLOW RD

B4033

1

30

74 | A | B | 75 | C | D | 76 | E | F

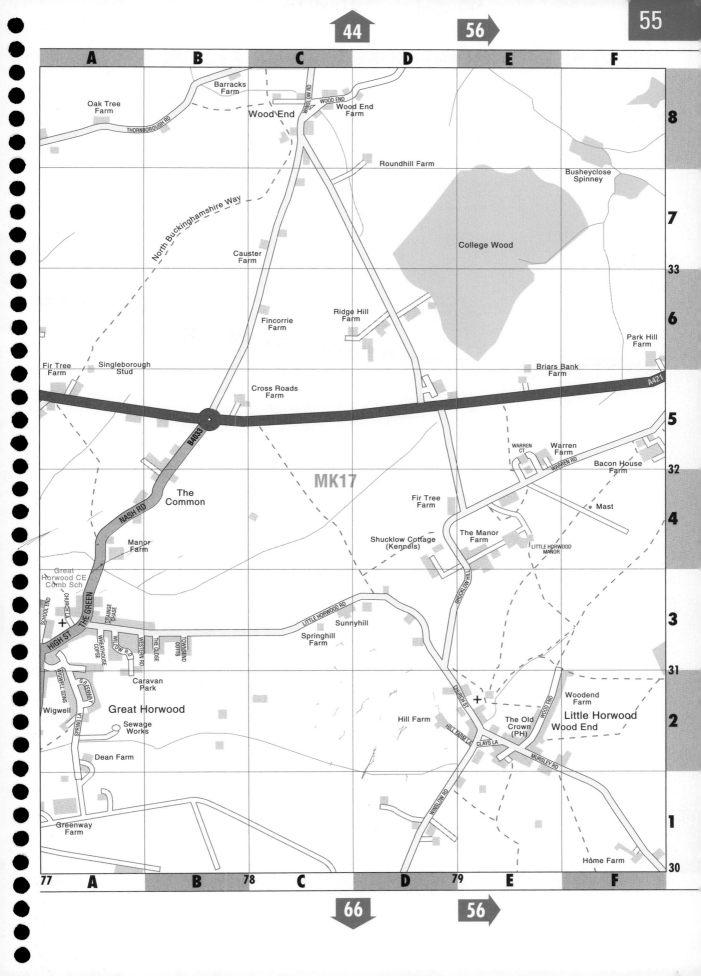

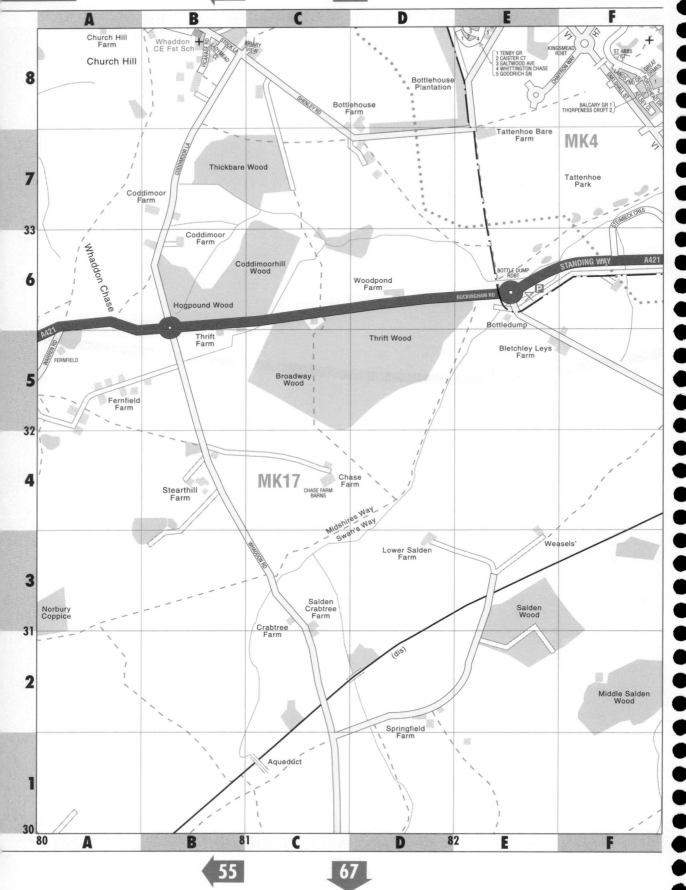

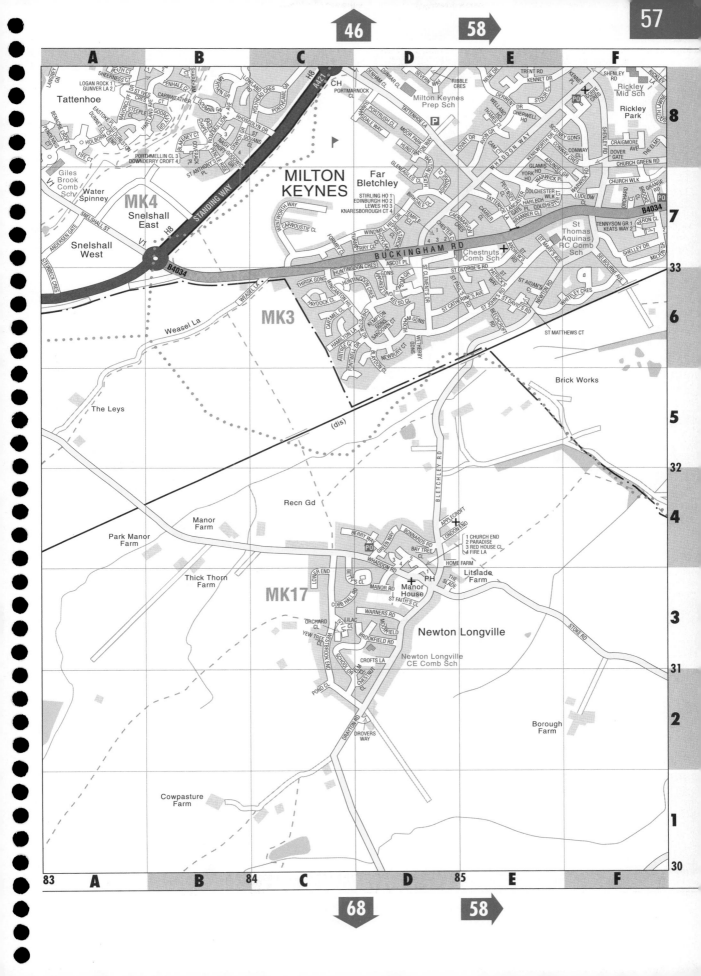

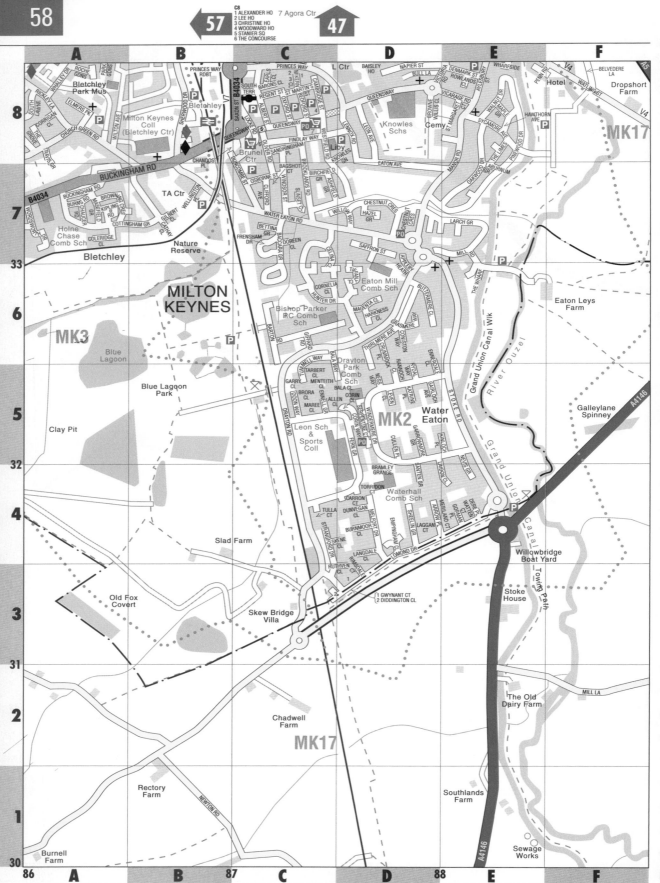

C8
1 ALEXANDER HO   7 Agora Ctr
2 LEE HO
3 CHRISTINE HO
4 WOODWARD HO
5 STANIER SQ
6 THE CONCOURSE

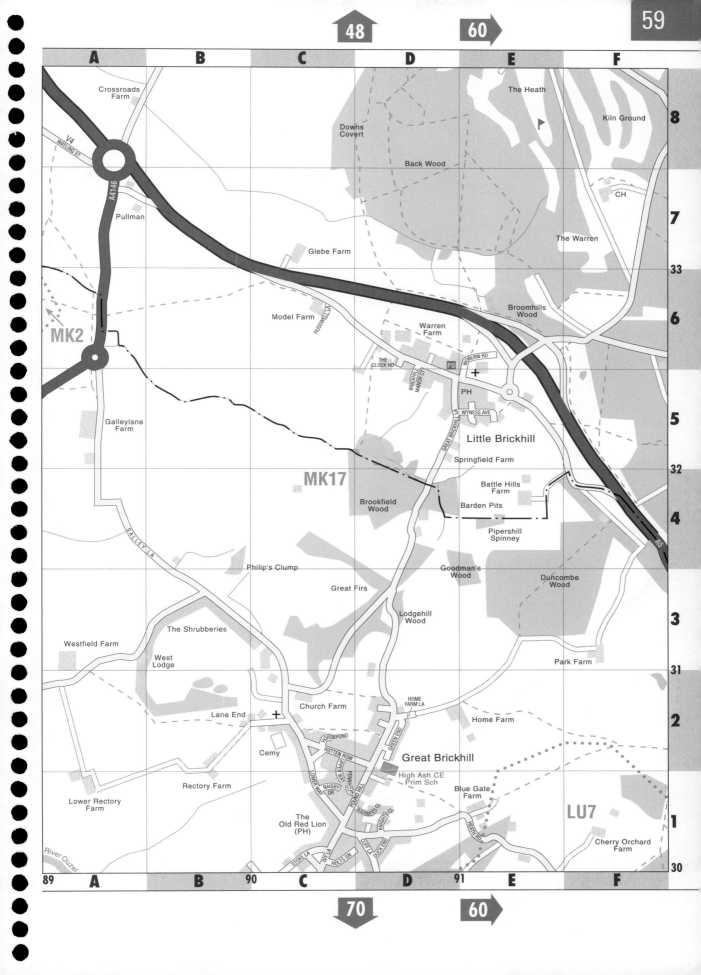

A B C D E F

8

Crossroads
Farm

The Heath

Kiln Ground

Downs
Covert

Back Wood

CH

V4
WATLING ST

A4146

7

Pullman

The Warren

33

Glebe Farm

Broomhills
Wood

6

MK2

Model Farm

RUSSWELLA

Warren
Farm

THE
CLOCK HO

PO

WOBURN RD

PH

GREAT BRICKHILL

WYNESS AVE

Little Brickhill

5

Galleylane
Farm

BRICKHILL MANOR CT

Springfield Farm

32

MK17

Brookfield
Wood

Battle Hills
Farm

Barden Pits

4

GALLEY LA

Pipershill
Spinney

A5

Philip's Clump

Goodman's
Wood

Duncombe
Wood

3

Great Firs

Lodgehill
Wood

The Shrubberies

Westfield Farm

Park Farm

31

West
Lodge

Lane End

Church Farm

HOME
FARM LA

Home Farm

2

Cemy

HORSEPOND

GREEN END

Great Brickhill

ROTTEN ROW

UPPER WAY

LOWER WAY

NAISBY
DR

PENNYCUCK HILL

High Ash CE
Prim Sch

Blue Gate
Farm

LU7

1

Rectory Farm

Lower Rectory
Farm

The
Old Red Lion
(PH)

KNIGHTS CL

WARNESS CL

CLIFF LA

DUCK END

HEATH RD

Cherry Orchard
Farm

River Ouzel

STOKE LA

IVY LA

HOLTS GN

30

A B C D E F

8

New Wavendon Heath

P

The Birch
(PH)

A5130 WOBURN RD

NEWPORT RD A5130

BIRCHMOOR GN

CRAWLEY RD A4012

DRAKELOE CL

ELEANOR CL

Dolton's
Farm

Horsemoor
Farm

Bells
Copse

Tollhouse
Grove

Hundreds
Farm

7

CASWELL LA

ELEANOR
WLK

BEDFORD ST

PO

STAUNTON
HO

MARQUIS CT

Woburn Lower
Sch

TH

Woburn

MARKET

PARK

A4012 Leighton Buzzard

Little Brickhill
Copse

33

Charle Wood

GEORGE ST

TIMBER LA

HOWLAND
PL

DUCK LA

LONDON END

Maryland
Coll

LEIGHTON ST

BLOOMSBURY
PL

6

Shire Oak

Pinfold Pond

Wayn Close

Pinfoldpond

Crowholt
Plantation

Lowe's Wood

Job's Farm

Greensand Ridge Wlk

5

Utcoate
Grange

Circuitt's
Covert

32

Buttermilk
Farm

MK17

4

Buttermilk Wood

A5

Bedfordshire STREET ATLAS

3

Nun Wood

Apesfield
Farm

Sheeplane
Belt

31

2

Rammamere
Farm

SHEEPLANE

The
Fox
& Hounds
(PH)

Bushycommon
Wood

Hill Farm

1

Sand Pit

King's Wood

WOBURN RD

LU7

Arnold's
Cottages

Bragenham Wood

A5

30

Rammamere
Heath

LU7

A5 Dunstable

92 A B 93 C D 94 E F

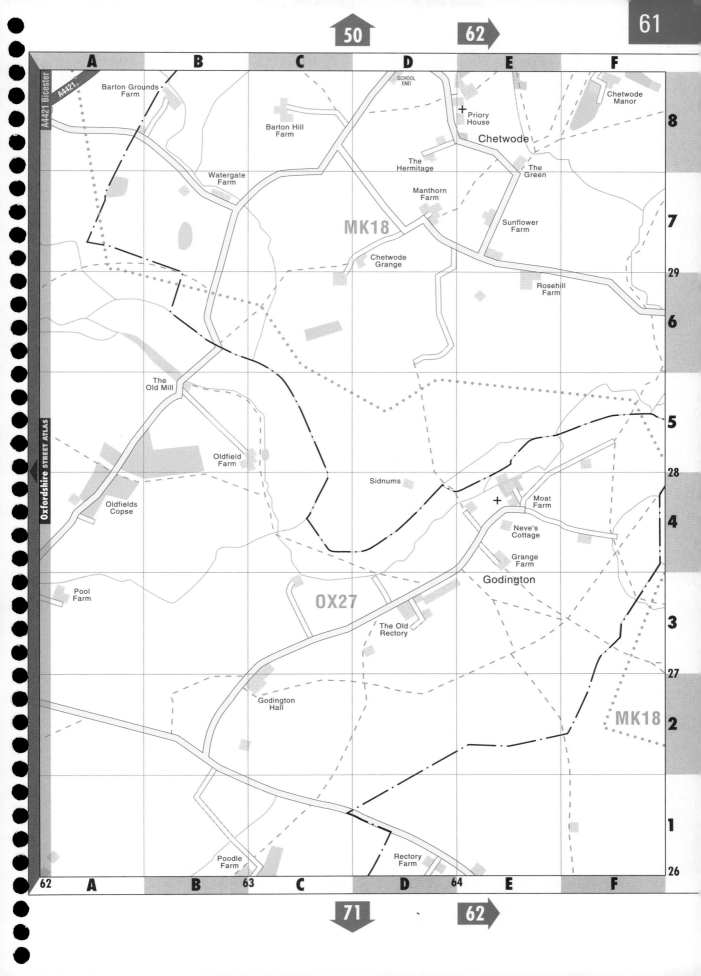

A4421 Bicester
A4421

Oxfordshire STREET ATLAS

A   B   C   D   E   F

Barton Grounds Farm

Barton Hill Farm

Watergate Farm

SCHOOL END

+ Priory House

Chetwode

The Hermitage

The Green

Manthorn Farm

Chetwode Manor

MK18

Sunflower Farm

Chetwode Grange

Rosehill Farm

The Old Mill

Oldfield Farm

Sidnums

Moat Farm

Oldfields Copse

+

Neve's Cottage

Grange Farm

Godington

Pool Farm

OX27

The Old Rectory

Godington Hall

MK18

Poodle Farm

Rectory Farm

62   A   B   63   C   D   64   E   F

8
7
29
6
5
28
4
3
27
2
1
26

61
51

A **B** **C** **D** **E** **F**

8

Church Farm
Old Hat (PH)
The Laurels
The Common
Preston Bissett
SCHOOL LA
THE SQUARE
Thorpes Farm
Poplars Farm

Jubilee Farm House
Jubilee Farm
College Farm

7

Fir Tree Cottage
Copperhouse Farm
Buryfield Spinney

29

6

Casemore Farm

Westfield Farm
Manor Farm

5

MK18

28

Cowley Farm

OX27

4

Cowley Old House

Cowley Lodge

3

Twyford Mill

Three Bridge Mill

27

Church View Farm

2

Seven Stars (PH)

Twyford CE Sch
GRANGE
CHURCH ST
SCHOOL LA
MILL LA
MAIN ST
Home Farm

OX27

1

Twyford
Hall
PO
Crown (PH)
BICESTER RD
PORTWAY RD
ROSEHILL CRES
Portway Cottages
MANOR CT

26

65 **A** **B** 66 **C** **D** 67 **E** **F**

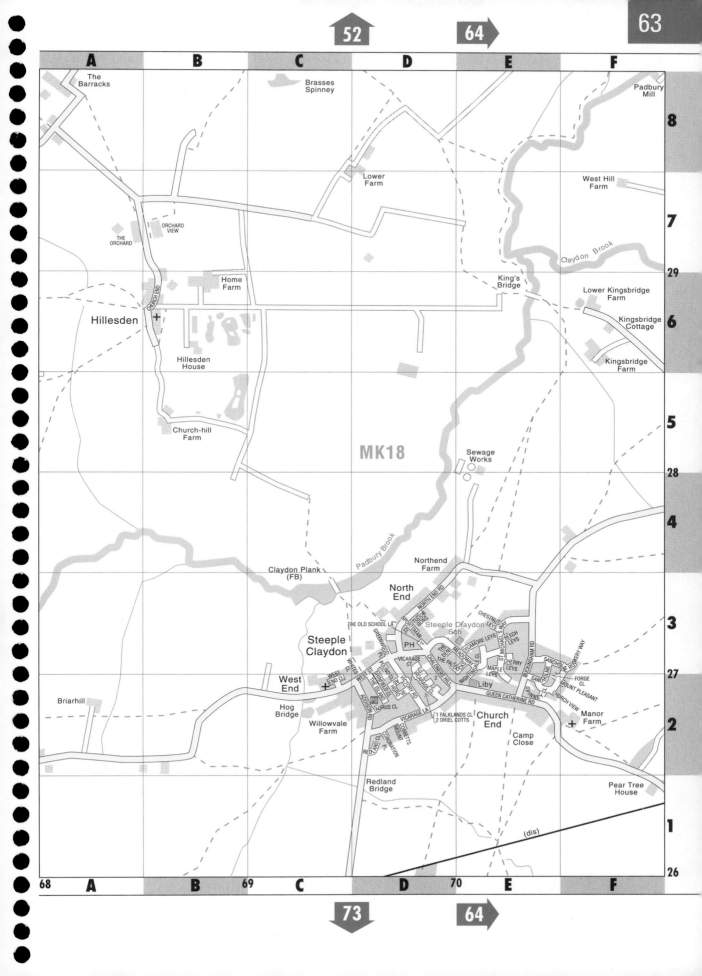

63
53

A **B** **C** **D** **E** **F**

A413

Folly Farm

Adstock Manor

A413

8

Wardens Farm

Padburyhill Farm

7

White Bridge

29

Hill Farm
Cottages

6

Hill Farm

Claydon Brook

MK18

5

Herd's Hill
Cottage

Claydon Hill Farm
No 6

Claydon Hill Farm
No 5

28

Claydon Hill Farm

Swan's Way

4

Jubilee Bridge

HERD'S HILL

Windmillhill Farm

Verney
Junction

Littleworth Farm

The Verney Arms
(Hotel)

JUBILEE
COTTS

3

Littleworth

(dis)

Ashmore Farm House

27

Greenacres

Sandhill

2

Mount Pleasant
Farm

Sandhill

Sandhill Farm

North Buckinghamshire Way

RAILWAY
COTTS

LC

Rectory Farm

1

26

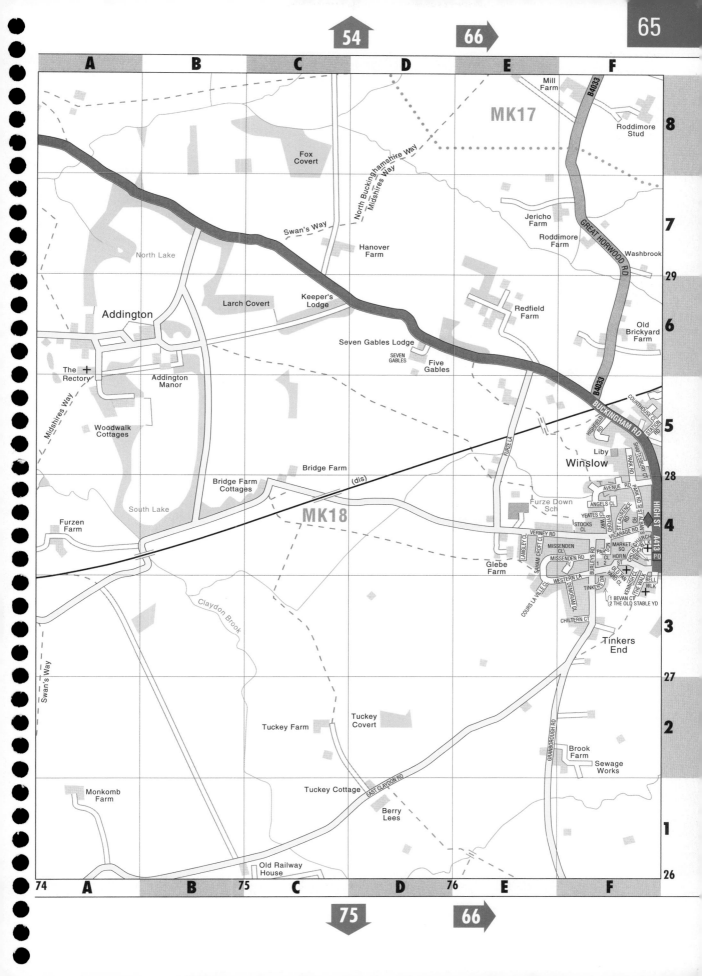

65
55

A   B   C   D   E   F

8

Greenway Farm

Mount Pleasant

The Hollows

Horwood House

7

Osierbed Spinney

Fishpond Spinney

29

The White House

(dis)

Moco Farm

Roddimore Covert

6

Clare Farm

Canada

Foxhole Farm

1 STATION COTTS
2 OLD STATION CL

TANK HOUSE RD

MAGPIE LAKE CL

Spring Corner

MK17

Dodley Hill Farm

Midshires Way

COMERFORD WAY

McLERNON WAY

THE SPINNEY

RUDDS CL

FLEDGELINGS WLK

INGWELL LA

TTS CL

5

Station Rd Ind Est

Station Rd

Old Mill Furlong

SCOTT EVANS CT

LONGLANDS CT

KEACH CL

LAM CL

SINS

MEETING OAK LA

Redhall Farm

Abovemead Farm

LOADES WAY

Winslow CE Comb Sch

BEAMISH WAY

28

CRICKETERS ROW

OAKWAY

ELMFIELDS GATE

NORTH CROFT

CAMPUS

MK18

P

P

4

GREYHOUND CT

FAIR MDN

SHEPHERDS ROW

ELMSIDE

ROVERS END

Winslow

Ivy Farm

COPSE GATE

Duck End

OLD END

CHARLTON CL

A413

SHEEP ST

Hotel

Shipton Mead Farm

CLAYCUTTERS

FENNY CL

LYNE CL

B4032

SHIPTON

Rands Farm

B4032

WINSLOW RD

3

Jubilee Cottages

Shipton Farm

27

Shipton Bridge

Swanbourne House Sch

2

Claydon Brook

Haybush Farm

1

Midshires Way

Swan's Way

26

Bennett's Hill

North Hill Farm

A413

77   A   B   78   C   D   79   E   F

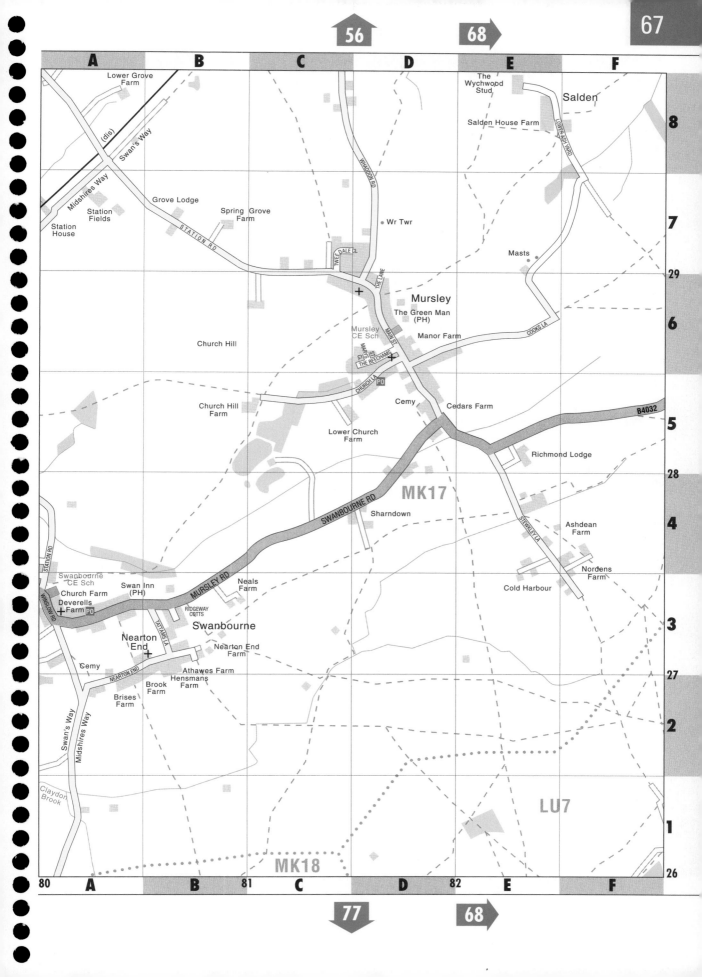

| A | B | C | D | E | F |

Lower Grove Farm

Swan's Way

(dis)

Midshires Way

Grove Lodge

Station Fields

Station House

STATION RD

Spring Grove Farm

WHADDON RD

Wr Twr

The Wychwood Stud

Salden

Salden House Farm

LOWER ASH YARD

8

7

29

TWEEDALE CL

THE LANE

Masts

COOKS LA

Mursley

The Green Man (PH)

Church Hill

Mursley CE Sch

THE BEECHAMS

MARY'S CL

Manor Farm

6

Church Hill Farm

CHURCH LA

PO

Cemy

Lower Church Farm

Cedars Farm

B4032

Richmond Lodge

5

28

MK17

SWANBOURNE RD

Sharndown

STEWKLEY LA

Ashdean Farm

Nordens Farm

4

Swanbourne CE Sch

Church Farm

Swan Inn (PH)

Deverells Farm PO

OLD WINDMILL

STATION RD

MURSLEY RD

Neals Farm

RIDGEWAY COTTS

TATTAMS LA

Swanbourne

Cold Harbour

3

27

Nearton End

Nearton End Farm

NEARTON END

Cemy

Athawes Farm

Hensmans Farm

Brook Farm

Brises Farm

2

Swan's Way

Midshires Way

Claydon Brook

LU7

1

MK18

8

Ash Farm

Highfield

Villiers Farm

NEWTON RD

Drayton Crossroad Farm

7

29

Prospect Farm

MK17

CARRINGTON HALL RD

HIGHWAY

PROSPECT CL

STONES WAY

6

NEWMANS CTYD

Drayton Parslow Village Sch

Chestnut Farm

The Lower Farm

LOVE ROW

Sewage Works

Manor Farm

BATES GDNS

CALDEN CL

BELL RD

NORTH CL

CHAPEL LA

NEW RD

NEW RD

PH

Drayton Parslow

Bungler's Hall

Kingsland Farm

MAIN RD

Church End

Stokeroad Farm

5

B4032

28

Merrymead

4

Old Leighton Farm

BLETCHLEY RD

Grange Farm

LU7

3

The Grange

HAYWOOD PK

North End

Heywood House

27

Lower Dean Farm

Lansdowne Farm

White Horse Lodge

Laurel Farm

Stewkley House

Upper Dean Farm

HIGH ST N

STOCKHALL CRES

SYCAMORE CL

Stewkley

2

DEAN RD

Stewkley Dean

Sycamore Farm

Bonham Farm

Dean Farm

St Michael's CE Comb Sch

PH

IVY LA

FISHWEIR

CHAPEL SQ

Liby

Church Farm

1

26

Dean Tithe Farm

Bury Farm

ST MICHAELS CL

SOULBURY RD B4032

TYTHE GDNS

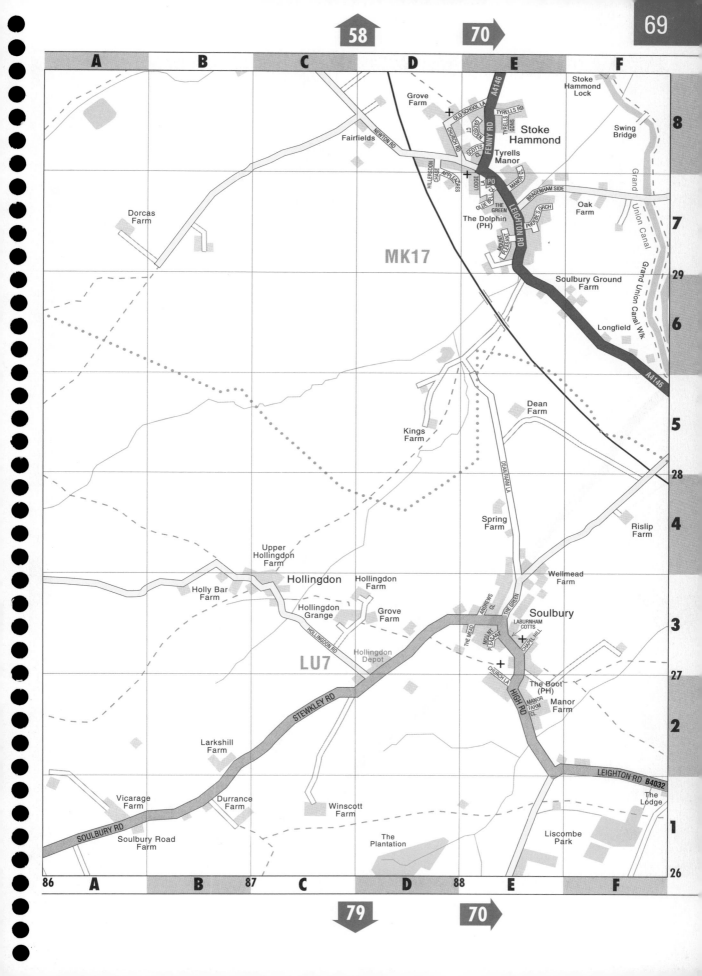

A B C D E F

8

7

29

6

5

28

4

3

27

2

26

Stoke Hammond Lock

Swing Bridge

Grand Union Canal

Grand Union Canal Wk

A4146

Grove Farm

Fairfields

OLD SCHOOL LA

TYRELLS RD

TYRELLS GDNS

Stoke Hammond

CHURCH RD

FENNY RD

SCOTTS CL

THE GREEN

Tyrells Manor

MANOR RD

BRAGENHAM SIDE

PROBE'S ORCH

The Dolphin (PH)

LEIGHTON RD

MOUNT PLEASANT

Oak Farm

Soulbury Ground Farm

Longfield

NEWTON RD

Dorcas Farm

MK17

Kings Farm

Dean Farm

DEAN FARM LA

Spring Farm

Rislip Farm

Upper Hollingdon Farm

Holly Bar Farm

Hollingdon

Hollingdon Farm

Hollingdon Grange

Grove Farm

HOLLINGDON RD

Hollingdon Depot

LU7

ANDREWS CL

THE GREEN

Wellmead Farm

Soulbury

LABURNHAM COTTS

CHAPEL HILL

THE MEAD

MOUNT PLEASANT

CHURCH LA

HIGH RD

The Boot (PH)

MANOR FARM CL

Manor Farm

Larkshill Farm

STEWKLEY RD

Winscott Farm

LEIGHTON RD B4032

The Lodge

Vicarage Farm

Durrance Farm

SOULBURY RD

Soulbury Road Farm

The Plantation

Liscombe Park

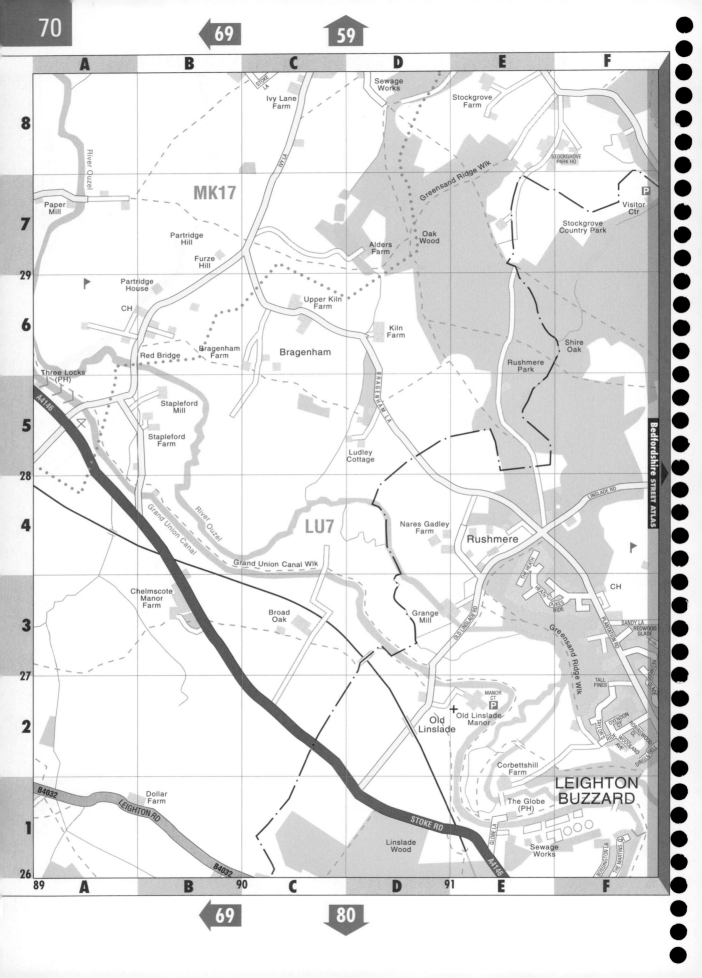

A B C D E F

8

River Ouzel

Paper Mill

MK17

STOKE LA

Ivy Lane Farm

Sewage Works

Stockgrove Farm

STOCKGROVE PARK HO

Greensand Ridge Wlk

P

Visitor Ctr

Stockgrove Country Park

7

Partridge Hill

Furze Hill

IVY LA

Alders Farm

Oak Wood

29

Partridge House

Upper Kiln Farm

CH

6

Bragenham Farm

Bragenham

Kiln Farm

Shire Oak

Red Bridge

Rushmere Park

Three Locks (PH)

A4146

Stapleford Mill

BRAGENHAM LA

5

Stapleford Farm

Ludley Cottage

28

Grand Union Canal

River Ouzel

4

LU7

Nares Gadley Farm

Rushmere

Grand Union Canal Wlk

CH

THE HEATH

HEATH CL

DUKES RIDE

LINSLADE RD

SANDY LA

REDWOOD GLADE

3

Chelmscote Manor Farm

Broad Oak

Grange Mill

Greensand Ridge Wlk

OLD LINSLADE RD

PLANTATION RD

TALL PINES

REDWOOD GLADE

27

MANOR CT P

OXENDON CT

ROBINSWOOD

DINGLE DELL

2

Old Linslade

Old Linslade Manor

TAYLORS RIDE

WOODLAND AVE

Corbettshill Farm

LEIGHTON BUZZARD

B4032

Dollar Farm

The Globe (PH)

1

LEIGHTON RD

STOKE RD

GLOBE LA

Sewage Works

BROGNINGTON LA

THE MARTINS

A4146

Linslade Wood

26

89 A B 90 C D 91 E F

Bedfordshire STREET ATLAS

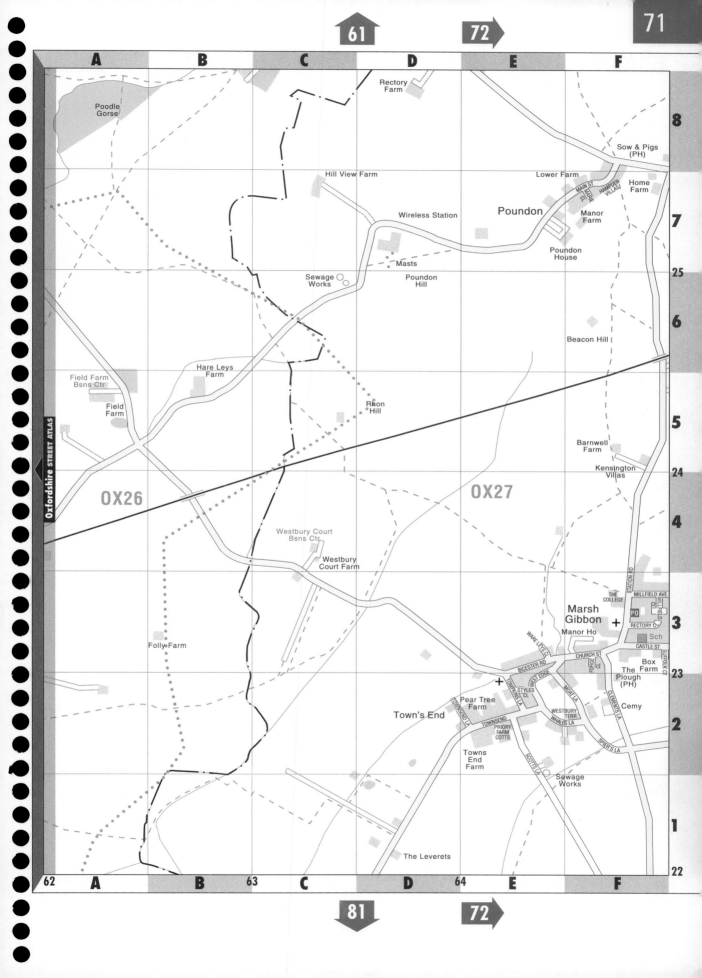

71
62

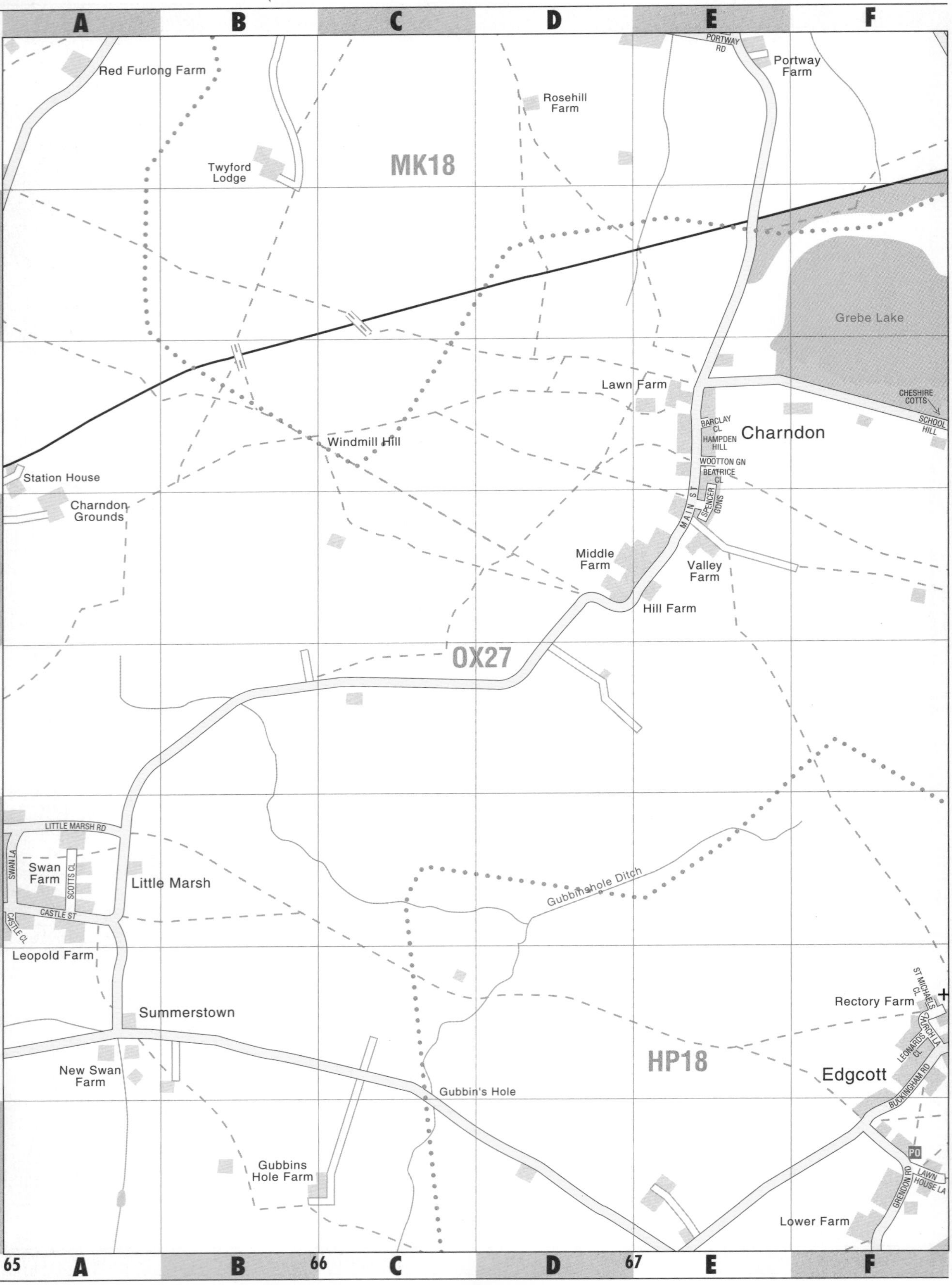

A   B   C   D   E   F

8

Red Furlong Farm

MK18

Twyford
Lodge

Rosehill
Farm

PORTWAY
RD

Portway
Farm

7

25

Grebe Lake

6

Windmill Hill

Lawn Farm

BARCLAY
CL
HAMPDEN
HILL

Charndon

CHESHIRE
COTTS

SCHOOL
HILL

Station House

Charndon
Grounds

WOOTTON GN
BEATRICE
CL

MAIN ST

SPENCER
GDNS

5

Middle
Farm

Valley
Farm

Hill Farm

24

OX27

4

3

LITTLE MARSH RD

SWAN LA

Swan
Farm

SCOTTS CL

Little Marsh

Gubbinshole Ditch

CASTLE ST

23

CASTLE CL

Leopold Farm

2

Summerstown

Rectory Farm

ST MICHAELS CL

CHURCH LA

HP18

Edgcott

LEONARDUS CL

BUCKINGHAM RD

New Swan
Farm

Gubbin's Hole

1

Gubbins
Hole Farm

PO

BRENDON RD

LAWN
HOUSE LA

Lower Farm

22

65   A   B   66   C   D   67   E   F

71
82

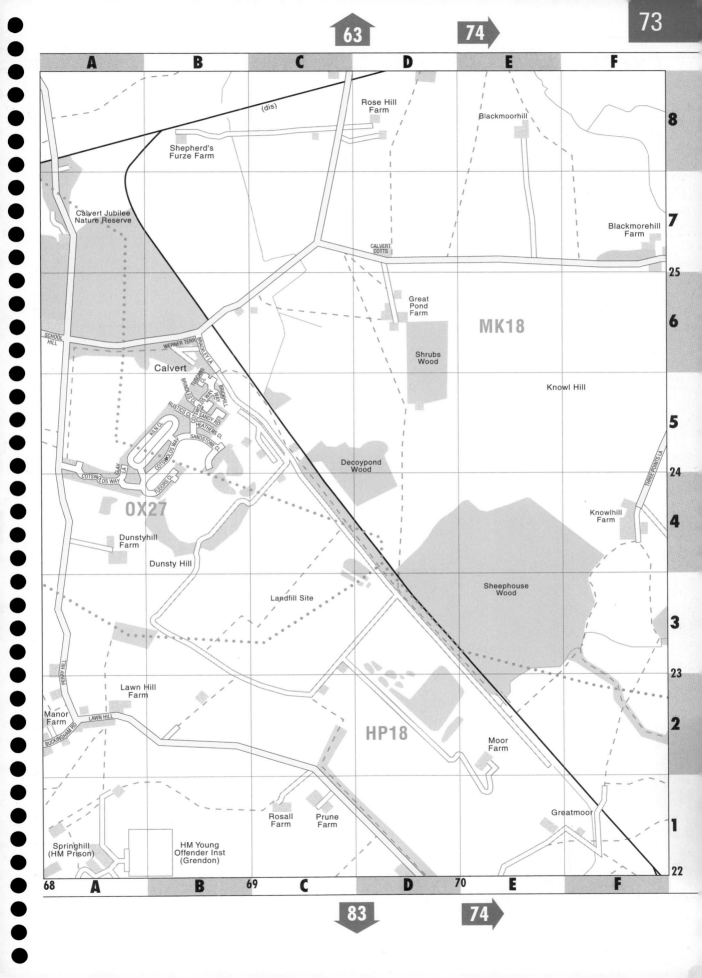

A B C D E F

8

Rose Hill
Farm

Blackmoorhill

(dis)

Shepherd's
Furze Farm

7

Calvert Jubilee
Nature Reserve

Blackmorehill
Farm

CALVERT
COTTS

25

Great
Pond
Farm

6

MK18

SCHOOL
HILL

WERNER TERR

BRACKLEY LA

Shrubs
Wood

Knowl Hill

Calvert

TUSCANS
WAY

BRICKHILL

BRINDLES CL

CLMLES WAY

RUSTICS CL

SANDY RD

HEATHERS CL

5

KILN CL

SANDSTONE CL

Decoypond
Wood

COTSWOLDS WAY

24

TUDORS CL

OX27

CLAY
LA

Knowlhill
Farm

THREE POINTS LA

4

COTSWOLDS WAY

Dunstyhill
Farm

Dunsty Hill

Sheephouse
Wood

Landfill Site

3

23

PERRY HILL

Lawn Hill
Farm

2

Manor
Farm

BUCKINGHAM RD

LAWN HILL

HP18

Moor
Farm

Greatmoor

1

Rosall
Farm

Prune
Farm

Springhill
(HM Prison)

HM Young
Offender Inst
(Grendon)

22

68 A B 69 C D 70 E F

73
64

A B C D E F

8

Home Farm
TOWNSEND COTTS
Cemy
Middle Claydon

Weir
The Old Brick Yard (disused)
Claydon Park
Catherine Farm

Swan's Way
New Farm
Verney Farm
East Claydon
SANDHILL RD
VERNEY FARM
EMERALD CL
CHESTNUT VIEW
ST MARYS CL
CHURCH WAY

7

Claydon House

25

South Lodge
Phoenix Fruit Farm
East Claydon Sch
Ivy Nook
ST MARYS RD
Botolph Farm

6

BOTYL RD
Botolph Farm
Botolph Claydon
ORCHARD WAY

MK18

5

Home Wood
Muxwell Farm
Bernwood Farm
WEIR LA

24

4

Claydon Lawn

3

Romer Wood
Balmore Wood
Runt's Wood
Coppice Lowhill Farm
Hogshaw Farm

23

Greatsea Wood
Three Points La
Hogshaw Farm

2

HP22

HP18
Finemerehill House

1

Kitehill Farm

22

71 A B 72 C D 73 E F

THREE POINTS LA

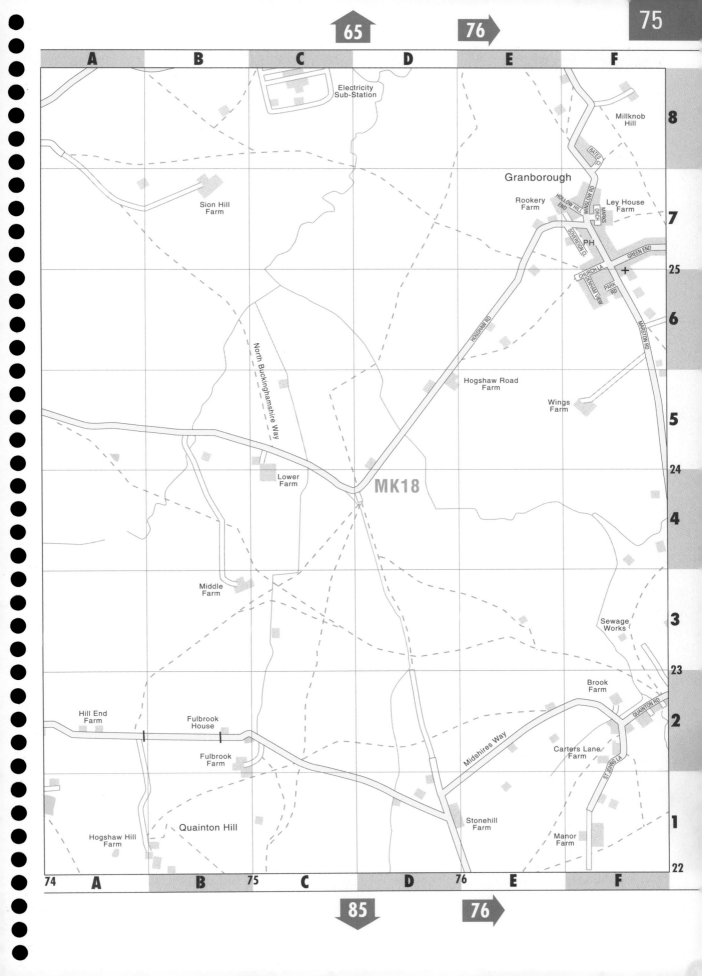

75
66

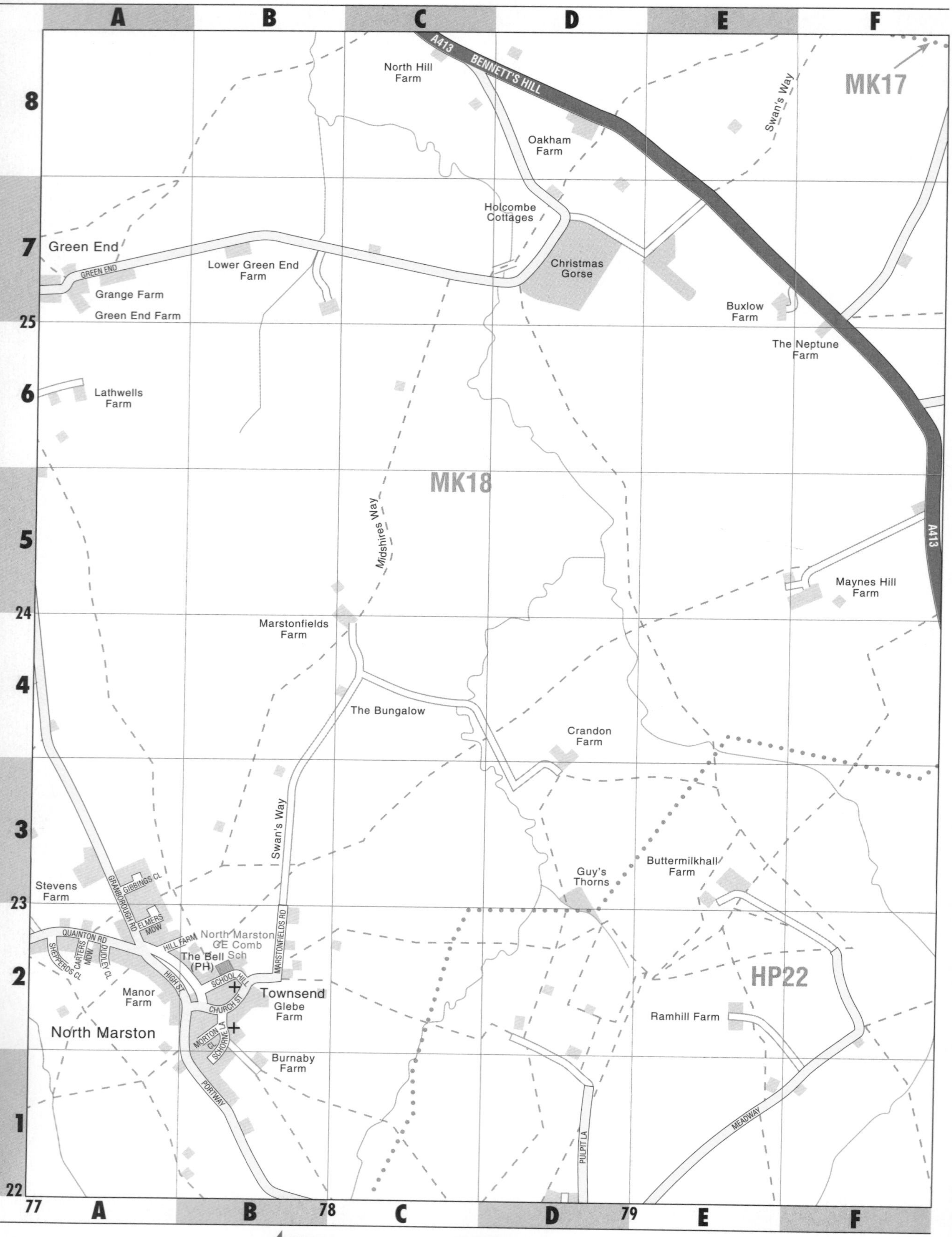

A B C D E F

8

North Hill Farm

A413 BENNETT'S HILL

Oakham Farm

Swan's Way

MK17

Holcombe Cottages

7

Green End

Lower Green End Farm

GREEN END

Christmas Gorse

Buxlow Farm

25

Grange Farm

Green End Farm

The Neptune Farm

6

Lathwells Farm

MK18

Midshires Way

5

A413

Maynes Hill Farm

24

Marstonfields Farm

4

The Bungalow

Crandon Farm

3

Swan's Way

Stevens Farm

Guy's Thorns

Buttermilkhall Farm

23

GRANBOROUGH RD

GIBBINGS CL

ELMERS

MDW

HILL FARM

North Marston C/E Comb Sch

MARSTONFIELDS RD

QUAINTON RD

CARTERS MDW

DUDLEY CL

SHEPPERDS CL

HIGH ST

The Bell (PH)

SCHOOL HILL

CHURCH ST

HP22

2

Manor Farm

Townsend

Glebe Farm

Ramhill Farm

North Marston

MOATON CL

SCHOOL LA

Burnaby Farm

MEADWAY

1

PORTWAY

PULPIT LA

22

77 A B 78 C D 79 E F

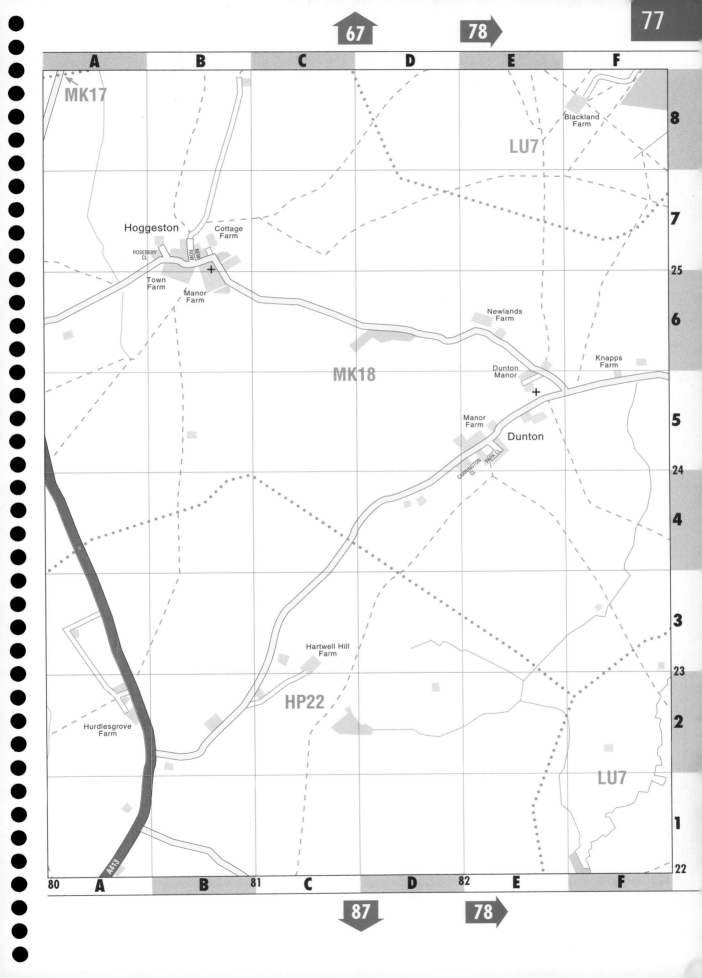

A   B   C   D   E   F

MK17

8

Blackland
Farm

LU7

7

Hoggeston   Cottage
                 Farm

ROSEBERY
CL   25

Town   NEW ROW
Farm   Newlands   6
Manor Farm   Farm

MK18   Dunton   Knapps
                     Manor   Farm

                     Manor   5
                     Farm
                              Dunton

                     CARRINGTON   PARK CL   24
                     CL.

                                                    4

                                                    3

Hartwell Hill
Farm   23

HP22   2

Hurdlesgrove
Farm   LU7

                                                    1

                                                    22

80   A   B   81   C   82   D   E   F

A413

A B C D E F

8

7

25

6

MK18

Littlecote

5

24

4

LU7

3

23

2

1

22

83 A B 84 C D 85 E F

TYTHE GDNS
PARSONS CL
SOULBURY RD
B4032
TYTHE CL
FOLDING CL
DOVE ST
ORKNEY CL
WALDUCKS CL
Red Barn Farm
OLD MANOR CH
MANOR DR
Manor House
LOVETTS END
HIGH ST
South End
MALTINGS CL
COURTMEIDGE CL
TAYLORS LA
ORCHARD LA
Breach Farm
FARM CL
KINGS ST
Carpenters' Arms (PH)
Wing Road Farm
SOUTH LA
Kiln Farm
WING RD
DUNTON RD
Sewage Works
Forge Farm
North Farm
Penton Farm
Warren Farm
Littlecote Dairy Farm
LIDCOTE
Mount Pleasant Farm
Kingsbridge Farm
Poultry Farm
Steart Farm
New Dairy Farm
Cedars Farm
South Tinkers Hole Farm
Lockharts
Poultry Farm
Acorn Bsns Ctr
Cublington
Neales Farm
ST NICHOLAS CL 1
CHENEY CL 2
MEADOW CL 3
READS LA
The Olde Manor
Old Manor Farm
CHURCH PATH
SILVER ST
STEWKLEY RD
Old House Farm
HIGH ST
BELL CL
WING RD
RIDING S WAY
PH
Manor Farm
WHITCHURCH RD
ROSES CL
ASTON ABBOTTS RD
Southend Farm

A B C D E F

8
7
25
6
5
24
4
3
23
2
1
22

Walducks Farm

Home Farm

Liscombe House

Liscombe Park

ROCKLANE FARM

Blackend Spinney

Ash Farm

CH

Burcott Lodge Farm

WING RD

Soulbury Road Farm

LU7

Burcott Hall Farm

Fox Covert

Poultry Farm

Mount Pleasant Farm

Burcott

SOULBURY RD

HIGH ST LA

Long Spinney

Kemsall Wood

STEWKLEY RD

HAWTHORN WAY

MEADOW WAY

MOORLANDS

RIDGE WAY

WILLIAM BANDY CL

CHESTERFIELD CRES

WILLOW WAY

LITTLEWORTH

M'GHULLS RD

WOODMAN WAY

COTTESLOE CL

CASTLE CL

DORMER AVE

WANTAGE CRES

MOORHILLS CRES

THE LANDS

COTES WAY

WANTAGE CL

Glebe Farm

OVERSTONE CL

WANTAGE CL

Glebe Close Farm

STEWKLEY RD

ROTHSCHILD

A418

LEIGHTON RD

WELL LA

Cottesloe Farm

Old Park

Castle Hill

WOOD DR

SEDWICK WARWICK RD

1 CHARLOTTE CL
2 GEORGE ST

Wing

VICARAGE LA

ORCHARD WAY

HIGH ST

CHURCH ST

PROSPECT PL

PH

PO

Overstone Comb Sch

EVELYN CL

1 GOLDEN MILLER CT
2 NEW ZEALAND GDNS

The Cottesloe Sch

AYLESBURY RD

PARK GATE

LOWER ASCOTT

A418

Wing Park Farm

86 A B 87 C D 88 E F 22

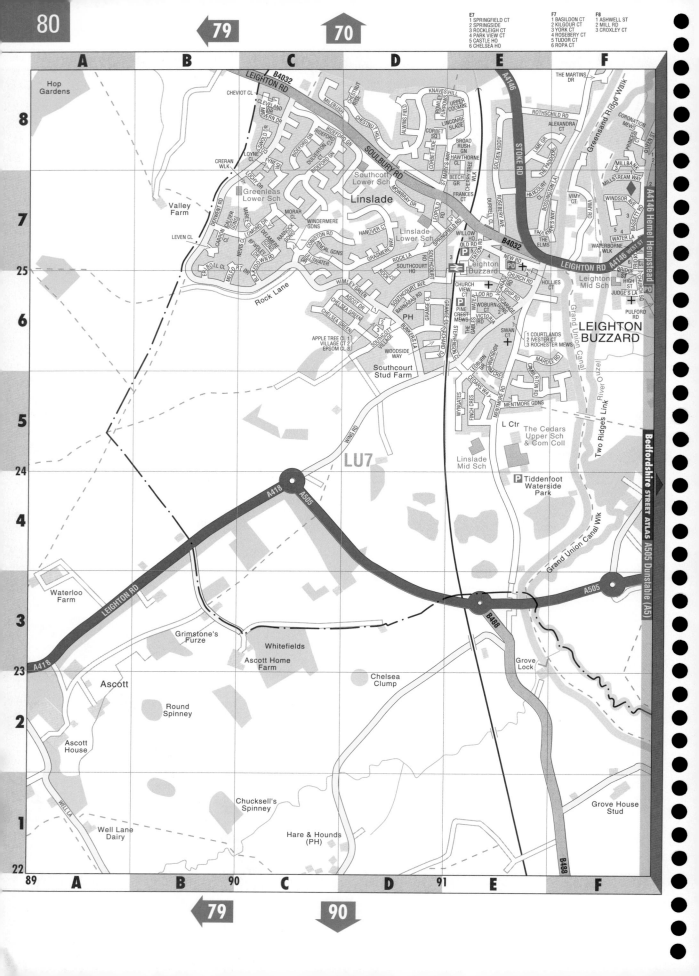

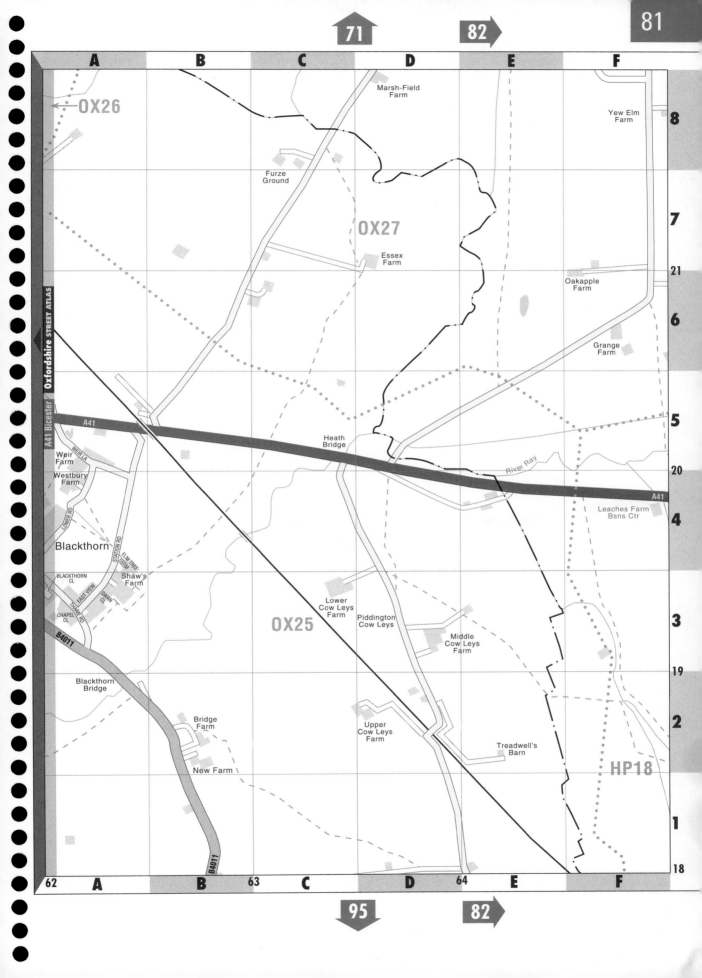

81
72

A **B** **C** **D** **E** **F**

8 Yew Elm Farm

PARK RD

SPRINGHILL RD

MARSH GIBBON RD

Dunmead Farm

Gubbinshole Ditch

Tudor Farm

HALL COTTS

OX27

7

EGGCOTT RD

21

MIDSUMMER DR

MILLERS CL

Manor Farm

THE BROADWAY

RUMPTON'S PADDOCKS

MAIN ST

SHAKESPEARE ORCH

SAVE & SELE CL

6

River Ray

Shakespeare Farm

Three Points

5

HP18

20

Winding Brook

White House Farm

Tetchwick Brook

A41

4

Cub Pond

Gallow's Bridge

A41

Tetchwick Farm

3

19

Tetchwick

2

New Barn Farm

Sewage Works

1

Tittershall Wood

18

65 **A** **B** 66 **C** **D** 67 **E** **F**

81
96

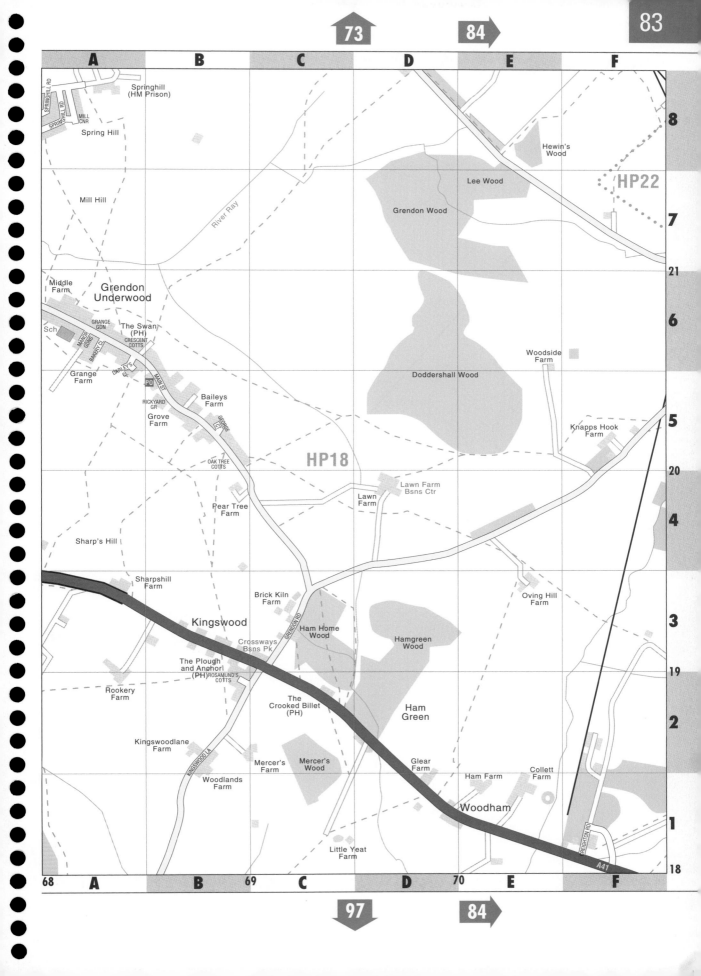

83
74

A **B** **C** **D** **E** **F**

HP18

Finemere Wood

Dry Leys Farm

River Ray

MK18

8

Shipton Lee

Woodlands Farm

7

Middle Farm

Hill Farm

Lee House

21

Woodlands Cottages

Lee Bridge Cottage

Grange Hill

North Farm

Grange Farm

6

LEE RD

5

Railway Cottage

Doddershall House

HP22

20

Fieldside Farm

Knapps Hook Wood

4

Lower South Farm

3

Upper South Farm

Factory

STATION RD

Binwell Farm

19

Quainton Road

HP18

P

2

Buckinghamshire Railway Centre

Mast

1

Lower Farm

18

UPPER BARN FARM

71 **A** **B** 72 **C** **D** 73 **E** **F**

83
98

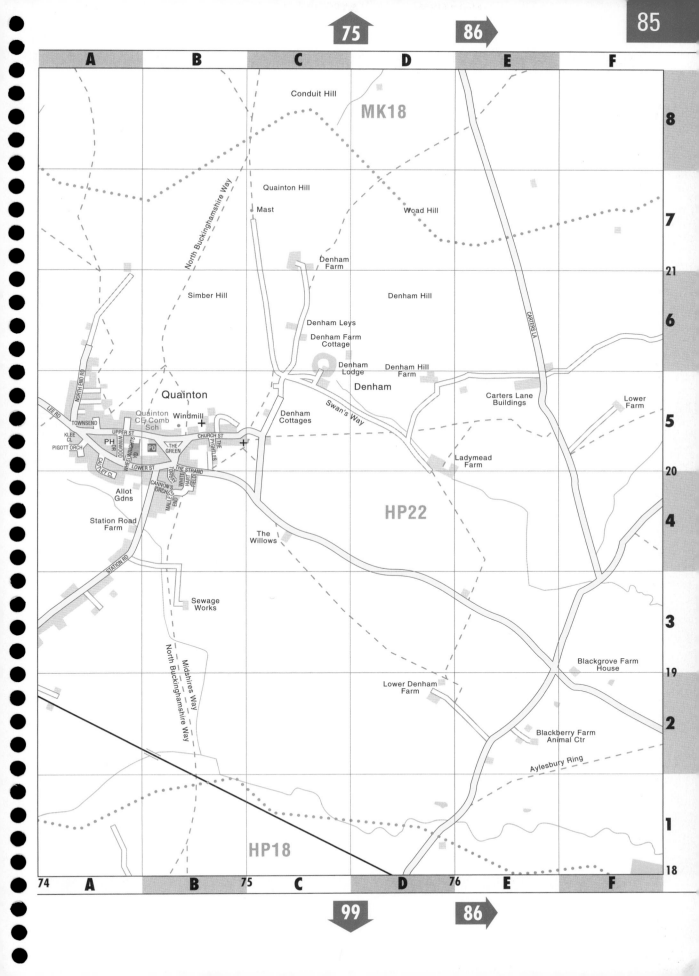

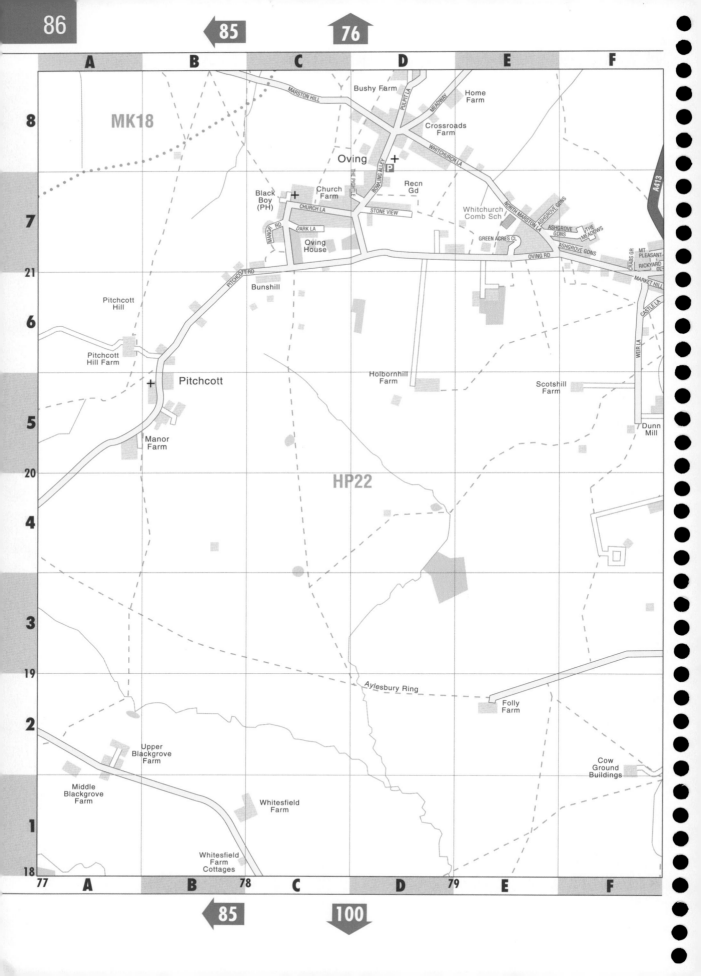

MK18

Oving

Bushy Farm

Home Farm

Crossroads Farm

Black Boy (PH)

Church Farm

Whitchurch Comb Sch

ASHGROVE GDNS

THE MEADOWS

ASHGROVE GDNS

Stone View

Oving House

Dark La

Green Acres Cl

Oving Rd

Crabs Gr

MT Pleasant

Rickyard Cl

Market Hill

Pitchcott Rd

Bunshill

Pitchcott Hill

Pitchcott Hill Farm

Pitchcott

Holbornhill Farm

Scotshill Farm

Weir La

Castle La

Dunn Mill

Manor Farm

HP22

Aylesbury Ring

Folly Farm

Upper Blackgrove Farm

Middle Blackgrove Farm

Whitesfield Farm

Cow Ground Buildings

Whitesfield Farm Cottages

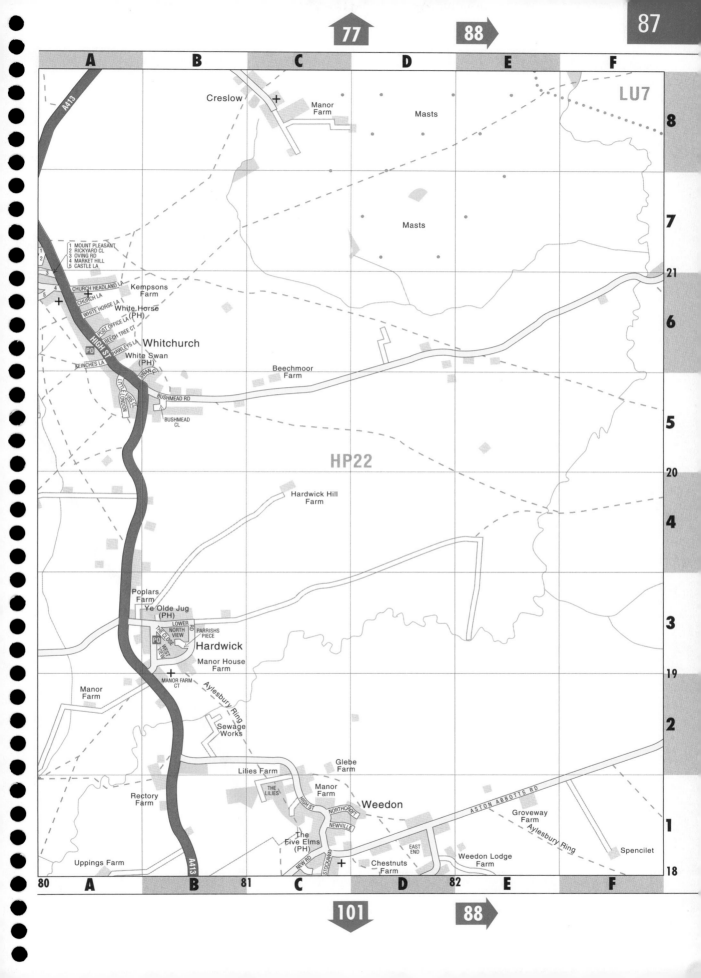

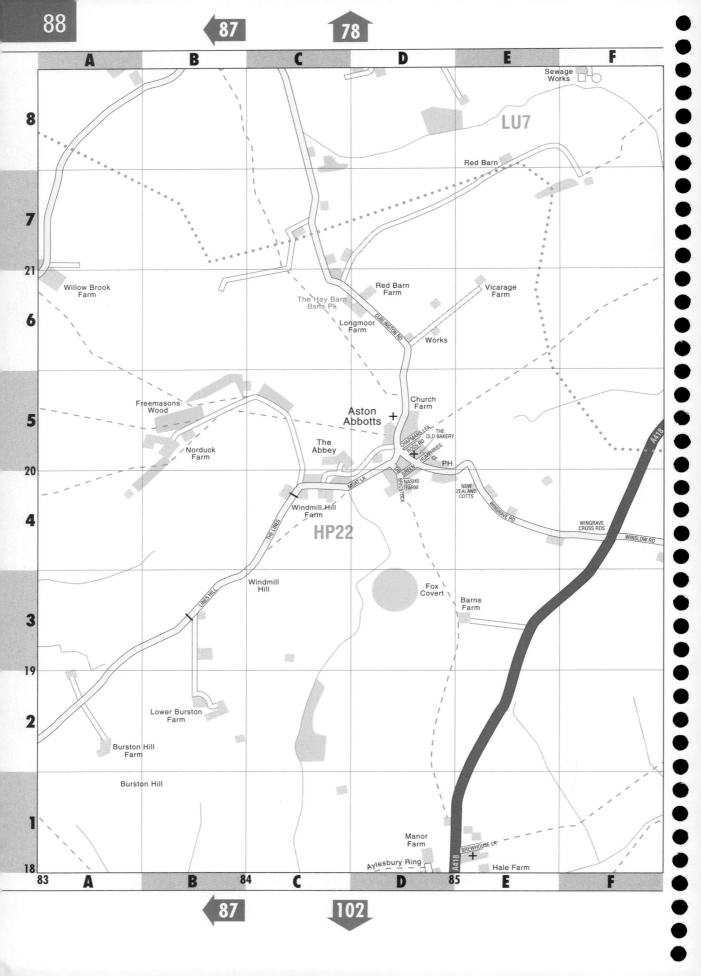

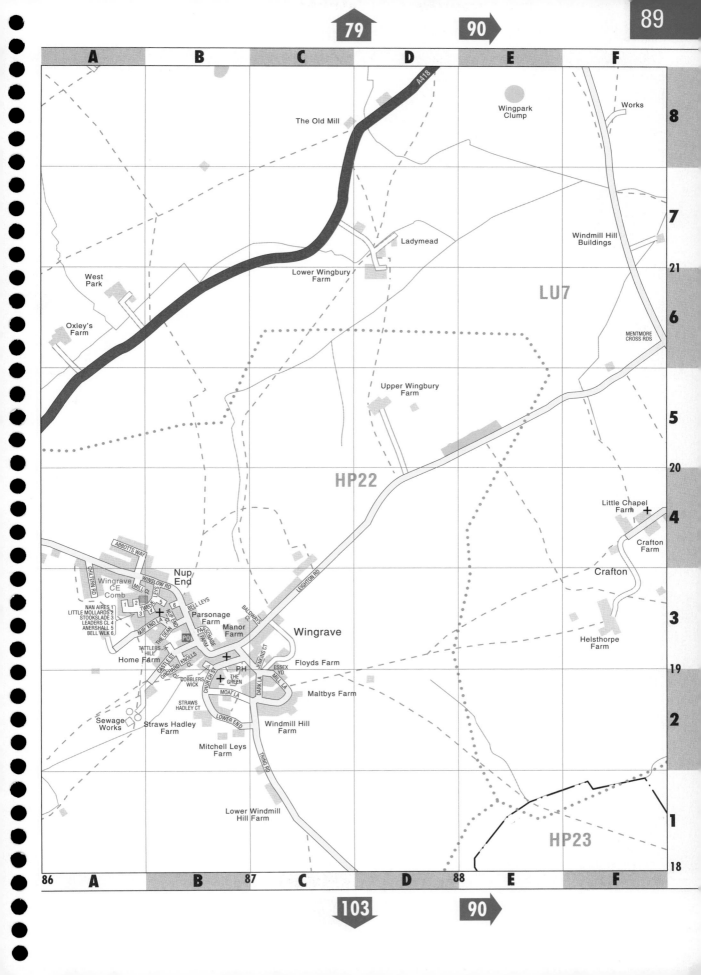

A B C D E F

8
7
21
6
5
20
4
3
19
2
1
18

A418

Works

Wingpark
Clump

The Old Mill

LU7

Windmill Hill
Buildings

Ladymead

West
Park

Lower Wingbury
Farm

MENTMORE
CROSS RDS

Oxley's
Farm

Upper Wingbury
Farm

HP22

Little Chapel
Farm

Crafton
Farm

ABBOTTS WAY

Crafton

CHILTERN RD

Nup
End

WINSLOW RD

MILL CL

Wingrave
CE
Comb

NAN AIRES 1
LITTLE MOLLARDS 2
STOOKSLADE 3
LEADERS CL 4
ANERSHALL 5
BELL WLK 6

TWELVE LEYS

1 2
3 4
5 6

BELL LEYS

Parsonage
Farm

Helsthorpe
Farm

NUP END LA

THE DEAN

PARSONAGE FARM LA

NUP END

Manor
Farm

BALDWAYS CL

LEIGHTON RD

Wingrave

PO

TATTLERS
HILL

CASTLE EST

ORCHARD
CL

KNOLLS

Home Farm

Floyds Farm

PH

THE
GREEN

CHURCH ST

COBBLERS
WICK

JENKINS CT

ESSEX
YD

DARK LA

MILL LA

MOAT LA

Maltbys Farm

Sewage
Works

STRAWS
HADLEY CT

LOWER END

Straws Hadley
Farm

Windmill Hill
Farm

THING RD

Mitchell Leys
Farm

Lower Windmill
Hill Farm

HP23

89
80

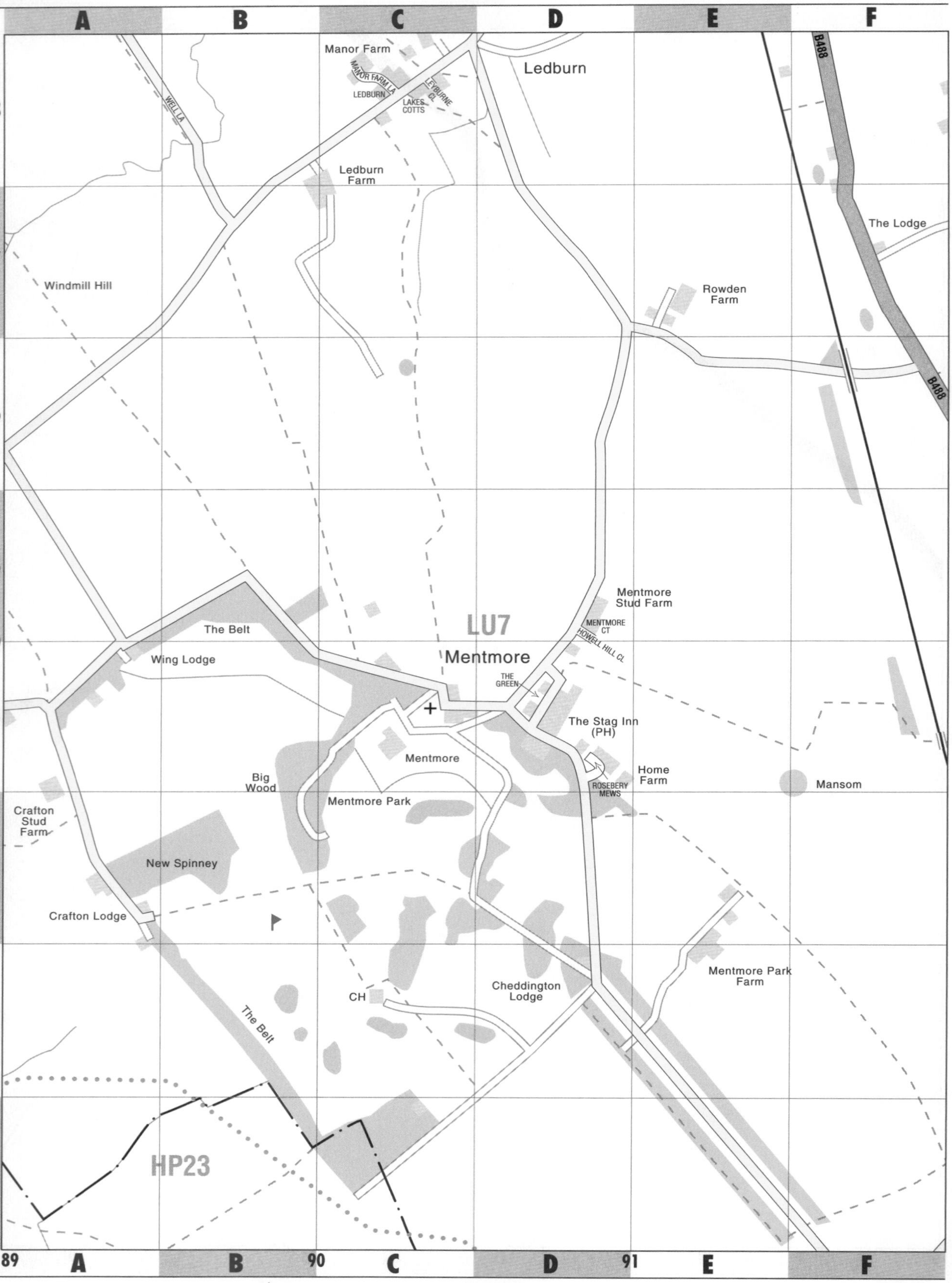

A **B** **C** **D** **E** **F**

Manor Farm

Ledburn

MANOR FARM
LEDBURN

LEDBURNE CL

LAKES COTTS

B488

8

Ledburn
Farm

The Lodge

7

Windmill Hill

Rowden
Farm

21

B488

6

5

Mentmore
Stud Farm

Mentmore
Stud Farm

LU7

The Belt

MENTMORE CT

20

HOWELL HILL CL

Wing Lodge

Mentmore

THE GREEN

4

The Stag Inn
(PH)

Big
Wood

Mentmore

Home
Farm

Mansom

Mentmore Park

ROSEBERY
MEWS

Crafton
Stud
Farm

3

New Spinney

Crafton Lodge

19

Mentmore Park
Farm

The Belt

2

CH

Cheddington
Lodge

1

HP23

18

A **B** **C** **D** **E** **F**

89 90 91

89
104

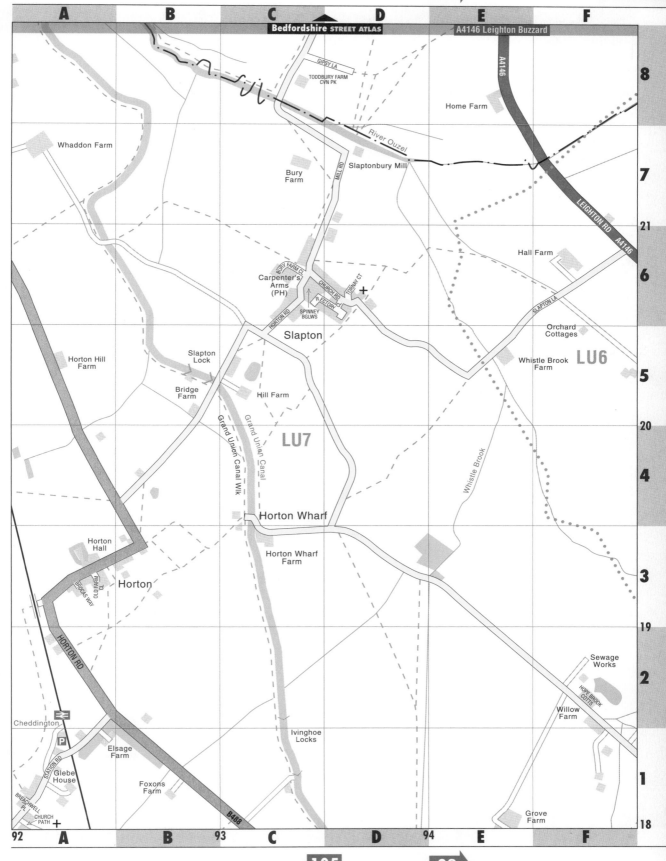

92 →

Bedfordshire STREET ATLAS

A4146 Leighton Buzzard

A **B** **C** **D** **E** **F**

GIPSY LA

TODDBURY FARM
CVN PK

Home Farm

A4146

Whaddon Farm

River Ouzel

Bury
Farm

MILL RD

Slaptonbury Mill

LEIGHTON RD A4146

8

7

21

Hall Farm

BURY FARM CL

Carpenter's
Arms
(PH)

CHURCH RD

TORBAY CT

SLAPTON LA

6

R.ECTORY

HORTON RD

SPINNEY
BGLWS

Slapton

Orchard
Cottages

Whistle Brook
Farm

LU6

5

Horton Hill
Farm

Slapton
Lock

Bridge
Farm

Hill Farm

Grand Union Canal Wlk

Grand Union Canal

LU7

20

Whistle Brook

4

Horton Wharf

Horton
Hall

Horton Wharf
Farm

3

Horton

BROCAS WAY

OLD FARM CL

19

HORTON RD

Sewage
Works

2

Cheddington

HOPS BROOK COTTS

Willow
Farm

P

Elsage
Farm

Glebe
House

Ivinghoe
Locks

1

STATION RD

BREACHWELL PL

Foxons
Farm

Grove
Farm

CHURCH
PATH

B488

18

A **B** 93 **C** **D** 94 **E** **F**

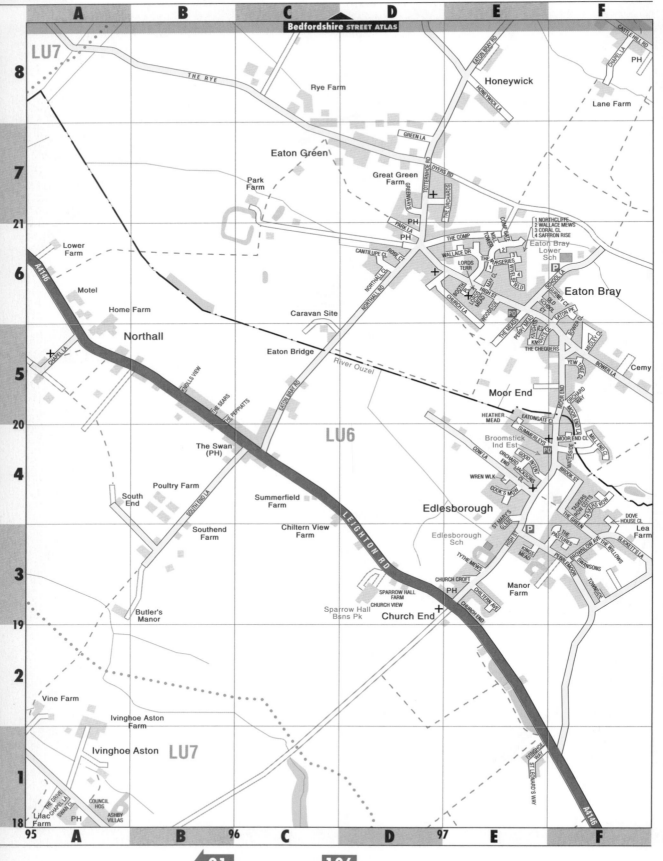

Bedfordshire STREET ATLAS

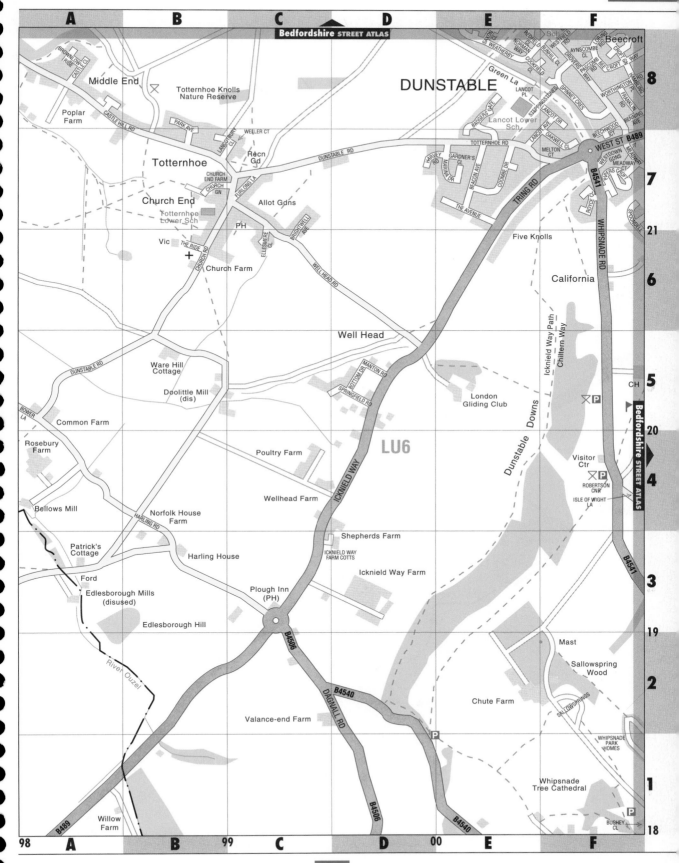

Bedfordshire STREET ATLAS

DUNSTABLE

Beecroft

Middle End

Totternhoe Knolls
Nature Reserve

Poplar
Farm

Totternhoe

Church End

Totternhoe
Lower Sch

Vic

Church Farm

Recn
Gd

Dunstable Rd

Allot Gdns

PH

Well Head Rd

Well Head

Lancot Lower
Sch

Totternhoe Rd

WEST ST

B489

B4541

Five Knolls

California

Icknield Way Path

Chiltern Way

Ware Hill
Cottage

Doolittle Mill
(dis)

Dunstable Rd

Common Farm

Rosebury
Farm

Bellows Mill

Patrick's
Cottage

Ford

Edlesborough Mills
(disused)

Edlesborough Hill

River Ouzel

Willow
Farm

B489

Poultry Farm

Wellhead Farm

Norfolk House
Farm

Harling Rd

Harling House

Plough Inn
(PH)

Valance-end Farm

B4506

B4540

Icknield Way

Manton Rd

Bottom Dr

Springfield Rd

LU6

Shepherds Farm

Icknield Way
Farm Cotts

Icknield Way Farm

B4506

Dagnall Rd

London
Gliding Club

Dunstable Downs

Visitor
Ctr

ROBERTSON
CNR

ISLE OF WIGHT
LA

Mast

Sallowspring
Wood

Chute Farm

Sallowsprings

Whipsnade
Park
Homes

Whipsnade
Tree Cathedral

Bushey
Cl

Whipsnade Rd

B4541

Bedfordshire STREET ATLAS

CH

21

8

7

6

5

20

4

3

19

2

1

18

Oxfordshire STREET ATLAS

Astley Bridge Farm

River Ray

Depot

Upper Arncott

The Plough (PH)

PALMER AVE

PLOUGHLEY RD

NORRIS RD

PATRICK HAUGH RD

LC

LC

LC

LC

LC

OX25

GREEN LA

FIELD CL

HOPCRAFT

HARPER CLOSE

CONSTABLE'S CROFT

MILL LA

HILLSIDE CL

BUCHANAN RD

WOODPIECE RD

GREENFIELDS

CH

Arncott Hill

Arncott Hill Farm

Arncott Wood

Arncott Hill

Depot

MURCOTT RD

ARNCOTT WOOD RD

LC

LC

LC

LC

LC

LGs

M40 Banbury

FIELD RD

M40

Boarstall Lane

New Park Farm

Red House Farm

Oxfordshire STREET ATLAS

Murcott

Marlake House

Latchmeads

OX5

Oldhouse Spinney

Four Winds Farm

Whitecross Green

Panshill Farms

Manor Farm

Upper Panshill Farm

Pans Hill

HP18

Whitecross Green Wood

OX33

Upper Wood

Oriel Wood

M40

59   60   61

8 7 17 6 5 16 4 3 15 2 1 14

A B C D E F

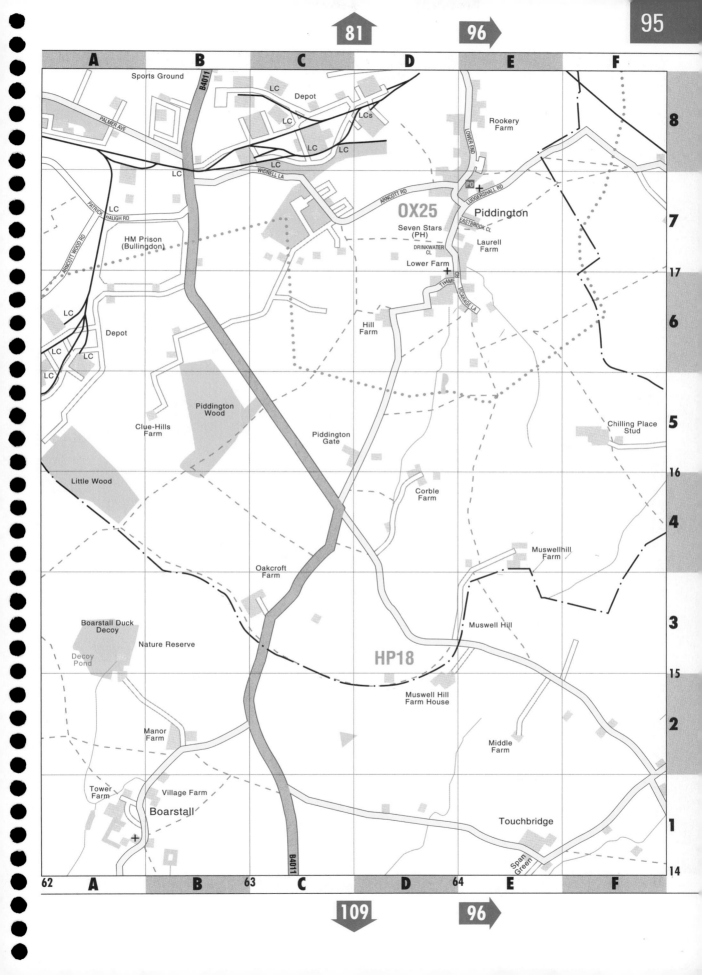

A B C D E F

8
7
17
6
5
16
4
3
15
2
1
14

Sports Ground
PALMER AVE
B4011
LC
Depot
LC
LCs
LC
LC
LC
WIDNELL LA
LC
Rookery Farm
LOWER END
ARNCOTT RD
LUDGERSHALL RD
PO
OX25
Piddington
Seven Stars (PH)
EASTBROOK CL
PATRICK HAUGH RD
LC
ARNCOTT WOOD RD
HM Prison (Bullingdon)
DRINKWATER CL
Laurell Farm
Lower Farm
THAME RD
VICARAGE LA
LC
Depot
LC
LC
LC
Hill Farm
Piddington Wood
Clue-Hills Farm
Piddington Gate
Chilling Place Stud
Little Wood
Corble Farm
Muswellhill Farm
Oakcroft Farm
Muswell Hill
Boarstall Duck Decoy
Nature Reserve
HP18
Decoy Pond
Muswell Hill Farm House
Manor Farm
Middle Farm
Tower Farm
Village Farm
Boarstall
Touchbridge
Span Green
B4011

62 A B 63 C D 64 E F

95
82

A B C D E F

8

Nursery
Kings Farm

D'Oyley's Farm
Rookery Farm
The Green

Tittershall Wood

Bridge Farm
Ludgershall

Bull & Butcher (PH)

PIDDINGTON RD
BICESTER RD
DUCK LA
SALTERS CL
BROOK CL
WHITE HART CL
HIGH ST
SALTERS LA

Manor Farm

Glebe Farm

7

Eastfield Farm

CHURCH LA

BRILL RD

Ludgershall Farm

WOTTON END

KINGSWOOD LA

17

6

Clearfields Farm

The Lake

5

Poletrees Farm

Lapland Farm

HP18

Long Wood

The Warrells

16

Fivearch Wood
Fivearch Bridge

4

Rushbeds Wood Nature Reserve

Grenville's Wood

Lawn Farm

3

Tramway Farm

Rid's Hill

15

Brillbury Hall Farm

Coldharbour Farm

2

Dorton Park Farm

TRAM HILL

Brill Common

Norcotts Kiln Cotts

Chinkwell Wood

1

Windmill

NORTH HILLS

Brill

Dorton

Brook Farm

SOUTH HILLS
WINDMILL ST
BRAE HILL
HIGH LAND CK
THE LAWNS
TEMPLE ST
GODFREYS CL
Ct

PH

Brill CE Comb Sch

14

65 A B 66 C D 67 E F

95
110

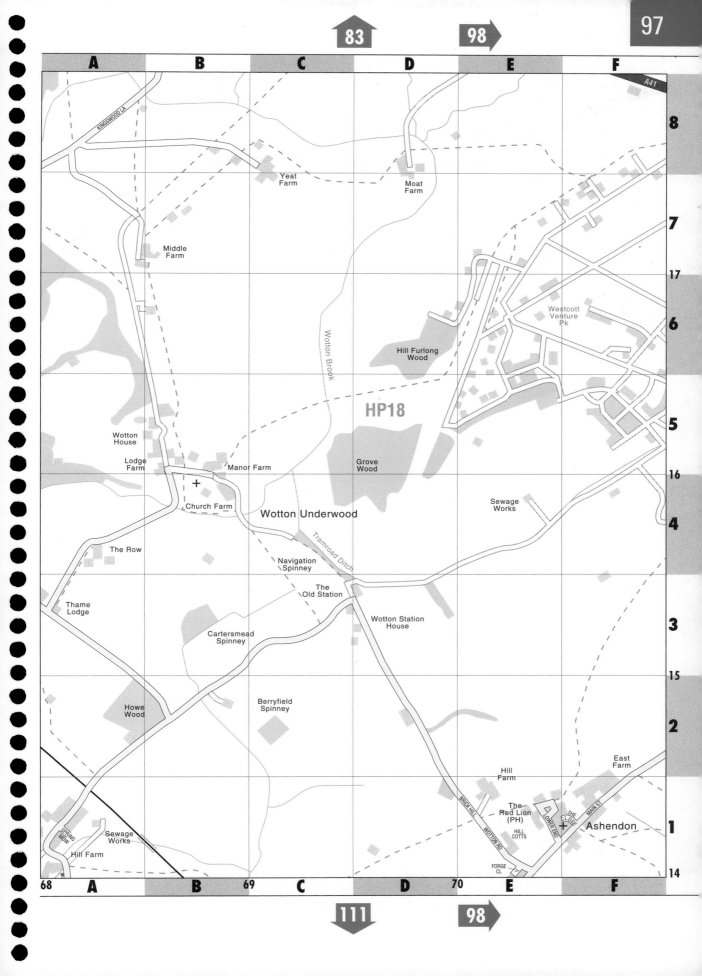

83
98
111
98

A41

A B C D E F

8
7
17
6
5
16
4
3
15
2
1
14

68 69 70

KINGSWOOD LA

Yeat
Farm

Moat
Farm

Middle
Farm

Westcott
Venture
Pk

Wotton Brook

Hill Furlong
Wood

HP18

Wotton
House

Grove
Wood

Lodge
Farm

Manor Farm

Sewage
Works

Church Farm

Wotton Underwood

The Row

Tramroad Ditch

Navigation
Spinney

Thame
Lodge

The
Old Station

Wotton Station
House

Cartersmead
Spinney

Berryfield
Spinney

Howe
Wood

East
Farm

Hill
Farm

SPRING MDW

Sewage
Works

Hill Farm

BRICK HILL

WOTTON RD

The
Red Lion
(PH)

HILL
COTTS

LOWER END

THE CLOSE

MAIN ST

Ashendon

FORGE
CL

A **B** **C** **D** **E** **F**

8

A41

Newhouse Farm

Littleton Middle Farm

South View Farm

7

Hall Farm

Westcott CE Sch

BURNHAM RD

HIGH ST

The White Swan (PH)

Westcott

Waddesdon Gardens

Waddesdon Farm

A41 HIGH ST

17

PO

WHITCHURCH CE

AYLESBURY CL

LOWER GREEN

KINGS CL

QUEEN ST

Waddesdon Dairy

6

Works

Westcott Farm

ASHENDON RD

RALPH CRES

JANET DR

Lodge Hill

WADDESDON MANOR FLATS

Waddesdon Manor (National Trust)

Westcott Venture Pk

Westcott Field Farm

5

Windmill Plantation

16

HP18

4

Gypsy Bottom

Windmill Hill Farm

Watbridge Farm Cottages

3

15

2

Grassy Dell

Decoy Farm

1

Watbridge Farm

Decoy Wood

14

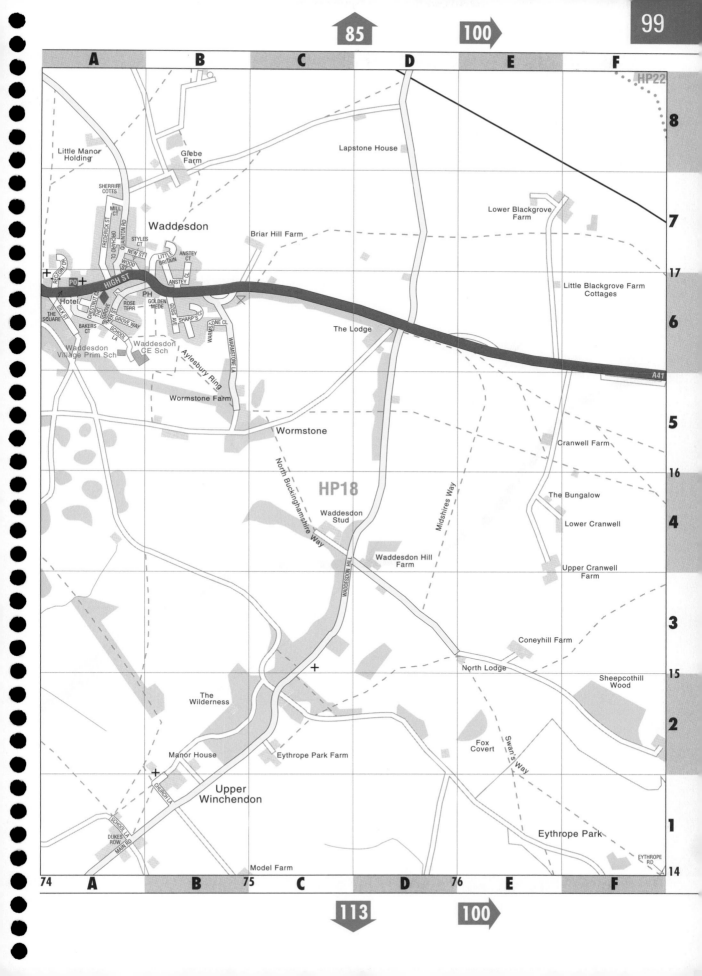

HP22

Little Manor
Holding

Glebe
Farm

Lapstone House

SHERRIFF
COTTS

Lower Blackgrove
Farm

MILL
CT

FREDERICK ST

QUAINTON RD

CHURCH ST

Waddesdon

Briar Hill Farm

STYLES
CT

NEW ST

ANSTEY
CT

LITTLE
BRITAIN

WOOD

ANSTEY CL

Little Blackgrove Farm
Cottages

ANSTEY

RECTORY DR

PO

HIGH ST

17

PH

CHESTNUT CL

GOLDEN
MEDE

GOSS AVE

SHARP'S CL

Hotel

THE GROVE

ROSE
TERR

GROVE WAY

The Lodge

6

SILK ST

THE
SQUARE

BAKERS
CT

BYE RD

SCHOOL
LA

Waddesdon
CE Sch

WARNSTONE CL

WARNSTONE LA

A41

Waddesdon
Village Prim Sch

Aylesbury Ring

Wormstone Farm

5

Wormstone

Cranwell Farm

North Buckinghamshire Way

16

HP18

The Bungalow

Waddesdon
Stud

Midshires Way

Lower Cranwell

4

Waddesdon Hill
Farm

Upper Cranwell
Farm

WADDESDON HILL

3

Coneyhill Farm

North Lodge

15

Sheepcothill
Wood

The
Wilderness

2

Manor House

Eythrope Park Farm

Fox
Covert

Swan's Way

CHURCH LA

Upper
Winchendon

1

SCHOOL LA

DUKES
ROW

MAIN RD

Eythrope Park

EYTHROPE
RD

Model Farm

14

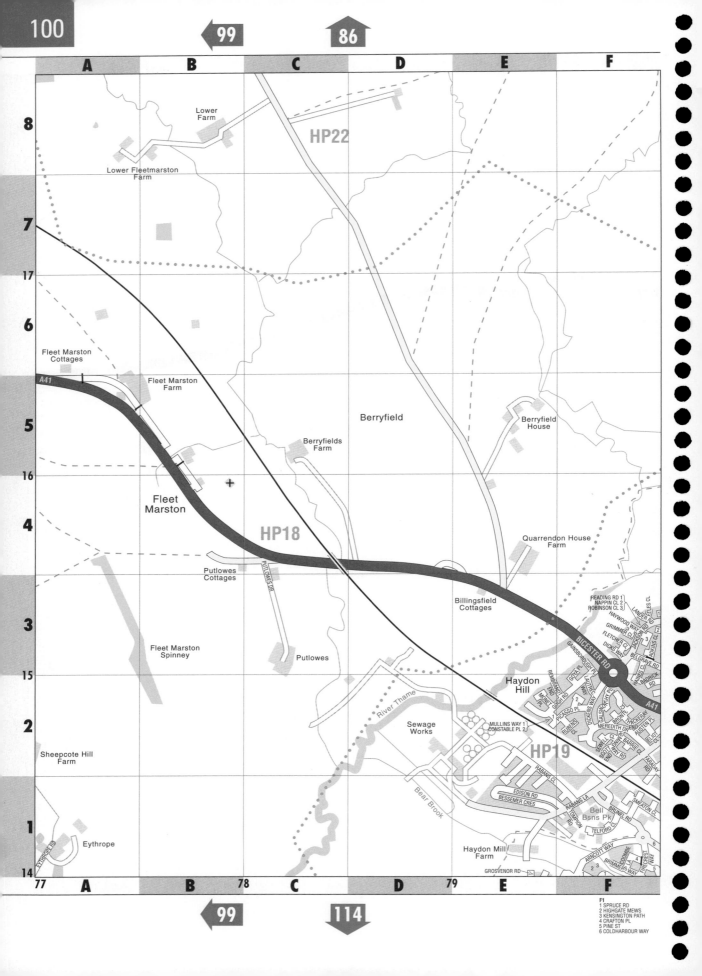

A | B | C | D | E | F

8

Lower Farm

HP22

Lower Fleetmarston Farm

7

17

6

Fleet Marston Cottages

A41

Fleet Marston Farm

5

Berryfield

Berryfield House

16

Berryfields Farm

Fleet Marston

4

HP18

Quarrendon House Farm

Putlowes Cottages

PUTLOWES DR

Billingsfield Cottages

READING RD 1
NAPPIN CL 2
ROBINSON CL 3

EELES CL
LANDER RD
HAYWOOD WAY
GRIMMER CL
FLETCHER CL
DICKS WAY
JACKSON CL
ADKINS CL
BELGRAVE RD

3

Fleet Marston Spinney

Putlowes

GAINSBOROUGH PL

BICESTER RD

HANES CL
BADRICK RD

15

Haydon Hill

A41

River Thame

REMBRANDT END
COGGH RD
MONET END
PICASSO PL
LAUTREC WAY
RUBENS CL
FALSWORTHY PL
DICKENS WAY
BRONTE
THACKERAY
MEREDITH DR END
BARRIE CL
AUSTEN PL
ELIOT CL

2

Sheepcote Hill Farm

Sewage Works

MULLINS WAY 1
CONSTABLE PL 2

SEWELL END
SCOTT ASHBY RD

HP19

FARELAM
WAY

Bear Brook

RABANS CL

EDISON RD
BESSEMER CRES

RABANS LA
TOMPION CL

Bell Bsns Pk

BRUNEL RD
SMEATON CL

1

EYTHROPE RD

Eythrope

TELFORD CL

ARNCOTT WAY
COMBE
BRIMMERS WAY

FIRCREST WAY
COLDHARBOUR WAY

14

Haydon Mill Farm

GROSVENOR RD

77 | A | B | 78 | C | D | 79 | E | F

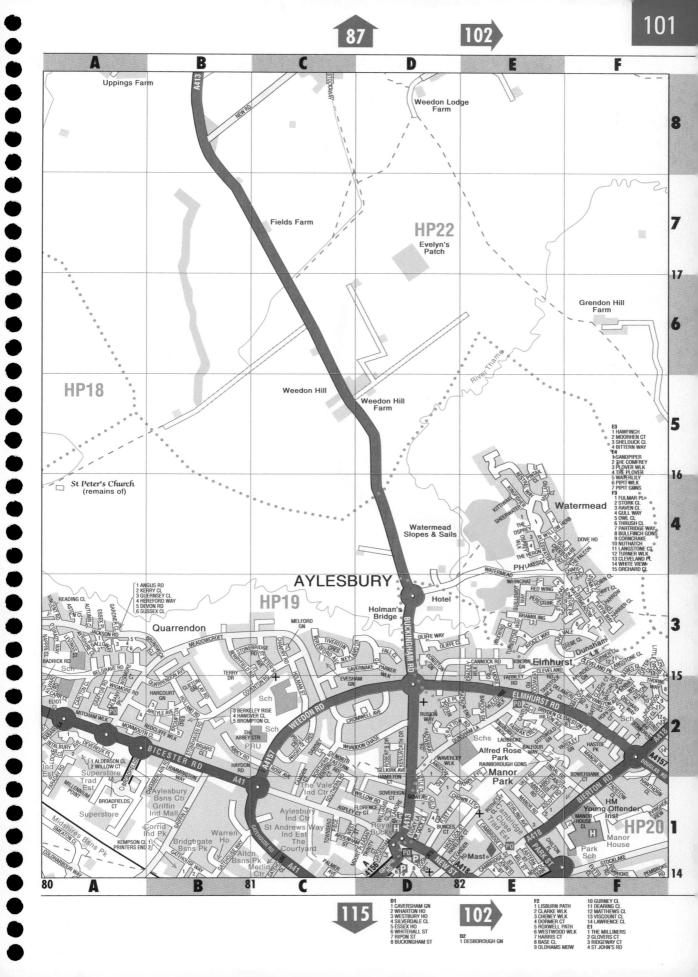

87
102

Uppings Farm

Weedon Lodge Farm

HP22

Evelyn's Patch

Fields Farm

Grendon Hill Farm

HP18

River Thame

Weedon Hill

Weedon Hill Farm

St Peter's Church
(remains of)

E3
1 HAWFINCH
2 MOORHEN CT
3 SHELDUCK CL
4 BITTERN WAY
E4
1 SANDPIPER
2 THE COMFREY
3 PLOVER WLK
4 THE PLOVER
5 WATERLILY
6 PIPIT WLK
7 PIPIT GDNS
F3
1 FULMAR PL
2 STORK CL
3 RAVEN CL
4 GULL WAY
5 OWL CL
6 THRUSH CL
7 PARTRIDGE WAY
8 BULLFINCH GDNS
9 CORNCRAKE
10 NUTHATCH
11 LANGSTONE CT
12 TURNER WLK
13 CLEVELAND PL
14 WHITE VIEW
15 ORCHARD CL

Watermead

Watermead
Slopes & Sails

AYLESBURY

Hotel

Holman's Bridge

HP19

1 ANGUS RD
2 KERRY CL
3 GUERNSEY CL
4 HEREFORD WAY
5 DEVON RD
6 SUSSEX CL

Quarrendon

MELFORD GN

READING CL

Elmhurst

Dunsham

3 BERKELEY RISE
4 HANOVER CL
5 BROMPTON CL

ELMHURST RD

BICESTER RD

Sch

THE ABBEY CTR
PRU

Aylesbury
Bsns Ctr
Griffin
Ind Mall

Superstore

1 ALDERSON CL
2 WILLOW CT

Broadfields
Superstore

BROADFIELDS
CT

Midshires Bsns Pk

Kempson Cl
Printers End 2

Bridgegate
Bsns Pk

Warren
Ho

Alton
Bsns Pk

Merlin
Ctr

Aylesbury
St Andrews Way
Ind Est
The
Courtyard

Corrib
Ind Pk

Royal
Buck

Alfred Rose
Park

RAINBOROUGH GDNS

Manor
Park

HM
Young Offender
Inst

Manor
House
Sch

Manor
House

Park
Sch

HP20

A4157

A41

A413

A4156

A418

A4157

PARK ST

A418

80

81

82

115

D1
1 CAVERSHAM GN
2 WHARTON HO
3 WESTBURY HO
4 SILVERDALE CL
5 ESSEX HO
6 WHITEHALL ST
7 RIPON ST
8 BUCKINGHAM ST

102

D2
1 DESBOROUGH GN

F2
1 LISBURN PATH
2 CLARKE WLK
3 CHENEY WLK
4 DORMER CT
5 ROXWELL PATH
6 WESTWOOD WLK
7 HARRIS CT
8 BASE CL
9 OLDHAMS MDW

10 GURNEY CL
11 DEARING CL
12 MATTHEWS CL
13 VISCOUNT CL
14 LAWRENCE CL
E1
1 THE MILLINERS
2 GLOVERS CT
3 RIDGEWAY CT
4 ST JOHN'S RD

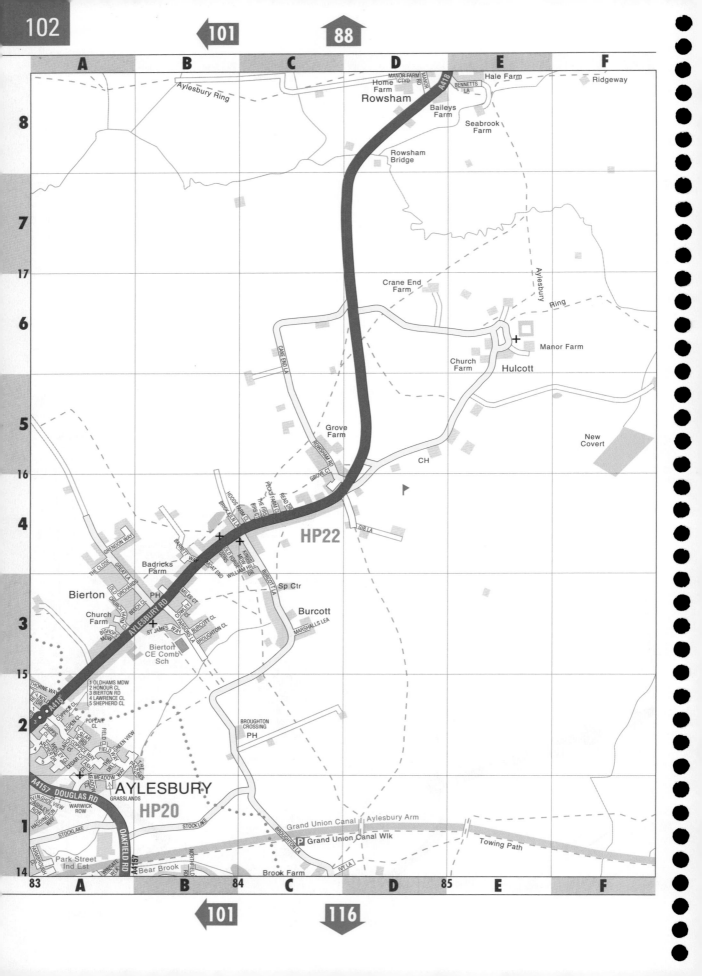

A B C D E F

8

7

17

6

5

16

4

HP22

3

15

2

1

14

83 84 85

Aylesbury Ring

MANOR FARM CTYD
Home Farm
Rowsham
A-418
BENNETTS LA
Hale Farm
Ridgeway

Baileys Farm
Seabrook Farm

Rowsham Bridge

Crane End Farm

Aylesbury Ring

Manor Farm

Church Farm
Hulcott

CANE END LA

Grove Farm

ROWSHAM RD

GROVE CT

CH

New Covert

PICOS FARM CT
THE FIRS CT
FIELD DR
GIB LA

HOODS FARM LA
BROOK END LA

BADNETT WAY
OLD FORGE
GIBBS MDW
KINGS MDW
WILLIAM HILL DR
BURCOTT LA

Sp Ctr

Badricks Farm

THE CLOSE
GREAT LA
OLD ORCHARDS
BEECH CL
PH
CHURCH FM LA

Bierton

Church Farm
BISHOPS MDW

AYLESBURY RD
ST JAMES WAY
COWLEY
PARSONS LA
MILLS CT
BURCOTT CL
BROUGHTON CL

Burcott

MARSHALLS LEA

Bierton CE Comb Sch

GRENDON WAY

THORNE WAY
LANGDON
NOLDER DR
A-418
COPPICE CL

1 OLDHAMS MDW
2 HONOUR CL
3 BIERTON RD
4 LAWRENCE CL
5 SHEPHERD CL

POPLAR CL
FIELD VIEW
THE GREEN VIEW

PHIPPS CL
ASPEN CL
S-LAR
ARCH CL
COBB CL
CEDAR CL
5
DEW WAY
THE PASTURES

BROUGHTON CROSSING
PH

BROUGHTON LA

A4157 DOUGLAS RD
IVINGHOE VIEW
ASHEVLON ROW
HADDINGTON WAY
STOCKLAKE
MEADOW WAY
AYLESBURY
GRASSLANDS
HP20

Stocklake

Grand Union Canal
Aylesbury Arm
P Grand Union Canal Wlk

IVY LA

Towing Path

A4157
OAKFIELD RD
WINGATE RD
HARBOROUGH
Park Street Ind Est
Bear Brook
NORTHFIELD RD
Brook Farm

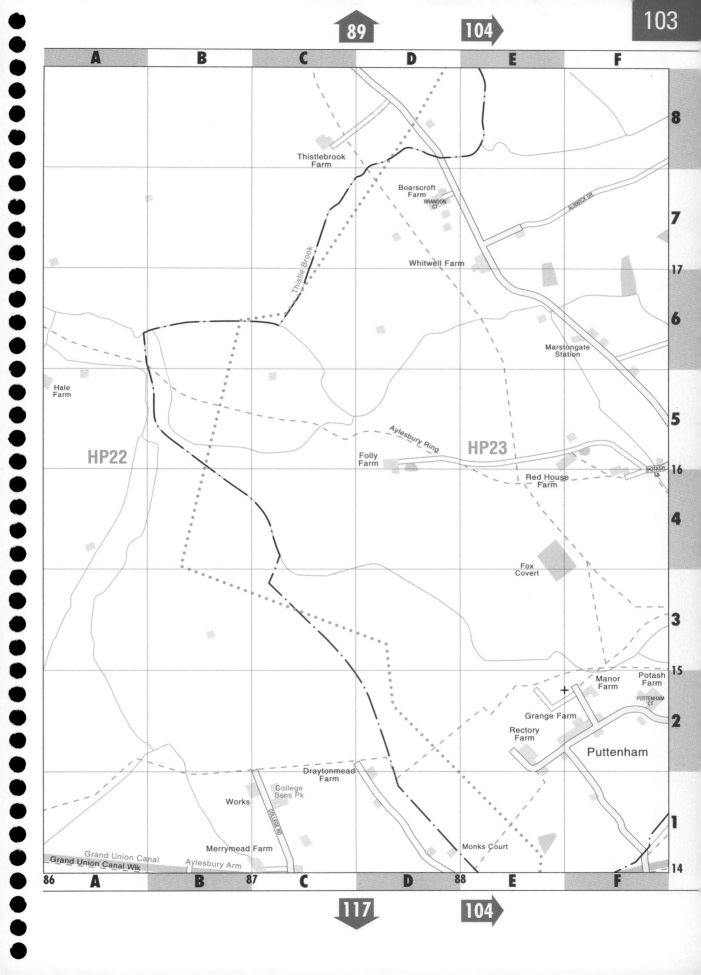

89
104

A   B   C   D   E   F

8

Thistlebrook
Farm

Boarscroft
Farm
BRANDON
CT

ALNWICK DR

7

Whitwell Farm

17

Thistle Brook

6

Marstongate
Station

Hale
Farm

5

HP22

Aylesbury Ring

HP23

Folly
Farm

Red House
Farm

POTASH
LA

16

Fox
Covert

4

3

15

Manor
Farm

Potash
Farm

PUTTENHAM
CT

Grange Farm

2

Rectory
Farm

Puttenham

Draytonmead
Farm

College
Bsns Pk

Works

COLLEGE RD

1

Merrymead Farm

Monks Court

Grand Union Canal
Grand Union Canal Wlk

Aylesbury Arm

14

86   A   B   87   C   D   88   E   F

117
104

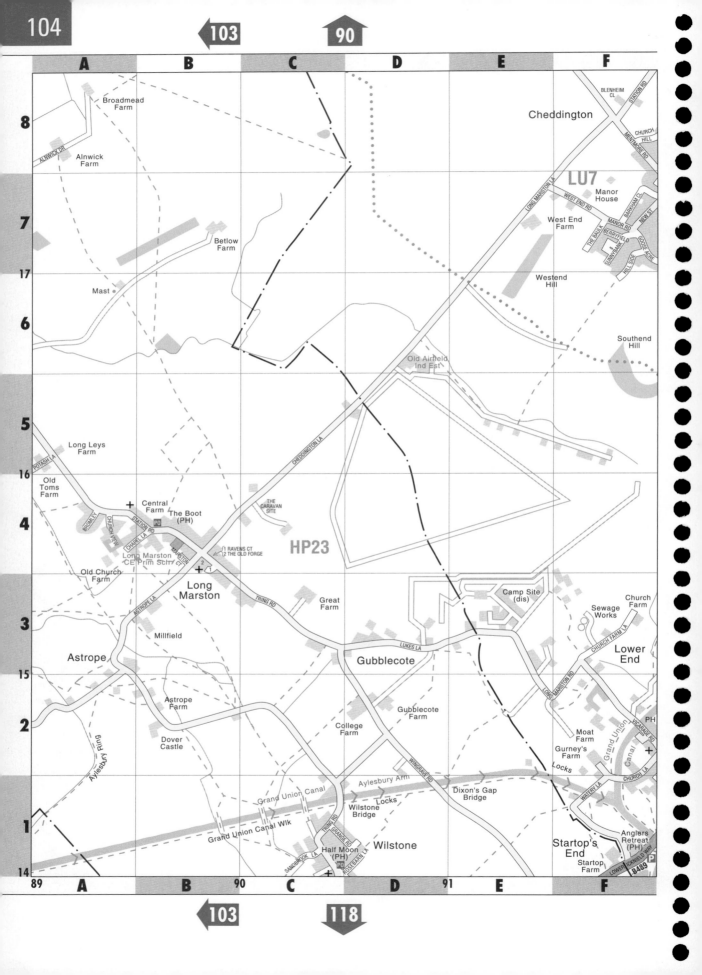

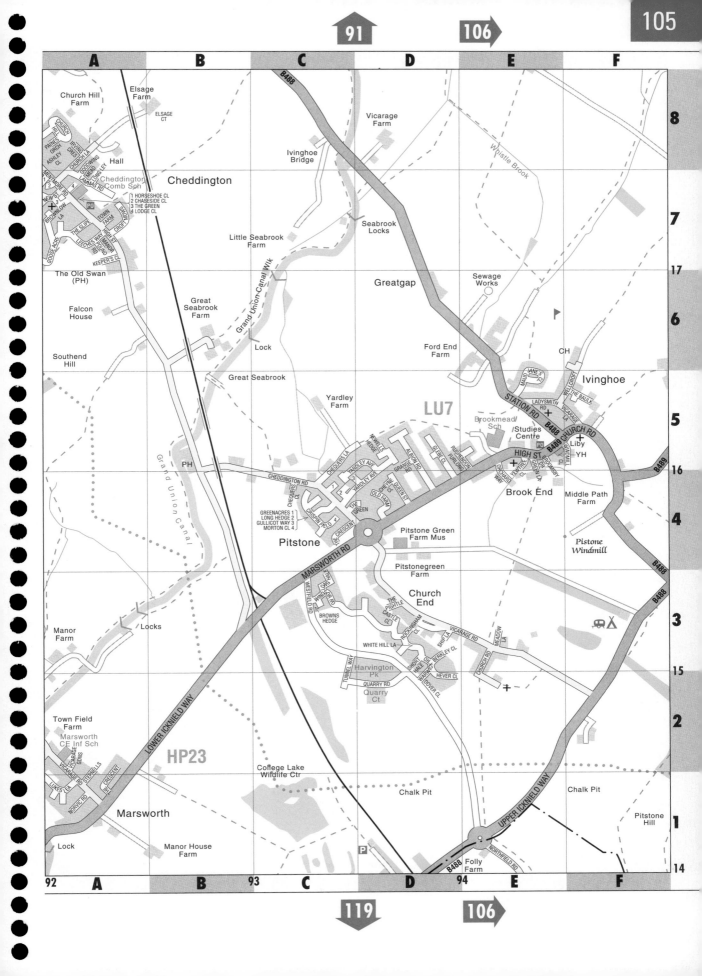

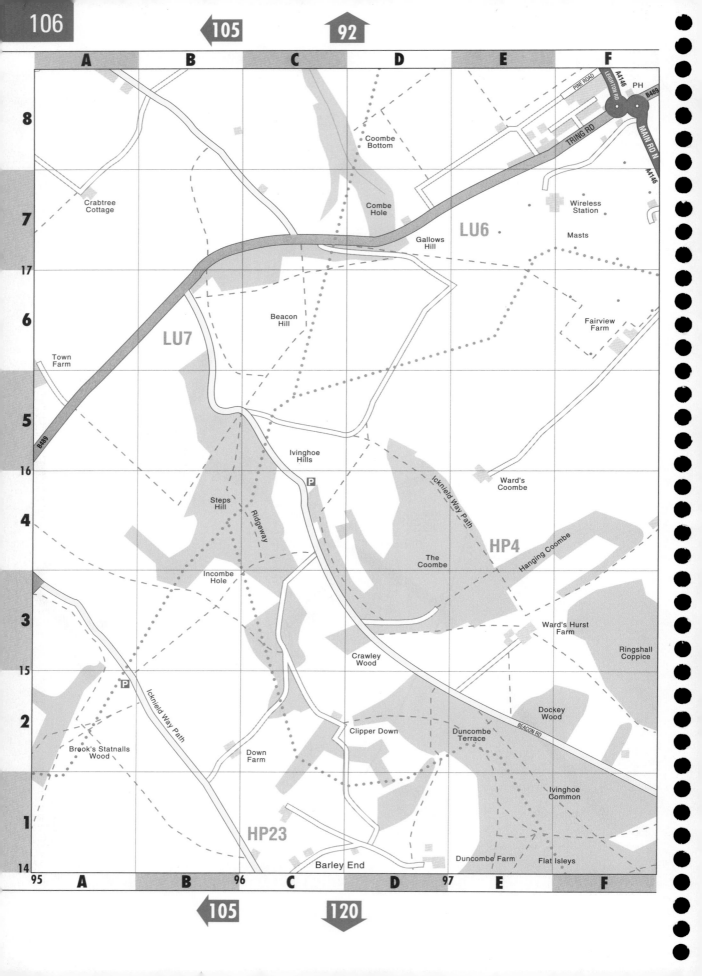

A B C D E F

8

Coombe
Bottom

Combe
Hole

LU6

Wireless
Station

Masts

PINE ROAD
LEIGHTON RD
A4146
B489
PH
TRING RD
MAIN RD N
A4146

7

Crabtree
Cottage

Gallows
Hill

Fairview
Farm

17

LU7

Beacon
Hill

6

Town
Farm

B489

Ward's
Coombe

5

Ivinghoe
Hills

P

Icknield Way Path

HP4

Hanging Coombe

16

Steps
Hill

The
Coombe

4

Ridgeway

Incombe
Hole

Ward's Hurst
Farm

Ringshall
Coppice

3

P

Icknield Way Path

Crawley
Wood

Dockey
Wood

15

BEACON RD

2

Brook's Statnalls
Wood

Down
Farm

Clipper Down

Duncombe
Terrace

Ivinghoe
Common

1

HP23

Duncombe Farm

Flat Isleys

14

Barley End

95 A B 96 C D 97 E F

93

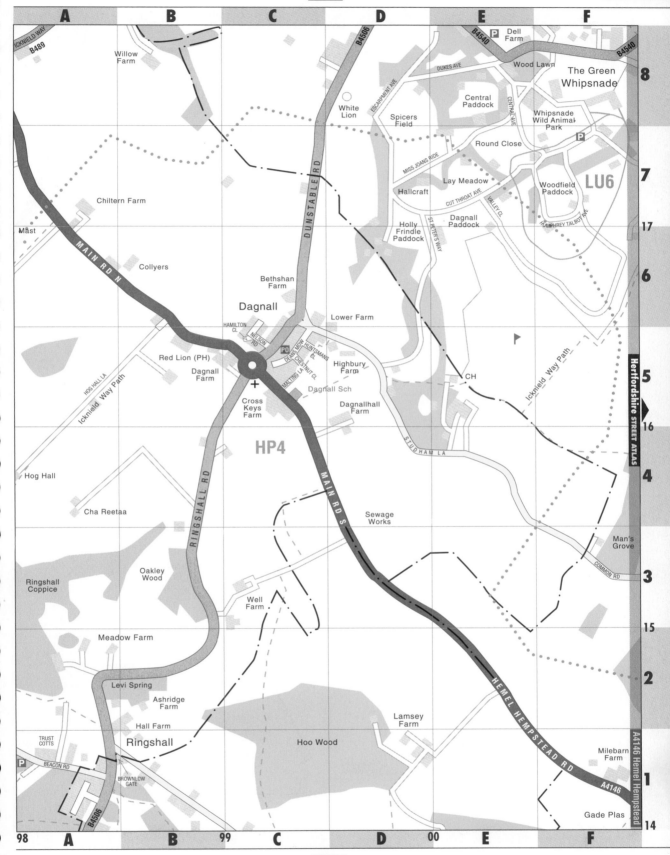

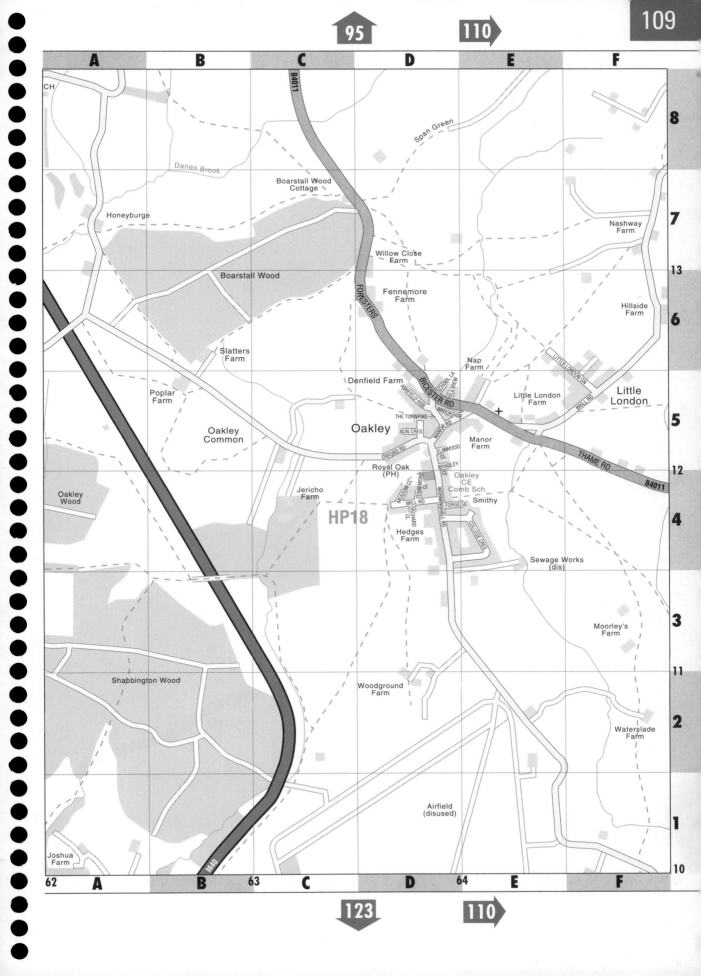

95
110

A B C D E F

8
7
13
6
5
12
4
3
11
2
1
10

CH

Danes Brook

Honeyburge

Boarstall Wood
Cottage

Span Green

Boarstall Wood

Willow Close
Farm

Nashway
Farm

Hillside
Farm

Slatters
Farm

FORSTERS

Fennemore
Farm

Nap
Farm

LITTLE LONDON GN

Denfield Farm

Poplar
Farm

ASHFIELD RISE

HILL VIEW
SCHOOL LA

BICESTER RD

Little London
Farm

Little
London

BRILL RD

Oakley
Common

THE TURNPIKE

BROOKSIDE

Oakley

SUN CRES

MANOR RD

OXFORD RD

ELMWOOD
CL

Manor
Farm

THAME RD

B4011

Royal Oak
(PH)

BRADLEY
CL

Jericho
Farm

MEADOW CL

FENNEMORE
CL

Oakley
CE
Comb Sch

HP18

MILL RD

ORCHARD
CL

WORMINGHALL RD

FORGE CL

Smithy

Oakley
Wood

Hedges
Farm

COLLEGE CRES

Sewage Works
(dis)

Moorley's
Farm

Shabbington Wood

Woodground
Farm

Waterslade
Farm

Airfield
(disused)

Joshua
Farm

M40

62 A B 63 C D 64 E F

123
110

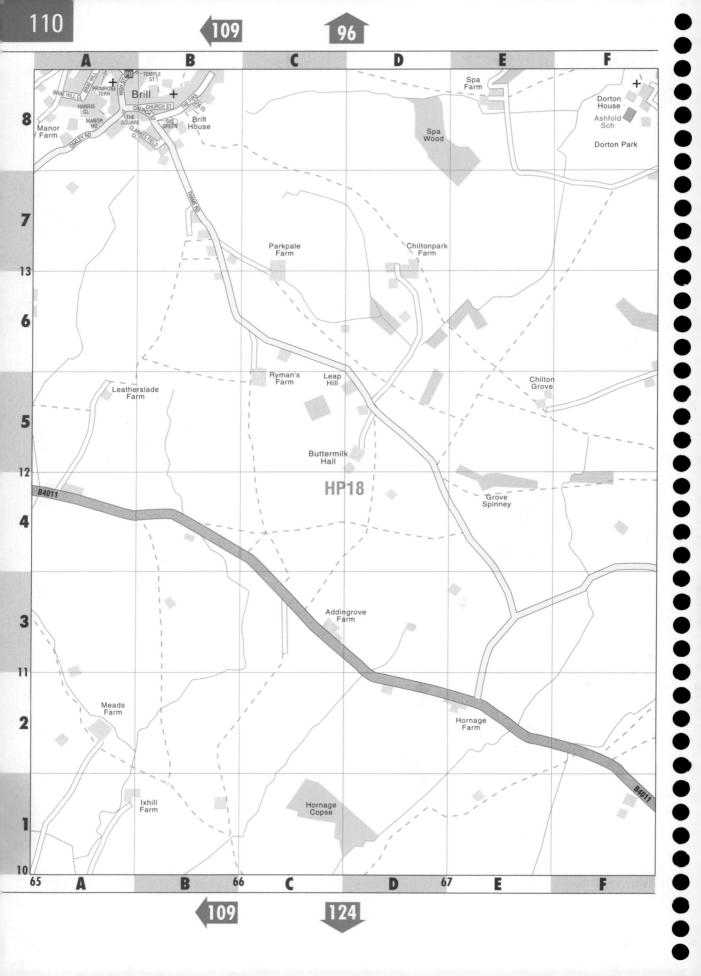

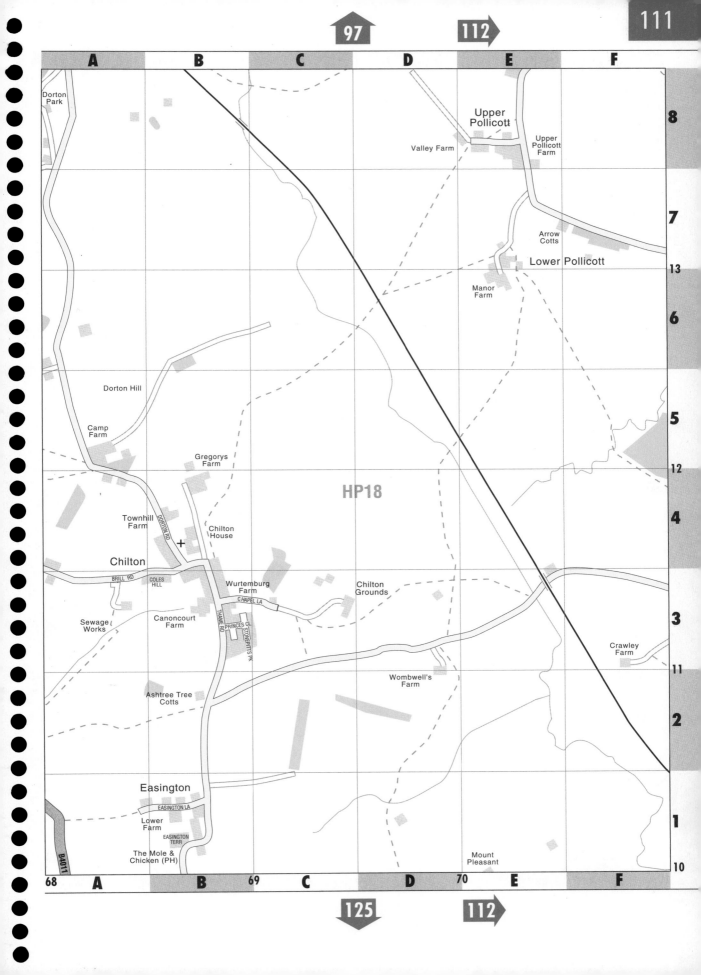

111
98

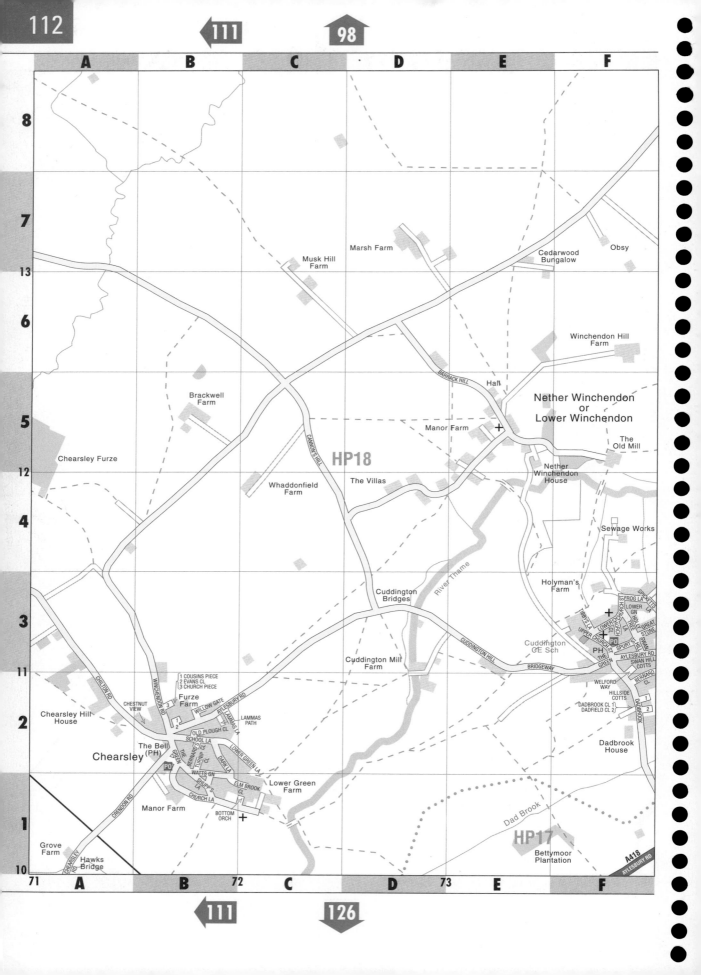

111
126

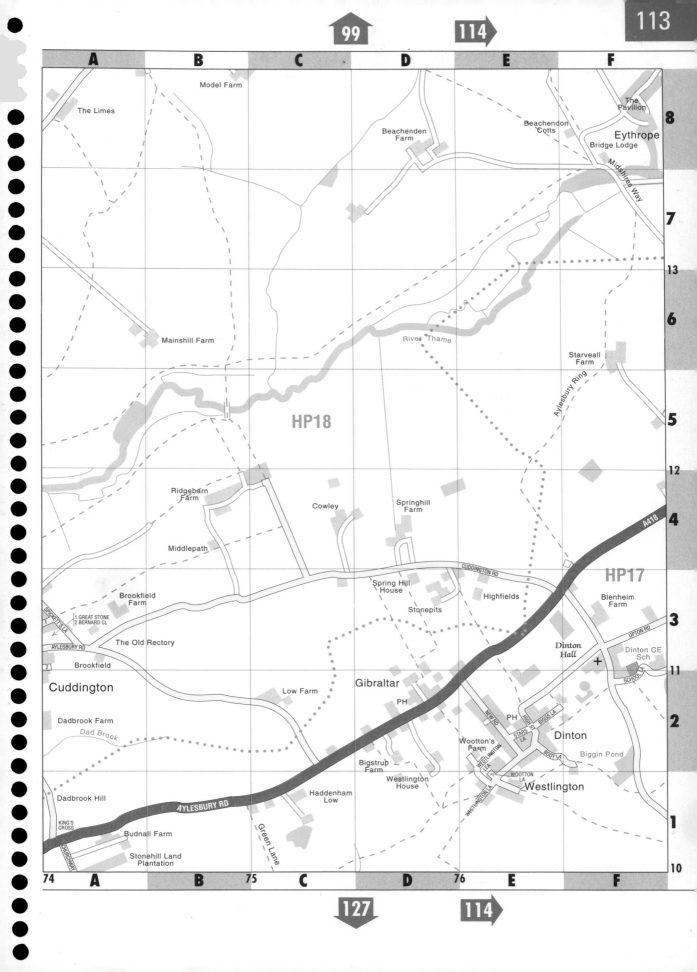

99
114

A B C D E F

The Pavilion

The Limes

Model Farm

Beachendon Cotts

8

Beachenden Farm

Eythrope

Bridge Lodge

Midshires Way

7

13

Mainshill Farm

6

River Thame

Starveall Farm

HP18

Aylesbury Ring

5

12

Ridgebarn Farm

Cowley

Springhill Farm

A418

4

Middlepath

CUDDINGTON RD

HP17

Spring Hill House

Highfields

Blenheim Farm

Brookfield Farm

Stonepits

UPTON RD

1 GREAT STONE
2 BERNARD CL

Dinton Hall

Dinton CE Sch

3

SPACKETTS LA

The Old Rectory

SCHOOL LA

AYLESBURY RD

11

2

Brookfield

Cuddington

Low Farm

Gibraltar

PH

PH

Dinton

NEW RD

STARS LA

BIGGS LA

2

Dadbrook Farm

Wootton's Farm

HIGH ST

BOOT LA

Biggin Pond

Dad Brook

Bigstrup Farm

Westlington House

WOOTTON LA

Dadbrook Hill

Haddenham Low

Westlington

WESTLINGTON LA

KING'S CROSS

Budnall Farm

1

CHURCHWAY

AYLESBURY RD

Green Lane

Stonehill Land Plantation

10

74 A B 75 C D 76 E F

127
114

A B C D E F

8

HP18

Eythrope Park

Weir Lodge

River Thame

Littleworth Farm

Midshires Way

North Buckinghamshire Way

Whaddon Hill Farm

HP19

GROSVENOR WAY
NAPIER RD
ARNCOTT WAY
SPRUCE RISE
BRIMMERS
SWALLOW LA
CUCKOO WAY
WARBLER CL
KINGFISHER CL
WREN
GREAT TICHDEN
COONS RD
LYSTERFIELD WAY

TREBAH SQ 1
WREN PATH 2
LOOSE PATH 3
WATERPERRY MEWS 4
CROWELL MEWS 5
LONGDOWN MEWS 6
ROSEMOOR MEWS 7
LOWNES PATH 8
WIXON PATH 9
PAKENHAM CL 10

7

Arthur's Gorse

Burn Hill

13

Lower Hartwell

Lower Hartwell Farm

6

The Nursery

Botts Furlong Farm

EYTHROPE RD

Cemy

Barnet's Close

Upper Hartwell

Park Hill

BELLE VUE
CHESTERFIELD CL
POPLARS CL
JEFFERIES RD
COTTAGE GROUNDS
CRAMHAMSTONE

THE SPIERT
PO
GRIFFITHS ACRE

Hartwell House (Hotel)

A418

5

LONG FURLONG
FAITHFULL CL
DARVILL RD
OXFORD RD
THE GLEBE
BADGERS RISE
CHURCH WAY
STONE CROFT
MANOR FARM CL
CORN CL
PH
Stone CE Comb Sch

Beech Wlk

WARREN CL
HAGGAR ST
BEACON CL
ST JOHNS
CRESLOW WAY
Stone
ROUND HILL
BISHOPSTONE RD
LEE CRES
CHILTERN CL
CHILTERN AVE

PH
MAYFLOWER
WAY
WILLOWMEAD
MEAD

12

Mast

HP17

Stone House

Midshires Way

BITTERHAM CL
PORTWAY RD
PORTWAY

Calley Farm

SEDRUP LA

4

A418

TEMPLECROFT TERR
Upton
HOMESTEAD CL
UPTON TERR
OLD MAIN RD

Lower Farm

Alwyn Lawn House

Sedrup

3

LOWER FARM GATE

Wallace Farm

Sewage Works

MEADOW COTTS

BISHOPSTONE RD

11

Pasture Farm

2

Chilboro Hill Farm

1

Aylesbury Ring

10

77 A 78 B C 78 78 D 79 E F

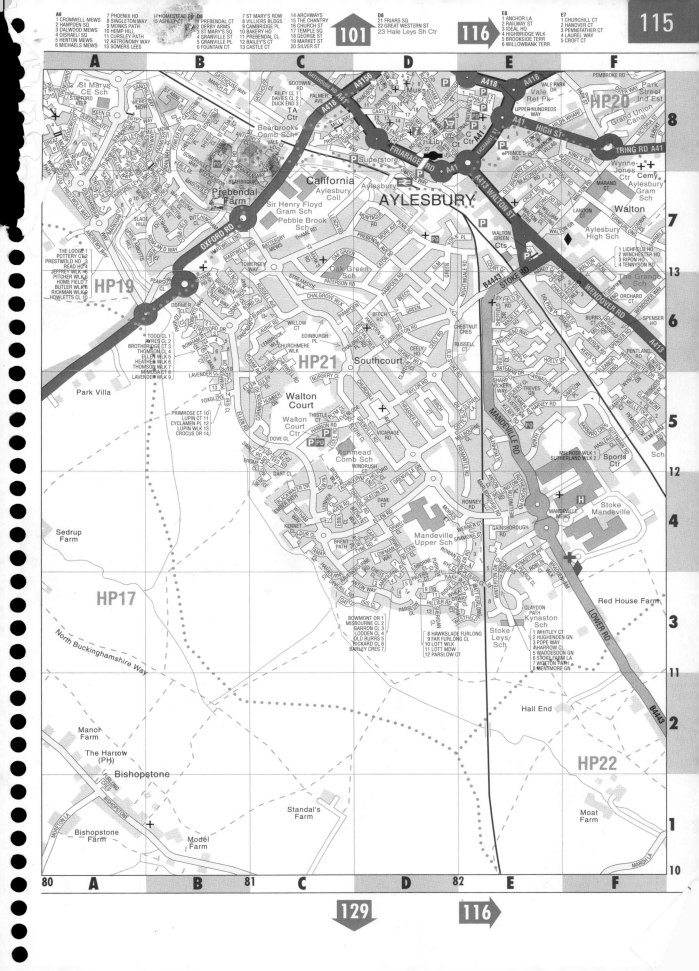

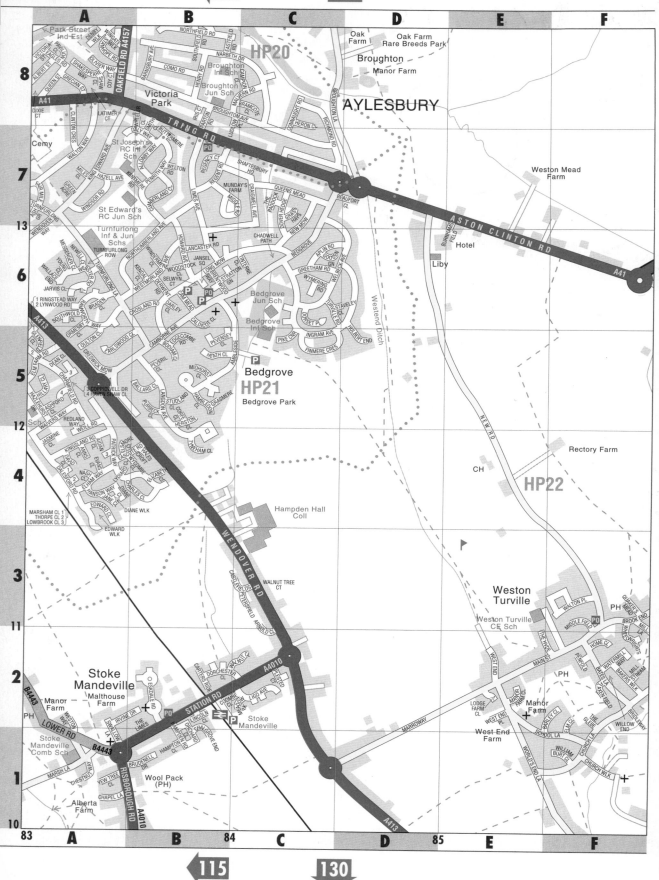

A B C D E

8
7
13
6
5
12
4
3
11
2
1
10

HP23

Grand Union Canal Wlk
Grand Union Canal
(Aylesbury Arm)

College
Farm

Dropshort
Farm

COLLEGE RD

Works

A41

Cherry
Farm

Lower
Farm

MODEL
ROW

Sunny Brook
Farm

BALLARDS
ROW

SUNNY BROOK CL

HP22

Aston Clinton

THE GREENWOOD 1
BROOK CL 2
BONHAM CT 3
MARSHMENT CL 4

Brook
Farm

ASTON CLINTON RD

NORMILL TERR

TURNER'S MDW

AYLESBURY RD

BROOK ST

LONG PLOUGH

PUTMANS DR

ARCHIVE CL

CHAPEL DR

GINGERS CL

GREEN END ST

TWITCHELL LA

TALBOT RD

THE ORCHARD

NEW RD

PLEASAUNCE WAY

THE GARTH

BEECHWOOD WAY

GARDEN

OVERSTRAND

ROTHSCHILD AVE

WATERY

Buckland

Moat
Farm

Church
Farm

PEGGS LA

Manor
Farm

Nield's
Farm

CHESTNUT CL

BEECHWOOD HO

Rothschild
Arms
(PH)

WESTON CT

WESTON RD

PARSLEY CL

THE RYE

WILLIAMS

PO

Sch

WARWICK CL

YORKE CL

TURVEY CL

ROSEBERY RD

MOUNT TILL RD

BEECHWOOD

BEACONSFIELD RD

LOWER ICKNIELD WAY

DEAN WAY

Park
Farm

CHURCH CL

CHURCH LA

PH

LONDON RD

ORCHARD DR

MOUNT CL

TOMPKINS CL

PH

VIRAGE

Rookery
Farm House

THE
COURTYARDS

Aston Clinton
Park

Old Rectory
Farm

STABLEBRIDGE RD

Splash
Covert

Green
Park

Wellonhead
Bridge

P

B4009

Bye
Green

BYE GN

BROOK END

ANSTEY
BROOK

LOWER GN

Brook End

Brook Farm

MILL LA

Mill
Farm

BROOKSIDE

Airfield

Sewage
Works

Grand Union Canal Wlk

CHILTERN WAY

UPPER ICKNIELD WAY

CH

Rosemead
Covert

Grand Union Canal
Wendover Arm

HAREBRIDGE LA

Marl
Copse

ROSEMEAD

B4009

Wendover
Woods

Church
Farm

Halton
Camp

Lower
Farm

THE
LEYS

BROOKSIDE

OLD
SCHOOL CL

CHESTNUT END

CHURCH
ST

MICHAEL CL

Halton

McEWEN RIDE

Halton
House

MANSION HILL

Aston
Hill

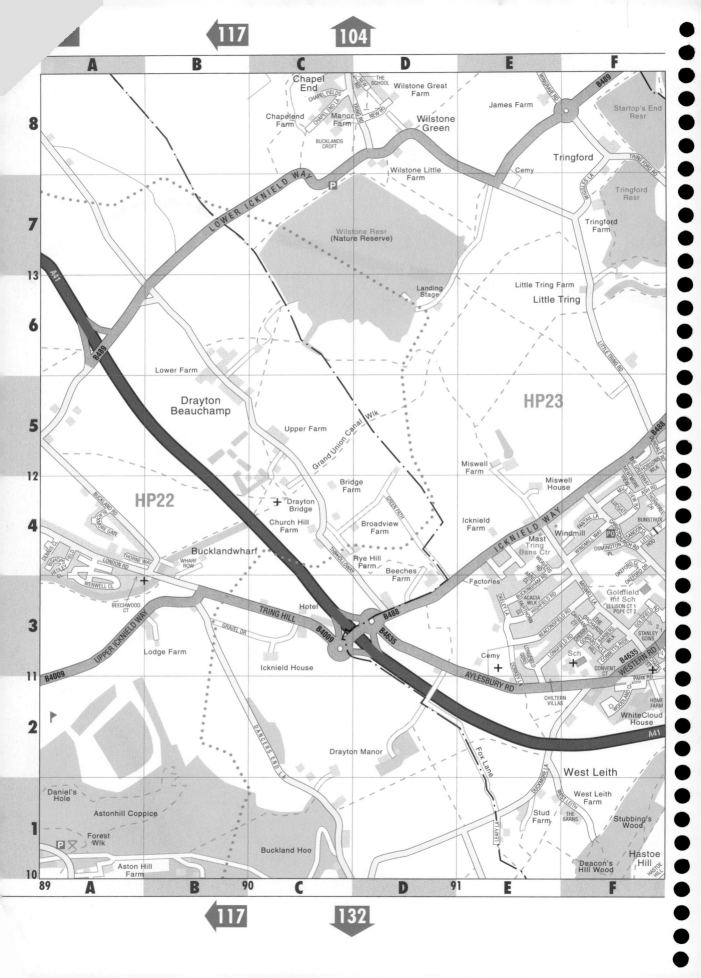

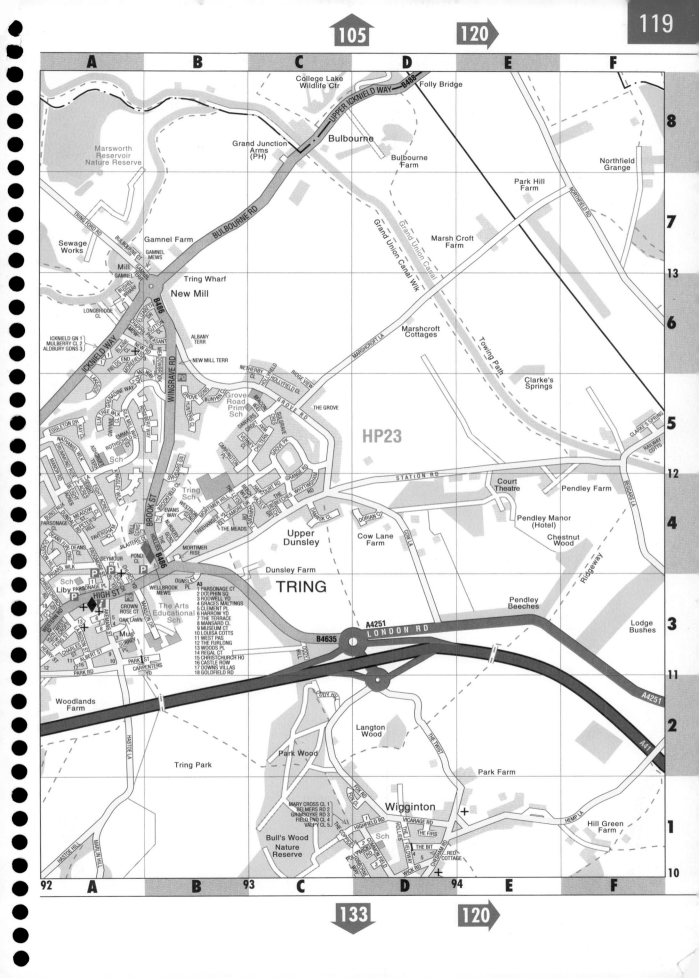

A B C D E F

Badger Wood

Church
Farm

Chiltern Way

BRIDGEWATER
CT

PO

Bridgewater
Arms
(PH)

GATESDENE CL

RINGSHALL DR

CHURCH RD

Chiltern Way

Chiltern Way

Hudnall Common
Plantation

Little Gaddesden
CE Prim Sch

Little
Gaddesden

Hudnall

Hudnall Common

8

7

Pitstone Park Copse

Ashridge

CH

The Green

HUDNALL LA

POND LA

13

Manor
House

THE LYE

CHAPEL CL

Hudnall
Farm

Old Park
Lodge

Prince's Riding

Golden Valley

Ashridge Park

Robin
Hood
Farm

Little
Brownlow
Farm

6

Thunderdell
Wood

Chiltern Way

LITTLE GADDESDEN
HO

Cromer
Wood

Gdns

Home Farm

Lady Grove

5

Ashridge Coll

Harding's
Rookery

HP4

ASHRIDGE
COTTS

CROMER CL

NETTLEDEN RD

12

Woodyard
Cottages

4

Toll

Pulridge
Wood

Little Coldharbour
Farm

Berkhamsted Common

Golden Valley
Farm

3

Coldharbour
Farm

11

Nettleden
Lodge

Furzefield
Wood

Hertfordshire Way

Webb's
Copse

2

Ashridge

Bluebell
Spring

HP1

Brickkiln
Cottage

Frithsden
Gardens

1

Frithsden Beeches

10

B4506

ALDERTON DR

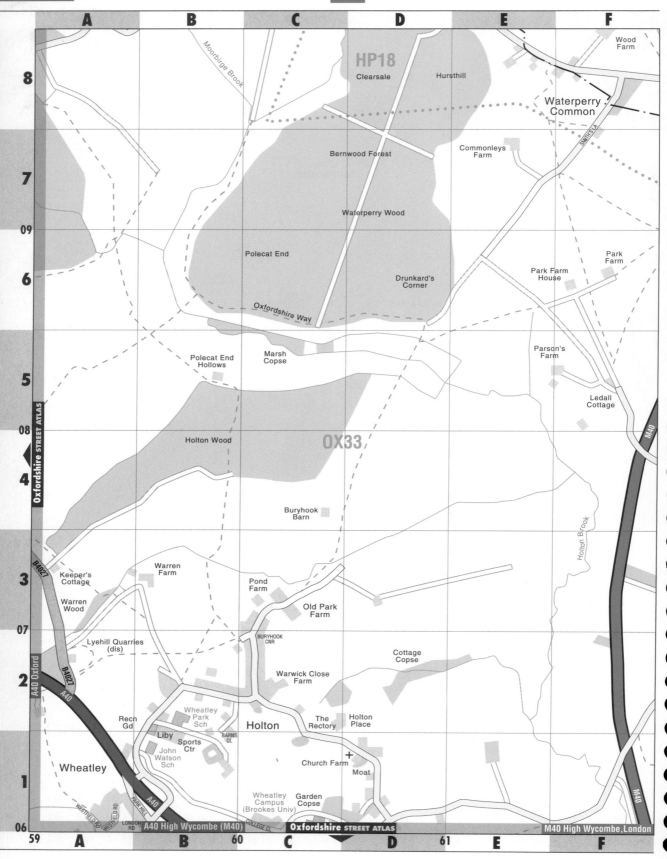

Wood Farm

HP18

Clearsale

Hursthill

Waterperry Common

Bernwood Forest

Commonleys Farm

Moorbirge Brook

Waterperry Wood

Polecat End

Park Farm

Park Farm House

Drunkard's Corner

Parson's Farm

Oxfordshire Way

Polecat End Hollows

Marsh Copse

Ledall Cottage

Holton Wood

OX33

M40

Buryhook Barn

Holton Brook

Keeper's Cottage

Warren Farm

Pond Farm

B4027

Warren Wood

Old Park Farm

Lyehill Quarries (dis)

BURYHOOK CNR

Cottage Copse

A40 Oxford

B4027

Warwick Close Farm

Recn Gd

Wheatley Park Sch

Holton

The Rectory

Holton Place

A40

Liby

Sports Ctr

BARNS CL

John Watson Sch

Wheatley

Church Farm

Moat

PARK HILL

Wheatley Campus (Brookes Univ)

Garden Copse

WESTFIELD RD

WESTFIELD RD

LONDON RD

COLLEGE CL

SMITH'S LA

Oxfordshire STREET ATLAS

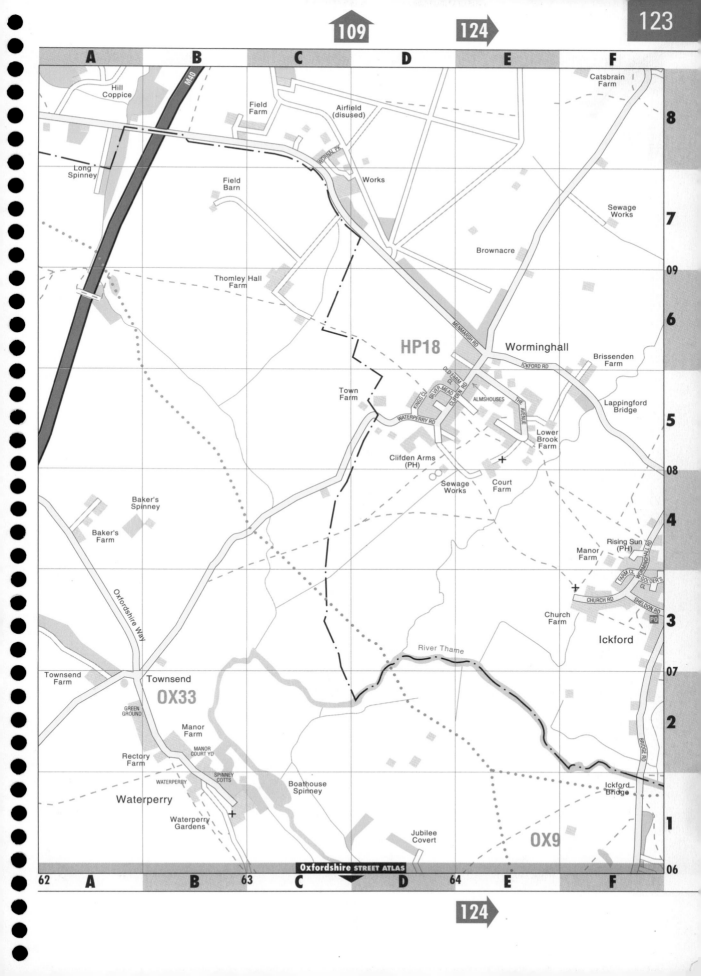

A B C D E F

8

Hill Coppice

M40

Field Farm

Airfield (disused)

Long Spinney

Field Barn

Works

Catsbrain Farm

7

Sewage Works

WORNAL PK

Thomley Hall Farm

Brownacre

09

MENMARSH RD

6

HP18

Worminghall

ICKFORD RD

Brissenden Farm

Town Farm

OLD FARM CL

KINGS CL

SILVER MEAD

CLIFDEN RD

ALMSHOUSES

THE AVENUE

Lappingford Bridge

5

WATERPERRY RD

Lower Brook Farm

Baker's Spinney

Clifden Arms (PH)

Sewage Works

Court Farm

08

Baker's Farm

Manor Farm

Rising Sun (PH)

4

WORMINGHALL RD

THAME RD

FARM CL

GOLDER'S CL

Oxfordshire Way

CHURCH RD

SHELDON RD

PO

Church Farm

Ickford

3

Townsend Farm

Townsend

OX33

River Thame

07

GREEN GROUND

BRIDGE RD

2

Manor Farm

MANOR COURT YD

Rectory Farm

WATERPERRY

SPINNEY COTTS

Boathouse Spinney

Ickford Bridge

Waterperry

Waterperry Gardens

Jubilee Covert

OX9

1

06

62 A B 63 C D 64 E F

123
110

Woodway Farm

Westfield Farm

Lower
Peppershill Farm

Peppershill

Crendon
House

Hill
Farm

Peppershill Farm

HP18

Peacehaven
Farm

Lower
Farm

Upper
Farm

Ickford

GOLDER'S CL
SCHOOL CL
FIELD CL
TURNFIELDS
SHELDON RD
Ickford
Comb Sch
BULL'S LA

Little
Ickford

Marsh
Farm

Sewage
Works

THE BURNHAMS
MARSH RD
LOWER
FARM
CL
LONG CRENDON RD
HOME CL
MORTON KING
CL

Shabbington

Rookery
Farm

Village
Farm

THE VINE

LIMES WAY
ICKFORD RD
DUKES CL
KIMBELLS CL
PO
SCHOOL LA

Franklins
Farm

Old
Fisherman
(PH)

River Thame

OX9

River Thame

OX9

Manor Farm

North
Weston

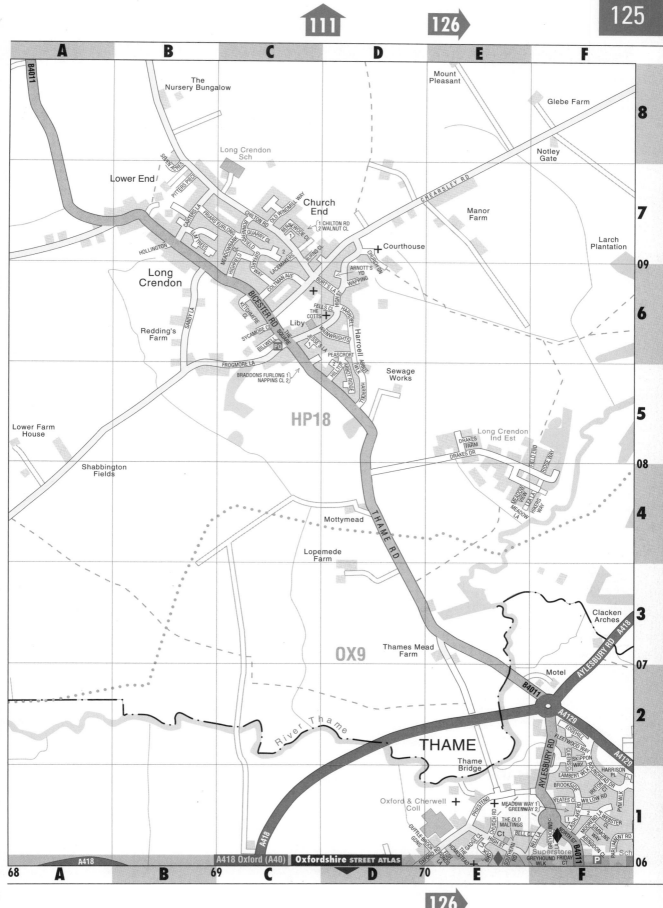

B4011

The Nursery Bungalow

Mount Pleasant

Glebe Farm

8

Long Crendon Sch

Notley Gate

Lower End

CHEARSLEY RD

Church End

7

Manor Farm

Larch Plantation

CHILTON RD
WALNUT CL

PITTERS PIECE

CARTERS LA

CHILTON RD

OLD WINDMILL WAY

BERKWODE CL

Courthouse

09

Long Crendon

FRIARS FURLONG

ELM TREES

MEADOWBANK

HIGHFIELD

STAFFORD WAY

QUARRY CL

ROTHWELLSFIELD

COLTMAN AVE

LACEMAKERS

BURNS CL

CHURCH GN

ARNOTT'S YD

WAPPING

BURT'S LA

SHORT CL

6

HOLLINGTON

BICESTER RD

THE SQUARE

SANDY LA

KETCHMERE CL

SYCAMORE CL

BILLWELL

PO

Liby

FELLS CL
THE COTTS

WAINWRIGHTS

JESSE'S LA

HILLTOP

PEASCROFT

ABBOT RIDGE

ABBOT TICK

HARROELL

HARROELL

Harroell

Sewage Works

Redding's Farm

FROGMORE LA

BRADDONS FURLONG 1
NAPPINS CL 2

Lower Farm House

HP18

5

Shabbington Fields

Long Crendon Ind Est

DRAKES FARM

DRAKES DR

FIELD END

RIDGE WAY

08

THAME RD

MEADOW VIEW

DELLA

MEADOW LA

HIKERS WAY

4

Mottymead

Lopemede Farm

OX9

3

Thames Mead Farm

Clacken Arches

A418

AYLESBURY RD

07

Motel

B4011

A4129

2

River Thame

THAME

A4129

Thame Bridge

EDGEHILL

FLEETWOOD WAY

AYLESBURY RD

DEENS CL

SKIPPON WAY

HARRISON PL

ROUNDHEAD DR

BROOKSIDE

IRETON CT

WILLOW RD

PYM WLK

Oxford & Cherwell Coll

PRIESTEND

MEADOW WAY 1
GREENWAY 2

YEATES CL

MOOREND LA

WEBSTER CL

LAMBERT WLK

1

THE OLD MALTINGS

CHURCH RD

BELL CL

SIMMONS CL

ABINGDON RD

CUTTLE BROOK GDNS

PRIESTEND

HIGH ST

BELL LA

GREYHOUND LA

NORTH ST

PARLIAMENT RD

CX CL

HOMESTEAD

BADGER'S CL

SOUTHERN RD

LASHLAKE RD

Ct

GREYHOUND FRIDAY CT

Superstore

GREYHOUND WLK

B4011

Sch

P

06

68

A

B

69

C

D

70

E

F

125 112

8

7

09

6

08

5

4

07

3

2

1

06

A B C D E F

CHEARSLEY RD

Dad Brook

Roundhill Farm

WINDMILL CT

A418

Long Mead Copse

Yolsum Plantation

HP18

NOTLEY FARM

Home Copse

Notley Abbey (remains of)

Aylesbury & Thame Airport

Haddenham Aerodrome Bsns Pk

HORSERN CL

DOLLICOTT

Crosse's Covert

AYLESBURY RD

Dovecote Cl 1
Marriotts Cl 2
South End 3
Croft Ctyd 4
Popes Acre 5

LONG FURLONG

WATERSIDE PENS

WINDMILL RD

THE BYRES

TACKS LA

ANXEY WAY

GREENS KEEP

YOLSUM CL

BRUCES WAY

DOVECOTE

Cvn Pk

Haddenham & Thame Parkway

P

MARRIOTTS LA

Mus

WYKEHAM WAY

WYKEHAM GATE

TOWNSIDE

THAME RD

Fowlers Field

SHEERSTOCK

Allot Gdns

GREENWAY

CLERKENWELL COTTS

CRABTREE RD

THE CROFT

STATION RD

SLAVE HILL

WHITECROSS RD

THE RUSH

LONG PLANS ST

THE WALL

HP17

Diggs

Grove End Barns

Grove End Farm

SCOTSGROVE COTTS

Dogkennel Covert

Scotsgrove House

SCOTSGROVE HILL

A418

MILL LA

OX9

Tythrop Park Farm

Scotsgrove Mill

Decoy Pond

Long Covert

Tythrop House

Sewage Works

MOOREND LA

Long Covert

Tythrop Lodge

1 ROUNDHEAD DR
2 RUSHALL RD
3 RUPERT WAY
4 SEDGEMOOR DR
5 DUNBAR DR
6 CHARLES DR
7 LUDLOW DR

A4129

THAME

8 STUART WAY
9 DIGBY CL
10 CAVENDISH WLK
11 PENNINGTON PL
12 PELHAM RD
13 GLENHAM RD

CHALGROVE RD

BERKELEY RD

CAVALIER RD

HAMILTON RD

CLARENDON DR

ORMOND RD

MARSTON RD

HIPTON CL

BLAKE CL

ONSLOW DR

OVERTON DR

GRENVILLE WAY

ASTLEY RD

NASBY CL

VANE RD

A4129

Pilmoor Arch

A4129

A4129 KINGSEY RD

WINDMILL RD

Whites Farm

Mast

71 A B 72 C D 73 E F

125

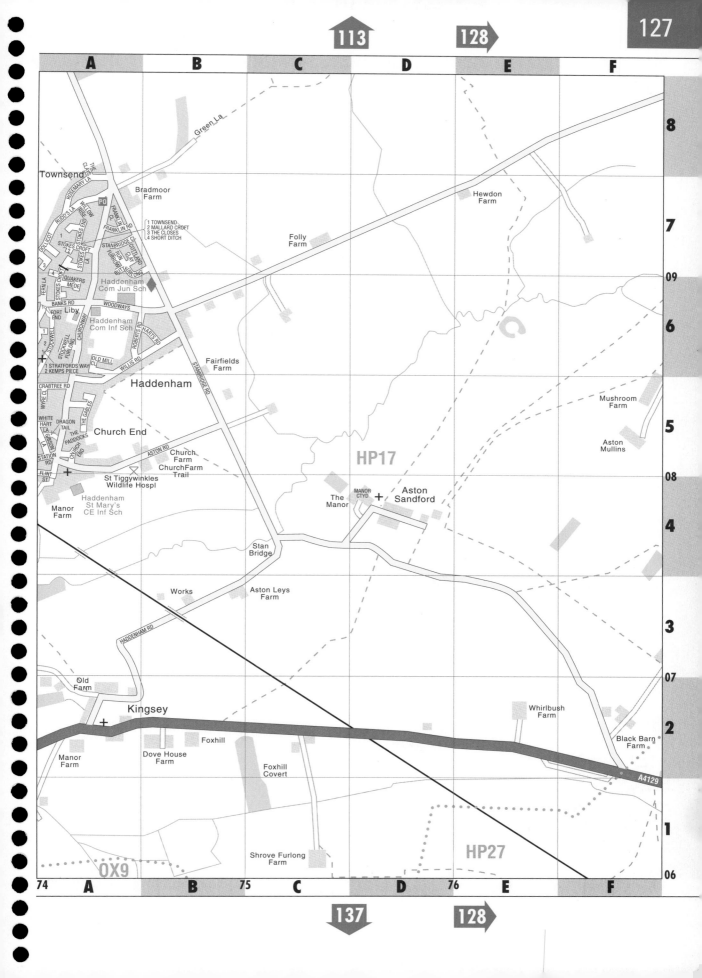

A B C D E F

8

7

09

6

5

08

4

3

07

2

06

Townsend

Bradmoor Farm

Green La

Hewdon Farm

1 TOWNSEND
2 MALLARD CROFT
3 THE CLOSES
4 SHORT DITCH

Folly Farm

PO

Haddenham Com Jun Sch

Haddenham Com Inf Sch

Fairfields Farm

Haddenham

Mushroom Farm

Aston Mullins

Church End

HP17

Church Farm
ChurchFarm Trail

Aston Sandford

The Manor

MANOR CTYD

St Tiggywinkles Wildlife Hospl

Haddenham St Mary's CE Inf Sch

Manor Farm

Stan Bridge

Works

Aston Leys Farm

HADDENHAM RD

Old Farm

Kingsey

Whirlbush Farm

Black Barn Farm

Manor Farm

Dove House Farm

Foxhill

Foxhill Covert

A4129

Shrove Furlong Farm

HP27

OX9

127 114

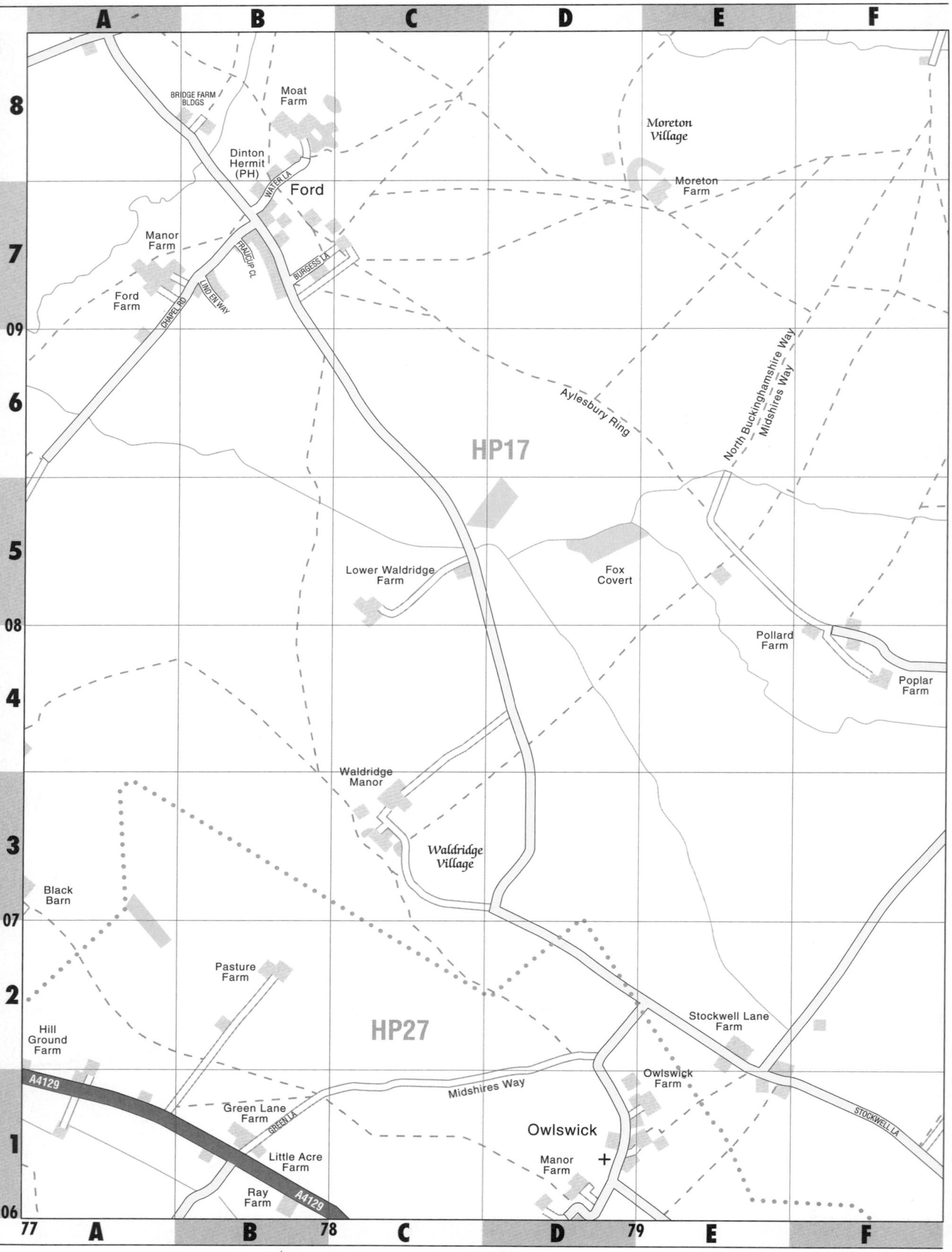

A B C D E F

8

Moat
Farm

BRIDGE FARM
BLDGS

Moreton
Village

Dinton
Hermit
(PH)

Moreton
Farm

Ford

7

WATER LA

BURGESS LA

Manor
Farm

FRANGUP CL

Ford
Farm

09

LINDEN WAY

CHAPEL RD

6

Aylesbury Ring

North Buckinghamshire Way

Midshires Way

HP17

5

Lower Waldridge
Farm

Fox
Covert

08

Pollard
Farm

4

Poplar
Farm

Waldridge
Manor

3

Waldridge
Village

Black
Barn

07

Pasture
Farm

2

Stockwell Lane
Farm

HP27

Hill
Ground
Farm

Owlswick
Farm

A4129

STOCKWELL LA

Green Lane
Farm

Midshires Way

GREEN LA

1

Owlswick

Little Acre
Farm

Manor
Farm

A4129

Ray
Farm

06

77 A B 78 C D 79 E F

127 138

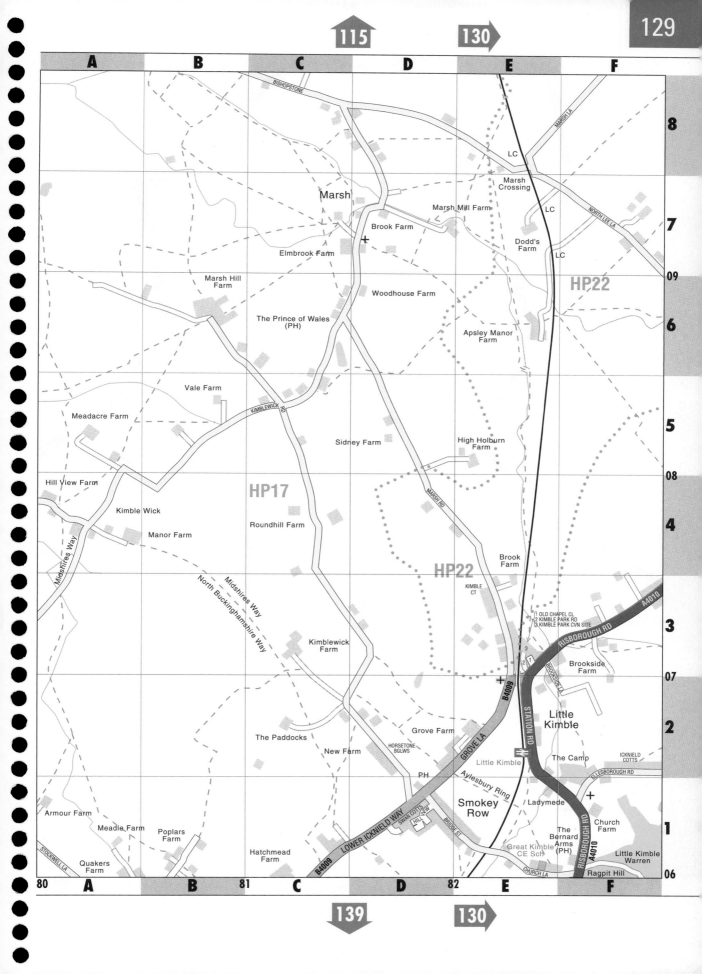

A B C D E F

8
7
09
6
5
08
4
3
07
2
1
06

BISHOPSTONE

Marsh

MARSH LA

LC

Marsh Crossing

Marsh Mill Farm

LC

NORTH LEE LA

Brook Farm

Dodd's Farm

LC

Elmbrook Farm

Marsh Hill Farm

Woodhouse Farm

HP22

The Prince of Wales (PH)

Apsley Manor Farm

Vale Farm

KIMBLEWICK RD

Meadacre Farm

Sidney Farm

High Holburn Farm

Hill View Farm

MARSH RD

HP17

Kimble Wick

Roundhill Farm

Manor Farm

Midshires Way

Brook Farm

HP22

KIMBLE CT

North Buckinghamshire Way

Midshires Way

1 OLD CHAPEL CL
2 KIMBLE PARK RD
3 KIMBLE PARK CVN SITE

A4010

Kimblewick Farm

RISBOROUGH RD

BROOKSIDE LA

Brookside Farm

B4009

STATION RD

Little Kimble

The Paddocks

Grove Farm

GROVE LA

The Camp

ICKNIELD COTTS

New Farm

HORSETONE BGLWS

Little Kimble

ELLESBOROUGH RD

PH

Aylesbury Ring

Smokey Row

Ladymede

LOWER ICKNIELD WAY

SWAN COTTS

HILL VIEW

BRIDGE ST

The Bernard Arms (PH)

RISBOROUGH RD

A4010

The Camp

Church Farm

Armour Farm

Meadle Farm

Poplars Farm

Great Kimble CE Sch

Little Kimble Warren

STOCKWELL LA

Hatchmead Farm

B4009

CHURCH LA

Ragpit Hill

Quakers Farm

129
116

A **B** **C** **D** **E** **F**

8

Belmore Hotel
Yew Tree Farm
Whitehorn Farm
Stoke House
A4010
WHITEHORN CL
OLD RISBOROUGH RD
Triangle Bsns Pk
A413
QUILTERS WAY
WENDOVER RD
Hideaway Farm
B4009
CHILTERNS
WORLD'S END LA
B4009

Bucks Goat Ctr
RISBOROUGH RD

7
World's End
Marquis of Granby (PH)
NASH LEE RD
Fox Close Farm
B4009

North Lee
09
North Lee Farm
Stoke Grove Farm
NASH LEE END
NASH LEE LA
Loudwater Farm

NORTH LEE LA
6
Nashlee Farm
NASH LEE RD
B4009

Nash Lee

Chiltern Brewery
HP22

5
Terrick House
TERRICK ROW
B4009
Terrick
ROYAL MEAD
A413

Grove Farm
08

4
Springfield Farm
CHALKSHIRE RD
CHALKSHIRE COTTS
Chalkshire
Wellwick Farm
Coneycroft Farm

Chalkshire Farm
Chalkshire
A4010
Home Close Farm
Aylesbury Ring
ELLESBOROUGH RD

3
Bushey Leys
HP17
SOUTHFIELD COTTS
ELDRIDGE LA
Butler's Cross
CH
WENDOVER RD
Bacombe Hill

The Springs
ELM CT
ELM CL
07
The Springs Farm
SPRINGS LA
ELLESBOROUGH RD
Russell Arms (PH)
Hill End Farm
Ridgeway

2
SPRINGS CL
CHURCH HILL
Ellesborough Manor
Mon
Combe Hill

Ellesborough
ELLESBOROUGH RD
MISSENDEN RD

1
Cymbeline's Castle
Ellesborough Plantation
Combe
Low Scrubs
Upper Bacombe

Beacon Hill
Combe Hill Farm
P

Ellesborough Warren
Lodge Hill
06
83 **A** **B** 84 **C** **D** 85 **E** **F**

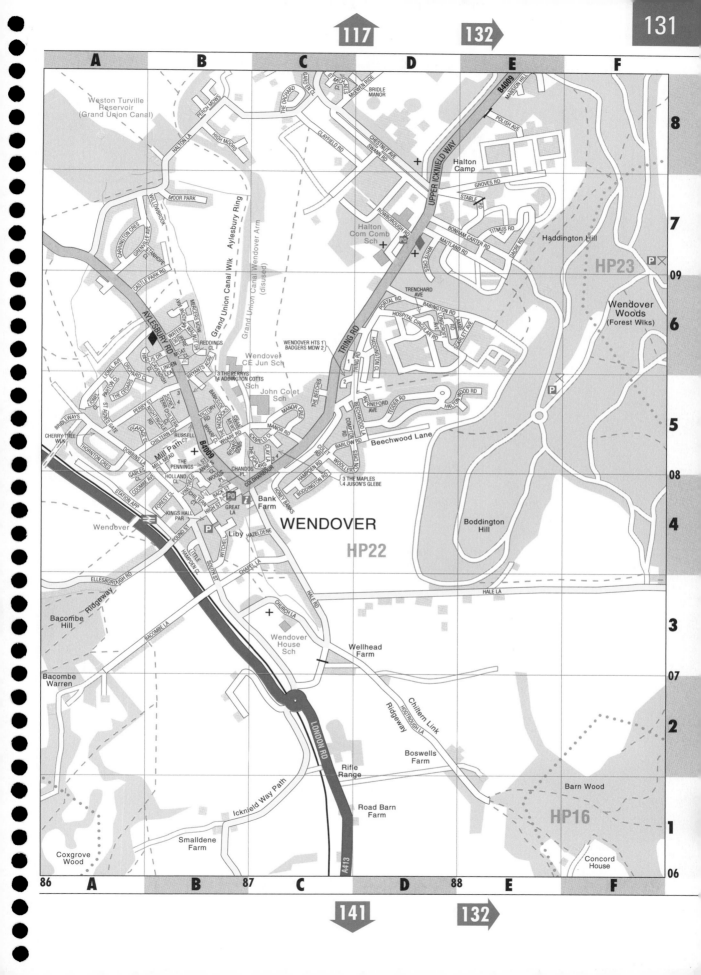

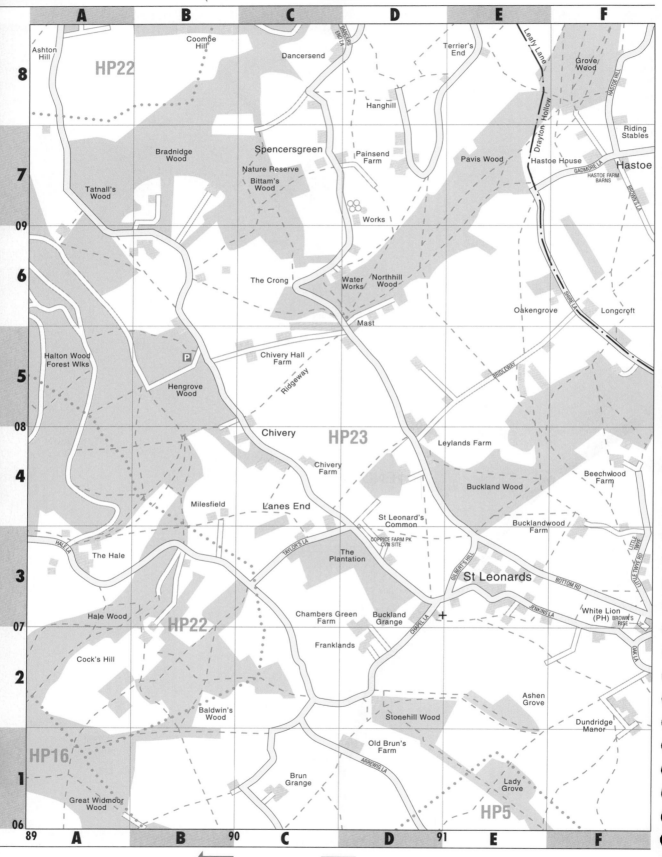

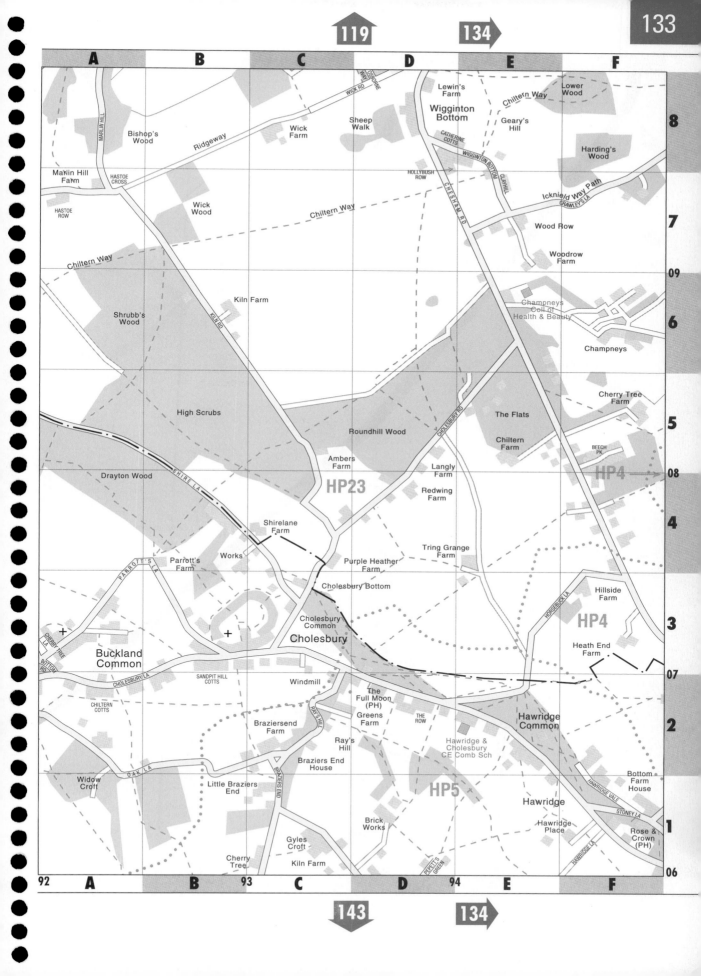

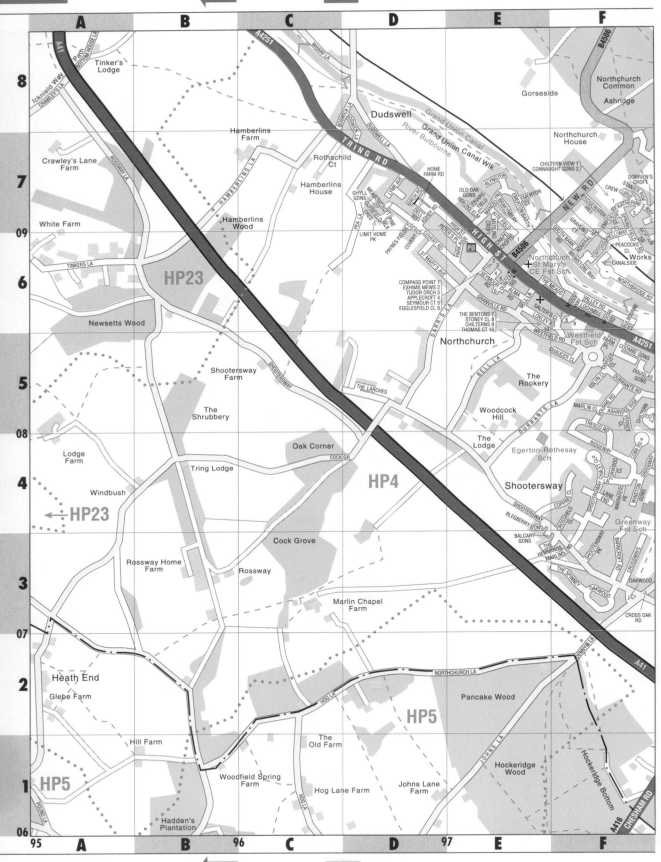

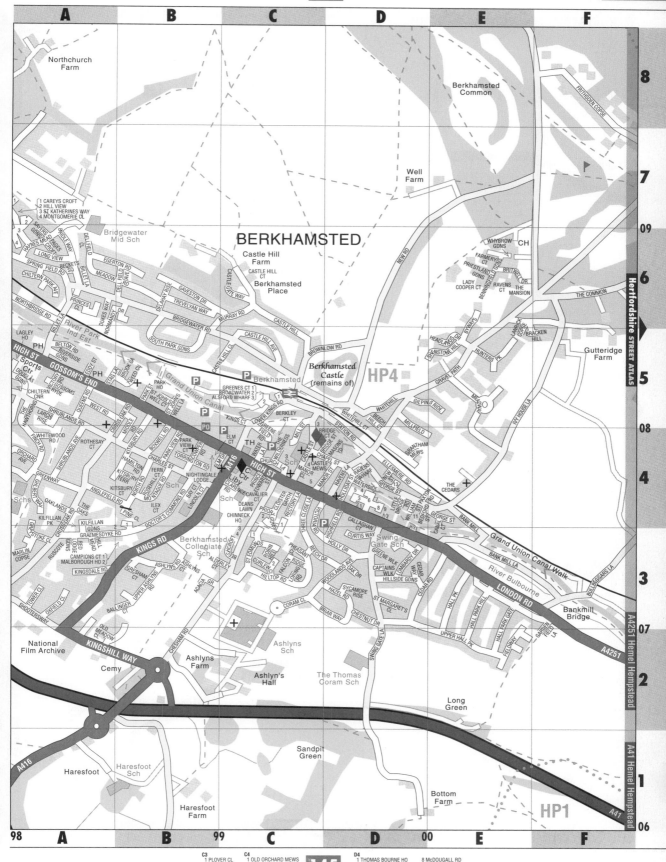

BERKHAMSTED

Northchurch Farm

Berkhamsted Common

Well Farm

1 CAREYS CROFT
2 HILL VIEW
3 ST KATHERINES WAY
4 MONTGOMERIE CL

Bridgewater Mid Sch

Castle Hill Farm

CASTLE HILL CT

Berkhamsted Place

WHYBROW GDNS
CH
FARMERY CT
PRIESTLANDS GDNS
BRITWELL DR
THE MANSION
LADY COOPER CT
RAVENS CT

Berkhamsted Castle (remains of)

HP4

Gutteridge Farm

BRACKEN HILL
HUNTERS PK
GRAVEL PATH

Berkhamsted

GREENES CT 1
BROADWATER 2
ALSFORD WHARF 3

Grand Union Canal

Sports Ctr
GOSSOM'S END
HIGH ST

PH
PH

Grand Union Canal Walk

HIGH ST
A416
Liby
Ctr

Swing Gate Sch

River Bulbourne

LONDON RD

Bankmill Bridge

National Film Archive

KINGSHILL WAY

Berkhamsted Collegiate Sch

KINGS RD

Cemy

Ashlyns Farm

Ashlyns Sch

Ashlyn's Hall

The Thomas Coram Sch

Long Green

A4251 Hemel Hempstead

A41 Hemel Hempstead

Haresfoot

Haresfoot Sch

Sandpit Green

Bottom Farm

HP1

Haresfoot Farm

A41

Hertfordshire STREET ATLAS

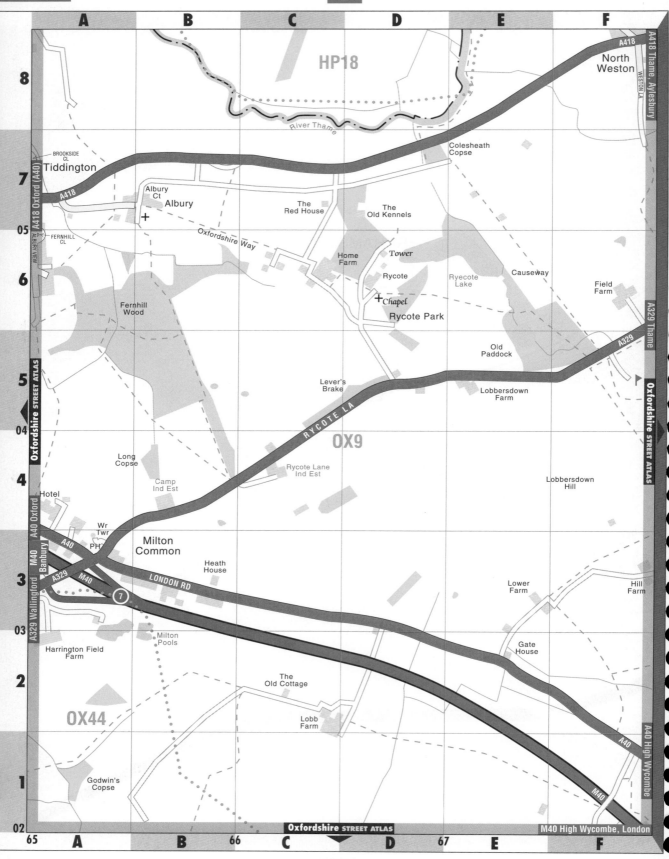

A B C D E F

8 HP18

North
Weston

A418 Thame, Aylesbury

WESTON LA

River Thame

Coleshealth
Copse

7 BROOKSIDE CL

Tiddington

A418 Oxford (A40)

A418

Albury Ct

Albury

The
Red House

The
Old Kennels

05 FERNHILL CL

Oxfordshire Way

ALBURYVIEW

Tower

Home
Farm

Rycote

Causeway

Field
Farm

6 Fernhill
Wood

Ryecote
Lake

A329 Thame

A329

Chapel

Rycote Park

Old
Paddock

Oxfordshire STREET ATLAS

5 Lever's
Brake

Lobbersdown
Farm

04 RYCOTE LA

OX9

Long
Copse

Rycote Lane
Ind Est

Lobbersdown
Hill

4 Camp
Ind Est

Hotel

Wr
Twr

PH

Milton
Common

Heath
House

A40 Oxford

A40

3 M40 Banbury

A329

M40

LONDON RD

Lower
Farm

Hill
Farm

A329 Wallingford

7

03 Milton
Pools

Gate
House

Harrington Field
Farm

2 The
Old Cottage

OX44

Lobb
Farm

A40 High Wycombe

1 Godwin's
Copse

M40

02

A B 66 C D 67 E F

65

M40 High Wycombe, London

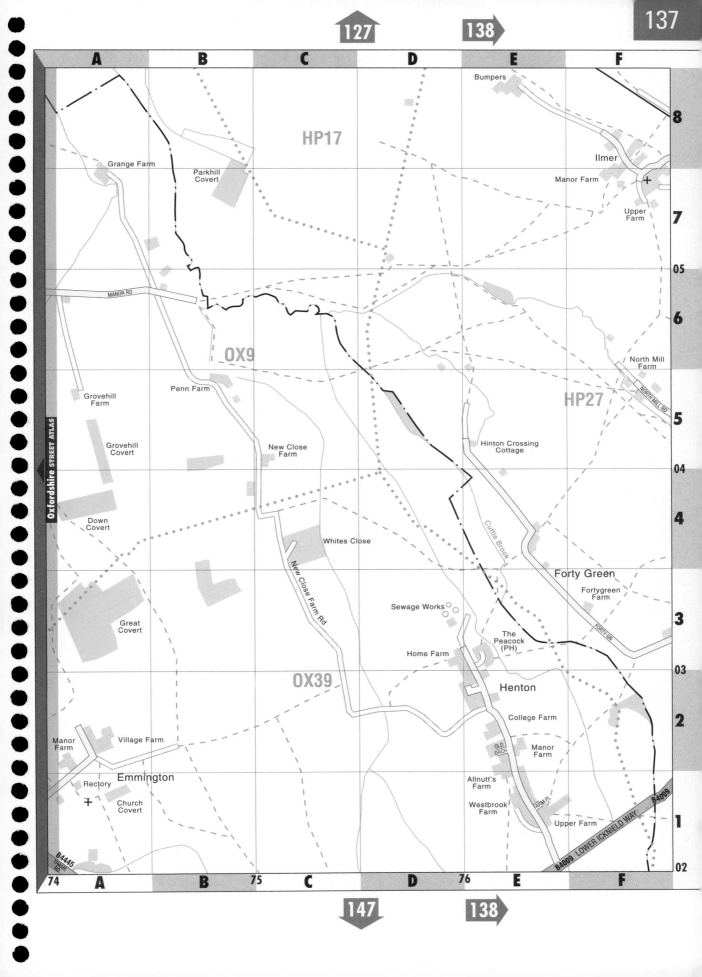

127
138
147
138

Oxfordshire STREET ATLAS

HP17

OX9

HP27

OX39

Bumpers

Ilmer

Manor Farm

Upper Farm

North Mill Farm

NORTH MILL RD

Grange Farm

Parkhill Covert

MANOR RD

Grovehill Farm

Penn Farm

Grovehill Covert

New Close Farm

Hinton Crossing Cottage

Down Covert

Cuttle Brook

Forty Green

Fortygreen Farm

FORTY GN

Whites Close

New Close Farm Rd

Great Covert

Sewage Works

The Peacock (PH)

Home Farm

Henton

College Farm

Manor Farm

Village Farm

OLD ORCH

Manor Farm

Rectory

Emmington

Church Covert

Allnutt's Farm

Westbrook Farm

FARM PL

Upper Farm

B4009

LOWER ICKNIELD WAY

B4009

B4445 THAME RD

74   75   76

8   7   05   6   5   04   4   3   03   2   1   02

A B C D E F

8

7

05

6

5

04

4

3

03

2

1

02

HP17

A4129

Lower Farm

Anderdons Farm

Tifnams

Buntings

Redhouse Farm

SPEX TYDN
BLACKSMITHS RD
WHEELWRIGHT RD
SAWMILL RD

Chadwell Hill Cottage

BAR LA

Longwick

Chadwell Hill

Rose Farm

CENTENARY COTTS

Swan's Way

TOLL BAR
CWR 3

B4009

PH

PO

THAME RD

Longwick CE Comb Sch

ORCHARD CL
WALNUT TREE
DOBBELLS RD
MEADOW DR

Laurels Farm

BLENHEIM CL 1
THE GREEN 2
CLAYDONS PL 3

PH

BOXER RD
BARN RD
WILLIAMS WAY

BELL CRES

B4444

CHESTNUT WAY

THE WILLOWS

Longwick RD A4129

LONGWICK RD

IVY CL

LITTLE ORCHARD CL

WOODBINE CL

Midshires Way

THE COTTS

Longwick Mill

Works

HP27

B4444

Little Horsenden Farm

The Ford

Sewage Works

Waltons Farm

Sandpit Farm

SUMMERLEYS RD

Summerleys

Park Mill

Holly Green Farm

Sandpit Lane Farm

SANDPIT LA

LOWER ICKNIELD WAY

HOLLY GREEN LA

Holly Green

Pitch Green Farm

Pitch Green

Chinnor & Princes Risborough Rly

Icknield Line

NORTH MILL

FIRS CT

CHAPEL LA

Skittle Green

Brew House Farm

Manor Farm

LC

Mast

Princes Risborough

SKITTLE GN

FORTY GN

RIDGEWAY MEADS

Horsenden

CHINNOR RD

THE VINEYARDS

Bledlow Bridge

HORSENDEN LA

P

CROSS LANES

WEST LA

B4009

Westfield Farm

PERRY LA

BLEDLOW COTTS

Bledlow

PICTS LA 1
SHOOTACRE LA 2

Cemy

LYDE END

Bledlow House

BLEDLOW RIDGE RD

MANOR CL

CHURCH END

Saunderton

BLEDLOW RD

NORTH MILL RD

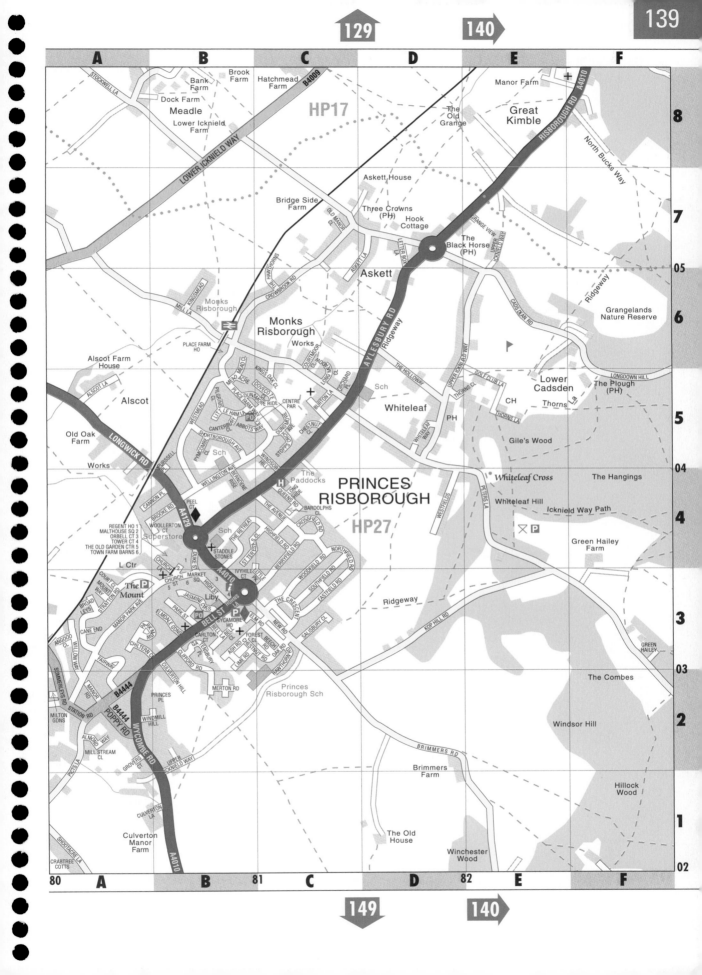

139
130

	A	B	C	D	E	F

8

The Dene

Whorley Wood

Chequers

Lodge Hill

Lodge Hill Farm

High Scrubs

Ridgeway

Linton's Wood

HP22

Fugsdon Wood

7

Ridgeway

Maple Wood

HP17

Goodmerhill Wood

05

Pulpit Hill

Brockwell Farm

LEE COTTS

Dunsmore Old Farm

6

Pulpit Wood

Pond Wood

Buckmoorend

Chisley Wood

Little Hampden Manor

5

Hobb's Hill

Longdown Farm

Hengrove Wood

Little Hampden Common

Ninn Wood

Weyburn's Wood

04

Blyth's Wood

Rising Sun (PH)

4

Sergeant's Wood

Cross Coppice

Dirtywood Farm

Little Hampden

Chiltern Way

Little Hampden Farm

Solinger House

HP27

Little Boy's Heath

Hampden Bottom Farm

Warren Wood

3

Knighton's Hill Wood

HP16

03

Kingsfield Wood

2

Chiltern Way

Hampden House

1

Hillock Wood

Barnes's Grove

Park Farm

The Glade

Oaken Grove

Redland End

02

83	A	B	84	C	D	85	E	F

139
150

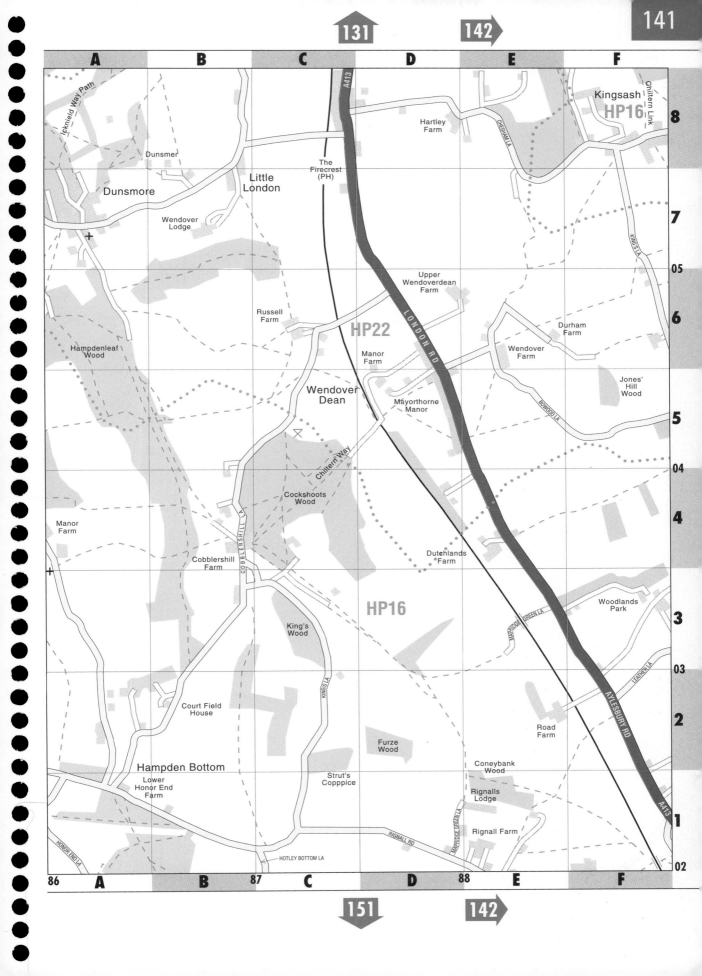

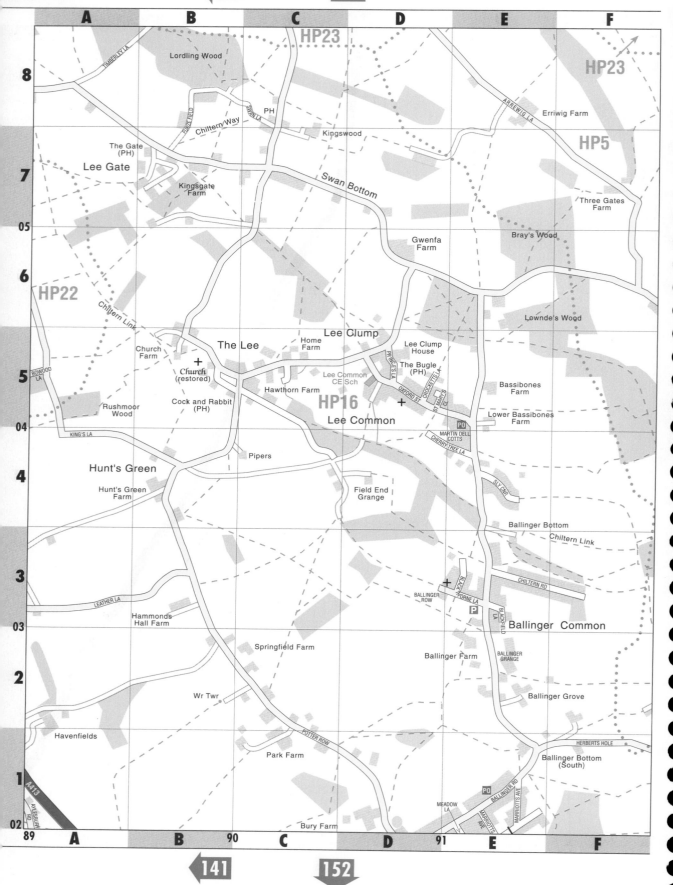

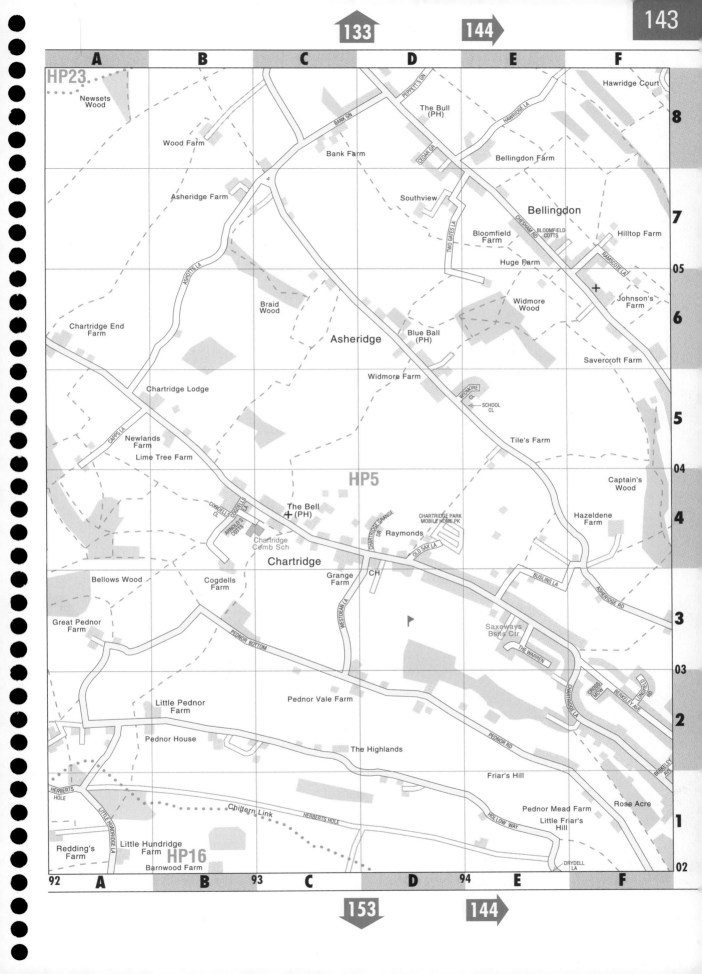

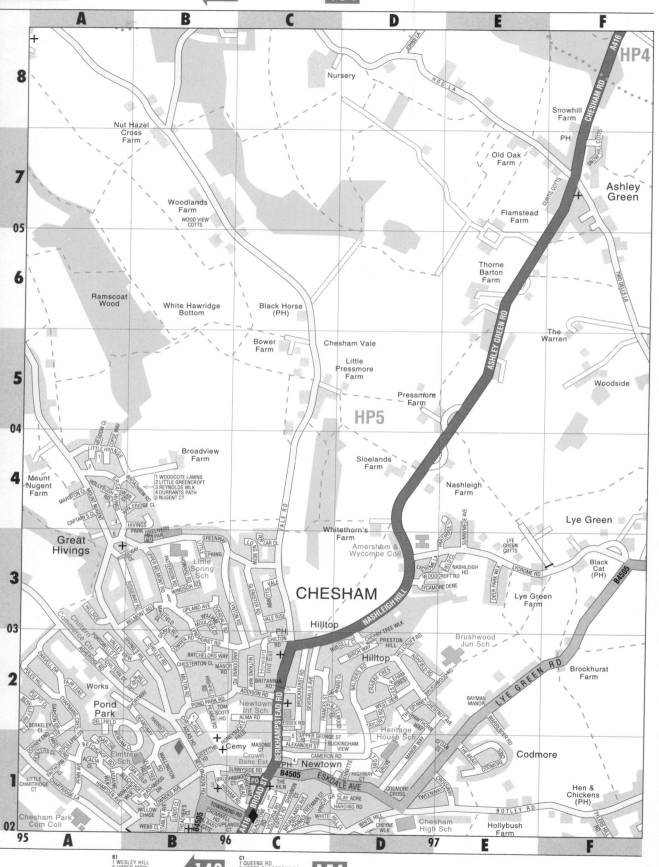

Nursery

Nut Hazel
Cross
Farm

Snowhill
Farm

PH

Ashley
Green

Old Oak
Farm

Woodlands
Farm

WOOD VIEW
COTTS

Flamstead
Farm

Ramscoat
Wood

White Hawridge
Bottom

Black Horse
(PH)

Chesham Vale

Thorne
Barton
Farm

The
Warren

Woodside

Bower
Farm

Little
Pressmore
Farm

Pressmore
Farm

HP5

Broadview
Farm

Sloelands
Farm

Mount
Nugent
Farm

1 WOODCOTE LAWNS
2 LITTLE GREENCROFT
3 REYNOLDS WLK
4 DURRANTS PATH
5 NUGENT CT

Nashleigh
Farm

Lye Green

Great
Hivings

Whitethorn's
Farm

LYE
GREEN
COTTS

Amersham &
Wycombe Coll

Black Cat
(PH)

Little
Spring
Sch

CHESHAM

Lye Green
Farm

Hilltop

Brushwood
Jun Sch

Brockhurst
Farm

PH

Hilltop

Britannia
Ind Est

Preston
Hill

Newtown
Inf Sch

Bayman
Manor

Codmore

Heritage
House Sch

Pond
Park

Works

Cemy

Crown
Bsns Est

Masons
Ct

Newtown

Codmore
Cross

Elmtree
Sch

PH

B4505

ESKDALE AVE

Chesham High Sch

Hen &
Chickens
(PH)

Hollybush
Farm

Little
Chartridge
Ct

Chesham Park
Com Coll

BOTLEY RD

95   A   B   96   C   D   97   E   F

B1
1 WESLEY HILL
2 UPPER MDW
3 Phoenix Bsns Ctr
B2
1 THE CHASE
2 NIGHTINGALE RD

C1
1 QUEENS RD
2 UPPER GLADSTONE RD
3 FRANCHISE ST
4 TURNERS WLK
5 GEORGE ST

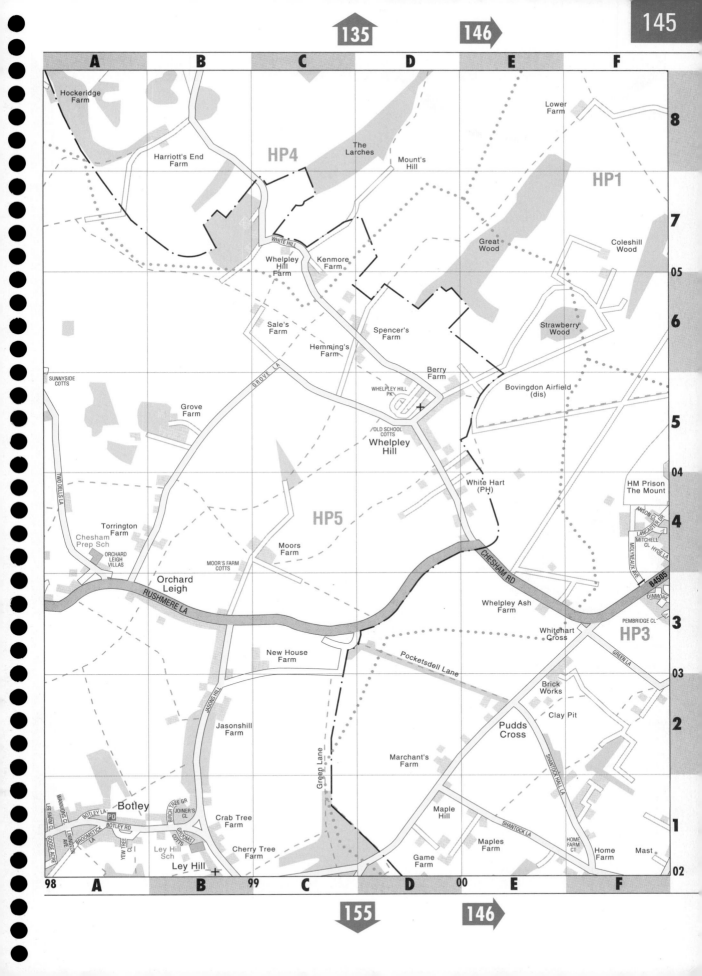

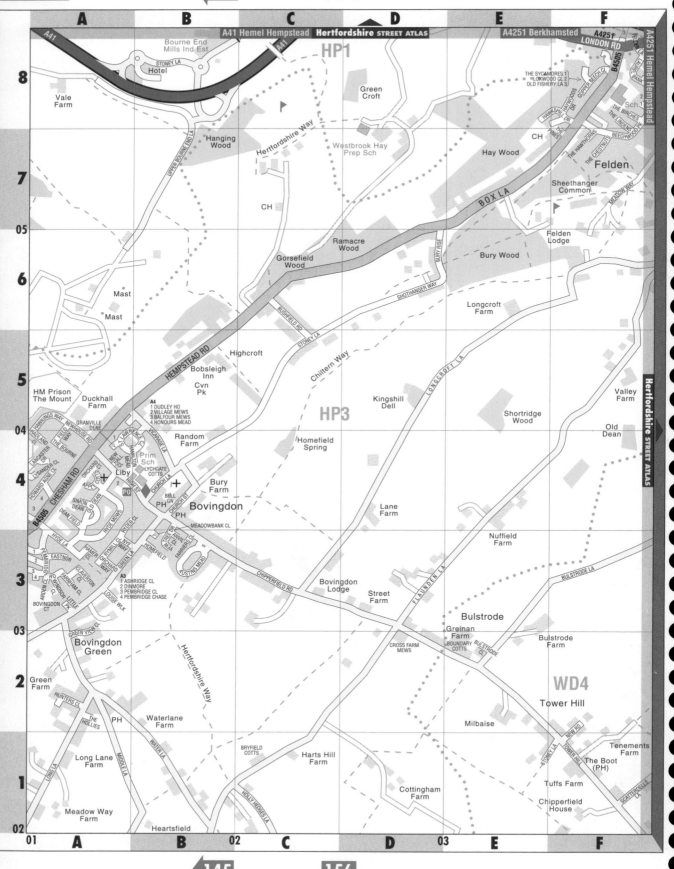

145

A41 Hemel Hempstead **Hertfordshire** STREET ATLAS A4251 Berkhamsted A4251

HP1

Bourne End Mills Ind Est

STONEY LA

Hotel

Vale Farm

Green Croft

THE SYCAMORES 1
LOKWOOD CL 2
OLD FISHERY LA 3

LONDON RD

B4505

Sch

The Birches

Hanging Wood

Hertfordshire Way

Westbrook Hay Prep Sch

Hay Wood

CH

THE LINDENS

BEECHWOOD CL

HP1

Felden

CH

Sheethanger Common

BOX LA

Felden Lodge

Ramacre Wood

BURY RISE

Bury Wood

Gorsefield Wood

SHOTHANGER WAY

Longcroft Farm

Mast

Mast

BUSHFIELD RD

STONEY LA

Chiltern Way

LONGCROFT LA

Valley Farm

HEMPSTEAD RD

Highcroft

Bobsleigh Inn Cvn Pk

HP3

Kingshill Dell

Shortridge Wood

Old Dean

HM Prison The Mount

Duckhall Farm

GRANVILLE DENE

A4
1 DUDLEY HO
2 VILLAGE MEWS
3 BALFOUR MEWS
4 HONOURS MEAD

Random Farm

Homefield Spring

HAWKINS WAY
NEWHOUSE RD
FIELD WAY
THE BOURNE
LANCASTER DR
LYSANDER CL
HOWARD AGNE CL

CHESHAM RD

B4505

Prim Sch

Liby

LYCHGATE COTTS

Bury Farm

Lane Farm

Nuffield Farm

PO

BELL GN

Bovingdon

PH

PH

MEADOWBANK CL

HYDE MDWS

AUSTINS MEAD

A3
1 ASHRIDGE CL
2 DINMORE
3 PEMBRIDGE CL
4 PEMBRIDGE CHASE

CHIPPERFIELD RD

Bovingdon Lodge

Street Farm

FLAUNDEN LA

BULSTRODE LA

EASTNOR

PEMBRIDGE RD

CLAVERTON

FARNHAM CL

WINDSOR

ARDEN CL

BOVINGDON CT

LITTLE

LOUISE WLK

HOMEFIELD

Bovingdon Green

GREEN VIEW CL

Bulstrode

Greinan Farm

BOUNDARY COTTS

BULSTRODE CL

Bulstrode Farm

WD4

Green Farm

HUNTERS CL

THE HOLLIES

PH

Waterlane Farm

WATER LA

Hertfordshire Way

CROSS FARM MEWS

Tower Hill

STONEY LA

NEW RD

Milbaise

TOWER HILL

Tenements Farm

The Boot (PH)

LONG LA

MIDDLE LA

Long Lane Farm

HOLLY HEDGES LA

BRYFIELD COTTS

Harts Hill Farm

Cottingham Farm

Tuffs Farm

Chipperfield House

SCATTERDELLS LA

Meadow Way Farm

Heartsfield

A B C D E F

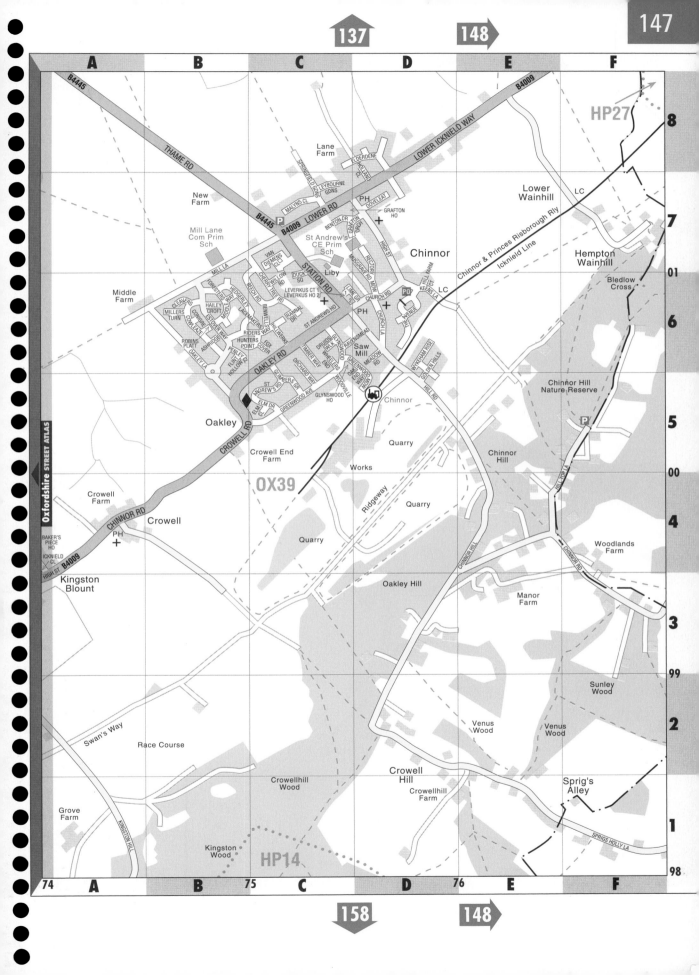

HP27

A B C D E F

B4445

THAME RD

LOWER ICKNIELD WAY

B4009

8

Lane
Farm

ELDERDENE

RICHLAND CL

Lower
Wainhill

LC

7

New
Farm

SPRINGFIELD GDNS

LEYBOURNE
GDNS

MALYNS CL

B4009 LOWER RD

PH

DOVELEAT

P

BENTON DR

GRAFTON
HO

01

Mill Lane
Com Prim
Sch

Mill La

VAN
DIEMENS CL

St Andrew's
CE Prim
Sch

GRAFTON CT

RECTORY RD

HIGH ST

Chinnor

Chinnor & Princes Risborough Rly

Icknield Line

Hempton
Wainhill

7

Middle
Farm

FORESTERS WAY

CHERRY TREE RD

BEECH RD

DUCK SQ

WILLOW RD

Liby

MUSGRAVE RD

LIME GR

CHURCH RD

Bledlow
Cross

01

CLEANERS

MILLERS
TURN

HAILEY
CROFT

HEDGERLEY

COWLANE

CROWELL RD

MIDDLE WAY

BENWELLS

LACEMAKERS

RANNA
DRI

ST ANDREWS HO

PH

HILL FARM

CHURCH LA

KEENS LA

LC

THE AVENUE

6

ROBINS
PLATT

ASHRIDGE

COVERT WAY

RIDERS
POINT

FOX
COVER

HUNTERS
POINT

STATION RD

OAKLEY RD

OAKLEY LA

PENLEY RD

FLINT
HOLLOW RD

DRUIDS
WALK

TIMBER WAY

ORCHARD WAY

GREENWOOD AVE

RAVENSMEAD

WYNWOOD

WHEELERS
END

WOODVILLE

Saw
Mill

MEADOW RD

GREENWOOD
END

WYCHAM RISE

SOMMER HILLS

HILL RD

Chinnor Hill
Nature Reserve

6

Oakley

GLYMBER GR

ST
ANDREW'S RD

ELM DR

ELM
CL

GREENWOOD RD

GLYNSWOOD
HO

GLYNSWOOD

Chinnor

HILL TOP LA

P

5

Crowell End
Farm

Quarry

Chinnor
Hill

Woodlands
Farm

OX39

Works

CHINNOR RD

Quarry

00

Crowell
Farm

CHINNOR RD

Crowell

Ridgeway

Quarry

CHINNOR HILL

CHINNOR RD

4

BAKER'S
PIECE
HO

PH

ICKNIELD
CL

B4009

HIGH ST

Quarry

Oakley Hill

Manor
Farm

3

Kingston
Blount

99

Sunley
Wood

Swan's Way

Race Course

Venus
Wood

Venus
Wood

2

Crowellhill
Wood

Crowell
Hill

Crowellhill
Farm

Sprig's
Alley

Grove
Farm

KINGSTON HILL

Kingston
Wood

HP14

SPRIGS HOLLY LA

1

98

74 **A** 75 **B** **C** 76 **D** **E** **F**

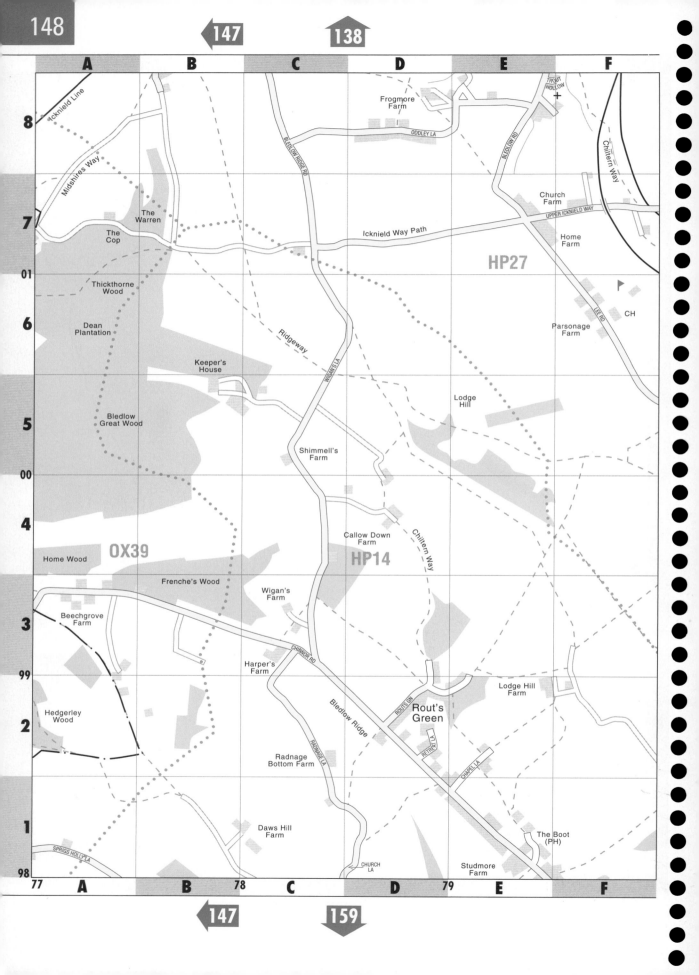

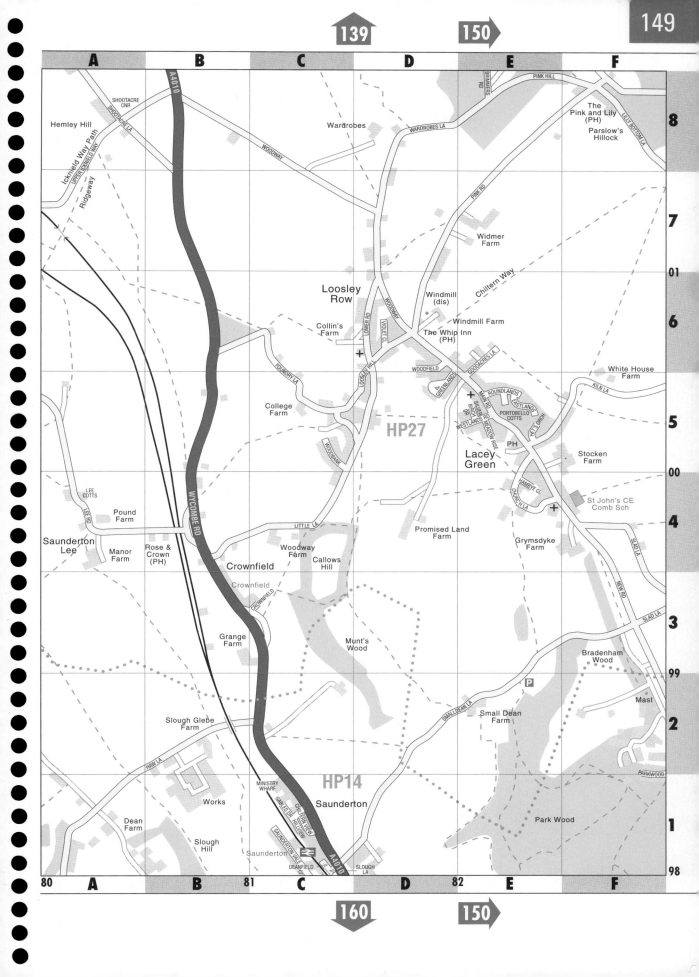

149
140

8

Chiltern Way

Ferns Farm

Coppice House

HOBART COTTS

Hampden Arms (PH)

Great Hampden

Keepershill Wood

Lily Farm

7

LILY BOTTOM LA

Hampden Coppice

01

Monkton Wood

Great Hampden Farm

Hampden Common

The Old Rectory

HP16

6

Kingswood House

Monkton

HP27

Monkton Farm

Denner Farm

5

HIGHWOOD BOTTOM

Redhouse Farm

GRUBBINS LA

College Plantation

SPRING COPPICE LA

Spring Coppice Farm

Denner Hill

HAMPDEN RD

HANGINGS LA

MOSES PLAT LA

CHERRY TREE CL

CORNERWAYS

MONKTON WAY

WOODVIEW DR

COLEHEATH BOTTOM

00

Turnip End

STUDRIDGE LA

ARCH WAY

PH

Spring Coppice

Dennerhill Farm

COTTAGE FARM WAY

VANSIDE

ABBOTSWOOD

4

Flowers Bottom

ST PETERS CL

DAIRYMEDE

Pye Corner

Bryant's Bottom

BRYANTS BOTTOM RD

Flowers Bottom Farm

WATER LA

LAUREL CL

Speen

Acrehill Wood

Darvillshill

FLOWERS BOTTOM LA

Speen CE Sch

SPRINGWOOD

CHAPEL HILL

The Gate (PH)

Inn

3

The Lodge

SLAD LA

Westcroft Stables

Guy's Spring

Bowley Wood

Speen Farm Firs

99

Old House Farm

SPEEN RD

Piggott's Wood

2

GREENWOOD

HP14

PARKWOOD

NEW RD

GREENWOOD

Wks

Upper North Dean Farm

Upper North Dean

PIGGOTT'S HILL

SILVER BIRCH CVN SITE

GRIMMS

Courns Wood

Naphill & Walters Ash Sch

MAIN RD

1

PARKSIDE 1 TEMPLEWOOD 2

BEECH

BRADENHAM WOODS LA

Walter's Ash

WOODCOCK AVE

CLAPPING LA

PRIMROSE COTTS

Home Farm

Sherwood Farm

98

BRADENHAM BEECHES

Lower North Dean

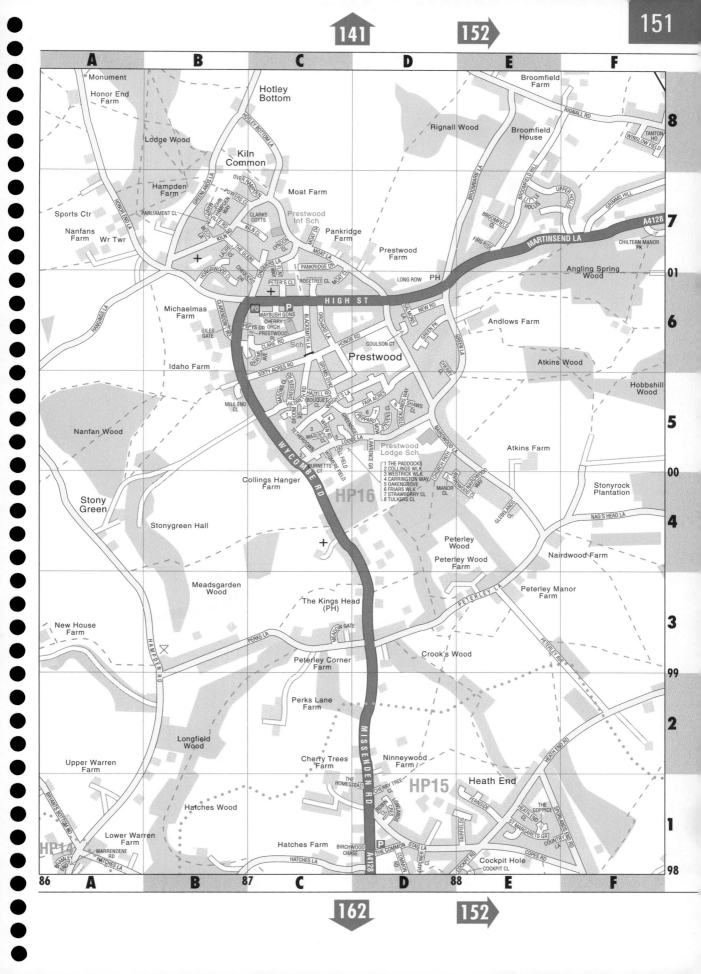

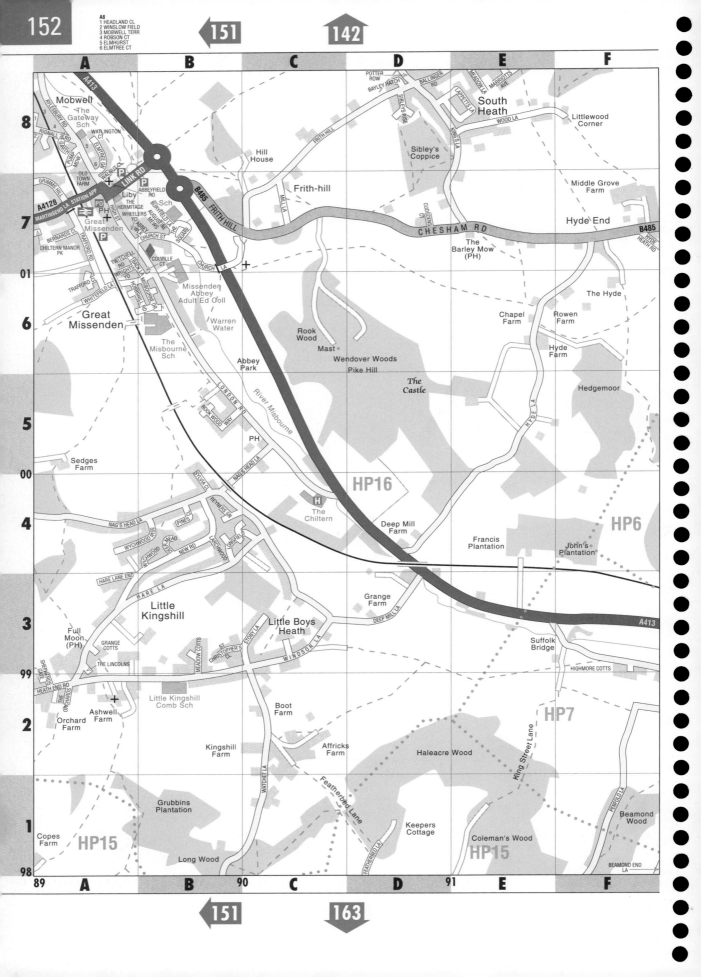

A8
1 HEADLAND CL
2 WINSLOW FIELD
3 MOBWELL TERR
4 ROBSON CT
5 ELMHURST
6 ELMTREE CT

151
142

A   B   C   D   E   F

Mobwell
The Gateway Sch
AYLESBURY RD
RIGNALL RD
PUMP MDW
WATLINGTON CT
ELMTREE GN
OLD TOWN FARM
WALNUT CL
LINK RD
ABBEYFIELD RD
B485
Hill House
FRITH HILL
Frith-hill
POTTER ROW
BAYLEY HATCH
SIBLEY'S RISE
BALLINGER RD
MEADOW LA
MARRIOTTS AVE
South Heath
Littlewood Corner
Sibley's Coppice
LIPPETTS LA
KING'S LA
WOOD LA
Middle Grove Farm
Hyde End
B485
HYDE HEATH RD

GRIMMS HILL
A4128
MARTINSEND LA
STATION APP
Liby
THE HERMITAGE
WHEELERS YD
AUGUSTINE
ABBEY VW
CHURCH ST
THE SQUARE
Great Missenden
PO
PH
High St
BURRFIELD CT
FRITH HILL
CHESHAM RD
The Barley Mow (PH)
BERNARDS CL
CHILTERN MANOR PK
TRAFFORD RD
TWITCHEL RD
WRIGHTS YD
COLVILLE CT
MISBOURNE DR
CHURCH LA
The Hyde

WHITEFIELD LA
TRAFFORD RD
MOBWELL RD
Missenden Abbey Adult Ed Coll
Warren Water
Chapel Farm
Rowen Farm
01

Great Missenden
The Misbourne Sch
LONDON RD
Abbey Park
River Misbourne
Rook Wood
Mast
Wendover Woods
Pike Hill
The Castle
Hyde Farm
HYDE LA
Hedgemoor
6

ROOK WOOD WAY
SYLVIA CL
NAG'S HEAD LA
PH
5

Sedges Farm
00
HP16
Deep Mill Farm
Francis Plantation
John's Plantation
HP6

NAG'S HEAD LA
WYCHWOOD
WYCHWOOD RISE
DEER MEAD
REYNERS GM
PINES CL
NEW RD
LARCHWOOD
LONGFIELD
The Chiltern
H
4

HARE LANE END
HARE LA
Little Kingshill
MEADOW COTTS
ST CHRISTOPHER'S CL
STONY LA
Little Boys Heath
Grange Farm
DEEP MILL LA
Suffolk Bridge
A413
3

Full Moon (PH)
GRANGE COTTS
THE LINCOLNS
WINDSOR LA
HIGHMORE COTTS
99

SHEPHERDS GATE
HEATH END RD
THE ORCHARDS
Ashwell Farm
Little Kingshill Comb Sch
Boot Farm
Affricks Farm
KING STREET LANE
HP7
2

Orchard Farm
Kingshill Farm
WATCHET LA
Haleacre Wood

Grubbins Plantation
FEATHERBED LANE
Keepers Cottage
Coleman's Wood
Beamond Wood
1

Copes Farm
HP15
Long Wood
FEATHERBED LA
HP15
BEAMOND END LA
98

89   A   B   90   C   D   91   E   F

151
163

8
7
6
5
4
3
2
1

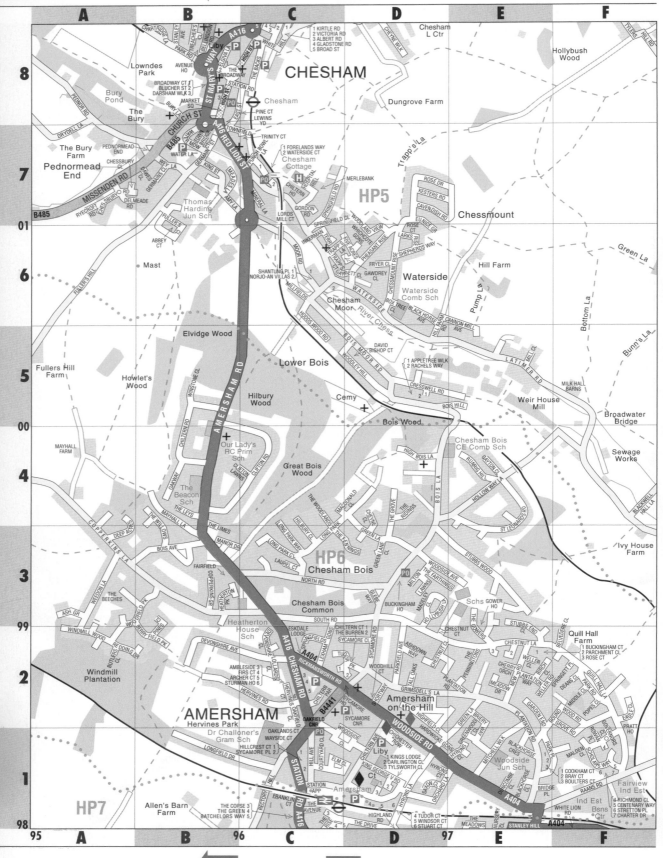

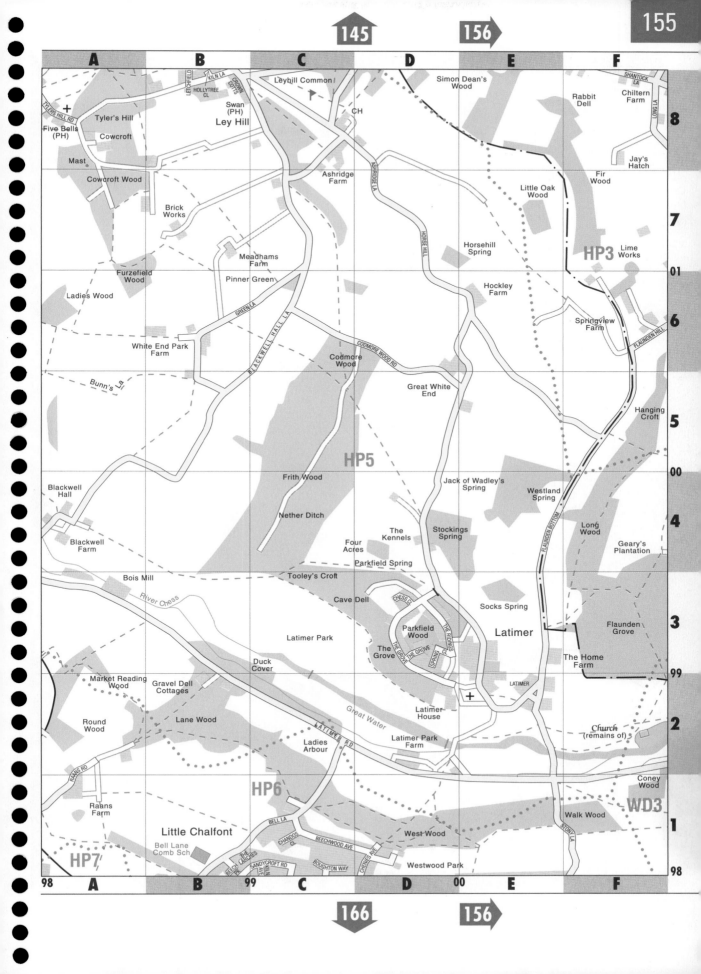

A | B | C | D | E | F

Tyler's Hill Rd
Five Bells (PH)
Tyler's Hill
Cowcroft
Mast
Cowcroft Wood
Brick Works
Furzefield Wood
Ladies Wood
White End Park Farm
Bunn's La

Letchfield
Kiln La
Hollytree Cl
Crown Cotts
Swan (PH)
Ley Hill
Meadhams Farm
Pinner Green
Green La
Blackwell Hall La

Leyhill Common
CH
Ashridge Farm
Codmore Wood
Codmore Wood Rd

Ashridge La
Horse Hill

Simon Dean's Wood
CH

Little Oak Wood
Horsehill Spring
Hockley Farm
Great White End

Rabbit Dell
Chiltern Farm
Shantock La
Long La
Jay's Hatch
Fir Wood
HP3
Lime Works
Springview Farm
Flaunden Hill
Hanging Croft

8
7
01
6

HP5
Frith Wood
Nether Ditch
Blackwell Hall
Blackwell Farm
Bois Mill
River Chess

Four Acres
The Kennels
Parkfield Spring
Tooley's Croft
Cave Dell

Jack of Wadley's Spring
Stockings Spring

Westland Spring
Long Wood
Geary's Plantation

5
00
4
3

Market Reading Wood
Gravel Dell Cottages
Round Wood
Lane Wood
Raans Rd
Raans Farm

Duck Cover
Latimer Park
Ladies Arbour
Latimer Rd
Great Water

Parkfield Wood
The Grove
The Grove
Spring Cl
The Ridings
Chess Cl
Socks Spring
Latimer
Latimer House
Latimer Park Farm

The Home Farm
Flaunden Grove
Flaunden Bottom
Church (remains of)

99
2

HP6
Little Chalfont
Bell Lane Comb Sch
Bell La
Chandos Cl
The Larches
Beech Rd
Sandycroft Rd
Kiln Way
Chenies Ave
Boughton Way
Beechwood Ave
West Wood
Westwood Park

Coney Wood
WD3
Walk Wood
Stony La

1
98

HP7

98 | A | B | 99 | C | D | 00 | E | F

A **B** **C** **D** **E** **F**

Oxgate Farm

Venus Hill

Venus Hill Dairy Farm

MOOR LA

VENUS HILL

Chiltern Way

Hollow Hedge

Woodman's Wood

Braziers Farm

TOWER HILL

Chipperfield

WD4

New Maulden Farm

Caravan Site

Hogpits Bottom

FLAUNDEN LA

LONG LA

HOGPITS BOTTOM

Bricklayers Arms (PH)

Lower Plantation

Woodman's Farm

Rose Farm

OLLEBERRIE LA

DUNNY LA

THE COMMON

WINDMILL HILL

Cherry Trees Farm

Holly Hedges

LITTLE WINDMILL HILL

Perman's Green

01

Sharlow's Farm

Green Dragon (PH)

BIRCH LA

Dale Farm

Whitedell Farm

FLAUNDEN LA

BELSIZE COTTS PH

Belsize

HP3

FLAUNDEN HILL

Flaunden

Newhouse Farm

Bragman's Farm

BRAGMANS LA

Rose Hall Farm

Rosehall Wood

POLESTL

PLOUGH LA

6

Hollin's Hall

Moonshine Farm

Wireless Station

Great Sarratt Hall

00

Mast

Mast

Mast

Hanginglane Wood

Oldcroft Wood

Chiltern Way

CHILTERN WAY

Sarratt

HP5

Martin Top Farm

Oldfield Spring

Bramble Croft

MOOR LA

DAWES LA

Dawes Common

DOWNER DR

3

Baldwin's Wood

Wallace's Wood

Limeshill Wood

Valley Farm

WD3

Old Rectory

Sarratt Bottom

99

Mill Farm

Chenies Bottom

River Chess

Ford

Mount Wood

The Cock (PH)

2

Chenies Place

HOLLOWAY LA

Church End

CHURCH END COTTS

Chenies

Manor House

Mountwood Farm

Nicholas Spring

Goldingtons

CHURCH LA

NEW RD

1

Greathouse Farm

Chenies Sch

BEDFORD CL

Bedford Arms (Inn)

Turveylane Wood

Wyburn Wood

98

Chiltern Way

A **B** **01** **02** **C** **D** **03** **E** **F**

Hertfordshire STREET ATLAS

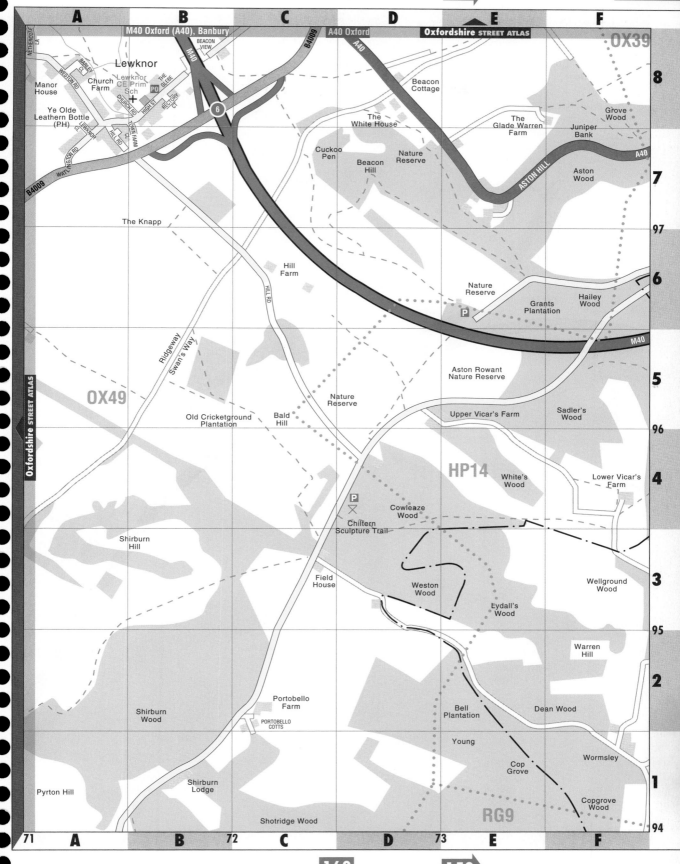

Oxfordshire STREET ATLAS

OX39

M40 Oxford (A40), Banbury

A40 Oxford

Oxfordshire STREET ATLAS

OX49

HP14

RG9

OX39

Kingston Grove

Collier's Lane

High Wood

Grove Wood

OX39

Crowell Wood

Lott Wood

Gurdon's Farm

Collier's Lane

A40

ASTON HILL

Aston Wood

KINGSTON HILL

Beechwood Shaw

Hawing Wood

Stockfield Wood

Hallbottom Farm

Hill Farm

Mast

Radio Station

Kiln Farm

Mallard's Court

Park La

OXFORD RD

Wood Farm

BOWLING GN 1
CHURCH PATH 2
LOWER CHURCH ST 3
PARK LANE CT 4
KARENZA 5

BRIARSWOOD CL

Stokenchurch

M40

North Remlets Wood

RED LION DR

COMM FARM

Stokenchurch Prim Sch

1 CURZON GATE CT
2 BRITNELL CT
3 MILESTONE CL
4 FERNDALE CL
5 OLD SCHOOL CL
6 HART MOOR CL
7 FOWLERS FARM RD

Hailey Wood

OXFORD RD

CHURCH ST

CRICKET GROUND
COOPER'S COURT RD

PH

Liby

PIGEON FARM RD

SPRINGFIELD HOLLOW

GEORGE RD

COVEFIELD

Stokenchurch

Langleygreen Plantation

MILL LA

GREEN LA

Independent Bsns Pk

ADKINS

ROSE CT

ANGLESEY CT

Ind Est

THE COPPICE

MUSGRAVE

WYCOMBE RD

A40

MILL RD

Coopers Court Farm

MEAD PLATT

HOMEFIELD CL

SLADE RD

B482

ST HUGH'S CL

Wallace Hill

STUDDRIDGE CT

HP14

Chiltern Way

Bissomhill Shaw

COLLYER RD

PARRS RD

SLADE RD

Stokenchurch Cty Fst Sch

SAUNDERS WOOD COPSE

THE DELL

Little Studdridge

BEECH CL

ELIZABETH RD

MARCOURT RD

JUBILEE RD

MARLOW RD

EASTWOOD RD

Wellground Farm

Studdridge Farm

Bowley's Wood

Coombe Wood

Commonhill Wood

Penley Farm

PENDLES PADDOCKS

M40

B482

Commonhill Wood

Hartmoor Wood

Penley Wood

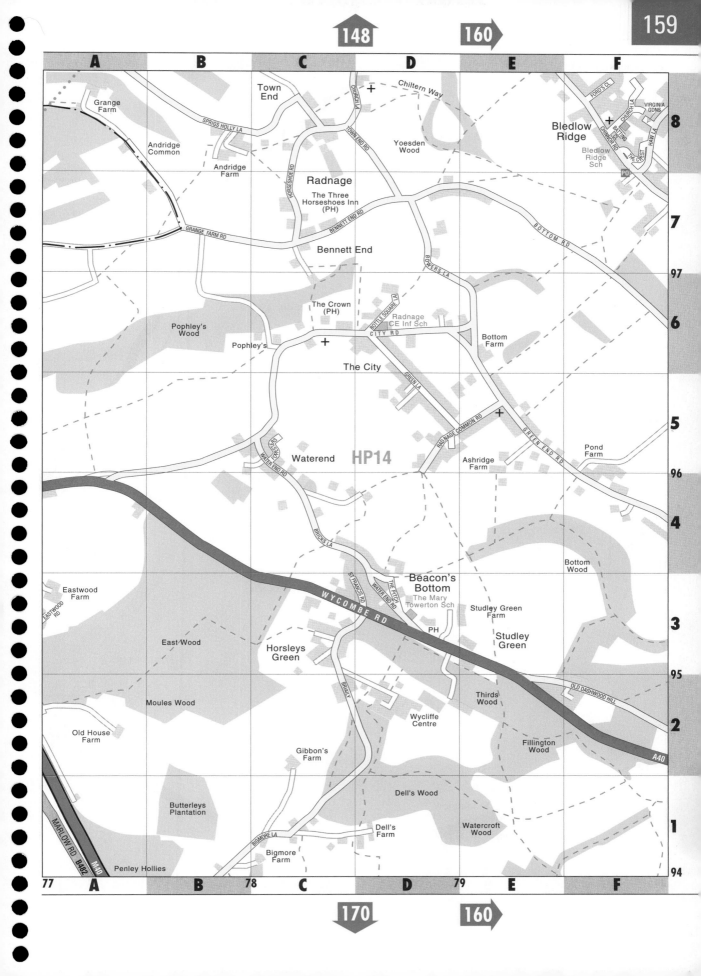

159
149

A B C D E F

8

Works

RIDGE SIDE

HAM LA

Orchard Farm

West Yard Ind Est

WYCOMBE RD

A4010

Yewtree Hill Plantation

DEANFIELD

7

The Old House

Slough Bottom Farm

Allnutt's Wood

Piper's Hanging Wood

Bradenham

YH

Manor Farm

The Red Lion (PH)

BRADENHAM WOOD LA

97

Morlands Farm

SCRUBB'S LA

Bradenham Manor

6

Loxborough House

Wayside Farm

Nobles Farm

The Old Rectory

SLOUGH LA

CHINNOR RD

BRADENHAM RD

5

Loxboro Wood

Hearnton Wood

Averingdown Farm

A4010

Wks

BOTTOM RD

96

Nature Reserve

HP14

Pond Wood

Chawley Manor Farm

4

Green End

GREEN END RD

HATCH LA

Chawley Green Farm

Loxboro Hill

Windyhaugh House

Chorley Farm

CHORLEY RD

3

Green End Farm

Chawley Wood

West Wycombe Hill

P

Plomer's Bottom

Cockshoot Farm

95

Little Cockshoots Wood

WEST WYCOMBE HILL RD

Hellfire Caves

2

P

Sch
P PO

A40 HIGH ST

Great Cockshoots Wood

Liby

OLD DASHWOOD HILL

West Wycombe

A40

Fillingdon Farm

WYCOMBE RD

Ham Farm

Piddington

1 TUDOR CT
2 GEORGE LEE CT

TOWERIDGE LA

West Wycombe Park

1

CHIPPS HILL

PH

PRINCES ST

QUEEN ST

KING ST

OLD OXFORD RD

PIDDINGTON LA

OXFORD RD

BULLOCKS FARM LA

Myze Farm

High Wood

94

80 **A** **B** 81 **C** **D** 82 **E** **F**

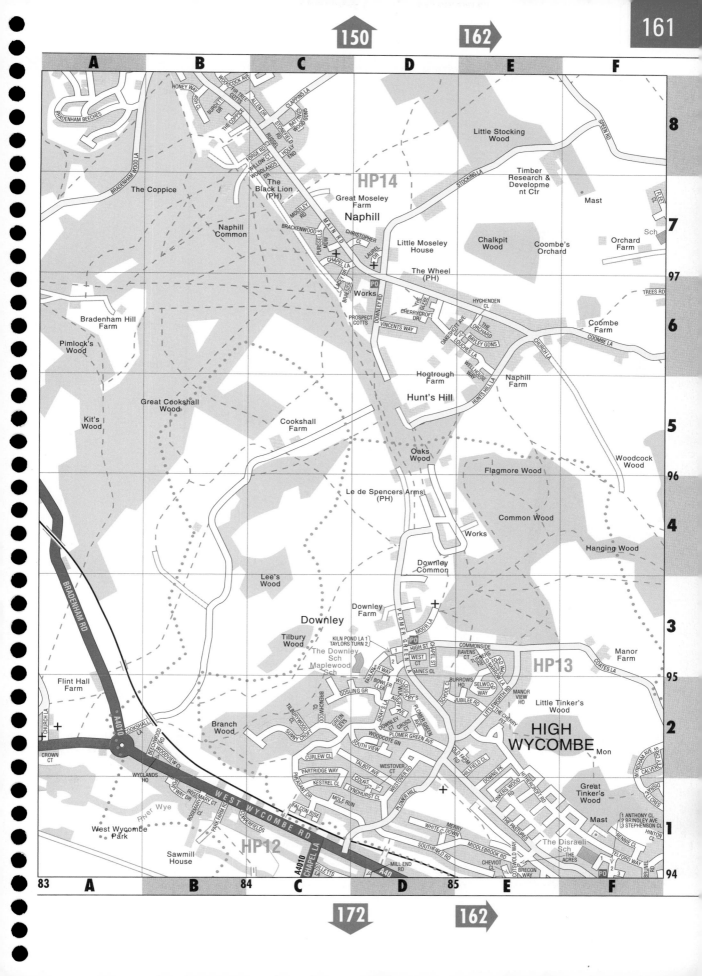

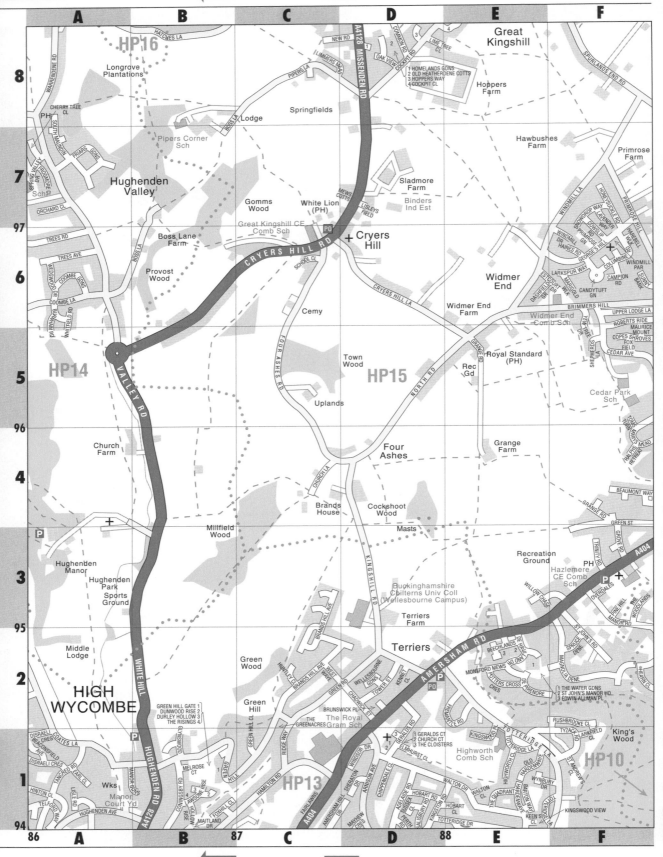

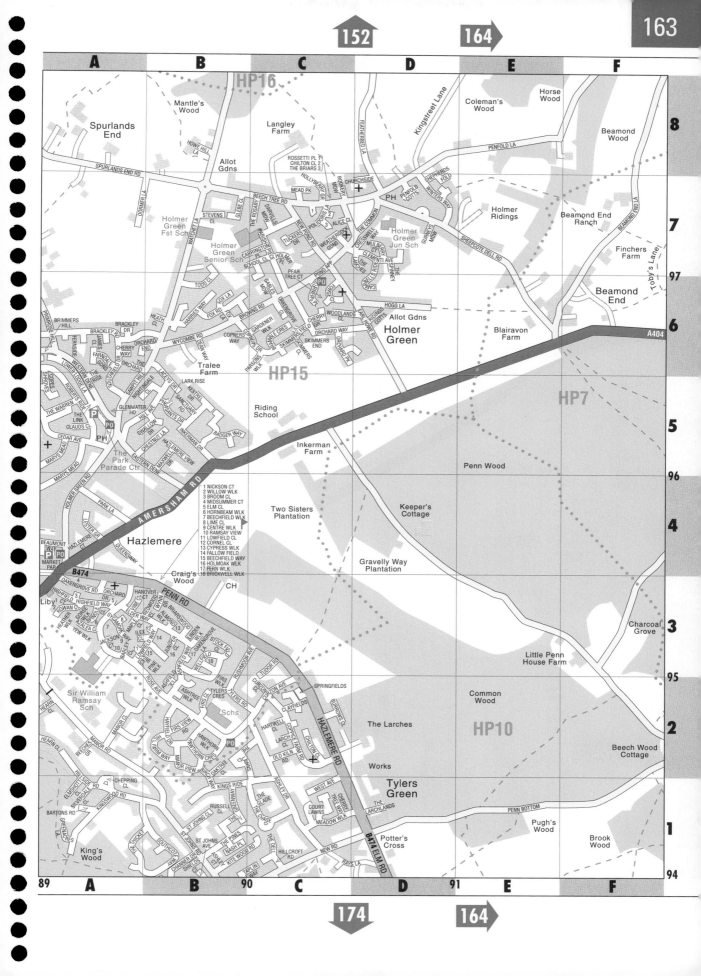

HP15

Toby's La

8

High Wood

SHARDELOES

Lower Park House

Lodges

SCHOOL LA

A413

Upper Park

MOP END LA

7

Mop End Farm

Summerville's Wood

Wheatley Wood

Shardeloes Farm

97

Mop End

The Rough Park

Model Farm

CHERRY LA

Second Wood

Crem

6

A404

Wycombe Lodge

Woodrow High House

Woodrow

Hundred Acres

A404

Curzon CE Comb Sch

CHANCELLORS CNR

SCHOOL LA

Childs Farm

WHIELDEN LA

5

CHANCELLORS

Vicarage

Woodrow Farm

NEW RD

96

Meml

Penn Street

HP7

PENN WOOD VIEW

The Squirrel (PH)

WHIELDEN GATE

Queen's Head (PH)

MDW

HILL

4

Ind Est

Hit or Miss (PH)

Priestlands Wood

Tragoe's Plantation

Coleshill

WHIELDEN LA

Coleshill Larches

West Wood

Penn Street Farm

MEADOW COTTS LA

VILLAGE RD

3

Cowley Cotts

Chiltern Way

Coleshill CE Inf Sch

1 ORCHARD COTTS
2 THE ROW

AMBER COTTS

Red Lion (PH)

Ferndale

NELSON CL

THE HILL

POND CL

Works

MANOR HILL

UNDERWOOD COTTS

95

Charcoal Grove

Penn House

ELM TREE COTTS 1
ROYAL COTTS 2

Winchmore Hill

COLESHILL LA

BARRACKS HILL

Coleshill Common

The Potters Arms (PH)

PO

WINDMILL HILL

CHALK HILL

2

Pennhouse Grove

HORSEMOOR LA

Fagnall Farm

SAMPSONS HILL

MAGPIE LA

Glory Farm

FAGNALL LA

HP10

Lowlands

Luckings Farm

1

Pennhouse Farm

Hertfordshire House

Penn Bottom

Branches Wood

Lodge

Little Hertfordshire House

94

92

93

94

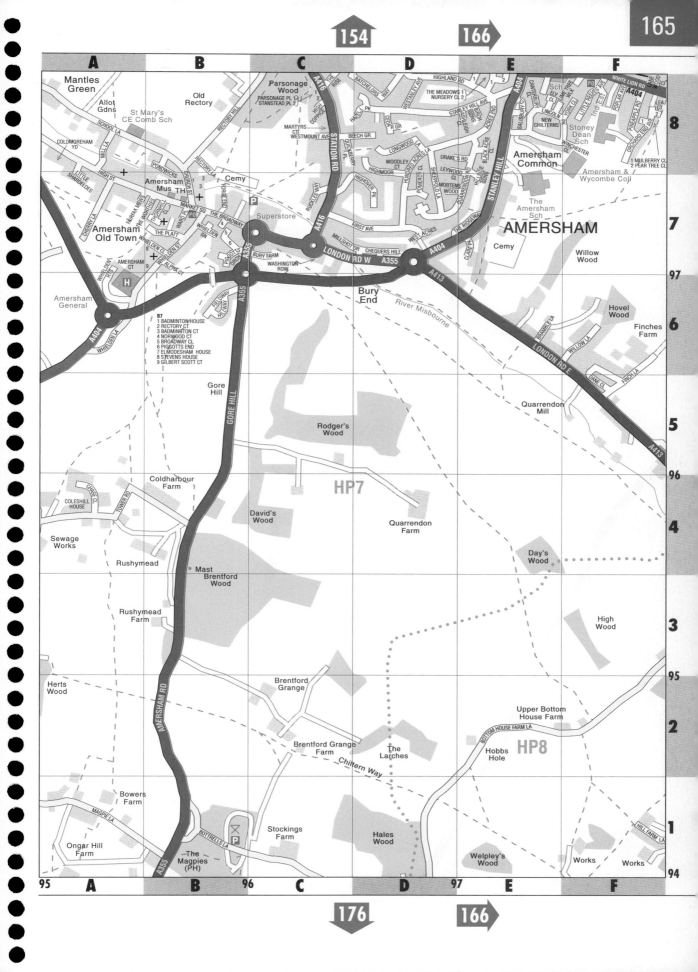

165 155

A B C D E F

8

A404
WHITE LION RD
Boughton Bsns Pk
ARBOUR VIEW
REPTON PL
WHITE LION RD
CHILTERN HTS
CHILCOTE LA
DERWENT CL
KENWAY
ST NICHOLAS CL
BEEL CL
CLAYTON WLK
CUMBERLAND
CAVENDISH
MARY OLD
CHAPEL CL
PAVILION
ELIZABETH AVE
LATIMER CL
SANDYCROFT RD
SANDYCROFT RD
KILN AVE
BEECHWOOD CL
FARM CL
CHENIES AVE
WESTWOOD DR
WOODSIDE CL
CHESSFIELD PK
CHESSFIELD PK
STONY LA
A404
AMERSHAM RD
AMERSHAM WAY
CHURCH GR
HP6
STATION APP
RUSSELL AVE
BEDFORD AVE
BEDFORD CT
CHALFONT CL
OAKINGTON AVE
OLD FIELD CL
THE RETREAT

Bendrose Farm
Works
Dr Challoner's High Sch
Beel House
Snell's Farm
Little Chalfont
Liby
P
P
PO
Halifax HO
APPLEFIELD
LOUDHAMS RD
CHALFONT STATION RD
B4442
CHENIES PAR
CHALFONT RD
Village Way
VILLAGE WAY
Chalfont & Latimer
Little Chalfont Comb Sch
CH
Netherground Spring
Lodge Copse
Lodge Farm

7
FINCH LA
SNELLS LA
SNELL'S WOOD CL
APPLETON CL
YARROWSIDE LA
LINEFIELDS
1 NIGHTINGALES CNR
2 NIGHTINGALES CT
3 THE HAWTHORNS
LOUDHAMS WOOD LA
LONG WLK
LODGE LA
NEW RD

97

6
HP7
Coke's Farm
MAPLEFIELD LA
COKE'S FARM LA
COKE'S LA
HAREWOOD RD
BURTON'S WAY
BIRKETT WAY
PARK GR
GARDEN REACH
BURTON'S LA
Burton's Farm
Burton's Wood
WD3

5
DOGGETT'S WOOD CL
DOGGETTS WOOD LA
CH
NIGHTINGALES LA

96
A413
LONDON RD

4
Ivy House (PH)
Harewood Downs House
Pollards Park House
Pollards Wood
HP8
ROUGHWOOD LA
Crosslane Wood
Roughwood Park

3
BOTTOM HOUSE FARM LA
Lower Bottom House Farm
AMERSHAM RD
River Misbourne
Warren Farm
Roughwood Farm
Roughwood Cottages
WD3

95
Bow Wood
Bailey Wood
Mon
Grovespring Wood

2
Chiltern Way
Misbourne Farm
The Vache
Kilnpond Wood
Shortenills Wood
Newland Gorse
Chiltern Way

1
HILL FARM LA
STRATTON CHASE DR
MILL LA
Chalfont Mill
For Mill Farm
MISBOURNE HO
A413
St Giles Lodge
VACHE LA
B4442
KINGS RD
GORELANDS LA
DEADHEARN LA
BARRINGTON PARK GDNS

94
98 A 99 B C D 00 E F

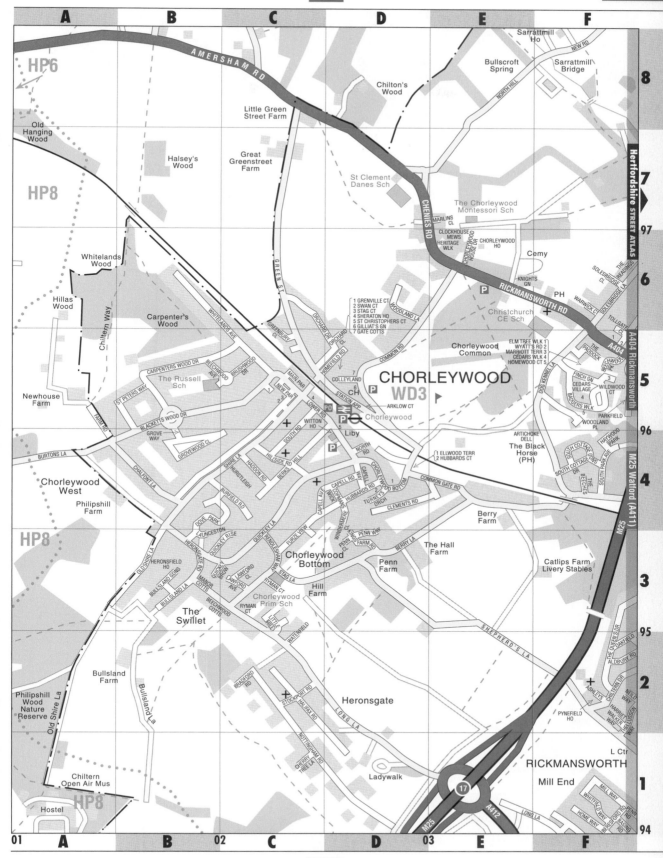

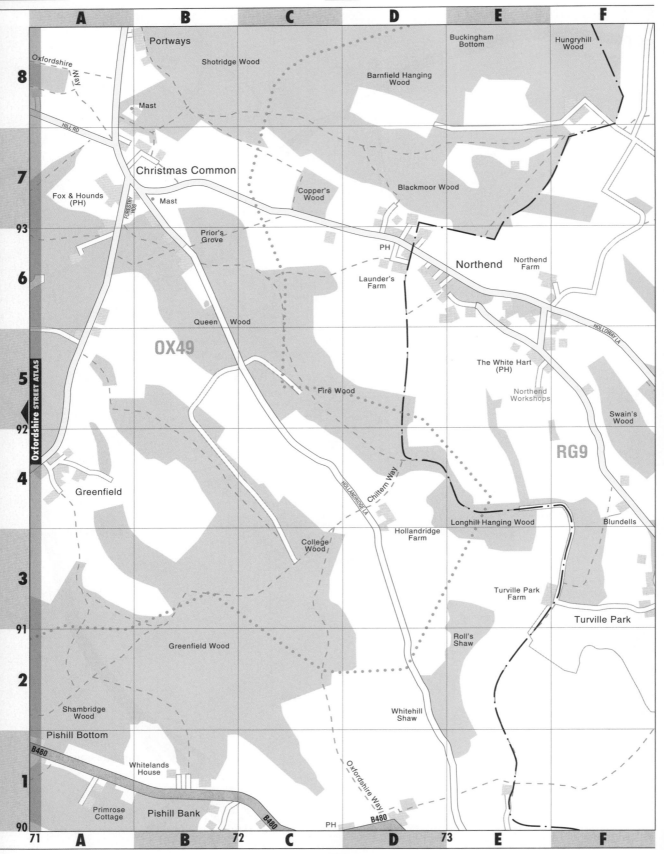

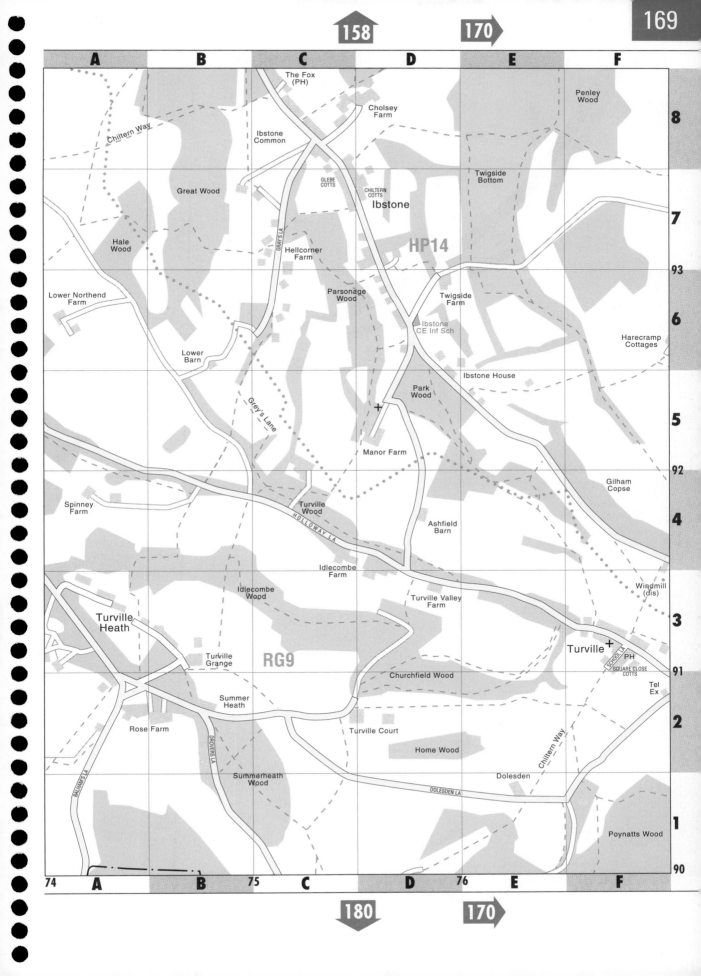

169
159

A B C D E F

8

7

93

6

5

92

4

3

91

2

1

90

B482
M40

Chequers Manor
Farm

BIGMORE LA

Blue Flag
(PH)

MARLOW RD

Pound
Wood

HP14

Barn
Wood

Leygrove's
Wood

Watercroft
Farm

Huckenden
Farm

Pound
Farm

Cadmore End
CE Sch

Cadmore
End

Kensham
Farm

Cadmore End
Common

M40

Old Ship
(PH)

Bolter
End

NEW RD

The
Peacock
(PH)

BOLTER END LA

CHEQUERS LA

Hanger
Wood

Hill
Farm

Rackley's
Farm

FININGS RD
B482

Priestley's
Farm

Gravesend

Manor
Farm

Mill Hanging
Wood

Hanger
Farm

FINGEST LA

Hanover
Hill

Long
Copse

Terville
Hill

Fingest

The Chequers Inn
(PH)

RG9

Fingest
Wood

Mousells Wood

Dovers
Farm

DOLESDEN
LA

Murrage
Farm

Chiltern Way

Maiden
House

Spurgrove

SPURGROVE LA

The
Prince Albert
(PH)

Little
Frieth

PERRIN SPRINGS
LA

ELLERY RISE

Poynatts
Farm

Goddard's
Wood

Adam's
Wood

Bottom
Wood

Frieth

PO

The Frog
(PH)

SHOGMOOR LA

Upper
Goddards

Colliers
Farm

INNINGS
GATE

HAYLESFIELD

Maiden
Farm

Frieth
CE Comb Sch

Stud
Farm

Lower
Goddards
Farm

PARMOOR LA

Skirmett

SHOGMOOR LA

77 A 78 B C 78 C D 79 E F

90

169
181

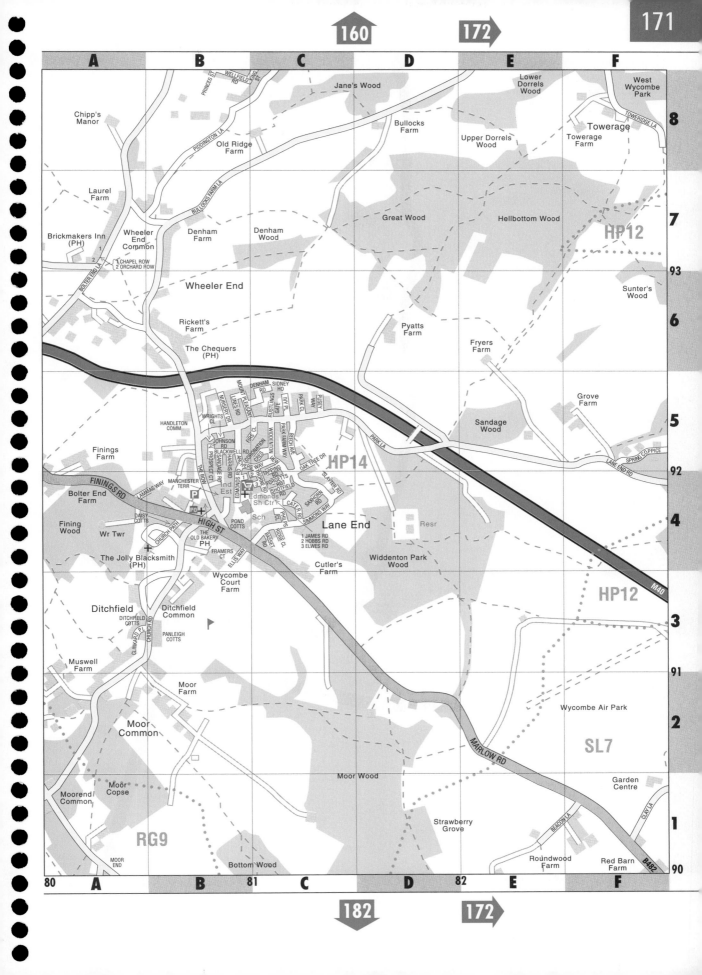

A B C D E F

8
Chipp's Manor
West Wycombe Park
Lower Dorrels Wood
Jane's Wood
Bullocks Farm
Upper Dorrels Wood
Towerage
Towerage Farm
TOWERIDGE LA

7
Laurel Farm
Old Ridge Farm
Denham Farm
Denham Wood
Great Wood
Hellbottom Wood
HP12
Brickmakers Inn (PH)
Wheeler End Common
1 CHAPEL ROW
2 ORCHARD ROW

93
Sunter's Wood

6
Wheeler End
Rickett's Farm
Pyatts Farm
Fryers Farm

The Chequers (PH)
Grove Farm
Sandage Wood
SPRING COPPICE

5
Finings Farm
HANDLETON COMM.
WRIGHTS CL
SIDNEY HO
PUSEY
LANE END RD

92
HP14
Bolter End Farm
FININGS RD
LAMMAS WAY
MANCHESTER TERR
Ind Est
Edmonds Sh Ctr
Sch
Lane End
Resr
92

4
Fining Wood
Wr Twr
HIGH ST
CHURCH PATH
THE OLD BAKERY PH
POND COTTS
Cutler's Farm
1 JAMES RD
2 HOBBS RD
3 ELWES RD
Widdenton Park Wood

The Jolly Blacksmith (PH)
FRAMERS CT
ELLIS WAY
HP12

3
Ditchfield
Ditchfield Common
DITCHFIELD COTTS
CHURCH RD
PANLEIGH COTTS
Wycombe Court Farm

91
Muswell Farm
GLINGARD
Moor Farm

2
Moor Common
Wycombe Air Park
MARLOW RD
SL7

Moor Copse
Moor Wood
Garden Centre

1
Moorend Common
RG9
Strawberry Grove
BEACON LA
Roundwood Farm
Red Barn Farm
CLAY LA
B482

MOOR END
Bottom Wood

90

80 A B 81 C D 82 E F 90

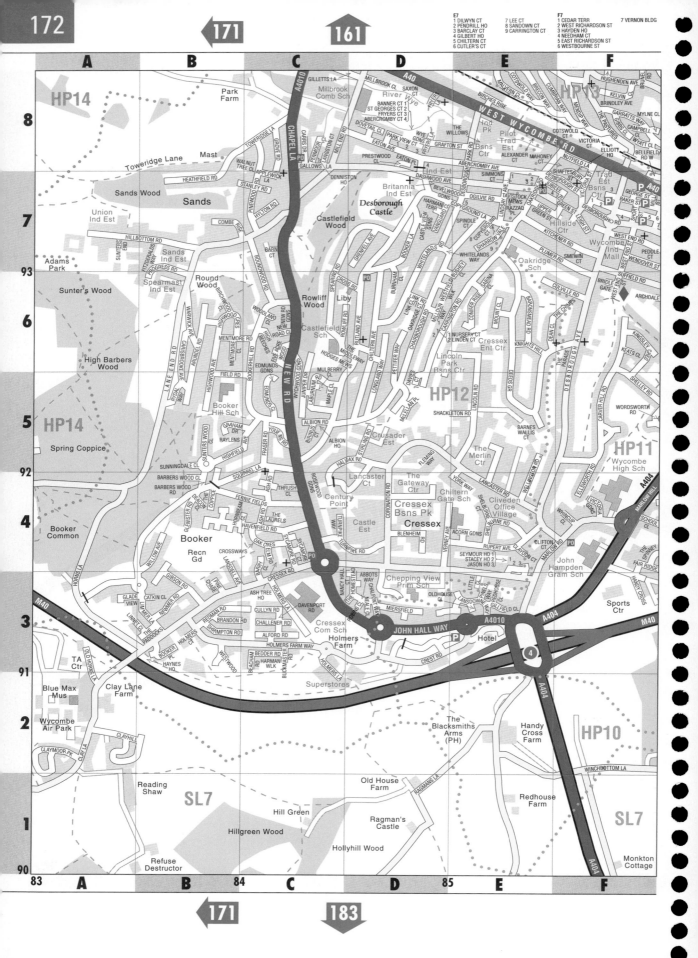

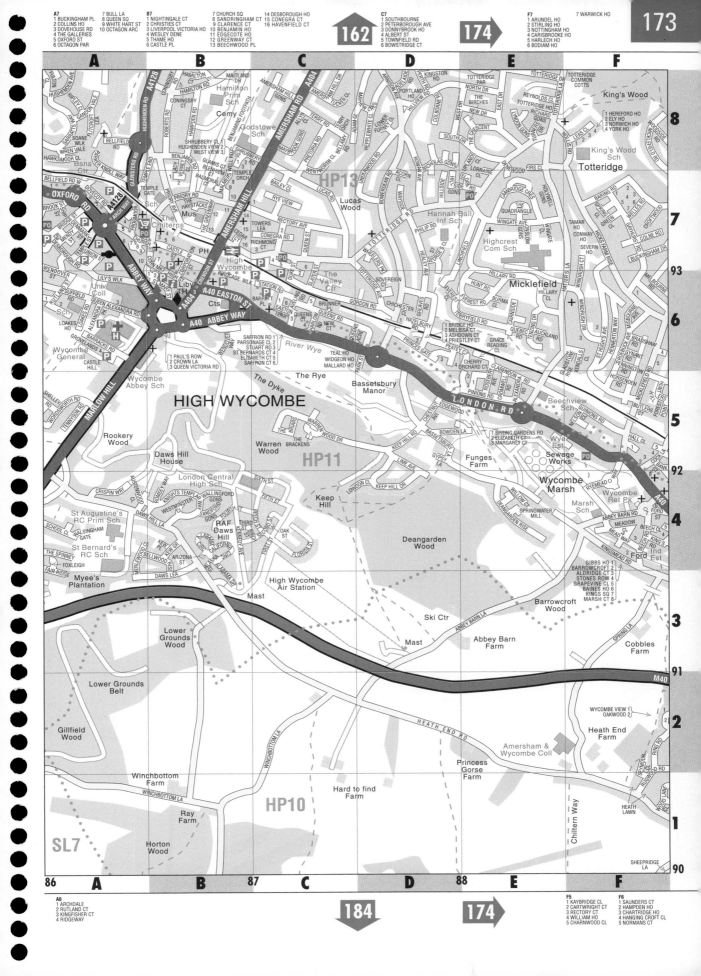

173 163

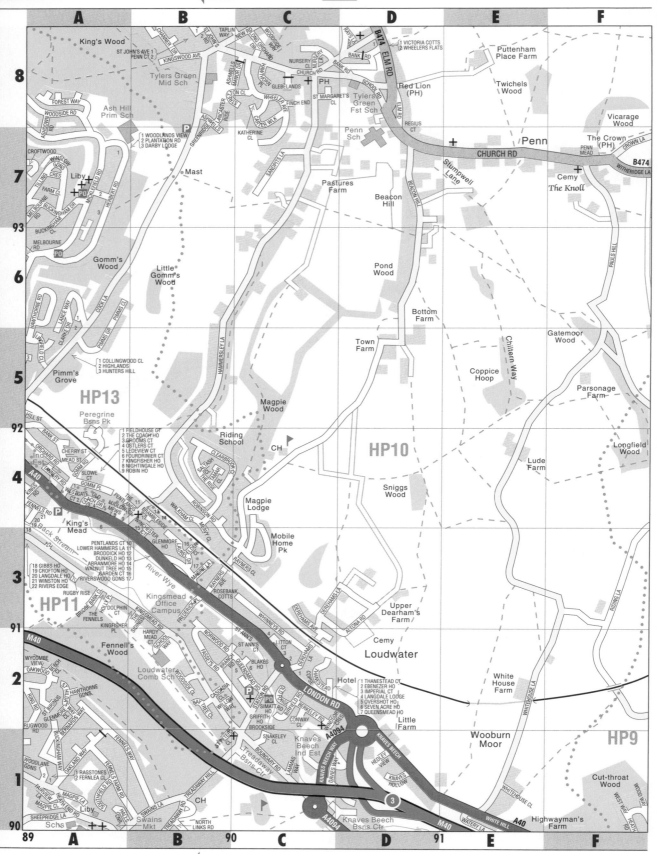

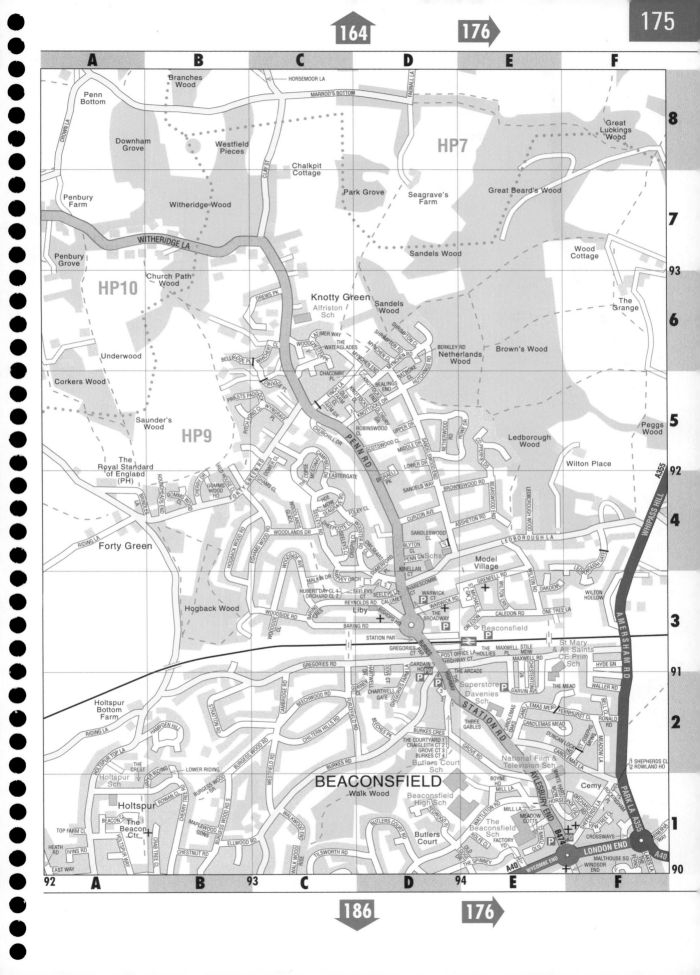

175
165

A B C D E F

8
7
93
6
5
92
4
3
91
2
1
90

95 A 96 B C 97 D E F

175
187

Hill's Wood
Barnhurst
HP7
Red Barn Farm
Owlsears Wood
AMERSHAM RD
A355
Starveacre Wood
Bottom Wood
South Lodge
Birchen Spring
WHIPASS HILL
A355
Oldfields Farm
Blue Close Wood
Drummer's Yard
Young's Wood

BOTTOM HOUSE FARM LANE
BOTTRELLS LA
Highfield Grove
Hodgemoor Woods
HP8
Three Households
Piggery
Newbarn
Highclere
THREE HOUSEHOLDS
CH
Butlers Cross
TWITCHELL'S LA
NEWBARN LA
RAWLINGS LA
Widmer Farm
Rawlings Farm
Big Copse
West Riding
The Princess Marina Centre
CHALFONT RD
PARK PL
Recreation Ground
Harmony Nurseries
Austens
HIGHLANDS RD
HOWARD CRES
HOWARD RD
MANOR CRES
MANOR RD
HEARNE'S CL
HEARNE'S MDW
BOTTOM LA
GURNELLS RD
WYNNSWICK RD
ORCHARD RD
ORCHARD CL
BASSDEN
CHERRYWOOD CL
CHURCH RD
WOOD POND CL
PEAR TREE CL
DELL LEES
GROVES WAY
GODOLPHIN RD
COLE WALKS
CULVERS CROFT
FARMERS WAY
BARRACKS WAY
LONG GROVE
STABLE
SEER MEAD
SEER GREEN LA
VICARAGE CL
BAYNE HILL
Seer Green CE Comb Sch
Hall Place
Cemy
PO
PH
Seer Green
HP9
Jordans Sch
PUERS FIELD
LONG WOOD DR
Jordans
PUERS LA
CRUTCHES LA
JORDANS WAY
WILTON LA
GREEN WEST RD
GREEN NORTH
GREEN EAST RD
COPSE LA
SEER GREEN LA
JORDANS LA
MEADOWSIDE
Crutches Wood
Jordans Farm
BEECH LA
LONGBOTTOM LA
Seer Green & Jordans CH
FARM LA
DEAN WOOD RD
YH
WELDERS LA
Meeting House
Welders House
SL9
The Mount
Walk Wood
Wheatsheaf Wood
Stone Dean Farm
Thirty Acre Knoll
MINERVA WAY
MAUDE RD
Wilton Park
GORELL RD
WAKALL RD
DUPRE CRES
BALVAIR
BERWICK CL
Sports Field
Wilton Park
POTKILN LA
Birchland Wood
LONDON END
A40 LONDON RD
BURNHAM AVE
A40

1 PADDOCKS END
2 MOSS CT
3 ORCHARD MEWS
4 MANOR FARM WAY
5 GREENWOOD CL
6 THE COPPICE

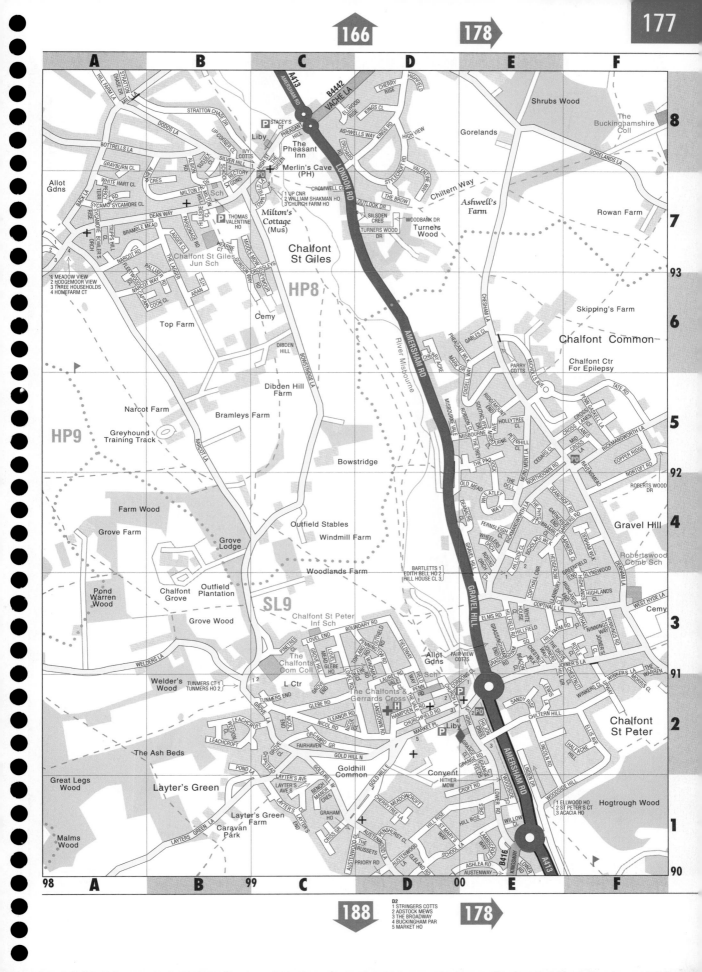

177
167

HP8

Bottom Wood

Ladywalk Wood

A412 NORTH ORBITAL RD

UXBRIDGE RD A412

Buckinghamshire Chilterns Univ Coll

Newland Park

Five Plantations

Pollardshill Wood

Woodoaks Farm

Froghall Farm

BASING RD

ROTHERLEY RD

KENWOOD DR

TONG LA

EASTWICK CRES

A412 Rickmansworth · Watford

GORELANDS LA

Model Farm

CHALFONT RD

Chalfont Shire Horse Ctr

93

Brawlings Farm

BRAWLINS LA

SHIRE LA

Hillview

Maple Cross

PH

PO

OAKHILL RD

OAKHILL CL

HAZEL CT

MAPLE LODGE CL

LONGMORE

DUMBLETONS

Maplelodge Farm

River Colne

Springwell Lake

6

Horn Hill

The Dumb Bell (PH)

Beechen Wood

LADYWALK

P

Recn Gd

Sewage Works

RICKMANSWORTH LA

Springview Farm

Longlees

LONGLEES

POLLARDS

BRADBERY

Long Croft RD

WOODOAKS WOOD

PINCH FIELD

TICHBORNE

Recn Gd

5

ROBERTS LA

Mast

HORSLEYS

HORNHILL RD

WOODLAND RD

Lynsters

BUTTLEHIDE

ASH VALE

BY-WOOD END

ROBERTS WOOD DR

THE HAWTHORNS

THE BIRCH DR

Franklin's Spring

Sch

92

SL9

WD3

4

Round Rocket Plantation

DENHAM WAY

Lynsters Lake

WEST HYDE LA

SUNNYHILL RD

Royal Oak (PH)

COPPERMILL LA

P

91

Cemy

Bloom Wood

CHALFONT LA

West Hyde

BUTTERFIELD COTTS

PLEASANT PL

Pynesfield Lake

UB9

Warren Farm

DENHAM LA

(NORTH ORBITAL RD)

OLD UXBRIDGE RD

TILEHOUSE LA

2

Chalfont Heights Scout Camp

UB9

1

Mopes Farm

West Hyde House

A412

M25

177
189

Hertfordshire STREET ATLAS

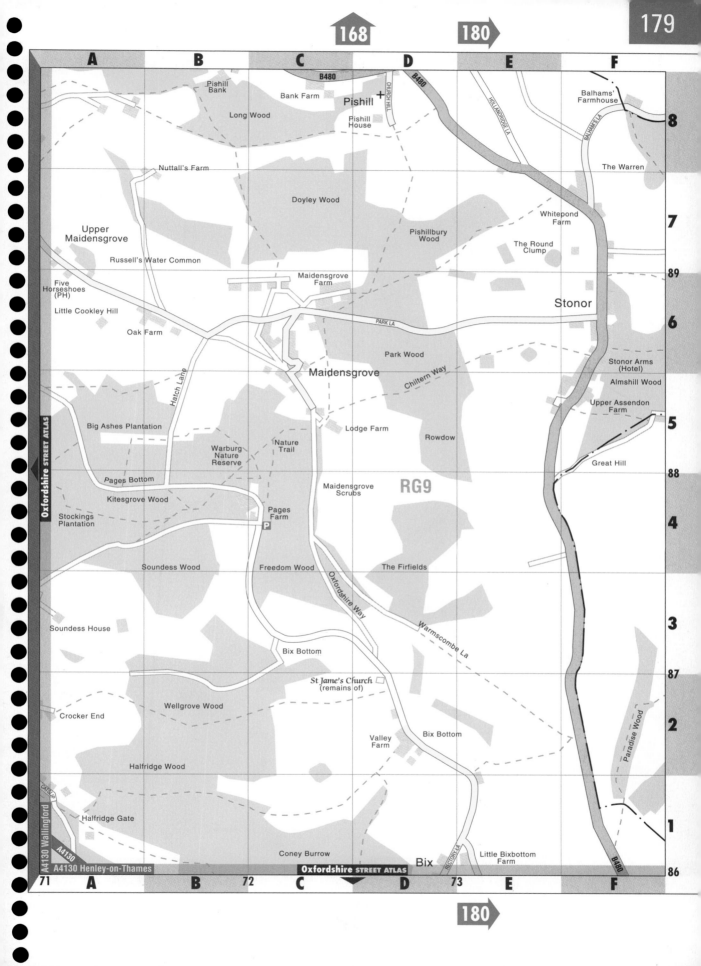

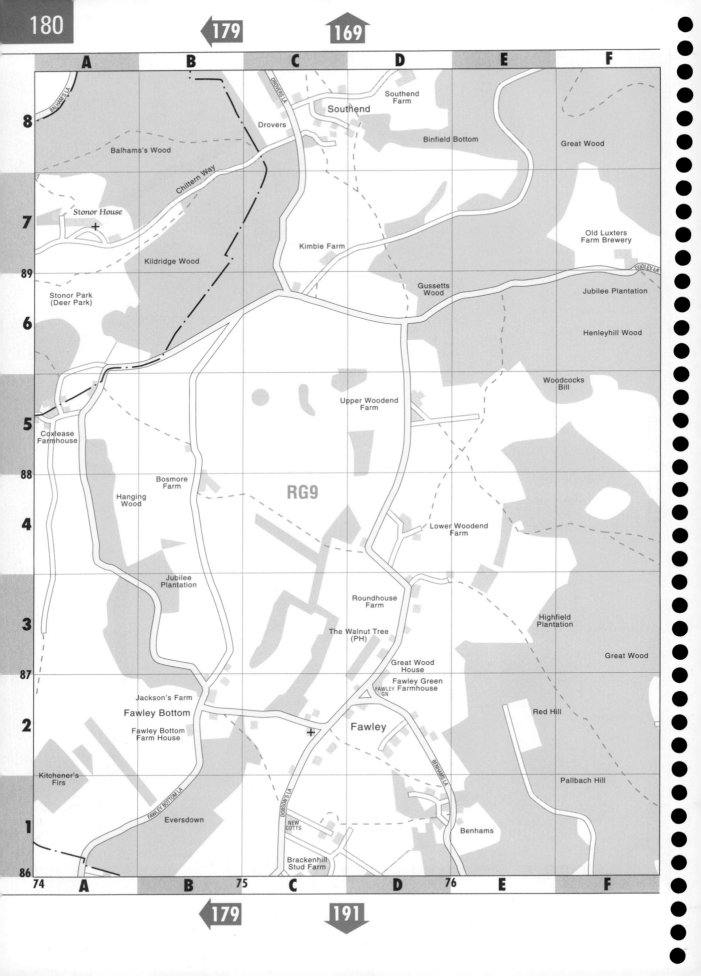

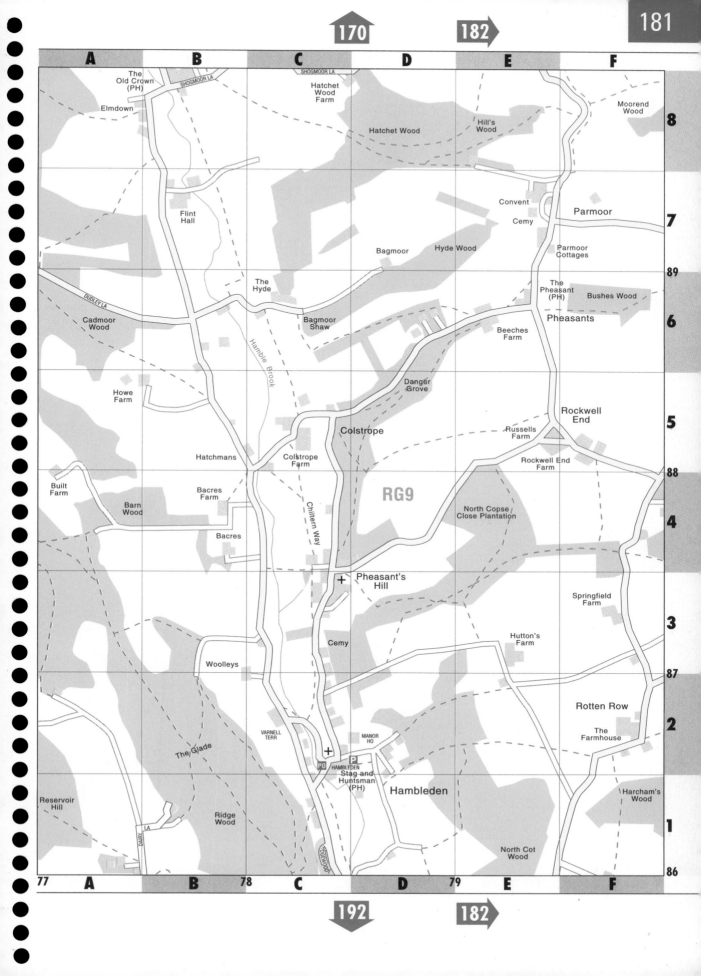

170
182

A B C D E F

8

7

89

6

5

88

4

87

3

2

1

86

192
182

77 A B 78 C D 79 E F

The Old Crown (PH)
SHOGMOOR LA
Elmdown
SHOGMOOR LA
Hatchet Wood Farm
Hill's Wood
Moorend Wood
Hatchet Wood
Flint Hall
Convent
Cemy
Parmoor
Bagmoor
Hyde Wood
Parmoor Cottages
The Hyde
DUDLEY LA
The Pheasant (PH)
Bushes Wood
Cadmoor Wood
Bagmoor Shaw
Pheasants
Beeches Farm
Hamble Brook
Danger Grove
Rockwell End
Howe Farm
Russells Farm
Colstrope
Hatchmans
Colstrope Farm
Rockwell End Farm
Built Farm
RG9
Barn Wood
Bacres Farm
Chiltern Way
North Copse Close Plantation
Bacres
Pheasant's Hill
Springfield Farm
Cemy
Hutton's Farm
Woolleys
Rotten Row
The Glade
VARNELL TERR
MANOR HO
The Farmhouse
PO
HAMBLEDEN
Stag and Huntsman (PH)
Reservoir Hill
DAIRY LA
Ridge Wood
Hambleden
Harcham's Wood
EDGEWOOD
North Cot Wood

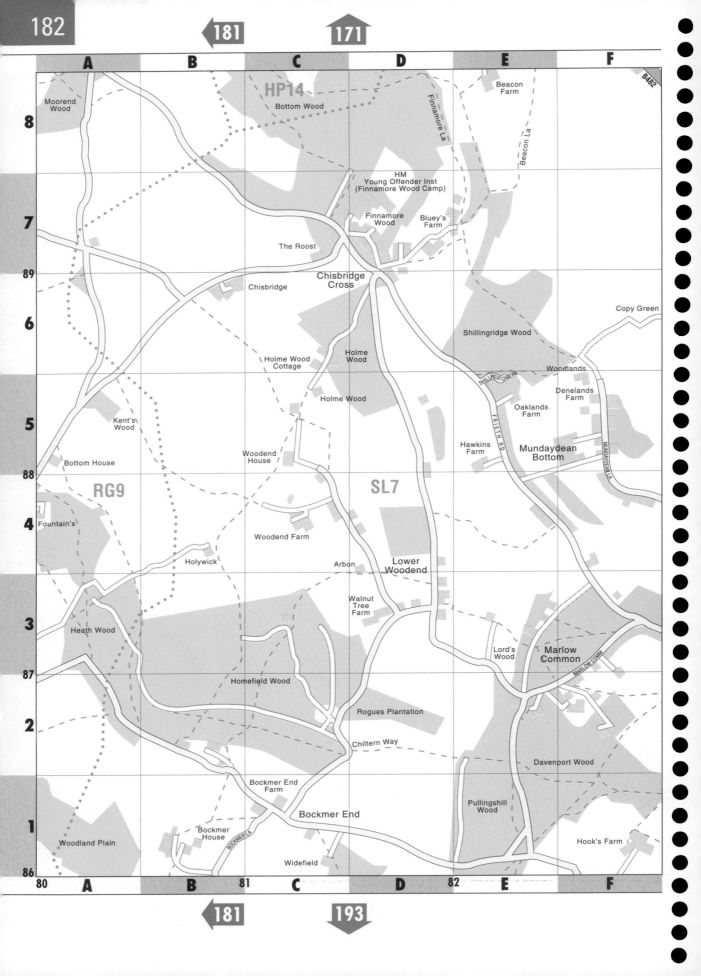

B482

A **B** **C** **D** **E** **F**

HP14

Moorend Wood

Bottom Wood

Beacon Farm

8

Beacon La

Finnamore La

HM Young Offender Inst (Finnamore Wood Camp)

7

Finnamore Wood

Bluey's Farm

The Roost

89

Chisbridge

Chisbridge Cross

Copy Green

6

Shillingridge Wood

Woodlands

Holme Wood Cottage

Holme Wood

SHILLINGRIDGE PK

Denelands Farm

Kent's Wood

Holme Wood

FRIETH RD

Oaklands Farm

5

Woodend House

Hawkins Farm

Mundaydean Bottom

MUNDAYDEAN LA

Bottom House

88

RG9

SL7

Fountain's

4

Woodend Farm

Holywick

Arbon

Lower Woodend

3

Heath Wood

Walnut Tree Farm

Lord's Wood

Marlow Common

87

MARLOW COMM

Homefield Wood

Rogues Plantation

2

Chiltern Way

Davenport Wood

Bockmer End Farm

Pullingshill Wood

Bockmer End

1

Bockmer House

BOCKMER LA

Hook's Farm

Woodland Plain

Widefield

86

A **B** **C** **D** **E** **F**

80 81 82

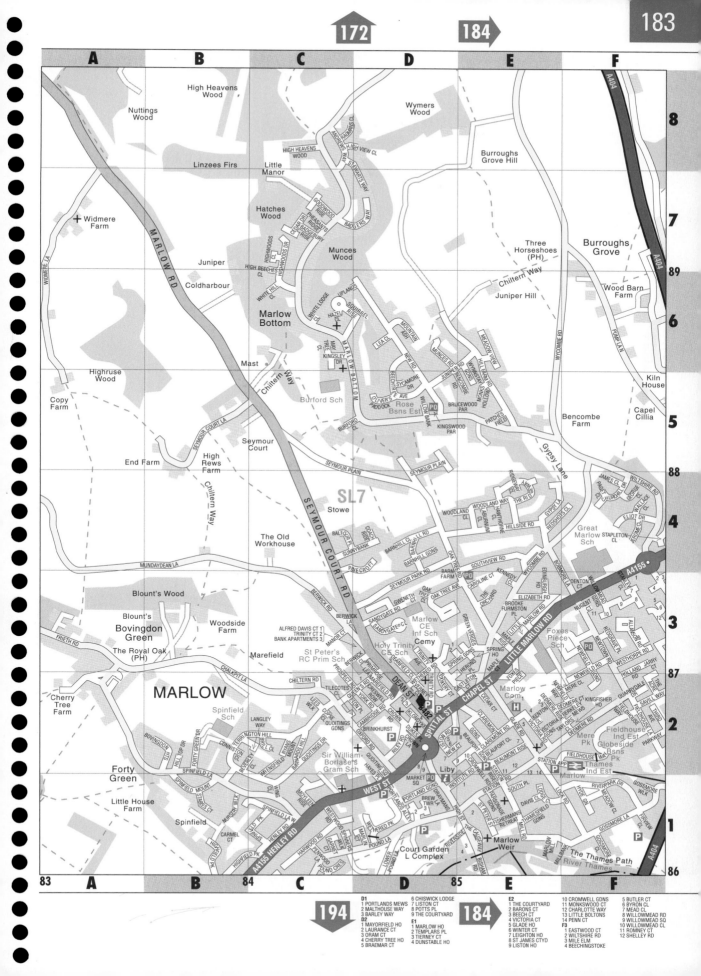

183
173

HP10

Chiltern Way

New Farm

Chiltern Way

PH

Sheepridge

Horton Wood

Bloom Wood

SHEEPRIDGE LA

Chiltern Way

Bloom Farm

WINCHBOTTOM LA

Merton's Hole Cottage

Pigeon House Farm

A404

Fern House

Cemy

FERN COTTS

FERN LA

Fern

SL7

Well End

ABBEY MEAD

Wilton Farm

Little Marlow CE Sch

ELM LA

ABBEY RD

Pump La N

MARLOW RD

Coronach

The Kings Head (PH)

CHURCH RD

SCHOOL LA

Little Marlow

WELL END COTTS

A4155

THE HEWTIE

Pump Farm

POUND LA

THE MOOR

Manor House

SL8

Thame Valley Falconry & Conservation Ctr

PUMP LA S

The Drive

The Abbey

STAPLETON CL

A4155

SPADE OAK

MILL LA

TO MARLOW RD

The Spade Oak (PH)

Abbotsbrook

P

MILE ELM

1 BUTLER CT
2 BRISTOW CT
3 GRATTON CT
4 DOUGLAS CT
5 RAVENSCOURT

Westhorpe Park CVN Site

Sewage Works

The Moor

SPADE OAK FARM

LC

LC

THE PHASE

WILTSHIRE RD

PEACOCK RD

GUNTHORPE RD

THE CROFT

GUILD CROFT CL

Westhorpe House

River Thames

SAVILL WAY

6 HOBART CT
7 MARCHANT CT
8 WASHINGTON CT
9 SWALLOW HO
10 SWIFT HO

Westhorpe Farm

The Thames Path

Noah's House

Cock Marsh

FOURTH AVE

Patches

FIRST AVE

SL6

Stone House

Coney Copse

PARKWAY

The Thames Path

A404

RIVERWOODS DR

RIVERWOOD AVE

GIBRALTAR LA

STONEHOUSE LA

WINTER HILL

Winter Hill

BRADCUTTS LA

TERRY'S LA

Harvest Moon

Greythatch

P

183
195

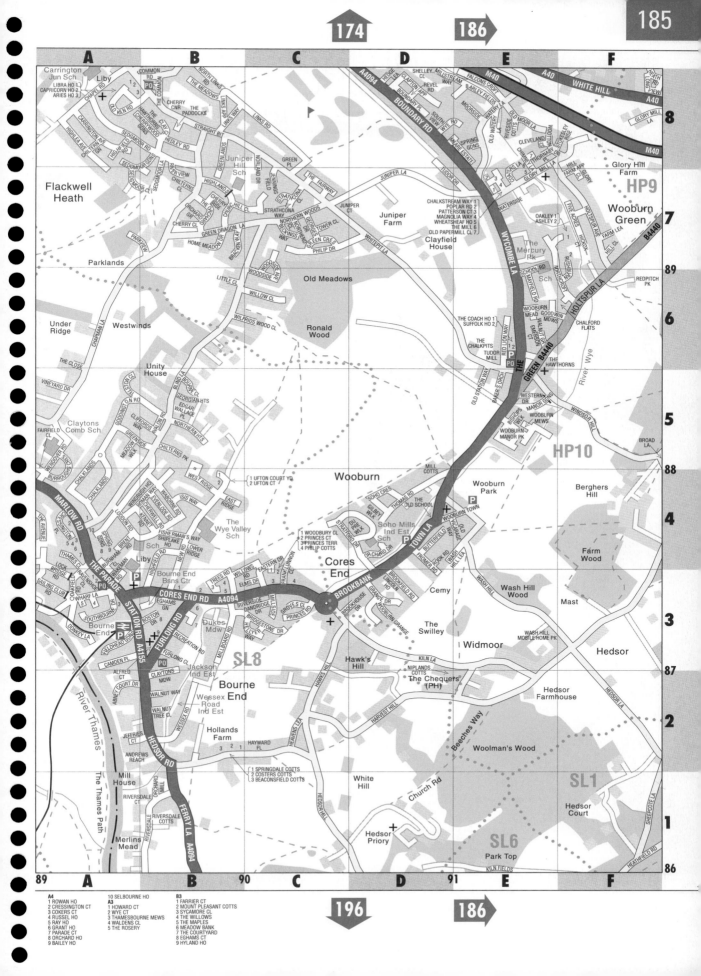

BEACONSFIELD

HP9

HP10

HP9

SL1

SL2

1 FREDERICKS CT
2 HOLTSPUR TOP LA
3 BEACONSFIELD MEWS
4 HOLTSPUR PAR
5 HOLTSPUR CT

Cemy

Springfield

Over's Farm

Mill Wood

Lillyfee Farm

Dipple Wood

Obelisk

Home Farm

The Grove

Hall Barn

The Bungalow

Fairview House

Hill Wood

Woodlands Farm

Hollybush Wood

Castleman's Farm

Odds Farm Park

SALTERS ROW

ODDS FARM EST

Dipple Lodge

GREEN COMMON LA

Hicknaham Plantation

Jennings Farm

The Royal Standard (PH)

Wooburn Common

Sheepcote Farm

Hales Cottage

Ashen Coppice

Hicknaham Farm

Little Jennings Farm

Boveney Wood

Akroyd Cottages

Healy's Gorse

Saw Mill

Bristles Wood

Abbey Park Farm

HEDSOR LA

Johnson's Coppice

HEATHFIELD RD

Hollybush Wood

Dropmore Inf Sch

LITTLEWORTH RD

DROPMORE RD

Jolly Woodman (PH)

BOVENEY WOOD LA

Boveney Wood Farm

Littleworth Common

DORNEY WOOD RD

COMMON LA

Dorney Wood

PARK LA

Staplefurze Wood

The Lake

Dropmore

176
188
198
188

BURNHAM AVE
A355
A40
LONDON RD
PYEBUSH LA
HEDGERLEY LA
POPKIN LA
Birchland Wood
Stampwell Farm
Pyebushes
Lower Pyebushes
Birch Wood
OXFORD RD
Mast
Hyde Farm
HP9
Hotel
Wapsey's Wood
A40
A355
Mast
Green Broom
Further Warren Wood
SL9
89
Burtley Wood
Bower Wood Cotts
Cave Wood
HEDGERLEY LA
Works
6
Moat Farm
Hillmotts Farm
Birchen Spring Coppice
Slade Farm
Slade Wood
5
Bower Wood
BEACONSFIELD COMMON LA
WAPSEYS LA
88
Hillmotts Furze
Manor Farm
Hedgerley Green
Dorney Bottom
SL1
Mount Pleasant Farm
Sutton's Wood
Nature Reserve
Sherley Close
4
DORNEY HILL N
DORNEY HILL S
Pennlands Wood
VILLAGE LA
White Horse (PH)
Hedgerley
THE CHURCH HOLT
Pennlands Farm
HAREHATCH LA
ANDREW HILL LA
KILN LA
SL2
HILLYVIEW
Court Farm
Church Wood
3
87
Summerlins Wood
The Yew Tree (PH)
Kiln Wood
Brick Mould (PH)
Hanging Wood
OLD NURSERY CT
GREGORY RD
STEVENSON RD
Black Grove Ho
ELKINS RD
Hedgerley Hill
Hedgerley Park
2
COLLINSWOOD RD
ROBERT RD
SPICE WAY
JONES WAY
COTTAGE PARK RD
Egypt Woods
EGYPT LA
HOLLYBUSH CNR
PARISH LA
One Pin Farm
LONGFIELD
TIMBER WOOD
Hedgerley Park Farm
Heathfield Wood
CHRISTMAS LA
School Wood
The One Pin (PH)
WOOD END CL
COLLUM GREEN RD
1
EGYPT WOOD COTTS
COLINSWOOD
WOODLAND GLADE
ONE PIN LA
HEATHERSIDE
GYPSY LA
COLLEY HILL LA
STOKE WOOD
ROMSEY DR
A355
86

95   A   B   96   C   D   97   E   F

A **B** **C** **D** **E** **F**

8

LAYTERS GREEN LA

St Joseph's RC Comb Sch
Austenwood

PRIORY RD
PRIORY WAY
THE ROWANS
LEWINS RD

SCHOOL LA
CLELAND RD
AUSTENWAY
CLAYTON END
CLAYTON LA
RUSSETT HILL

KINGSWAY B416
A413

River Misbourne
CH

Chalfont Park

Siblet's Wood

Maltmans Green Sch
MALTMANS LA

Gayhurst Sch

AUSTENWOOD LA
WOODBINE COTTS
SOUTH SIDE
THE GREENWAY
ACREFIELD RD
THE QUEENSWAY
FIRST END
CEDAR
HUBERTS WAY
NORTH PK

Schs
CROSSFIELD HO
St Mary's Sch

7

Mumford's Farm

A40 89

BULL LA

MILTON AVE
SOUTH VIEW RD
LATCHMOOR DR
LATCHMOOR WAY
ORCHEHILL AVE
OVAL WAY
HERITAGE GATE

NORGROVE PK
PENN HAVEN
SOUTH PARK CRES
SOUTH PARK
THE CHYNE
SOUTH PK

PACKHORSE RD

O WER RD
PARSIDE

A413

RAYLANDS MEAD
LAYTERS WAY
BENTINCK CL
BULSTRODE WAY

ORCHEHILL RISE
HAMILTON PL
THORPE CRES
THORPE CL
Gerrards Cross

STATION APP

1 2
DORCHESTER BEN MORE

WOODHILL AVE
ROUSE CT

6

Jarretts Hill

MAIN DR
WEST COMM

OXFORD RD

MILLER PL
WEST COMM

ETHORPE HO 1
THE GRANGE 2
SOUTH PARK CT 3
WEST COMM

Station Rd
Liby
EUROPA HO

MAPLE CT
MERSHAM LA

MARSHAM WAY
MARSHAM LODGE

WOODLANDS

89

Bulstrode Park

Bulstrode

TOP PK
VALLEY WAY
WOODBINE WAY
PORTLAND PK
ROMAND CL

B416

Gerrards Cross Common

GERRARDS CROSS

HARTLEY COLSTON CT
FULMER WAY
MARGARET SMYTHE HO

VICARAGE WAY
EAST COMM

MILL LA
HILL WAVE
HILLCREST WAVE
BEECH WAVE

5

M40 88

Grove Plantation

Ponders

HEDGERLEY LA

Crab Hill

SL9

CAMP RD

MANOR LA
DENMEAD

ST HUBERTS COTTS
PINEWOOD CL

The Gerrards Cross CE Sch

WOODHILL CT

Woodhill Lodge

WOODHILL

4

SL2

STONEYFIELD

Upper Meadows

WINDSOR RD

MAYSIDE GDNS

MEADAWAY PK

DUKES LA
DUKES CL
DUKES VALE
DUKES RIDE
DUKES WOOD AVE

GAVIOTS WAY
GAVIOTS CL

A40
HEUSDEN WAY

3

Hedgerley Park

High Meadows

MOUNT HILL LA

DUKES KILN DR

DUKES WOOD DR
THE SPINNEY
BIRCHDALE

CHEYNE CL
THE GLADE
HIGH BEECHES

ELMWOOD PK
ST HUBERTS CL
THE UPLANDS

FULMER RD
ST HUBERTS LA

The Rancho
St Huberts

The Home Farm

87

Mount Hill Farm

HOWARDS THICKET

DALE SIDE

FULMER DR

2

Mounthill Wood
Park House

DUKES VALLEY

HOWARDS WOOD DR

Fulmerfields

The Oldhouse Farm

1

Cemy

B416

Pickeridge Wood

Low Farm

SL3

M40

FULMER LA

Alderbrook

86

98 **A** **B** 99 **C** **D** 00 **E** **F**

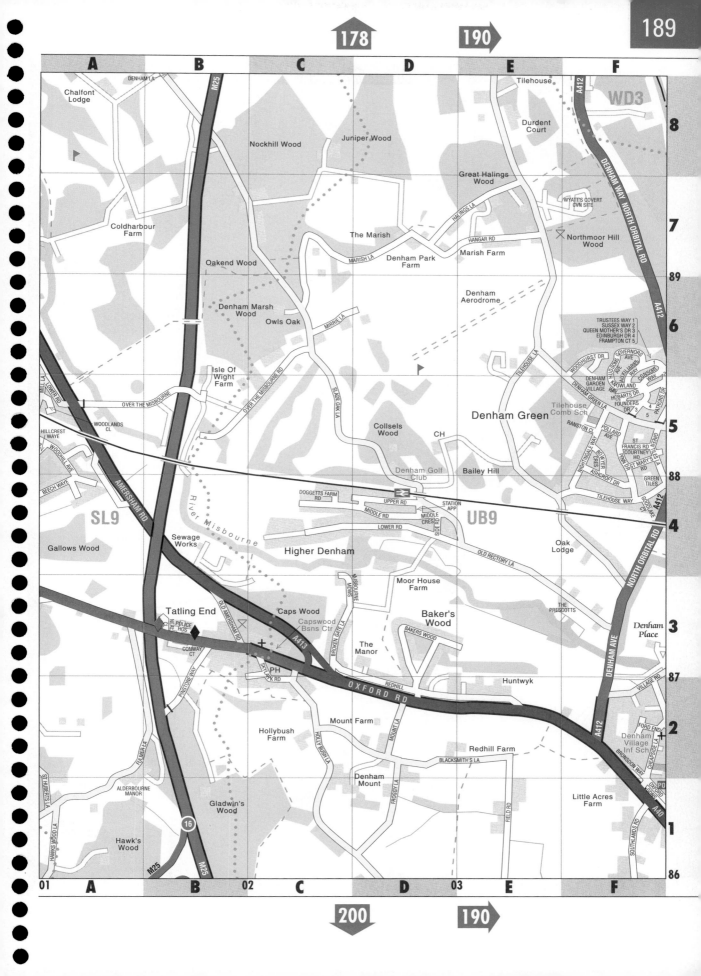

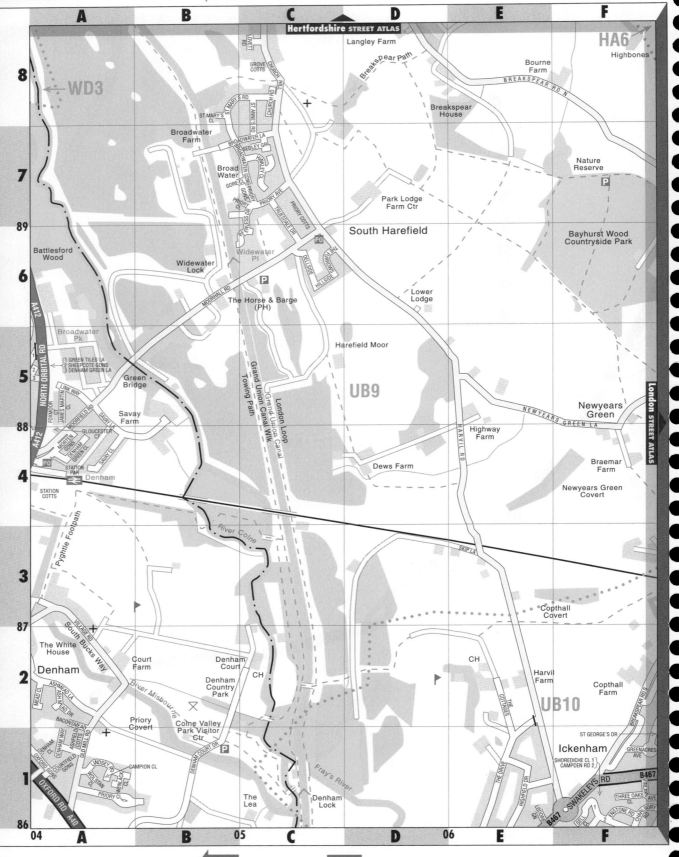

Hertfordshire STREET ATLAS

HA6

Langley Farm

Breakspear Path

Highbones

Bourne
Farm

BREAKSPEAR RD N

8

WD3

LOVETT RD

GROVE
COTTS

CHURCH HILL

Breakspear
House

Broadwater
Farm

ST MARY'S RD

ST MARY'S
CL

ST ANNE'S RD

SEDLEY GRI

BROADWATER LA

Nature
Reserve

P

7

Broad
Water

GORE CL

PRIORY CL

GDNS

HUXLEY CL

PRIORY

PRIORY AVE

PRIORY COTTS

Park Lodge
Farm Ctr

South Harefield

Bayhurst Wood
Countryside Park

89

PO

Widewater
PI

THE ROWANS

DELLSIDE

HILLSIDE

TRUESDALE DR

Battlesford
Wood

Widewater
Lock

P

6

MOORHALL RD

The Horse & Barge
(PH)

Lower
Lodge

Broadwater
Pk

1 GREEN TILES LA
2 SHEEPCOTE GDNS
3 DENHAM GREEN LA

Harefield Moor

NORTH ORBITAL RD

A412

LINK WAY

FOXMOOR
CT

Green
Bridge

Grand Union Canal
Towing Path

Grand Union Canal

London Loop

UB9

Newyears
Green

NEWYEARS GREEN LA

5

JAMES MARTIN CL

MOORFIELD RD

Savay
Farm

London

STREET ATLAS

88

A412

MORTEN
GDNS

DENHAM
GREEN CL

GLOUCESTER
CT

SAVAY CL

Highway
Farm

HARVIL RD

Braemar
Farm

PO

STATION
PAR

Dews Farm

Newyears Green
Covert

4

STATION
COTTS

Denham

SKIP LA

Pyghtle Footpath

River Colne

3

Copthall
Covert

87

VILLAGE RD

South Bucks Way

CH

Harvil
Farm

The White
House

Court
Farm

Denham
Court

CH

Copthall
Farm

2

Denham

River Misbourne

Denham
Country
Park

THE COTTAGES

UB10

MEAD CL

ASHMEAD LA

ASH MEAD DR

BACONSMEAD

Priory
Covert

Colne Valley
Park Visitor
Ctr

St George's Dr

THE DRIVE

HIGHFIELD DR

ST GEORGE'S DR

GREENACRES
AVE

DENHAM
GDNS

DENHAM WAY

ASHFIELD
GDNS

OLD MILL RD

DENHAM COURT DR

P

Ickenham

SHOREDICHE CL 1
CAMPDEN RD 2

1

OXFORD GDNS

COURTFIELD GDNS

LINDSEY RD

WOLSTAN CL

WENLACK CL

CAMPION CL

PRIORY CL

The
Lea

Fray's River

Denham
Lock

HIGHFIELD DR

THE DRIVE

LOVEDAY CL

GELL CL

B467

SWAKELEYS RD

B467

THREE OAKS AVE

ENSTONE RD

CHALSBURY

OXFORD RD A40

86

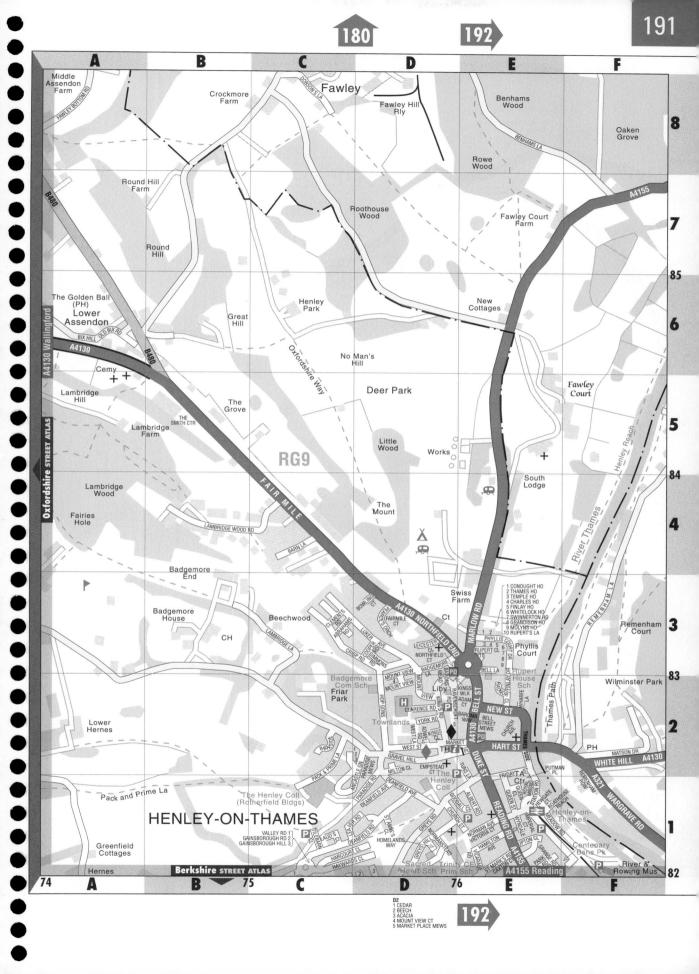

HENLEY-ON-THAMES

RG9

Fawley

Middle Assendon Farm

Crockmore Farm

Fawley Hill Rly

Benhams Wood

Oaken Grove

Round Hill Farm

Roothouse Wood

Rowe Wood

Fawley Court Farm

Round Hill

Henley Park

The Golden Ball (PH) Lower Assendon

Great Hill

No Man's Hill

New Cottages

Cemy

Deer Park

Fawley Court

Lambridge Hill

The Grove

Lambridge Farm

Little Wood

Works

South Lodge

Lambridge Wood

Fairies Hole

The Mount

Lambridge Wood Rd

Barn La

Badgemore End

Beechwood

Swiss Farm

1 CONOUGHT HO
2 THAMES HO
3 TEMPLE HO
4 CHARLES HO
5 FINLAY HO
6 WHITELOCK HO
7 SWINNERTON HO
8 GRANDISON HO
9 MOLYNS HO
10 RUPERT'S LA

Remenham Court

Badgemore House

CH

Phyllis Court

Wilminster Park

Friar Park

Badgemore Com Sch

Liby

Rupert House Sch

Townlands

Clarence Rd

NEW ST

Lower Hernes

BELL ST

HART ST

PH

Matson Dr

WHITE HILL A4130

Pack & Prime La

The Henley Coll (Rotherfield Bldgs)

DUKE ST

READING RD

WARGRAVE RD

Henley-on-Thames

HENLEY-ON-THAMES

Greenfield Cottages

VALLEY RD 1
GAINSBOROUGH RD 2
GAINSBOROUGH HILL 3

Homelands Way

Centenary Bsns Pk

Hernes

Sacred Heart Sch

Trinity CE Prim Sch

A4155 Reading

River & Rowing Mus

D2
1 CEDAR
2 BEECH
3 ACACIA
4 MOUNT VIEW CT
5 MARKET PLACE MEWS

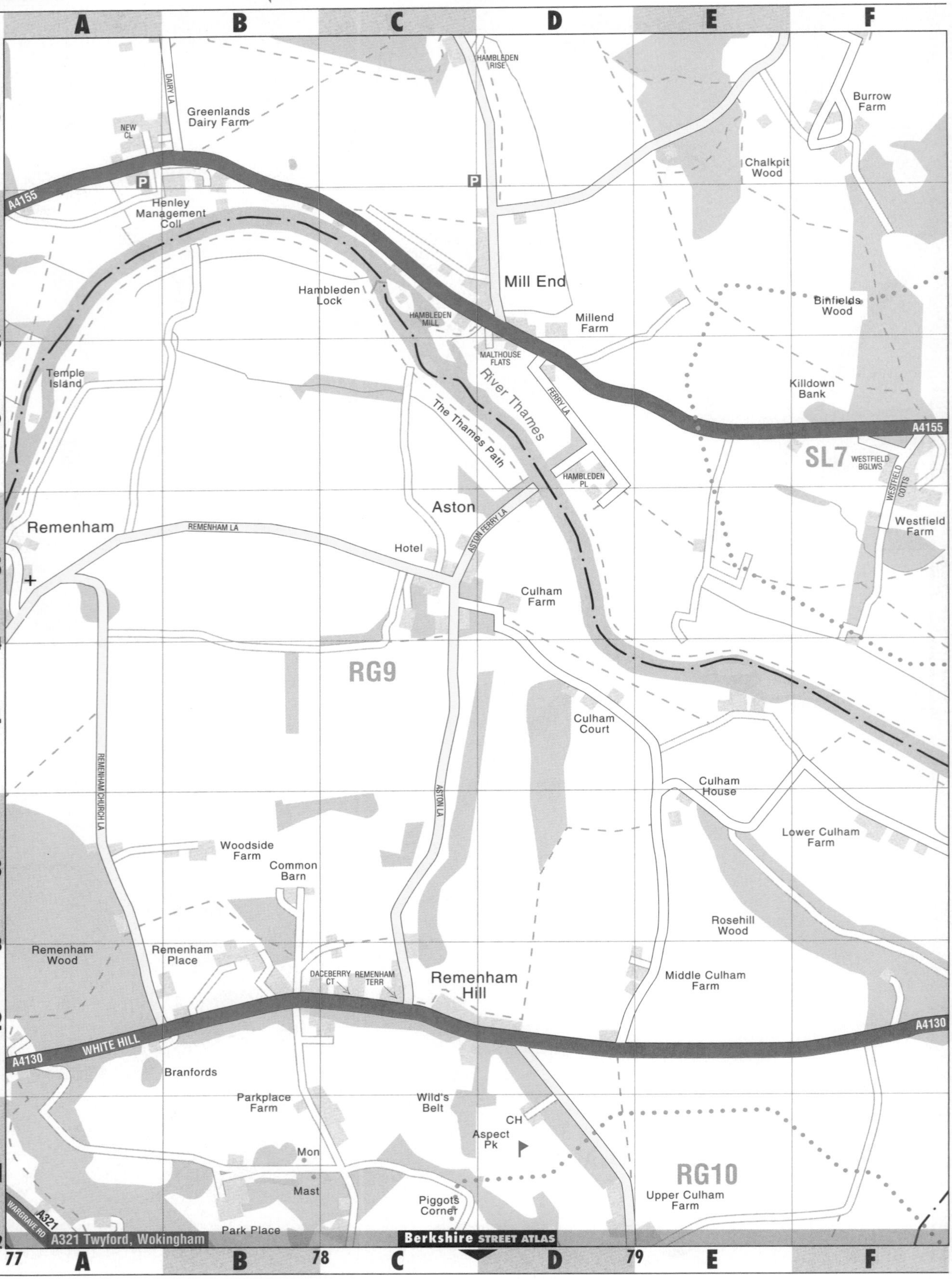

← 191
↑ 181

Grid references / Map labels

8

New Cl

Greenlands Dairy Farm

HAMBLEDEN RISE

Burrow Farm

Chalkpit Wood

7

P

A4155

Henley Management Coll

Mill End

Binfields Wood

Hambleden Lock

HAMBLEDEN MILL

Millend Farm

85

MALTHOUSE FLATS

Killdown Bank

Temple Island

River Thames

FERRY LA

6

The Thames Path

SL7

A4155

WESTFIELD BGLWS

HAMBLEDEN PL

WESTFIELD COTTS

Aston

ASTON FERRY LA

Westfield Farm

5

Remenham

REMENHAM LA

Hotel

Culham Farm

+

84

RG9

4

Culham Court

REMENHAM CHURCH LA

ASTON LA

Culham House

Lower Culham Farm

3

Woodside Farm

Common Barn

Rosehill Wood

83

Remenham Wood

Remenham Place

DACEBERRY CT

REMENHAM TERR

Remenham Hill

Middle Culham Farm

2

WHITE HILL

A4130

Branfords

A4130

1

A321

WARGRAVE RD

Parkplace Farm

Mon

Wild's Belt

CH

Aspect Pk

RG10

Upper Culham Farm

Mast

Piggots Corner

Park Place

82

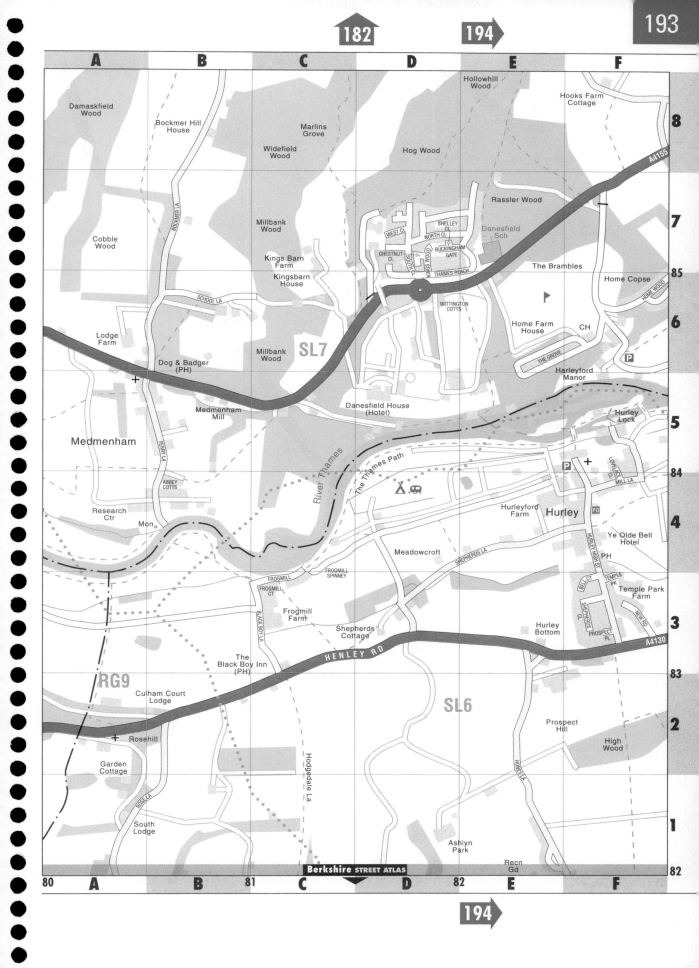

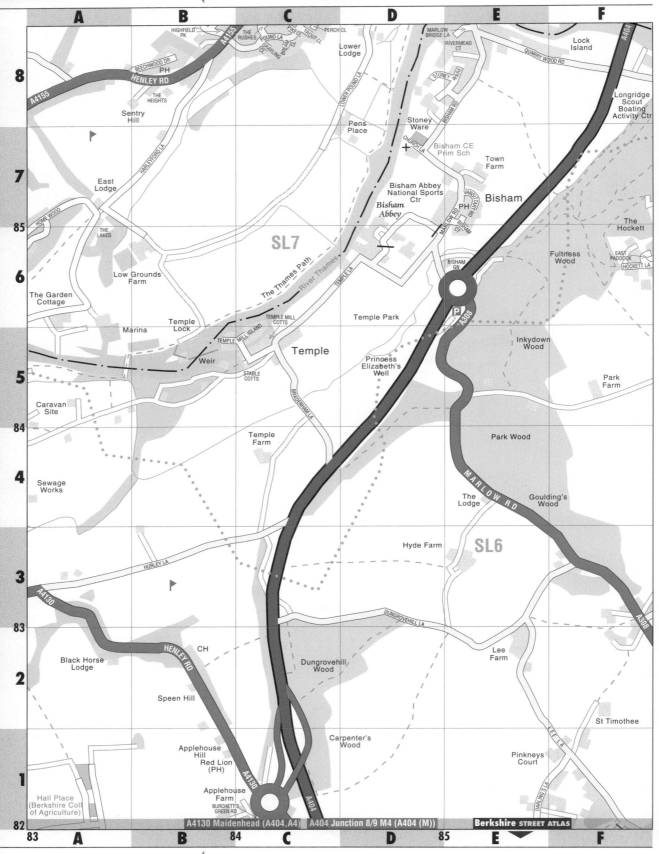

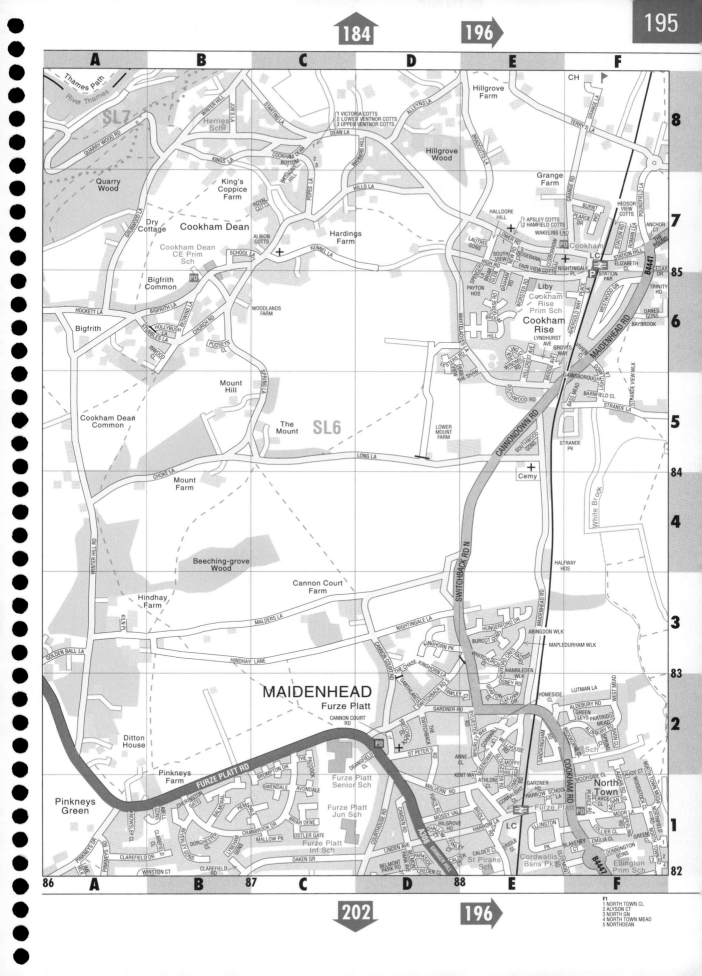

Grid columns: A B C D E F

Row numbers: 8 7 85 6 5 84 4 3 83 2 1 82

Bottom coordinates: 86 87 88

Thames Path
River Thames
SL7
Quarry Wood Rd
Quarry Wood
GroveWood La
Winter Hill La
Job's La
Herries Sch
Kings La
Starting's La
Cookham Dean Bottom
Wesonic Hill
Popes La
Dean La
1 Victoria Cotts
2 Lower Ventnor Cotts
3 Upper Ventnor Cotts
Alleyns La
Hillgrove Farm
CH
Hillgrove Wood
Bracotts La
Terry's Rd
Grange La
King's Coppice Farm
Royal Cotts
Hills La
Grange Farm
Grange Rd
Burnt Wd
Pearce Dr
Hedsor View Cotts
Anchor Ct
The Pound
Dry Cottage
Cookham Dean
Albion Cotts
Hardings Farm
Kennel La
Halldore Hill
1 Apsley Cotts
2 Hamfield Cotts
Wakelins End
Lower Rd
Cookham
PO
Station Hill
Cedar Dr
B4447
Cookham Dean CE Prim Sch
School La
Bigfrith Common
PO
Lautree Gdns
Spencers Rd
Lark La
High Rd
South View
Fair View Cotts
Nightingale Pl
Rosebank
Codbrow
Elizabeth Cl
Station Par
Trinity Ho
Station Rd
Roman Lea
Hockett La
Bigfrith La
Browns La
Church Rd
Woodlands Farm
Gorse Rd
Webster Rd
Graham Rd
Liby
Cookham Rise Prim Sch
Peace La
Shergold Way
Westwood Gn
Maidenhead Rd
Danes Gdns
Baybrook
Bigfrith
Hollybush La
Stubbles La
Inwood Cl
Pudseys Cl
Payton Hos
Broom Hill
Cookham Rise
Lyndhurst Ave
Groves Way
Vivien Cl
Gainsborough
Baggs Mead
Strande View Wlk
Church Rd
Spring La
Mount Hill
The Shaw
Whiteladys La
Lesters Rd
Dean Cl
Hillcrest Ave
Windmill Rd
Bridge Rd
Barnfield Cl
Strande La
Cookham Dean Common
The Mount
SL6
Long La
Lower Mount Farm
Southwood Gdns
Southwood Rd
Cannondown Rd
Strande Pk
Choke La
Mount Farm
Cemy
White Brook
Winter Hill Rd
Beeching-grove Wood
Kiln Pl
Hindhay Farm
Cannon Court Farm
Malders La
Nightingale La
Switchback Rd N
Maidenhead Rd
Halfway Hos
Golden Ball La
Hindhay Lane
Cannon Court Rd
The Chase
Kinghorn La
Kinghorn Pk
Abingdon Wlk
Mapledurham Wlk
Hungerford Dr
Burcot Gdns
Whitchurch Cl
Shefford Cres
Radcot Cl
Hambleden Wlk
Osney Rd
MAIDENHEAD
Furze Platt
Garthlands
Switchback Rd S
Fawley Cl
Gardner Rd
Sylvesters Way
Grafton Cl
Calvin Dr
Homeside Cl
Lutman La
West Mead
Aldebury Rd
Green Leys
Partridge Mead
Cannon Court Rd
Switchback Cl
The Switchback
St Peter's Rd
Anne Cl
Queensway
Cornwall Cl
Wellhouse Rd
Sandringham
Gardner Ho
Altwood Cl
Barn Cl
Sch
Ditton House
PO
Deansfield Cl
Kent Way
Athloner Rd
Gloucester Cl
Moffy Cl
Connaught
Harrow School La
Moorside Cl
North Town Moor
Woodstock Cl
Pinkneys Farm
Furze Platt Rd
Brompton Dr
Paddock
Gwendale
Avondale
Furze Platt Senior Sch
Malvern Rd
Harrow La
Mossy Vale
Gardner Rd
Cookham Rd
Harrow Cl
Pearce Rd
North Town
Furze Platt
PO
Moor La
Green Cl
San Sq
Northfield Rd
Pinkneys Green
Knowsley Cl
Cherington Gate
Balmoral
Heacone
Briar Dene
Furze Platt Jun Sch
Courthouse Rd
Camden Rd
Hilgrove Rd
Challow Cl
Fenley Cl
Ellington Rd
LC
Cordwallis Bsns Pk
Hedsavoy Cl
Emilia Cl
Donnington Gdns
Ellington Prim Sch
B4447
Abell Gdns
Clarefield Cl
Beverley Gdns
Dorchester Ct
Lyleham Gdns
Cranbrook Dr
Mallow Pk
Ostler Gate
Furze Platt Inf Sch
Oaken Gr
Linden Ave
A308
Ginger Hill
St Pirans Sch
Bridle Cl
Blakeney Ct
Pinkneys Dr
Lime Wlk
Clarefield Dr
Clarefield Rd
Winston Ct
Belmont Park Rd
Parkside Rd
Belmont
Creden Cl
Calder Cl
Calder Rd
Pearce Rd

A B C D E F

8

Sewage Wks

SL8

RIVERSDALE

A4094 FERRY LA

Lock Cut

Hedsor Hill

Hedsor House

Hedsor Park

Upper Lodge

Gully Farm

HEATHFIELD RD

BOURNE END RD

Cookham Bridge

Cookham Lock

7

GLEBE RD

BERRIES RD

VICARAGE CL

TERRY'S LA

THE POUND

B4447

HIGH ST B4447

POCKETTS YD

SCHOOL LA

P

P

Moor Hall

Holy Trinity CE Prim Sch

Cookham

ST GEORGES LODGE

DONEY LA

FERRY LA

Stanley Spencer Art Gall & Mus

WOODMOOR END

BLACK BUTT COTTS

SUTTON CL

Lulle Brook

MILL LA

Formosa Court

Cliveden

The Feathers (PH)

Gulley Wood

85

CEDAR DR

Triangle Cottages

6

SUTTON RD

Garden Cottages

Sutton Farm

Lodge

Widbrook House

White Place Farm

Green Dr

ORKNEY CT

Burwood House

TAPLOW COMMON RD

NASHDOM LA 1
NASHDOM 2

1
2

84

STRANDE LA

Strand Water

Widbrook Common

White Brook

SL6

Thames Path

River Thames

Towing Path

PARLIAMENT LA

HUNTSWOOD LA

5

Maidenhead Court

Whitebrook Pk

Hunt's Wood

4

ELMWOOD

OAK HURST

CUBA COTTS

MAIDENHEAD COURT PK

ASHDOWN

WIDBROOK RD

BATTLEMEAD CL

ISLET

PARK DR

ISLET PK

ISLET PARK HO

SL1

Hitchambury

CLIVEDEN RD

3

83

Sheephouse Farm

THE AVENUE

ISLET RD

LOVETT GDNS

EBSWORTH CL

HIGH MDW

HERONS PL

COURT DR

AMBERLEY CT

Somerlea

HUNT'S LA

Hitchambury Farm

2

MAIDENHEAD

SHEEPHOUSE RD

FULLERS YD

CLIVEDEN MEAD

POPLARS GR

ASHLEY PK

LOWER COOKHAM RD

LOCK MEAD

MEAD CL

TUDOR DR

HAZELL

LOCK AVE

Weir

Boulter's Lock

HILL FARM RD

HITCHAM LA

1

LAKESIDE

SUMMERLEAZE RD

THE PAGE

BOULTERS LA

RAY MEAD CT 1
BOULTERS CL 2

HORSHAM REACH

P

BOULTERS GDNS

Taplow Vineyard

St Nicholas' CE Comb Sch

BREEMS

1 CHURCH COTTS
2 COLD GROVE COTTS

Hill Farm

Hitcham Grange

HITCHAM RD

LAKE VIEW

BLACKAMOOR LA

LONSDALE CL

RAY MDW

PRINCE ANDREW CL 1
PRINCE ANDREW RD 2
WHITEHALL 3

WHITE ROCK

CHESTNUT CL

SUNNYMEDE COTTS

RAY MILL RD E

CYGNET HO

HORTON CL

CLAPPERS MDW

BOULTERS CT

CAMBER DOWN

A4094 RAY MEAD RD

HORTON GRANGE

St

Taplow Court

HILL HO

RECTORY RD

BERRY HILL

P

HIGH ST

WELLBANK

Hitcham Grange

82

WATERS REACH

THE FALLOWS

BEECHWOOD

RAY LEA RD

ADDISON CT

LEIGHTON GDNS

WOODHURST RD

LONGWORTH DR

WOODHURST SOUTH

FRANCES AVE

Stockwells

SAXTON GDNS

SAXON GDNS

CEDAR CHASE

Taplow

BOUNDARY RD

Poplar Farm

A 89 B 90 C D 91 E F

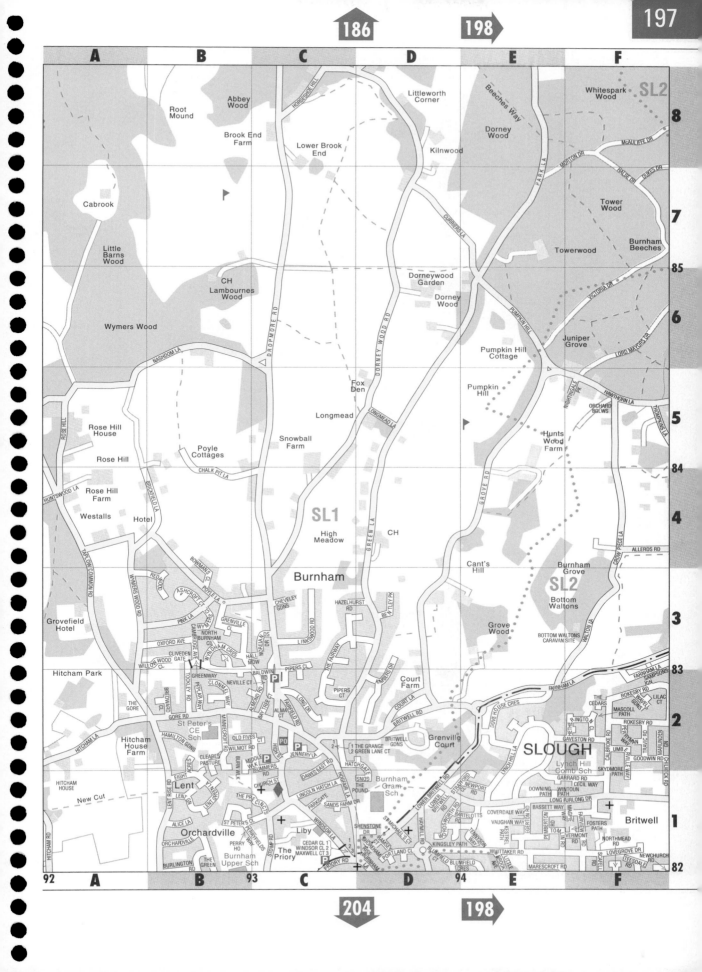

A B C D E F

SL2

Whitespark Wood

8

Root Mound

Abbey Wood

Littleworth Corner

Beeches Way

Dorney Wood

Brook End Farm

Lower Brook End

Kilnwood

McAuliffe Dr

Morton Dr

Cabrook

Tower Wood

7

CURRIERS LA

PARK LA

Little Barns Wood

Burnham Beeches

Towerwood

HALSE DR

DUKES DR

85

CH Lambournes Wood

Dorneywood Garden

VICTORIA DR

6

Dorney Wood

Juniper Grove

LORD MAYORS DR

Wymers Wood

NASHDOM LA

Pumpkin Hill Cottage

DROPMORE RD

DORNEY WOOD RD

PUMPKIN HILL

HAWTHORN LA

ROSE HILL

Fox Den

Pumpkin Hill

NIGHTINGALE PK

ORCHARD BGLWS

THOMPKINS LA

5

Rose Hill House

Longmead

LONGMEAD LA

Hunts Wood Farm

Poyle Cottages

Snowball Farm

Rose Hill

CHALK PIT LA

84

HUNTSWOOD LA

Rose Hill Farm

GROVE RD

4

Westalls

Hotel

BROOKFIELD LA

High Meadow

GREEN LA

CH

SL1

Cant's Hill

Burnham Grove

CROW PIECE LA

ALLERDS RD

TARTON COMMON RD

Burnham

Bottom Waltons

SL2

3

Grovefield Hotel

WINTERS WOOD RD

REDWOOD

POYLE LA

ASHCROFT CT

Grove Wood

BOTTOM WALTONS CARAVAN SITE

WALTON LA

BOWMAN'S CL

Hazelhurst Rd

LINKSWOOD RD

BENTLEY PK

CHEVELEY GDNS

Oxford Ave

PINK LA

CAMBRIDGE RD

North Burnham CC

WYNDHAM CRES

HALL MDW

THE FAIRWAY

FARNHAM LA

FARNHAM RD

83

Hitcham Park

CLIVEDEN GATE

WILLOW WOOD CL

PIPERS CL

KIPPERS RD

Court Farm

DOVE HOUSE CRES

THE CEDARS

ROKESBY RD

MANOR CT

LILAC CT

2

THE GORE

BRENTWOOD CL

GORE RD

TOOKLEY RD

GREENWAY

PEPLAR WAY

ALMOND RD

BALDWIN RD

NEVILLE CT

CLONMEL WAY

FAIRFIELD RD

LONG DR

PIPERS CT

COURT LA

BRITWELL RD

Grenville Court

LYNCH HILL LA

MASCOLL PATH

ROKESBY RD

SAMPSONS IGN

FERNMAN

MARVILLE WAY

CHUXLOCK RD

SLOUGH

HAMILTON GDNS

MINNIECROFT RD

St Peter's CE Sch

OLD FIVES CT

WILMOT RD

ALMA CT

JENNERY LA

Britwell GDNS

SLOUGH

Lynch Hill Comb Sch

GARRARD RD

CECIL WAY

SKYDMORE PATH

GAVESTON RD

GOODWIN RD

HITCHAM LA

Hitcham House Farm

CLEARES PASTURE

MIDDLE WLK

BURN WLK

SUMMERS RD

HIGHER RD

DAWES EAST RD

HATCHGATE

THE POUND

Burnham Gram Sch

LOWER BRITWELL RD

STAFFERTON

NEWPORT RD

DOWNING PATH

WINTOUN PATH

Bassett Way

VAUGHAN WAY

PEMBERTON RD

VERMONT RD

FOSTERS PATH

1

HITCHAM RD

EIGHT ACRES RD

Lent

Lent Rise Rd

LENT RD

ALICE LA

Orchardville

ST PETER'S CL

PERRYFIELDS

Liby

STOMP RD

WINDSOR LA

SHENSTONE DR

ST MICHAEL'S CT

HAYMILL RD

KINGSLEY PATH

Coverdale Way

KESTREL PATH

WHITTAKER RD

FAIRLIN LN RD

NORTHMEAD RD

Britwell

New Cut

Hitcham House

ORCHARDVILLE

BURLINGTON

THE GREEN

PERRY HO

Burnham Upper Sch

CEDAR CL 1 WINDSOR CL 2 MAXWELL CT 3

The Priory

PRIORY RD

PORTLAND CL

BLUMFIELD CRES

LOVEGROVE DR

MARESCROFT RD

SCAFELL RD

TEESDALE RD

NEWCHURCH RD

82

92 A 93 B C 94 D E F

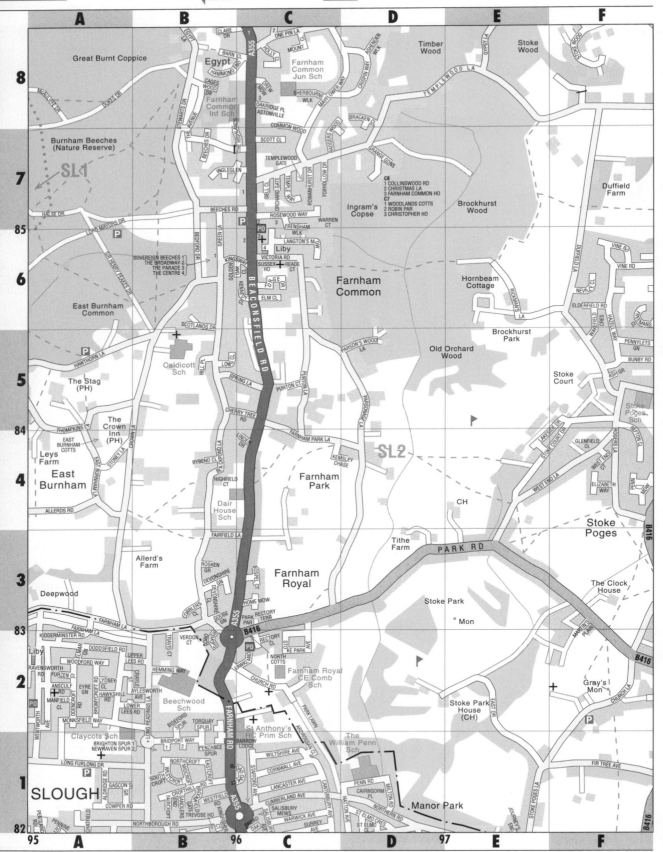

199
189

A B C D E F

8

7

85

6

5

84

4

3

83

2

1

82

01 02 03

HAWKSWOOD LA

M40

M25

1a

16

Alderbourne
Arches

SL9

Brown's
Wood

Ways
Farm

Alderbourne
Farm

ALDERBOURNE LA

FULMER COMMON RD

Strawberry
Wood

Gossams
Wood

Blanchards
Farm

Belle
Farm

Sevenhills
Farm

Long
Coppice

SEVENHILLS RD

The
Clump

Dromenagh
Farm

LADY YORKE PK

SL0

Black Park
Country Park

PEACE RD

Pinewood
Film Studios

BOND
CL

PINEWOOD GR

PINEWOOD CL

PINEWOOD RD

CEDAR CL

FIRS CL

Park Lodge
Farm

PEACE RD

Park
Lodge

ASHFORD RD

THORNBRIDGE RD

HEATHERDEN
GN

LONGSTO NE

THE PARKWAY

ROSTREVOR GDNS

ST DAVID'S CL

ST
DAVID'S
PAR

Recn
Gd

BIRCH CL

ANSLOW GDNS

TREWARDEN AVE

COPSE WOOD

LAUREL CT

DENHAM RD

Iver
Heath

BANGORS RD N

Round
Coppice
Farm

Mansfield
Farm

M25

A4007

Chandlers
Hill

SL3

CHURCH RD

WARREN
GDNS

ROWAN
GDNS

OAK END

ALDER RD

GLAISER

Bodley
HO

WAY

ST MARGARET'S

Liby

PO

HEATH WAY

LAURELS RD

KEENS CSE

1 ST MARGARET'S GATE
2 ST MARGARETS CT

1 2

SLOUGH RD

Warren
House

HAWTHORN CL

A4007

A412

Iver Heath
Jun Sch

Sch

POTTERS CROSS

MEAD
HO

MUD

POST

LOWER
MEAD

GROSVENOR RD

Moorwards
Farm

UXBRIDGE RD

A412

FIVE POINTS

Beeches Way

PLEASANT
COTTS

PH

WOOD
LANE
CL

WOOD LA

THE CLOSE

White
Lodge

HARDINGS
CL

WHITEHOUSE

SWALLOW WAY

LOWMALL

Home
Cottage
Farm

BANGORS RD S

Bangors Park
Farm

HARDINGS ROW

COOPERS ROW

SWALLOW ST

BANGOR
COTTS

NORWOOD LA

MARTINDALE

COPPINS LA

Langley Park
Country Park

BILLET LA

P

P

SL0

SOUTHLANDS RD

M40

Rush
Green

FIELD RD

FIELD RD

HOLLYBUSH LA

New House
Farm

WILLETTS LA

UB9

WILLETTS LA

Kingcup
Farm

A412

Oldhouse
Wood

Alder Bourne

Southlands
Manor

Southlands
Manor

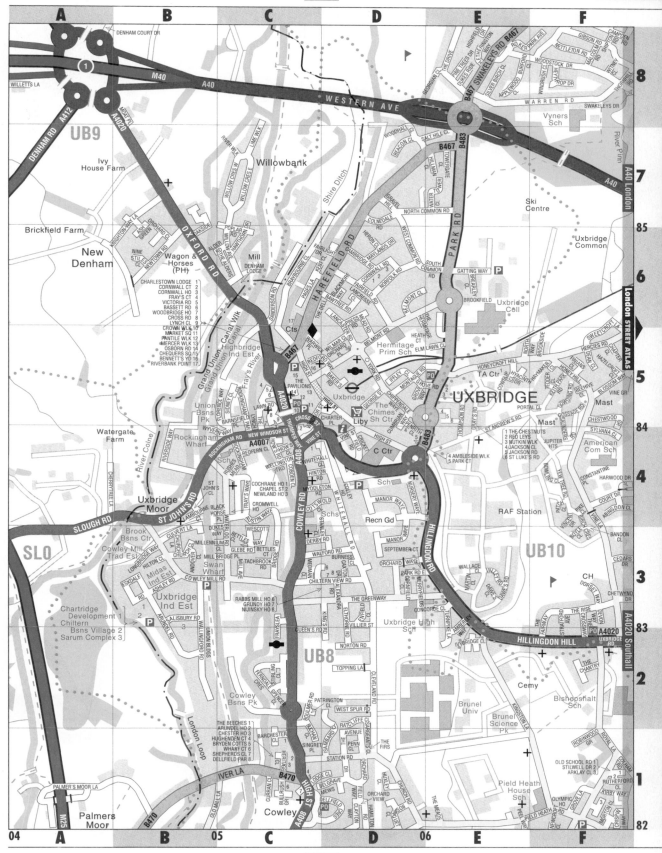

F]
1 WHITE HART RD
2 Nicholsons Sh Ctr
3 REGENT CT
4 FROGMORE CT
5 WHITCHURCH HO
6 KINGSWAY HO
7 WILBERFORCE MEWS
8 SYGNUS CT
9 PROVIDENCE PL
10 ST MARY'S WLK
11 OLD POST OFFICE LA
12 QUEEN'S LA

F6
1 BERKSHIRE LODGE
2 WILTSHIRE LODGE
3 SOMERSET LODGE
4 BUCKINGHAM HO
5 MARLBOROUGH HO
6 KENT LODGE
7 SUSSEX LODGE
8 HAMPSHIRE LODGE
9 DORSET LODGE
10 DEVONSHIRE LODGE
11 CORNWALL LODGE
12 HENLEY LODGE
13 MARLOW LODGE
14 COURTLANDS
15 COOKHAM LODGE

MAIDENHEAD

SL6

86 A 87 B C 88 D E F

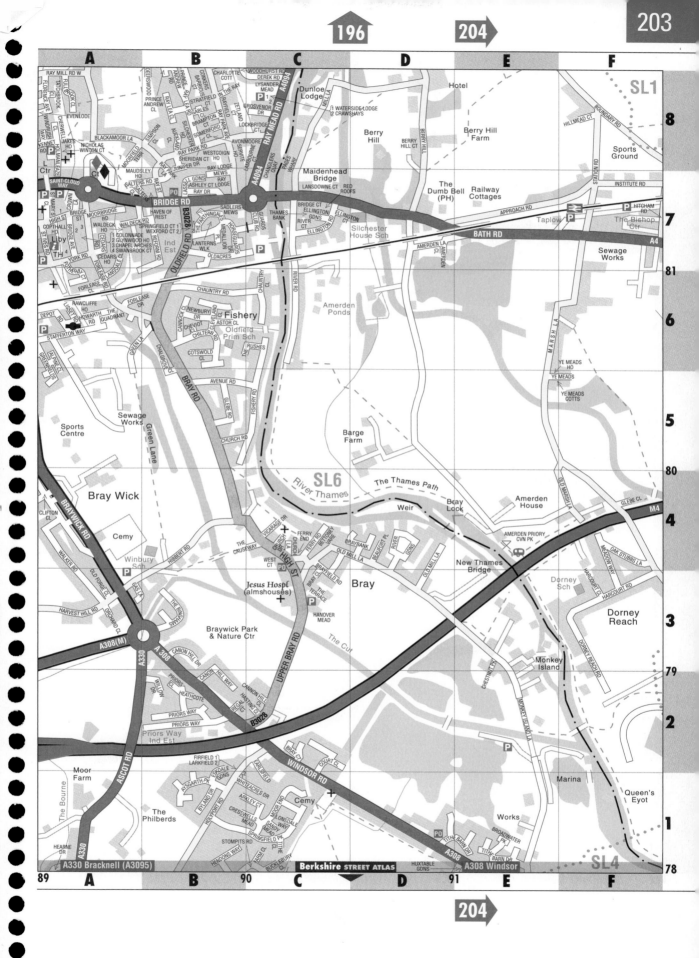

SL1

8

7

81

6

5

80

4

79

2

1

78

A   B   C   D   E   F

SL6

River Thames

The Thames Path

Bray Wick

Sports Centre

Cemy

Braywick Park & Nature Ctr

Moor Farm

The Philberds

Fishery

Oldfield Prim Sch

Sewage Works

Maidenhead Bridge

Dunloe Lodge

Berry Hill

Berry Hill Farm

Hotel

The Dumb Bell (PH)

Railway Cottages

Sewage Works

Sports Ground

The Bishop Ctr

Taplow

BATH RD

A4

Amerden Ponds

Barge Farm

Bray Lock

Weir

Amerden House

Amerden Priory CVN PK

New Thames Bridge

Bray

Dorney Sch

Dorney Reach

Monkey Island

Marina

Queen's Eyot

Works

SL4

Jesus Hospl (almshouses)

Hanover Mead

The Cut

Priors Way Ind Est

Cemy

203 197

A B C D E F

8

7

81

6

Lent Rise

THE GREEN
Burnham Upper Sch

HANBURY CL
BYWAYS
HITCHAM RD
EASTFIELD RD
MAYPOLE RD
FAIRVIEW RD
BINGHAM RD
BATLEY
MILNER RD
ST JAS
HARKNESS RD
STOMP RD
CHILTERN RD
WENDOVER RD
COULSON WAY
LENT RISE RD
TAPLOW RD
GREEN CL
Lent Rise Comb Sch
PO

Marshgate Trad Est

HAG HILL RISE
HAG HILL LA
CAVENDISH
A4
NURSERY RD
BRIAR DR
FERN DR
CONWAY RD
RAMBLER CL
MILTON RISE
HUNTERS RD
Lake End Ct
STAFFORD CL
ALVISTA AVE
CHILTON CT
B3026
Superstore

SL6

Pondleys Cottage

Huntercombe Manor

Burnham Abbey

LAKE END RD

PRIORY RD
STOMP RD
IMPERIAL RD
Ct
THIRLMERE AVE
CORISTON CRES
ULLSWATER RD
DERWENT DR
WINDERMERE WAY
HUNTERCOMBE LA
ST JAMES PL
CLARE AVE
GREENFERN AVE
CARDINALS
KINNAIRD
WALK
BATH RD
BOSWORTH CT
ST GEORGES CRES
ANTHONY WAY
FRANCIS LA
ABBOTTS WAY
HARRISON WAY
QUOMAN LA
LANGTON CL
WEST POINT

M4
HUNTERCOMBE SPUR

LEAHOLME GDNS
LAMMAS RD
Priory Sch
Our Lady of Peace Schl
HURST RD
HAMILTON RD
PHIPPS RD
BLUME CRES
BURFORD GDNS
TUDOR GDNS
ROYSTON WAY
WEST AVE
MEAD WAY
WALPOLE RD
WHITTLE PARKWAY
Burnham Hts
Progress Bsns Ctr
Burnham
STANHOPE RD
STATION RD
Works
HOLYHEAD MEWS
Lincoln Way
WASHINGTON DR
Cippenham Inf & Jun Schs
DENNIS WAY
PLACKETT WAY
BLYTHE HOS
BARNFIELD
MORETON WAY
MERCIAN WAY
Recn Gd
1 Kennedy Ho
2 Harborough Cl

Liby

SL1

SL2
MARESCROFT
GREYSTOKE
SCAFELL RD
NEWCHURCH
NORTHMEAD RD
TEESDALE RD
AMBERLEY
PLYMOUTH RD
YEOVIL RD
WESTON RD
DOVER RD
BANBURY AVE
OXFORD AVE
Slough Trad Est
BUCKINGHAM AVE
DUNDEE
DEAL AVE
HENLEY
CARDIGAN CL
BOWER CT
Western House Inf Sch
Cippenham
Recn Gd
COMPTON CT
PETTY CROSS
IONA CRES
MARLBOROUGH
PO
MASON'S RD
MASONS CT
BRIDGE RD
SAXON LODGE
SHAKESPEARE LODGE
EARLS LA

5

80

4

Lake End

PH
Lake End Farm

Ashford La

The Palmer Arms (PH)
Dorney

Elm View Farm
Dorney Court
Court La
VILLAGE RD
SOUTH FIELD LA

MARSH LA

79

2

Pigeonhouse Farm
Riding School

SL4
Court Farm
Manor Farm
COMMON RD
Roundmoor Ditch
Sewage Works
M4

Dorney Common
Elm Farm Bungalow
BOVENEY RD

ALMA CT 1
VAUGHAN GDNS 2
BELLSFIELD CT 3
THE WHEATBUTTS 4
GLENORTON CRES
BOVENEY NEW RD
INKERMAN
ALMA RD
PO
Eton Wick Rd
VICTORIA RD
QUEENS RD
TILSTONE AVE
CORNWALL
LEESON GDNS
PRINCES CL
HAYWARDS MEAD
B3026
Liby
Recn Gd

1

78

SL6

Dorney Lake Rowing Ctr

River Thames

Cress Brook
Roasthill La
Boveney Ditch
Eton Wick

92 A B 93 C D 94 E F

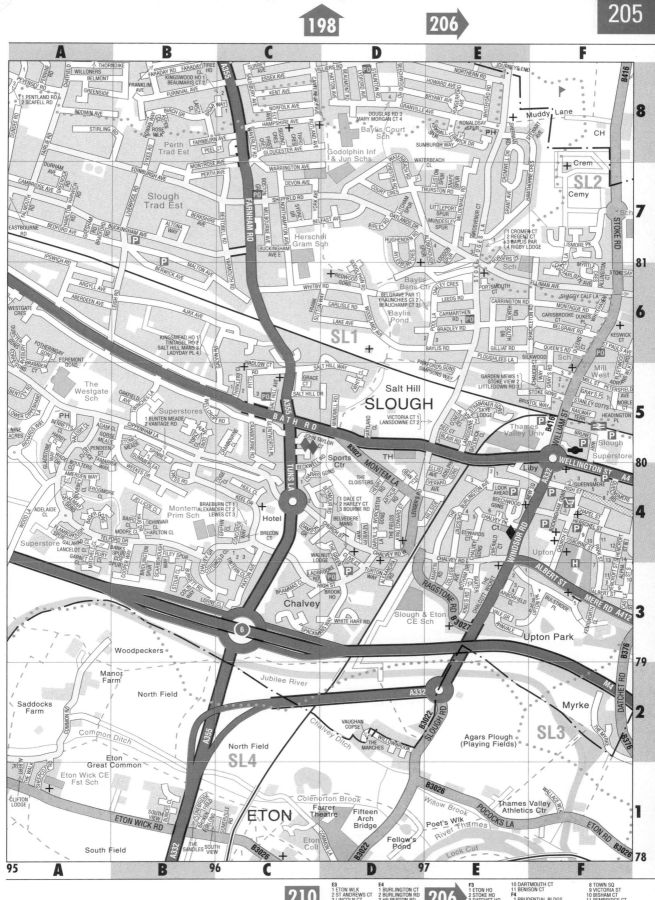

E3
1 ETON WLK
2 ST ANDREWS CT
3 LINCOLN CT
4 LOCKSLEY CT

E4
1 BURLINGTON CT
2 BURLINGTON HO
3 HILPERTON RD
4 WINDSOR HO
5 UPTON CL
6 MANOR CT
7 SPRUCE CT
8 CHARTER CL
9 ALBERT CL

F3
1 ETON HO
2 STOKE HO
3 DATCHET HO
4 ASHBOURNE HO
5 SHAFTESBURY CT
6 MOORSTOWN CT

F4
1 PRUDENTIAL BLDGS
2 MACKENZIE ST
3 MACKENZIE MALL
4 The Village Sh Ctr
5 LEOPOLD MALL
6 CURZON MALL
7 CHANDOS MALL

10 DARTMOUTH CT
11 BENISON CT

8 TOWN SQ
9 VICTORIA ST
10 BISHAM CT
11 BEMBRIDGE CT
12 STEPHENSON CT
13 SHAMAA HO
14 HENCROFT MEWS

Grid columns: **A B C D E F**

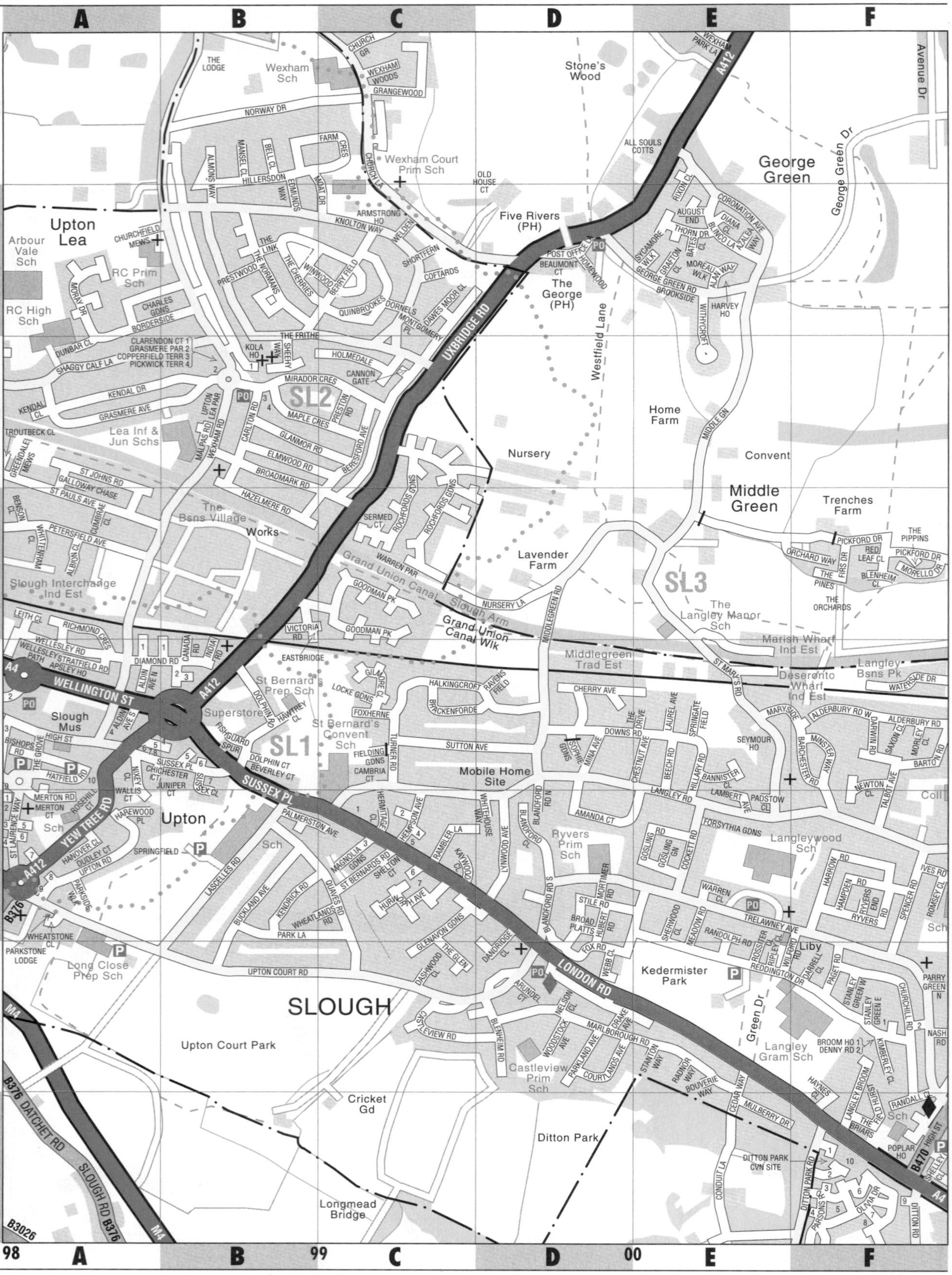

Grid rows: **8 7 81 6 5 80 4 3 79 2 1 78**

SL2 · **SL1** · **SL3**

Upton Lea · Arbour Vale Sch · George Green · Stone's Wood · Five Rivers (PH) · The George (PH) · Home Farm · Convent · Middle Green · Trenches Farm · The Pippins · Nursery · Lavender Farm · Westfield Lane · The Langley Manor Sch · Marish Wharf Ind Est · Langley Bsns Pk · Deseronto Wharf Ind Est · Middlegreen Trad Est

Slough Interchange Ind Est · Grand Union Canal · Slough Arm · Grand Union Canal Wlk · Goodman Pk

WELLINGTON ST · Slough Mus · Superstore · St Bernard's Prep Sch · St Bernard's Convent Sch · Mobile Home Site · Ryvers Prim Sch · Langleywood Sch

SUSSEX PL · Upton · Kedermister Park · Libby · Langley Gram Sch

SLOUGH

Upton Court Park · Long Close Prep Sch · Parkstone Lodge · Castleview Prim Sch · Cricket Gd · Ditton Park · Longmead Bridge · Ditton Park Cvn Site

UXBRIDGE RD · A412 · LONDON RD · B470 · A4 · M4 · B376 DATCHET RD · SLOUGH RD · YEW TREE RD

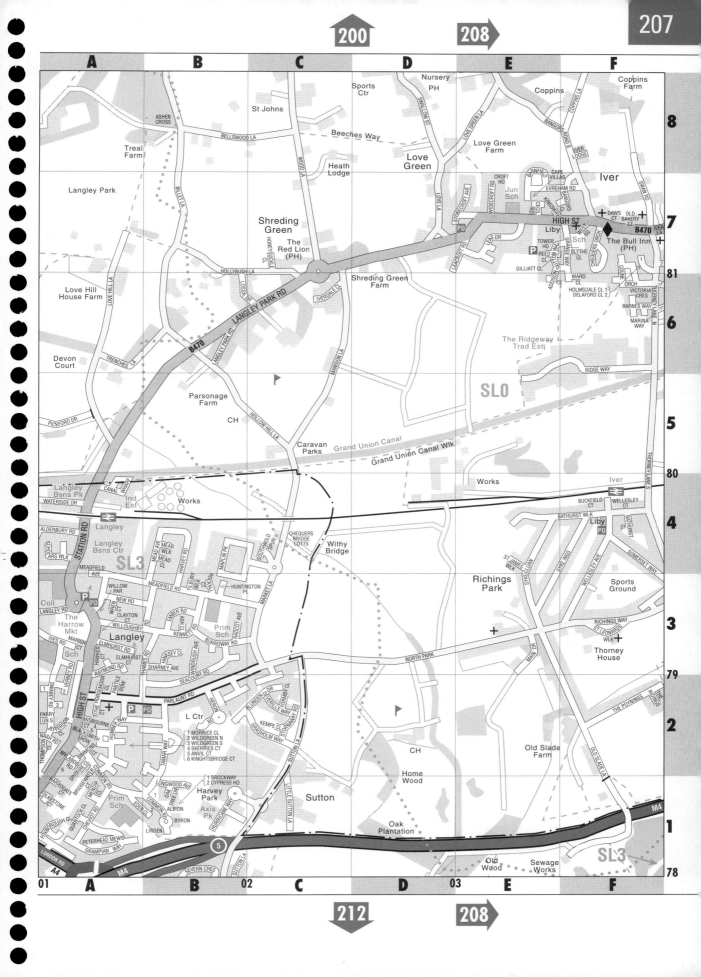

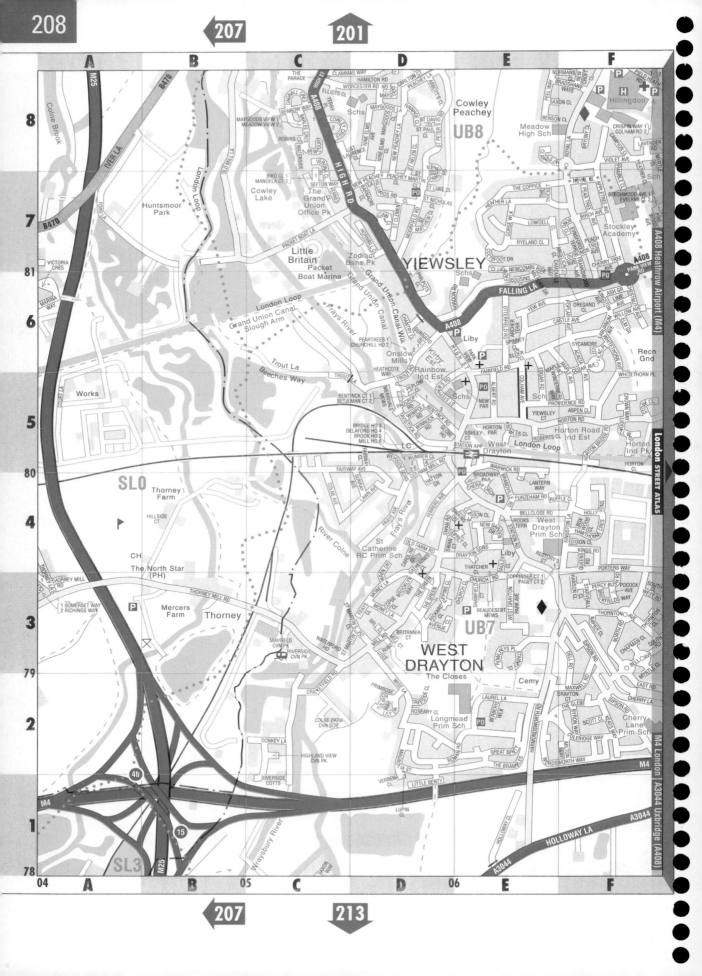

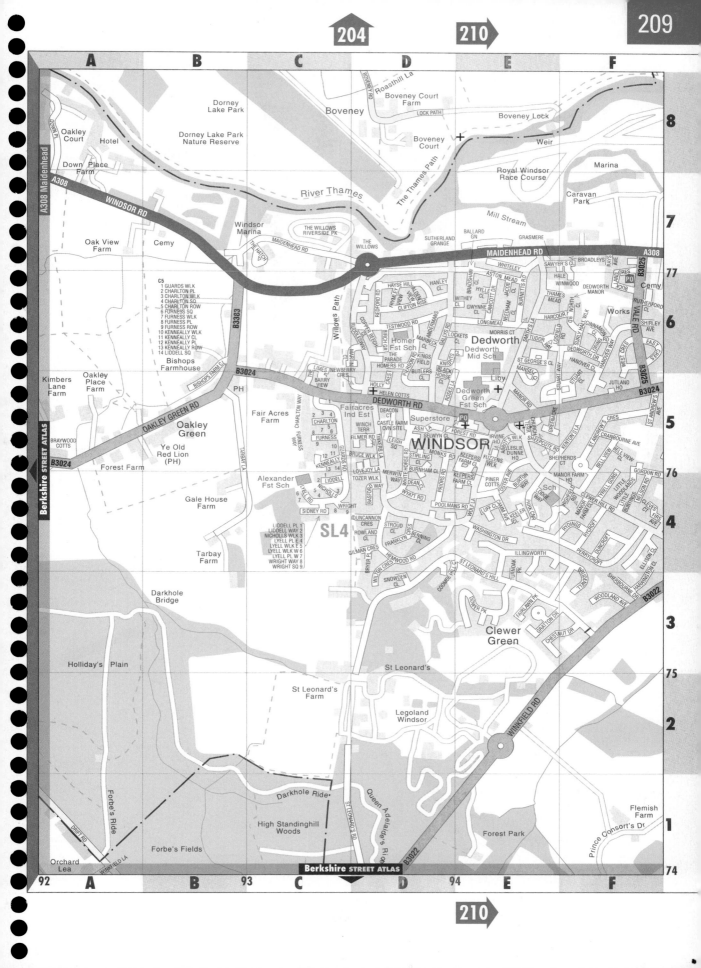

A B C D E F

8

7

77

6

Boveney

Roasthill La
Boveney Court Farm
LOCK PATH
Boveney Court
Boveney Lock
Weir

Dorney Lake Park
Dorney Lake Park Nature Reserve

Oakley Court Hotel
Down Place Farm

River Thames
The Thames Path
Mill Stream

Royal Windsor Race Course
Marina
Caravan Park

A308 Maidenhead
A308
WINDSOR RD

Oak View Farm
Cemy
Windsor Marina
THE HATCH
MAIDENHEAD RD
THE WILLOWS RIVERSIDE PK
THE WILLOWS

MAIDENHEAD RD
A308

SUTHERLAND GRANGE
BALLARD GN
GRASMERE

WHITELEY
SAWYER'S CL
BROADLEYS
RAVS CL
LAND CRES
B3025
PO
Cemy

C5
1 GUARDS WLK
2 CHARLTON PL
3 CHARLTON WLK
4 CHARLTON SQ
5 CHARLTON ROW
6 FURNESS SQ
7 FURNESS WLK
8 FURNESS PL
9 FURNESS ROW
10 KENNEALLY WLK
11 KENNEALLY CL
12 KENNEALLY PL
13 KENNEALLY ROW
14 LIDDELL SQ

B3383

Willows Path

HAYSE HILL
HANLEY CL
BRADSHAW
ASTON MEAD
HYLLE CL
JACOB
HALE
WINNWOOD
DEDWORTH MANOR
BUCK LANE
RUTHERFORD

Kimbers Lane Farm
Oakley Place Farm

Bishops Farmhouse
B3024
OAKLEY GREEN RD
BISHOPS FARM CL
PH
Oakley Green

REDFORD RD
FRIMLEY CL
CLIFTON RISE
TESTWOOD RD
COPPER BEECH
RUDDLESWAY
WITHEY CL
GWYNNE CL
LONGMEAD
NEEDHAM
BURNETTS RD
THAMES MEAD
HARCOUR

LOSFIELD
Works
SHIRLEY AVE
EAST

Dedworth
MORRIS CT
Dedworth Mid Sch
TUDOR
DEDWORTH DR
HANOVER CL
GREEN
WEST CRES
JUTLAND HO
B3025

Braywood Cotts
B3024

Fair Acres Farm

THE LIMES
NEWBERRY CRES
BARRY VIEW
HOLLY
HELEN COTTS
HOMERS RD
THE PARADE
BIRCH GR
LOCKETS RD
GILLYS RD
MARBECK
KINGS FIELD
KNIGHTS
BUTLERS
BLACK HORSE CL
ROSES CL
ST GEORGE'S CL
Liby
Dedworth Green Fst Sch
MANSEL
STUART WAY
ST JAMES CL
GIRING RD

Forest Farm
Ye Old Red Lion (PH)

TARBAY LA

FURNESS WAY

Fairacres Ind Est
CHARLTON
FURNESS
GUARDS RD
FILMER RD
WINCH TERR
BRUCE WLK
LOVEJOY LA
KENNEALLY
TOZER WLK
LYELL RD
NICHOLLS
SIDNEY RD
WRIGHT

DEACON CT
ASH LA
SELWYN CL
TINKERS
LEIGH
MONKS RD
HORSE CL
STIRLING CL
BURNHAM CL
MERWIN WAY
W DEAN
WYATT RD
BASFORD WAY

Superstore
PO
WINDSOR
IRVINE HO
LESLIE DUNNE HO
FUZZENS WLK
KEEPERS FARM CL
PINER COTTS
KEEPERS RD

ST ANDREW'S CRES
Cranbourne Ave
KENTON'S LA
ST ANDREW'S CL
SHEEPCOTE RD
BELL VIEW
BELL VIEW RD
SHEPHERDS CT
MANOR FARM HO
GORDON CL

76

Gale House Farm
Alexander Fst Sch

SL4
LIDDELL PL 1
LIDDELL WAY 2
NICHOLLS WLK 3
LYELL PL E 4
LYELL WLK E 5
LYELL WLK W 6
LYELL PL W 7
WRIGHT WAY 8
WRIGHT SQ 9

DUNCANNON CRES
ROWLAND CL
GILMAN CRES
BRYER PL
WILTON CRES

STROUD CL
FRANKLYN CL
HEMWOOD RD
CRESWOOD
SNOWDEN CL
COOMBE HILL

BENNING CL
POOLMANS RD
LIFE CL
WASHINGTON DR
ILLINGWORTH
TURNOAK PK

CLEWER HILL RD
HIGHFIELD
MANOR CL
RIVERS
PERRYCROFT
DUNGROFT
ELLISON CL

Sch
DODGE WAY
MANOR WAY
RYDINGS
RYCROFT
SHERBOURNE RD
WOODLAND AVE
B3022

75

Tarbay Farm

Darkhole Bridge

St Leonard's Farm
St Leonard's

LOWER PK
ST LEONARD'S HILL
FAIRLAWN PK
GRATTON DR
CHESTNUT DR

Clewer Green

3

Holliday's Plain

St Leonard's Farm

Legoland Windsor

WINKFIELD RD

Forest Park

2

Darkhole Ride
High Standinghill Woods
ST LEONARD'S RD
Queen Adelaide's Ride
B3022

Flemish Farm

Forbe's Ride
Forbe's Fields

Orchard Lea
DRIFT RD
WINKFIELD LA

Prince Consort's Dr

1

74

92 A 93 B C 93 D 94 E F 94 F 74

Berkshire STREET ATLAS B3024

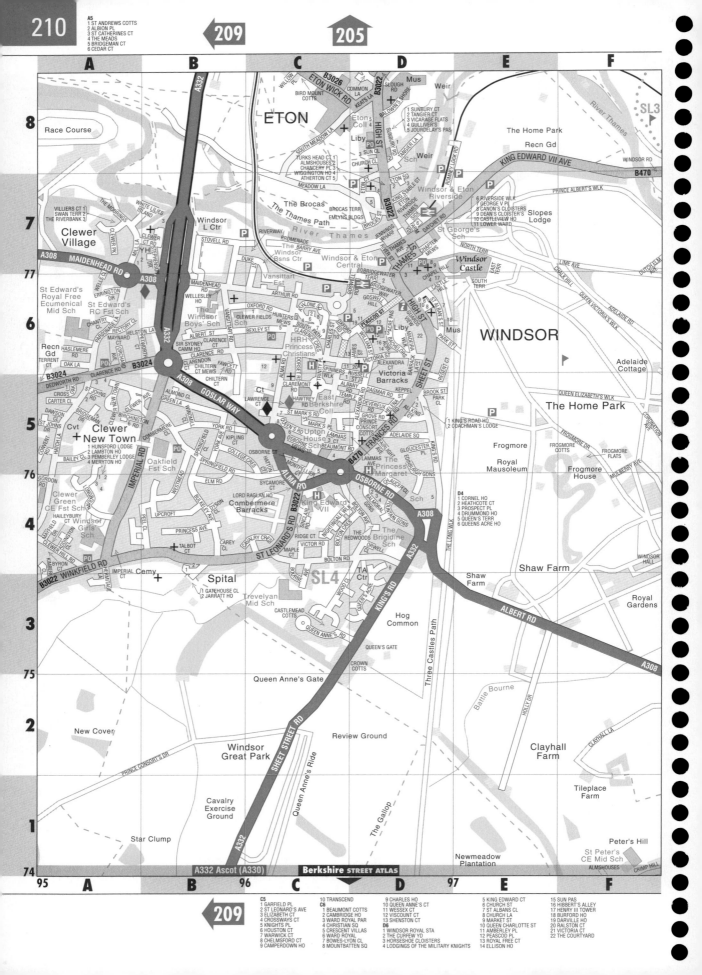

A5
1 ST ANDREWS COTTS
2 ALBION PL
3 ST CATHERINES CT
4 THE MEADS
5 BRIDGEMAN CT
6 CEDAR CT

C5
1 GARFIELD PL
2 ST LEONARD'S AVE
3 ELIZABETH CT
4 CROSSWAYS CT
5 KNIGHTS PL
6 HOUSTON CT
7 WARWICK CT
8 CHELMSFORD CT
9 CAMPERDOWN HO

10 TRANSCEND
C6
1 BEAUMONT COTTS
2 CAMBRIDGE HO
3 WARD ROYAL PAR
4 CHRISTIAN SQ
5 CRESCENT VILLAS
6 WARD ROYAL
7 BOWES-LYON CL
8 MOUNTBATTEN SQ

9 CHARLES HO
10 QUEEN ANNE'S CT
11 WESSEX CT
12 VISCOUNT CT
13 SHENSTON CT
D6
1 WINDSOR ROYAL STA
2 THE CURFEW YD
3 HORSESHOE CLOISTERS
4 LODGINGS OF THE MILITARY KNIGHTS

5 KING EDWARD CT
6 CHURCH ST
7 ST ALBANS CL
8 CHURCH LA
9 MARKET ST
10 QUEEN CHARLOTTE ST
11 AMBERLEY PL
12 PEASCOD PL
13 ROYAL FREE CT
14 ELLISON HO

15 SUN PAS
16 HIBBERT'S ALLEY
17 HENRY III TOWER
18 BURFORD HO
19 DARVILLE HO
20 RALSTON CT
21 VICTORIA CT
22 THE COURTYARD

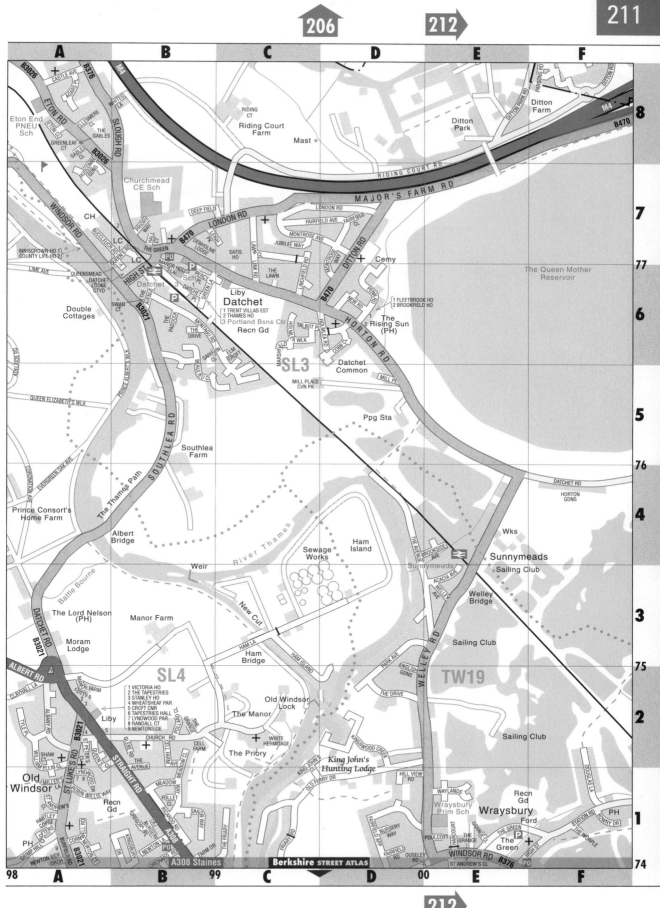

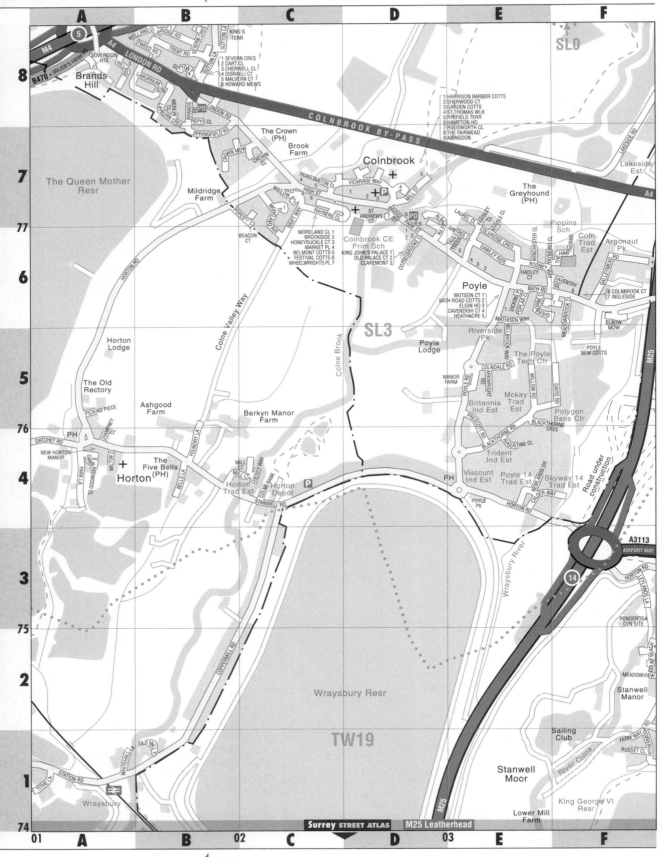

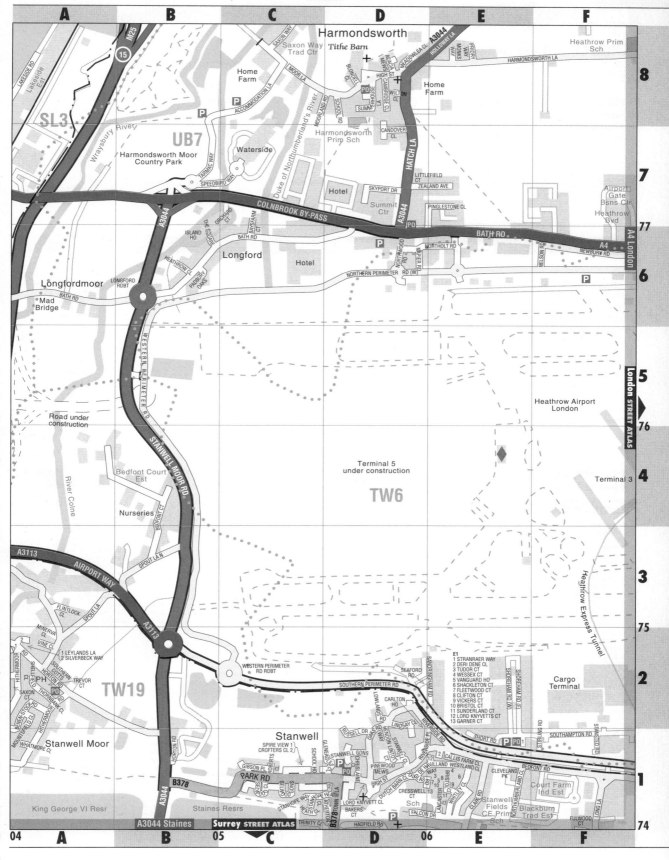

Index

Church Rd 6 Beckenham BR2..........**53** C6

Place name	**Location number**	**Locality, town or village**	**Postcode district**	**Page and grid square**
May be abbreviated on the map	Present when a number indicates the place's position in a crowded area of mapping	Shown when more than one place has the same name	District for the indexed place	Page number and grid reference for the standard mapping

Public and commercial buildings are highlighted in magenta   **Places of interest** are highlighted in blue with a star★

Abbreviations used in the index

Acad	**Academy**	Comm	**Common**	Gd	**Ground**	L	**Leisure**	Prom	**Prom**
App	**Approach**	Cott	**Cottage**	Gdn	**Garden**	La	**Lane**	Rd	**Road**
Arc	**Arcade**	Cres	**Crescent**	Gn	**Green**	Liby	**Library**	Recn	**Recreation**
Ave	**Avenue**	Cswy	**Causeway**	Gr	**Grove**	Mdw	**Meadow**	Ret	**Retail**
Bglw	**Bungalow**	Ct	**Court**	H	**Hall**	Meml	**Memorial**	Sh	**Shopping**
Bldg	**Building**	Ctr	**Centre**	Ho	**House**	Mkt	**Market**	Sq	**Square**
Bsns, Bus	**Business**	Ctry	**Country**	Hospl	**Hospital**	Mus	**Museum**	St	**Street**
Bvd	**Boulevard**	Cty	**County**	HQ	**Headquarters**	Orch	**Orchard**	Sta	**Station**
Cath	**Cathedral**	Dr	**Drive**	Hts	**Heights**	Pal	**Palace**	Terr	**Terrace**
Cir	**Circus**	Dro	**Drove**	Ind	**Industrial**	Par	**Parade**	TH	**Town Hall**
Cl	**Close**	Ed	**Education**	Inst	**Institute**	Pas	**Passage**	Univ	**University**
Cnr	**Corner**	Emb	**Embankment**	Int	**International**	Pk	**Park**	Wk, Wlk	**Walk**
Coll	**College**	Est	**Estate**	Intc	**Interchange**	Pl	**Place**	Wr	**Water**
Com	**Community**	Ex	**Exhibition**	Junc	**Junction**	Prec	**Precinct**	Yd	**Yard**

Index of localities, towns and villages

A

Addington 65 A6
Adstock 53 F1
Akeley 41 E8
Albury 136 B7
Aldbury 120 D5
Alderton 9 A2
Alscot 139 A5
Amersham 154 B2
Amersham Common ..165 E8
Amersham Old Town ..165 A7
Amersham on the Hill ..154 D2
Ascott 80 A2
Ashendon 97 F1
Asheridge 143 C6
Ashley Green 144 F7
Ashton 9 E8
Askett 139 D6
Aspley Guise 49 F4
Aspley Heath 49 A2
Aston 192 C5
Aston Abbotts 88 D5
Aston Clinton 117 C6
Aston Sandford 127 D4
Astrope 104 A3
Astwood 16 A3
Atterbury 36 A4
Austenwood 188 C8
Aylesbury 115 D7

B

Baker's Wood 189 D3
Ballinger Common 142 E3
Bancroft 33 F5
Barretts End 42 F7
Barton Hartshorn 50 D2
Beachampton 44 B6
Beacon's Bottom 159 D3
Beaconsfield 175 D1

Beamond End 163 F6
Beanhill 47 B4
Bedgrove 116 C5
Bedlam 14 C1
Beecroft 93 F8
Bellingdon 143 E7
Belsize 156 F6
Bennett End 159 C7
Berkhamsted 135 C4
Berryfield 100 D5
Biddlesden 27 D5
Bierton 102 A3
Birchmoor Green 60 E8
Bisham 194 E7
Bishopstone 115 A1
Bix 179 D1
Blackthorn 81 A4
Blakelands 22 B1
Bleak Hall 46 F5
Bledlow 138 B1
Bledlow Ridge 159 F8
Bletchley 58 A7
Boarstall 95 B1
Bockmer End 182 C1
Bolbeck Pk 35 A7
Bolter End 170 F5
Booker 172 B4
Botley 145 A1
Botolph Claydon 74 F6
Bourne End 185 B2
Bourton 52 F8
Boveney 209 D8
Bovingdon 146 B4
Bovingdon Green 146 A2
Bow Brickhill 48 C1
Boyne Hill 202 D6
Brackley 38 A8
Bradenham 160 F7
Bradville 34 B7
Bradwell 34 A4
Bradwell Abbey 33 F3
Bradwell Common ...34 B3
Bragenham 70 C6
Brands Hill 212 A8

Bray 203 D3
Bray Wick 203 A4
Brill 96 B1
Britwell 197 F1
Broad Green 25 B3
Brook End
  Ivinghoe 105 E4
  North Crawley 23 F5
  Weston Turville ..117 A3
Broughton
  Aylesbury 116 D8
  Milton Keynes 36 A3
Browns Wood 48 C4
Bryant's Bottom 150 F4
Buckingham 41 D2
Buckland 117 F6
Buckland Common ...133 A3
Bucklandwharf 118 B4
Buckmoorend 140 D6
Buffler's Halt 40 C3
Bulbourne 119 C8
Bullington End 20 C7
Bulstrode 146 E3
Burcott 79 E4
Burnham 197 C3
Bury End 165 D6
Butlers Cross 176 F1
Butler's Cross 130 C3
Bye Green 117 A3

C

Cadmore End 170 C6
Caldecote 22 E1
Caldecotte 48 A2
California
  Aylesbury 115 C7
  Dunstable 93 F6
Calvert 73 B6
Calverton 32 E3
Campbell Park 35 A3
Castlethorpe 19 E5

Central Milton Keynes ...34 D1
Chackmore 41 B4
Chalfont Common ...177 F6
Chalfont St Giles ..177 C7
Chalfont St Peter ..177 C7
Chalkshire 130 C4
Chalvey 205 C4
Chandlers Hill 200 E3
Chapel End 118 C8
Charndon 72 E6
Chartridge 143 C4
Chearsley 112 A2
Cheddington 105 B7
Chenies 156 B2
Chenies Bottom 156 B2
Chesham 154 C8
Chesham Bois 154 C3
Chessmount 154 E7
Chetwode 61 E8
Chicheley 23 C8
Chilton 111 A4
Chinnor 147 D7
Chipperfield 156 F8
Chisbridge Cross ..182 D6
Chivery 132 C4
Cholesbury 133 C3
Chorleywood 167 D5
Chorleywood Bottom ..167 C3
Chorleywood West ..167 A4
Christmas Common ..168 B7
Church End
  Chorley Wood 156 F1
  Drayton Parslow ...68 B5
  Haddenham 127 A5
  Hanslope 11 A2
  Long Crendon ...125 C7
  Pitstone 105 D3
  Steeple Claydon ..63 E2
  Totternhoe 93 B7
Church Hill 56 A8
Cippenham 204 F4
Clewer Green 209 E3
Clewer New Town ..210 A5
Clewer Village 210 A7

Clifton Reynes 7 C3
Codmore 144 E1
Coffee Hall 46 F7
Cold Brayfield 8 B5
Coleshill 164 F3
Colnbrook 212 D7
Colstrope 181 D5
Combe 130 C1
Common The 55 B4
Conniburrow 34 C4
Cookham 196 A7
Cookham Dean 195 B7
Cookham Rise 195 E6
Cores End 185 C4
Cosgrove 19 D2
Cowley 201 C1
Cowley Peachey ...208 E8
Cow Roast 120 B1
Cox Green 202 C3
Crafton 89 F3
Cranfield 25 B1
Creslow 87 B8
Cressex 172 D4
Crofts End 14 A1
Crowell 147 B4
Crowell Hill 147 D2
Crowfield 26 B3
Crownfield 149 B4
Crownhill 45 D7
Cryers Hill 162 D6
Cublington 78 B1
Cuddington 113 A2

D

Dadford 28 D1
Dagnall 107 C6
Darvillshill 150 A4
Datchet 211 C6
Deanshanger 31 D4
Dedworth 209 E6

Denham
Denham Green 190 A2
Quainton 85 D5
Denham Green 189 E5
Denner Hill 150 E4
Diggs 126 F5
Dinton 113 F2
Ditchfield 171 A3
Dorney 204 C3
Dorney Reach 203 F3
Dorton 96 F1
Downhead Park 35 B5
Downley 161 C3
Downs Barn 35 A5
Drayton Beauchamp 118 B5
Drayton Parslow 68 C6
Duck End
Akeley 42 A8
Swanbourne 66 F4
Dudswell 134 D8
Dunsmore 141 A7
Dunstable 93 E8
Dunton 77 E5

E

Eaglestone 47 B7
Eakley Lanes 4 D2
Easington 111 B1
East Burnham 198 A4
East Claydon 74 E8
East End
Cranfield 25 C1
North Crawley 24 F6
Eaton Bray 92 F6
Eaton Green 92 C7
Edgcott 72 F2
Edlesborough 92 E4
Egypt 198 B8
Ellesborough 130 B2
Elmhurst 101 E3
Emberton 13 E8
Emerson Valley 46 B2
Emmington 137 A1
Eton 210 C8
Eton Wick 204 F1
Eythrope 113 F8

F

Far Bletchley 57 D7
Farnham Common 198 D6
Farnham Park 198 C4
Farnham Royal 198 C3
Fawley 191 C8
Fawley Bottom 180 B2
Felden 146 F7
Fenny Lock 47 E2
Fern 184 E6
Filgrave 13 C5
Finmere 50 D7
Fishermead 35 A1
Flackwell Heath 185 A7
Flaunden 156 A6
Fleet Marston 100 B4
Flowers Bottom 150 A4
Ford 128 B7
Forty Green
Beaconsfield 175 A4
Princes Risborough 137 F3
Foscote 42 B4
Four Ashes 162 D4
Fox Milne 35 F4
Franklin's Spring 178 D5
Frieth 170 F1
Frith-hill 152 C7
Fullers Slade 33 A4
Fulmer 199 C8
Fulwell 39 A2
Furtho 19 A3
Furze Platt 195 C2
Furzton 46 D4

G

Gawcott 51 F4
Gayhurst 12 D2
George Green 206 E8
Gerrards Cross 188 E5
Gibraltar 113 D2
Giffard Park 22 A2
Godlington 61 E3
Gossard's Green 25 C4
Grafton Regis 9 D2
Granborough 75 E7
Granby 47 B3
Gravel Hill 177 F4

Great Brickhill 59 D2
Greatgap 105 D6
Great Hampden 150 D7
Great Hivings 144 A3
Great Holm 45 E8
Great Horwood 55 A1
Great Kimble 139 E8
Great Kingshill 162 E8
Great Linford 34 E8
Great Missenden 152 A6
Green End
Granborough 76 A7
High Wycombe 160 A4
Greenfield 168 A4
Greenleys 33 B5
Grendon Underwood 83 A6
Gubblecote 104 D3

H

Haddenham 127 B5
Halton 117 D1
Hambleden 181 D1
Ham Green 83 D2
Hampden Bottom 141 B2
Hanslope 11 B3
Hardmead 15 D3
Hardwick 87 B3
Harmondsworth 213 D8
Harrold 3 F6
Hartwell 10 D8
Hastoe 132 F7
Haversham 20 E2
Hawridge 133 E1
Hawridge Common 133 E2
Haydon Hill 100 E2
Hazeley 45 D5
Hazelmere 163 B4
Heath End
Cholesbury 134 A2
Prestwood 151 E1
Hedgerley 187 D3
Hedgerley Green 187 E4
Hedgerley Hill 187 E2
Hedsor 185 F3
Heelands 34 C4
Hempton Wainhill 147 F7
Henley-on-Thames 191 B1
Henton 137 E2
Heronsgate 167 D2
Higham Cross 10 D3
Higher Denham 189 C4
Highway 202 B7
High Wycombe 173 B5
Hillesden 63 A6
Hillesden Hamlet 51 F1
Hilltop 144 D2
Hoggeston 77 B7
Hogpits Bottom 156 B7
Hollingdon 69 C3
Holly Green 138 A3
Holmer Green 163 D6
Holton 122 C2
Holtspur 175 A1
Honeywick 92 E8
Horn Hill 178 B6
Horsenden 138 E2
Horsleys Green 159 C3
Horton
Cheddington 91 B3
Wraysbury 212 A4
Horton-cum-Studley 108 B6
Horton Wharf 91 C4
Hotley Bottom 151 C8
Hughenden Valley 162 B7
Hulcote 37 E2
Hulcott 102 E6
Huntgate End 10 D2
Hunt's Hill 161 D5
Hurley 193 E4
Hurst End 24 A3
Hyde End 152 F7
Hyde Heath 153 C5

I

Ibstone 169 D7
Ickenham 190 F1
Ickford 124 A3
Ilmer 137 F8
Iver 207 F7
Iver Heath 200 D4
Ivinghoe 105 F5
Ivinghoe Aston 92 A1

J

Jordans 176 F3

K

Kents Hill 48 A7
Kiln Common 151 B8
Kiln Farm 33 B3
Kingsey 127 B2
Kingston 36 C2
Kingston Blount 147 A3
Kingswood 83 B3
Knotty Green 175 C6
Knowlhill 46 D6

L

Lacey Green 149 E5
Lake End 204 B4
Lane End 171 C4
Lanes End 132 C4
Langley 207 A3
Lathbury 22 C7
Latimer 155 E3
Lavendon 7 F7
Layter's Green 177 B1
Leadenhall 47 A8
Leckhampstead 42 E7
Ledburn 90 D8
Lee Common 142 D5
Lee Gate 142 A7
Leighton Buzzard 80 F6
Lenborough 52 D3
Lent 197 B1
Lent Rise 204 A8
Lewknor 157 B8
Ley Hill 145 B1
Lillingstone Dayrell 29 F4
Lillingstone Lovell 30 B5
Linslade 80 D7
Little Boys Heath 152 C3
Little Brickhill 59 E5
Little Britain 208 C2
Little Chalfont 155 B1
Littlecote 78 A5
Little End 23 B8
Little Frieth 170 E1
Little Gaddesden 121 D7
Little Hampden 140 F4
Little Horwood 55 F2
Little Kimble 129 E2
Little Kingshill 152 B3
Little Linford 21 C5
Little London
Oakley 109 F5
Wendover 141 C7
Little Marlow 184 D5
Little Marsh 72 A3
Little Missenden 153 A2
Little Row 202 B5
Little Tingewick 50 E6
Little Tring 118 F6
Littleworth Common 186 D1
Long Crendon 125 B6
Longford 213 C6
Longfordmoor 213 A6
Long Marston 104 A3
Long Street 10 F4
Longwick 138 C5
Loosley Row 149 C6
Loudwater 174 C2
Loughton 46 A8
Love Green 207 D8
Lower Assendon 191 A6
Lower Bois 154 C5
Lower Cadsden 139 E5
Lower End
Long Crendon 125 B7
Marsworth 104 F3
Thornborough 53 F8
Woburn Sands 49 C8
Lower Hartwell 114 E6
Lower North Dean 150 E1
Lower Pollicott 111 F7
Lower Wainhill 147 E7
Lower Weald 32 E2
Lower Woodend 182 D4
Ludgershall 96 D8
Lye Green 144 F4

M

Maidenhead 202 F4
Maidenhead Court 196 C4
Maidensgrove 179 C5

Maids Moreton 41 E4
Manor Park
Aylesbury 101 E2
Slough 198 D1
Mantles Gn 165 A8
Maple Cross 178 D6
Marlow 183 B2
Marlow Bottom 183 C6
Marlow Common 182 F3
Marsh 129 C7
Marsh Gibbon 71 F3
Marsworth 105 A1
Meadle 139 B8
Medbourne 45 E5
Medmenham 193 A5
Mentmore 90 D4
Micklefield 173 E6
Middle Claydon 74 C8
Middle End
Leckhampstead 42 D8
Totternhoe 93 A8
Middle Green 206 E5
Middleton 35 E3
Middle Weald 32 E1
Mill End
Henley-on-Thames 192 D7
Little Missenden 153 A3
Rickmansworth 167 F1
Milton Common 136 B3
Milton Keynes 34 D5
Milton Keynes Village 35 E2
Mixbury 38 D1
Mobwell 152 A8
Monks Risborough 139 C6
Monkston 36 A1
Monkston Park 35 E1
Moor Common 171 A2
Moor End
Eaton Bray 92 E5
Yardley Gobion 18 D6
Mop End 164 B7
Moulsoe 36 D8
Mount Pleasant
Buckingham 52 D7
Stoke Goldington 12 B7
Mundaydean Bottom 182 E5
Murcott 94 A4
Mursley 67 D6
Myrke 205 F2

N

Naphill 161 D7
Nash 44 C1
Nash Lee 130 C5
Nearton End 67 A3
Neath Hill 34 F6
Netherfield 47 C6
New Bradwell 33 F8
New Denham 201 A6
New Ground 120 A2
Newland Park 178 A4
New Mill 119 B6
Newport Pagnell 22 B5
Newton 144 C1
Newton Blossomville 8 A4
Newton Longville 57 D3
Newton Purcell 50 B2
Newyears Green 190 F5
Norcott Hill 120 D2
Northall 92 B5
Northchurch 134 E5
North End
Stagsden 16 E8
Steeple Claydon 63 D3
Stewkley 68 D3
Northfield 35 F5
North Lee 130 E4
North Marston 76 A2
North Town 195 F1
North Weston 136 F8
Nup End 89 B3

O

Oakgrove 35 D2
Oakhill 45 D4
Oakley
Brill 109 D5
Chinnor 147 B5
Oakley Green 209 B5
Oldbrook 46 E8
Old Farm Park 48 E5
Old Linslade 70 D2
Old Stratford 32 B7
Old Town 38 A7
Old Windsor 211 A1

Old Wolverton 33 D8
Olney 6 E4
Orchard Leigh 145 B3
Orchardville 197 B1
Oving 86 D8
Owlswick 128 D1
Oxley Park 45 E3

P

Padbury 53 B2
Page Hill 41 F2
Palmers Moor 201 A1
Parmoor 181 F7
Passenham 32 C4
Paulerspury 17 B7
Pednormead End 154 A7
Penn 174 E7
Penn Street 164 B5
Pennyland 35 A6
Peppershill 124 D6
Petsoe End 14 A7
Pheasants 181 E6
Pheasant's Hill 181 D3
Piddington
Blackthorn 95 E7
High Wycombe 160 B1
Northamptonshire 4 B8
Pimlico 26 F6
Pindon End 10 C4
Pineham 35 E7
Pinfoldpond 60 E6
Pinkneys Green 195 A1
Pishill 179 D8
Pishill Bank 168 B1
Pishill Bottom 168 A1
Pitchcott 86 B5
Pitch Green 138 B3
Pitstone 105 C4
Plumpton End 17 C7
Pond Park 144 A2
Portways 168 B8
Potterspury 18 D2
Poundon 71 E7
Poyle 212 E6
Prebendal Farm 115 B7
Preston Bissett 62 B8
Prestwood 151 D6
Princes Risborough 139 D4
Pudds Cross 145 E2
Pury End 17 A7
Puttenham 103 F2
Puxley 31 D7

Q

Quainton 85 B5
Quainton Hill 75 B1
Quarrendon 101 B3

R

Radclive 51 E8
Radnage 159 C7
Radstone 26 A6
Ram Alley 12 B5
Ravenstone 5 D2
Redmoor 47 A4
Remenham 192 A5
Remenham Hill 192 C2
Richings Park 207 E3
Rickmansworth 167 F1
Ringshall 107 B1
Rockwell End 181 F5
Rooksley 34 B2
Rotten Row 181 F2
Rout's Green 148 D2
Rowsham 102 D8
Rush Green 200 E8
Rushmere 70 E4

S

St Leonards 132 E3
Salcey Green 11 B7
Salden 67 F8
Salford 37 C3
Salt Hill 205 D5
Sandhill 64 E2
Sands 172 B7
Sarratt 156 F4
Saunderton
Bledlow Ridge 149 C1
Princes Risborough 138 E1
Saunderton Lee 149 A4

Sedrup 114 F3
Seer Green 176 D4
Shabbington 124 D3
Shalstone 39 E6
Sheeplane 60 C2
Sheepridge 184 E7
Shenley Brook End 46 A2
Shenley Church End ...45 E6
Shenley Lodge 46 C5
Shenley Wood 45 F4
Sherington 14 A2
Shipton 66 B3
Shipton Lee 84 D7
Shootersway 134 E4
Shreding Green 207 C7
Singleborough 54 F5
Skirmett 170 A1
Skittle Green 138 A3
Slapton 91 D5
Slough 205 D5
Snelshall East 57 B7
Snelshall West 57 A7
Soulbury 69 E3
Southcourt 115 D6
Southend 180 C8
South End
  Leckhampstead 42 E7
  Stewkley 78 E8
South Harefield 190 D6
South Heath 152 E8
Speen 150 C4
Spencersgreen 132 C7
Spital 210 B3
Sprig's Alley 147 F1
Springfield 35 B2
Spurgrove 170 E2
Spurlands End 163 A8
Stacey Bushes 33 E4
Stagsden 16 F6
Stagsden West End 16 F4
Stantonbury 34 D7
Stanwell 213 C1
Stanwell Moor 212 E1
Startop's End 104 F1
Steeple Claydon 63 C3
Stewkley 68 E2
Stewkley Dean 68 B1
Stoke Bruerne 9 B8
Stoke Goldington 12 A6
Stoke Green 199 B1
Stoke Hammond 69 E8
Stoke Mandeville 116 A2

Stokenchurch 158 E5
Stoke Poges 198 F4
Stone 114 C5
Stonebridge 33 F7
Stonor 179 F6
Stony Green 151 A4
Stowe Park 40 F7
Studley Green 159 E3
Summerstown 72 B2
Sunnymeads 211 E4
Sutton 207 C1
Swanbourne 67 B3
Syresham 27 B8

T

Taplow 196 E1
Tathall End 11 E2
Tatling End 189 B3
Tattenhoe 57 A8
Temple 194 C5
Terrick 130 C5
Terriers 162 D2
Tetchwick 82 F2
Tew's End 17 C8
Thame 125 E2
The City 159 D6
The Green
  Milton Keynes 47 D8
  Newport Pagnell 22 C3
  Whipsnade 107 F8
The Swillet 167 B3
Thornborough 54 A8
Thorney 208 B3
Thornton 43 C4
Three Households 176 F7
Tickford End 22 F4
Tiddington 136 A7
Tilbrook 48 C3
Tingewick 51 B7
Tinkers Bridge 47 D6
Tinkers End 65 F3
Tongwell 35 C8
Totteridge 173 F8
Totternhoe 93 B7
Touchbridge 95 E1
Towerage 171 F8
Tower Hill 146 F2
Town End 159 C8

Townsend
  Haddenham 127 A7
  North Marston 76 B2
Town's End 71 D2
Tring 119 C3
Tringford 118 F8
Turvey 8 F6
Turville 169 F3
Turville Heath 169 A3
Turweston 38 C8
Two Mile Ash 33 D2
Twyford 62 C1
Tylers Green 163 D1
Tyringham 12 F2

U

Up End 24 A8
Upper Arncott 94 E7
Upper Dunsley 119 C4
Upper Maidensgrove ..179 A7
Upper North Dean 150 E2
Upper Pollicott 111 E8
Upper Winchendon 99 B1
Upton
  Slough 206 B3
  Stone 114 A4
Upton Lea 206 A7
Upton Park 205 F3
Uxbridge 201 E5
Uxbridge Moor 201 B4

V

Venus Hill 156 B8
Verney Junction 64 F4
Victoria Park 116 B8

W

Waddesdon 99 B7
Walnut Tree 48 C6
Walter's Ash 150 C1
Walton
  Aylesbury 115 F7
  Milton Keynes 47 F5

Walton Court 115 C5
Walton Manor 48 A6
Walton Park 48 A4
Warrington 2 B1
Water Eaton 58 D5
Waterend 159 C5
Watermead 101 F4
Waterperry 123 B1
Waterperry Common ...122 F8
Waterside 154 D6
Water Stratford 40 A1
Wavendon 48 E7
Wavendon Gate 48 D6
Weedon 87 D1
Well End 184 F5
Well Head 93 D5
Wendover 131 C4
Wendover Dean 141 C5
Westbury 39 B4
Westcott 98 C7
Westcroft 45 E2
West Drayton 208 D3
West End 63 C2
West Hyde 178 E3
West Leith 118 F2
Westlington 113 E1
Weston Turville 116 E3
Weston Underwood 6 B1
West Wycombe 160 F2
Wexham Street 199 C4
Whaddon 45 A1
Wharley End 24 D1
Wheatley 122 A1
Wheeler End 171 B6
Whelpley Hill 145 D5
Whipsnade 107 F8
Whitchurch 87 B6
Whiteleaf 139 D5
Whitfield 26 D3
Wicken 31 B3
Widmer End 162 E6
Widmoor 185 E3
Wigginton 119 D1
Wigginton Bottom 133 D8
Willen 35 D7
Willen Park 35 C6
Willowbank 201 C7
Wilstone 104 D1
Wilstone Green 118 D8
Wilton Park 176 B1
Winchmore Hill 164 D2
Windsor 210 E6

Wing 79 F2
Wingrave 89 C3
Winslow 66 B4
Winterhill 46 D8
Woburn 60 F7
Woburn Sands 49 A5
Wolverton 33 C5
Wolverton Mill 33 A6
Wooburn 185 D4
Wooburn Green 185 F7
Wooburn Moor 174 E1
Woodburn Common 186 B3
Wood End
  Little Horwood 55 E2
  Nash 55 C8
Wood Green 27 F2
Woodham 83 E1
Woodrow 164 D5
Woolstone 35 D3
Wootton Bourne End ..25 F8
World's End 130 F7
Worminghall 123 E6
Wormstone 99 C5
Wotton Underwood ...97 C4
Woughton On The Green 47 D8
Woughton Park 47 E6
Wraysbury 211 E1
Wycombe Marsh 173 F4
Wymbush 33 F2

Y

Yardley Gobion 18 E5
Yardley Hastings 1 B6

A

Abbey Barn La HP10 173 E3
Abbey Barn Rd HP11 173 F4
Abbey Cl SL1 204 E6
Abbey Cotts SL7 193 B4
Abbey Ct HP5 154 B6
Abbey Ctr The HP19 101 B2
Abbey Gate SL6 204 A7
Abbey Mead SL8 184 F5
Abbey Park La SL1 186 E2
Abbey Rd Aylesbury HP19 101 B2
Bourne End SL8 184 F5
Milton Keynes,Bradwell MK13 34 A4
Milton Keynes,Simpson MK6 47 E5
Syresham NN13 27 C7
Abbey Sq MK43 8 E5
Abbey Terr MK16 22 D4
Abbey Way
High Wycombe HP11 173 A6
Milton Keynes MK13 34 B6
Ravenstone MK46 5 E2
Abbey Wlk HP16 152 B7
Abbey's Comb Sch MK3 47 A2
Abbeydore Gr MK10 35 F1
Abbeyfield Ho HP16 152 A7
Abbeyhill Rdbt MK12 33 E4
Abbot Ridge HP18 125 D5
Abbot Wlk HP18 125 D5
Abbot's Wlk SL4 209 E5
Abbots Cl MK13 34 B6
Abbots Way
High Wycombe HP12 172 D3
Monks Risborough HP27 139 C5
Abbotsbury MK4 45 E2
Abbotsfield MK6 47 B8
Abbotswood HP27 150 C4
Abbott's Cl UB8 208 D8
Abbotts Cl HP20 101 E1
Abbotts Rd HP20 101 E1
Abbotts Vale HP5 144 C3
Abbotts Way Slough SL1 204 D5
Wingrave HP22 89 A4
Abell Gdns SL6 195 B1
Abercromby Ave HP12 172 E8
Abercromby Ct HP12 172 D8
Aberdeen Ave SL1 205 A6
Aberdeen Cl MK3 46 F2
Abingdon Cl Thame OX9 125 F1
Uxbridge UB10 201 F4
Abingdon Wlk SL6 195 E3
Abington SL3 212 D7
Abney Court Dr SL8 185 A2
Abraham Cl MK15 35 C6
Abrahams Rd RG9 191 C3
Abstacle Hill HP23 118 F3
Acacia 3 RG9 191 D2
Acacia Ave
West Drayton UB7 208 F6
Wraysbury TW19 211 E3
Acacia Cl HP5 144 A1
Acacia Gr HP4 135 B3
Acacia Ho SL9 177 E2
Acacia Mews UB7 213 D8
Acacia Wlk HP23 118 E3
Accommodation La UB7 213 C8
Ackerman Cl MK18 52 F8
Ackroyd Pl MK5 46 B5
Acorn Bsns Ctr LU7 78 F1
Acorn Cl HP13 173 D7
Acorn Gdns HP12 172 E4
Acorn Ho MK9 34 D2
Acorn Wlk MK9 34 E2
Acre Pas SL4 210 D6
Acre The SL7 183 F2
Acrefield Rd SL9 188 D8
Acres End HP7 165 E8
Acres The HP13 161 E1
Adam Cl
High Wycombe HP13 173 D8
Slough SL1 205 A5
Adam Ct RG9 191 E2
Adams Cl MK18 41 C1
Adams Ct MK6 47 C8
Adams Way HP23 119 B6
Addington Cl SL4 210 A4
Addington Cotts HP22 131 B5
Addington Rd MK18 41 D1
Addington Terr MK18 41 D1
Addison Cl SL0 207 E6
Addison Ct SL6 196 B1
Addison Rd
Chesham HP5 144 C2
Steeple Claydon MK18 63 D2
Adelaide Cl SL1 205 A4
Adelaide Rd
High Wycombe HP13 162 D1
Windsor SL4 210 F6
Adelaide Sq SL4 210 D5
Adelphi Gdns SL1 205 E4
Adelphi St MK9 34 F4
Adkins Cl HP19 100 F3
Adkins Ct HP14 158 E5
Admiral Way HP4 134 F6
Adrians Wlk SL2 205 F5
Adstock Mews 2 SL9 177 D2
Adwell Sq RG9 191 D2
Agars Pl SL3 211 A8
Agora Ctr
7 Milton Keynes MK2 58 C8
Milton Keynes,Wolverton MK12 33 D7
Aidan Cl HP21 116 A4
Ailward Rd HP19 101 A2
Ainsdale Cl MK3 46 D1
Aintree Cl
Milton Keynes MK3 57 C6
Poyle SL3 212 E6
Airport Gate Bsns Ctr UB7 213 F7
Airport Way TW19 213 A3
Aiston Pl HP20 101 F2
Ajax Ave SL1 205 B6
Akeley Wood Jun Sch MK19 31 A1
Akeley Wood Lower Sch MK18 29 B4
Akeley Wood Sch MK18 41 C7
Akeman St HP23 119 A3
Akerman Cl MK12 33 B5
Akister Cl MK18 52 E8
Alabama Circ HP11 173 B4
Alabama Dr HP11 173 B3
Alan Way SL3 206 E7
Alaska St HP11 173 B4
Albany Ct MK14 34 D7
Albany Gate HP5 144 B1
Albany Pk SL3 212 D7
Albany Pl HP19 101 A2
Albany Rd
Old Windsor SL4 211 A2
Windsor SL4 210 D5
Albany Terr HP23 119 B6
Albert Cl 9 SL1 205 F3
Albert Pl SL4 205 A1
Albert Rd Chesham HP5 154 C8
Henley-on-T RG9 191 E1
West Drayton UB7 208 E5
Windsor SL4 210 E3
Albert St Aylesbury HP20 116 A8
4 High Wycombe HP13 173 C7
Maidenhead SL6 202 F7
Milton Keynes MK2 58 C8
Slough SL1 205 F3
Tring HP23 119 A3
Windsor SL4 210 B6
Albion SL3 207 B1
Albion Cl SL2 206 A5
Albion Cotts SL6 195 C7
Albion Cres HP8 177 B7
Albion Ho HP12 172 C5
Albion Pl
Milton Keynes MK9 35 A3
2 Windsor SL4 210 A5
Albion Rd
Chalfont St Giles HP8 177 B8
High Wycombe HP12 172 C5
Pitstone LU7 105 D5
Albion St HP20 115 E8
Albury Ct 3 MK8 33 F1
Albury View OX9 136 A6
Aldborough Spur SL1 205 E7
Aldbourne Rd SL1 204 B8
Aldbury CE Prim Sch HP23 120 C6
Aldbury Gdns HP23 119 B6
Aldbury Rd WD3 167 F2
Aldebury Rd SL6 195 F2
Alden View SL4 209 D6
Aldene Rd MK19 11 B3
Aldenham MK6 47 D5
Alder Cl SL1 204 F5
Alder Rd Iver Heath SL0 200 D3
New Denham UB9 201 C6
Alderbourne La SL3 199 E8
Alderbourne Manor SL9 189 A1
Alderbury Rd SL3 207 A4
Alderbury Rd W SL3 206 F4
Aldergill MK13 34 C5
Alderley Ct HP4 135 C3
Aldermead MK12 33 E5
Alderney Pl MK5 45 F4
Alders The UB9 201 C6
Alderson Cl HP19 101 A2
Alderton Dr HP4 121 B8
Aldin Ave N SL1 206 A4
Aldin Ave S SL1 206 A4
Aldrich Dr MK15 35 E7
Aldridge Ct HP11 173 F4
Aldridge Rd SL2 198 A1
Aldwick Dr SL6 202 D6
Aldwycks Cl MK5 45 F6
Alexander Ct
High Wycombe HP12 172 E8
Slough SL1 205 C4
Alexander Fst Sch SL4 209 C4
Alexander Ho 1 MK2 58 C8
Alexander Rd HP20 101 D1
Alexander St HP5 144 C1
Alexandra Ct
Leighton Buzzard LU7 80 F8
Milton Keynes MK13 34 A4
Windsor SL4 210 D5
Alexandra Dr MK16 22 C2
Alexandra Pk HP11 173 A6
Alexandra Rd
High Wycombe HP13 173 E5
Maidenhead SL6 202 D8
Slough SL1 205 D3
Uxbridge UB8 201 D3
Windsor SL4 210 D5
Alford Rd HP12 172 C3
Alfred Ct SL8 185 B3
Alfred Davis Ct SL7 183 D3
Alfriston Sch HP9 175 C6
Alham Rd HP21 115 C6
Alice Cl HP15 163 C7
Alice La SL1 197 B1
All Saints CE Jun Sch SL6 202 C6
All Saints View MK5 46 B8
All Saints' Ave SL6 202 D7
All Souls Cotts SL3 206 E8
Alladale Pl MK12 33 D4
Allanson Rd SL7 183 F3
Allen Cl MK2 58 C5
Allen Dr HP14 161 C8
Allenby Rd SL6 202 B7
Allerds Rd SL2 198 A4
Allerford Ct MK4 46 C4
Alleyns La SL6 195 D8
Allhusen Gdns SL3 199 E8
Allington Circ MK4 45 E1
Allington Ct SL2 205 F6
Allison Ct MK15 35 C1
Allkins Ct SL4 210 D5
Allonby Way HP21 116 B7
Allyn Cl HP13 173 C8
Alma Ct Burnham SL1 197 C2
Eton Wick SL4 204 F2
Alma Rd
Berkhamsted HP4 134 E6
Chesham HP5 144 C2
Eton Wick SL4 204 F2
Windsor SL4 210 C6
Almhouses MK14 21 E1
Almond Cl
Newport Pagnell MK16 22 B3
Windsor SL4 210 B5
Almond Rd SL1 197 C2
Almond Way HP27 139 A2
Almond Wlk HP15 163 B3
Almons Way SL2 206 B8
Almshouses Eton SL4 210 D7
Old Windsor SL4 210 F1
Worminghall HP18 123 E5
Almshouses The MK46 5 E2
Alnwick Dr HP23 103 F7
Alpha Ct HP7 165 B7
Alpha St N 3 SL1 206 A4
Alpha St S SL1 205 F3
Alpine Cl SL6 203 A6
Alpine Croft MK5 46 A3
Alscot La HP27 139 A5
Alsford Wharf HP4 135 C5
Alston Dr MK13 33 F3
Alston Gdns SL6 202 E7
Alstonefield 1 MK4 46 B3
Althorpe Cres MK13 34 B6
Alton Bsns Pk HP19 101 B1
Alton Gate MK4 45 F3
Altona Rd HP10 174 D3
Altona Way SL1 205 B7
Altwood Bailey SL6 202 B5
Altwood CE Sec Sch SL6 202 B5
Altwood Cl
Maidenhead SL6 202 B5
Slough SL1 204 E8
Altwood Dr SL6 202 B5
Altwood Rd
Maidenhead SL6 202 B5
Maidenhead SL6 202 C5
Alverton MK14 34 F8
Alvista Ave SL6 204 B7
Alwin Cl HP21 115 C4
Alwins Field LU7 80 D8
Alwyn Inf Sch SL6 202 C8
Alwyn Rd SL6 202 B8
Alyngton HP4 134 E7
Alyson Ct 2 SL6 195 F1
Amanda Ct SL3 206 D3
Amber Cotts HP7 164 F3
Ambergate MK16 36 B4
Amberley Ct SL6 196 C3
Amberley Pl 11 SL4 210 D6
Amberley Rd SL2 204 E8
Amberley Way UB10 201 E3
Amberley Wlk MK4 45 E1
Amblers Way MK18 53 A1
Ambleside
Amersham HP6 154 C2
Aylesbury HP21 116 B5
Ambleside Wlk UB8 201 D4
Ambridge Gr MK6 35 C1
Ambrose Ct MK15 35 C2
Amelias La MK9 35 A3
Amerden Cl SL6 203 D7
Amerden La SL6 203 D7
Amerden Priory Cvn Pk SL6 203 E4
Amerden Way SL1 205 A4
American Com Sch UB10 201 F4
Amersham & Wycombe Coll
Amersham HP7 165 F8
Chesham HP5 144 D3
Flackwell Heath HP10 173 E2
Amersham Ct HP7 165 A7
Amersham General Hospl HP7 165 A6
Amersham Hill HP13 173 B7
Amersham Hill Dr HP13 173 C8
Amersham Hill Gdns HP13 173 C8
Amersham Mus★ HP7 165 B7
Amersham Pl HP7 166 C8
Amersham Rd
Beaconsfield HP7 176 A6
Chalfont Common HP8,SL9 177 D6
Chalfont St Giles HP8 166 B2
Chalfont St Peter SL9 177 E2
Chesham HP6 154 B5
Chorleywood WD3 167 C8
Denham Green SL9 189 A4
Gerrards Cross SL9 188 C7
Hazlemere HP15 162 E5
High Wycombe HP13 173 C8
Little Chalfont HP6 166 E8
Amersham Sch The HP7 165 E7
Amersham Way HP6 166 E8
Ames Cl MK6 46 F8
Amherst Ct MK15 35 C7
Amos Ct MK13 34 A6
Ampleforth MK10 36 A1
Amy La HP5 154 B7
Ancastle Gn RG9 191 D1
Ancell Rd MK11 32 E5
Anchor Ct SL6 195 F7
Anchor La 1 HP20 115 E8
Ancona Gdns MK5 45 F3
Andermans SL4 209 D6
Andersen Gate MK4 57 A7
Anderson Cl HP14 158 F4
Anding Cl MK46 6 E4
Andover Cl UB8 201 B3
Andrew Hill La SL2 187 C3
Andrewes Croft MK14 34 F8
Andrews Cl LU7 69 E3
Andrews Reach SL8 185 A2
Andrews Way
Aylesbury HP19 115 A7
Marlow Bottom SL7 183 C8
Anershall HP22 89 B3
Angel Cl MK15 35 A7
Angelica Cl UB7 208 F7
Angelica Ct MK7 48 A5
Angels Cl MK18 65 F4
Anglefield Rd HP4 135 B4
Anglesey Ct
Milton Keynes MK8 46 A8
Stokenchurch HP14 158 E5
Angood Cl HP27 139 A3
Angora Cl MK5 46 A3
Angstrom Cl MK5 46 B5
Angus Dr MK3 46 F2
Angus Rd HP19 101 A3
Anne Cl SL6 195 E2
Annes Gr MK14 21 D1
Annesley Rd MK16 22 B3
Anns Cl Aylesbury HP21 116 A4
Tring HP23 118 E3
Ansculf Rd SL2 198 A2
Anslow Gdns SL0 200 D3
Anslow Pl SL1 204 C8
Anson Cl Aylesbury HP21 115 E4
Bovingdon HP3 145 F4
Anson Rd MK12 33 C6
Anstey Brook HP22 117 A3
Anstey Cl HP18 99 B6
Anstey Ct HP18 99 B7
Anthony Cl HP13 161 F1
Anthony Ct MK11 32 D5
Anthony Way SL1 204 D6
Anton Way HP21 115 D3
Anvil Cl HP3 146 B3
Anvil Ct SL3 207 A2
Anxey Way HP17 126 F6
Aplin Rd HP21 116 C6
Apple Cotts HP3 146 A4
Apple Tree Cl LU7 80 D6
Appleacres MK17 69 D8
Appleby Heath MK2 58 D6
Applecroft
Berkhamsted HP4 134 E6
Maidenhead SL6 202 C3
Newton Longville MK17 57 D4
Applefield HP7 166 C7
Appleton Cl HP7 166 B7
Appleton Mews 4 MK4 46 B3
Appletree Ave UB7,UB8 208 F7
Appletree La 3 SL3 206 C3
Appletree Wlk HP5 154 D5
Applewick La HP12 172 C8
Applewood Cl UB10 201 E8
Appleyard Pl 1 MK6 34 E1
Approach Rd SL6 203 E7
Approach The MK8 33 E2
Apsley Cotts SL6 195 E7
Apsley Ho SL1 206 A4
Aran Hts HP8 177 B6
Arborfield Cl SL1 205 E3
Arbour Vale Sch SL2 205 F7
Arbour View HP7 166 B8
Arbroath Cl MK3 46 E3
Arbrook Ave MK13 34 D3
Arcade The HP9 175 E3
Arch Way
High Wycombe HP13 173 A7
Speen HP27 150 B4
Archdale 1 HP11 173 A6
Archer Cl SL6 202 D8
Archer Ct HP6 154 C2
Archer Dr HP20 102 A2
Archer Terr UB7 208 E6
Archers Way HP14 171 B5
Archers Wells MK3 47 B2
Archford Croft MK4 46 C3
Archive Cl HP22 117 D5
Archways 14 HP20 115 D8
Arden Cl HP3 146 A3
Arden Pk MK12 33 B7
Ardenham La HP19 101 D1
Ardenham St HP19 101 C1
Ardley Mews MK10 36 B3
Ardrossan Cl SL2 198 C1
Ardwell La MK12 33 B5
Ardys Ct MK5 46 B8
Argonaut Pk SL3 212 F6
Argyle Ave HP19 101 B2
Argyll Ave SL1 205 A6
Argyll Ho MK3 46 F1
Aries Ho HP10 185 A8
Aris Way MK18 52 D6
Arizona St HP11 173 B4
Arklay Cl UB8 201 F1
Arkley Ct SL6 203 C1
Arklow Ct WD3 167 D5
Arkwright Rd SL3 212 E5
Arlington Cl SL6 202 A8
Arlington Ct MK4 46 E3
Arlott Cres MK6 46 F8
Armourer Dr MK14 34 F6
Armstrong Cl MK8 45 E7
Armstrong Ho SL2 206 C7
Arncliffe Dr MK13 34 B5
Arncott Rd OX25 95 D7
Arncott Way HP19 100 F1
Arncott Wood Rd OX25 94 E6
Arne La MK7 48 D5
Arnison Ave HP13 162 D1
Arnold Cl HP22 116 C2
Arnold Cott MK19 32 C7
Arnold Ct HP21 115 F6
Arnold's Cotts HP5 143 B4
Arnolds Cl MK18 53 A1
Arnott's Yd HP18 125 D6
Arranmore Ho HP11 174 B4
Arrewig La HP5 142 E8
Arrow Pl MK2 58 D4
Arthur Rd Slough SL1 205 D4
Windsor SL4 210 C6
Artichoke Dell WD3 167 E4
Arts Educational Sch HP23 119 B3
Arundel Cl SL6 202 A8
Arundel Ct SL3 206 D2
Arundel Gn HP20 101 F2
Arundel Gr MK3 57 E7
Arundel Ho
1 High Wycombe HP13 173 F7
Uxbridge UB8 201 C1
Arundel Rd
High Wycombe HP12 172 B6
Uxbridge UB8 201 B2
Ascot Dr LU7 80 D6
Ascot Ho MK9 34 C2
Ascot Pl MK3 57 D7
Ascot Rd SL6 203 A1
Ascott Ct HP20 101 E1
Ascott Ho★ LU7 80 A2
Ascott Rd HP20 101 E1
Ash Cl Aylesbury HP20 102 A2
Slough SL3 207 B3
Walter's Ash HP14 161 B8
Ash Gn UB9 201 B6
Ash Gr Amersham HP6 154 A3
Aylesbury HP21 116 A7
Stoke Poges SL2 198 F5
West Drayton UB7 208 F6
Ash Hill Prim Sch HP13 174 A7
Ash Hill Rd MK16 22 B4
Ash La SL4 209 D5
Ash Mead Dr UB9 190 A2
Ash Rd
High Wycombe HP12 172 C4
Princes Risborough HP27 139 B3
Tring HP23 118 F4
Ash Tree Ho HP12 172 C4
Ash Vale WD3 178 D5
Ashbourne End HP21 115 D4
Ashbourne Gr SL6 202 C3
Ashbourne Ho 5 SL1 205 E4
Ashbrook Fst Sch MK8 33 E1
Ashburnham Cl 2 MK3 46 D1
Ashburnham Cres LU7 80 E6
Ashby MK6 47 A8
Ashby Rd HP4 134 D7
Ashby Villas LU7 92 A1
Ashcroft Ct SL1 197 B3
Ashcroft Dr UB9 189 F4
Ashcroft Rd SL6 202 C8
Ashcroft Terr HP23 119 A5
Ashdown SL6 196 B3
Ashdown Cl MK14 35 A8
Ashdown Ct HP13 173 D6
Ashdown Rd HP13 174 A8
Ashdown Way HP6 154 D2
Ashen Cross SL3 207 B8
Ashenden Wlk SL2 198 D8
Ashendon Rd HP18 98 C6
Asheridge Rd HP5 144 A2
Ashfield MK14 34 D8
Ashfield Cl HP15 163 B2
Ashfield Cotts UB9 190 A1
Ashfield Gr MK2 58 C7
Ashfield Rd HP5 144 D2
Ashfield Rise HP18 109 D5
Ashfield Way HP15 163 B3
Ashfold Sch HP18 110 F8
Ashford Cl HP21 116 A5
Ashford Cres MK8 45 D6
Ashford La SL4 204 B4
Ashford Rd SL0 200 C4
Ashgrove MK18 63 D2
Ashgrove Gdns HP22 86 E7
Ashlea MK46 6 E3
Ashlea Rd SL9 177 E1
Ashleigh Cl HP7 165 E8
Ashley HP10 185 F7
Ashley Cl LU7 105 A8
Ashley Ct
15 Aylesbury HP19 115 A8
Maidenhead SL6 203 B7
Tylers Green HP10 163 B1
West Drayton UB7 208 E5
Ashley Dr HP10 163 C1
Ashley Green Rd HP5 144 E5
Ashley Pk SL6 196 B2
Ashley Rd UB8 201 B3
Ashley Row HP20 102 A1

Ashleys WD3 ....167 F2
Ashlyns Ct HP4 ....135 B3
Ashlyns Rd HP4 ....135 B3
Ashlyns Sch HP4 ......135 C2
Ashmead Comb Sch
  HP21 ....115 C5
Ashmead La UB9 ......190 A4
Ashotts La HP5 ....143 B6
Ashpole Furlong MK5 ..46 B7
Ashridge OX39 ....147 B6
Ashridge Cl
  1 Bovingdon HP3 ......146 A3
  Milton Keynes MK3 ....57 D7
Ashridge Coll Gdns★
  HP4 ....121 D5
Ashridge Cotts HP4 ...121 C5
Ashridge Est Visitor Ctr★
  HP4 ....120 E6
Ashridge La HP5 ......155 D7
Ashridge Man Coll HP4 121 C5
Ashridge Rise HP4 ....134 F3
Ashton Pl SL6 ....202 A6
Ashton Rd NN12 ....9 D8
Ashtree Wlk HP15 .....163 B2
Ashwell St **1** LU7 ....80 F8
Ashwells HP10 ....174 B8
Ashwells Manor Dr
  HP10 ....174 C8
Ashwells Way HP8 ....177 D8
Ashwood MK13 ....34 A7
Ashwood Dr HP5 ......144 B1
Askett La HP27 ....139 D7
Aspen Cl Aylesbury HP20 .102 A2
  Slough SL2 ....205 B8
  West Drayton UB7 ....208 F5
Asplands Cl MK17 ......49 B4
Aspley Ct Aylesbury HP19 101 C1
  Woburn Sands MK17 ...49 C3
Aspley Guise Lower Sch
  MK17 ....49 E4
Aspley Guise Sta MK17 49 D6
Aspley Hill MK17 ....49 C4
Aspley La MK17 ....49 E2
Aspreys MK46 ....6 E4
Assheton Rd HP9 .....175 E4
Astlethorpe MK8 ....33 F2
Astley Rd OX9 ....126 B1
Aston Abbotts Rd
  Cublington LU7 ....78 C1
  Weedon HP22 ....87 E1
Aston Cl Aylesbury HP19 101 A3
  Milton Keynes MK5 ....46 B5
Aston Clinton Rd HP22 116 A6
Aston Clinton Sch HP22 117 D5
Aston Ferry La RG9 ...192 D5
Aston Hill OX49 ......157 E7
Aston La RG9 ....192 C3
Aston Mead SL4 ......209 E6
Aston Rd HP17 ....127 B5
Aston Rowant Nature
  Reserve★ HP14 ......157 E5
Astonville SL2 ....198 C8
Astor Cl SL6 ....203 B6
Astronomy Way **12**
  HP19 ....115 A8
Astrope La HP23 ......104 B3
Astwood Rd MK43 ......25 C7
Atherstone Ct MK8 ....33 C2
Atherton Cl TW19 ....213 D1
Atherton Ct SL4 .....210 D7
Athlone Cl SL6 ....195 E1
Athlone Sq SL4 ......210 C5
Atkins Cl MK13 ....34 B3
Atlas Ho HP5 ....144 B1
Atterbrook MK13 ....34 A4
Attingham Hill MK8 ....34 A1
Atwell Cl MK8 ....45 E7
Auckland Cl SL6 .....203 B8
Auckland Pk MK1 ......47 D4
Auckland Rd HP13 ....173 E6
Auden Cl MK16 ....22 A5
Audley Dr SL6 ....202 B6
Audley Mead MK13 .....34 B3
August End SL3 ......206 E7
Augustine Cl SL3 ....212 E4
Augustine Mews HP16 ..22 E7
Augustus Rd MK11 .....32 E4
Augustus Smith Ho **2**
  HP4 ....135 D4
Austen Ave MK46 ....7 A4
Austen Pl HP19 ....100 F2
Austenway SL9 ....188 E8
Austenwood Cl
  Chalfont St Peter SL9 .177 C1
  High Wycombe HP11 ..173 A4
Austenwood La
  Chalfont St Peter SL9 .177 D1
  Gerrards Cross SL9 ..188 D8
Austin Waye UB8 .....201 C4
Austins Mead HP3 ....146 B3
Australia Ave SL6 ....202 F8
Australia Rd **1** SL1 ..206 B4
Austwick La MK4 ......46 B2
Autumn Cl
  Aylesbury HP19 ......101 A3
  Slough SL1 ....204 F5
Autumn Wlk SL6 .....202 A5
Auxiliaries Way UB9 ..189 F6
Avalon Rd SL8 ....185 B5
Avant Bsns Ctr MK1 ...47 C2
Avebury SL1 ....205 A6
Avebury Bvd MK9 ......34 E2
Avebury Rdbt MK9 .....34 D1
Aveling Rd HP13 .....173 C6
Avenue Cl UB7 ....208 D3

Avenue Dr
  Iver Heath SL3 ....199 F1
  Slough SL3 ....206 F8
Avenue Ho HP5 ....154 B8
Avenue Rd
  Buckingham MK18 .....41 E3
  Maidenhead SL6 .....203 B5
  Winslow MK18 ....65 F4
Avenue The
  Amersham HP7 ....154 C1
  Bourne End SL8 .....184 F4
  Chinnor OX39 ....147 D6
  Datchet SL3 ....211 B6
  Dunstable LU6 ....93 E7
  Farnham Common SL2 .198 B8
  Maidenhead SL6 .....196 C3
  Old Windsor SL4 ....211 B2
  Princes Risborough HP27 139 C2
  Uxbridge UB8 ....201 D1
  Whitfield NN13 ....26 D4
  Worminghall HP18 ...123 E5
  Wraysbury TW19 .....211 B1
Averil Ct SL4 ....204 C7
Avery Ave HP13 ......161 D2
Avery Ct MK16 ....22 C2
Avington MK8 ....33 E1
Avocet Way HP19 .....101 C4
Avon Cl
  Newport Pagnell MK16 .22 D3
  Slough SL1 ....204 E6
Avon Gr MK3 ....57 E8
Avon Pl HP21 ....115 D4
Avonbury Ct NN13 .....38 A5
Avondale SL6 ....195 C1
Avonmoore SL6 ......203 B8
Axis Pk SL3 ....207 B1
Aylesbury & Thame Airport
  HP17 ....126 E7
Aylesbury Bsns Ctr
  HP19 ....101 B1
Aylesbury Coll HP21 ..115 C7
Aylesbury Cres SL1 ..205 D6
Aylesbury End HP9 ...175 E1
Aylesbury Gram Sch
  HP21 ....115 F7
Aylesbury High Sch
  HP21 ....115 F7
Aylesbury Ind Ctr HP19 101 C1
Aylesbury Rd
  Aston Clinton HP22 ..117 B5
  Bierton HP22 ....102 B3
  Chearsley HP18 .....112 B2
  Cuddington HP18 ....113 A3
  Great Missenden HP16 142 F2
  Haddenham HP17,OX9 126 C6
  Monks Risborough HP27 139 D6
  Thame OX9 ....125 F2
  Tring HP23 ....118 E2
  Wendover HP22 .....131 B6
  Wing LU7 ....79 E1
Aylesbury St
  Milton Keynes,Bletchley
  MK2 ....58 E8
  Milton Keynes,Wolverton
  MK12 ....33 D6
Aylesbury St W MK12 ..33 C6
Aylesbury Sta HP20 ..115 D7
Aylesbury Vale PRU
  HP19 ....101 C2
Aylesford Gr MK10 .....36 A1
Ayless Cl HP18 ....98 B7
Ayleswater HP19 .....101 C1
Aylesworth Ave SL2 ..198 B2
Aylward Gdns HP5 ...144 A1
Aynho Ct MK8 ....45 F8
Aynscombe Cl LU6 .....93 F8
Ayr Way MK3 ....46 E2
Ayres Cl HP21 ....115 B6
Ayrshire Ct HP19 ....101 A1
Ayrton Cl MK8 ....45 D6
Aysgarth Pk MK8 ....203 B1
Azalea Cl HP15 ......163 A3
Azalea Way SL3 ......206 E7

B

Babington Cl MK10 ....36 A3
Babington Rd HP22 ..131 D6
Baccara Gr MK2 ....58 C7
Bachelors Acre SL4 ..210 D6
Back Dr MK16 ....12 F3
Back La
  Chalfont St Giles HP8 .177 A7
  Great Missenden HP16 152 B7
  Tingewick MK18 ....51 A6
Back St Gawcott MK18 ..51 F4
  Thornborough MK18 ..54 A8
  Wendover HP22 .....131 B4
Backleys MK7 ....48 A4
Backs The HP5 ....154 C8
Bacombe La HP22 ....131 B3
Bacon Hill MK46 ....6 E3
Baconsmead UB9 ....190 A2
Bad Godesberg Way
  SL6 ....202 F7
Bader Gdns SL1 .....205 A4
Badgemore Rise SL7 183 C7
Badgemore Com Sch
  RG9 ....191 D2
Badgemore Ct MK8 ....33 C2
Badgemore La RG9 ...191 D3
Badger Cl SL6 ....202 D4
Badger Way HP15 ....163 B5
Badgers Mdw HP22 ..131 C5
Badgers Oak MK7 .....48 B7
Badgers Rise HP17 ..114 C5

Badgers Way
  Buckingham MK18 .....52 E7
  Marlow Bottom SL7 ..183 D7
Badgers Wlk WD3 ....167 F5
Badgers Wood SL2 ...198 C7
Badmington Ct **3** HP7 165 B7
Badminton Ho **1** HP7 165 B7
Badminton Rd SL6 ...202 B6
Badminton View MK6 ..34 A1
Badrick Rd HP19 .....100 F3
Bagley Cl UB7 ....208 E4
Bagshot St MK2 ....58 C7
Bailey Cl
  High Wycombe HP13 ..173 C2
  Maidenhead SL6 .....202 C7
  Windsor SL4 ....210 A5
Bailey Ho **9** SL8 ....185 A4
Bailey's Ct **12** HP20 ..115 D8
Baily Ct MK5 ....46 A5
Baines Ho HP11 ......173 F4
Baird Cl SL1 ....205 B4
Baisley Ho MK2 ....58 D8
Baker St
  High Wycombe HP11 ..172 F7
  Waddesdon HP18 ......99 A6
Baker's Orch HP10 ...185 C6
Baker's Piece Ho OX39 147 D6
Baker's Rd UB8 .....201 D5
Bakers Cl
  Stoke Goldington MK16 12 B5
  Turvey MK43 ....8 E5
Bakers Ct Stanwell TW19 213 D1
  Waddesdon HP18 ......99 A6
Bakers La NN12 ....9 A8
Bakers Wlk HP22 .....116 F2
Bakers Wood SL8 ....195 B7
Bakery Cl Cranfield MK43 25 B1
  Grendon Underwood HP18 83 A6
Bakery Ho **10** HP20 .115 D8
Bala Cl MK2 ....58 D5
Bala Way MK2 ....58 C5
Balcary Gdns HP4 ...134 F3
Balcary Rd MK4 ....56 F8
Baldways Cl HP22 .....89 C3
Baldwin Cres HP21 ..115 F5
Baldwin Pl SL6 ......202 C7
Baldwin Rd
  Beaconsfield HP9 ...176 B1
  Burnham SL1 ....197 C2
Baldwin's Shore SL4 210 D8
Balfe Mews MK7 ....48 D4
Balfour Mews HP3 ...146 A4
Balfour Pl SL7 ......183 D4
Balfour Way SL3 .....206 D3
Balham's La RG9 ....179 F8
Ball Moor MK18 ....52 D6
Ballard Cl HP21 .....116 B5
Ballard Gn SL4 ......209 E7
Ballards Row HP22 ..117 D6
Ballinger Ct HP4 ....135 B3
Ballinger Grange HP16 142 E2
Ballinger Rd HP16 ..142 E1
Ballinger Row HP16 .142 D3
Balmer Bridge MK18 ..52 E5
Balmer Cut MK18 .....52 E6
Balmerino Cl MK10 ...36 B2
Balmoral SL1 ....195 B1
Balmoral Cl SL1 ....204 E7
Balmoral Ct
  High Wycombe HP13 ..173 B7
  Newport Pagnell MK16 .22 D4
Balmoral Gdns SL4 ..210 D4
Balsam Cl MK7 ....48 B6
Bamfords Cl MK43 .....8 E6
Bamfords Yd MK43 .....8 E5
Bampton Cl MK4 ....46 E2
Banburies Cl MK10 ....47 A3
Banbury Ave SL1 ....204 F8
Bancroft Rdbt MK13 ..34 A5
Bandon Cl UB10 .....201 F3
Bangor Cotts SL0 ...200 D1
Bangors Cl SL0 .....207 F7
Bangors Rd N SL0 ...200 D3
Bangors Rd S SL0 ...200 E1
Bangors Road S SL0 207 E8
Bank Apartments SL7 183 D3
Bank Court Mews MK12 33 D7
Bank Gn HP5 ....143 C8
Bank Mill HP4 ....135 E4
Bank Mill La HP4 ...135 E3
Bank Rd HP10 ....174 D8
Bank St HP13 ....174 A4
Bankfield Rdbt MK9 ...35 A2
Banks Rd HP17 ......127 A6
Banks Spur SL1 .....205 B4
Bankside HP22 ......131 B5
Banktop Pl MK4 ....46 C3
Bannard Rd SL6 .....202 A5
Banner Ct HP12 .....172 D8
Bannister Cl SL3 ...206 E4
Bantock Cl MK7 ....48 C5
Bar La HP27 ....138 E7
Barbers Mews MK14 ..34 F6
Barbers Wlk HP23 ..118 F3
Barbers Wood Cl HP12 172 B4
Barbers Wood Rd HP12 172 B4
Barbicus Ct SL6 ....203 B8
Barbury Ct MK14 .....35 A8
Barchester Cl UB8 ..201 C1
Barchester Rd SL3 ..206 F4
Barclay Ct OX27 ......72 E6
Barclay St **3** HP12 ..172 E7
Bardney Cl SL6 .....202 D3
Bardolphs Cl HP27 .139 C4
Bardon Gn HP20 ....101 C2
Bardsey Ct MK10 .....36 A2
Barford MK11 ....32 F4
Bargeman Rd SL6 ...202 E5

Barham Lodge MK18 ...52 C8
Baring Cres HP9 .....175 C3
Baring Rd
  Beaconsfield HP9 ...175 D3
  High Wycombe HP13 ..173 F7
Barkers Croft MK12 ...33 C4
Barkestone Cl MK4 ...46 C1
Barkham Cl LU7 .....104 F7
Barkus Way HP14 ....158 F5
Barlee Cres UB8 ....208 C8
Barley Cl
  Hazlemere HP15 ....163 A3
  Lewknor OX49 ......157 A8
  Weston Turville HP22 116 F2
Barley Cres HP21 ....115 D3
Barley Fields HP10 ..185 E8
Barley Hill Prim Sch
  OX9 ....126 A1
Barley Mead SL6 ....202 A5
Barley Way **3** SL7 ..183 D1
Barleycroft MK4 ......46 E4
Barlow Rd HP22 ....131 C5
Barn Cl
  Farnham Common SL2 198 B8
  Maidenhead SL6 ....195 F2
Barn Ct HP12 ....172 C7
Barn Dr SL6 ....202 A4
Barn Farm SL7 .....183 D3
Barn La RG9 ....191 C4
Barn Rd HP27 ....138 E6
Barnabas Rd LU7 .....80 D6
Barnacre Cl UB8 ....208 D7
Barnard Cres HP21 ..115 F5
Barnards Hill SL7 ...183 C2
Barncroft MK43 ....8 E6
Barncroft Rd HP4 ...134 F3
Barnes Ave HP5 ....144 C1
Barnes Pl MK6 ....46 E8
Barnes Wallis Ct HP12 172 E5
Barnes Way SL0 ....207 F6
Barnet Cl MK5 ....45 D5
Barnett Way HP22 ...102 B4
Barnfield Iver SL0 ..207 E2
  Slough SL1 ....204 D5
Barnfield Cl SL6 ....195 F5
Barnfield Dr MK6 ....47 C5
Barnhill Cl SL7 .....183 D4
Barnhill Gdns SL7 ..183 D4
Barnhill Rd SL7 ....183 D4
Barns Cl OX33 ......122 B1
Barns The HP23 ....118 F1
Barnsbury Ave HP16 116 B8
Barnsbury Gdns MK16 22 C3
Barnsdale Dr MK4 ....45 F2
Barnsfield Pl UB8 ...201 C5
Barnstable Ct MK4 ...46 D3
Baroma Way RG9 ...191 E2
Barons Cl MK2 ....58 C8
Barons Ct **2** SL7 ..183 E2
Barons Mead RG9 ..191 D2
Baronsmead RG9 ...191 D2
Baronsmead Rd HP12 172 E6
Barr's Rd SL6 ....204 B7
Barrack Hill HP18 ...112 E5
Barrack La SL4 .....210 D6
Barracks Hill HP7 ..164 F2
Barracks Rd HP11 ..173 A6
Barrards Way HP9 ..176 C4
Barrett Pl
  High Wycombe HP11 ..173 C6
  Milton Keynes MK5 ...45 F6
Barrie Ct HP14 ......100 F2
Barrington Ct NN13 ...38 A5
Barrington Mews **4** MK6 34 E1
Barrington Park Gdns
  HP8 ....166 D1
Barrow Lodge SL2 ..198 C1
Barrowcroft HP11 ...173 F4
Barry Ave Eton SL4 ..210 C7
  Milton Keynes MK14 ..34 C7
Barry Cl HP12 ......172 C4
Barry View SL4 .....209 C5
Bartelotts Rd SL2 ..197 E1
Bartholomew Cl MK7 ..48 A5
Bartholomew Tipping Way
  HP14 ....158 F5
Bartlett Cl **1** MK18 ...41 E2
Bartletts SL9 ....177 E3
Barton Rd
  Milton Keynes MK2 ...58 C6
  Slough SL3 ....206 F4
Barton Way HP13 ...162 E1
Bartons Rd HP10 ...163 A1
Bascote MK6 ....47 D5
Base Cl **8** HP20 ....101 F2
Basford Way SL4 ...209 D4
Basildon Ct
  1 Leighton Buzzard LU7 80 F7
  Milton Keynes MK8 ...45 F8
Basing Rd WD3 .....167 F1
Baskerfield Gr MK6 ...47 C8
Bass Mead SL6 .....195 F5
Basset Rd HP14 ....171 C4
Bassetsbury La HP11 173 D5
Bassett Ct MK16 .....22 C4
Bassett Rd
  Leighton Buzzard LU7 80 F7
  Uxbridge UB8 ....201 C5
Bassett Way SL2 ...197 E1
Batchelor Cl HP20 ..101 F2
Batchelors Way
  Amersham HP7 .....165 D8
  Chesham HP5 ......144 D8
Bateman Croft MK5 ..45 F6
Bateman Dr HP21 ...115 E5
Bates Cl
  Granborough MK18 ...75 F8
  Milton Keynes MK15 ..35 D7

Bates Cl *continued*
  Slough SL3 ....206 E7
Bates Ct HP20 ......101 F2
Bates Gdns MK17 .....68 B6
Bates La HP22 ......116 F2
Bath Cl SL6 ....202 C6
Bath La MK18 ....52 C8
Bath Lane Terr MK18 .52 C8
Bath Rd
  Harmondsworth UB7 213 C6
  Harmondsworth UB7 213 E6
  Maidenhead SL6 ...202 C6
  Poyle SL3 ....212 E6
  Slough SL1,SL6 ....204 D6
  Taplow SL6 ....203 E7
Bath Road Cotts SL3 212 E6
Bathurst Cl SL0 ....207 F4
Bathurst Wlk SL0 ..207 F4
Batt Furlong HP21 ..115 E3
Battersby Mews HP21 115 C7
Batting Cl HP14 ....159 F4
Battings Wood Gdns
  HP14 ....161 C8
Battle Cl MK46 ....13 F8
Battlemead Cl SL6 ..196 C3
Battoney Vare SL6 ..203 C4
Baulk The
  Cheddington LU7 ...104 F7
  Ivinghoe LU7 ....105 F5
Bawtree Rd UB8 ....201 D6
Baxter Cl
  Milton Keynes MK8 ...45 E7
  Slough SL1 ....205 E3
Bay Ct HP4 ....135 B4
Bay La MK46 ....5 D2
Bay Tree Ct
  Loudwater HP11 ....174 B2
  Newton Longville MK17 57 D4
Bay Tree Ct SL1 ....197 C2
Baybrook SL6 ......195 F6
Bayhurst Wood Countryside
  Pk★ UB9 ....190 F6
Bayley Cres SL1 ....204 A8
Bayley Gdns HP14 ..161 E6
Bayley Hatch HP15 .152 B8
Baylis Bsns Ctr SL1 205 D6
Baylis Court Sch SL1 205 D8
Baylis Par SL1 .....205 E7
Baylis Rd SL1 ......205 E6
Bayman Manor HP5 144 E2
Bayne Hill HP9 .....176 D3
Bayne Hill Cl HP9 ..176 D3
Baynham Mead MK7 ..48 B8
Baysfarm Ct UB7 ...213 C6
Beacham Rd HP12 ..172 C3
Beachampton Bsns Pk
  MK19 ....44 C4
Beachborough Sch NN13 39 A4
Beacon Ave LU6 ......93 E7
Beacon Cl
  Beaconsfield HP9 ..175 A1
  Chalfont St Peter SL9 177 E3
  Stone HP17 ....114 C5
  Uxbridge UB8 ......201 D1
Beacon Ct Colnbrook SL3 212 C7
  Milton Keynes MK4 ..46 D2
Beacon Hill HP10 ..174 D7
Beacon La SL7 .....171 E1
Beacon Rd HP4 ....106 E2
Beacon Sch The HP6 154 B4
Beacon View OX49 ..157 B8
Beacon Way HP23 ..119 C5
Beaconsfield Ave HP13 162 A1
Beaconsfield Common La
  SL2 ....187 C5
Beaconsfield Cotts SL8 185 B2
Beaconsfield High Sch
  HP9 ....175 D1
Beaconsfield Mews
  HP9 ....186 A8
Beaconsfield Pl MK16 22 C4
Beaconsfield Rd
  Aston Clinton HP22 117 F4
  Aylesbury HP21 ...115 E8
  Farnham Common SL2 198 C5
  Tring HP23 ....118 E3
Beaconsfield Sch The
  HP9 ....175 E1
Beaconsfield Sta HP9 175 E3
Beadlemead MK6 ....47 C6
Beales La MK7 ....48 A5
Bealings End HP9 ..175 D5
Beamish Way MK18 ..66 B5
Beamond End La HP7,
  HP15 ....163 F7
Beanfare MK6 ....47 B4
Bearbrook Rd HP21 115 C7
Bearbrook Comb Sch
  HP19 ....115 C8
Bearswood End HP9 175 D5
Beatrice Cl OX27 .....72 E6
Beauchamp MK14 ...34 E6
Beauchamp Ct SL1 .205 E6
Beaudesert Mews UB7 208 E4
Beaufort Cl
  Aylesbury HP21 ....116 D7
  Marlow SL7 ....183 E2
Beaufort Dr MK15 ...35 C7
Beaufort Gdns SL7 183 E2
Beaufort Pl SL6 ....203 D4
Beaulieu Cl SL3 ...211 B5
Beaumaris Ct SL1 ..205 C8
Beaumaris Gr MK5 ..46 A6
Beaumont Cl SL6 ...202 A6
Beaumont Cotts **1** SL4 210 C6
Beaumont Ct SL3 ..206 D7
Beaumont Rd
  Slough SL2 ....205 D8

Beaumont Rd *continued*
Windsor SL4 .210 C5
Beaumont Rise SL7 .183 E2
Beaumont Way HP15 .162 F4
Beaver Cl MK18 .52 E7
Beaverbrook Ct MK3 .47 A1
Bec La MK15 .35 B7
Beckets Sq HP4 .135 A6
Beckett Chase 5 SL3 .206 F1
Beckings Way HP10 .185 C7
Beckinsale Gr MK8 .45 E7
Beckwell Rd SL1 .205 C4
Bedder Rd HP12 .172 C3
Beddoes Croft MK5 .45 E4
Bede Ct HP4 .121 C8
Bedfont Court Est TW19 .213 B4
Bedfont Rd TW19 .213 F1
Bedford Ave
Little Chalfont HP6 .166 D8
Slough SL1 .205 A7
Bedford Cl Chenies WD3 .156 B1
Maidenhead SL6 .202 A3
Bedford Ct HP6 .166 D8
Bedford Dr SL2 .198 B6
Bedford Rd
Aspley Guise MK17 .49 F5
Cold Brayfield MK46 .8 B5
Cranfield MK43 .25 C2
Sherington MK16 .14 A1
Bedford Rd E NN7 .1 D5
Bedford Rd W NN7 .1 A6
Bedford St
Berkhamsted HP4 .135 D4
Milton Keynes,Bletchley MK2 .58 C8
Milton Keynes,Wolverton MK12 .33 D6
Woburn MK17 .60 F7
Bedgebury Pl MK7 .48 A8
Bedgrove HP21 .116 C6
Bedgrove Inf Sch HP21 .116 C5
Bedgrove Jun Sch HP21 .116 C6
Bedlam La MK16 .14 C1
Bedlam Wlk MK16 .14 C1
Bedwins La SL6 .195 B6
Bedwyn Wlk HP21 .115 D4
Beech 2 RG9 .191 D2
Beech Ave
Lane End HP14 .171 C5
Olney MK46 .6 E3
Beech Cl Bierton HP22 .102 B3
Buckingham MK18 .41 D2
Flackwell Heath HP10 .174 A2
High Wycombe HP11 .173 F4
Maidenhead SL6 .202 B8
Stokenchurch HP14 .158 F3
Beech Ct
Berkhamsted HP4 .135 D4
3 Marlow SL7 .183 E2
Beech Dr HP4 .135 C3
Beech Fern MK7 .48 A5
Beech Gn HP21 .115 D6
Beech Gr Amersham HP7 165 D8
Leighton Buzzard LU7 .80 E7
Tring HP23 .119 C4
Beech Hill Ct HP4 .135 D5
Beech House Dr NN12 .18 F4
Beech La
Prestwood HP16 .151 B7
Seer Green HP9 .176 E3
Beech Leys MK18 .63 E3
Beech Pk
Little Chalfont HP6 .155 B1
Naphill HP14 .150 A1
Wigginton HP23 .133 F5
Beech Rd
Aylesbury HP21 .115 D6
Chinnor OX39 .147 C6
High Wycombe HP11 .173 F4
Newport Pagnell MK16 .22 B3
Princes Risborough HP27 .139 C3
Slough SL3 .206 E4
Beech St HP11 .173 C4
Beech Tree Cl MK19 .20 D2
Beech Tree Ct HP22 .87 A6
Beech Tree Rd HP15 .163 C7
Beech Waye SL9 .189 A4
Beech Wlk HP23 .119 B4
Beechams The MK17 .67 D6
Beechcroft HP4 .135 C3
Beechcroft Rd
Chesham HP5 .144 B1
Milton Keynes MK3 .57 E6
Beeches Dr SL2 .198 B7
Beeches Gr HP10 .163 A2
Beeches Pk HP9 .175 D2
Beeches Rd SL2 .198 B7
Beeches The
Amersham HP6 .154 A3
Chorleywood WD3 .167 F4
Deanshanger MK19 .31 E3
Milton Keynes MK1 .47 E1
Tring HP23 .119 C4
Uxbridge UB8 .201 C1
Wendover HP22 .131 C5
Beeches Way SL1 .197 C2
Beechfield Pl SL6 .202 C4
Beechfield Way HP15 .163 B3
Beechfield Wlk HP15 .163 A3
Beechingstoke 4 SL7 .183 F3
Beechlands HP15 .162 E2
Beechtree Ave SL7 .183 D5
Beechview Sch HP13 .173 E5
Beechwood Ave
Chorleywood WD3 .167 B5
Little Chalfont HP6 .155 C1

Beechwood Ave *continued*
Uxbridge UB8 .208 F7
Beechwood Cl HP6 .166 C8
Beechwood Cotts WD3 .167 B3
Beechwood Ct
Aston Clinton HP22 .118 A3
Dunstable LU6 .93 F7
Beechwood Dr
Aldbury HP23 .120 D5
Maidenhead SL6 .202 A6
Marlow SL7 .194 B8
Beechwood Gdns SL1 .205 E4
Beechwood Ho HP22 .117 F5
Beechwood La HP22 .131 D5
Beechwood Pk
Chorleywood WD3 .167 F5
Felden HP3 .146 F7
Beechwood Pl 13 HP13 .173 B7
Beechwood Rd
Beaconsfield HP9 .175 C2
High Wycombe HP12 .161 B2
Slough SL2 .205 D8
Beechwood Sch SL2 .198 B2
Beechwood Way HP22 .117 F5
Beecroft Lower Sch LU6 .93 F8
Beecroft Way LU6 .93 F8
Beehive Cl UB10 .201 F5
Beel Cl HP7 .166 C8
Beethoven Cl MK7 .48 E4
Beeward Cl MK12 .33 A5
Beggars La HP23 .119 F4
Bekonscot Ct MK14 .21 F1
Bekonscot Model Village★ HP9 .175 E4
Belfast Ave SL1 .205 D7
Belgrave Mews UB8 .201 D1
Belgrave Par SL1 .205 E6
Belgrave Pl 6 SL1 .206 A4
Belgrave Rd
Aylesbury HP19 .101 A3
Slough SL1 .205 F6
Bell Ave UB7 .208 F3
Bell Bsns Ctr SL6 .202 F6
Bell Bsns Pk HP19 .100 F1
Bell Cl Beaconsfield HP9 .175 F2
Cublington LU7 .78 B1
Drayton Parslow MK17 .68 B6
Princes Risborough HP27 .139 B3
Slough SL2 .206 B8
Thame OX9 .125 E1
Bell Cres HP27 .138 E6
Bell Ct SL6 .193 F3
Bell Gn HP3 .146 B4
Bell La Berkhamsted HP4 .134 E5
Eton Wick SL4 .204 F2
Henley-on-T RG9 .191 E3
Little Chalfont HP6 .155 C1
Princes Risborough HP27 .139 B3
Syresham NN13 .27 B8
Thame OX9 .125 F1
Bell Lane Comb Sch HP6 .155 B1
Bell Leys HP22 .89 B3
Bell St Henley-on-T RG9 .191 E2
Maidenhead SL6 .202 F6
Princes Risborough HP27 .139 B3
Bell Street Mews RG9 .191 E2
Bell View SL4 .209 F5
Bell View Cl SL4 .209 F5
Bell Wlk Wingrave HP22 .89 B3
Winslow MK18 .65 F3
Bellamy Rd HP13 .173 C8
Bellclose Rd UB7 .208 E4
Belle Vue HP17 .114 C5
Bellfield Rd HP13 .173 A8
Bellfield Rd W HP11 .172 F7
Bellfounder Ho MK13 .34 B4
Bellingdon Rd HP5 .144 B1
Bellini Cl MK7 .48 D5
Bellis Gr MK6 .47 C8
Bellridge Pl HP9 .175 B6
Bells Hill SL2 .199 A4
Bells Hill Gn SL2 .199 A5
Bells La SL3 .212 B4
Bells Mdw MK15 .35 B7
Bellsfield Ct SL4 .204 F2
Bellswood La SL0 .207 B8
Bellway MK17 .49 A6
Bellwether MK11 .33 A4
Bellwood Rise HP11 .173 B4
Belmers Rd HP23 .119 D1
Belmont SL2 .205 A8
Belmont Cl UB8 .201 D6
Belmont Cotts SL3 .212 C7
Belmont Cres SL6 .202 D8
Belmont Ct MK8 .33 C2
Belmont Dr SL6 .202 D8
Belmont Park Ave SL6 .202 D8
Belmont Park Rd SL6 .202 D8
Belmont Rd
Chesham HP5 .144 B3
Maidenhead SL6 .202 D8
Uxbridge UB8 .201 D5
Belmont Vale SL6 .202 D8
Belsize Ave MK6 .35 B1
Belsize Cotts WD3 .156 E6
Belton Rd HP4 .135 A5
Belvedere Cl HP6 .154 F2
Belvedere La MK17 .58 F8
Belvedere Mans SL1 .205 D4
Belvedere Rdbt MK9 .34 F4
Belvoir Ave MK4 .46 C1
Bembridge Ct 11 SL1 .205 F4
Ben More SL9 .188 F6
Benacre Croft MK4 .57 A8
Benbow Ct MK5 .46 A7
Benbow Way UB8 .208 C8
Bench Manor Cres SL9 .177 C1

Bencombe Rd SL7 .183 E5
Benen-Stock Rd TW19 .213 A2
Benham Cl HP5 .144 B1
Benhams La RG9 .180 D2
Benison Ct 11 SL1 .205 F3
Benjamin Ho 10 HP13 .173 B7
Benjamin Rd HP13 .173 B8
Benjamins Footpath HP13 .173 B8
Bennet Cl MK11 .32 D4
Bennet's Yd UB8 .201 D5
Bennett End Rd HP14 .159 C7
Bennett's Hill MK18 .76 C8
Bennetts HP5 .144 D1
Bennetts Cl Padbury MK18 53 B1
Slough SL1 .205 A5
Bennetts La HP22 .102 E8
Benning Ave LU6 .93 F8
Benning Cl SL4 .209 D4
Benningfield Gdns HP4 .135 E6
Bens Cl MK19 .19 F5
Benson Cl Slough SL2 .206 A5
Uxbridge UB8 .208 E8
Bentall Cl MK15 .35 C7
Bentinck Cl SL9 .188 D6
Bentinck Ct UB7 .208 D5
Bentinck Rd UB7 .208 D5
Bentley Ct SL6 .202 D5
Bentley Pk SL1 .197 D3
Bentley Rd SL1 .205 A5
Benton Dr OX39 .147 C7
Bentons The HP4 .134 F6
Benwell Cl MK13 .33 F5
Benwells OX39 .147 C6
Berberis Cl MK7 .48 A5
Berberis Wlk UB7 .208 E2
Bercham MK8 .33 E2
Beresford Ave
Aylesbury HP19 .101 C3
Slough SL2 .206 C6
Beresford Cl MK4 .46 B3
Beresford Rd WD3 .167 F1
Beretun MK8 .33 E1
Bereville Ct MK10 .35 E3
Berevilles La MK10 .35 E3
Bergamot Gdns MK7 .48 B5
Berkeley Ave HP5 .143 F1
Berkeley Cl
Chesham HP5 .144 A1
Stoke Goldington MK16 .12 B6
Berkeley Mews
Marlow SL7 .183 F2
Slough SL1 .204 E7
Berkeley Rd
Loudwater HP10 .174 C2
Thame OX9 .126 A1
Berkeley Rise HP19 .101 B2
Berkhampstead Rd HP5 144 C2
Berkhamsted Castle★ HP4 .135 D5
Berkhamsted Collegiate Sch
Berkhamsted HP4 .135 B4
Berkhamsted HP4 .135 C4
Berkhamsted Sta HP4 .135 C5
Berkley Cl
Maidenhead SL6 .202 A8
Pitstone LU7 .105 D3
Berkley Ct HP4 .135 C4
Berkley Rd HP9 .175 D6
Berks Hill WD3 .167 C4
Berkshire Ave SL1 .205 B7
Berkshire Gn MK5 .45 F3
Berkshire Lodge 1 SL6 202 F6
Berling Rd MK8 .33 F2
Bernard Cl HP18 .112 F2
Bernard's Cl HP18 .112 B2
Bernardines Way MK18 .52 E7
Bernards Cl HP16 .152 A7
Bernards Way HP10 .174 A2
Bernay Gdns MK15 .35 B7
Berndene Rise HP27 .139 B4
Berners Cl SL1 .204 E6
Bernewode Cl HP18 .125 C7
Bernstein Cl MK7 .48 C4
Bernwood Forest Nature Reserve HP18 .108 E3
Berrell's Ct MK46 .6 F3
Berries Rd SL6 .196 A8
Berry Field SL2 .206 C7
Berry Field Pk HP6 .154 B2
Berry Hill SL6 .203 D8
Berry Hill Ct SL6 .203 D8
Berry La
Aspley Guise MK17 .49 F6
Chorleywood WD3 .167 D3
Berry Way MK17 .57 D4
Berryfield LU7 .104 F7
Berryfield Rd
Aylesbury HP19 .101 B3
Princes Risborough HP27 .139 C4
Berrystead MK7 .48 B3
Bertram Cl MK13 .34 B8
Berwald Cl MK7 .48 D4
Berwick Ave SL1 .205 B6
Berwick Cl
Beaconsfield HP9 .176 B1
Marlow SL7 .183 D3
Berwick Dr MK3 .46 F2
Berwick La SL7 .183 D3
Berwick Rd SL7 .183 C3
Bessemer Cl 2 SL3 .206 F1
Bessemer Cres HP19 .100 E1
Bessemer Ct MK14 .22 A1
Bestobell Rd SL1 .205 C7
Betjeman Ct UB7 .208 D5
Bettina Gr MK2 .58 C7
Bettles Cl UB8 .201 C3
Bettles Ct UB8 .201 C3

Betty's Cl MK17 .57 D3
Betty's La HP23 .119 A4
Bevan Ct MK18 .65 F4
Bevan Hill HP5 .144 B2
Bevelwood Gdns HP12 .172 D7
Beverley Cl SL7 .183 B2
Beverley Ct SL1 .206 B4
Beverley Gdns SL6 .195 B1
Beverley Pl MK6 .35 B2
Bewcastle Row MK4 .45 E1
Bewdley Dr LU7 .80 C7
Bexley St SL4 .210 C6
Bicester Rd
Aylesbury HP19 .101 B2
Long Crendon HP18 .125 C6
Ludgershall HP18 .96 C8
Marsh Gibbon OX27 .71 E3
Oakley HP18 .109 D5
Twyford MK18 .62 C1
Bickleigh Cres MK4 .46 D3
Biddles Cl SL1 .204 E5
Biddlesden Rd NN13 .39 A5
Bideford Ct LU7 .80 C8
Bideford Gn LU7 .80 C8
Bideford Spur SL2 .198 B2
Bierton CE Comb Sch HP22 .102 B3
Bierton Rd HP20 .101 F1
Bigfrith La SL6 .195 B6
Biggs La HP17 .113 E2
Bigmore La
Beacon's Bottom HP14 .170 B8
Stokenchurch HP14 .159 C1
Bignell Croft MK5 .34 B1
Biko Cl UB8 .208 C7
Bilbrook La MK4 .46 C4
Billet La
Berkhamsted HP4 .135 A6
Iver SL0,SL3 .207 B7
Billings Cl HP14 .158 F5
Billingwell Pl MK6 .35 B2
Billwell HP18 .125 C6
Bilton Rd MK1 .47 D2
Binders Ind Est HP15 .162 D7
Bingham Cl MK4 .46 C1
Bingham Rd SL1 .204 A8
Binghams The SL6 .203 B3
Birch Ave UB7 .208 F7
Birch Cl Amersham HP6 .154 E2
Iver Heath SL0 .200 D3
Birch Cres UB10 .201 F4
Birch Ct HP21 .115 D5
Birch Dr WD3 .178 D5
Birch Gdns HP7 .165 E8
Birch Gr Slough SL2 .205 B8
Windsor SL4 .209 D6
Birch La HP3 .156 B7
Birch Rd HP4 .134 D7
Birch St HP11 .173 B3
Birch Tree Gr HP5 .145 B1
Birch Way Chesham HP5 .144 D2
Tylers Green HP10 .163 B1
Birchdale SL9 .188 D3
Birchen Lee MK4 .46 C2
Birches Rise HP12 .172 E8
Birches The Felden HP3 .146 F8
High Wycombe HP13 .173 E8
Birchfield Gr MK2 .58 C7
Birchington Rd SL4 .210 A5
Birchmoor Gn MK17 .60 F8
Birchwood Chase HP15 151 D1
Birchwood Cl HP12 .172 B6
Bird Mount Cotts SL4 .210 C8
Birdcage Wlk HP13 .173 B6
Birdlip La MK7 .48 B7
Birds La MK16 .12 B6
Birdwood Rd SL6 .202 B7
Birfield Rd HP10 .174 C2
Birinus Ct HP12 .172 C5
Birkdale Cl MK3 .57 D7
Birkett Way HP8 .166 D6
Birley Rd SL1 .205 D7
Bisham Abbey National Sports Ctr SL7 .194 D7
Bisham CE Prim Sch SL7 .194 D7
Bisham Ct Bisham SL7 .194 E6
10 Slough SL1 .205 F4
Bisham Gn SL7 .194 E6
Bisham Rd Bisham SL7 .194 E8
Marlow SL7 .183 E1
Bishop Ct SL6 .202 D6
Bishop Ctr The SL6 .203 F7
Bishop Parker RC Comb Sch MK2 .58 C6
Bishop Wood CE Jun Sch HP23 .119 A3
Bishops Ct MK18 .52 C7
Bishops Farm Cl SL4 .209 B6
Bishops Field HP22 .118 A4
Bishops Ho HP9 .175 D3
Bishops Mdw HP22 .102 A3
Bishops Orch SL2 .198 B2
Bishops Rd SL1 .206 A4
Bishops Wlk
Aylesbury HP21 .115 F6
Woburn Sands MK17 .49 B3
Wooburn Green HP10 .185 E5
Bishopshalt Sch UB8 .201 F2
Bishopstone
Milton Keynes MK13 .34 B5
Stone HP17 .115 A1
Bishopstone Rd HP17 .114 D5
Bissley Dr SL6 .202 A3
Bit The HP23 .119 D1
Bittenham Cl HP17 .114 D4
Bittern Way 4 HP20 .101 E3
Bix Hill RG9 .191 A6

Bix La SL6 .194 F1
Black Acre Cl HP7 .165 E8
Black Boy La SL6 .193 C3
Black Butt Cotts SL6 .196 B7
Black Horse Ave HP5 .154 D6
Black Horse Cl SL4 .209 D5
Black Horse Pl UB8 .201 C4
Black Park Ctry Pk★ SL0,SL3 .200 A4
Black Park Ctry Pk Visitor Ctr★ SL3 .199 F2
Black Park Rd SL3 .199 E4
Blackamoor La SL6 .203 A8
Blackberry Ct MK7 .48 B6
Blackburn Trad Est TW19 .213 F1
Blackdown MK11 .32 F4
Blacketts Wood Dr WD3 .167 B5
Blackfield La HP16 .142 E3
Blackham Ct MK6 .46 E7
Blackheath Cres MK13 .34 D3
Blackhill Dr MK12 .33 A6
Blackhorse Cl HP6 .154 E1
Blackhorse Cres HP6 .154 E1
Blackmoor Gate MK4 .46 E2
Blackmore Gate HP22 .118 A4
Blackmore Way UB8 .201 D6
Blackpond La SL2 .198 B4
Blacksmith La HP16 .151 C6
Blacksmith Row SL3 .207 A2
Blacksmith's La UB9 .189 D2
Blacksmiths Rd HP27 .138 D7
Blackthorn Cl OX25 .81 A3
Blackthorn Dell 2 SL3 .206 C3
Blackthorn Gr MK17 .49 A4
Blackthorne Cres SL3 .212 E5
Blackthorne Ind Pk SL3 .212 E5
Blackthorne La HP16 .142 E3
Blackthorne Rd SL3 .212 E4
Blackwater Dr HP21 .115 C4
Blackwell End NN12 .18 C3
Blackwell Hall La HP5 .155 C6
Blackwell Pl MK5 .46 A4
Blackwell Rd HP14 .171 B5
Blackwells Yd NN7 .1 B6
Blackwood Cres MK13 .33 E6
Blaine Cl HP23 .119 A6
Blair Rd SL1 .205 E5
Blairmont St MK9 .34 F4
Blake Way OX9 .126 A1
Blakedown Rd LU7 .80 C6
Blakeney Ct
Maidenhead SL6 .195 F1
Milton Keynes MK4 .57 B8
Blakes Ho HP10 .174 C2
Blanchland Circ MK10 .36 A1
Blandford Cl SL3 .206 D3
Blandford Ho SL6 .202 C8
Blandford Rd N SL3 .206 D3
Blandford Rd S SL3 .206 D3
Blansby Chase MK4 .46 C3
Blatherwick Ct MK5 .45 F7
Blaydon Cl MK3 .57 D6
Bleak Hall Rdbt MK6 .47 A5
Bleasdale MK13 .34 C5
Bledlow Bridge Halt★ HP27 .138 C2
Bledlow Cotts HP27 .138 C1
Bledlow Rd HP27 .148 E8
Bledlow Ridge Rd HP14 148 C8
Bledlow Ridge Sch HP14 .159 F8
Blegberry Gdns HP4 .134 E4
Blenheim Ave MK11 .32 E4
Blenheim Cl
Cheddington LU7 .104 F8
Longwick HP27 .138 D6
Slough SL3 .206 F5
Blenheim Ct HP13 .173 B7
Blenheim Pl
Aylesbury HP21 .115 E5
Syresham NN13 .27 C7
Blenheim Rd
High Wycombe HP12 .172 D4
Maidenhead SL6 .202 B8
Slough SL3 .206 D2
Bletcham Rdbt MK1 .47 E3
Bletcham Way
Milton Keynes MK1 .47 C2
Milton Keynes MK1 .47 E2
Walton Park MK7 .48 B4
Bletchley Com Hospl MK3 .47 A1
Bletchley Park Mus★ MK3 .58 A8
Bletchley Rd
Milton Keynes MK5 .46 B4
Newton Longville MK17 .57 D4
Stewkley LU7 .68 D3
Bletchley Sta MK3 .58 B8
Blinco La SL3 .206 E7
Blind La
Bourne End HP10,SL8 .185 B5
South Heath HP16 .153 B8
Blind Pond Ind Est MK17 48 D2
Bliss Ave MK43 .25 C2
Bliss Ct MK7 .48 C4
Blisworth MK6 .47 D5
Blondell Cl UB7 .213 D8
Bloomfield Cotts HP5 .143 E7
Bloomfield Rd SL6 .202 A5
Bloomsbury Cl MK17 .60 F6
Blossom Way UB10 .201 F5
Blucher St HP5 .154 B8

Blue Max Mus★ SL7 ....172 A2
Bluebell Cl MK18 ....52 C7
Bluebell Croft MK7 .....48 B6
Blumfield Cres SL1 .....204 E8
Blumfield Ct SL1 ....197 D1
Blundells Rd MK13 ......34 C6
Blunden Dr SL3 ....207 C2
Blyth Ct MK4 ....57 A8
Blythe Cl Aylesbury HP21 115 C5
Iver SL0 ....207 F7
Newport Pagnell MK16 ....22 D3
Blythe Hos SL1 ....204 D5
Blyton Cl HP9 ....175 D4
Boadicea Cl SL1 ....204 E5
Boarlands Cl SL1 ....204 F6
Boarstall Duck Decoy★
HP18 ....95 A3
Boathouse Reach RG9 ...191 E1
Bobmore La SL7 ....183 F3
Bockmer La SL7 ....193 B7
Boddington Rd HP22 ....131 C4
Bodenham Cl MK18 ......52 F8
Bodiam Cl
Aylesbury HP21 ....116 B5
Milton Keynes MK5 ......46 A5
Bodiam Ho 6 HP13 ......173 F7
Bodle Cl MK15 ....35 A7
Bodley Ho SL0 ....200 D3
Bodmin Ave SL2 ....205 A8
Bodnant Cl MK4 ....45 F2
Bois Ave HP6 ....154 B3
Bois Hill HP5 ....154 E5
Bois La HP6 ....154 D4
Bois Moor Rd HP5 ....154 D5
Bolan Ct MK8 ....45 E6
Bold's Ct SL2 ....199 A5
Bolter End La HP14 .....171 A6
Bolton Ave SL4 ....210 D4
Bolton Cl MK3 ....47 A2
Bolton Cres SL4 ....210 C4
Bolton Rd SL4 ....210 C4
Boltwood Gr MK5 ....45 E5
Bond Ave MK1 ....47 D3
Bond Cl Aylesbury HP21 ..115 B6
Iver Heath SL0 ....200 B5
West Drayton UB7 ....208 F7
Bone Hill MK18 ....52 C7
Bonham Carter Rd
HP22 ....131 E7
Bonham Cl HP21 ....115 B6
Bonham Cl HP22 ....117 D5
Bonnards Rd MK17 ......57 D4
Bonnersfield HP18 ......125 C7
Booker Ave MK13 ....34 D4
Booker Hill Sch HP12 ...172 B5
Booker La HP12 ....172 D7
Booker Pl HP12 ....172 B3
Bookerhill Rd HP12 .....172 C6
Boot La HP17 ....113 E2
Booth Pl LU6 ....92 E6
Borderside SL2 ....206 A7
Borodin Ct MK7 ....48 D5
Boroma Way RG9 ....191 E2
Borough Ct NN13 ....38 A5
Borough Rd NN13 ....38 A5
Borough Wlk MK9 ....34 E3
Bosanquet Cl UB8 ......201 D1
Boss La
Great Kingshill HP15 ....162 B8
Hughenden Valley HP14 ..162 B6
Bossiney Pl MK6 ....34 F1
Bossington La LU7 ......80 E7
Bostock Ct MK18 ....52 C8
Boston Dr SL8 ....185 B3
Boston Gr SL1 ....205 C7
Boswell Ct MK18 ....41 E2
Boswell La MK19 ....31 E4
Boswick La HP4 ....134 D8
Bosworth Cl MK3 ....46 E2
Bosworth Ct SL1 ....204 C6
Botham Dr SL1 ....205 E3
Botley La HP5 ....145 A1
Botley Rd HP5 ....144 E1
Bottesford Cl MK3 ......46 D1
Bottle Dump Rdbt MK17 .56 E6
Bottle Square La HP14 ..159 D6
Bottom Dr LU6 ....93 D5
Bottom House Farm La
HP8 ....165 E2
Bottom House La HP23 ..120 A1
Bottom La HP9 ....176 C5
Bottom Orch HP18 ......112 C1
Bottom Rd
Bledlow Ridge HP14 .....160 B5
Buckland Common HP23 ..132 C4
Bottom Waltons Caravan Site
SL2 ....197 D3
Bottrells La HP8 ....176 E8
Botyl Rd MK18 ....74 C6
Boughton Bsns Pk HP6 ..166 B8
Boughton Way SL6 ......155 C1
Boulevard The MK9 ......34 E2
Boulmer Rd UB8 ....201 C2
Boulters Cl
Maidenhead SL6 ....196 C1
Slough SL1 ....205 A4
Boulters Ct
Amersham HP6 ....154 E1
Maidenhead SL6 ....196 C1
Boulters Gdns SL6 ......196 C1
Boulters La SL6 ....196 C1
Boulters Lock SL6 ......196 C1
Boundary Cotts WD4 ....146 E2
Boundary Cres MK11 ....32 E6
Boundary Pl HP10 ......185 D8

Boundary Rd
Brackley NN13 ....38 A6
Chalfont St Peter SL9 ...177 D3
Loudwater HP10 ....174 C1
Taplow SL6 ....203 F8
Wooburn Green HP10 ....185 D8
Boundary The MK6 ......46 F8
Bounds Croft MK12 .....33 C4
Bounty St MK13 ....33 F7
Bouquet Cl HP16 ....151 C5
Bourbon St HP20 ....115 D8
Bourton Ave MK18 ......41 D2
Bourne Cl SL8 ....185 B5
Bourne End MK43 ....25 C6
Bourne End Bsns Ctr
SL8 ....185 B3
Bourne End Mills Ind Est
HP1 ....146 B8
Bourne End Rd
Bourne End SL6,SL8 .....196 E8
Cranfield MK43 ....25 C4
Bourne End Sta SL8 .....185 A3
Bourne Rd
Berkhamsted HP4 ......134 F5
Slough SL1 ....205 D4
Bourne The SL8 ....146 A4
Bourton Low MK7 ......48 B5
Bourton Meadow Sch
MK18 ....52 F8
Bourton Rd MK18 ......52 E8
Bourtonville MK18 ......52 D8
Bouverie Way SL3 .....206 E2
Boveney Cl SL1 ....205 A4
Boveney New Rd SL4 ...204 C2
Boveney Rd SL4 ....204 D1
Boveney Wood La SL1 ..186 A1
Bovingdon Ct HP3 ......146 A3
Bovingdon Hts SL7 .....183 B2
Bovingdon Prim Sch
HP3 ....146 B4
Bow Brickhill CE Fst Sch
MK17 ....48 D2
Bow Brickhill Rd MK17 ..48 F3
Bow Brickhill Sta MK7 ..48 B2
Bowden La HP11 ....173 D5
Bowen Cl MK7 ....48 C5
Bower Cl SL1 ....204 F6
Bower Ct SL1 ....204 F6
Bower La LU6 ....92 F5
Bower Way SL1 ....204 E6
Bowerbank Ct HP20 ....101 F1
Bowerdean Rd HP13 ....173 D7
Bowers La HP14 ....159 D7
Bowes Cl MK16 ....22 C3
Bowes-Lyon Cl 7 SL4 ..210 C6
Bowl Rdbt The MK6 ....46 D5
Bowland Dr MK4 ....46 B1
Bowler Lea HP16 ......161 D2
Bowler Rd HP21 ....115 E4
Bowler's Orch HP8 .....177 A7
Bowles Pl MK6 ....47 D7
Bowling Alley HP21 ....86 D7
Bowling Cl UB10 ......201 F4
Bowling Ct RG9 ....191 D3
Bowling Gn HP14 ......158 D5
Bowling Green Rd MK43 .25 C1
Bowling Leys MK10 ....36 A2
Bowmans Cl SL1 ....197 B3
Bowmont Dr HP21 .....115 D4
Bowood Ct 8 MK8 .....33 F1
Bowood Rd HP22 ......141 E5
Bowry Dr TW19 ....211 F1
Bowstridge Ct 6 HP13 ..173 C7
Bowstridge La HP8 .....177 C5
Bowyer Cres UB9 ......189 F5
Bowyer Dr SL1 ....204 E6
Bowyers Mews MK14 ...34 F6
Box La HP3 ....146 E7
Box Tree Cl HP15 ......154 D6
Boxberry Gdns MK7 ....48 A6
Boxer Rd HP27 ....138 E6
Boxgrove Ct MK10 .....36 A1
Boxmoor House Com Specl
Sch HP3 ....146 F8
Boxwell Rd HP4 ....135 B4
Boxwood Cl UB7 ......208 F4
Boyce Cres MK7 ....48 E5
Boycott Ave MK6 ......34 E1
Boyle Cl UB10 ....201 F3
Boyn Hill Ave SL6 .....202 D6
Boyn Hill Cl SL6 ......202 D6
Boyn Hill Rd SL6 ......202 D6
Boyn Valley Rd SL6 ....202 D5
Boyndon Rd SL6 ......202 D7
Boyne Hill CE Inf Sch
SL6 ....202 D6
Boyne Ho HP9 ....175 C1
Bozenham Mill La NN7 ..9 F5
Bracken Cl SL2 ....198 D8
Bracken Hill HP4 ......135 E5
Bracken Rd SL6 ....202 C4
Bracken Way
Aylesbury HP21 ....115 B8
Flackwell Heath HP10 ...185 B7
Brackenforde SL3 ......206 C4
Brackens The HP11 .....173 C5
Brackenwood HP14 .....161 C7
Brackley Dr HP15 ......163 A6
Brackley La MK18 ......73 B6
Brackley Rd
Chackmore MK18 ....41 B1
Hazelmere HP15 ....163 A6
Westbury NN13 ....39 B5
Bradbery WD3 ....178 D5
Bradbourne Dr MK7 ....48 C3
Bradbury Cl MK13 .....34 A3
Bradbury Gdns SL3 ....199 D8
Bradcutts La SL6 ......195 E8

Braddenham Wlk HP21 ..115 E4
Braddons Furlong HP18 .125 C6
Braden Cl HP21 ....116 A6
Bradenham Beeches
HP14 ....161 A8
Bradenham La SL7 .....194 C5
Bradenham Rd HP14 ...161 A3
Bradenham Wood La
Naphill HP14 ....150 B1
Walter's Ash HP14 .....161 A7
Bradfield Ave MK18 ....41 D2
Bradford Gdns MK5 ....46 B4
Bradford Rd
Heronsgate WD3 ....167 C2
Slough SL1 ....205 A7
Bradley Cl HP18 ....109 D5
Bradley Gr MK2 ....46 B2
Bradley Rd SL1 ....205 E6
Bradshaw Cl SL4 ......209 E6
Bradshaw Rd HP13 ....173 F6
Bradshawe Waye UB8 ..208 F8
Bradvue Cres MK13 ....34 B6
Bradwell Common Bvd
MK13 ....34 C3
Bradwell Rd
Milton Keynes MK5,MK8 .34 A1
Milton Keynes,Bradville
MK13 ....34 A4
Milton Keynes,Loughton
MK5 ....46 B8
Bradwell Village Mid Sch
MK13 ....34 B4
Bradwell Village YH★
MK13 ....34 A3
Brae Hill HP18 ....110 A8
Brae Hill Cl HP18 .....110 A8
Braeburn Cl SL1 ......205 C4
Braemar Ct 5 SL7 .....183 D2
Braemar Gdns SL1 ....205 A4
Braeside HP14 ....161 C6
Braford Gdns MK5 ....46 B4
Bragenham La LU7,MK17 .70 D5
Bragenham Side MK17 ..69 F7
Bragmans La WD4 .....156 E6
Brahms Cl MK7 ....48 C5
Braid The HP5 ....144 E1
Brakynbery HP4 ....134 E7
Bramber Cl MK3 ......57 E7
Bramber Cl SL1 ....205 A5
Bramble Ave MK14 ....34 E4
Bramble Cl
Chalfont St Peter SL9 ..177 E4
Uxbridge UB8 ....208 F7
Bramble Cres HP15 ....163 C6
Bramble Dr SL6 ....202 A4
Bramble La HP7 ......165 E6
Bramble Mead HP8 ....177 B7
Brambles The UB7 .....208 B2
Brambleside HP11 .....174 B4
Brambling HP19 ......101 E3
Bramcote Cl HP20 ....116 C8
Bramley Chase SL6 ...202 C4
Bramley Cl SL6 ....202 C3
Bramley Ct MK43 ......3 F6
Bramley End HP14 ....151 A1
Bramley Grange MK2 ...58 D4
Bramley Mdws MK16 ...22 B3
Bramley Rd MK1 ......47 D3
Brammas Cl SL1 ......205 C3
Brampton Ct
Maidenhead SL6 ......203 B8
Milton Keynes MK13 ...34 A6
Branch Rd HP10 ......174 B2
Brandon Ct HP23 .....103 D7
Brandon Rd HP12 .....172 B3
Brands Hill Ave HP13 ..162 C4
Brands Rd SL3 ....212 B8
Brandville Rd UB7 ....208 E4
Bransgill Ct MK13 ....34 B4
Bransome Ave MK10 ..48 C8
Brantham Cl MK7 ....48 A3
Braunston MK6 ......47 D6
Bravenfield MK18 ....53 D7
Brawlings La SL9 .....178 A6
Bray Cl SL6 ....203 C3
Bray Ct Amersham HP6 .154 E1
Maidenhead SL6 ......203 C3
Bray Rd SL6 ....203 B5
Braybank SL6 ....203 D4
Braybourne Cl UB8 ...201 C6
Braybrooke Dr MK4 ...46 E4
Brayfield Ho MK46 .....8 B5
Brayfield Rd SL6 .....203 C4
Brays Cl HP6 ....153 C4
Brays Green La HP6 ...153 C4
Brays La HP6 ....153 C5
Brays Mdw HP6 ......153 C4
Brayton Ct MK5 ......46 C6
Braywick Park & Nature Ctr★
SL6 ....203 B3
Braywick Rd SL6 .....203 A4
Braywood Cotts SL4 ..209 A5
Braziers End HP5 .....133 C1
Breachwell Pl LU7 ....91 A1
Breakspear Rd N UB9 .190 E8
Breakspear Rd S UB10 .190 F2
Bream Cl SL7 ....194 C8
Breamore Cl MK8 .....45 F8
Brearley Ave MK6 ....46 E7
Brearley Cl UB8 ......201 E6
Breckland MK14 ......34 D6
Brecon Ct
Milton Keynes MK10 ...35 F1
Slough SL1 ....205 C4
Brecon Way HP13 ....172 E8
Bredward Cl SL1 .....197 B2
Bremen Gr MK5 ......46 A4
Brenchwood Cl HP13 ..161 C2

Brendon Ct MK4 ......46 D2
Brent MK6 ....47 D5
Brent Path HP21 .....115 D4
Brent Rd SL8 ....185 A4
Brentwood Way HP21 ..116 B6
Bretby Chase MK4 ....45 F3
Breton MK11 ....32 E6
Brew Twr SL7 ....183 D1
Brewhouse La HP22 ...88 E1
Brewster Cl MK5 .....45 D5
Briaily MK7 ....159 C2
Briar Cl SL6 ....204 B7
Briar Dene SL6 ......195 C1
Briar Glen SL6 ......195 E6
Briar Hill MK12 ......33 E4
Briar Lodge MK12 ....33 C8
Briar Way
Berkhamsted HP4 .....135 D3
Slough SL2 ....205 B8
Briars Cl HP19 ....101 B2
Briars The
High Wycombe HP11 ...173 C5
Holmer Green HP15 ...163 C7
Slough SL3 ....206 F1
Briarswood HP15 .....163 B3
Briarswood Cl HP14 ..158 E5
Briary View MK17 ....56 C8
Brices Mdw MK5 .....46 A3
Brick Cl MK11 ....33 C2
Brick Hill HP18 ......97 E1
Brick Kiln La HP22 ...102 B4
Brickfield La SL1 ....197 B4
Brickfields Way UB7 ..208 F3
Brickhill Manor Ct MK17 59 D5
Brickhill St
Giffard Park MK14 .....22 A1
Milton Keynes,Monkston Park
MK10 ....35 B2
Milton Keynes,Willen Park
MK15 ....35 C6
Walton Park MK7 .....48 A4
Brickhill Way MK18 ...73 B5
Bricks La HP14 ......159 C4
Brickwell Wlk HP15 ..163 B3
Bricstock HP22 ......88 D4
Bridens Way HP17 ...126 F6
Bridge Ave
Cookham Rise SL6 ....195 E6
Maidenhead SL6 .....203 A7
Bridge Bank Cl HP11 ..174 A3
Bridge Cl SL1 ....204 F6
Bridge Ct
Berkhamsted HP4 .....135 D4
Maidenhead SL6 .....203 C7
Bridge Farm Bldgs
HP17 ....128 B8
Bridge Ho
High Wycombe HP13 ..173 D6
West Drayton UB7 ....208 D5
Bridge Pl HP6 ....154 F1
Bridge Rd Cosgrove MK19 .19 E2
Ickford HP18 ....123 F2
Maidenhead SL6 .....203 B7
Stoke Bruerne NN12 ...9 A8
Uxbridge UB8 ....201 C3
Bridge St
Berkhamsted HP4 .....135 D4
Buckingham MK18 .....52 D8
Colnbrook SL3 ....212 D7
Great Kimble HP17 ...129 D1
High Wycombe HP11 ..173 A7
Leighton Buzzard LU7 ..80 F7
Olney MK46 ....6 F2
Thornborough MK18 ...54 B8
Turvey MK43 ....8 D5
Bridge Wlk MK19 .....31 E4
Bridgeford Ct MK6 ....46 E8
Bridgegate Bsns Pk
HP19 ....101 B1
Bridgeman Ct 5 SL4 ..210 A5
Bridgeman Dr SL4 ....210 A5
Bridgestone Dr SL8 ..185 C3
Bridgeturn Ave MK12 .33 D8
Bridgewater Ct
Little Gaddesden HP4 .121 C8
Slough SL3 ....207 A2
Bridgewater Hill HP4 ..134 C7
Bridgewater Ho MK18 ..52 C8
Bridgewater Mid Sch
HP4 ....135 A6
Bridgewater Monument★
HP4 ....120 E7
Bridgewater Rd HP4 ..135 B5
Bridgewater Terr SL4 ..210 D6
Bridgewater Way SL4 ..210 D6
Bridgeway
Cuddington HP18 .....112 C2
Milton Keynes MK13 ...34 A7
Bridgnorth Dr MK4 ...45 E1
Bridle Cl Maidenhead SL6 195 E1
Milton Keynes MK13 ...34 B6
Bridle Gate LU7 ......172 F6
Bridle Manor HP22 ...131 C8
Bridle Rd SL6 ....195 E1
Bridle Way HP4 ......135 A6
Bridleway
Buckland Common HP22 132 E5
Weston Turville HP22 ..116 F2
Bridleways MK13 .....131 K5
Bridlington Cres MK10 .36 A1
Bridlington Spur SL1 ..205 B4
Bridport Way SL2 ....198 B1
Briery Way HP6 ......154 E1
Brighton Spur SL2 ....198 B1
Brightwell Ave LU6 ...93 C7
Brightwell Ave MK5 ...46 A4
Brigidine Sch The SL4 .210 D4

Brill CE Comb Sch HP18 .96 B1
Brill Cl Maidenhead SL6 .202 D3
Marlow SL7 ....183 C2
Brill Ho SL6 ....202 C3
Brill Pl MK13 ....34 C3
Brill Rd Chilton HP18 ..111 A3
Horton-cum-S OX33 ...108 C6
Ludgershall HP18 .....96 B7
Oakley HP18 ....109 F5
Brimmers Hill HP15 ...162 F6
Brimmers Rd HP27 ...139 D2
Brimmers Way HP19 ..114 F8
Brimstone Way HP4 ...134 F6
Brindlebrook MK8 ....33 E1
Brindles Cl MK18 .....73 B5
Brindles La HP9 ......175 A4
Brindley Ave HP13 ....161 F1
Brinkburn Chase MK10 .36 A1
Brinkhurst SL7 ....183 D2
Brinklow Rdbt MK10 ..36 C1
Briskman Way HP21 ..115 B6
Bristle Hill HP18 .....52 C8
Bristol Ct TW19 ......213 E1
Bristol Ct 10 TW19 ...213 E1
Bristol Way SL1 ......205 F5
Bristow Ct MK2 ......47 C1
Britannia Ct UB7 .....208 D3
Britannia Ind Est
High Wycombe HP12 ..172 D7
Poyle SL3 ....212 E1
Britannia Rd 6 HP5 ..144 C2
Britannia St HP20 ....115 E8
Britnell Ct HP14 .....158 E5
Britten Gr MK7 ......48 D5
Brittens Ct MK46 ......7 C3
Brittons Cl MK17 .....37 C3
Britwell Dr HP4 ......135 E6
Britwell Gdns SL1 ....197 D2
Britwell Rd SL1 ......197 D2
Broad Arrow Cl MK14 .34 E7
Broad Dean MK6 .....47 A8
Broad Gn MK43 ......25 C3
Broad Leys HP9,HP10 ..186 A6
Broad Leys HP27 .....139 A3
Broad Oak SL2 ....198 C1
Broad Oak Ct SL2 ....198 C1
Broad Platts SL3 .....206 D3
Broad Rush Gn LU7 ...80 E8
Broad St Chesham HP5 .144 C1
Newport Pagnell MK16 .22 C4
Syresham NN13 ....27 B8
Broadfields HP19 .....101 A1
Broadfields Ct HP19 ..101 A1
Broadlands MK6 .....47 C5
Broadlands Ave HP5 ..144 C1
Broadleys SL4 ....209 F7
Broadmark Rd SL2 ...206 B6
Broadpiece MK15 ....35 A7
Broadview Rd HP5 ...144 B4
Broadwater
Berkhamsted HP4 .....135 C5
Milton Keynes MK6 ...47 D6
Broadwater Gdns UB9 .190 C7
Broadwater La UB9 ..190 C7
Broadwater Pk
Denham Green UB9 ...190 A5
Maidenhead SL6 .....203 E1
Broadway SL6 ....202 F7
Broadway Ave MK14 ..21 F2
Broadway Cl 5 HP7 ..165 B7
Broadway Ct HP5 ....154 B8
Broadway Par UB7 ...208 E4
Broadway The
Amersham HP7 ....165 B7
Beaconsfield HP9 ....175 D3
3 Chalfont St Peter SL9 177 D2
Chesham HP5 ....154 B8
Farnham Common SL2 .198 C6
Grendon Underwood HP18 .82 F6
Brocas St SL4 ....210 D7
Brocas Terr SL4 .....210 D7
Brocas Way LU7 ......91 A3
Brock La SL6 ....202 F7
Brockhampton MK15 ..35 B6
Brockhurst Rd SL6 ...144 C2
Brockton Ct SL2 .....202 F6
Brockway SL3 ....207 B1
Brockwell MK16 .....22 C4
Broddick Ho HP11 ...174 B4
Broken Furlong SL4 ..205 B1
Broken Gate La UB9 ..189 C3
Bromham Mill MK14 ..21 F2
Bromley HP23 ....104 A4
Bromley La HP6 .....153 C5
Brompton Cl HP19 ...101 B2
Brompton Cres HP19 .101 B2
Brompton Dr SL6 ....195 C2
Bromycroft Rd SL2 ..198 A2
Bronsdon Way UB9 ..189 F2
Bronte Cl HP19 ......100 F2
Brook Bsns Ctr UB8 ..201 B3
Brook Cl
Aston Clinton HP22 ...117 D5
Ludgershall HP18 .....96 C8
Brook Cres SL1 ......204 E7
Brook End
North Crawley MK16 ...24 A6
Weston Turville HP22 ..117 A3
Brook Ho Slough SL1 ..205 D3
West Drayton UB7 ....208 D5
Brook La
Berkhamsted HP4 .....135 B5
Harrold MK43 ....8 B3
Newton Blossomville MK43 .8 B3
Thame OX9 ....125 E1
Brook Path SL1 ......204 F6
Brook St
Aston Clinton HP22 ...117 D5

Brook St continued
Edlesborough LU6 ....92 F4
High Wycombe HP11 .173 A7
Tring HP23 ....119 B4
Windsor SL4 ....210 D5
Brookbank HP10 ....185 D3
Brookdene Cl SL6 ....195 F2
Brooke Cl MK3 ....57 F7
Brooke Furmston Pl
SL7 ....183 E3
Brooke Rd HP27 ....139 B4
Brookfield UB8 ....201 E6
Brookfield HP23 ....119 B4
Brookfield Ho SL3 ....211 D6
Brookfield La MK18 ....52 D7
Brookfield Rd
Haversham MK19 ....20 D2
Newton Longville MK17 ....57 D3
Wooburn HP10 ....185 D3
Brookhouse Dr HP10 ....185 C3
Brooklands Rd MK2 ....58 C7
Brooklyn Way UB7 ....208 D3
Brookmead Sch LU7 ....105 C5
Brooks Cl MK18 ....52 D8
Brookside Colnbrook SL3 212 C5
Halton HP22 ....117 C1
Lillingstone Lovell MK18 ....30 A6
Loudwater HP10 ....174 C2
Milton Keynes MK12 ....33 D4
Oakley HP18 ....109 D5
Slough SL3 ....206 E7
Thame OX9 ....125 F1
Uxbridge UB10 ....201 F5
Weston Turville HP22 ....117 A2
Brookside Ave TW19 ....211 E4
Brookside Cl
Old Stratford MK19 ....32 B6
Tiddington OX9 ....136 A2
Brookside La HP17 ....129 E3
Brookside Terr 5 HP21 .115 E8
Brooksward Comb Sch
MK14 ....34 F7
Brookway MK19 ....31 E4
Broom Cl HP15 ....163 A3
Broom Hill
Cookham Rise SL6 ....195 E6
Stoke Poges SL2 ....199 A5
Broom Ho SL3 ....206 F2
Broombarn La HP16 ....151 E7
Broomfield MK12 ....33 D4
Broomfield Cl HP16 ....151 E7
Broomfield Gate SL2 ....198 B1
Broomfield Hill HP16 ....151 E7
Broomlee MK13 ....34 A5
Broomstick Ind Est LU6 ....92 F4
Broomstick La HP5 ....145 A1
Brora Cl MK2 ....58 C5
Brotheridge Ct HP21 .115 B6
Brough Cl MK5 ....46 A5
Broughton Ave HP20 ....116 B8
Broughton Dr HP22 ....102 B3
Broughton Crossing
HP22 ....102 C2
Broughton Fields Comb Sch
MK10,MK16 ....36 A4
Broughton Grounds Com
Woodlands ★ MK16 ....36 E6
Broughton Inf Sch
HP20 ....116 B8
Broughton Jun Sch
HP20 ....116 B8
Broughton La HP20,
HP22 ....116 C8
Broughton Manor Bsns Pk
MK16 ....36 B4
Broughton Rd MK17 ....37 C3
Brow The HP8 ....177 D7
Brown's La HP23 ....132 F1
Brown's Rise HP23 ....132 F3
Brownbaker Ct MK14 ....34 F6
Browne Willis Cl MK2 ....58 D8
Brownfield Gdns SL6 ....202 E5
Browning Cl MK16 ....22 A4
Browning Cres MK3 ....58 A7
Brownlow Ave LU6 ....92 F3
Brownlow Gate HP4 ....107 A1
Brownlow La LU7 ....105 A4
Brownlow Rd HP4 ....135 C5
Brownlow Rise LU6 ....93 A8
Browns Ct SL1 ....204 E6
Browns Hedge LU7 ....105 C3
Browns Rd
Holmer Green HP15 ....163 C6
South Heath HP16 ....153 E5
Browns Way MK17 ....49 E5
Browns Wood Rdbt MK7 .48 C5
Brownset Dr MK4 ....45 E1
Brownsfield Rd NN12 ....18 E6
Brownswood Dr NN12 ....18 D3
Brownswood Rd HP9 .175 E4
Broxbourne Cl MK14 ....21 F2
Bruce Cl SL1 ....205 A5
Bruce Wlk SL4 ....209 D5
Brucewood Par SL7 ....183 E4
Bruckner Gdns MK7 ....48 D5
Brudenell SL4 ....209 F3
Brudenell Dr
Milton Keynes MK10 ....48 C8
Stoke Mandeville HP22 .116 B1
Brunel Cl SL6 ....202 E5
Brunel Ctr
Maidenhead SL6 ....202 D5
Milton Keynes MK2 ....58 C8
Brunel Rd
Aylesbury HP19 ....100 F1
High Wycombe HP13 ....161 F1
Maidenhead SL6 ....202 D5
Brunel Science Pk UB8 .201 E2

Brunel Univ UB8 ....201 E2
Brunel Way SL1 ....205 F5
Brunleys MK11 ....33 B3
Brunner Rd HP13 ....173 C6
Brunswick Cl HP19 ....101 B3
Brunswick Pl HP13 ....162 D2
Brushford MK4 ....46 A3
Brushwood Jun Sch
HP5 ....144 A2
Brushwood Rd HP5 ....144 B1
Bryans Cres MK18 ....24 A6
Bryanston Ave HP20 ....101 F2
Bryant Ave SL2 ....205 E8
Bryants Acre HP22 ....131 B6
Bryants Bottom Rd
HP16 ....150 F4
Bryden Cotts UB8 ....201 C1
Bryer Pl SL4 ....209 D4
Bryfield Cotts HP3 ....146 C1
Bryne La MK18 ....53 B2
Bryony Cl UB8 ....208 F3
Bryony Pl MK14 ....34 E5
Bsns Ctr The HP6 ....154 E1
Bsns Village The SL2 .206 B5
Buccleuch Rd SL3 ....211 B7
Buchan Cl UB8 ....201 C2
Buchanan Rd OX25 ....94 E7
Buckby MK6 ....47 B6
Buckfast Ave MK3 ....47 A2
Buckfield SL0 ....207 F4
Buckingham Ave E SL1 .205 C5
Buckingham Ave E SL1 .205 B2
Buckingham Canal Nature
Reserve ★ MK18 ....42 D3
Buckingham Cl HP13 ....174 A7
Buckingham Ct
Amersham HP6 ....154 E2
Brackley NN13 ....38 A6
Newport Pagnell MK16 ....22 B2
Buckingham Dr HP13 ....174 A7
Buckingham Gate
Medmenham SL7 ....193 D7
Milton Keynes MK6 ....35 D3
Buckingham Gdns SL1 .205 F4
Buckingham Ho
Amersham HP6 ....154 D3
4 Maidenhead SL6 ....202 F6
Buckingham Hospl MK18 41 D1
Buckingham Ind Pk
MK18 ....52 D6
Buckingham Par 4 SL9 177 D2
Buckingham Pl 1 HP13 173 A7
Buckingham Prim Sch
MK18 ....41 E2
Buckingham Rd
Aylesbury HP19,HP20 ....101 D3
Brackley NN13 ....38 A6
Deanshanger MK19 ....31 E2
Edgcott HP18 ....72 F2
Gawcott MK18 ....52 A5
Milton Keynes MK3 ....57 D7
Milton Keynes,Church Hill
MK17 ....56 E6
Steeple Claydon MK18 ....63 E3
Tring HP23 ....118 E3
Winslow MK18 ....65 F5
Buckingham Road Ind Est
NN13 ....38 A6
Buckingham Sch MK18 ....52 D6
Buckingham Sq MK9 ....34 C2
Buckingham St
8 Aylesbury HP20 ....101 D1
Milton Keynes MK12 ....33 D7
Tingewick MK18 ....51 B6
Buckingham View HP5 .144 C1
Buckingham Way HP10 .174 A1
Buckinghamshire Chilterns
Univ Coll
Chalfont St Peter HP8 .178 A7
High Wycombe HP11 ....173 A6
Buckinghamshire Chilterns
Univ Coll (Wellesbourne
Campus) HP13 ....162 D3
Buckinghamshire County
Mus ★ HP22 ....115 D8
Buckinghamshire Railway
Ctr ★ HP22 ....84 F2
Buckland Ave SL3 ....206 B3
Buckland Cres SL4 ....209 F6
Buckland Dr MK6 ....47 C6
Buckland Gate SL3 ....199 B2
Buckland Lodge MK6 ....47 B6
Buckland Rd HP22 ....118 A4
Bucklands Croft HP23 .118 E6
Bucklebury Cl SL6 ....203 C1
Buckley St MK11 ....32 F4
Buckman Cl MK12 ....33 B5
Buckmaster Rd MK18 ....172 C3
Buckthorn MK12 ....33 E5
Budge Rd NN12 ....18 F5
Buffins SL6 ....196 E2
Bulbourne Cl HP4 ....134 F6
Bulbourne Ct HP23 ....119 A7
Bulbourne Rd HP23 ....119 B7
Bulkeley Ave SL4 ....210 B4
Bull La
Gerrards Cross SL9 ....188 C7
7 High Wycombe HP11 .173 A7
Milton Keynes MK2 ....58 D8
Bullbarto La HP6 ....153 B5
Bullbeggars La HP4 ....134 F6
Bullfinch Gdns 8 HP19 .101 F3
Bullington End Rd MK19 ....20 B7
Bullocks Farm La HP14 .171 B7
Bullrush Gr UB8 ....201 C1

Bulls La HP18 ....124 A3
Bullsland Gdns WD3 .167 B3
Bullsland La WD3 ....167 B3
Bulmer MK18 ....36 B3
Bulstrode Cl WD4 ....146 A4
Bulstrode Ct SL9 ....188 D5
Bulstrode La WD4 ....146 F3
Bulstrode Pl SL1 ....205 A1
Bulstrode Way SL9 ....188 D6
Bunby Rd SL2 ....198 F5
Bunces Cl SL4 ....205 B1
Bunces Ct HP20 ....101 C1
Bungalows The MK18 ....51 A6
Bunhill Cl LU6 ....93 F8
Bunkers La LU7 ....80 D6
Bunsen Pl MK5 ....46 C4
Bunstrux HP23 ....119 A3
Bunten Meade SL1 ....205 B5
Bunyan Cl HP23 ....119 B5
Burano Cl MK7 ....48 C6
Burchard Cres MK5 ....46 A6
Burchett's Green Rd
SL6 ....194 C1
Burcot Gdns SL6 ....195 C6
Burcott Cl HP22 ....102 B3
Burcott La HP22 ....102 C3
Burdeleys La MK5 ....46 A4
Burdett Dr MK18 ....161 B8
Burdock Ct MK16 ....21 F4
Burewelle MK8 ....33 D1
Burfield Rd
Chorleywood WD3 ....167 C4
Old Windsor SL4 ....211 A1
Burford Cl
Ickenham UB10 ....201 E8
Marlow Bottom SL7 ....183 C5
Burford Gdns SL1 ....204 C8
Burford Ho 18 SL4 ....210 D6
Burford Sch SL3 ....183 C5
Burgess Gdns MK16 ....22 B2
Burgess La HP17 ....128 B7
Burgess Wood Gr HP9 .175 B1
Burgess Wood Rd HP9 .175 B2
Burgess Wood Rd S
HP9 ....175 B1
Burgett Rd SL1 ....205 B3
Burghley Ct MK8 ....45 F8
Burholme MK4 ....46 C3
Burke Rd HP22 ....131 C5
Burkes Cl HP9 ....186 B8
Burkes Cres HP9 ....175 D2
Burkes Par HP9 ....175 D2
Burkes Par HP9 ....175 D3
Burkes Rd HP9 ....175 C2
Burleigh Ct MK18 ....52 F8
Burleigh Piece MK18 ....41 F1
Burleys Rd MK18 ....65 F4
Burlington Ave SL1 ....205 E4
Burlington Ct 1 SL1 .205 E4
Burlington Rd
Burnham SL1 ....197 B1
2 Slough SL1 ....205 E4
Burma Cl HP13 ....173 E6
Burn Wlk SL1 ....197 B1
Burners La MK11 ....33 B4
Burners Lane S MK11 .33 B3
Burness Cl UB8 ....201 D3
Burnet MK14 ....34 C7
Burnetts Ct HP16 ....151 C5
Burnetts Rd SL4 ....209 E6
Burnham Ave HP9 ....176 A1
Burnham Beeches (Nature
Reserve) ★ SL2 ....198 A7
Burnham Cl
Bourne End SL8 ....185 A4
High Wycombe HP12 ....172 D6
Windsor SL4 ....209 D5
Burnham Ct SL6 ....202 F8
Burnham Dr MK13 ....34 C3
Burnham Gram Sch
SL1 ....197 D1
Burnham Hts SL1 ....204 C7
Burnham La SL1 ....204 E7
Burnham Pl NN13 ....27 B8
Burnham Rd
Beaconsfield HP9 ....186 F6
Hughenden Valley HP14 .162 A6
Westcott HP18 ....98 B7
Burnham Sta SL1 ....204 D7
Burnham Upper Sch
SL1 ....204 B8
Burnhams Field HP22 .116 E7
Burnhams The
Aston Clinton HP22 ....117 C5
Shabbington HP18 ....124 D3
Burnmoor Cl MK2 ....58 D4
Burns Cl
Long Crendon HP18 ....125 D7
Newport Pagnell MK16 ....22 A4
Burns Ct HP21 ....115 F6
Burns Rd MK3 ....58 A7
Burnt Oak SL6 ....195 F7
Burrell Cl HP21 ....115 C6
Burren The HP6 ....154 D2
Burroughs Cres SL8 .185 A4
Burroway Rd SL3 ....207 B3
Burrows Cl
Tylers Green HP10 ....163 C2
Woburn Sands MK17 ....49 B5
Burrows Ho HP13 ....161 E2
Burt's La HP18 ....125 D6
Burton La HP27 ....139 C5
Burton Way SL4 ....209 E4
Burton's La HP8 ....166 E5
Burton's Way HP8 ....166 C7
Burtons La WD3 ....167 A4
Burtree MK12 ....33 D5

Bury Ave MK16 ....22 C4
Bury Cl MK16 ....22 C4
Bury Farm HP7 ....165 C7
Bury Farm Cl LU7 ....91 C6
Bury La HP5 ....154 B8
Bury Lawn Sch MK14 ....34 D7
Bury Rise HP3 ....146 D6
Bury St MK16 ....22 C4
Buryfield La HP16 ....152 B7
Buryhook Cnr OX33 ....122 C2
Busby Cl MK18 ....41 F1
Buscot Pl MK8 ....45 F8
Bush The HP7 ....126 F5
Bushel Wharf HP23 ....119 A6
Bushes La MK18 ....51 C1
Bushey Bartrams MK5 .46 A3
Bushey Cl
Buckingham MK18 ....41 F1
High Wycombe HP12 ....172 E7
Whipsnade LU6 ....93 F1
Bushfield Mid Sch MK12 .33 D6
Bushfield Rd HP3 ....146 C6
Bushfields MK12 ....33 D6
Bushmead Rd HP22 ....87 B5
Bushmead Rd HP22 ....87 B5
Bushy Cl MK3 ....47 A3
Buslins La HP5 ....143 E3
Butcher La MK5 ....45 F3
Bute Brae MK4 ....46 C2
Butler Ct 5 SL7 ....183 F3
Butler Wlk HP19 ....115 A7
Butlers Cl
Amersham HP6 ....154 A2
Windsor SL4 ....209 D6
Butlers Court Rd HP9 .175 D1
Butlers Court Sch HP9 .175 D1
Butlers Ct HP13 ....173 F5
Butlers Gr MK14 ....34 D8
Butterfield HP10 ....185 D4
Butterfield Cl MK15 ....35 C2
Butterfield Cotts WD3 .178 A3
Butterly Rd HP14 ....158 F4
Buttermere HP21 ....116 B7
Buttermere Ave SL1 .204 C8
Buttermere Cl MK2 ....58 D6
Buttfurlong HP17 ....127 A7
Buttlehide WD3 ....178 D5
Button Gr MK6 ....47 A4
Buzzacott La MK4 ....46 C3
By-Wood End SL9 ....178 A5
Bybend SL2 ....198 B4
Bycell Rd MK18 ....41 C6
Bye Gn HP22 ....117 A3
Byerly Ho MK14 ....34 F5
Byerly Pl MK14 ....34 F5
Byford Way MK18 ....65 F4
Byland Dr SL6 ....203 B1
Byrd Cres MK7 ....48 D6
Byres The HP17 ....126 F6
Byron SL3 ....207 A3
Byron Cl 6 Marlow SL7 .183 F3
Milton Keynes MK3 ....57 F7
Byron Ct SL4 ....210 A4
Byron Dr MK16 ....22 A4
Byron Rd HP21 ....115 F6
Byron Way UB7 ....208 F2
Byward Cl MK14 ....21 E2
Byways Berkhamsted HP4 135 E5
Burnham SL1 ....204 C5

C

Cadeby Ct MK10 ....36 B3
Cadman Sq MK5 ....46 C5
Cadmore End CE Sch
HP14 ....170 C6
Cadsdean Rd HP27 .139 C6
Cadwell Dr SL6 ....202 D3
Caernarvon Cres MK3 .57 E7
Caesars Cl MK13 ....34 A5
Caesars Gate SL2 ....38 A6
Cages Wood Dr SL2 .198 B8
Cairngorm Gate MK6 ....46 D8
Cairngorm Pl SL2 ....198 D1
Cairnside HP13 ....173 E6
Caister Ct MK4 ....56 E8
Caithness Ct MK3 ....46 E2
Calamus Ct MK7 ....48 B6
Calbroke Rd SL2 ....197 F2
Caldecote La MK16 ....22 F2
Caldecote St MK16 ....22 C4
Caldecotte La MK7 ....48 A3
Caldecotte Lake MK7 .48 A3
Caldecotte Rdbt MK7 ....47 F3
Calder Cl SL6 ....195 E1
Calder Ct
Maidenhead SL6 ....195 D1
1 Slough SL3 ....206 D1
Calder Gdns LU7 ....80 B7
Calder Vale MK3 ....46 E1
Calder Way SL3 ....212 E4
Caldwell MK8 ....33 D1
Caldicot Cl HP21 ....116 B6
Caldicott Sch SL2 ....198 B5
Caledon Cl HP9 ....175 E3
Caledon Rd HP9 ....175 E3
Caledonian Rd MK13 ....33 E7
Calewen MK8 ....33 E1
California Circ HP11 .173 B4
Callaghan Ct HP4 ....135 D4
Callis Farm Cl TW19 .213 E1
Calluna Dr MK3 ....47 A3
Calumet HP9 ....175 D3
Calvards Croft MK12 ....33 C4
Calverleigh Cres MK4 .46 D3
Calverley Cres HP13 .161 F2
Calvert Cotts MK18 ....73 D7

Calvert Jubilee Nature
Reserve ★ MK18,OX27 .73 A7
Calverton La MK19 ....33 B1
Calverton La Rdbt MK11 .33 B2
Calverton Rd MK11 ....32 D4
Calves Cl MK5 ....46 A3
Cam Ct MK3 ....57 E8
Cam Mead HP21 ....116 B6
Camber Cl MK3 ....57 E7
Camberton Rd LU7 ....80 E6
Camborne Ave HP21 .116 B5
Cambria Cl SL3 ....206 C4
Cambridge Ave
Burnham SL1 ....197 B3
Slough SL1 ....205 A7
Cambridge Cl
Aylesbury HP20 ....101 E1
Harmondsworth UB7 ....213 D8
Cambridge Close Trad Est
HP20 ....101 E1
Cambridge Cres HP13 .173 E7
Cambridge Ho 2 SL6 .202 F6
Cambridge Pl 9 HP20 .115 D8
Cambridge Rd
Beaconsfield HP9 ....175 C2
Marlow SL7 ....183 C2
Uxbridge UB8 ....201 D6
Cambridge St
Aylesbury HP20 ....101 E1
Milton Keynes,Bletchley
MK2 ....58 C8
Milton Keynes,Wolverton
MK12 ....33 C6
Cambridge Terr 13 HP4 .135 D4
Cambron MK8 ....33 D2
Camden Ct HP19 ....101 C1
Camden Pl SL8 ....185 A3
Camden Rd SL6 ....195 C6
Cameron Rd HP5 ....144 C1
Camfield Ct SL6 ....202 A8
Camlet Gr MK14 ....34 D7
Camley Gdns SL6 ....202 A8
Camm Ave SL4 ....209 E4
Camomile Ct MK7 ....48 C5
Camomile Way UB7 .208 E6
Camp Ind Est OX9 ....136 B4
Camp Rd SL2 ....188 C4
Campania Cl MK10 ....36 A2
Campbell Cl
Buckingham MK18 ....52 F8
High Wycombe HP13 ....172 F8
Campbell Dr HP9 ....175 C5
Campbell Park Rdbt MK9 .34 F3
Campbells Ride HP15 .163 D7
Campden Rd UB10 ....190 F1
Camperdown SL6 ....196 B1
Camperdown Ho 9 SL4 .210 D7
Campion MK14 ....21 E2
Campion Cl
Aylesbury HP20 ....116 C8
Denham UB9 ....190 A1
Uxbridge UB8 ....208 F8
Campion Rd HP15 ....162 F6
Campions Ct HP4 ....135 E3
Canada Rd SL1 ....206 B4
Canal Ct HP4 ....135 E4
Canal Mus The ★ NN12 ....9 A8
Canal Wharf SL3 ....207 A4
Canalside
Berkhamsted HP4 ....134 F6
Old Stratford MK19 ....32 C7
Stoke Bruerne NN12 ....9 A8
Canalside Rdbt MK9 ....35 B4
Candlemas La HP9 ....175 E2
Candlemas Mead HP9 .175 E2
Candlemas Oaks HP9 .175 E2
Candlewicks MK7 ....48 B6
Candover Cl UB7 ....213 D7
Candy La MK5 ....46 B4
Candytuft Gn HP15 ....162 F6
Cane End HP27 ....139 A3
Cane End La HP22 ....102 C6
Canford Ct HP21 ....115 F5
Cannock Cl SL6 ....203 B6
Cannock Rd HP20 ....101 E3
Cannon Court Rd SL6 .195 D3
Cannon Gate SL2 ....206 C6
Cannon Hill Cl SL6 ....203 C2
Cannon La SL6 ....202 A6
Cannon Mill Ave HP5 .154 E5
Cannon Pl HP27 ....139 B4
Cannon's Hill HP18 ....112 C5
Cannon's Orch HP27 ....85 B4
Cannondown Rd SL6 .195 E5
Canon Harnett Ct MK12 .33 B8
Canon Hill Dr SL6 ....203 B3
Canon Hill Way SL6 .203 B2
Canon's Cloisters SL4 .210 D7
Canons Rd MK12 ....33 C7
Canons The MK16 ....22 E3
Cantell Cl MK18 ....41 D1
Canterbury Ave SL2 .198 C1
Canterbury Cl
Amersham HP6 ....165 C2
Monks Risborough HP27 .139 B5
Cantilupe Cl LU6 ....92 D6
Cantle Ave MK14 ....35 A5
Cantley Cl HP20 ....101 E2
Cape Villas SL0 ....207 D2
Capel Cl MK18 ....41 F7
Capel Dr MK14 ....34 F5
Capell Ave WD3 ....167 C4
Capell Rd WD3 ....167 D4
Capell Way WD3 ....167 D4
Capian Wlk MK8 ....33 E1

Capital Dr MK14 ....34 E6
Capps La HP5 ....143 A5
Capricorn Ho HP10 ..185 A8
Capron MK6 ....47 B5
Capswood Bsns Ctr
UB9 ....189 C3
Captain Cook Cl HP8 ..177 B6
Captain's Cl HP5 ......144 A4
Captains Wlk HP4 ....135 D3
Caravan Site The HP23 .104 C4
Caraway Ct MK7 ......48 B4
Cardain Ho HP9 ......175 D3
Cardigan Cl
Milton Keynes MK3 ....46 F1
Slough SL1 ....204 F6
Cardinals Wlk SL6 ....204 C7
Cardwell Cl MK4 ......46 C2
Carey Cl Aylesbury HP21 .115 D4
Windsor SL4 ....210 B4
Carey Way MK46 ......7 A4
Careys Croft HP4 ....135 A7
Careys Rd NN12 ......17 A8
Carhampton Ct MK4 ..46 D3
Carisbrooke Ave MK7 .172 B6
Carisbrooke Cl SL6 ..202 C6
Carisbrooke Ct
Buckingham MK18 ....41 E2
Slough SL1 ....205 F6
Carisbrooke Ho 4
HP13 ....173 F7
Carisbrooke Way MK4 .45 F7
Carleton Gate MK15 ..35 E7
Carlina MK14 ....34 D3
Carlisle Rd SL1 ......205 D6
Carlton Cl
Aylesbury HP19 ......101 A2
Newport Pagnell MK16 ..22 E4
Carlton Ct HP27 ....139 B3
Carlton Ho TW19 ....213 D2
Carlton Rd Slough SL2 .206 B6
Turvey MK43 ....8 E7
Carlyle Ave HP21 ....115 F7
Carlyle Cl MK16 ......22 A4
Carman Ct HP23 ....118 F3
Carmarthen Rd SL1 ..205 E6
Carmel Ct SL7 ......183 E1
Carnation Way HP21 .115 D6
Carne The MK11 ......32 E5
Carnot Ct MK5 ......46 C4
Carnoustie Cl MK3 ..57 C7
Carnweather Ct MK4 .57 B8
Caroline Cl UB7 ....208 D4
Caroline Ct SL7 ....183 E3
Caroline Haslett Comb Sch
MK5 ....46 B4
Carolus Creek MK15 ..35 A4
Carpenter Ct MK14 ..34 F6
Carpenters Wood Dr
WD3 ....167 B5
Carpenters Yd HP23 .119 B3
Carr Cl HP10 ......101 A2
Carrick Rd MK6 ......34 F1
Carriers Cl MK19 ....11 A2
Carrington Ave HP10 .185 A8
Carrington Cl MK18 ..77 E5
Carrington Cres HP22 .131 A7
Carrington Ct 9 HP12 .172 E7
Carrington Hall Rd MK17 68 C6
Carrington Inf Sch The
HP10 ....174 A1
Carrington Jun Sch
HP10 ....185 A8
Carrington Pl
Holmer Green HP15 ..163 C7
Tring HP23 ....119 B5
Carrington Rd
Aylesbury HP21 ......115 D6
High Wycombe HP12 ..172 E7
Newport Pagnell MK16 ..22 B3
Slough SL1 ....205 D6
Carrington Way HP16 .151 C5
Carroll Cl MK16 ......22 A5
Carron Cl LU7 ......80 B7
Carron Ct MK2 ......58 C4
Carrs Dr HP12 ......172 C8
Carter Cl SL4 ......210 A5
Carter Wlk HP10 ....174 A1
Carteret Cl MK15 ....35 E7
Carters Cl MK16 ....13 F1
Carters La
Long Crendon HP18 ..125 B7
Milton Keynes MK11 ..33 A3
Quainton HP22,MK11 ..85 E6
Carters Mdw MK18 ..76 A2
Carters Ride HP22 ..116 B2
Cartmel Cl MK3 ....57 C6
Cartwright Ct 2 HP23 .173 F5
Cartwright Pl MK6 ..46 E8
Carver Hill Rd HP12 .172 F6
Carvers Mews MK14 ..34 F6
Cascadia Cl HP11 ....174 B2
Cashmere Cl MK5 ....46 A4
Casterton Cl MK13 ..34 C4
Castle Acre MK10 ....35 F1
Castle Ashby Rd NN7 ..1 B7
Castle Ave Datchet SL3 .211 A8
West Drayton UB7 ....208 F6
Castle Cl
Marsh Gibbon OX6 ....72 A3
Pitstone LU7 ....105 D3
Totternhoe LU6 ......93 A8
Wing LU7 ....79 E3
Castle Ct
13 Aylesbury HP20 ..115 D8
Buckingham MK18 ....52 D8

Castle Ct *continued*
Maidenhead SL6 ......202 D7
Castle Dr SL6 ......202 D7
Castle Est HP12 ....172 D4
Castle Farm Cvn Site
SL4 ....209 D5
Castle Gate Way HP4 .135 C6
Castle Hill
Berkhamsted HP4 ....135 C5
High Wycombe HP11 ..173 A6
Maidenhead SL6 ......202 E7
Windsor SL4 ....210 B6
Castle Hill Ave HP4 ..135 C5
Castle Hill Cl HP4 ..135 C5
Castle Hill Ct HP4 ..135 C6
Castle Hill Rd LU6 ..93 A8
Castle Hill Terr SL6 .202 E7
Castle Ho 5 LU7 ....80 E7
Castle La HP22 ......86 F6
Castle Lodge SL6 ....202 F7
Castle Meadow Cl MK16 .22 C4
Castle Mews
Berkhamsted HP4 ....135 C4
Maidenhead SL6 ......202 E7
Castle Park Rd HP22 .131 D6
Castle Pl 6 HP13 ....173 B7
Castle Rd MK46 ......2 F1
Castle Rose MK6 ....47 D6
Castle Row 16 HP23 ..119 A3
Castle St Aylesbury HP20 115 D8
Berkhamsted HP4 ....135 C4
Buckingham MK18 ....52 D8
High Wycombe HP13 ..173 B7
Marsh Gibbon OX27 ..72 A3
Slough SL1 ....205 F3
Wingrave HP22 ....89 B3
Castle View Gdns HP12 .172 D7
Castlefield Sch HP12 .172 C6
Castlefields HP22 ....116 C3
Castlemead Cotts SL4 .210 C3
Castlesteads MK13 ..33 F5
Castlethorpe Fst Sch
MK19 ....19 F5
Castlethorpe Rd MK19 ..11 A2
Castleton Ct SL7 ....183 E2
Castleview Ho SL4 ..210 D7
Castleview Prim Sch
SL3 ....206 D2
Castleview Rd SL3 ..206 C2
Caswell La MK17 ....60 F7
Catchpole Cl MK12 ..33 B5
Cater Rd HP14 ......171 C4
Catesby Croft MK5 ..46 C8
Cathay Cl MK5 ......58 B7
Catherine Cotts HP23 .133 E8
Catherine Ct MK18 ..41 E2
Catherines Cl UB7 ..208 D4
Catkin Cl HP12 ......172 B3
Catslip RG9 ....179 A1
Causeway The Bray SL6 .203 C4
Marlow SL7 ....183 E1
Cautley Cl HP22 ....85 A5
Cavalier Ct HP4 ....135 C4
Cavalier Rd OX9 ....126 A1
Cavalry Cres SL4 ..210 C4
Cavendish Cl
Burnham SL6 ....204 A7
Little Chalfont HP6 ..166 B8
Wendover HP22 ......131 B6
Cavendish Ct
Milton Keynes MK5 ..46 A7
Poyle SL3 ....212 A6
Cavendish Rd HP5 ..154 D7
Cavendish Wlk OX9 .126 B1
Cavenham MK8 ......33 F2
Caversham Gn 1 HP20 .101 D1
Cawardon MK14 ....34 C7
Cawcott Dr SL4 ....209 E6
Cawdor Rise MK4 ..45 E2
Cawkwell Way MK2 ..58 C8
Caxton Ct RG9 ......191 E1
Caxton Dr UB8 ......201 D3
Caxton Rd MK12 ....33 B7
Cecil Ct SL0 ......207 E2
Cecil Way SL2 ......197 B1
Cecily Ct MK5 ......46 A5
Cedar 1 RG9 ......191 D2
Cedar Ave
Hazelmere HP15 ....163 A5
West Drayton UB7 ..208 F6
Cedar Chase SL6 ....196 D1
Cedar Cl Aylesbury HP20 .102 A3
Burnham SL1 ....197 C1
Chesham HP5 ......144 B1
Iver SL0 ....200 C4
Cedar Ct
Gerrards Cross SL9 ..188 E7
High Wycombe HP13 ..173 B7
Maidenhead SL6 ....202 E7
Marlow SL7 ....183 E2
6 Windsor SL4 ....210 A5
Cedar Dr Chesham HP5 .144 A1
Cookham SL6 ....196 A7
Cookham Rise SL6 ..195 F7
Marlow Bottom SL7 ..183 C7
Cedar Gr Amersham HP7 .165 D8
Bellingdon HP5 ......143 D8
Cedar Lodge Dr MK12 ..33 D2
Cedar Park Sch HP15 .162 F5
Cedar Rd HP4 ......135 D3
Cedar Terr 1 HP11 ..172 F7
Cedar Way
Berkhamsted HP4 ....135 D3
Slough SL3 ....206 D2
Cedars Cl Akeley MK18 ..41 F8
Chalfont St Peter SL9 .177 E5
Cedars Comb Sch MK16 .22 C4

Cedars Dr UB10 ....201 F3
Cedars Ho SL6 ......203 A7
Cedars Rd SL6 ......203 A7
Cedars The
Berkhamsted HP4 ....135 E4
Slough SL2 ....197 F2
Wendover HP22 ......131 A5
Cedars Upper Sch & Com
Coll The LU7 ....80 E5
Cedars Village WD3 ..167 F5
Cedars Way
Leighton Buzzard LU7 ..80 E5
Newport Pagnell MK16 ..22 C4
Ceely Ho HP21 ......115 D6
Ceely Rd HP21 ......115 D6
Celandine Ct MK7 ..48 A5
Celina Cl MK2 ......58 C7
Cell Farm SL4 ......211 B2
Cell Farm Ave SL4 ..211 B2
Centenary Bsns Pk RG9 .191 F1
Centenary Cotts HP27 .138 D7
Centenary Way HP6 .154 F1
Central Ave
Cranfield MK43 ......24 E2
Whipsnade LU6 ......107 E8
Central Dr SL1 ......204 F6
Central Est SL6 ....202 E7
Central Park Bsns Ctr
HP13 ....173 A8
Centre Par HP27 ....139 C5
Centre The SL2 ......198 C6
Centre Wlk HP15 ....163 A3
Centurion Ct MK11 ..33 C2
Century Ave MK6 ....46 E8
Century Point HP12 ..172 A4
Cestreham Cres HP5 .144 D2
Chackmore CE Sch MK18 41 B4
Chacombe Pl HP9 ..175 D5
Chadbone Cl MK18 ..115 D8
Chadds La MK6 ......47 C8
Chadwell Path HP21 .116 C6
Chadwick Dr MK6 ..47 B7
Chadwick St HP13 ..162 D2
Chaffinch HP19 ....101 F4
Chaffron Way
Leadenhall MK6 ......46 F7
Milton Keynes,Oakgrove
MK6,MK10,MK15 ....35 D1
Milton Keynes,Shenley Lodge
MK4,MK5,MK6 ......46 C5
Chairborough Rd HP12 .172 D6
Chalcot Pl MK8 ....45 F8
Chalcott SL1 ......205 E3
Chalet Cl HP4 ......134 F4
Chalfont & Latimer Sta
HP7 ....166 C8
Chalfont Ave HP6 ..166 D8
Chalfont Cl MK13 ..34 A6
Chalfont Ho HP7 ..166 D7
Chalfont La
Chorleywood WD3 ..167 B4
Maple Cross WD3 ..178 C7
Chalfont Rd
Maple Cross SL9 ..178 C7
Seer Green HP9 ....176 D5
Chalfont Shire Horse Ctr★
HP8 ....178 A7
Chalfont St Giles Inf Sch
HP8 ....177 B7
Chalfont St Giles Jun Sch
HP8 ....177 B7
Chalfont St Peter CE Sch
SL9 ....177 D2
Chalfont St Peter Inf Sch
SL9 ....177 C3
Chalfont Station Rd
HP7 ....166 C7
Chalfont Way HP12 ..172 D3
Chalfonts & Gerrards Cross
Hospl The SL9 ......177 D2
Chalfonts Com Coll The
SL9 ....177 C3
Chalford Flats HP10 .185 F6
Chalford Way HP19 ..114 F8
Chalgrove Cl SL6 ..203 B6
Chalgrove End HP22 .116 B1
Chalgrove Rd OX9 ..126 A1
Chalgrove Wlk HP21 .115 C6
Chalk Farm Rd HP14 .158 F3
Chalk Hill Chesham HP5 .144 B2
Coleshill HP7 ......164 F7
Windsor SL4 ......210 F6
Chalk La HP6,HP7 ..153 D5
Chalk Pit La SL7 ..197 B4
Chalkdell Dr MK5 ..45 F4
Chalkpit La SL7 ....183 B3
Chalklands SL8 ....185 A4
Chalkpits The HP10 ..130 C4
Chalkshire Cotts HP17 .130 C4
Chalkshire Rd HP17 ..130 C4
Chalkstream Way HP10 .185 E7
Challacombe MK4 ..46 D3
Challener Rd HP12 ..172 C3
Challenge Ho MK3 ..47 B1
Challow Ct SL6 ......195 D1
Chalmers Ave MK19 ..20 D2
Chaloner Pl HP21 ..115 D6
Chaloner Rd HP21 ..115 D6
Chaloners Hill MK18 ..63 D8
Chalvey Gdns SL1 ..205 E4
Chalvey Gr SL1 ....205 B4
Chalvey Pk SL1 ....205 E4
Chalvey Rd E SL1 ..205 E4
Chalvey Rd W SL1 ..205 D4
Chamberlain Rd HP19 .101 B1
Champflower MK4 ..46 D3

Champney Cl SL3 ..212 A4
Champneys Coll of Health &
Beauty HP23 ......133 E6
Chancellors HP7 ....164 B5
Chancellors Cnr HP7 .164 B5
Chancery Ct MK13 ..34 A6
Chancery Pl SL4 ....210 D7
Chandlers Ct MK6 ..47 C5
Chandlers Quay SL6 .203 C8
Chandos Cl
Buckingham MK18 ....52 D7
Little Chalfont HP6 ..155 C1
Chandos Ct MK18 ..52 D7
Chandos Mall 7 SL1 .205 F4
Chandos Pl
Milton Keynes MK2 ..58 B8
Wendover HP22 ....131 B4
Chandos Rd MK18 ..52 D8
Channer Dr HP10 ..163 B1
Channory Ct MK4 ..46 A1
Chantry Cl
West Drayton UB7 ..208 D6
Windsor SL4 ....210 A6
Woburn Sands MK17 ..49 A6
Chantry Rd HP19 ..101 C3
Chantry Sch UB7 ..208 E6
Chantry The
15 Aylesbury HP20 ..115 D8
Uxbridge UB8 ......201 F2
Chapel Arches SL6 ..203 A7
Chapel Cl Blackthorn OX25 81 A3
Little Gaddesden HP4 .121 D6
Chapel Cotts SL2 ..199 B5
Chapel Ct SL6 ......202 D4
Chapel Dr HP22 ....117 E5
Chapel End La HP23 ..118 C8
Chapel Farm NN7 ..10 C6
Chapel Fields HP23 .118 C8
Chapel Hill Soulbury LU7 .69 E3
Speen HP27 ....150 C7
Windsor SL4 ......210 D6
Chapel Ho HP6 ....153 C5
Chapel La Akeley MK18 ..41 B4
Chilton HP18 ....111 B3
Drayton Parslow MK17 ..68 B5
High Wycombe HP12 ..172 C8
Ivinghoe Aston LU7 ..92 A1
Long Marston HP23 ..104 B4
Northall LU6 ....92 A5
Pitch Green HP27 ..138 B3
Rout's Green HP14 ..148 E2
St Leonards HP23 ..132 D3
Stoke Bruerne NN12 ..9 A8
Stoke Mandeville HP22 116 A1
Stoke Poges SL2 ....199 B5
Thornborough MK18 ..54 B8
Totternhoe LU6 ......92 F8
Turweston NN13 ....38 B7
Walter's Ash HP14 ..161 C7
Wendover HP22 ......131 B4
Whitfield NN13 ......26 D3
Chapel Rd
Flackwell Heath HP10 .185 A8
Ford HP17 ....128 A7
Chapel Row HP14 ..171 A7
Chapel Sq LU7 ......68 C3
Chapel St
Berkhamsted HP4 ..135 D4
High Wycombe HP13 ..161 D3
Marlow SL7 ....183 E2
Slough SL1 ....205 F4
Tring HP23 ....118 F3
Uxbridge UB8 ......201 C4
Woburn Sands MK17 ..49 B4
Chapels Cl SL1 ....204 B5
Chaplin Gr MK8 ....45 D7
Chaplin Mews 7 SL3 .206 F1
Chapman Ave MK14 ..35 A6
Chapman Cl
Aylesbury HP21 ......115 B6
West Drayton UB7 ..208 F3
Chapman La HP8,HP10 .185 A6
Chapmans Cres HP5 .144 A2
Chapmans Dr MK19 ..32 B7
Chapmans Lea HP22 ..88 D5
Chappel Mdw HP23 ..119 B6
Chapter MK6 ....47 A5
Chapter Cl UB10 ....201 F5
Chapter Ho MK6 ....47 A5
Chapter Mews SL4 ..210 D7
Charbray Cres MK5 ..46 A4
Chardacre MK8 ....33 E1
Charlbury Rd UB10 ..190 F1
Charles Cl HP21 ....116 B4
Charles Dr OX9 ....126 A1
Charles Gdns SL2 ..206 A7
Charles Ho
Henley-on-T RG9 ..191 E3
9 Windsor SL4 ....210 C6
Charles St
Berkhamsted HP4 ..135 B4
Tring HP23 ....119 A3
Windsor SL4 ......210 C6
Charles Way MK16 ..22 C4
Charlestown Lodge
UB8 ....201 D6
Charleswood Ho MK17 .49 B3
Charlock Ct MK16 ..21 F4
Charlotte Ave SL2 ..205 F6
Charlotte Cl SL7 ..183 D8
Charlotte Cott SL6 ..203 B8
Charlotte Way 12 SL7 .183 E2
Charlton SL4 ......209 C5
Charlton Cl Slough SL1 .205 B4
Swanbourne MK17 ..66 F3
Charlton Pl 2 SL4 ..209 C5
Charlton Row 5 SL4 .209 C5

Charlton Sq 4 SL4 ..209 C5
Charlton Way SL4 ..209 C5
Charlton Wlk 3 SL4 .209 C5
Charmfield Rd HP23 ..116 A5
Charnwood Cl 5 HP13 .173 F5
Charsley Cl HP6 ....166 C8
Charter Cl 8 SL1 ..205 F3
Charter Dr HP6 ....154 F1
Charter Pl UB8 ....201 D5
Charter Rd SL1 ....204 E6
Chartley Ct MK5 ..46 B4
Chartridge Comb Sch
HP5 ....143 C4
Chartridge Development
UB8 ....201 B3
Chartridge Grange Dr
HP5 ....143 D4
Chartridge Ho 3 HP13 .173 D4
Chartridge La HP5 ..143 F2
Chartridge Park Mobile
Home Pk HP5 ......143 D4
Chartwell Gate HP9 .175 D2
Chartwell Rd MK16 ..22 E4
Chase Ave MK7 ....48 A4
Chase Cl HP7 ......165 A4
Chase Farm Barns MK17 .56 C4
Chase Park Rd NN7 ..1 A5
Chase The
1 Chesham HP5 ....144 B2
Maidenhead SL6 ....195 D3
Marlow SL7 ......184 A3
Tylers Green HP10 ..163 C1
Chaseport Cl MK46 ..5 D2
Chaseside Cl LU7 ..105 A7
Chatfield SL2 ......205 A8
Chatham Ct 2 SL1 ..206 A3
Chatsworth MK8 ....33 F1
Chatsworth Cl SL6 ..202 C5
Chaucer Cl
Berkhamsted HP4 ..134 F5
Newport Pagnell MK16 ..22 A4
Windsor SL4 ......210 D4
Chaucer Dr HP21 ..115 F6
Chaucer Rd MK3 ..58 A7
Chaucer Way SL1 ..205 F5
Chauntry Cl SL6 ..203 C6
Chauntry Rd SL6 ..203 B6
Chawton Cres MK8 ..33 F1
Cheapside La UB9 ..189 C7
Cheddington Comb Sch
LU7 ....105 A7
Cheddington La HP23 .104 C5
Cheddington Rd LU7 .105 C4
Cheddington Sta LU7 ..91 A2
Chelmsford Ct 8 SL4 .210 C5
Chelsea Gn LU7 ....80 D6
Chelsea Ho 6 LU7 ..80 E7
Cheltenham Gdns MK3 .57 D6
Cheney Cl LU7 ....78 B1
Cheney Way HP20 ..101 E1
Cheney Wlk 3 HP20 .101 F2
Cheneys Wlk MK3 ..47 A2
Chenies Ave HP6 ..166 D8
Chenies Manor Ho★
WD3 ....156 A1
Chenies Par HP7 ..166 C7
Chenies Rd WD3 ..167 D7
Chenies Sch WD3 ..156 B1
Chepping Cl HP10 ..163 A1
Chepping View Prim Sch
HP12 ....172 D3
Chepstow Dr MK3 ..57 D6
Chequers Bridge Cotts
SL0 ....207 C4
Chequers Cl LU7 ..105 C4
Chequers Ct HP21 ..115 E4
Chequers Dr HP16 ..151 C6
Chequers End MK46 ..66 A4
Chequers Hill HP7 ..165 C6
Chequers La
Ibstone HP14,RG9 ..170 A5
North Crawley MK16 ..24 B6
Pitstone LU7 ......105 C5
Prestwood HP16 ....151 C7
Chequers Orch SL0 .207 C4
Chequers Sq UB8 ..201 C5
Chequers The
Castlethorpe MK19 ..19 F5
Eaton Bray LU6 ....92 F5
Cherington Gate SL6 .195 B1
Cheriton MK4 ......46 E3
Cherleton MK8 ....33 E1
Cherries The SL2 ..206 B7
Cherry Acre SL9 ..177 D6
Cherry Ave SL3 ..206 D4
Cherry Cl
Flackwell Heath HP10 .185 B7
Prestwood HP16 ....151 D6
Cherry Cnr HP10 ..185 B8
Cherry Dr HP9 ....175 B4
Cherry Gdns HP23 ..118 F3
Cherry Gr HP15 ..163 C6
Cherry La Amersham HP7 .165 A4
West Drayton UB7 ..208 F2
Woodrow HP7 ......164 D6
Cherry Lane Prim Sch
UB7 ....208 F2
Cherry Leys MK18 ..63 E3
Cherry Orch
Amersham HP6 ....154 C2
Olney MK46 ....6 E4
Prestwood HP16 ....151 C6
Stoke Poges SL2 ..199 A5
West Drayton UB7 ..208 E4
Cherry Orchard Ct
HP13 ....173 E6
Cherry Pit The HP13 .161 E2

Cherry Rd MK16 ......22 B3
Cherry Rise
  Chalfont St Giles HP8 ....177 D8
  Flackwell Heath HP10 ...185 B7
Cherry St HP13 ......174 A4
Cherry Tree Ave UB7 ...208 F7
Cherry Tree Cl
  Great Kingshill HP15 .....151 E1
  Hughenden Valley HP14 ..162 A7
  Speen HP27 ....150 B5
Cherry Tree Ho 4 SL7 .183 D2
Cherry Tree La
  Buckland Common HP23 ..133 A3
  Fulmer SL3 ....199 F6
  Heronsgate WD3 ....167 C1
  Lee Common HP16 ......142 E4
Cherry Tree Rd
  Beaconsfield HP9 ....175 B1
  Chinnor OX39 ....147 C6
  Farnham Common SL2 ...198 C5
Cherry Tree Way HP10 .163 C1
Cherry Tree Wlk
  Chesham HP5 ....144 D2
  Leighton Buzzard LU7 ....80 E7
  Wendover HP22 ....131 A5
Cherry Way
  Hazlemere HP15 ....163 A6
  Horton SL3 ....212 C4
Cherrycroft Dr HP14 ...161 D6
Cherrytree La
  Chalfont St Peter SL9 ...177 D1
  Iver Heath SL0 ....201 A4
Cherrywood Cl HP9 ....176 D5
Cherrywood Gdns HP10 185 B8
Chervil MK6 ....47 B5
Cherwell Cl
  Maidenhead SL6 ....203 A8
  Slough SL3 ....212 B8
Cherwell Ho MK3 ....57 E8
Cherwell Rd
  Aylesbury HP21 ....115 C6
  Bourne End SL8 ....185 B4
Chesham Ave MK13 .....34 C3
Chesham Bois CE Comb Sch
  HP6 ....154 D4
Chesham Cottage Hospl
  HP5 ....154 C7
Chesham High Sch HP5 144 C1
Chesham La
  Chalfont St Peter SL9 ...177 E6
  Wendover HP22,HP16 ...141 E8
Chesham Park Com Coll
  HP5 ....144 A4
Chesham Prep Sch HP5 145 A4
Chesham Rd
  Amersham HP6 ....154 C2
  Ashley Green PH4,PH5 ..144 F8
  Bellingdon HP5 ....143 D4
  Berkhamsted HP4 ......135 B2
  Bovingdon HP3,HP5 ....145 E4
  Hyde Heath HP16 ....153 C7
  Wigginton HP23 ....133 D7
Chesham Sta HP5 ....154 C8
Cheshire Cotts OX27 ...72 F6
Cheshire Ct 6 SL1 .....206 B4
Cheshire Rise MK3 .....46 E1
Cheslyn Gdns MK14 ....35 A8
Chesney Wold MK6 .....46 F5
Chess Cl Aylesbury HP21 .115 D3
  Latimer HP5 ....155 D3
Chessbury Cl HP5 ....154 A1
Chessbury Rd HP5 ......154 A1
Chessfield Pk HP6 ......166 E8
Chessmount Rise HP5 ..154 D6
Chester Cl MK3 ....57 D7
Chester Ho UB8 ....201 C1
Chester Rd SL1 ....205 D7
Chesterfield Cl HP17 ...114 C5
Chesterfield Cres HP14 ..79 E3
Chesterfield Pl HP19 ...115 B8
Chesterholm MK13 ......33 F5
Chesterton Cl HP5 ......144 B2
Chesterton Gn HP9 .....175 E2
Chestnut Ave
  Chesham HP5 ....144 E2
  Halton HP22 ....131 D8
  High Wycombe HP11 ....173 D5
  Slough SL3 ....206 E4
  West Drayton UB7 ......208 F6
Chestnut Cl
  Amersham HP6 ....154 B4
  Aston Clinton HP22 .....117 F5
  Chalfont St Peter SL9 ...177 D1
  Dagnall HP4 ....107 C5
  Maidenhead SL6 ....196 B1
  Medmenham SL7 ....193 D4
  Milton Keynes MK11 .....32 D5
  Monks Risborough HP27 .139 C4
  Newton Longville MK17 ..57 D2
  Waddesdon HP18 ....99 A6
Chestnut Cotts MK18 ...52 C7
Chestnut Cres
  Aylesbury HP21 ....115 D6
  Milton Keynes MK2 ......58 D7
Chestnut Ct HP6 ....154 C7
Chestnut Dr
  Berkhamsted HP4 ......135 D3
  Windsor SL4 ....209 F3
Chestnut End HP22 .....117 C1
Chestnut Gn NN13 ......26 E4
Chestnut Hill LU7 ....80 D8
Chestnut La
  Amersham HP6 ....154 B4
  Hazlemere HP15 ....163 B5
Chestnut Lane Sch HP6 154 B4
Chestnut Leys MK18 ....63 D6
Chestnut Pk SL6 ....203 E3

Chestnut Rd
  Beaconsfield HP9 ....175 B1
  Princes Risborough HP27 .139 C3
  Yardley Gobion NN12 ....18 F6
Chestnut Rise LU7 ......80 D8
Chestnut View
  Chearsley HP18 ....112 B2
  East Claydon MK18 ......74 F7
Chestnut Way
  Longwick HP18 ....138 C6
  Stoke Mandeville HP22 ..116 A1
Chestnut Wlk SL9 ......177 E3
Chestnuts Comb Sch
  MK3 ....57 E7
Chestnuts The
  Castlethorpe MK19 ......19 E5
  Felden HP3 ....146 F7
  Uxbridge UB10 ....201 E5
Chestwood Gr UB10 ....201 F5
Chettle Pl NN12 ....18 E2
Chetwode Ave MK10 ....36 B1
Chetwode Cl MK18 .....41 E2
Chetwynd Dr UB10 .....201 F3
Chevalier Gr MK8 ....45 D7
Cheveley Gdns SL1 .....197 B3
Cheviot Cl
  High Wycombe HP13 ....161 E1
  Leighton Buzzard LU7 ....80 C8
  Maidenhead SL6 ....203 B6
Cheviot Rd SL3 ....207 A1
Cheyne Cl
  Amersham HP6 ....154 D3
  Buckingham MK18 ....41 F1
  Gerrards Cross SL9 .....188 E3
  Pitstone LU7 ....105 D4
Cheyne Wlk HP5 ....154 D8
Chicheley Hall MK16 ....23 D8
Chicheley Hill MK16 .....23 A8
Chicheley Rd MK16 .....23 E7
Chicheley St MK16 ......22 E4
Chichester Cl HP13 ....173 D6
Chichester Ct SL1 ......206 A4
Chichester Row HP6 ...154 D2
Chicksands Ave MK10 ..36 A2
Chievely Ct MK4 ....46 C1
Chilcote La HP7 ....166 A4
Childs Way MK4,MK5,MK6,
  MK10 ....46 C7
Chillery Leys MK15 ......35 E7
Chillingham Ct MK5 .....46 A4
Chiltern Ave
  Amersham HP6 ....154 D1
  Edlesborough LU6 ....92 E3
  High Wycombe HP12 ...172 D6
  Stone HP17 ....114 D5
Chiltern Brewery ★
  HP17 ....130 C5
Chiltern Bsns Village
  UB8 ....201 B3
Chiltern Cl
  Berkhamsted HP4 ......134 F5
  Princes Risborough HP27 .139 D4
  Stone HP17 ....114 D5
  Wendover HP22 ....131 B4
Chiltern Cnr HP4 ....135 A5
Chiltern Commerce Ctr
  HP5 ....144 A2
Chiltern Cotts
  Buckland Common HP23 .133 A2
  Ibstone HP14 ....169 D7
Chiltern Court Mews
  SL4 ....210 B6
Chiltern Ct
  Amersham HP6 ....154 C2
  Chesham HP5 ....144 A1
  5 High Wycombe HP12 .172 E7
  Wendover HP22 ....131 B4
  Windsor SL4 ....210 B6
  Winslow MK18 ....65 F3
Chiltern Dr WD3 ....167 F2
Chiltern Gate Sch HP12 172 E4
Chiltern Gn HP10 ......185 B8
Chiltern Hill SL9 ....177 E2
Chiltern Hills Rd HP9 ..175 C2
Chiltern Ho HP5 ....154 C7
Chiltern Hospl The
  HP16 ....152 C4
Chiltern Manor Pk
  HP16 ....152 A7
Chiltern Open Air Mus ★
  HP8 ....167 A1
Chiltern Par HP6 ....154 C2
Chiltern Park Ave HP4 .135 A6
Chiltern Rd
  Amersham HP6 ....154 B4
  Ballinger Common HP16 .142 E3
  Burnham SL1 ....204 B8
  Maidenhead SL6 ....203 B6
  Marlow SL7 ....183 C2
  Wendover HP22 ....131 B5
  Wingrave HP22 ....89 A3
Chiltern Ridge HP14 ...158 C4
Chiltern Sculpture Trail ★
  OX49 ....157 D4
Chiltern St HP21 ....115 E6
Chiltern View
  Berkhamsted HP4 ......134 F7
  Saunderton HP14 ....149 C5
Chiltern View Rd UB8 ..201 D3
Chiltern Villas HP23 ....118 E2
Chiltern Way
  Aston Clinton HP22 .....117 F2
  Tring HP23 ....119 C5
Chilterns
  Berkhamsted HP4 ......134 F6
  World's End HP22 ....130 F7
Chilterns Cl HP10 ......185 B7

Chilterns Pk SL8 ....185 B5
Chilterns The HP13 ....173 A7
Chilton Cl
  Holmer Green HP15 .....163 C7
  Tylers Green HP10 .....163 C2
Chilton Ct SL6 ....204 C7
Chilton Pl HP20 ....101 E1
Chilton Rd
  Chearsley HP18 ....112 A2
  Chesham HP5 ....144 C2
  Long Crendon HP18 ....125 C7
Chilwick Rd SL2 ....197 F1
Chimes Sh Ctr The UB8 201 D5
Chimes The HP12 ......172 E6
Chimney La HP10 ......185 E8
Chinalls Cl MK18 ....50 D6
Chingle Croft MK4 ......46 C2
Chinneck Ho HP4 ....135 C4
Chinnor & Princes
  Risborough Rly Icknield
  Line ★ OX39 ....147 E2
Chinnor Hill OX39 ......147 E4
Chinnor Hill Nature
  Reserve ★ OX39 .....147 F5
Chinnor Rd
  Bledlow HP27 ....138 A2
  Bledlow Ridge HP14 ...148 A3
  Chinnor OX39 ....147 A4
  Chinnor Sta ★ OX39 ...147 C3
Chippendale Cl HP13 ..162 D1
Chippendale Waye UB8 201 D5
Chippenham Dr MK10 ..36 C1
Chipperfield Cl SL1 .....34 A7
Chipperfield Rd HP3 ...146 C3
Chipping Vale MK6 .....46 C2
Chipstead SL9 ....177 C2
Chirbury Cl MK10 ....35 F1
Chislehampton MK15 ...35 C3
Chiswick Cl MK4 ....45 F2
Chiswick Lodge 6 SL7 .183 D2
Choke La SL6 ....195 B4
Cholesbury La HP23 ....133 A4
Cholesbury Rd HP23 ...133 D5
Chorley Rd HP14 ....160 E3
Chorleywood Bottom
  WD3 ....167 D4
Chorleywood Ho WD3 ..167 E6
Chorleywood House Dr
  WD3 ....167 E6
Chorleywood Montessori Sch
  The WD3 ....167 E6
Chorleywood Prim Sch
  WD3 ....167 F6
Chorleywood Sta WD3 ..167 D5
Chrislaine Cl TW19 .....213 D1
Christ the King RC Fst Sch
  TW19 ....213 D1
Christchurch CE Sch
  WD3 ....167 F6
Christchurch Gr MK12 ..33 B6
Christchurch Ho 15
  HP23 ....119 A3
Christchurch Rd HP23 .118 F4
Christian Ct MK15 ......35 F3
Christian Sq 4 SL4 ....210 C6
Christian Smith Ho SL6 202 A1
Christie Cl MK16 ....58 C8
Christies Ct HP13 ......173 B7
Christmas La SL2 ....187 C1
Christine Ho 3 MK2 ....58 C8
Christopher Cl HP14 ...161 D7
Christopher Ho 3 SL2 .198 C7
Church Ave RG9 ....191 E2
Church Cl
  Aston Clinton HP22 .....117 D5
  Cuddington HP18 ......112 F3
  Eton SL4 ....210 D8
  Maidenhead SL6 ....202 D6
  Maids Moreton MK18 ....41 F3
  Uxbridge UB8 ....201 B3
  West Drayton UB7 .....208 E3
  Wicken MK19 ....31 B3
Church Cotts SL6 ......196 E2
Church Croft LU6 ....92 E3
Church Ct HP13 ....162 D1
Church Dr SL6 ....203 C4
Church End Adstock MK18 53 F1
  Bledlow HP27 ....138 A2
  Drayton Parslow MK17 ..68 B5
  Edlesborough LU6 ......92 E3
  Haddenham HP17 ......127 A5
  Hillesden MK18 ....63 B6
  Leckhampstead MK18 ...42 D8
  Newton Longville MK17 ..57 D3
  Pottersbury NN12 ......18 E3
  Sherington MK16 ....14 A2
  Syresham NN13 ....27 C8
  Wavendon MK17 ....48 E7
Church End Cotts WD3 .156 F1
Church End Farm LU6 ..93 B7
Church End Rd MK5 ....46 A4
Church Farm Cl HP22 ..102 B3
Church Farm Cres MK14 .34 E8
Church Farm Ho HP8 ...177 C7
Church Farm La HP23 ..104 F3
Church Farm Trail ★
  HP17 ....127 B5
Church Gn
  Long Crendon HP18 ....125 D7
  Totternhoe LU6 ....93 B7
Church Gr
  Little Chalfont HP6 .....166 E8
  Slough SL3 ....206 C8
Church Green Rd MK3 ..58 A8
Church Headland La
  HP22 ....87 A6
Church Hill Akeley MK18 ..41 F8
  Aspley Guise MK17 .....49 E5

Church Hill continued
  Cheddington LU7 ......105 A8
  Ellesborough HP17 .....130 B2
  Milton Keynes MK8 .....33 C7
  Pishill RG9 ....179 D1
  South Harefield UB9 ...190 C8
  Whaddon MK17 ....45 B1
Church Holt The SL2 ...187 E3
Church La Alderton NN12 ..9 A2
  Aston Clinton HP22 .....117 D4
  Berkhamsted HP4 ......135 C4
  Bisham SL7 ....194 D7
  Bledlow Ridge HP14 ...159 F8
  Bovingdon HP3 ....146 B4
  Bray SL6 ....203 C4
  Chalfont St Peter SL9 ..177 C5
  Chearsley HP18 ....112 B1
  Cheddington LU7 ......105 A8
  Chinnor OX39 ....147 D6
  Clifton Reynes MK46 ....7 C3
  Cryers Hill HP15 ....162 C4
  Deanshanger MK19 .....31 E4
  Eaton Bray LU6 ....92 E6
  Edgcott HP18 ....72 F2
  Emberton MK46 ....13 C7
  Grafton Regis NN12 ....9 D2
  Granborough MK18 .....75 F6
  Great Horwood MK17 ...55 A3
  Great Kimble HP17 .....129 C1
  Great Missenden HP16 ..152 B7
  Hastoe HP23 ....133 C4
  Horton-cum-S OX33 ...108 A5
  Lacey Green HP27 ......149 E4
  Lillingstone Lovell MK18 ..30 A6
  Ludgershall HP18 ......96 C7
  Marsworth HP23 ....104 F1
  Milton Keynes MK5 .....46 B8
  Mixbury NN13 ....38 D1
  Mursley MK17 ....67 D5
  Newport Pagnell MK16 ..22 D7
  Oving HP22 ....86 C7
  Padbury MK18 ....53 C2
  Pottersbury NN12 ......18 E3
  Princes Risborough HP27 .139 B4
  Radnage HP14 ....159 D8
  Sarratt WD3 ....156 F1
  Slough SL2,SL3 ....206 C8
  Soulbury LU7 ....69 E2
  Stoke Bruerne NN12 ....9 A8
  Stoke Goldington MK16 ..12 A7
  Stoke Poges SL2 ....198 F2
  Thornborough MK18 ....54 A8
  Tingewick MK18 ....38 D1
  Upper Winchendon HP18 .99 B1
  Uxbridge UB8 ....201 B3
  Walter's Ash HP14 .....161 E6
  Walton MK7 ....47 F6
  Wendover HP22 ....131 C3
  West Wycombe HP14 ...161 A2
  Weston Turville HP22 ...116 F1
  Whaddon MK17 ....45 B1
  Whitchurch HP22 ......87 A6
  Wicken MK19 ....31 B3
  8 Windsor SL4 ....210 D6
  Yardley Hastings NN7 ...1 B7
Church Lees MK12 ......21 D1
Church Pas MK16 ......22 D4
Church Path
  Cheddington LU7 ......91 A1
  Cublington LU7 ....78 B1
  Lane End HP14 ....171 B4
  Prestwood HP16 ....151 D5
  Stokenchurch HP14 ....158 D5
Church Piece HP18 ....112 B2
Church Rd
  Aspley Heath MK17 .....49 B3
  Bow Brickhill MK17 .....48 D1
  Brackley NN13 ....38 A7
  Chinnor OX39 ....147 D6
  Cookham Dean SL6 ....195 B6
  Farnham Royal SL2 .....198 C2
  Ickford HP18 ....123 F3
  Iver Heath SL0 ....200 C3
  Ivinghoe LU7 ....105 F5
  Lane End HP14 ....171 B3
  Leighton Buzzard LU7 ...80 E6
  Lewknor OX49 ....157 B8
  Little Gaddesden HP4 ..121 D8
  Little Marlow SL7 ......184 C5
  Maidenhead SL6 ....203 B5
  Old Windsor SL4 ....211 B2
  Penn HP10 ....174 E7
  Pitstone LU7 ....105 E3
  Seer Green HP9 ....176 D4
  Sherington MK16 ....13 F2
  Slapton LU7 ....91 D6
  South Harefield UB9 ...190 C8
  Stoke Hammond MK17 ..69 D8
  Stokenchurch HP14 ....158 D5
  Thame OX9 ....125 E1
  Totternhoe LU6 ....93 B6
  Tylers Green HP10 .....174 C8
  Uxbridge UB8 ....201 D1
  West Drayton UB7 .....208 E3
Church Row SL3 ....199 D8
Church Sq
  7 High Wycombe HP11 .173 B7
  Leighton Buzzard LU7 ...80 F6
Church St
  Amersham HP7 ....165 B7
  Aspley Guise MK17 .....49 E5
  16 Aylesbury HP20 ....115 D8
  Bovingdon HP3 ....146 B4
  Brill HP18 ....110 B8
  Buckingham MK18 ......52 C8
  Burnham SL1 ....197 C1
  Chesham HP5 ....154 B7
  Gawcott MK18 ....52 A4

Church St continued
  Great Missenden HP16 ..152 B7
  Henley-on-T RG9 ......191 D1
  High Wycombe HP11 ...173 B7
  Little Horwood MK17 ....55 E2
  Maids Moreton MK18 ....41 F3
  Marsh Gibbon OX27 ....71 F3
  Milton Keynes,Fenny Stratford
    MK2 ....47 E1
  Milton Keynes,New Bradwell
    MK13 ....33 F7
  Milton Keynes,Stony Stratford
    MK11 ....32 D5
  Milton Keynes,Wolverton
    MK12 ....33 D7
  North Marston MK18 ....76 B2
  Olney MK46 ....7 A3
  Princes Risborough HP27 .139 B3
  Quainton HP22 ....85 B5
  Slough,Chalvey SL1 ....205 D4
  Slough,Upton Park SL1 .205 F4
  Stokenchurch HP14 ....158 D5
  Twyford MK18 ....62 C2
  6 Windsor SL4 ....210 D6
  Wing LU7 ....79 E2
  Wingrave HP22 ....89 B2
  Winslow MK18 ....65 F4
Church Terr Turvey MK43 ..8 E5
  Windsor SL4 ....209 E5
Church View
  Brackley NN13 ....38 A7
  Edlesborough LU6 ......92 D3
  Halton HP22 ....117 C1
  Long Marston HP23 ....104 A4
  Newport Pagnell MK16 ..22 D4
  9 Slough SL1 ....206 A3
  Steeple Claydon MK18 ..63 E2
Church Views Ct LU7 ...80 E6
Church Views SL6 ......202 F6
Church Way
  East Claydon MK18 .....74 F8
  Stone HP17 ....114 C5
Church Wlk
  Milton Keynes MK3 .....57 F7
  North Crawley MK16 ....24 B6
  Weston Turville HP22 ...116 F1
  Wing LU7 ....79 E2
  Winslow MK18 ....65 F4
Church Yd HP23 ....119 A3
Churchfield Mews SL2 ..206 A7
Churchfield Rd SL9 ....177 D2
Churchgates 3 HP4 ....135 C4
Churchill Ave HP21 ....115 D5
Churchill Cl HP10 ......185 B7
Churchill Ct 1 HP21 ...115 E7
Churchill Dr
  Beaconsfield HP9 ......175 C5
  Marlow SL7 ....183 F4
Churchill Ho UB7 ......208 D6
Churchill Rd SL3 ......206 F2
Churchmead CE Sch
  SL3 ....211 B7
Churchmere Wlk HP21 .115 C6
Churchside SL5 ....163 D7
Churchway HP17 ....127 A6
Chyne The SL9 ....188 F6
Cinnamon Cl SL4 ......209 F6
Cinnamon Gr MK7 .....48 A5
Cippenham Cl SL1 .....204 F6
Cippenham Inf Sch SL1 204 D6
Cippenham Jun Sch
  SL1 ....204 D6
Cippenham La SL1 .....205 B5
City Rd HP14 ....159 D6
Clailey Ct MK11 ....32 F5
Claires Court Sch SL6 .196 D1
Clammas Way UB8 .....208 D6
Clapham Pl MK13 ......34 C2
Clappers Mdw SL6 .....196 B1
Clappins La Naphill HP14 150 D1
  Walter's Ash HP14 .....161 C8
Clapton App HP10 .....185 D8
Clare Croft MK10 ......36 A3
Clare Dr SL2 ....198 B8
Clare Pk HP7 ....165 E7
Clare Rd Maidenhead SL6 202 D6
  Prestwood HP16 ....151 C6
  Slough SL6 ....204 C7
  Stanwell TW19 ....213 E1
Clarefield Cl SL6 ......195 B1
Clarefield Dr SL6 ......195 A1
Clarefield Rd SL6 ......195 A1
Claremont SL3 ....212 D6
Claremont Ave MK11 ...32 E4
Claremont Cl HP21 ....115 F5
Claremont Gdns SL7 ..183 E2
Claremont Rd
  Marlow SL7 ....183 E2
  Windsor SL4 ....210 C5
Clarence Cres SL4 .....210 C6
Clarence Ct
  9 High Wycombe HP13 .173 B7
  Maidenhead SL6 ....202 E8
  Windsor SL4 ....210 B6
Clarence Ho MK9 ......34 C2
Clarence Rd
  Berkhamsted HP4 ......135 C4
  Henley-on-T RG9 ......191 E2
  Milton Keynes MK11 ....32 E5
  Windsor SL4 ....210 B6
Clarendon Copse SL6 ..202 D6
Clarendon Ct Slough SL2 206 B6
  Windsor SL4 ....210 B6
Clarendon Dr
  Milton Keynes MK8 .....33 F2

Clarendon Dr *continued*
Thame OX9 126 A1
Clarendon Rd
High Wycombe HP13 173 E5
Prestwood HP16 151 B6
Claridge Dr MK10 36 A2
Clarke Ct HP20 101 F2
Clarke Dr HP13 174 A6
Clarke Rd MK1 47 D4
Clarke Wlk 2 HP20 101 F2
Clarke's Spring HP23 119 F5
Clarkes Dr UB8 208 E8
Clarkes Field Cl HP18 110 B8
Clarks Cotts HP16 151 C7
Classon Cl UB7 208 E4
Clauds Cl HP15 163 A5
Claverton Cl HP3 146 A3
Clay Acre HP5 144 D1
Clay Cl HP10 185 B8
Clay Hill MK8 33 E2
Clay La Calvert OX27 73 A5
Marlow Bottom SL7 172 A2
Wendover HP22 131 C5
Clay St HP7,HP9 175 C7
Claycots Sch SL2 198 A1
Claycutters MK18 66 A4
Claydon Cl HP21 115 D6
Claydon Ct HP12 172 E4
Claydon End SL9 188 E8
Claydon Ho★ MK18 74 C7
Claydon La SL9 188 E8
Claydon Path HP21 115 E3
Claydons Pl HP27 138 D7
Clayfield Rd HP22 131 C8
Clayfields HP10 163 C2
Clayhall La SL4 210 F2
Clayhill
Marlow Bottom SL7 172 A2
Wigginton HP23 133 E7
Claymoor Pk SL7 172 A2
Clays La MK17 55 E2
Clays The HP17 127 A7
Clayton Ct SL3 207 A3
Clayton Gate MK14 35 A8
Clayton Way UB8 201 D1
Clayton Wlk HP7 166 C8
Claytons Comb Sch SL8 185 A5
Claytons Mdw SL8 185 B2
Clearbrook Cl HP13 174 B4
Cleares Pasture SL1 197 B2
Cleavers OX39 147 B6
Cleavers Ave MK14 34 E3
Cleeve Cres MK3 47 A2
Clegg Sq MK5 46 B5
Cleland Rd SL9 177 D1
Clement Pl 5 HP23 119 A3
Clementi Ave HP15 163 D7
Clements Cl 5 SL1 206 B4
Clements La OX27 71 F2
Clements Rd
Chorleywood WD3 167 D4
Henley-on-T RG9 191 C3
Clerkenwell Cotts HP17 126 F5
Clerkenwell Pl MK6 35 B2
Clevehurst Cl SL2 199 A6
Cleveland MK13 34 B6
Cleveland Cl
Maidenhead SL6 203 B6
Wooburn Green HP10 185 E8
Cleveland Dr LU7 80 C8
Cleveland Pk
Aylesbury HP20 101 F3
Stanwell TW19 213 E1
Cleveland Pl 13 HP20 101 F3
Cleveland Rd
Aylesbury HP20 101 E3
Uxbridge UB8 201 D2
Cleves Ct SL4 209 F4
Clewer Ave SL4 210 A5
Clewer Court Rd SL4 210 B7
Clewer Fields SL4 210 C6
Clewer Green CE Fst Sch
SL4 210 A4
Clewer Hill Rd SL4 209 F4
Clewer New Town SL4 210 A5
Clewer Pk SL4 210 A7
Clickers Yd MK46 6 F4
Clifden Rd HP18 123 E5
Clifford Ave MK2 58 C7
Clifford Rd HP27 139 B3
Cliffords Way SL8 185 B5
Clifton Cl SL6 203 A4
Clifton Ct
High Wycombe HP11 172 E4
Olney MK46 7 A3
8 Stanwell TW19 213 E1
Clifton Gn HP19 101 B2
Clifton Lawns HP6 154 C4
Clifton Lodge
Eton Wick SL4 205 A1
7 Slough SL1 206 A4
Clifton Moor MK5 45 D5
Clifton Rd
Amersham HP6 154 C4
Newton Blossomville MK43 8 A4
5 Slough SL1 206 A4
Clifton Rise SL4 209 D6
Cline Ct MK8 45 E6
Clinkard Pl HP14 171 A3
Clinton Cres HP21 116 A8
Clive Ct SL1 205 D4
Cliveden★ SL6 196 E7
Cliveden Gate SL1 197 B3
Cliveden Mead SL6 196 C2
Cliveden Office Village
HP12 172 E4
Cliveden Rd SL6 196 E4
Clivemont Rd SL6 202 F8
Clock Ho The MK17 59 D6
Clockhouse Mews WD3 167 E6
Cloebury Paddock MK15 35 C3
Cloister Garth HP4 135 C4
Cloisters The
High Wycombe HP13 162 D2
Slough SL1 205 D4
Clonmel Way SL1 197 B2
Close The Akeley MK18 42 A8
Ashendon HP18 97 F1
Bierton HP22 102 A4
Bourne End SL8 185 A6
Great Horwood MK17 55 B3
Hardmead MK16 15 D4
Hardwick HP22 87 B3
Iver Heath SL0 200 C2
Lathbury MK16 22 D7
Milton Keynes,Bradwell
MK13 34 A4
Milton Keynes,The Green
MK6 47 D7
Newton Blossomville MK43 7 F3
Ravenstone MK46 5 E2
Slough SL1 204 D6
Weston Underwood MK46 6 A1
Closes The HP17 127 A7
Cloudberry MK7 48 A6
Cloutsham Cl MK4 46 D3
Clover Cl MK5 46 B8
Clover End MK18 52 C7
Clover La HP21 115 E5
Club Cotts MK17 49 B4
Cluny Ct MK7 48 D6
Clyde Pl MK3 46 E1
Clydesdale Pl MK14 34 F4
Coach Ho The
Loudwater HP11 174 A4
Wooburn Green HP10 185 E6
Coach Ride SL7 183 D4
Coach Yd NN12 18 E3
Coachmaker Ct MK14 34 F6
Coachman's Lodge SL4 210 D5
Coalmans Way SL1 204 A8
Coat Wicks HP9 176 C4
Coaters La HP10 185 E7
Coates La HP13 162 A1
Cobb Cl SL3 211 D6
Cobb Hall Rd MK17 57 C3
Cobb Rd HP4 134 F4
Cobbetts Mount MK18 63 D2
Cobbetts Ride HP23 118 F3
Cobblers Cl SL2 198 B3
Cobblers Wick HP22 89 B3
Cobblershill La HP16 141 B4
Cobbs Gdn MK46 6 F4
Cobden Cl UB8 201 C4
Coberley Cl MK15 35 B6
Cobham Cl
Buckingham MK18 41 C1
Slough SL1 204 F5
Cochran Cl MK8 45 E7
Cochrane Ho UB8 201 C4
Cock Gr HP4 134 D4
Cock La HP10 174 A6
Cockerell Gr MK5 46 C5
Cockett Rd SL3 206 E3
Cockpit Cl HP15 151 E1
Cockpit Rd HP15 162 D8
Coddimoor La MK17 56 B7
Codmore Cres HP5 144 E1
Codmore Cross HP5 144 D1
Codmore Wood Rd HP5 155 D6
Coe Spur SL1 205 B3
Coffee Hall Rdbt MK6 47 B6
Cofferidge Cl MK11 32 D5
Coftards SL2 206 C7
Cogan Ct MK8 45 E7
Cogdells Cl HP5 143 B4
Cogdells La HP5 143 B4
Coggeshall Gr MK7 48 C7
Coin Cl MK10 35 F3
Coke's Farm La HP8 166 B6
Coke's La HP8 166 B6
Cokers Ct 3 SL8 185 A4
Colborne Rd HP13 173 D8
Colchester Ct MK3 57 E7
Colchester Wlk MK3 57 E7
Cold Grove Cotts SL6 196 E2
Cold Harbour CE Comb Sch
MK3 46 F3
Coldeaton La MK4 46 B3
Coldharbour HP22 131 C4
Coldharbour Way HP19 115 A7
Coldmoorholme La SL8 184 E4
Coldmoreham Yd 165 A8
Cole Rd HP21 115 C5
Coleheath Bottom
HP27 150 C5
Colenorton Cres SL4 204 E2
Coleridge Cl
Milton Keynes MK3 58 A7
Newport Pagnell MK16 21 F4
Coleridge Cres SL3 212 E6
Coleridge Way UB7 208 F2
Coles Hill HP18 111 B3
Colesbourne Dr MK15 35 B6
Coleshill CE Inf Sch
HP7 164 F3
Coleshill Ho HP7 165 A4
Coleshill La HP7 164 D2
Coleshill Pl MK13 34 C3
Colet Rd HP22 131 C5
Colgrain St MK9 35 A4
Colham Ave UB7 208 E5
Colham Mill Rd UB7 208 D5
Colham Rd UB8 201 F1
Colin Way SL1 205 B3
Colindale St MK9 35 E1
Colinswood SL2 187 B1
College Ave
Maidenhead SL6 202 E7
Slough SL1 205 E3
College Bsns Pk HP22 103 C1
College Cl OX33 122 C1
College Cres
Oakley HP18 109 E4
Windsor SL4 210 B5
College Glen SL6 202 D7
College Lake Wildlife Ctr★
HP23 105 C1
College Rd
Aston Clinton HP22 117 C7
Cranfield MK43 24 E2
Maidenhead SL6 202 E7
Slough SL1 204 F5
College Rise SL6 202 D7
College The OX27 71 F3
Colley Hill MK13 34 A4
Colley Hill La SL2 187 F1
Colley Ho UB8 201 D4
Colleyland WD3 167 D5
Collier Cl SL6 195 F1
Collings Wlk HP16 151 C5
Collingwood Cl HP13 174 A6
Collins Ho 2 HP11 173 A7
Collins Wlk MK16 22 A4
Collinswood Rd SL2 187 B2
Collum Green Rd SL2 187 E1
Collyer Rd HP14 158 E4
Coln Cl SL6 202 F8
Coln Trad Est SL3 212 F6
Colnbrook By-Pass
Colnbrook SL3 212 D7
Harmondsworth UB7 213 C7
Colnbrook CE Prim Sch
SL3 212 D6
Colnbrook Ct SL3 212 F6
Colndale Rd SL3 212 E5
Colne MK6 47 D6
Colne Ave UB7 208 C4
Colne Bank SL3 212 C4
Colne Orch SL0 207 F6
Colne Park Cvn Site
UB7 208 C2
Colne Rd HP13 173 F7
Colne Reach TW19 212 F2
Colne Valley Park Visitor
Ctr★ UB9 190 B1
Colnedale Rd UB8 201 D7
Colonial Rd 1 SL1 206 A4
Colonnade SL6 203 A7
Colsons Way MK46 6 F5
Colston Bassett MK4 46 C1
Colston Ct SL9 188 E5
Coltman Ave HP18 125 C6
Colts Holm Rd MK12 33 C8
Coltsfoot Dr UB7 208 E7
Coltsfoot Pl MK14 34 D3
Columbia Pl MK9 35 A3
Columbine Rd HP15 162 F6
Colville Ct HP16 152 B7
Colville Rd HP11 172 F6
Combe Martin MK4 46 D3
Combe Rise HP12 172 B7
Combermere Cl SL4 210 B5
Comerford Way MK18 66 A5
Comfrey Cl MK7 48 A5
Comfrey The 2 HP19 101 E4
Common Field HP23 119 D1
Common Gate Rd WD3 167 E4
Common La Eton SL4 205 D1
Hedgerley SL1 186 D1
Milton Keynes MK5 46 C8
Milton Keynes,Bradwell
MK13 34 A4
Common Rd
Chorleywood WD3 167 D5
Dagnall LU6 107 F3
Dorney SL4 204 D2
Eton Wick SL4 205 A2
Flackwell Heath HP10 185 B8
Great Kingshill HP15 151 D1
Slough SL3 207 A1
Common St MK46 5 D1
Common The
Berkhamsted HP4 135 F6
Chipperfield WD4 156 F7
Flackwell Heath HP10 185 B8
Great Kingshill HP15 151 D1
Holmer Green HP15 163 D7
Stokenchurch HP14 158 E5
Common Wood SL2 198 C8
Commonside HP13 161 E3
Como Rd HP20 116 B8
Comp Gate LU6 92 E6
Comp The LU6 92 E6
Compass Point HP4 134 E6
Compton Ct
Moulsoe MK16 36 D8
Slough SL1 204 E7
Compton Dr SL6 202 A8
Compton Rd HP22 131 D5
Concorde Cl UB10 201 E3
Concorde Rd SL6 202 D4
Concorde Way SL1 205 C4
Concourse The 6 MK2 58 C8
Concra Pk MK17 49 C4
Concrete Cows★ MK13 33 F4
Condor Cl MK6 47 A8
Conduit La SL3 206 E1
Conegar Ct SL1 205 E5
Conegra Ct 15 HP13 173 B7
Conegra Rd HP13 173 C7
Coneygere MK46 7 A3
Congreve MK6 47 D5
Conifer Rise HP12 172 E6
Conifers The SL6 202 A8
Conigre OX39 147 B6
Coningsby Cl SL6 202 D3
Coningsby Ct HP13 173 B8
Coningsby Rd HP13 162 B1
Coniston Cres SL1 204 C8
Coniston Gn HP20 101 D3
Coniston Rd LU7 80 C7
Coniston Way MK2 58 D6
Conkers SL6 203 B8
Connaught Cl SL6 195 E1
Connaught Gdns HP4 134 F7
Connaught Rd
Aylesbury HP20 116 C8
3 Slough SL1 206 B4
Conniburrow Bvd MK14 34 E4
Conniston Cl SL7 183 B2
Conought Ho RG9 191 E3
Consort Way UB9 189 F6
Constable Cl MK14 34 F7
Constable Pl HP19 100 F2
Constable's Croft OX25 94 E7
Constantine Pl UB10 201 F4
Constantine Way MK13 33 F5
Convent Ct HP23 118 F3
Convent Rd SL4 210 A5
Conway Cl
Aylesbury HP21 115 F7
Loudwater HP10 174 C2
Milton Keynes MK3 57 F8
Conway Cres MK3 57 E8
Conway Ct SL9 189 B3
Conway Ho HP13 173 F7
Conway Rd SL6 204 B7
Cook Cl MK7 48 B4
Cook's Mdw LU6 92 E4
Cookfield Cl LU6 93 E8
Cookham Ct HP6 154 E1
Cookham Dean Bottom
SL6 195 C8
Cookham Dean CE Prim Sch
SL6 195 B7
Cookham Lodge 15 SL6 202 F6
Cookham Rd SL6 195 F1
Cookham Rise Prim Sch
SL6 195 E6
Cookham Sta SL6 195 F7
Cooks Cl NN7 9 F8
Cooks La MK17 67 E6
Cooks Rd HP19 114 F8
Cookshall La HP12 161 A2
Coombe Ave HP22 131 B4
Coombe Cl HP22 116 C2
Coombe Dr LU6 93 E7
Coombe Gdns
Berkhamsted HP4 134 F5
Hughenden Valley HP14 162 A6
Coombe Hill Ct SL4 209 D4
Coombe La
Aylesbury HP19 100 F1
Walter's Ash HP14 161 F6
Coombe Vale SL9 188 E3
Cooper Rd RG9 191 D3
Cooper Way
3 Berkhamsted HP4 135 D4
Slough SL1 205 B3
Cooper's Court Rd
HP14 158 D5
Cooper's Yd HP20 101 D1
Coopers Ct MK16 22 C4
Coopers Mews MK14 34 F6
Coopers Row SL0 200 D1
Coots Cl MK18 52 E7
Cope Ct SL6 202 C7
Copeland Cl MK7 48 C5
Copes Haven MK5 46 B3
Copes Rd HP15 151 E1
Copes Shroves HP15 162 F5
Copmans Wick WD3 167 D4
Copners Dr HP15 163 C6
Copners Way HP15 163 B6
Copper Beech Cl
Felden HP3 146 F8
Windsor SL4 209 D6
Copper Ridge SL9 177 F5
Copperfield Terr SL2 206 B6
Copperfields
Beaconsfield HP9 175 E5
High Wycombe HP12 161 B1
Copperkins Gr HP6 154 B3
Copperkins La HP6 154 A3
Coppermill La WD3 178 F3
Coppermill Rd TW19 212 B2
Coppice Cl HP20 102 A2
Coppice Farm Pk Cvn Site
HP23 132 D3
Coppice Farm Rd HP10 163 C2
Coppice The
Great Kingshill HP15 151 E1
High Wycombe HP12 172 B4
Seer Green HP9 176 D4
Stokenchurch HP14 158 E5
Walter's Ash HP14 161 B8
West Drayton UB7 208 E7
Wigginton HP23 119 C1
Coppice Way
Aylesbury HP20 102 A2
Hedgerley SL2 187 D2
Coppidwell Dr HP21 116 A5
Coppin La MK13 34 A3
Coppinger Ct UB7 208 E4
Coppins Cl HP4 134 F4
Coppins La SL0 207 F8
Copse Cl Marlow SL7 183 C2
Copse Cl *continued*
Slough SL1 204 F5
West Drayton UB7 208 D3
Copse Gate MK18 66 A4
Copse La HP9 176 E3
Copse The
Amersham HP7 154 C1
Beaconsfield HP9 175 C4
Copse Way HP5 144 A4
Copse Wood SL0 200 D4
Copthall Cl SL9 177 F3
Copthall Cnr SL9 177 E3
Copthall Ho SL6 203 A7
Copthall La SL9 177 E3
Copthorn Cl SL6 202 A4
Copthorne Pl MK7 48 B8
Copyground Ct HP12 172 E7
Copyground La HP12 172 E7
Coral Cl LU6 92 E6
Coram Cl HP4 135 C3
Corbet Ride LU7 80 D8
Corbet Sq LU7 80 D8
Corbett Cl MK15 35 D7
Cordons Cl SL9 177 D2
Cordwainer Ct MK14 34 F6
Cordwallis Bsns Pk SL6 195 E1
Cordwallis Est SL6 202 F8
Cordwallis Rd SL6 202 F8
Cordwallis St SL6 202 E8
Cores End Rd SL8 185 B3
Corfe Cl HP21 116 B5
Corfe Cres MK3 57 F8
Corfe Gdns SL1 205 A6
Corfe Pl SL6 202 C7
Coriander Ct MK7 48 B5
Corin Cl MK2 58 D5
Corin Way MK2 58 D5
Corinium Ind Est HP6 154 F1
Cork Pl MK3 46 E2
Corn Cl HP17 114 D5
Corn Hill MK8 33 E1
Corn Mkt HP11 173 B7
Cornbrook Rd HP21 115 C5
Cornbury Cres MK15 35 A6
Corncrake 9 HP19 101 F3
Cornel Cl HP15 163 B3
Cornel Ho 1 SL4 210 D4
Cornelia Cl MK2 58 C6
Cornerways HP27 150 C5
Cornfield Cl UB8 201 D3
Cornfield Cres HP4 134 D7
Cornflower Pl MK18 52 C7
Cornhill Cty Fst Sch MK6 47 A6
Cornwall Ave SL2 198 C1
Cornwall Cl
Eton Wick SL4 204 E1
Maidenhead SL6 195 E2
Cornwall Ct UB8 201 D6
Cornwall Gr MK3 46 F1
Cornwall Ho UB8 201 D6
Cornwall Lodge 11 SL6 202 F6
Cornwall Rd UB8 201 D6
Cornwalls Ctr The MK18 41 D1
Cornwalls Mdw MK18 41 D1
Cornwell Rd SL4 211 A1
Coronation Ave
Slough SL3 206 E7
Windsor SL4 211 A4
Coronation Cotts MK18 41 F8
Coronation Cres HP14 171 C5
Coronation Mews LU7 80 F8
Coronation Pl MK18 63 D2
Coronation Rd
Cranfield MK43 25 B1
High Wycombe HP12 172 D4
Milton Keynes MK11 32 E5
Coronation Villas HP21 115 E8
Corporation St HP13 173 B7
Corrid Ind Pk HP19 101 B1
Corrigan Cl MK3 58 A8
Corsewall Pl MK4 45 F1
Corsham Ct 4 MK8 33 F1
Cosgrove Leisure Pk★
MK19 19 F1
Cosgrove Rd MK19 32 C7
Cosgrove Village Prim Sch
MK19 19 E2
Costers Cotts SL8 185 B2
Costins Wlk 7 HP4 135 D4
Cosway Pl MK8 45 D6
Cotes Way LU7 79 F3
Cotman Cl MK12 33 B5
Cotswold Cl
Maidenhead SL6 203 B6
Slough SL1 205 B3
Uxbridge UB8 201 C4
Cotswold Ct HP12 172 F8
Cotswold Dr LU7 80 C8
Cotswold Gn HP20 101 E2
Cotswold Way HP13 172 E8
Cotswolds Way MK18,
OX27 73 B5
Cottage Comm MK5 46 B8
Cottage Farm Way
HP27 150 C4
Cottage Grounds HP17 114 D5
Cottage Park Rd SL2 187 D2
Cottages The
Ickenham UB10 190 E2
Syresham NN13 27 C5
Cottesbrooke Cl SL3 212 D6
Cottesloe Cl LU7 79 E3
Cottesloe Ct MK11 32 F5
Cottesloe Rd HP21 115 E5
Cottesloe Sch The LU7 79 D1
Cottingham Gr MK3 58 A7
Cottisford Cres MK14 21 F1
Cottland Clay HP17 127 A7

Cotts The
Long Crendon HP18 ....125 C6
Longwick HP27 ....138 E5
Coulson Ave MK8,MK5 ...45 E6
Coulson Ct HP16 ......151 D6
Coulson Way SL1 .....204 B8
Council Hos LU7 ....92 A1
Countisbury MK4 ....46 D2
Country La HP15 ......151 F1
Country Life Ho SL3 ...211 B7
County Rd NN13 ....38 A6
Cours La Ville Cl MK18 ..65 E3
Court Cl Aylesbury HP21 ..115 E7
  High Wycombe HP13 ...161 E1
  Maidenhead SL6 ......203 D2
  Princes Risborough HP27 ..139 A3
Court Cnr MK46 ....6 E3
Court Cres SL1 ....205 D7
Court Dr Maidenhead SL6 196 C3
  Uxbridge UB10 ....201 F4
Court Farm Ind Est
  TW19 ....213 F1
Court La Burnham SL1 ..197 D2
  Dorney SL4 ....204 C8
  Iver SL0 ....208 A5
Court Lawns HP10 .....163 C1
Court Rd Cranfield MK43 ..25 B1
  Maidenhead SL6 ......196 C3
Court The MK17 ....37 C3
Courteneys Lodge MK4 ..46 E3
Courtfield Dr SL6 .....202 C6
Courtfield Gdns UB9 ...190 A1
Courthouse★ HP18 .....125 D7
Courthouse Cl MK18 ....65 F5
Courthouse Jun Sch
  SL6 ....202 B8
Courthouse Mews MK16 ..22 C4
Courthouse Rd SL6 ....202 C8
Courtlands
  Leighton Buzzard LU7 ...80 E6
  14 Maidenhead SL6 ....202 F6
Courtlands Ave SL3 ...206 D2
Courtmoor Cl HP27 ....139 C6
Courtneidge Cl LU7 .....78 E8
Courtney Ho UB9 ......189 F5
Courtyard Arts Ctr★
  MK14 ....21 E1
Courtyard Cl HP6 ......154 C1
Courtyard The
  Aylesbury HP19 ......101 C1
  Beaconsfield HP9 ....175 D2
  7 Bourne End SL8 ....185 B3
  9 Marlow SL7 ....183 D2
  1 Marlow SL7 ....183 E2
  22 Windsor SL4 ......210 D6
Courtyards The HP22 ..117 E4
Cousins Cl UB7 ....208 E6
Cousins Dr HP20 ......101 F2
Cousins Piece HP12 ....112 B2
Coverack Pl MK4 ....57 B8
Coverdale MK13 ....34 C5
Coverdale Way SL2 ....197 E1
Covert Cl HP4 ....134 D6
Covert Rd HP4 ....134 D6
Cow La Edlesborough LU6 ..92 E4
  Gawcott MK18 ....51 F4
  Tring HP23 ....119 D4
Cowdray Cl MK15 ....35 C3
Cowleaze OX39 ....147 B6
Cowley Bsns Pk UB8 ...201 C2
Cowley Cl HP22 ....102 B3
Cowley Cotts HP7 .....164 C3
Cowley Cres SL6 ......208 C8
Cowley Inf Sch UB8 ...208 D8
Cowley Mill Rd UB8 ...201 B3
Cowley Mill Trad Est
  UB8 ....201 B3
Cowley Rd UB8 ....201 C4
Cowper & Newton Mus The★
  MK46 ....6 F3
Cowper Cl MK16 ....22 A4
Cowper Rd
  Berkhamsted HP4 .....135 B4
  Chesham HP5 ....144 B2
  Slough SL1 ....198 A1
Cowper St MK46 ....7 A5
Cowpers Orch MK46 .....6 A1
Cowslip UB10 ....201 E5
Cowslip Rd HP15 ......162 F6
Cox Green La SL6 .....202 C3
Cox Green Rd SL6 .....202 D3
Cox Green Sch SL6 ....202 A4
Coxborrow Cl SL6 .....195 E7
Coxfield Cl SL6 ....158 F5
Coxwell Cl MK18 ....41 F1
Coy Ct HP20 ....116 A8
CR Bates Ind Est HP14 ..158 E5
Crab Tree Cl
  Beaconsfield HP9 ....175 B1
  Olney MK46 ....6 F5
Crabbe Cres HP5 ......144 D2
Crabs Gr HP22 ....86 F7
Crabtree Cotts HP27 ..139 A1
Crabtree Rd MK17 ......49 C8
Crabtree Rd HP27 .....127 A5
Craddocks Cl MK13 .....34 B3
Cradley Wlk HP10 .....101 E3
Crafton Pl 4 HP19 ....100 F1
Craigleith Ct HP9 .....175 D2
Craigmore Ave MK3 .....57 F8
Craigwell Ave HP21 ...116 C7
Cranberry Cl MK7 ......48 B6
Cranborne Ave
  Milton Keynes MK4 .....45 F1
  Milton Keynes MK4 .....45 F1
Cranbourne Ave SL4 ...209 F5
Cranbourne Cl SL1 ....205 C5

Cranbourne Rd SL1 ....205 C5
Cranbrook MK17 ....49 B5
Cranbrook Dr SL6 .....195 C1
Crane Ct MK5 ....34 B1
Crane Way MK43 ....25 C2
Cranes MK43 ....8 E5
Cranesbill Pl MK14 .....34 E4
Cranfield Innovation Ctr
  MK43 ....37 D8
Cranfield Lower Sch
  MK43 ....25 B1
Cranfield Rd
  Astwood MK16,MK43 ....16 B2
  Cranfield MK43 ....25 F3
  Moulsoe MK16 ....36 E8
  Salford MK17 ....37 D5
  Wavendon MK17 ....37 B2
Cranfield Tech Pk MK43 ..37 C8
Cranfield Univ MK43 ....24 E2
Cranwell Cl MK5 ....46 B3
Craufurd Ct SL6 ......202 E8
Craufurd Rise SL6 ....202 E8
Craven The MK13 ....34 C4
Crawley Rd
  Cranfield MK43 ....25 B3
  Woburn MK17 ....60 F8
Crawley's La HP23 ....133 F7
Crawshays SL6 ....203 C8
Crayle St SL2 ....198 B2
Creden Cl SL6 ....195 D1
Creed St MK12 ....33 D7
Creighton Rd HP18 .....83 F1
Crendon Rd HP18 ......112 A1
Crendon St HP13 ......173 B7
Creran Wlk LU7 ....80 C7
Crescent Cotts HP18 ...83 A6
Crescent Dale SL6 ....202 F6
Crescent Dr SL6 ......202 E7
Crescent The
  Cranfield MK43 ....24 E2
  Haversham MK19 ....20 E2
  High Wycombe HP13 ...173 E8
  Maidenhead SL6 ......202 E7
  Marsworth HP23 .....105 A1
  Milton Keynes,Fenny Stratford
   MK2 ....47 C1
  Milton Keynes,Giffard Park
   MK14 ....21 E2
  Pitstone LU7 ....105 C4
  Princes Risborough HP27 ..139 C3
  Slough SL1 ....205 E4
Crescent Villas 5 SL4 ..210 C6
Creslow Ct MK11 ....32 F5
Creslow Way HP17 .....114 B3
Cress Rd SL1 ....205 B4
Cressex Bsns Pk HP12 ..172 D4
Cressex Com Sch HP12 ..172 C3
Cressex Ent Ctr HP12 ..172 C3
Cressex Rd HP12 ......172 C3
Cressey Ave MK5 ....46 B4
Cressington Ct 2 SL8 ..185 A4
Cressington Pl SL8 ....185 A4
Cresswell Ct TW19 ....213 D1
Cresswell Rd HP5 .....154 D5
Cresswell Way HP15 ...163 D7
Cresswells Mead SL6 ..203 C1
Crest Rd HP11 ....172 D3
Crest The
  Beaconsfield HP9 ....175 A1
  Bledlow Ridge HP14 ..159 F8
  Maidenhead SL6 ......203 A7
  Marlow SL7 ....183 D2
  Penn HP10 ....174 F7
Cricket Field Rd UB8 ..201 D4
Cricket Green Rdbt MK9 ..35 B4
Cricket Ground HP14 ..158 D5
Cricketers Row MK14 ...66 A4
Cricketfield Rd UB7 ...208 C2
Cricklebeck MK13 ....34 B5
Crimp Hill SL4 ....211 A1
Crisp Rd RG9 ....191 C3
Crispin Cl HP9 ....175 C4
Crispin Field LU7 .....105 C4
Crispin Rd MK13 ....34 B7
Crispin Way
  Farnham Common SL2 ..198 D8
  High Wycombe HP11 ...173 A4
  Uxbridge UB8 ....208 F8
Criss Gr SL9 ....177 C1
Crocketts La HP16 ....142 D5
Crocus Dr HP15 ....115 B5
Croft Cl SL4 ....211 A2
Croft Ct 5 HP21 ......115 E7
Croft Ctyd HP17 ......126 F6
Croft Gn LU6 ....93 F8
Croft Ho SL0 ....207 E7
Croft Mdws LU7 ....105 A7
Croft Rd Aylesbury HP21 ..115 E7
  Chalfont St Peter SL9 ..177 E1
Croft The
  Haddenham HP17 ......126 F5
  Maidenhead SL6 ......202 C5
  Marlow SL7 ....184 A3
Crofters SL4 ....211 A1
Crofters Cl TW19 .....213 D1
Crofthill Rd SL2 ......198 B1
Crofton Ho HP11 ......174 A4
Crofts End MK6 ....14 A1
Crofts La MK17 ....57 D3
Croftwood HP13 ....173 F7
Cromarty Ct MK3 ....46 E3
Cromer Cl HP4 ....121 E5
Cromer Ct SL1 ....205 E2
Cromhamstone HP17 ...114 C8
Cromwell Ave
  Aylesbury HP19 ......101 D2
  Newport Pagnell MK16 ..22 A3
  Thame OX9 ....126 A1

Cromwell Cl HP8 ......177 C7
Cromwell Ct MK18 ....41 E2
Cromwell Dr SL1 ......205 E7
Cromwell Gdns 10 SL7 ..183 E2
Cromwell Ho
  Chesham HP5 ....144 B1
  Uxbridge UB8 ....201 C4
Cromwell Mews 1
  HP19 ....115 A8
Cromwell Rd
  High Wycombe HP13 ...173 E5
  Maidenhead SL6 ......202 D7
  Marlow SL7 ....183 E2
Cropredy Ct MK18 ......41 E2
Cropton Rise MK4 ....46 A2
Cropwell Bishop MK4 ...46 C1
Crosby Cl HP9 ....186 F8
Crosby Ct MK8 ....45 E6
Crosland Rd HP21 .....116 B6
Cross Ct HP13 ....161 D2
Cross End MK17 ....48 F7
Cross Farm Mews HP3 ..146 E2
Cross La
  Beaconsfield HP9 ....186 F8
  Tingewick MK18 ....51 B6
  Weston Underwood MK46 ...6 B2
Cross Lanes
  Bledlow HP27 ....138 A2
  Chalfont St Peter SL9 ..177 F5
Cross Lanes Cl SL9 ...177 F5
Cross Oak SL4 ....210 A5
Cross Oak Rd HP4 .....135 A4
Cross Rd
  High Wycombe HP12 ...172 C6
  Uxbridge UB8 ....201 C5
Cross St
  Newport Pagnell MK16 ..22 A4
  Uxbridge UB8 ....201 C5
Cross Tree Rd MK19 ....31 B3
Crossfield Cl HP4 .....134 F4
Crossfield Ho SL9 .....188 E7
Crossfield Rd HP27 ...139 C4
Crosshills MK11 ....32 D4
Crosslands MK14 ....34 E4
Crossleys 4 MK7 ......177 C7
Crossley UB7 ....207 D8
Crosslow Bank MK4 .....46 C3
Crossway MK5 ....144 E1
Crossway The UB10 ...201 F1
Crossways
  Beaconsfield HP9 ....175 F1
  Berkhamsted HP4 ....134 F3
  High Wycombe HP12 ...172 C4
Crossways Bsns Pk HP18 83 C3
Crossways Ct 4 SL4 ...210 C5
Crosthwaite Way SL1 ..204 D8
Crow La MK11 ....49 B8
Crow Piece La SL2 ....197 E4
Crowborough La MK7 ...48 A8
Crowbrook Rd HP27 ...139 C6
Crowell Mews HP19 ...114 F8
Crowell Rd OX39 ......147 B5
Crown Bsns Est HP5 ...144 C1
Crown Cl SL3 ....212 C7
Crown Cotts Botley HP5 ..155 B8
  Windsor SL4 ....210 D3
Crown Ct MK14 ....161 A2
Crown La
  East Burnham SL2 ....198 A4
  High Wycombe HP11 ...173 B6
  Maidenhead SL6 ......203 A7
  Marlow SL7 ....183 D2
  Penn HP10 ....174 F7
Crown Leys HP20 ......101 E1
Crown Mdw SL3 ....212 B7
Crown Rd SL7 ....183 D2
Crown Rose Ct HP23 ..119 A3
Crown Way UB7 ....208 F5
Crown Wlk
  Milton Keynes MK9 .....34 F2
  Uxbridge UB8 ....201 C5
Crownfield HP27 ......149 C3
Crownhill Rdbt MK8 ....45 E8
Crowther Ct MK5 ....46 C5
Croxley Ct 3 LU7 ......80 F8
Croxley Rise SL6 .....202 D6
Croydon Cl MK4 ....46 C3
Cruickshank Gr MK8 ....45 E7
Crummock Cl SL1 ......204 C7
Crummock Pl MK2 ....58 D6
Crusader Est HP12 ....172 D5
Crutches La HP4 ......176 E4
Cryers Hill La HP15 ..162 D8
Cryers Hill Rd HP15 ..162 C6
Cuba Cotts SL6 ....196 B3
Cubb Field HP19 ......115 B7
Cublington Rd HP22 ....88 D6
Cuckoo Way HP19 .....114 F8
Cuddington CE Sch
  HP18 ....112 F3
Cuddington Hill HP18 ..112 E3
Cuddington Rd HP17,
  HP18 ....113 E3
Cudsdens Ct HP16 ....152 D7
Cuff La MK17 ....59 D1
Culbertson La MK13 ....33 E6
Culham Dr SL6 ....195 E2
Cullen Rd MK2 ....58 D5
Culley Way SL6 ....202 A4
Cullyn Rd HP12 ....172 C3
Culmstock Cl MK4 ......46 D2
Culrain Rd SL3 ....212 A4
Culross Gr MK10 ....36 A2
Culvers Croft HP9 .....176 C4
Culvert La UB8 ....201 D1
Culverton Hill HP27 ..139 B3
Culverton La HP27 ....139 B1

Cumberland Ave SL2 ..198 C1
Cumberland Cl
  Aylesbury HP21 ......116 B7
  Little Chalfont HP7 ..166 B8
Cumbrae Cl SL2 ....206 A5
Cumbria Cl
  Maidenhead SL6 ......202 C3
  Milton Keynes MK3 ....46 F1
Cumbrian Way
  High Wycombe HP13 ...172 F8
  Uxbridge UB8 ....201 D5
Curfew Yd The 2 SL4 ..210 D6
Curlew HP19 ....101 F3
Curlew Cl
  Berkhamsted HP4 ....135 C3
  High Wycombe HP13 ...161 C3
Curls La SL6 ....202 E4
Curls Rd SL6 ....202 D6
Curran Cl UB8 ....201 C1
Currier Dr MK14 ....34 F6
Curriers La SL1 ......197 D7
Cursley Path 11 HP19 ..115 A8
Curtis Cotts HP5 .....144 F7
Curtis Croft MK5 ....46 B3
Curtis Way HP4 ....135 C3
Curzon Ave
  Beaconsfield HP9 ....175 D4
  Tylers Green HP15 ...163 C2
Curzon CE Comb Sch
  HP7 ....164 A5
Curzon Cl HP15 ....163 C2
Curzon Gate MK14 ....158 E5
Curzon Mall 6 SL1 ....205 E6
Curzon Pl MK7 ....48 E4
Cut Throat Ave HP4 ...107 E7
Cutler's Ct 6 HP12 ...172 E7
Cutlers Mews MK14 ....34 F6
Cuttle Brook Gdns OX9 ..125 E1
Cyclamen Pl HP21 .....115 B5
Cygnet Ho SL6 ....196 C1
Cypress MK16 ....22 A3
Cypress Ho SL3 ......207 B1
Cypress Wlk HP15 ....163 B3

D

Daceberry Ct RG9 .....192 C5
Dacre Rd HP22 ....131 E7
Dadbrook HP18 ....112 F2
Dadbrook Cl HP18 .....112 F2
Dadfield Cl HP18 .....112 F2
Dag La
  Stoke Goldington MK16 ...12 A7
  Stoke Goldington MK16 ...12 B6
Dagmar Rd SL4 ....210 D5
Dagnall Cres UB8 .....208 C8
Dagnall Rd Olney MK46 ...6 F4
  Whipsnade LU6 ....93 D2
Dagnall Sch HP4 ......107 C5
Dair House Sch SL2 ...198 B4
Dairy La RG9 ....192 B8
Dairymede HP27 ......150 C4
Daisy Cotts HP14 ....171 B4
Dale Cl NN13 ....38 A7
Dale Ct SL1 ....205 C4
Dale Side SL9 ....188 E2
Dalesford Rd HP21 ...116 A4
Dalgin Pl MK9 ....35 A3
Dalston Cl HP20 ......101 F2
Dalton Gate MK10 .....35 F4
Dalvina Pl MK12 ....33 D4
Dalwood Mews 3 HP19 115 A4
Daly Way HP20 ....116 B7
Damask Cl HP21 ......119 C4
Damson Gr SL1 ....205 C4
Danbury Ct MK14 ....34 E5
Dancers End La HP22,
  HP23 ....118 C2
Dandridge Cl SL3 .....206 D3
Dandridge Ct MK8 .....45 C6
Dandridge Dr SL8 .....185 C3
Dane Cl HP7 ....165 F6
Dane Ct MK7 ....115 D4
Dane Rd MK1 ....47 D3
Danes Ct SL6 ....202 D7
Danes Gdns SL6 ......195 F6
Danesborough Dr MK17 ..49 A2
Danesbrook Cl MK4 ....46 D6
Danesfield MK17 ....49 A1
Danesfield Sch SL7 ...193 E7
Daneswood MK17 ....49 A1
Daniels Welch MK6 .....47 A6
Dansteed Way
  Milton Keynes,Bradwell Common
   MK8,MK13,MK14,MK5 ...34 C4
  Milton Keynes,Crownhill
   MK8 ....45 D7
Danvers Croft HP23 ...119 C3
Darby Cl MK5 ....46 B5
Darby Lodge HP13 ....174 F7
Darin Ct MK8 ....45 F8
Dark La Chearsley HP18 ..112 B2
  Oving HP22 ....86 C7
  Wingrave HP22 ....89 C2
Darley Cl HP21 ....116 B6
Darley Gate MK14 .....35 A5
Darley's La MK14 ......83 A6
Darling's La SL6 .....194 E1
Darlington Cl HP6 ....154 C1
Darnel Cl MK6 ....47 A5
Darr's La HP4 ....134 C4
Darrell Cl SL3 ....206 F2
Darsham Wlk HP4 .....158 B8
Dart Cl Aylesbury HP21 ..115 C5
  Newport Pagnell MK16 ..22 C4
  Slough SL3 ....212 B8
Dartington Pl MK4 .....45 F1
Dartmouth Ct 10 SL1 ..205 F3

Dartmouth Rd MK46 .....6 F4
Darvell Dr HP5 ....144 A2
Darvill Rd HP17 ......114 B5
Darvill's La SL1 ......205 D4
Darville Ho 19 SL4 ...210 D6
Darvills Mdw HP15 ....163 C7
Darwin Cl MK5 ....45 E5
Darwin Rd SL3 ....206 F4
Dashfield Gr HP15 ....162 F6
Dashwood Ave MK12 ...172 D7
Dashwood Cl SL3 .....206 C2
Dashwood Ind Est HP12 172 D7
Datchet Ho 3 SL1 .....205 F3
Datchet Lodge Ctyd
  SL3 ....211 B6
Datchet Pl 3 SL3 .....211 B6
Datchet Rd Eton SL4 ..205 F2
  Horton SL3 ....211 F4
  Old Windsor SL4 .....211 A3
  Windsor SL4 ....210 D7
Datchet St Mary's CE Prim
  Sch SL3 ....211 B6
Datchet Sta SL3 ......211 B6
Daubeney Gate MK5 ....45 F6
Davenies Sch HP9 ....175 C2
Davenport Lea MK7 ....48 E5
Davenport Rd HP12 ...172 C3
Daventry Cl SL3 ......212 F6
David Bishop Ct HP5 ..154 D5
David Cl HP21 ....116 A4
David Rd SL3 ....212 A4
Davidge Pl HP9 ....175 C5
Davidson Rd 6 SL3 ...206 F1
Davies Ct HP12 ......172 B4
Davies La HP20 ....115 D8
Davies Way HP10 .....174 C1
Davis Cl SL7 ....183 E1
Davis Ho 3 HP4 ....135 C3
Davison Ct MK8 ....45 D6
Davy Ave MK5 ....46 D6
Dawe's Cl SL1 ....201 E3
Dawe's Rd UB10 ......201 E3
Dawes Ct HP5 ....154 B7
Dawes East Rd SL1 ...197 C2
Dawes La WD3 ....156 F3
Dawes Moor Cl SL2 ...206 C7
Dawley Ride SL3 .....212 E6
Dawn Redwood Cl SL3 212 A4
Dawney Cl HP19 ......101 C2
Daws Cl SL0 ....207 F2
Daws Hill La HP11 ....173 A4
Daws Lea HP11 ....173 B3
Dawson Cl SL4 ....210 A5
Dawson Rd MK1 ....47 D3
Daylesford Ct MK15 ...35 B5
De Clare Ct MK18 .....41 E1
De Havilland Dr HP15 ..162 E2
De Havilland Way TW19 213 E1
De Montfort Univ MK7 ..48 E4
De Pirenore HP15 ....162 E2
Deacon Cl HP12 ......172 B4
Deacon Ct SL4 ....209 D5
Deacon Pl MK10 ....35 F3
Deadhearn La HP8 ....166 E1
Deal Ave SL1 ....204 F7
Dean Cl Aylesbury HP21 ..116 A4
  High Wycombe HP12 ...172 E6
  Uxbridge UB10 ......201 E5
  Windsor SL4 ....209 D4
Dean Farm La LU7 .....69 E4
Dean Field HP3 ....146 A4
Dean La SL6 ....195 C8
Dean Rd LU7 ....68 D3
Dean St SL7 ....183 D2
Dean The HP22 ....89 E3
Dean View SL6 ....195 D6
Dean Way
  Aston Clinton HP22 ...117 F4
  Chalfont St Giles HP8 ..177 D7
  Holmer Green HP15 ...163 B6
Dean Wood Rd HP9 ...176 D2
Dean's Cloisters SL4 ..210 D7
Dean's Rd MK12 ....33 C7
Deanacre Cl SL9 .....177 C4
Deancroft Rd SL9 ....177 E4
Deanfield HP14 ....160 B8
Deanfield Ave RG9 ....191 D1
Deanfield Cl Marlow SL7 183 D2
  Saunderton HP14 .....149 C1
Deanfield Rd RG9 ....191 D1
Deangarden Rise HP11 173 D4
Deans Cl Amersham HP6 ..154 F2
  Tring HP23 ....119 C4
  Wexham Street SL2 ...199 B4
Deans Furlong HP23 ..119 C4
Deans Lawn HP4 ......135 C4
Deans Mdw HP4 ......107 C4
Deansfield Cl SL6 ....195 D2
Deanshanger Dr NN12 ..17 F1
Deanshanger Prim Sch
  MK19 ....31 E1
Deanshanger Rd
  Old Stratford MK19 ....32 B6
  Wicken MK19 ....31 B3
Deansway HP5 ....144 B2
Dearing Cl 11 HP20 ...101 C2
Debbs Cl MK11 ....32 E5
Deben Cl MK16 ....22 C4
Decies Way SL2 ......199 A4
Dedmere Ct SL7 ......183 F2
Dedmere Rd SL7 ......183 F2
Dedmere Rise SL7 ....183 E2
Dedworth Dr SL4 .....209 F6
Dedworth Green Fst Sch
  SL4 ....209 E5

Dedworth Manor SL4 . .209 F6
Dedworth Mid Sch SL4 .209 E6
Dedworth Rd SL4 . . . .209 D5
Deeds Gr HP12 . . . . . .172 E5
Deena Cl SL1 . . . . . . .204 E6
Deep Acres HP6 . . . . .154 A3
Deep Field SL3 . . . . . .211 B8
Deep Mill La HP16 . . . .152 D3
Deepdale MK13 . . . . . .34 C5
Deer Park Wlk HP5 . . .144 E3
Deer Wlk MK9 . . . . . . .34 F3
Deerfern Cl MK14 . . . . .21 E1
Deerfield Cl MK18 . . . . .52 E7
Deermead HP16 . . . . . .152 B4
Deerswood SL6 . . . . . .196 A1
Deethe Cl MK17 . . . . . .49 B6
Delafield HP14 . . . . . .158 F4
Delaford Cl SL0 . . . . . .207 F7
Delaford Ho HP7 . . . . .208 D5
Delahay Rise HP4 . . . .135 B6
Delamere Cl HP20 . . . .101 F2
Delamere Gdns LU7 . . .80 C7
Delaware Dr
  Milton Keynes MK15 . . .35 F4
  Tongwell MK15,MK16 . . .22 B1
Delius Cl MK7 . . . . . . .48 C4
Dell Cl SL2 . . . . .198 C7
Dell Field SL1 . . . . . . .151 C5
Dell Field Ave HP4 . . .135 C6
Dell Lees HP9 . . . . . . .176 C4
Dell Rd Berkhamsted HP4 134 D7
  West Drayton UB7 . . . .208 F3
Dell The Aylesbury HP20 .102 A2
  Chalfont St Peter SL9 . .177 E4
  Maidenhead SL6 . . . . .202 A3
  Stokenchurch HP14 . . .158 F3
  Tylers Green HP10 . . . .163 B5
  Uxbridge UB8 . . . . . .201 C6
Dellfield HP5 . . . . . . .144 A4
Dellfield Cl HP4 . . . . .135 C6
Dellfield Cres UB8 . . . .201 C1
Dellfield Par UB8 . . . . .201 C1
Dells MK46 . . . . .6 F4
Dellside UB9 . . . . . . .190 C6
Delmeade Rd HP5 . . . .154 A7
Deltic Ave MK13 . . . . . .34 B2
Demoram Cl MK18 . . . . .65 D2
Denbigh East Ind Est
  MK1 . . . . .47 D2
Denbigh Hall MK3 . . . . .46 F3
Denbigh Hall Dr MK3 . . .46 F3
Denbigh Hall Ind Est
  MK3 . . . . .46 F3
Denbigh Rd
  Milton Keynes MK1 . . . .47 D4
  Thame OX9 . . . . .126 A1
Denbigh Sch MK5 . . . . .46 A4
Denbigh Way MK2 . . . . .47 C1
Denbigh West Ind Est
  MK1 . . . . .47 B2
Denby Wlk HP20 . . . . .116 A8
Denchworth Ct **2** MK4 . .46 C2
Dene Cl Winslow MK18 . . .66 A3
  Woburn Sands MK17 . . .49 C4
Dene The MK18 . . . . . . .63 D3
Denewood HP13 . . . . . .173 E8
Denham Ave UB9 . . . . .189 F3
Denham Cl Denham UB9 .190 A1
  Maidenhead SL6 . . . . .202 C6
  Milton Keynes MK3 . . . .57 D8
Denham Court Dr UB9 . .190 B1
Denham Ctry Pk★ UB9 .190 B2
Denham Garden Village
  UB9 . . . . .189 F5
Denham Golf Club Sta
  UB9 . . . . .189 D4
Denham Green Cl UB9 . .190 A4
Denham Green La UB9 . .189 F5
Denham La SL9 . . . . . .178 A4
Denham Lodge UB9 . . . .201 C6
Denham Rd
  Iver Heath SL0 . . . . . .200 E5
  Lane End HP14 . . . . . .171 C5
Denham Sta UB9 . . . . .190 A4
Denham View MK18 . . . .75 F6
Denham Village Inf Sch
  UB9 . . . . .189 F2
Denham Way UB9 . . . . .190 A1
Denham Way (North Orbital
Rd) WD3 . . . . .178 E4
Denham Way North Orbital
Rd UB9 . . . . .189 F7
Denham Wlk SL9 . . . . .177 F4
Denholme Lodge SL3 . . .211 B7
Denison Ct MK7 . . . . . . .48 D6
Denmark St
  High Wycombe HP11 . . .173 A7
  Maidenhead SL6 . . . . .202 E8
  Milton Keynes MK2 . . . .58 E8
Denmead MK8 . . . . .33 E2
Denmead Cl SL9 . . . . .188 E4
Dennis Cl HP22 . . . . . .118 A4
Dennis Way SL1 . . . . . .204 D6
Denniston Ho HP12 . . . .172 C8
Denny Rd SL3 . . . . . . .206 F2
Denny's La HP4 . . . . . .134 F2
Denton Cl SL7 . . . . . . .183 F3
Depot Rd SL6 . . . . . . .203 A6
Derby Arms **2** HP20 . .115 D8
Derby Rd UB8 . . . . . . .201 D3
Dere Pl MK2 . . . . .58 E4
Derehams Ave HP10 . . .174 C3
Derehams La HP10 . . . .174 C2
Derek Rd SL6 . . . . . . .203 C8
Deri Dene Cl **2** TW19 . .213 E1

Derwent Cl
  Little Chalfont HP7 . . . .166 B8
  Newport Pagnell MK16 . . .22 D4
Derwent Dr
  Maidenhead SL6 . . . . .202 D8
  Milton Keynes MK3 . . . .57 E8
  Slough SL1 . . . . .204 C8
Derwent Rd
  Aylesbury HP21 . . . . .116 B6
  Leighton Buzzard LU7 . . .80 B7
Desborough Ave HP11 . .172 F6
Desborough Cres SL6 . .202 D5
Desborough Gn **1**
  HP20 . . . . .101 D2
Desborough Ho **14**
  HP13 . . . . .173 B7
Desborough Ind Pk
  HP12 . . . . .172 E8
Desborough Park Rd
  HP12 . . . . .172 E8
Desborough Rd HP11 . .172 F7
Desborough Sch SL6 . .202 E5
Desborough St HP11 . . .172 F7
Deseronto Wharf Ind Est
  SL3 . . . . .206 E4
Develin Cl MK14 . . . . . .34 F7
Devereux Pl HP19 . . . .101 A2
Devereux Rd SL4 . . . . .210 D5
Deverill Rd HP21 . . . . .115 C3
Deverills Way SL3 . . . .207 C2
Devon Ave SL1 . . . . . .205 C5
Devon Cl MK3 . . . . .46 F1
Devon Pk HP20 . . . . . .101 A3
Devon Way UB10 . . . . .201 F3
Devonshire Ave HP6 . . .154 B2
Devonshire Cl
  Amersham HP6 . . . . . .154 C2
  Farnham Royal SL2 . . .198 B3
Devonshire Gn SL2 . . . .198 B3
Devonshire Lodge **10**
  SL6 . . . . .202 F6
Dexter Ave MK6 . . . . . .46 F8
Dexter Ho MK6 . . . . . . .46 F8
Dhoon Rise SL6 . . . . . .202 F6
Diamond Rd SL1 . . . . .206 A4
Diana Cl SL3 . . . . .206 E2
Diane Cl HP21 . . . . . . .116 A4
Dibden Hill HP8 . . . . . .177 C3
Dickens Cl MK43 . . . . . . .3 F6
Dickens Dr MK19 . . . . . .32 B6
Dickens Rd MK12 . . . . . .33 C8
Dickens Spinney MK46 . . .6 E4
Dickens Way HP19 . . . .100 F2
Dickins Pl SL3 . . . . . . .212 E6
Dicks Way HP19 . . . . . .100 F3
Diddington Cl MK2 . . . . .58 C3
Digby Cl OX9 . . . . . . .126 B1
Digby Croft MK10 . . . . .35 C3
Dilwyn Ct **1** HP12 . . .172 E7
Dingle Dell LU7 . . . . . . .70 F2
Dingleberry MK46 . . . . . .6 F4
Dinmore HP3 . . . . .145 F3
Dinton CE Sch HP17 . . .113 F3
Disraeli Cres HP13 . . . .161 F1
Disraeli Ct SL3 . . . . . .212 B8
Disraeli Pk HP9 . . . . . .175 D4
Disraeli Sch The HP13 . .161 F1
Disraeli Sq **4** HP19 . .115 A8
Diswell Brook Way MK19 31 E5
Ditchfield Cotts HP14 . . .171 A3
Ditchingham Cl HP19 . . .115 B7
Ditton Park Cvn Site
  SL3 . . . . .206 F1
Ditton Park Rd SL3 . . . .211 B8
Ditton Rd Datchet SL3 . .211 D7
  Slough SL3 . . . . .211 F8
Dixie Cl HP20 . . . . . . .116 A8
Dixie La MK7 . . . . .48 C6
Dixon Cl HP21 . . . . . . .115 B6
Dobbins La HP22 . . . . .131 B5
Dobson's La RG9 . . . . .191 C8
Doctor's Commons Rd
  HP4 . . . . .135 B4
Dodds La HP8 . . . . . . .177 B8
Doddsfield Rd SL2 . . . .198 A2
Dodkin MK6 . . . . .47 B5
Dodman Gn MK4 . . . . . .57 B8
Dog Kennel La WD3 . . .167 F5
Doggetts Farm Rd UB9 .189 C4
Doggetts Wood Cl HP8 .166 B6
Doggetts Wood La HP8 .166 B5
Dolben Ct MK15 . . . . . .35 D8
Dolesden La RG9 . . . . .169 D1
Dollicot HP17 . . . . . . .126 F6
Dolphin Ct
  Loudwater HP11 . . . . .174 A3
  Slough SL1 . . . . .206 B4
Dolphin Pl HP21 . . . . . .115 B5
Dolphin Rd SL1 . . . . . .206 B4
Dolphin Sq **2** HP23 . .119 A3
Don The MK3 . . . . .46 D1
Donkey Dr SL8 . . . . . .185 A3
Donkey La
  Bourne End SL8 . . . . .185 A3
  Tring HP23 . . . . .118 E2
  West Drayton UB7 . . . .208 C2
Donnay Cl SL9 . . . . . .188 D5
Donnington MK16 . . . . . .34 B6
Donnington Gdns HP14 .195 F1
Donnybrook Ho **3**
  HP13 . . . . .173 C7
Doon Way MK2 . . . . . . .58 C5
Dorchester Ave MK3 . . . .47 A2
Dorchester Ho
  Maidenhead SL6 . . . . .195 B1
  Stoke Mandeville HP22 . .116 B2

Dorchester Ho SL9 . . . .188 F6
Doreen Cl MK2 . . . . . . .58 C7
Dorian Ct HP23 . . . . . .119 D4
Dorking Pl MK5 . . . . . . .46 B4
Dormans Cl MK10 . . . . . .36 A2
Dormer Ave HP11 . . . . . .79 E3
Dormer Cl HP21 . . . . . .115 B6
Dormer Ct **4** HP20 . . .101 F2
Dormer La HP15 . . . . . .163 B7
Dornels SL2 . . . . .206 C7
Dorney End SL4 . . . . . .144 A1
Dorney Hill N SL1,HP9 . .187 A4
Dorney Hill S SL2 . . . . .187 A4
Dorney Lake Park Nature
  Reserve★ SL4 . . . . . .209 B8
Dorney Lake Pk★ SL4 . .209 B8
Dorney Lake Rowing Ctr★
  SL4 . . . . .204 A1
Dorney Pl MK13 . . . . . . .34 C3
Dorney Reach Rd SL6 . .203 F3
Dorney Sch SL6 . . . . . .203 F3
Dorney Wood Rd
  Burnham SL1 . . . . . . .197 D6
  Littleworth Common SL1 .186 C1
Dorneywood Gdn★ SL1 .197 D6
Dorrells Rd HP27 . . . . .138 D6
Dorrien's Croft HP4 . . .134 F7
Dorset Cl
  Berkhamsted HP4 . . . .134 F5
  Milton Keynes MK3 . . . .46 F1
Dorset Lodge **9** SL6 . .202 F6
Dorset Pl HP21 . . . . . .116 C6
Dorset Rd SL4 . . . . . . .210 C6
Dorset Way SL0 . . . . . .201 F3
Dorton Cl MK8 . . . . .33 F1
Dorton Rd HP18 . . . . . .111 B4
Douglas Ct SL7 . . . . . .184 A3
Douglas Gdns HP4 . . . .135 A5
Douglas La TW19 . . . . .211 F1
Douglas Pl MK6 . . . . . . .46 E8
Douglas Rd
  Aylesbury HP20 . . . . .102 A1
  Slough SL2 . . . . .205 D8
  Stanwell TW19 . . . . . .213 D1
Doune Ho MK3 . . . . . . .46 F2
Dove Cl Aylesbury HP21 .115 C5
  Buckingham MK18 . . . . .52 E7
  Newport Pagnell MK16 . . .22 D4
Dove Ct SL9 . . . . .175 D3
Dove Ho HP19 . . . . . . .101 F1
Dove House Cl
  Edlesborough LU6 . . . . .92 F4
  Winslow MK18 . . . . . . .66 A4
Dove House Cres SL2 . .197 E1
Dove Pk WD3 . . . . . . .167 B4
Dove St LU7 . . . . .78 E8
Dovecot Rd HP13 . . . . .173 A7
Dovecote
  Haddenham HP17 . . . .126 F6
  Newport Pagnell MK16 . . .22 C4
Dovecote Cft MK14 . . . .21 E1
Dovecote Cl
  Haddenham HP17 . . . .126 F6
  Monks Risborough HP27 .139 C5
Dovecote Cotts MK5 . . . .46 A4
Dovehouse Mews MK16 . .12 B6
Dovehouse Rd **3** HP11 .173 A7
Doveleat OX39 . . . . . .147 D7
Dover Cl LU7 . . . . .105 D2
Dover Gate MK3 . . . . . .57 F8
Dover Hedge HP21 . . . .116 C7
Dover Rd SL1 . . . . . . .204 F7
Dowding Rd UB10 . . . .201 F5
Dower Cl HP9 . . . . . . .175 D3
Dower Mews **5** HP4 . .135 C4
Dower Pk SL4 . . . . . . .209 E4
Down Pl SL4 . . . . .209 A8
Downdean MK6 . . . . . . .47 A8
Downderry Croft MK4 . . .57 B8
Downer Cl MK18 . . . . . .52 F8
Downer Dr WD3 . . . . . .156 F3
Downham Rd MK17 . . . . .49 C4
Downing Path SL2 . . . .197 E1
Downings Wood WD3 . .178 D5
Downland MK8 . . . . . . .33 E2
Downley Ave MK13 . . . . .34 C3
Downley Cl HP13 . . . . .161 D2
Downley Rd HP14 . . . . .161 D6
Downley Sch The HP13 .161 D3
Downs Barn Bvd MK14 . .34 F5
Downs Barn Fst Sch
  MK14 . . . . .34 F5
Downs Barn Rdbt MK14 . .34 F5
Downs Pk HP13 . . . . . .161 E2
Downs View MK17 . . . . .48 C2
Downs Villas **17** HP23 .119 A3
Dr Challoner's Gram Sch
  HP6 . . . . .154 C1
Dr Challoner's High Sch
  HP7 . . . . .166 B7
Dragon Tail HP17 . . . . .127 A5
Drake Ave SL3 . . . . . .206 D4
Drake Cl HP21 . . . . . . .115 B6
Drake's Rd HP7 . . . . . .165 B3
Drakeloe Cl MK17 . . . . . .60 F8
Drakes Dr HP18 . . . . . .125 E5
Drakes Farm HP18 . . . .125 E5
Drakes Mews MK8 . . . . .45 F7
Drakewell Rd MK17 . . . . .48 D1
Draymans La **1** SL7 . .183 D1
Drayton Ct UB7 . . . . . .208 F2
Drayton Gdns UB7 . . . .208 E4
Drayton Park Comb Sch
  MK2 . . . . .58 D5

Drayton Parslow Village Sch
  MK17 . . . . .68 C6
Drayton Rd
  Aylesbury HP20 . . . . .101 D2
  Milton Keynes MK2 . . . .58 C5
  Newton Longville MK17 . .57 E2
Dresser Rd HP16 . . . . .151 C5
Drew Cl MK3 . . . . .47 A4
Drew Mdw SL2 . . . . . .198 C8
Drews Pk HP9 . . . . . . .175 C6
Drey The SL9 . . . . .177 E5
Drift Rd SL4 . . . . .209 A1
Drift Way SL3 . . . . . . .212 C7
Drinkwater Cl OX25 . . . .95 D7
Drive The
  Amersham HP7 . . . . . .154 D1
  Bourne End SL8 . . . . .184 F4
  Chalfont St Peter SL9 . .177 F3
  Cranfield MK43 . . . . . .24 D2
  Datchet SL3 . . . . .211 B6
  Ickenham UB10 . . . . . .190 E1
  Ivinghoe Aston LU7 . . . .92 A1
  Slough SL3 . . . . .206 F4
  Wraysbury TW19 . . . . .211 D2
Dropmore Inf Sch SL1 . .186 C1
Dropmore Rd
  Burnham SL1 . . . . . . .197 C5
  Littleworth Common SL1 .186 C1
Drovers Croft MK12 . . . .33 D4
Drovers La RG9 . . . . . .169 B2
Drovers Way
  Dunstable LU6 . . . . . . .93 F8
  Newton Longville MK17 . .57 D2
  Seer Green HP9 . . . . . .176 C4
Druce End NN12 . . . . . .18 E6
Druids Wlk OX39 . . . . .147 C6
Drummond Ho **4** MK4 . .57 B8
Drummond Ride HP23 . .119 A5
Drummond Hay MK15 . . .35 C7
Drydell La HP5 . . . . . . .153 F8
Dryden Cl
  Aylesbury HP20 . . . . .101 E2
  Newport Pagnell MK16 . . .22 A4
Du Pre Wlk HP9 . . . . . .185 D4
Duchess Gdns NN12 . . . .18 D3
Duchess Pk MK7 . . . . . .48 C7
Duchess St SL1 . . . . . .204 E5
Duck End
  Aylesbury HP20 . . . . .115 C8
  Great Brickhill MK17 . . . .59 D1
Duck La Ludgershall HP18 . .96 C6
  Woburn MK17 . . . . . . .60 F7
Duck Lake MK18 . . . . . .41 E3
Duck Lake Cl MK18 . . . .41 E4
Duck Sq OX39 . . . . . . .147 C6
Duckmore La HP23 . . . .118 C2
Duckworth Ct MK6 . . . . .46 E7
Dudley Cl SL6 . . . . . . .206 A3
Dudley Ct SL1 . . . . . . .206 A3
Dudley Hill MK5 . . . . . .46 A4
Dudley Ho HP3 . . . . . . .146 A4
Dudley La RG9 . . . . . . .181 A6
Dudswell La HP4 . . . . . .134 D7
Duffield La SL2 . . . . . .198 F6
Duffield Pk SL2 . . . . . .199 A2
Duke St Aspley Guise MK17 49 D4
  Eton SL4 . . . . .210 C7
  Henley-on-T RG9 . . . . .191 E2
  High Wycombe HP13 . . .173 C6
  Princes Risborough HP27 .139 B4
Dukes Ave LU6 . . . . . . .107 C5
Dukes Cl
  Gerrards Cross SL9 . . .188 E3
  Shabbington HP18 . . . .124 C2
Dukes Kiln Dr SL9 . . . . .188 D3
Dukes La
  Farnham Common SL2 . .198 A8
  Milton Keynes MK3 . . . .47 C1
Dukes Mdw SL8 . . . . . .185 B3
Dukes Piece MK18 . . . . .52 F8
Dukes Pl Marlow SL7 . . .183 D2
  Slough SL1 . . . . .205 F6
Dukes Ride
  Gerrards Cross SL9 . . .188 E3
  Ickenham UB10 . . . . . .201 E8
  Leighton Buzzard LU7 . . .70 F3
Dukes Row HP18 . . . . . .99 A1
Dukes Valley SL9 . . . . .188 B2
Dukes Way
  Berkhamsted HP4 . . . .135 A6
  Uxbridge UB8 . . . . . . .201 C4
Dukes Wood Ave SL9 . .188 E3
Dukes Wood Dr SL9 . . .188 D3
Dulverton Ct **2** SL0 . . .80 C8
Dulverton Dr MK4 . . . . . .46 D8
Dulwich Cl MK18 . . . . . .22 C2
Dumbletons WD3 . . . . .178 E6
Dumfries Cl MK3 . . . . . .46 F3
Dunbar Cl
  Milton Keynes MK3 . . . .57 D8
  Slough SL2 . . . . .206 A6
Dunbar Dr OX9 . . . . . .126 A1
Duncan Gr MK5 . . . . . . .45 F6
Duncan Rd MK43 . . . . . .24 E2
Duncannon Cres SL4 . . .209 D4
Dunchurch Dale MK7 . . . .48 B5
Duncombe Ho HP6 . . . .154 C1
Duncombe Rd HP4 . . . .134 E6
Duncombe St MK2 . . . . .58 C7
Duncroft SL4 . . . . .209 F4
Dundale Prim Sch
  HP23 . . . . .119 A5
Dundale Rd HP23 . . . . .119 A4
Dundee Rd SL1 . . . . . .205 A8
Dungeness Ct MK4 . . . . .46 A1
Dungrovehill La SL7 . . .194 D3

Dunholme End SL6 . . . .202 D3
Dunkeld Ho HP11 . . . . .174 B4
Dunkery Beacon MK4 . . .46 D3
Dunnet Cl MK4 . . . . .57 A8
Dunny La WD4 . . . . . . .156 F7
Dunsby Rd MK5 . . . . . . .47 A4
Dunsham La HP20 . . . . .101 E2
Dunsley Pl HP23 . . . . . .119 B3
Dunsmore Ave HP27 . . .139 C5
Dunsmore Ride HP27 . . .139 C5
Dunstable Downs★ LU6 . .93 E4
Dunstable Ho **4** SL7 . .183 E1
Dagnall HP4 . . . . .107 C7
  Eaton Bray LU6 . . . . . . .93 A5
  Totternhoe LU6 . . . . . . .93 D7
Dunster Ct MK4 . . . . . . .46 E3
Dunster Gdns SL1 . . . .205 A6
Dunston Hill HP23 . . . . .119 A4
Dunthorne Way MK8 . . . .45 D6
Dunton Rd LU7 . . . . . . .78 D6
Dunvedin Pl MK12 . . . . .33 D4
Dunvegan Cl MK2 . . . . .58 D4
Dunwood Ct SL6 . . . . .202 D5
Dunwood Rise HP13 . . .162 B1
Duparc Cl MK7 . . . . . . .48 C5
Dupre Cl SL1 . . . . .204 E4
Dupre Cres HP9 . . . . . .176 B1
Durgate MK7 . . . . .48 A8
Durham Ave SL1 . . . . .205 A7
Durham Ho **1** MK3 . . . .46 F1
Durley Hollow HP13 . . .162 B1
Durlston End MK4 . . . . . .57 A8
Durrans Ct MK2 . . . . . .47 E1
Durrans Ho MK2 . . . . . .47 E1
Durrants La HP4 . . . . . .134 F5
Durrants Path HP5 . . . .144 A4
Durrants Rd HP4 . . . . .134 F5
Durrell Cl LU7 . . . . .80 E7
Dutch Barn Cl TW19 . . .213 D1
Dutch Elm Ave SL4 . . . .210 E7
Dutton Way SL0 . . . . . .207 E7
Dyers Mews MK14 . . . . .34 F6
Dyers Rd LU6 . . . . .92 D7
Dyersdale MK13 . . . . . .34 C5
Dyson Cl SL4 . . . . .210 B4

E

Eagle Cl HP6 . . . . .154 F2
Eagle Way MK43 . . . . . . .3 F6
Eagle Wlk MK9 . . . . . . .34 F3
Eagles Rd HP20 . . . . . .116 A8
Eaglestone Rdbt MK6 . . .47 A8
Ealing Chase MK10 . . . . .47 F8
Eames Cl HP20 . . . . . .101 F3
Eardley Pl MK8 . . . . . . .45 D6
Earl Cl HP13 . . . . .162 A1
Earl Howe Rd HP15 . . .163 D6
Earls Cl MK3 . . . . .58 C8
Earls La SL1 . . . . .204 F5
Earls Willow MK13 . . . . .34 A8
Earlsfield SL6 . . . . .203 C2
Earlswood Cl HP21 . . . .116 A5
Easby Gr MK10 . . . . . . .36 A1
Eascote Rd HP21 . . . . .116 B4
Easington La HP18 . . . .111 B1
Easington Terr HP18 . . .111 B1
East Berkshire Coll
  Maidenhead SL6 . . . . .202 D6
  Slough SL3 . . . . .207 A3
  Windsor SL4 . . . . . . .210 C5
East Burnham Cotts
  SL2 . . . . .198 A4
East Burnham La SL2 . .198 A4
East Chapel MK4 . . . . . .57 B8
East Claydon Rd MK18 . .65 D2
East Claydon Sch MK18 . .74 E7
East Comm SL9 . . . . . .188 E5
East Cres SL4 . . . . . . .209 F6
East Dales MK13 . . . . . .34 C5
East Dr
  High Wycombe HP13 . . .173 E8
  Stoke Poges SL2 . . . . .198 E2
East End HP22 . . . . .87 D1
East Green Cl MK5 . . . . .45 F6
East Hills MK43 . . . . . . .25 B1
East La MK7 . . . . .47 F7
East Paddock SL6 . . . . .194 F6
East Rd Cranfield MK43 . .24 D1
  Maidenhead SL6 . . . . .202 F7
  West Drayton UB7 . . . .208 F2
East Richardson St **5**
  HP11 . . . . .172 F7
East Ridge SL8 . . . . . . .185 B4
East Spur MK7 . . . . .47 F7
East St Adstock MK18 . . .53 F1
  Chesham HP5 . . . . . . .154 B8
  Olney MK46 . . . . .7 A4
East Terr SL4 . . . . . . .210 E7
East View OX25 . . . . . . .81 A3
East Way HP9 . . . . . . .175 A1
East Wlk N MK9 . . . . . . .34 E2
East Wlk S MK9 . . . . . . .34 E2
Eastbourne Rd SL1 . . . .205 A7
Eastbridge SL2 . . . . . .206 B5
Eastbrook Cl OX25 . . . . .95 E7
Eastbury Ct 46 D1
Eastcroft SL2 . . . . .198 B1
Eastgate HP9 . . . . .175 C4
Eastern Dene HP15 . . . .163 B5
Eastern Dr SL8 . . . . . . .185 C4
Eastern St HP20 . . . . . .101 E1
Eastfield Cl **3** SL1 . . .206 A3
Eastfield Cres NN12 . . . .18 F5
Eastfield Dr MK19 . . . . .11 A3

Eastfield Rd
Aylesbury HP20 . . . . .116 B8
Burnham SL1 . . . . .204 A8
Princes Risborough HP27 .139 C3
Eastlands HP27 . . . . .149 E5
Eastnor HP3 . . . . .146 A3
Eastoke Pl MK4 . . . . .57 A8
Easton St HP11 . . . . .173 B6
Easton Terr HP13 . . . . . . .173 C6
Eastwick Cres WD3 . . . . .178 F8
Eastwood Ct 1 SL7 . . . . . .183 F3
Eastwood Rd HP14 . . . . . .158 F3
Eaton Ave
High Wycombe HP12 . . . .172 D8
Milton Keynes MK2 . . . . . .58 D7
Eaton Bray Lower Sch
LU6 . . . . .92 F6
Eaton Bray Rd
Edlesborough LU6 . . . . . . .92 C5
Honeywick LU6 . . . . .92 E8
Eaton Mill Comb Sch
MK2 . . . . .58 D6
Eaton Pk LU6 . . . . .92 F6
Eaton Pl HP12 . . . . .172 D8
Eaton Rd HP21 . . . . .115 D7
Eatongate Cl LU6 . . . . . . .92 E5
Ebble Cl HP21 . . . . .115 C4
Ebbsgrove MK5 . . . . .34 B1
Ebenezer Ho HP10 . . . . . .174 C2
Ebsworth Cl SL6 . . . . . . .196 C3
Eddy St HP4 . . . . .135 A5
Eden Cl Aylesbury HP21 . .115 D4
Slough SL3 . . . . .207 A1
Eden Wlk MK3 . . . . .46 E1
Edgar Rd UB7 . . . . .208 E5
Edgar Wallace Pl SL8 . . . .185 B5
Edge Hill St MK18 . . . . . . .41 E6
Edgecombe Rd HP21 . . . .116 B5
Edgecote MK8 . . . . .46 A8
Edgecote Ho 11 HP13 . . . .173 B7
Edgecott Rd HP18 . . . . . . .82 F7
Edgehill OX9 . . . . .125 F2
Edgewood HP13 . . . . .173 D5
Edinburgh Ave SL1 . . . . . .205 B7
Edinburgh Dr UB9 . . . . . .189 F5
Edinburgh Gdns SL4 . . . .210 D5
Edinburgh Ho MK3 . . . . . . .57 D7
Edinburgh Pl HP21 . . . . . .115 C6
Edinburgh Rd
Maidenhead SL6 . . . . . . .195 E1
Marlow SL7 . . . . .183 E3
Edison Cl UB7 . . . . .208 F4
Edison Rd HP19 . . . . .100 E1
Edison Sq MK5 . . . . .46 C5
Edith Bell Ho SL9 . . . . . . .177 E4
Edith Rd SL6 . . . . .202 A7
Edlesborough Sch LU6 . . . .92 E3
Edlyn Cl HP4 . . . . .134 F5
Edmonds Cl MK18 . . . . . . .41 F1
Edmonds Rd HP14 . . . . . .171 B4
Edmonds Sh Ctr HP14 . . .171 B4
Edmund Ct
Beaconsfield HP9 . . . . . .186 A8
Milton Keynes MK5 . . . . . .45 F7
Edmunds Cl HP12 . . . . . .172 C5
Edmunds Gdns HP12 . . . .172 C5
Edmunds Way SL2 . . . . . .206 B7
Edrich Ave MK6 . . . . .46 F8
Edstone Pl MK4 . . . . .46 C3
Edward Cl HP21 . . . . .116 A4
Edward Wlk HP21 . . . . . . .116 A4
Edwards Ct SL1 . . . . .205 E4
Edwin Allman Pl HP15 . . .162 E2
Edwin Cl MK17 . . . . .48 D2
Edy Ct MK5 . . . . .34 A1
Edzell Cres MK4 . . . . .45 E2
Eeles Cl HP4 . . . . .100 F3
Eelbrook Ave MK13 . . . . . .34 C2
Egerton Cl NN13 . . . . .38 A7
Egerton Gate MK5 . . . . . . .46 B4
Egerton Rd
Berkhamsted HP4 . . . . . .135 B6
Slough SL1 . . . . .197 E1
Egerton-Rothesay Lower Sch
HP4 . . . . .135 B4
Egerton-Rothesay Sch
HP4 . . . . .134 E6
Egglesfield Cl HP4 . . . . . .134 E6
Eggleton Dr HP23 . . . . . . .119 A5
Eghams Cl HP9 . . . . .175 C4
Eghams Ct 8 SL8 . . . . . . .185 B3
Eghams Gn SL8 . . . . .185 B3
Eghams Wood Rd HP9 . . .175 C4
Egmont Ave MK11 . . . . . . .32 E4
Egremont Gdns SL1 . . . . .205 A5
Egypt La SL2 . . . . .187 E1
Egypt Way HP19 . . . . .115 A8
Egypt Wood Cotts SL2 . . .187 B1
Eider Cl MK18 . . . . .52 E8
Eight Acres Burnham SL1 .197 B1
Tring HP23 . . . . .119 A4
Elangeni Sch HP6 . . . . . . .154 E3
Elbow Mdw SL3 . . . . .212 F6
Elder Cl Loudwater HP11 . .174 B3
West Drayton UB7 . . . . . .208 E6
Elder Gate
Milton Keynes,Rooksley
MK9 . . . . .34 C1
Milton Keynes,Winterhill
MK9 . . . . .46 C8
Elder Way HP15 . . . . .163 B3
Elderdene OX39 . . . . .147 D8
Elderfield Rd SL2 . . . . . . .198 F6
Eldridge La HP17 . . . . . . .130 C3
Eleanor Cl MK17 . . . . .60 F7
Eleanor Gdns HP21 . . . . .115 F6
Eleanor Rd SL9 . . . . .177 C2

Eleanor Wlk MK17 . . . . . . .60 F7
Elfords MK6 . . . . .47 A6
Elgar Gr MK7 . . . . .48 C4
Elgin Ho SL3 . . . . .212 E6
Eliot Cl Aylesbury HP19 . . .100 F2
Newport Pagnell MK16 . . . .21 F5
Eliot Dr SL7 . . . . .183 F4
Elizabeth Ave HP6 . . . . . .166 C8
Elizabeth Cl
Aylesbury HP21 . . . . .116 A4
Cookham Rise SL6 . . . . . .195 F7
Elizabeth Ct
High Wycombe HP13 . . . .173 C6
High Wycombe, Wycombe Marsh
HP13 . . . . .173 E5
10 Slough SL1 . . . . .206 A4
3 Windsor SL4 . . . . .210 C5
Elizabeth Dr HP23 . . . . . .119 B6
Elizabeth Rd Marlow SL7 .183 E3
Stokenchurch HP14 . . . . .158 F4
Elizabeth Way SL2 . . . . . .198 F4
Elkins Rd SL2 . . . . .187 E2
Ellen Pl HP21 . . . . .115 C5
Ellen Rd HP21 . . . . .115 C5
Ellen Wlk HP21 . . . . .115 B6
Ellenstow MK13 . . . . .34 A4
Ellerburn Pl MK4 . . . . .46 B3
Ellery Rise RG9 . . . . .170 F1
Ellesborough Gr MK8 . . . . .33 D3
Ellesborough Rd
Butler's Cross HP17 . . . . .130 C2
Ellesborough HP17 . . . . .130 A1
Wendover HP17 . . . . .131 A3
Ellesmere Cl
Datchet SL3 . . . . .211 A8
Totternhoe LU6 . . . . .93 C6
Ellesmere Rd HP4 . . . . . . .135 D4
Elliman Ave SL2 . . . . .205 F6
Ellington Ct SL6 . . . . .203 C7
Ellington Gdns SL6 . . . . . .203 C7
Ellington Pk SL6 . . . . .195 E1
Ellington Prim Sch SL6 . . .195 F1
Ellington Rd SL6 . . . . .203 C7
Elliots Cl UB8 . . . . .208 C8
Elliott Ho HP11 . . . . .172 F8
Ellis Ave
Chalfont St Peter SL9 . . . .177 F2
Slough SL1 . . . . .205 E4
Ellis Way HP14 . . . . .171 B4
Ellisgill Ct MK13 . . . . .34 A4
Ellison Cl SL4 . . . . .209 F4
Ellison Ho 14 SL4 . . . . . . .210 D6
Ellsworth Rd HP11 . . . . . .172 F4
Ellwood Ho SL9 . . . . .177 E2
Ellwood Rd HP9 . . . . .175 B1
Ellwood Rise HP8 . . . . . . .177 C8
Ellwood Terr WD3 . . . . . . .167 D4
Elm Brook Cl HP18 . . . . . .112 C1
Elm Cl Amersham HP6 . . . .154 C1
Butler's Cross HP17 . . . . .130 C3
Chinnor OX39 . . . . .147 C5
Farnham Common SL2 . . .198 C6
Hazelmere HP15 . . . . . . .163 A3
Newton Longville MK17 . . . .57 C2
Weston Turville HP22 . . . .116 F2
Elm Croft SL3 . . . . .211 C6
Elm Ct Berkhamsted HP4 . .135 B4
Butler's Cross HP17 . . . . .130 C3
Elm Dr Chinnor OX39 . . . .147 C5
Deanshanger MK19 . . . . . .31 D5
Elm Farm Rd HP21 . . . . . .116 A5
Elm Gn HP21 . . . . .115 D7
Elm Gr Berkhamsted HP4 . .135 C4
Maidenhead SL6 . . . . . . .202 E7
West Drayton UB7 . . . . . .208 F6
Woburn Sands MK17 . . . . .49 B4
Elm La SL6 . . . . .184 F5
Elm Lawn Cl UB8 . . . . . . .201 C6
Elm Rd
High Wycombe HP12 . . . .172 C4
Princes Risborough HP27 .139 C3
Tylers Green HP10 . . . . . .174 D8
Windsor SL4 . . . . .210 B4
Elm St MK18 . . . . .52 D8
Elm Tree Cotts HP7 . . . . . .164 C2
Elm Tree Farm OX25 . . . . .81 A4
Elm Tree Wlk
Chorleywood WD3 . . . . . .167 F5
Tring HP23 . . . . .119 A5
Elm Trees HP18 . . . . .125 B7
Elmar Gn SL2 . . . . .198 A2
Elmdale Gdns HP27 . . . . .139 B3
Elmers Cl MK19 . . . . .44 A6
Elmers Mdw MK18 . . . . . . .76 A2
Elmers Pk MK18 . . . . .58 A8
Elmfield Cl NN12 . . . . .18 D3
Elmfields Gate MK18 . . . . .66 A4
Elmhurst 5 HP16 . . . . . . .152 A8
Elmhurst Cl
High Wycombe HP13 . . . .162 D1
Milton Keynes MK4 . . . . . .46 F4
Elmhurst Ct SL3 . . . . .207 A8
Elmhurst Inf Sch HP20 . . .101 E2
Elmhurst Jun Sch HP20 . .101 E2
Elmhurst Rd
Aylesbury HP20 . . . . .101 E2
Slough SL3 . . . . .207 A8
Elmlea Dr SL6 . . . . .202 A7
Elmodesham Ho 7 HP7 . .165 B7
Elmridge Ct MK4 . . . . .46 C2
Elms Dr SL8 . . . . .185 C4
Elms Rd SL9 . . . . .177 E3
Elms The
Leighton Buzzard LU7 . . . .80 E7
Milton Keynes MK3 . . . . . .57 F8

Elms The continued
Preston Bissett MK18 . . . .51 B1
Elmshott Cl HP10 . . . . . . .163 A1
Elmshott La SL1 . . . . .204 E6
Elmside MK18 . . . . .66 A4
Elmslie Cl SL6 . . . . .202 E7
Elmtree Ct 6 HP16 . . . . . .152 A8
Elmtree Gn HP16 . . . . . . .152 A8
Elmtree Hill HP5 . . . . .144 B1
Elmtree Sch HP5 . . . . . . .144 B1
Elmwood
Maidenhead SL6 . . . . . . .196 B4
Turvey MK43 . . . . .8 E6
Elmwood Cl HP18 . . . . . . .109 D5
Elmwood Pk SL9 . . . . .188 E3
Elmwood Rd SL2 . . . . .206 B6
Elora Rd HP13 . . . . .173 E7
Elruge Cl UB7 . . . . .208 D3
Elsage Ct LU7 . . . . .105 B8
Elsmore Cl HP21 . . . . .116 A4
Eltham Ave SL1 . . . . .204 E4
Elthorne Rd UB8 . . . . .201 D3
Elthorne Way MK16 . . . . . .22 C2
Elton MK6 . . . . .47 D7
Elton Dr SL6 . . . . .202 D8
Elwes Rd HP14 . . . . .171 C4
Ely Ave SL1 . . . . .205 C8
Ely Cl HP7 . . . . .165 E8
Ely Ho HP13 . . . . .173 F8
Ember Path HP21 . . . . . . .115 C4
Ember Rd SL3 . . . . .207 B3
Emberton Ctry Pk ★ MK46 .6 E1
Emberton Ctry Pk Visitors
Ctr ★ MK46 . . . . .6 E1
Emberton Fst Sch SL6 . . . . .7 F8
Embleton Way MK18 . . . . . .52 C5
Emerald Cl MK18 . . . . .74 F8
Emerald Ct SL1 . . . . .205 E4
Emerald Gate MK15 . . . . . .35 E5
Emerson Ct HP10 . . . . . . .185 E6
Emerson Valley Sch MK4 . .46 C2
Emerton Ct HP4 . . . . .134 E4
Emerton Garth HP4 . . . . . .134 F4
Emerton Gdns MK11 . . . . .32 E5
Emilia Cl SL6 . . . . .195 F1
Emlyns Bldgs SL4 . . . . . . .210 D7
Emma Rothschild Ct
HP23 . . . . .119 A5
Emmett Cl MK4 . . . . .46 C1
Emperor Cl MK4 . . . . .134 F7
Empingham Cl MK2 . . . . . .58 D4
Empstead Ct RG9 . . . . . . .191 D2
Enborne Ct HP21 . . . . .115 D4
Enfield Chase MK14 . . . . . .34 C5
Enfield Cl UB8 . . . . .201 D3
Engaine Dr MK5 . . . . .45 F7
English Gdns TW19 . . . . . .211 D2
Enmore Gate MK9 . . . . . . .35 A3
Enmore Rdbt MK9 . . . . . . .35 A3
Ennell Gr MK2 . . . . .58 C5
Ennerdale Cl MK2 . . . . . . .58 D6
Ennerdale Cres SL1 . . . . .204 C8
Ensbury Path HP20 . . . . . .101 E2
Enstone Ct MK10 . . . . .190 F1
Enterprise La MK9 . . . . . . .35 A3
Epsom Cl LU7 . . . . .80 D6
Epsom Gr MK3 . . . . .57 D6
Eriboll Cl LU7 . . . . .80 B6
Erica Cl SL1 . . . . .204 E6
Erica Rd MK12 . . . . .33 E4
Eridge Gn MK7 . . . . .48 A8
Errington Dr SL4 . . . . .210 A6
Escarpment Ave LU6 . . . . .107 D8
Esk Way MK3 . . . . .46 E1
Eskan Ct MK9 . . . . .35 A4
Eskdale Ave HP5 . . . . .144 D1
Eskdale Gdns SL6 . . . . . . .203 B2
Eskdale Lodge HP6 . . . . . .154 C2
Eskdale Rd
Stoke Mandeville HP22 . . .116 B2
Uxbridge UB8 . . . . .201 B3
Eskdale Way MK10 . . . . . . .36 B3
Essenden Ct MK11 . . . . . . .32 F5
Essex Ave SL2 . . . . .205 C8
Essex Cl MK3 . . . . .46 F1
Essex Ho 5 HP20 . . . . . . .101 D1
Essex Pl HP19 . . . . .101 A4
Essex Rd HP5 . . . . .144 C2
Essex Yd HP22 . . . . .89 C2
Estcourt Dr HP15 . . . . .162 F6
Esther Cl MK13 . . . . .34 A6
Eston Ct MK13 . . . . .34 A5
Estover Way MK10 . . . . . . .147 B6
Etheridge Ave MK10 . . . . .48 C8
Ethorpe MK8 . . . . .33 E1
Ethorpe Cl SL9 . . . . .188 E6
Ethorpe Cres SL9 . . . . . . .188 E6
Ethorpe Ho SL9 . . . . .188 E6
Eton Cl SL3 . . . . .211 A8
Eton Cres MK12 . . . . .33 C6
Eton Ct SL4 . . . . .210 D7
Eton Coll SL4 . . . . .210 D8
Eton End PNEU Sch
SL3 . . . . .211 A8
Eton Ho 1 SL1 . . . . .205 F3
Eton Porny CE Fst Sch
SL4 . . . . .210 D8
Eton Rd SL3 . . . . .211 A8
Eton Riverside SL4 . . . . . .210 D7
Eton Sq SL4 . . . . .210 D7
Eton Wick CE Fst Sch
SL4 . . . . .205 A1
Eton Wick Rd SL4 . . . . . . .205 B1
Eton Wlk SL1 . . . . .205 E3
Eunice Gr HP5 . . . . .154 D1
Europa Bsns Pk MK10 . . . .36 C3
Europa Ho SL9 . . . . .188 E6

Evans Cl Aylesbury HP21 . .116 A4
Chearsley HP18 . . . . .112 A1
Evans Gate MK6 . . . . .46 E8
Evans Way HP23 . . . . .119 B4
Evelyn Cl LU7 . . . . .79 E1
Evelyn Pl MK13 . . . . .34 A7
Evelyns Cl UB8 . . . . .208 F7
Evenley Rd NN13 . . . . .38 D1
Evenlode SL6 . . . . .202 F8
Evenlode Cl HP21 . . . . . . .115 C5
Evenlode Rd SL8 . . . . .185 B4
Everard Ave SL1 . . . . .205 E4
Everest Cl HP13 . . . . .173 D6
Everest Rd HP13 . . . . .173 E6
Everglade MK6 . . . . .47 C3
Evergreen Oak Ave SL4 . .211 A4
Everley Cl MK4 . . . . .46 C3
Evesham Gn HP19 . . . . . . .101 C3
Evesham Way MK5 . . . . . . .45 D5
Evett Cl HP20 . . . . .101 F1
Evreham Rd SL0 . . . . .207 E7
Exbury La MK4 . . . . .45 F1
Exchange Ho MK9 . . . . . . .34 E2
Exchange St HP20 . . . . . . .115 E8
Exebridge MK4 . . . . .46 C3
Exhims Mews HP4 . . . . . . .134 E6
Exmoor Gate MK4 . . . . . . .46 E4
Eynsford Ct 4 SL7 . . . . . .208 F7
Eynsham Ct MK15 . . . . . . .35 C2
Eyre Cl HP19 . . . . .114 F8
Eyre Gn SL2 . . . . .198 A2
Eythrope Rd
Eythrope HP18 . . . . .100 A1
Stone HP17 . . . . .114 C6

F

Factory Yd HP9 . . . . .175 C1
Fadmoor Pl 3 MK4 . . . . . . .46 B3
Fagnall La HP7 . . . . .164 D2
Fair Acres HP16 . . . . .151 D5
Fair Leas HP5 . . . . .144 A2
Fair Mdw MK18 . . . . .66 A4
Fair Mile Aylesbury HP21 .116 A7
Henley-on-T RG9 . . . . . . .191 C4
Fair Ridge HP11 . . . . .172 F4
Fair View Cotts
Chalfont St Peter SL9 . . . .177 E3
Cookham Rise SL6 . . . . . .195 E7
Fairacre SL6 . . . . .202 C6
Fairacres Ind Est SL4 . . . .209 D5
Faircroft SL2 . . . . .198 B1
Fairfax MK13 . . . . .34 C4
Fairfax Cres UB8 . . . . .201 E2
Fairfax Mews HP7 . . . . . . .165 A7
Fairfield HP6 . . . . .154 B3
Fairfield App TW19 . . . . . .211 D1
Fairfield Ave SL3 . . . . .211 D7
Fairfield Cl
Bourne End SL8 . . . . .185 A5
Datchet SL3 . . . . .211 D7
Olney MK46 . . . . .7 A3
Fairfield La SL2 . . . . .198 B3
Fairfield Rd
Burnham SL1 . . . . .197 C2
Paulerspury NN12 . . . . . . .17 B3
Uxbridge UB8 . . . . .201 D6
West Drayton UB7 . . . . . .208 E6
Wraysbury TW19 . . . . . . .211 D1
Fairfields HP15 . . . . .151 E1
Fairford Cres MK15 . . . . . .35 B6
Fairford Leys Way HP19 . .115 A4
Fairford Rd SL6 . . . . .202 F8
Fairhaven SL6 . . . . .177 C2
Fairlawn Pk SL4 . . . . .209 E3
Fairlawns HP13 . . . . .162 C1
Fairlea SL6 . . . . .202 B3
Fairlie Rd SL1 . . . . .205 A8
Fairlight Ave SL4 . . . . .210 D5
Fairlight Dr UB8 . . . . .201 D6
Fairmead The SL3 . . . . . . .212 D7
Fairmile Ct RG9 . . . . .191 D3
Fairthorn Cl HP23 . . . . . . .118 E3
Fairview Ind Est
Amersham HP6 . . . . .154 F1
High Wycombe HP11 . . . .173 F4
Fairview La HP10 . . . . .174 A1
Fairview Rd
Burnham SL6 . . . . .204 A7
Slough SL2 . . . . .197 F1
Fairway HP27 . . . . .139 C3
Fairway Ave UB7 . . . . .208 D5
Fairway Cl UB7 . . . . .208 D5
Fairway The
Burnham SL1 . . . . .197 C3
Flackwell Heath HP10 . . . .185 C7
Maidenhead SL6 . . . . . . .202 B3
Uxbridge UB10 . . . . .201 F3
Fairways MK8 . . . . .33 C4
Fairways Rdbt MK8 . . . . . . .33 C6
Faith Terr MK19 . . . . .11 A2
Faithful Cl HP17 . . . . .114 C5
Faithorn Cl HP5 . . . . .144 A1
Falaise MK15 . . . . .35 A7
Falcon Ave MK6 . . . . .35 B2
Falcon Dr TW19 . . . . .213 E1
Falcon Ridge HP4 . . . . . . .135 C3
Falcon Rise HP13 . . . . . . .161 C5
Falcon The HP19 . . . . .101 F4
Falconhurst Comb Sch
MK6 . . . . .47 B8
Falcons Croft HP10 . . . . . .185 E8
Falkland Ho SL6 . . . . .202 F5
Falklands Cl MK18 . . . . . . .63 D2
Fall Cl HP19 . . . . .101 C4
Falling La UB7 . . . . .208 E6
Fallow Field HP15 . . . . . . .163 B3

Eas – Fer 227

Fallows The SL6 . . . . .196 A1
Falmouth Pl MK6 . . . . .34 F1
Falmouth Rd SL1 . . . . .205 A7
Fane Way SL6 . . . . .202 D5
Fantail La HP23 . . . . .118 F4
Far Furlong Cl HP21 . . . . .115 D3
Faraday Cl SL2 . . . . .205 B8
Faraday Rd
Aylesbury HP19 . . . . .101 A1
Slough SL2 . . . . .205 B8
Farington MK8 . . . . .33 F2
Farjeon Ct MK7 . . . . .48 D4
Farm Cl
High Wycombe HP13 . . . .174 A7
Ickford HP18 . . . . .123 F3
Little Chalfont HP6 . . . . . .166 D8
Maidenhead SL6 . . . . . . .203 C1
Maidenhead, Highway SL6 .202 A7
Stewkley LU7 . . . . .78 E7
Farm Cres SL2 . . . . .206 C8
Farm Dr SL4 . . . . .211 B1
Farm Gr HP9 . . . . .175 C5
Farm La HP9 . . . . .176 D3
Farm Lea HP10 . . . . .185 F7
Farm Pl Berkhamsted HP4 .134 F5
Henton OX39 . . . . .137 E1
Farm Rd Bourne End SL8 . .184 F4
Brackley NN13 . . . . .38 A6
Burnham SL6 . . . . .204 A5
Chorleywood WD3 . . . . . .167 A5
Maidenhead SL6 . . . . . . .202 A7
Farm Way TW19 . . . . .212 F1
Farm Yd SL4 . . . . .210 D7
Farmborough MK6 . . . . . . .47 C6
Farmbrough Cl HP20 . . . . .102 A1
Farmers SL6 . . . . .202 A4
Farmers Way
Maidenhead SL6 . . . . . . .202 A4
Seer Green HP9 . . . . .176 C4
Farmery Cl HP4 . . . . .135 C6
Farndale Gdns HP15 . . . . .163 A6
Farnell Ct MK5 . . . . .46 C8
Farnham Cl HP3 . . . . .146 A3
Farnham Common Ho 3
SL2 . . . . .198 C8
Farnham Common Inf Sch
SL2 . . . . .198 B8
Farnham Common Jun Sch
SL2 . . . . .198 C8
Farnham Ct MK8 . . . . .33 F1
Farnham La SL2 . . . . .198 A2
Farnham Park La SL2 . . . . .198 C4
Farnham Rd SL1,SL2 . . . . .205 C7
Farnham Royal CE Comb Sch
SL2 . . . . .198 C8
Farnley Rd HP20 . . . . .101 C2
Farrer Rd NN13 . . . . .26 D4
Farrier Ct 1 SL8 . . . . .185 B3
Farrier Pl MK14 . . . . .35 A5
Farriers Cl HP3 . . . . .146 B3
Farthing Ent Ctr The
MK6 . . . . .47 C6
Farthing Gr MK6 . . . . .47 C6
Farthing Green La SL2 . . . .199 B4
Farthingales The SL6 . . . . .203 B7
Farthings The HP6 . . . . . . .154 A3
Fassets Rd HP10 . . . . .174 B2
Faulkner Way HP11 . . . . . .161 D3
Faulkner's Way LU7 . . . . . . .80 E7
Favell Dr MK4 . . . . .46 F4
Faversham Cl HP23 . . . . . .119 A4
Fawcett Rd SL4 . . . . .210 B6
Fawley Bottom La RG9 . . .180 B1
Fawley Cl SL3 . . . . .195 D2
Fawley Ct ★ RG9 . . . . .191 E5
Fawley Gn RG9 . . . . .180 D2
Fawley Hill Rly ★ RG9 . . . .191 D4
Fawsley Cl SL3 . . . . .212 E7
Featherbed La HP15 . . . . .163 D8
Featherstone Rd MK12 . . . .33 A5
Fedden Ho MK3 . . . . .24 D3
Fegans Ct MK11 . . . . .32 D6
Felbridge MK7 . . . . .48 A7
Felden La HP3 . . . . .146 F8
Fells Cl HP18 . . . . .125 D6
Fellstead Ct SL6 . . . . .202 C6
Fences La MK16 . . . . .13 A2
Fennel Dr MK14 . . . . .34 E4
Fennels Farm Rd HP10 . . .174 A1
Fennels La HP11 . . . . .174 A4
Fennels The HP11 . . . . . . .174 A3
Fennels Way HP10 . . . . . . .174 A1
Fennemore Cl HP18 . . . . . .109 D4
Fenny House Tuition Service
MK6 . . . . .47 A6
Fenny Rd MK17 . . . . .69 E8
Fenny Stratford Sta MK1 . .47 E1
Fennymere MK8 . . . . .33 D1
Fenton Ct MK8 . . . . .45 F8
Fern Cotts SL7 . . . . .184 E5
Fern Cl HP4 . . . . .135 B4
Fern Dr SL6 . . . . .204 B7
Fern Gr MK2 . . . . .58 D5
Fern La Fern SL7 . . . . .184 E5
Haddenham HP17 . . . . . .127 A6
Fern Wlk HP15 . . . . .163 B3
Fernan Dell MK8 . . . . .45 D7
Fernborough Haven 4
MK4 . . . . .46 C2
Ferndale MK6 . . . . .35 B1
Ferndale Cl HP14 . . . . .158 F4
Ferndale Cres UB8 . . . . . .201 C2

Ferne Furlong MK46 ......6 F5
Fernes Cl UB8 ....208 C7
Fernfield MK17 ....56 A5
Fernhill Cl OX9 ....136 A6
Fernhurst Cl HP9 .....175 F2
Fernie Fields HP12 ...172 C4
Fernlea Cl HP10 ......174 A1
Fernley Ct SL6 ....195 D1
Ferns The HP9 ....175 F1
Fernside
  Great Kingshill HP15 ....151 E1
  Hazelmere HP15 ......163 A6
Fernsleigh Cl SL9 ....177 E4
Fernwood Sch MK17 ...49 B2
Ferrers Ave UB7 .....208 D4
Ferrers Cl SL1 ....204 C5
Ferry End SL6 ....203 C4
Ferry La Bourne End SL8 .196 B8
  Medmenham SL7 .....193 B5
  Mill End RG9 ....192 D6
Ferry Rd SL6 ....203 C4
Festival Cotts SL3 ....212 C7
Fetty Pl SL2 ....202 D4
Field Cl Aylesbury HP20 .102 A2
  Chesham HP5 ....144 E3
  Ickford HP18 ....124 A3
  Sherington MK16 .....14 A2
Field Ct MK5 ....46 B8
Field End HP18 ......125 F5
Field End Cl HP23 ....119 D1
Field Farm Bsns Ctr
  OX26 ....71 A5
Field Hurst SL3 ......211 A6
Field La MK12 ....33 B5
Field Rd Denham UB9 .189 C1
  Denham,Rush Green UB9 .208 E8
  High Wycombe HP12 ..172 B5
  Murcott OX5 ....94 A5
Field Way
  Aylesbury HP20 ......102 A2
  Bovingdon HP3 ......146 A4
  Chalfont St Peter SL9 ...177 D2
  Uxbridge UB8 ....201 D1
Field Wlk MK9 ....34 F3
Fieldfare HP19 ....101 E4
Fieldhead Gdns SL8 ..185 A3
Fieldhouse Ct HP13 ..174 A4
Fieldhouse Ind Est SL7 .183 F2
Fieldhouse La SL7 ....183 F2
Fieldhouse Way SL7 ..183 F2
Fielding Gdns SL3 ....206 C4
Fielding Rd SL6 ......202 B8
Fields End HP23 .....119 A6
Fields The SL1 ......205 D4
Fieldway Amersham HP7 .165 B6
  Berkhamsted HP4 ....135 E2
  Chalfont St Peter SL9 ...177 D3
  Wigginton HP23 .....119 D1
Fife La SL7 ....57 A8
Fife Ho MK3 ....46 F1
Fifth St HP11 ....173 C4
Filey Spur SL1 ....205 B4
Filgrave Sch MK16 ....13 C5
Filmer Rd SL4 ....209 D5
Finch Cl MK10 ....35 F3
Finch Cres LU7 ......80 E5
Finch Ct SL6 ....202 D5
Finch End HP10 .....174 C8
Finch Gn WD3 ......167 F5
Finch La Amersham HP7 .165 F5
  Beaconsfield HP9 ....175 C5
  Little Chalfont HP7 ...166 B7
Finch Rd HP4 ....135 A4
Findlay Way MK2 ....58 C8
Fingest La RG9 ......170 D3
Fingle Dr MK13 ......33 E7
Finians Cl UB10 .....201 E5
Finings Rd HP14 .....171 A4
Finlay Dr RG9 ....191 E2
Finlay Ho RG9 ......191 E3
Finmere CE Prim Sch
  MK18 ....50 D6
Finmere Cres HP21 ..116 C5
Fir Tree Ave SL2 .....198 F1
Fir Tree Cotts HP14 ..161 B8
Fircroft Cl SL2 ......199 A6
Fircroft Ct SL2 ......199 A6
Fire La MK17 ....57 D4
Firecrest Way HP19 ..100 F1
Firfield SL6 ....203 B1
Firs Ave SL4 ....209 F4
Firs Cl Hazelmere HP15 .163 B2
  High Wycombe HP13 ..173 E8
  Iver Heath SL0 ......200 C4
  Lane End HP14 ......171 C4
  Whitchurch HP22 ....87 A5
Firs Ct Amersham HP6 .154 C2
  Bierton HP22 ....102 C4
  Princes Risborough HP27 .138 F3
Firs Dr SL3 ....206 F5
Firs End SL9 ....188 D8
Firs Rise HP16 ......151 E7
Firs The Bierton HP22 .102 C4
  Brill HP18 ....110 B8
  Maidenhead SL6 .....202 E7
  Uxbridge UB8 ....201 D1
  Wigginton HP23 .....119 D1
Firs View Rd HP15 ...163 B2
Firs Wlk HP15 ......163 B2
First Ave Amersham HP7 .165 D7
  Marlow SL7 ....184 A2
  Milton Keynes MK1 ..47 C1
First Cres SL1 ......205 C8
First St HP11 ....173 C3
Firview Cl SL7 ......183 F1

Fish Ponds La OX9 ...125 E1
Fisherman's Way SL8 .185 B4
Fishermans Cl MK46 ..6 E4
Fishermans Retreat SL7 183 E1
Fishermead Bvd MK6 .35 A1
Fishers Field MK18 ...52 C8
Fishery Rd SL6 ......203 C5
Fishguard Spur SL1 ..206 B4
Fishweir LU7 ....68 D1
Fitzgeralds Way MK18 .41 E2
Fitzhamon Ct MK12 ..33 A5
Five Acre Wood HP12 .172 C6
Five Acres Chesham HP5 154 D6
  Wooburn Green HP10 .185 F7
Five Points SL0 .....200 C2
Flaggs Mdw MK46 ...6 E4
Flambard Cl HP3 ....156 E6
Flamborough Spur SL1 205 A4
Flamingo Zoo Gardens Pk★
  MK46 ....6 D6
Flaunden Bottom HP5 155 E4
Flaunden Hill HP3 ...156 A6
Flaunden La
  Bovingdon HP3 ......146 D3
  Chipperfield WD3 ....156 E6
Flavius Gate NN13 ...38 A7
Flaxbourne Ct MK7 ..48 C7
Flaxen Field HP22 ...116 F2
Flaxley Gate MK10 ..36 A3
Fledgelings Wlk MK18 .66 A5
Fleet Cl Buckingham MK18 .41 F7
  Walter's Ash HP14 ...161 F7
Fleet St HP20 ....101 D1
Fleet The MK6 ......35 B2
Fleetbrook Ho SL3 ...211 D6
Fleetwood Cl HP8 ...177 A6
Fleetwood Ct TW19 ..213 E1
Fleetwood Rd SL2 ...205 F6
Fleetwood Way OX9 .125 F2
Fleming Ct SL3 .....206 C3
Fleming Dr MK6 ....47 B6
Fleming Way HP12 ..172 D5
Fletcher Cl HP19 ....100 F3
Fletchers Mews MK14 .34 F6
Flint Ho MK3 ....46 F1
Flint Hollow OX39 ...147 B6
Flint St HP17 ....127 A5
Flint Way HP16 .....151 C7
Flintergill Ct MK13 ..34 B4
Flintlock Cl TW19 ...213 A3
Flitcroft Lea HP13 ...173 A8
Flitton Ct MK11 .....32 F5
Flora Thompson Dr
  MK16 ....21 F6
Florence Ave SL6 ....203 A8
Florence Cl HP19 ....101 D1
Florence Way UB8 ...201 C5
Florida St HP11 .....173 C4
Florin Cl MK15 .....35 A7
Flowers Bottom La
  HP27 ....150 B4
Fog Cotts HP23 .....120 A5
Folding Cl LU7 ......78 E8
Foley Cl HP9 ....175 C4
Foliejohn Way SL6 ..202 A1
Folkestone Ct SL3 ...207 A1
Follet Cl SL4 ....211 B1
Folly La Hartwell NN7 .11 F4
  North Crawley MK16 ..24 B5
Folly Rd MK19 ......31 D4
Fontwell Cl SL6 .....202 A8
Fontwell Dr MK3 ....57 C6
Forbes Pl MK5 .....45 E4
Forches Cl MK4 ....46 D2
Ford End UB9 ......189 F2
Ford La SL0 ....208 A7
Ford St Buckingham MK18 .52 D8
  High Wycombe HP11 ..173 F4
Ford Way HP13 ......161 E3
Ford's Cl HP14 .....159 F8
Fordcombe Lea MK4 .48 B8
Forelands Way HP5 ..154 C7
Forest Cl
  Princes Risborough HP27 .139 B3
  Wendover HP22 .....131 B4
Forest Point HP13 ...173 F5
Forest Rd Hanslope MK19 .10 F5
  Piddington (Northants) NN7 .4 A8
  Windsor SL4 ....209 C5
Forest Rise MK6 ....47 B8
Forest Way HP13 ....174 A8
Foresters
  Beacon's Bottom HP14 .159 C5
  Chinnor OX39 ....147 B6
  Oakley HP18 ....109 D6
Forestry Hos OX49 ..168 A7
Forfar Dr MK3 ......46 F2
Forge Cl Ashendon HP18 .97 E1
  Holmer Green HP15 ..163 C6
  Horton-cum-S OX33 .108 B5
  Marsh Gibbon OX27 ..71 F3
  Oakley HP18 ....109 D4
  Steeple Claydon MK18 .63 E2
Forge Dr SL2 ....198 C6
Forge End HP7 .....165 B7
Forge Rd HP14 .....161 C8
Forge The MK46 ....13 F8
Forgetts Rd HP14 ...171 C4
Forlease Cl SL6 .....203 A6
Forlease Dr SL6 ....203 A6
Forlease Rd SL6 ....203 A6
Formby Cl
  Milton Keynes MK3 ..57 C7
  Slough SL3 ....207 C2
Forrabury Ave MK13 .34 E4
Forsythia Gdns SL3 ..206 E3
Fort End HP17 .....127 A6
Fortescue Dr MK5 ...46 B6

Forthill Pl MK5 .....45 F7
Fortuna Ct MK7 ....48 C6
Forty Gn HP27 .....137 F3
Forty Green Dr SL7 ..183 B2
Forty Green Rd HP9 .175 C4
Forum The MK14 ....34 E5
Foscot Way MK18 ...41 E2
Foscote Cotts MK18 ..42 B4
Foscote Rd MK18 ...41 E7
Fossey Cl MK5 .....45 F3
Foster Ave SL4 .....209 E4
Foster Cl HP20 .....101 F3
Fosters La MK13 ....34 A3
Fosters Path SL2 ...197 F1
Fotherby Ct SL6 ....203 A6
Fotheringay Gdns SL3 .205 A6
Fotherley Rd WD3 ..178 F8
Founders Dr UB9 ...189 F5
Founders Mews MK14 .34 E7
Foundry La Horton SL3 .212 B4
  Lacey Green HP27 ...149 C5
Fountain Ct
  ⑥ Aylesbury HP20 ...115 D8
  Olney MK46 ....6 F3
Fountain Gdns SL4 ..210 D4
Fountaine Cl MK14 ..34 E7
Four Ashes Rd HP15 .162 C5
Four Oaks HP5 .....144 A4
Fourth Ave SL7 .....184 A2
Fourth St HP11 .....173 B4
Fowler MK14 ....34 C4
Fowler Rd HP19 ....115 B8
Fowlers Farm Rd HP14 .158 E4
Fox Cl HP23 ....119 D1
Fox Cover OX39 ....147 C6
Fox Field HP15 .....162 F5
Fox La HP15 ....163 B6
Fox Milne Rdbt MK10 .35 C4
Fox Rd
  Holmer Green HP15 ..163 B6
  Slough SL3 ....206 D2
  Wiggington HP23 ....119 C2
Fox Way MK18 .....52 E7
Foxborough Cl SL3 ..207 A1
Foxborough Prim Sch
  SL3 ....207 A1
Foxcovert Rd MK5 ..45 F4
Foxdell Way SL9 ....177 E5
Foxes Piece SL7 ....183 E5
Foxes Piece Sch SL7 .183 E3
Foxgate MK16 ......22 B4
Foxglove HP21 .....115 B5
Foxglove Cl MK18 ...52 C7
Foxglove Ct MK16 ...21 F4
Foxgoles Cl MK19 ...31 F5
Foxherne SL3 ......206 C4
Foxhill MK46 ....6 E5
Foxhill Cl HP13 .....162 B1
Foxhollow Dr SL2 ...198 C7
Foxhunter Dr MK14 .34 E6
Foxleigh HP11 .....173 A4
Foxley Pl MK5 .....46 C8
Foxmoor Ct UB9 ....190 A5
Foxton MK4 ....47 D6
Fraderica Cotts MK16 .22 C3
Framers Ct MK4 ....46 D2
Framewood Manor SL2 199 C6
Framewood Rd SL2,SL3 .199 C6
Framlingham Ct MK5 .46 A5
Frampton Ct UB9 ...189 F5
France Furlong MK14 .34 F8
Frances Ave SL6 ....196 C1
Frances Ct LU7 .....80 E7
Frances Rd SL4 ....210 D5
Frances St MK5 ....144 C2
Franchise St ❸ HP5 .144 C1
Francis St HP5 .....144 C1
Francis Edmonds Comb Sch
  HP14 ....171 B4
Francis Way SL1 ....204 D6
Frank Atter Croft MK12 .33 C5
Frank Howe Ct MK5 .35 A1
Frank Lunnon Cl SL8 .185 C5
Frank Sutton Way SL1 .205 D6
Franklin Ave SL2 ...205 B8
Franklin Cl HP17 ...127 A4
Franklin Cl HP7 ....154 C1
Franklin Rd Dunstable LU6 93 F8
  Haddenham HP17 ...127 A4
Franklins Croft MK12 .33 C5
Franklyn Cres SL4 ..209 D4
Frankston Ave MK11 .32 E5
Frankswood Ave UB7 .208 F7
Frantons The SL6 ...202 A7
Frascati Way SL6 ...202 F7
Fraser Rd HP12 ....172 C5
Fraucup Cl HP17 ...128 B7
Fraunchies Ct SL1 ..205 E6
Fray's Ct UB8 ......201 C5
Fray's Waye UB8 ...201 C4
Frays Ave UB7 .....208 D4
Frays Cl UB7 ....208 D3
Frayslea UB8 ......201 C3
Frederick Pl HP11 ..174 B3
Frederick Smith Ct MK12 33 D4
Frederick St HP11 ..99 A7
Fredericks Ct HP9 ..186 A8
Freeman Cl MK12 ...33 B5
Freeman Ct MK5 ...144 C1
Freemans Cl SL2 ...199 A6
Freemans Cl MK46 ..7 A3
Fremantle Rd
  Aylesbury HP21 ....115 C5
  High Wycombe HP13 .162 E2
Frenchum Gdns SL1 .204 E5
Frensham Dr MK2 ...58 C7

Frensham Wlk SL2 ..198 C6
Friarage Rd HP20 ...115 D8
Friars Field HP4 ....134 E7
Friars Furlong HP18 .125 B7
Friars Gdns HP14 ...162 A7
Friars Sq ⑦ HP20 ..115 D8
Friars Wlk
  Prestwood HP16 ....151 D5
  Tring HP23 ....119 A4
Friarscroft Way HP20 .115 C8
Friary Gdns MK16 ..22 C2
Friary Rd TW19 ....211 C1
Friary The SL4 .....211 C1
Friday Ct OX9 .....125 F1
Friday St
  Henley-on-T RG9 ....191 E2
  Leighton Buzzard LU7 .80 F7
Frieth CE Comb Sch
  RG9 ....170 F1
Frieth Rd SL7 ......182 E5
Fripp Gdns HP8 ....45 D6
Frith Hill
  Great Missenden HP16 .152 B7
  South Heath HP16 ..152 C8
Frithe The SL2 .....206 B4
Frithsden Copse HP4 .135 F8
Frithwood Cres MK7 .48 C8
Frog La HP18 ......112 F3
Froggy La UB9 .....189 D1
Frogmill Cl SL6 .....185 B3
Frogmill Ct SL6 ....193 C3
Frogmill Spinney SL6 .193 C3
Frogmoor HP13 ....173 A7
Frogmore Cl
  Hughenden Valley HP14 .162 A7
  Slough SL1 ....205 A4
Frogmore Cotts SL4 .210 E5
Frogmore Ct ❹ SL6 .202 E5
Frogmore Dr SL4 ...210 F5
Frogmore Flats SL4 .210 F5
Frogmore La HP18 ..125 C5
Frogmore St HP23 ..119 A3
Frome Cl HP21 .....115 C5
Fromer Rd HP10 ...185 D4
Frost Ho ❹ HP4 ...135 D4
Froxfield Ct MK4 ...46 C1
Fryday St MK6 .....46 E7
Fryer Cl HP5 ....154 D6
Fryers Ct HP12 ....172 D8
Fryers La HP12 ....172 D8
Frymley View SL4 ..209 D6
Fulbrook Mid Sch MK17 .49 B5
Fullbrook Cl SL6 ...203 A8
Fuller's Cl HP5 ....154 B6
Fuller's Hill HP5,HP6 .154 A6
Fullers Yd SL6 .....196 B2
Fulmar Pl ❶ HP11 .101 F3
Fulmer Chase SL3 ..199 C8
Fulmer Common Rd
  SL3,SL0 ....199 E6
Fulmer Dr SL9 .....188 D2
Fulmer Inf Sch SL3 .199 E8
Fulmer La SL9 .....189 A2
Fulmer Rd SL2 .....188 F2
Fulmer St
  Milton Keynes,Emerson Valley
  MK4 ....46 C3
  Milton Keynes,Medbourne
  MK8,MK5 ....45 E6
Fulmer Way SL9 ...188 E5
Fulton Cl HP13 .....173 A8
Fulwell Ct MK14 ...34 E8
Fulwell Rd Finmere MK18 .50 C7
  Westbury NN13 .....39 A4
Fulwood Ct TW19 ..213 F1
Fulwoods Dr MK6 ..47 A8
Furlong Cl SL8 .....185 B3
Furlong Cres HP17 .115 A1
Furlong La LU6 ....93 C7
Furlong Rd SL8 ....185 B3
Furlong The ⑫ HP23 .119 A3
Furness SL4 ....209 C5
Furness Cres MK3 ..47 A1
Furness Pl ❽ SL4 ..209 C5
Furness Row ❾ SL4 .209 C5
Furness Sq ❻ SL4 .209 C5
Furness Way SL4 ...209 C5
Furness Wlk ❼ SL4 .209 C5
Furnival Ave SL2 ...205 B8
Furrow Cl HP21 ....115 D4
Furrow Way SL6 ...202 A4
Furrows The UB9 ..190 C6
Furtho Ct MK19 ....32 B7
Furtho La NN12 ....18 E3
Fury Ct MK8 ....45 F7
Furze Down Sch MK18 .65 E4
Furze Field HP16 ...142 B8
Furze La MK18 ....65 E5
Furze Platt Halt SL6 .195 C1
Furze Platt Inf Sch SL6 .195 C1
Furze Platt Jun Sch
  SL6 ....195 C1
Furze Platt Rd SL6 .195 B1
Furze Platt Senior Sch
  SL6 ....195 D1
Furze Rd SL6 ......195 C1
Furze View WD3 ...167 C4
Furze Way MK2 ....33 C6
Furzefield Rd HP9 ..175 C2
Furzeham Rd UB7 ..208 E4
Furzen Cl SL2 .....198 A2
Furzton Rdbt MK4 ..46 C4
Fuzzens Wlk SL4 ...209 E5
Fyfield Barrow MK7 .48 C6
Fyne Dr LU7 ....80 C8

G

Gable Thorne MK7 ..48 D6
Gables Cl
  Chalfont St Peter SL9 .177 E6
  Datchet SL3 ....211 A8
  Maidenhead SL6 ....203 B8
  Wendover HP22 .....131 A4
Gables Dr HP14 ....149 C1
Gables Mdw HP15 ..163 C6
Gables The Datchet SL3 .211 A8
  Haddenham HP17 ...127 A5
  Leighton Buzzard LU7 .80 E6
Gabriel Cl MK7 ....48 C5
Gaddesden Cres MK7 .48 C6
Gadge Cl OX9 .....125 E1
Gadmore La HP23 ..132 F7
Gadsden Cl MK43 ..25 D3
Gadsden Ct MK17 ..69 E8
Gage Cl SL6 ....202 E4
Gainsborough SL6 ..195 F5
Gainsborough Cl MK8 ..45 D6
Gainsborough Dr SL6 .202 D3
Gainsborough Hill RG9 .191 D1
Gainsborough Pl MK10 .100 F3
Gainsborough Rd
  Aylesbury HP21 ....115 C8
  Henley-on-T RG9 ...191 D1
Gairloch Ave MK2 ..58 D5
Galahad Cl SL1 ....205 A4
Gallagher Cl MK8 ..45 E8
Galleries The ❹ HP13 .173 A7
Galley Hill MK11 ...32 F5
Galley La MK17 ....59 A4
Galleymead Rd SL3 .212 F6
Galloway Pl HP21 ..101 A3
Galloway Chase SL2 .206 A6
Galloway Cl MK3 ...46 F2
Gallows La HP12 ...172 C8
Gallys Rd SL4 .....209 D6
Galsworthy Pl HP19 .100 F2
Galvin Rd SL1 .....205 C6
Gamnel HP23 ......119 A6
Gamnel Mews HP23 .119 B7
Gamnel Terr HP23 ..119 A6
Gandon Vale HP13 .173 A8
Ganton Cl MK3 ....46 D1
Garamonde Dr MK8 .33 F2
Garbo Cl MK8 .....45 D7
Garden Cl Halton HP22 .131 C8
  Maidenhead SL6 ....202 A5
Garden Cotts SL3 ..212 D7
Garden Ct HP11 ...174 B3
Garden End HP6 ...154 C2
Garden Field La HP4 .135 F2
Garden Mews SL1 ..205 F5
Garden Reach HP8 .166 D6
Gardener Wlk HP15 .163 C6
Gardens Cl HP14 ...158 F4
Gardens The MK18 .53 F1
Gardiner Ct MK13 ..33 E6
Gardner Cl
  Aylesbury HP19 ....101 A3
  Great Kingshill HP15 .151 D1
Gardner Ho SL6 ...195 E1
Gardner Rd SL6 ...195 D2
Gardner's Cl LU6 ..93 E7
Garfield Pl ❶ SL4 .210 C5
Garland Ct MK8 ...45 E8
Garland Way HP22 .117 E5
Garner Ct ⑬ TW19 .213 E1
Garners End SL9 ..177 F4
Garners Rd SL9 ...177 F4
Garnet Cl SL1 .....205 A4
Garnet Ct SL7 .....183 C1
Garrard Rd SL2 ...197 F1
Garraways MK6 ....47 A6
Garrett Cl HP5 ....154 D6
Garrick Wlk MK9 ..34 F3
Garron Cl HP21 ...115 D3
Garrowmore Gr MK2 .58 D5
Garry Cl MK2 .....58 C5
Garson Gr HP5 ....144 A2
Garston MK8 ......33 F1
Garth The HP16 ...152 A8
Garthlands SL6 ....195 D2
Garthwaite Cres MK5 .46 A4
Garvin Ave HP9 ...175 C4
Garwood Cres
  Milton Keynes MK8 ..45 C6
  Milton Keynes MK8 ..45 D6
Gas La SL6 ....203 A3
Gascon's Gr SL2 ...198 A3
Gaskin Ct MK14 ...35 A5
Gatcombe MK8 ....33 F1
Gate Cotts WD3 ...167 D5
Gatehouse Cl
  Aylesbury HP19 ....115 C8
  Windsor SL4 ....210 B4
Gatehouse Sch The
  MK14 ....34 D7
Gatehouse Way HP19 .101 B1
Gatesbury Pl HP27 .139 B3
Gatesdene Cl HP4 ..121 C8
Gateway Ctr The HP12 .172 D4
Gateway Sch The HP16 .152 A8
Gatewick Cl SL1 ...205 E5
Gatewick La MK7 ..48 A3
Gatting Way UB8 ..201 E6
Gatward Ave SL6 ..202 A4
Gaveston Dr HP4 ..135 B6
Gaveston Rd SL2 ..197 F2
Gaviots Cl SL9 ....188 F3
Gaviots Gn SL9 ...188 F3
Gaviots Way SL9 ..188 E4

Gawcott Com Inf Sch
MK18 ....51 F4
Gawcott Fields MK18 ....52 B7
Gawcott Rd MK18 ....52 B6
Gawdrey Cl HP5 ....154 D6
Gayal Croft MK5 ....46 B4
Gayhurst Ho MK16 .....12 D1
Gayhurst Rd HP13 ....173 F7
Gayhurst Sch SL9 .....188 C7
Gayton Cl HP14 ......154 E4
Gees Farm Cl NN7 ....1 A5
Gell Cl SL9 ....190 F1
George Cl SL7 ....183 F4
George Ct HP18 ....83 B5
George Green Dr SL3 ..206 F7
George Green Rd SL3 ..206 E7
George Inn Pl MK16 ...12 B6
George Lee Ct HP14 ..160 C1
George Rd HP14 ......158 E5
George St
18 Aylesbury HP20 ...115 D4
Berkhamsted HP4 ....135 D4
Berkhamsted HP4 ....135 E4
5 Chesham HP5 ....144 C1
High Wycombe HP11 ..172 E1
Milton Keynes MK2 ....47 E1
Uxbridge UB8 ....201 D5
Wing LU7 ....79 E2
Woburn MK17 ....60 F7
George V Pl SL4 ......210 D7
George Yd MK11 ....32 D5
George's Hill HP15 ...162 F6
Georges Dr HP10 .....185 C7
Georgian Cl UB10 ....201 E8
Georgian Hts SL8 ....185 B5
Geralds Ct HP13 .....162 D2
Geralds Rd HP13 .....162 D2
Gerard Cl MK13 ....34 A7
Germain St HP5 ......154 B7
Germains Cl HP5 .....154 B7
Germander Park Fst Sch
MK14 ....34 D4
Germander Pl MK14 ...34 D4
Gerrards Cross CE Sch The
SL9 ....188 F4
Gerrards Cross Rd SL3 .199 A6
Gerrards Cross Sta SL9 .188 E6
Gershwin Ct MK7 ......48 C4
Gervaise Cl SL1 .....204 F5
Ghlbert Way HP4 .....135 A4
Ghyll Gdns HP4 .....134 C2
Gib La HP22 ....102 D4
Gibbings Cl MK18 .....76 A3
Gibbs Cl HP13 ......172 F8
Gibbs Ho HP11 ......173 F4
Gibbwin MK14 ....34 E8
Gibraltar La SL6 ....184 C1
Gibson Ct 9 SL3 ....206 F7
Gibson La HP17 .....127 A5
Gibson Pl TW19 .....213 C1
Gibson Rd
High Wycombe HP12 ..172 B3
Ickenham UB10 ......201 F8
Gibsons Gn
Milton Keynes MK13 ..34 C4
Milton Keynes MK13 ..34 C4
Giffard Park Comb Sch
MK14 ....22 A2
Giffard Park Rdbt MK14 .21 F3
Giffard Rd MK2 ....58 C6
Giffard Way HP18 ...125 C0
Gifford Gate MK14 ....34 E7
Gifford Pl MK18 ......41 E1
Gilbert Cl MK3 ....58 B7
Gilbert Ho 4 HP11 ..172 E7
Gilbert Scott Ct 9 HP7 .165 B7
Gilbert Scott Rd MK18 ..41 D2
Gilbert's Hill HP23 ..132 E3
Gilbey Wlk HP10 .....185 D4
Gilders Mews MK14 ...34 F6
Giles Brook Comb Sch
MK4 ....57 A7
Giles Gate HP16 ....151 B6
Gillamoor Cl 2 MK4 ...46 B3
Gilletts La HP12 ....161 C1
Gillfield Cl HP11 ...172 E3
Gilliad Rd SL1 ......205 E6
Gilliat's Gn WD3 ....167 D5
Gilliatt Cl SL0 .....207 E7
Gillott Cl SL6 ......202 F8
Gilman Cres SL4 ....209 D4
Gilmore Cl SL3 .....206 C4
Gilmore Rd HP20 ....101 E3
Gilpin Way MK46 ......7 A4
Gilpin's Ride HP4 ..135 D5
Gingers La LU7 ....91 D8
Gipsy La LU7 ....91 D8
Gisburn Cl MK13 .....34 E5
Glade Ho 5 SL7 .....183 E2
Glade Rd SL7 ....183 E2
Glade The
Gerrards Cross SL9 ..188 D2
Tylers Green HP10 ..163 C1
Glade View HP12 ...172 A3
Gladstone Cl MK16 ...22 D3
Gladstone Ind Est SL6 .202 E8
Gladstone Rd HP5 ...144 C1
Gladstone Rise HP13 .173 F6
Gladstone Way SL1 ..205 A5
Glaisyer Way SL0 ...200 D3
Glamis Cl HP13 .....173 B8
Glamis Ho MK3 ......57 E7
Glamorgan Cl MK3 ...46 F1
Glanmor Rd SL2 .....206 B6
Glassmill Ho 4 HP4 .135 D4
Glastonbury Cl MK3 ..47 A2
Glastonbury Thorn Fst Sch
MK5 ....46 B6

Glaven Rd HP21 .....115 C4
Glazier Dr MK14 ......34 F6
Glebe Cl
Chalfont St Peter SL9 .177 D3
Dorney SL6 ....203 F4
Holmer Green HP15 ..163 B7
Maids Moreton MK18 ..41 F3
Pitstone LU7 ....105 D5
Glebe Cotts HP14 ...169 C7
Glebe Dr NN13 ....38 A7
Glebe Ho SL9 ....177 D3
Glebe House Dr MK18 ..39 E6
Glebe La MK19 ....10 E5
Glebe Rd
Chalfont St Peter SL9 .177 C2
Deanshanger MK19 ...31 E5
Maidenhead SL6 ....203 B5
Old Windsor SL4 ....211 B2
Uxbridge UB8 ....201 C3
Glebe Rdbt MK9 ......35 B4
Glebe Terr MK18 .....41 F3
Glebe The Lavendon MK46 ..7 F8
Lewknor OX49 ....157 B8
Prestwood HP16 ....151 D2
Stone HP17 ....114 C5
Walter's Ash HP14 ..161 D4
West Drayton UB7 ..208 F2
Weston Turville HP22 .116 C2
Glebe Way MK4 .....154 D3
Glebelands HP10 ....174 C8
Glebelands 1 HP16 ..151 E4
Gledfield Pl MK12 ...33 D4
Gleeman Cl MK12 ...33 A5
Glen The SL3 ......206 C2
Glenavon Gdns SL3 .206 C3
Gleneagles Cl
Milton Keynes MK3 ..57 D7
Stanwell TW19 .....213 D1
Glenfield Cl
Aylesbury HP21 ....116 A5
Stoke Poges SL2 ...198 F4
Glenham Rd OX9 ....126 B1
Glenister Rd
Hazlemere HP15 ....163 A3
Chesham HP5 ......144 C3
High Wycombe HP12 .172 B4
Glenisters Rd HP13 .173 A8
Glenmore Cl HP10 ..174 A2
Glenmore Ho HP11 ..174 B3
Glenore SL6 ....196 A8
Glenstal Pl MK9 .....35 A3
Glentworth Pl SL1 ..205 C5
Glenwater Ho HP15 .163 A5
Glenwoods MK16 .....22 A4
Glimbers Gr OX39 ..147 C5
Globe Ho UB7 ......208 D5
Globe La 1 SL1 .....70 E1
Globeside Bsns Pk SL7 .183 F2
Glory Cl HP10 ......185 F7
Glory Mill La
Beaconsfield HP9 ..185 F8
Wooburn Green HP10 .185 E7
Gloucester Ave SL1 .205 C8
Gloucester Ct UB9 ..190 A4
Gloucester Pl SL4 ..210 C5
Gloucester Rd
Maidenhead SL6 ...195 E2
Milton Keynes MK15 .35 C3
Glovers Ct 2 HP20 .101 C3
Glovers La MK13 .....34 B4
Glyn Sq MK12 ....33 D7
Glyn St MK13 ....34 A7
Glynswood
Chalfont St Peter SL9 .177 F3
Chinnor OX39 .....147 C6
High Wycombe HP13 .162 B1
Glynswood Ho OX39 .147 C6
Glynswood Rd MK18 ..41 C1
Goathland Croft 2 MK4 ..46 B2
Goddards Croft MK12 ..33 C5
Goddington Rd SL8 .185 A5
Godfreys Cl HP18 ....96 B1
Godolphin Inf Sch SL1 .205 C7
Godolphin Jun Sch SL1 205 D7
Godolphin Rd
Seer Green HP9 ...176 C4
Slough SL1 ....205 D6
Godrevy Gr MK4 .....57 B8
Godstowe Sch HP13 .173 B8
Godwin Cl MK7 ......48 C7
Gogh Rd HP19 ......100 F2
Gold Crest HP19 ....101 F4
Gold Hill E SL9 ....177 D1
Gold Hill N SL9 ....177 C2
Gold Hill W SL9 ....177 C1
Gold Oak Wlk MK9 ...11 A2
Gold St MK19 ....11 A2
Golden Ball La SL6 .195 A3
Golden Dr MK6 ......47 B8
Golden Hills OX39 .147 D6
Golden Mede HP18 ..99 B6
Golden Miller Ct LU7 ..79 E2
Golden Oak Cl SL2 .198 C6
Golden Riddy LU7 ...80 E8
Golder's Cl HP18 ..123 F3
Goldfield Inf Sch HP23 .118 F3
Goldfield Rd HP23 ..118 F3
Goldilocks MK7 ......48 B6
Goldmark Cl MK7 ....48 D5
Goldsmith Dr MK16 ..21 F4
Goldsworthy Way SL1 .204 F4
Golf Club La HP27 ..139 E5
Golspie Croft MK12 ...33 C4
Gomm Pl HP13 ......174 A4
Gomm Rd HP13 ......174 A4
Gomms Wood Cl HP9 .175 B4
Gomms Wood Ho HP9 .175 B4

Good Intent LU6 ......92 E4
Goodacres La HP27 .149 E6
Goodall Cl RG9 .....191 E1
Goodlake Ct UB9 ...189 F4
Goodman Gdns MK6 ..47 D8
Goodman Pk SL2 ....206 C5
Goodrich Gn MK4 ....56 E8
Goodwick Gr MK4 ....57 B8
Goodwin Mdws HP10 .185 E6
Goodwin Rd
Aylesbury HP19 ....115 C8
Slough SL2 ....197 F2
Goodwin Villas SL1 .204 F5
Goodwins Mead LU7 .105 A4
Goodwood MK8 ....45 F8
Goodwood Rise SL7 ..183 D3
Goose Acre Botley HP5 ..145 A1
Cheddington LU7 ...105 A4
Goose Gn SL2 ......198 B3
Goosemere MK19 .....31 E4
Goosen Gn HP21 ...116 C6
Goran Ave MK11 .....32 E4
Gordale MK13 ....34 C5
Gordon Rd Chesham HP5 154 C7
High Wycombe HP13 .173 D6
Maidenhead SL6 ...202 D7
West Drayton UB7 .208 E6
Windsor SL4 ....209 F5
Gordon Way MK8 ...177 B7
Gore Cl UB9 ....190 C7
Gore Hill HP7 ......165 B5
Gore Rd SL1 ....197 B2
Gore The SL1 ......197 A2
Gorelands La HP8 ..177 F8
Gorell Rd HP9 .....176 B1
Goring MK14 ....34 C7
Gorman MK2 ....58 E4
Gorrell Cl MK18 ....51 B6
Gorrell La MK18 ....51 B6
Gorricks MK11 ......32 E4
Gorse Meade SL1 ..205 B5
Gorse Rd SL6 .....195 E6
Gorse Wlk
Hazlemere HP15 ..163 A3
West Drayton UB7 .208 E7
Goslar Way SL4 ...210 B5
Gosling Gn SL3 ...206 A5
Gosling Rd HP13 ..161 D2
Gosling Rd SL3 ...206 B5
Goslington MK1 .....47 C2
Goss Ave HP18 .....99 B6
Gossage Rd UB10 ..201 F5
Gossmore Cl SL7 ..183 F1
Gossmore La SL7 ..183 F1
Gossmore Wlk SL7 .183 F1
Gossom's End HP4 ..135 B4
Gossoms Ryde HP4 .135 A5
Goswell Hill SL4 ...210 D6
Goswell Rd SL4 ....210 D6
Goudhurst Ct MK7 ..48 B7
Governors Ave UB9 .189 F6
Governors Cl HP6 ..154 F1
Gower Ho HP6 .....154 E3
Gowers Field HP19,
HP20 ....101 D1
Gowers The HP16 ..154 E2
Gowers Yd MK19 ....32 B7
Gowings Gn SL1 ...204 E4
Goya Pl HP19 ......100 F3
Grace Ave MK6 .....46 E8
Grace Ct SL1 ......205 C5
Grace Reading Cl HP13 173 E6
Graces Cl MK43 ....25 C3
Graces Maltings 4
HP23 ....119 A3
Graeme Ave HP16 ..151 C6
Grafham Cl MK14 ...35 A8
Grafton Cl
Maidenhead SL6 ...195 E2
Potterspury NN12 ...18 E3
Slough SL3 ....206 F7
Grafton Ct NN7 ......4 A8
Grafton Gate MK9 ...34 C1
Grafton Ho SL7 ....147 C7
Grafton Orch OX39 .147 D7
Grafton Pk MK9 ....34 D1
Grafton Rd
Aylesbury HP19 ...101 A2
Yardley Gobion NN12 .18 F6
Grafton St
High Wycombe HP12 .172 D8
Milton Keynes,Bradwell
MK13 ....34 B4
Milton Keynes,Granby MK1 ..47 B3
Milton Keynes,New Bradwell
MK12,MK13,MK13 ...33 E8
Milton Keynes,Winterhill
MK6 ....46 E7
Graham Cl SL6 .....202 C5
Graham Dr HP12 ...172 B5
Graham Ho SL9 ....177 C1
Graham Rd SL6 ....195 E6
Grainge Chase MK17 .55 A3
Grainge Cl NN13 ....39 A5
Grampian Gate MK6 .46 E7
Grampian Way SL3 .207 A1
Gramwell MK5 ......45 F7
Granary Cl MK11 ....21 A3
Granborough Rd
North Marston MK18 ..76 A2
Winslow MK18 ......65 E2
Granby Ct MK1 ......47 A3
Granby Ind Est MK1 ..47 B3
Granby Rdbt MK1 ...47 C3
Grand Union Office Pk The
UB8 ....208 C7
Grandison Ho RG9 .191 E3
Granes End MK14 ...34 E8

Grange Cl
Chalfont St Peter SL9 .177 E2
Leighton Buzzard LU7 ..80 C4
Maids Moreton MK18 ..41 E3
Twyford MK18 ......62 D2
Wraysbury TW19 ...211 E1
Grange Cotts HP16 .152 A3
Grange Dr HP10 ....185 D3
Grange Farm Rd HP14 .159 F8
Grange Farm Rdbt MK8 ..45 D2
Grange Fields SL9 .177 E2
Grange Gdn HP18 ..83 A6
Grange Gdns
Farnham Common SL2 .198 D7
Wendover HP22 ...131 B5
Grange La SL6 ....195 B5
Grange Rd
Chalfont St Peter SL9 .177 E2
Cookham Rise SL6 .195 F7
Hazlemere HP15 ..162 F6
Hazlemere,Widmer End
HP15 ....162 E5
Henley-on-T RG9 ..191 E1
Milton Keynes MK3 ..57 F7
Pitstone LU7 ......105 D5
Tring HP23 ....119 C4
Wilstone HP23 ....104 D1
Grange Sch The HP21 .115 F6
Grange The
Burnham SL1 .....197 C2
Gerrards Cross SL9 .188 E6
Old Windsor SL4 ..211 B3
Wraysbury TW19 ..211 E1
Grange View HP27 .139 E7
Grange Way SL0 ..207 F7
Grangelands Nature
Reserve ★ HP27 ...139 F6
Grangers Croft MK12 .33 C4
Grangewood SL3 ..206 C8
Grant Ave SL1 ....205 E4
Grant Ho 6 SL8 ...185 A4
Grantham Ct MK5 ..46 C5
Grantham Mews HP4 .135 C4
Granville Ave SL2 .205 D8
Granville Dene HP3 .146 A8
Granville Pl 5 HP20 .115 D8
Granville Rd HP4 ..134 C6
Granville Sq MK15 ..35 C3
Granville St 4 HP20 .115 D8
Grapevine Cl HP11 .173 F4
Grasholm Way SL3 .207 C2
Grasmere
Aylesbury HP21 ...116 B3
Windsor SL4 ......209 E7
Grasmere Ave SL2 .206 A6
Grasmere Par SL2 .206 B6
Grasmere Way
Leighton Buzzard LU7 ..80 D7
Milton Keynes MK2 ..58 D6
Grass Hays HP21 ..116 C7
Grasscroft MK4 .....46 E4
Grassingham End SL9 .177 E3
Grassingham Rd SL9 .177 E3
Grassington MK13 ..34 A5
Grasslands HP20 ..102 A1
Grassy La SL6 ....202 E7
Grattan Ct SL7 ....184 A3
Gratton Ct MK5 ....46 C3
Gratton Dr SL4 ...209 D3
Gravel Dr HP23 ...118 B3
Gravel Hill
Chalfont St Peter SL9 .177 E3
Henley-on-T RG9 ..191 D2
Uxbridge UB8 .....201 D7
Gravel Path HP4 ..135 E5
Gravel Wlk MK46 ...13 F7
Graveney Pl MK6 ...35 B2
Gray's La
High Wycombe HP13 .161 D2
Ibstone HP14 ......169 C7
Gray's Mon ★ SL2 .198 F2
Gray's Pl SL2 .....205 F5
Gray's Rd Slough SL1 .205 F5
Uxbridge UB8 .....201 E5
Grayburn Cl HP8 ..177 A8
Grayling Cl SL7 ..194 C8
Grayling Ct HP4 ..134 F6
Grays Cl NN12 .....17 B8
Grays La Paulerspury NN12 ..17 D8
Yardley Gobion NN12 .18 E6
Grays Park Rd SL2 .199 A3
Grays Wlk HP5 ....144 B2
Greamesdyke Rd MK4 .135 A3
Great Benty UB7 ..208 E2
Great Brickhill La MK17 ..59 D5
Great Denson MK6 .47 A8
Great Ground MK4 ..34 E7
Great Hill Cres SL6 .202 C6
Great Hivings HP5 ..144 A4
Great Horwood CE Comb Sch
MK17 ....55 A3
Great Horwood Rd MK18 .65 F7
Great Kimble CE Sch
HP17 ....139 A1
Great Kingshill CE Comb Sch
HP15 ....162 C6
Great La Bierton HP22 .102 A4
Wendover HP22 ...131 B4
Great Linch MK10 ...36 A2
Great Linford Comb Sch
MK14 ....34 E8
Great Linford Lakes Wildfowl
Ctr ★ MK14 ....34 D7
Great Marlow Sch SL7 .183 F4
Great Meadow Way
Aylesbury HP19 ...114 F8
Aylesbury HP19 ...115 A8

Gaw – Gre 229

Great Missenden CE Comb
Sch HP16 ....152 B7
Great Missenden Sta
HP16 ....152 A7
Great Monks St
Milton Keynes,Wolverton
MK12 ....33 C5
Milton Keynes,Wymbush
MK8 ....33 E2
Great Ormes MK4 ...56 F8
Great Pasture MK10 .35 F3
Great Slade MK18 ...52 D6
Great Stone HP18 ..112 F3
Great Western St 22
HP20 ....115 D8
Greatchesters MK13 .33 F5
Greathead Dell MK7 .48 E6
Greaves Rd HP13 ..173 D6
Grebe Cl HP19 .....101 F3
Grecian St HP20 ...116 A8
Green Acre MK4 ....57 B8
Green Acres Cl HP22 .86 E7
Green Cl Burnham SL6 .204 A7
High Wycombe HP13 .173 C1
Maidenhead SL6 ..195 F1
Green Common La
HP10,HP9,SL1 .....186 C4
Green Cres HP10 ..185 C7
Green Dragon La HP10 .185 B7
Green East Rd HP9 .176 E3
Green End
Aylesbury HP19 ...115 D8
Granborough MK18 ..76 A7
Great Brickhill MK17 .59 D2
Green End La MK19 .11 A3
Green End Rd HP14 .159 E5
Green End St HP22 .117 E5
Green Farm Rd MK16 .22 C4
Green Ground OX33 .123 A2
Green Hailey HP27 .139 F3
Green Hill HP13 ...162 B1
Green Hill Cl HP13 .162 C1
Green Hill Gate HP13 .162 B1
Green La Amersham HP6 .154 C4
Aspley Guise MK17 ..49 E4
Botley HP5 ....155 B6
Bovingdon HP3 ...146 A3
Burnham SL1 .....197 D4
Chesham Bois HP6 .154 D3
Datchet SL3 ......211 B6
Eaton Bray LU6 ....92 D7
Farnham Common SL2 .198 B6
Ivinghoe LU7 .....105 E5
Maidenhead SL6 ..203 A6
Milton Keynes MK12 ..33 D6
Owlswick HP27 ...128 B3
Prestwood HP16 ..151 E6
Radnage HP14 ....159 D5
Stokenchurch HP14 .158 C5
Upper Arncott OX6 ..94 E7
Windsor SL4 ......210 B5
Green Lane Cl HP6 .154 D3
Green Lane Ct SL1 .197 C2
Green Lane Rdbt MK9 .35 B5
Green Leys
High Wycombe HP13 .161 C2
Maidenhead SL6 ..195 F2
Green North Rd HP9 .176 E4
Green Park Comb Sch
MK16 ....22 B3
Green Park Dr MK16 .22 C3
Green Path HP20,HP23 .118 C4
Green Pk HP16 ....151 D6
Green Pl HP10 ....185 C8
Green Rd HP13 ....162 C2
Green St
Chorleywood WD3 .167 C6
Hazlemere HP15 ..162 F4
High Wycombe HP12 .172 F7
Green The
Amersham HP7 ....154 C1
Aston Abbotts HP22 ..88 D4
Brill HP18 ....110 B8
Burnham SL1 .....197 B1
Chalfont St Giles HP8 .177 C8
Chearsley HP18 ..112 B2
Cheddington LU7 .105 A7
Cosgrove MK19 ....19 F2
Cranfield MK43 ....24 E2
Cuddington HP18 .112 F3
Deanshanger MK19 .31 E4
Edlesborough LU6 ..92 F4
Great Horwood MK17 .55 A3
Hanslope MK19 ....11 A2
Horton-cum-S OX33 .108 A5
Hyde Heath HP6 ..153 C5
Little Missenden HP7 .153 A2
Longwick HP27 ...138 D6
Mentmore LU7 .....90 D4
Milton Keynes,Loughton
MK5 ....46 A8
Milton Keynes,The Green
MK6 ....47 C8
Newport Pagnell MK16 .22 C4
Paulerspury NN12 ..17 B7
Pitstone LU7 .....105 D4
Quainton HP22 ....85 B5
Slough SL1 ....205 D4
Soulbury LU7 ......69 E3
Stoke Hammond MK17 .69 E7
Thornborough MK18 .54 A8
Turvey MK43 ....8 C2
West Drayton UB7 .208 D3
Wingrave HP22 ....89 B2
Wooburn Green HP10 .185 E5

Green The continued
Wraysbury TW19 ....211 E1
Green Tiles UB9 ....189 F4
Green Tiles La UB9 ......189 F5
Green Verges SL7 ......183 E3
Green View HP20 ......102 A3
Green View Cl HP3 .....146 A2
Green Way HP1 ....57 D4
Green West Rd HP9 .....176 E3
Greenacre SL7 ....209 E5
Greenacres LU7 ....105 C4
Greenacres Ave UB10 ...190 F1
Greenacres La HP10 ....163 A1
Greenacres The HP13 ...162 C1
Greenbury Cl WD3 ......167 C5
Greendale Mews SL2 ....206 A6
Greene Field Rd HP4 ...135 C4
Greene Wlk HP4 ....135 D3
Greenes Ct HP4 ....135 C5
Greenfern Ave SL1 ......204 C7
Greenfield End SL9 ......177 F3
Greenfield Rd MK16 ......22 A4
Greenfields Adstock MK18 .53 F1
Maidenhead SL6 ....203 A5
Upper Arncott OX6 ....94 D7
Greenhill Cl MK5 ....46 A8
Greenlands
Flackwell Heath HP10 ....185 B8
Lacey Green HP27 ....149 D1
Greenlands MK16 ....22 A3
Greenlands Ct SL6 ......202 B8
Greenlands La HP16 .....151 B7
Greenlaw Pl MK3 ....47 A3
Greenleaf Ct SL3 ....211 A8
Greenleas Lower Sch
LU7 ....80 C7
Greenleys Fst Sch MK12 .33 C5
Greenleys La MK12 ....33 C4
Greenleys Mid Sch MK12 .33 C5
Greenleys Rdbt MK12 .....33 B6
Greenock Rd SL1 ....205 A7
Greenridge HP10 ....174 B8
Greens Keep HP17 ......126 F6
Greenside
Bourne End SL8 ....185 A5
Prestwood HP16 ....151 C4
Slough SL2 ....205 A8
Greenside Hill MK4 ....46 B1
Greenway
Berkhamsted HP4 ....135 A4
Burnham SL1 ....197 B3
Chesham HP5 ....144 B3
Great Horwood MK17 ......55 A2
Haddenham HP17 ....126 F5
Thame OX9 ....125 F1
Greenway Ct [12] HP13 ...173 B7
Greenway Fst Sch HP4 ...134 F4
Greenway Par HP5 ....144 B3
Greenway The
Gerrards Cross SL9 ......188 D8
High Wycombe HP13 ......173 B7
Slough SL1 ....204 D5
Tring HP23 ....118 F5
Tylers Green HP10 ......163 B1
Uxbridge UB8 ....201 D3
Greenway Wlk MK18 ......41 F1
Greenways
Bow Brickhill MK17 ....48 C2
Eaton Bray LU6 ....92 D7
Greenways Dr MK16 ......202 A8
Greenwich Gdns MK16 ....22 C4
Greenwood HP14 ....150 A2
Greenwood Ave OX39 ...147 C5
Greenwood Cl
Amersham HP6 ....154 C1
Seer Green HP9 ....176 D4
Greenwood Mdw OX39 ...147 D6
Greenwood Pl MK18 ......63 D3
Greenwood The HP27 ....117 D5
Greenyard The NN7 ....1 B7
Greetham Rd HP21 ......116 C6
Gregories Ct HP9 ....175 D3
Gregories Dr MK7 ....48 D6
Gregories Farm La HP9 .175 D2
Gregories Rd HP9 ....175 C3
Gregory Dr SL4 ....211 B1
Gregory Rd SL2 ....187 D2
Grenadine Way HP23 ....119 A5
Grendon Rd Edgcott HP18 .72 F1
Kingswood HP18 ....83 C3
Grendon Underwood Comb
Sch HP18 ....83 A6
Grendon Way HP22 ......102 A4
Grenfell Ave
High Wycombe HP12 .....172 D7
Maidenhead SL6 ....202 F6
Grenfell Pl SL6 ....202 F6
Grenfell Rd
Beaconsfield HP9 ....175 D3
Maidenhead SL6 ....202 E6
Grenville Ave HP22 ......131 A4
Grenville Cl SL1 ....197 B3
Grenville Comb Sch
MK18 ....52 D1
Grenville Ct WD3 ....167 C5
Grenville Gn HP21 ......115 D4
Grenville Rd
Aylesbury HP21 ....115 D5
Buckingham MK18 ....41 C1
Grenville Way OX9 ......126 B1
Gresham Ct HP4 ....135 B3
Gresham Rd SL1 ....205 A4
Greyfriars Ct MK10 ....36 B2
Greyhound Ct MK18 .....66 A4

Greyhound La
Thame OX9 ....125 F1
Winslow MK18 ....66 A4
Greyhound Wlk OX9 .....125 F1
Greys Hill RG9 ....191 D1
Greys Rd RG9 ....191 D1
Greystoke Cl MK4 ....135 A3
Greystoke Rd SL2 ......204 D5
Greystonley [1] MK4 ......46 C2
Griffin Cl
Maidenhead SL6 ....202 E5
Slough SL4 ....205 C4
Griffin La HP19 ....101 B1
Griffin Gate Rdbt MK10 ..36 A2
Griffiths Acre HP17 .....114 E5
Griffiths Yd HP5 ....144 B1
Griffon Cl MK6 ....47 A7
Grigby Rise MK6 ....47 A7
Griggs Orch MK16 ....14 A2
Grimbold Ct MK15 ....35 C7
Grimmer Cl HP19 ....100 F3
Grimms Hill HP16 ....151 F7
Grimms Mdw HP14 .....150 B1
Grimsdell's La HP6 .....154 D2
Grimsdyke Rd HP23 .....119 D1
Gringer Hill SL6 ....202 E8
Grizedale MK13 ....34 B5
Groom Rd MK16 ....151 C5
Groombridge MK7 ....48 A7
Grooms Cotts HP5 ......145 B1
Grooms Ct HP11 ....174 A4
Groomsby Dr LU7 ....105 E5
Grosmont Cl [1] MK4 .....46 B2
Grosvenor Cl SL0 ......200 D2
Grosvenor Ct SL1 ......205 E7
Grosvenor Dr SL6 ......203 C8
Grosvenor Way HP19 ...114 E8
Groundsel Cl MK7 ....48 B6
Grove
Chalfont St Peter SL9 ....177 C2
[1] Slough SL1 ....206 A3
Grove Cotts UB9 ....190 C8
Grove Ct
Beaconsfield HP9 ....175 D2
Bierton HP22 ....102 C5
Maidenhead SL6 ....202 D7
Turvey MK43 ....8 E6
Grove End SL9 ....177 C2
Grove End Barns OX9 ...126 B4
Grove Gdns HP23 ....119 B5
Grove Hill SL9 ....177 C3
Grove Ind Sch The MK5 ..46 C7
Grove La
Ashley Green HP5 ......145 C5
Chalfont St Peter SL9 ....177 C2
Little Kimble HP17 ......129 E2
Uxbridge UB8 ....201 F1
Grove Pk HP23 ....119 C5
Grove Rd Amersham HP6 .154 F1
Beaconsfield HP9 ....175 C2
Burnham SL1,SL2 ....197 E4
Hazlemere HP15 ....162 F3
High Wycombe HP12 ....172 C8
Maidenhead SL6 ....202 F7
Tring HP23 ....119 C5
Turvey MK43 ....8 E6
Uxbridge UB8 ....201 D5
Windsor SL4 ....210 D5
Grove Road Prim Sch
HP23 ....119 C5
Grove The
Amersham HP6 ....154 D4
Latimer HP5 ....155 D3
Medmenham SL7 ....193 E6
Milton Keynes,Bradwell
MK13 ....34 A4
Milton Keynes,Rickley Park
MK3 ....58 A8
Newport Pagnell MK16 ....22 B3
Slough SL1 ....206 A4
Tring HP23 ....119 C5
Waddesdon HP18 ....99 A6
Grove Way
Chorleywood WD3 ....167 B4
Uxbridge UB8 ....201 D5
Waddesdon HP18 ....99 A6
Grovelands HP11 ....173 A6
Grovers Ct HP27 ....139 A2
Groves Cl SL8 ....185 C3
Groves Rd HP22 ....131 E2
Groves Way SL6 ....195 C6
Grovesbrook MK17 ....48 D2
Groveway
Bow Brickhill MK7 ....48 B7
Milton Keynes,Redmoor
MK3 ....47 A3
Milton Keynes,Simpson
MK6 ....47 D5
Growewood WD3 ....167 B4
Grubbins La HP27 ......150 B5
Grubwood La SL6 ......195 A4
Gryms Dyke HP16 ......151 D6
Grundy Ho UB8 ....201 D3
Guards Club Rd SL6 ....203 C7
Guards Rd SL4 ....209 C5
Guards View SL4 ....210 D6
Guards Wlk [1] SL4 .....209 C5
Guernsey Cl HP19 ......101 A3
Guest Gdns MK13 ....34 B8
Guildford Ave MK4 ....45 E1
Guildford Cl MK18 ....52 A4
Guillemot Way HP19 ....101 E3
Guinea Orch MK46 ....6 E4

Guinions Rd HP13 ......173 F5
Guise Ct MK17 ....49 F4
Gull Way [4] HP19 ......101 F3
Gullicot Way LU7 ....105 C4
Gulliver's SL4 ....210 D8
Gulliver's Land ★ MK15 ..35 C4
Gun La MK16 ....14 A2
Gundale Ct MK4 ....46 B2
Gunmaker Ct MK14 ....34 F6
Gunthorpe Rd SL7 ......184 A3
Gunver Ave MK4 ....57 B8
Gurnard Cl UB7 ....208 D6
Gurnards Ave MK6 ....35 A2
Gurnells Rd HP9 ....176 C5
Gurney Cl
[10] Aylesbury HP20 .....101 F2
Beaconsfield HP9 ....175 D2
Milton Keynes MK5 ....46 A2
Gurney Ct LU6 ....92 F6
Gurneys Mdw HP15 .....163 D3
Guttmann Rd HP21 .....115 F5
Gwendale SL6 ....195 C1
Gweneth Ct SL7 ....183 D3
Gwent Cl SL6 ....202 B4
Gwynant Ct MK2 ....58 C3
Gwynne Cl Tring HP23 ...119 A5
Windsor SL4 ....209 E6
Gynant Rd HP13 ....173 F6
Gyosei International Sch UK
MK15 ....35 C5
Gypsy La
Aspley Guise MK17 ....49 F3
High Wycombe HP11 .....173 D5
Marlow SL7 ....183 E4
Stoke Poges SL2 ....187 E1

H

Haberley Mead MK13 ....34 B3
Hackett Pl MK16 ....24 A6
Haddenham & Thame
Parkway Sta HP17 .....126 E6
Haddenham Aerodrome Bsns
Pk HP17 ....126 E6
Haddenham Com Inf Sch
HP17 ....127 A6
Haddenham Com Jun Sch
HP17 ....127 A6
Haddenham Mus ★ 126 F6
Haddenham Rd HP17 ....127 A3
Haddenham St Mary's CE Inf
Sch HP17 ....126 F6
Haddington Cl
Milton Keynes MK3 ....46 E2
Wendover HP22 ....131 D6
Haddington Way HP20 ...102 A1
Haddon MK8 ....45 F8
Haddon Rd
Chorleywood WD3 ....167 C4
Maidenhead SL6 ....202 C5
Hadfield Rd TW19 ....213 D1
Hadland Cl HP3 ....146 A4
Hadley Ct SL3 ....212 E6
Hadley Pl MK13 ....34 C3
Hadlow Ct SL1 ....205 C6
Hadrian's Gate NN13 .....38 A7
Hadrians Dr MK13 ....34 A5
Hag Hill La SL6 ....204 A7
Hag Hill Rise SL6 ....204 A7
Haggar St HP17 ....114 B5
Haglis Dr HP22 ....131 B6
Haig Dr SL1 ....205 A4
Hailey Croft OX39 ......147 B6
Hailey Ct SL6 ....202 F5
Haileybury St SL4 ......210 A4
Hainault Ave MK14 ......22 A4
Haines Cl HP19 ....100 F2
Haines Rd HP15 ....162 F6
Haithewaite MK8 ....33 D1
Haldene MK8 ....33 E2
Hale SL4 ....209 F6
Hale Ave MK11 ....32 E5
Hale La HP22 ....131 E3
Hale Leys Ctr HP20 .....115 D8
Hale Leys Sh Ctr [23]
HP20 ....115 D8
Hale Rd HP22 ....131 D5
Hale St HP20 ....115 E8
Hales Croft HP21 ....116 B4
Halfacre Hill SL9 ....177 F2
Halfway Hos
Hanslope MK19 ....10 F4
Maidenhead SL6 ....195 E4
Halfway House La HP5 ...153 F7
Halifax Cl SL6 ....202 A8
Halifax Ho HP7 ....166 C6
Halifax Rd
Heronsgate WD3 ....167 C2
High Wycombe HP12 ....172 D5
Maidenhead SL6 ....202 A8
Halifax Way SL6 ....202 A8
Halings La UB9 ....189 E7
Halkingcroft SL3 ....206 C4
Hall Cl
High Wycombe HP13 .....173 F5
Maids Moreton MK18 .....41 F3
Old Stratford MK19 ......32 B6
Hall Cotts HP18 ....82 B7
Hall Ct SL3 ....211 B7
Hall La MK16 ....23 C8
Hall Mdw SL1 ....197 C3
Hall Park Gate HP4 .....135 C3
Hall Park Hill HP4 ......135 C3
Hall Pk HP4 ....135 C3
Hall Place (Berkshire Coll of
Agriculture) SL6 ......194 A1

Halldore Hill SL6 ....195 E7
Halls Cnr HP10 ....174 A1
Halse Dr SL1 ....197 F7
Halswell Pl HP15 ....36 A3
Halton Com Comb Sch
HP22 ....131 D7
Halton Pl MK8 ....131 B8
Halton Wood Forest Wlks ★
HP22 ....132 A3
Halton Wood Rd HP22 ...132 A3
Haltonchesters MK13 ....33 F6
Haly Cl MK13 ....34 B4
Ham Island SL4 ....211 C3
Ham La SL4 ....211 C3
Hamberlins La HP4,
HP23 ....134 B7
Hamble Dr HP21 ....115 C6
Hambleden RG9 ....181 C2
Hambleden Mill RG9 .....192 C7
Hambleden Pl RG9 ......192 D6
Hambleden Rise RG9 ....192 D8
Hambleden Wlk SL6 .....195 E3
Hambleden Cl HP21 .....116 B5
Hambleton Gr MK4 ....46 B2
Hambling Pl LU6 ....93 F8
Hamburg Croft MK5 ......46 B3
Hambye Cl HP27 ....149 E4
Hamer Cl HP3 ....146 A3
Hamfield Cotts SL6 .....195 E7
Hamilton Ave RG9 ......191 C1
Hamilton Cl HP4 ....107 C5
Hamilton Ct
Aylesbury HP19 ....101 D1
High Wycombe HP13 .....173 B8
Hamilton Gdns SL1 .....197 B2
Hamilton La MK3 ....57 C6
Hamilton Mead HP3 ....146 A4
Hamilton Pk SL6 ....202 A6
Hamilton Pl HP18 ....188 E6
Hamilton Prim Sch
HP13 ....173 B7
Hamilton Prim Sch (Annexe)
HP13 ....173 B8
Hamilton Rd
Berkhamsted HP4 ....135 B4
High Wycombe HP13 .....162 C1
Slough SL1 ....205 A7
Thame OX9 ....126 A1
Uxbridge UB8 ....201 D1
Hamlins MK4 ....47 A6
Hammersley La HP10,
HP11 ....174 B5
Hammerwood Gate MK7 ..48 A7
Hammond Cres MK15 ....35 B6
Hammond End SL2 ......198 B8
Hampden Ave HP5 ......144 A1
Hampden Cl
Aylesbury HP21 ....115 D6
Stoke Poges SL2 ....199 A2
Hampden Gdns HP21 ....115 D6
Hampden Hall Coll
HP22 ....116 C4
Hampden Hill
Beaconsfield HP9 ....175 D2
Charndon OX27 ....72 E6
Hampden Ho [2] HP13 ...173 F6
Hampden Rd
Aylesbury HP21 ....115 D6
Chalfont St Peter SL9 ....177 D2
High Wycombe HP13 .....173 B8
Hughenden Valley HP16 ..151 B3
Maidenhead SL6 ....206 A6
Slough SL3 ....206 F3
Speen HP27 ....150 C5
Stoke Mandeville HP22 ...116 B1
Wendover HP22 ....131 C5
Hampden Sq [2] HP19 ...115 A8
Hampden Villas OX27 ....71 F7
Hampshire Ave SL1 .....205 C8
Hampshire Ct MK3 ....46 F2
Hampshire Lodge [8]
SL6 ....202 F6
Hampson Cl MK13 ....34 A5
Hampstead Gate MK13 ..34 C3
Hampton SL6 ....46 A8
Hampton Cl HP21 ....116 B1
Hampton Ho SL3 ....212 D7
Hanbury Cl SL1 ....204 A8
Handel Mead MK7 ....48 C5
Handley Comm HP14 ....171 B5
Handley Page Cl MK43 ..24 C7
Handy Cross HP11 ......172 F3
Hangar Rd UB9 ....189 F7
Hanging Croft Cl [4]
HP13 ....173 F6
Hangings La HP16 ......151 A6
Hanley Cl SL4 ....209 D6
Hanmer Rd MK6 ....47 E5
Hannah Ball Inf Sch
HP13 ....173 D7
Hannon Rd HP21 ....115 C5
Hanover Cl
Aylesbury HP19 ....101 A2
Slough SL1 ....206 A3
Windsor SL4 ....209 F6
Hanover Ct
[2] Aylesbury HP21 .....115 E7
Hazlemere HP15 ....163 B3
Leighton Buzzard LU7 ....80 C7
Milton Keynes MK14 ......34 C1
Hanover Gate SL1 ......204 F5
Hanover Mead SL6 ......203 C3
Hanover Way SL4 ......209 F6
Hanscomb Cl MK15 .....35 C2
Hansen Croft MK5 ....46 B5
Hanslope Comb Sch
MK19 ....11 A3
Hanslope Rd MK19 ......19 F6

Hanson Cl UB7 ....208 F3
Hanson Way HP21 ......116 A4
Harborne Ct MK8 ....33 C2
Harborough Cl SL1 ......204 D5
Harbourne Cl HP21 .....115 C3
Harby Cl MK4 ....46 C1
Harcourt
Milton Keynes MK13 ......34 A3
Wraysbury TW19 ....211 E1
Harcourt Cl Dorney SL6 .203 F3
Henley-on-T RG9 ....191 C1
Harcourt Gn HP19 ......101 B2
Harcourt Rd Dorney SL4 .203 F3
Tring HP23 ....119 C4
Windsor SL4 ....209 F6
Hardenwaye HP13 ......162 E1
Harding Rd
Chesham HP5 ....144 D1
Milton Keynes MK10 ......48 C8
Hardings Cl SL0 ....200 C2
Hardings Row SL0 ......200 D2
Hardmead Rd MK43 ....8 A3
Hardwick Cl SL6 ....202 A8
Hardwick Mews MK17 ...49 B3
Hardwick Pl MK3 ....49 B4
Hardwick Rd MK17 ......49 B4
Hardwicke Gdns HP6 ....154 E1
Hardy Cl Aylesbury HP21 .115 E7
Slough SL1 ....205 A5
Hardy Mead Ct HP11 ....174 B2
Hare Cl MK18 ....52 E7
Hare La MK16 ....152 B3
Hare Lane End HP16 ....152 A3
Hare Shoots SL6 ....202 E5
Harebell Cl MK7 ....48 B5
Harebell Wlk HP15 ......162 F6
Harebridge La HP22 .....117 E1
Hareden Croft MK4 ......46 B2
Harefield Rd
Maidenhead SL6 ....202 A7
Uxbridge UB8 ....201 D6
Harehatch La SL1 ....186 F3
Harescombe Ct MK9 ....175 D3
Haresfoot Sch HP4 .....135 B1
Harewood Pl SL1 ....206 A3
Harewood Rd HP8 ......166 C6
Hargrave Rd SL6 ....202 D8
Hargreaves Nook MK14 ..22 B2
Harkness Cl MK2 ....58 C6
Harkness Rd SL1 ....204 B8
Harlans Cl MK6 ....47 B8
Harle Stone Ct MK14 .....22 A1
Harlech Ho [5] HP13 ....173 F7
Harlech Pl MK3 ....57 E7
Harlequin Pl MK5 ....45 F3
Harley Ct SL1 ....205 C4
Harleyford La SL7 ......194 B7
Harling Rd LU6 ....93 B4
Harlow Rd HP13 ....173 C6
Harman Terr HP12 ......172 D7
Harman Wlk HP12 ......172 C1
Harmondsworth La UB7 .213 E8
Harmondsworth Prim Sch
UB7 ....213 D8
Harmondsworth Rd
UB7 ....208 E2
Harnett Dr MK12 ....32 F6
Harper Cl OX25 ....94 D7
Harpers La MK14 ....34 F8
Harrier Cl HP20 ....101 E3
Harrier Ct MK6 ....47 A8
Harrier Dr MK6 ....47 A8
Harries Cl HP5 ....144 B1
Harries Way HP15 ......163 B6
Harriet Walker Way
WD3 ....167 C2
Harrington Cl SL4 ......209 F3
Harris Cl HP18 ....110 A8
Harris Ct [7] HP20 .....101 F2
Harris Gdns SL1 ....205 C4
Harris Rd HP14 ....171 B5
Harrison Barber Cotts
SL3 ....212 D7
Harrison Cl MK5 ....46 D6
Harrison Pl OX9 ....125 F1
Harrison Way SL1 ......204 D5
Harroell
Long Crendon HP18 .....125 D5
Long Crendon,Church End
HP18 ....125 D6
Harrogate Ct SL3 ......207 A1
Harrold Lower Sch MK43 ..3 F6
Harrold Priory Mid Sch
MK43 ....3 F6
Harrold Rd MK46 ....3 B1
Harrow Cl
Aylesbury HP21 ....115 E4
Maidenhead SL6 ....195 E1
Harrow La SL6 ....195 E1
Harrow Mkt The SL3 ....207 A3
Harrow Rd SL3 ....206 F3
Harrow Yd [6] HP23 .....119 A3
Harrowden MK13 ....34 B7
Hart Moor Cl HP14 ......158 E4
Hart St RG9 ....191 E2
Hartdames MK5 ....46 A3
Hartfield Cl MK7 ....48 A7
Hartington Gr MK4 ....46 B3
Hartland Ave MK4 ....57 B8
Hartland Cl SL1 ....205 C6
Hartley MK14 ....34 E8
Hartley Cl SL3 ....199 C4
Hartley Ct SL3 ....199 C4
Hartley Copse SL4 ......211 A1
Hartley Ct SL9 ....188 E5
Harts Rd HP17 ....127 B6
Hartwell Cl HP10 ....163 C2
Hartwell Dr HP9 ....175 D3

Hartwell End HP21 . . . . . .115 B7
Hartwell Rd Ashton NN7 . . . . .9 F8
　Hanslope MK19 . . . . .10 E5
Hartwort Cl MK7 . . . . .48 B5
Harvard Cl MK14 . . . . .21 F2
Harvest Bank HP6 . . . . . .153 C4
Harvest Hill HP10 . . . . . .185 D2
Harvest Hill Rd SL4 . . . . .202 F3
Harvester Cl MK12 . . . . . . .33 B5
Harvey Dr MK46 . . . . .6 F1
Harvey Ho SL3 . . . . .206 A4
Harvey Orch HP9 . . . . . .175 C3
Harvey Rd
　Aylesbury HP21 . . . . .115 E5
　Dunstable LU6 . . . . .93 D7
　Slough SL3 . . . . .207 B4
Harvil Rd UB9,UB10 . . . . .190 E4
Harvington Pk LU7 . . . . . .105 D3
Harwich Rd SL1 . . . . .205 A7
Harwood Dr UB10 . . . . . .201 F4
Harwood Rd SL7 . . . . . . .183 C1
Harwood St MK13 . . . . . . .34 A7
Hasgill Ct MK13 . . . . .34 B4
Haslemere Rd SL4 . . . . . .210 A6
Haslerig Cl HP21 . . . . . . .115 F5
Haslow Ct MK8 . . . . .33 E3
Hasting Cl SL6 . . . . .203 C2
Hastings MK11 . . . . .32 E5
Hastings Mdw SL2 . . . . . .199 A4
Hastoe Cross HP23 . . . . .133 A7
Hastoe Farm Barns
　HP23 . . . . .132 F7
Hastoe Hill HP23 . . . . . . .132 F8
Hastoe La HP23 . . . . .119 A2
Hastoe Pk HP20 . . . . . . .101 F2
Hastoe Row HP23 . . . . . .133 A7
Hatch La
　Harmondsworth UB7 . . . . .213 D7
　Radnage HP14 . . . . .160 B4
　Windsor SL4 . . . . .210 A5
Hatch The SL4 . . . . .209 C7
Hatches La
　Great Kingshill HP15 . . . . .151 C1
　Hughenden Valley HP15 . . .162 B8
Hatchet Leys La MK18 . . . .53 F8
Hatchgate Gdns SL1 . . . . .197 D1
Hatchlands MK8 . . . . .33 F1
Hatfield Cl SL6 . . . . .202 C6
Hatfield Rd SL1 . . . . .206 A4
Hathaway Ct MK8 . . . . . . .45 E8
Hatter's La HP13 . . . . . . .173 F6
Hatton MK6 . . . . .47 D6
Hatton Ave SL2 . . . . .198 D1
Hatton Ct SL4 . . . . .210 C5
Hatton Gr UB7 . . . . .208 D4
Hauksbee Gdns MK5 . . . . .46 D5
Havelock Bsns Pk SL6 . . . .202 C7
Havelock Cres SL6 . . . . . .202 B7
Havelock Ct HP20 . . . . . .101 D1
Havelock Rd SL6 . . . . . . .202 B7
Havelock St HP20 . . . . . . .101 D1
Haven Of Rest SL6 . . . . . .203 B7
Haven Shaw Cl HP21 . . . .116 A5
Havenfield Ct HP13 . . . . . .173 B7
Havenfield Rd HP12 . . . . .172 C4
Haversham Fst Sch MK19 . .20 E2
Haversham Rd MK19 . . . . .20 D1
Haw La HP14 . . . . .149 A2
Hawfinch HP19 . . . . .101 E3
Hawker Ct SL3 . . . . .207 A3
Hawkhurst Gate MK7 . . . . .47 F7
Hawkings Way HP3 . . . . .146 A5
Hawkins Cl MK11 . . . . . . .32 C5
Hawkmoor Cl MK6 . . . . . . .47 B8
Hawkridge MK4 . . . . .46 E3
Hawks Hill SL8 . . . . .185 C3
Hawkshead Dr MK4 . . . . . .46 C3
Hawkshill Dr HP3 . . . . . . .146 B8
Hawkshill Rd SL2 . . . . . . .198 A2
Hawkslade Furlong
　HP21 . . . . .115 D3
Hawksmoor Cl HP13 . . . . .173 A8
Hawkswood MK46 . . . . .6 F5
Hawkswood Gr SL3 . . . . .199 F6
Hawkswood La SL3,SL9 . . .199 F3
Hawkwell Dr HP23 . . . . . .119 C4
Hawkwell Est MK19 . . . . . .32 B7
Hawley's La HP22 . . . . . . .87 A6
Hawridge & Cholesbury CE
　Comb Sch HP5 . . . . .133 E2
Hawridge La HP5 . . . . . . .143 E8
Hawridge Vale HP5 . . . . . .133 F1
Hawthorn Ave MK2 . . . . . .58 E3
Hawthorn Cl
　Aylesbury HP20 . . . . .101 C2
　Iver Heath SL0 . . . . .200 C6
　Turvey MK43 . . . . .8 E6
Hawthorn Cres HP15 . . . .163 B2
Hawthorn Dr UB9 . . . . . . .201 C6
Hawthorn Gdns SL6 . . . . .202 E5
Hawthorn La SL2 . . . . . . .198 A5
Hawthorn Pl HP10 . . . . . .174 C8
Hawthorn Rd HP27 . . . . . .139 C3
Hawthorn Way
　Chesham HP5 . . . . .144 D2
　Wing LU7 . . . . .79 C3
Hawthorn Wlk HP15 . . . . .163 B2
Hawthorne Cl
　Leighton Buzzard LU7 . . . . .80 E8
　Marlow SL7 . . . . .183 E4
Hawthorne Cres
　Slough SL1 . . . . .205 F7
　West Drayton UB7 . . . . . .208 F4
Hawthorne Gdns HP10 . . .174 A2
Hawthorne Rd HP13 . . . . .174 A6
Hawthorns The
　Berkhamsted HP4 . . . . . .135 A5
　Cranfield MK43 . . . . .25 B1

Hawthorns The continued
　Felden HP3 . . . . .146 F7
　Little Chalfont HP8 . . . . . .166 C7
　Maple Cross WD3 . . . . . .178 D5
　Monks Risborough HP27 . .139 C6
　Poyle SL3 . . . . .212 F6
　Wooburn Green HP10 . . . .185 E6
Hawtrey Cl SL1 . . . . .206 B4
Hawtrey Rd SL4 . . . . .210 C5
Hay Barn Bsns Pk The
　HP22 . . . . .88 C6
Hay La SL3 . . . . .199 D8
Hayden Ho 3 HP11 . . . . .172 F7
Haydon Abbey Comb Sch
　HP19 . . . . .101 C2
Haydon Ct SL6 . . . . .202 E6
Haydon Rd HP19 . . . . . . .101 C2
Hayes Pl SL2 . . . . .183 D1
Hayes Rd MK19 . . . . .31 F5
Hayfield Dr HP15 . . . . . . .163 B2
Hayles Field RG9 . . . . . . .170 E1
Haymaker Cl UB10 . . . . . .201 F5
Hayman Rise MK8 . . . . . . .45 D6
Haymill Rd SL1,SL2 . . . . .197 D1
Haynes Cl
　Bow Brickhill MK17 . . . . . .48 D2
　Slough SL3 . . . . .206 F1
Haynes Ho HP12 . . . . . . .172 B3
Haynes Mead HP4 . . . . . .135 A6
Hayse Hill SL4 . . . . .209 D6
Haythorp Cl HP15 . . . . . . .35 B6
Hayward Pl SL8 . . . . .185 C2
Haywards Cl RG9 . . . . . . .191 C1
Haywards Croft MK12 . . . . .33 C5
Haywards Mead SL4 . . . . .204 F1
Haywood Pk
　Chorleywood WD3 . . . . . .167 F4
　Stewkley LU7 . . . . .68 C3
Haywood Way HP19 . . . . .100 F3
Haywoods Dr HP3 . . . . . .146 F8
Hazel Cl SL7 . . . . .183 C6
Hazel Ct WD3 . . . . .178 E5
Hazel Gr MK2 . . . . .58 D7
Hazel Rd HP4 . . . . .135 D3
Hazelbury Rd HP13 . . . . .173 D6
Hazelcroft Cl UB10 . . . . . .201 F5
Hazeldene HP22 . . . . . . .131 C4
Hazeley Sch MK8 . . . . . . .45 D6
Hazelhurst 7 MK4 . . . . . .46 B2
Hazelhurst Rd SL1 . . . . . .197 D3
Hazell Ave HP21 . . . . . . .116 A7
Hazell Cl SL6 . . . . .202 F8
Hazell Pk HP16 . . . . .165 D8
Hazell Way SL2 . . . . .198 F6
Hazelwood MK14 . . . . . . .34 F8
Hazelwood Cl HP5 . . . . . .144 D2
Hazely HP23 . . . . .119 C4
Hazlemere CE Comb Sch
　HP15 . . . . .162 F3
Hazlemere Ct HP15 . . . . .163 A4
Hazlemere Rd
　Slough SL2 . . . . .206 B5
　Tylers Green HP10 . . . . . .163 C6
Hazlemere View HP15 . . . .163 B5
Hazley Wlk MK18 . . . . . . .41 F1
Headington Cl SL6 . . . . . .202 A7
Headington Pl SL2 . . . . . .205 F5
Headington Rd SL6 . . . . .202 A7
Headland Cl 1 HP16 . . . .152 A8
Headlands Dr HP4 . . . . . .135 E5
Healey Ave HP13 . . . . . . .173 D7
Heaney Cl MK16 . . . . .22 A5
Hearn Ct HP10 . . . . .162 F2
Hearne Cl HP8 . . . . .177 B7
Hearne Dr SL6 . . . . .203 A1
Hearne Pl MK6 . . . . .46 F8
Hearne's Mdw HP9 . . . . . .176 D5
Hearnes Cl HP9 . . . . .176 D5
Heath Cl
　Aylesbury HP21 . . . . .116 A7
　Holmer Green HP15 . . . . .163 B6
　Stanwell TW19 . . . . .213 C1
　Wooburn Sands MK17 . . . .49 C3
Heath Ct
　Leighton Buzzard LU7 . . . . .70 E3
　Uxbridge UB8 . . . . .201 D5
Heath End Cl HP15 . . . . . .151 E1
Heath End Rd
　Flackwell Heath HP10 . . . .174 A1
　Great Kingshill HP15,HP16 .151 E2
　Little Marlow HP10 . . . . . .173 C2
Heath La MK17 . . . . .49 A2
Heath Lawn HP10 . . . . . . .173 F1
Heath Rd
　Beaconsfield HP9 . . . . . . .186 A8
　Great Brickhill MK17,LU7 . .59 E1
　Hyde Heath HP6 . . . . . . .153 C5
Heath The LU7 . . . . .70 E4
Heath Way SL0 . . . . .200 D3
Heathacre SL3 . . . . .212 E6
Heathcote Ct 2 SL4 . . . . .210 D4
Heathcote Way UB7 . . . . .208 D5
Heather Cl
　Buckingham MK18 . . . . . . .52 C7
　Uxbridge UB8 . . . . .208 F8
Heather La UB7 . . . . .208 E7
Heather Mead LU6 . . . . . . .92 E5
Heather Wlk
　Aylesbury HP21 . . . . .115 B6
　Hazelmere HP15 . . . . . . .163 A3
Heathercroft MK14 . . . . . .34 E7
Heatherden Gn SL0 . . . . .200 D4
Heathers Cl MK18 . . . . . . .73 B5
Heatherside Gdns SL2 . . .187 D1

Heatherton House Sch
　HP6 . . . . .154 C3
Heatherton Pk HP6 . . . . . .154 B3
Heathfield MK12 . . . . .33 E4
Heathfield Rd
　High Wycombe HP12 . . . . .172 B7
　Taplow SL1 . . . . .186 A1
Heathlands Dr SL6 . . . . . .202 A6
Heathrow Bvd UB7 . . . . . .213 F7
Heathrow Cl UB7 . . . . . . .213 B6
Heathrow Prim Sch
　UB7 . . . . .213 F8
Heavens Lea SL8 . . . . . . .185 C2
Hedge Lea HP10 . . . . . . .185 D6
Hedgerley OX3 . . . . .147 B6
Hedgerley Hill SL2 . . . . . .187 D2
Hedgerley La
　Beaconsfield HP9 . . . . . . .186 A6
　Gerrards Cross SL9 . . . . .188 B4
　Hedgerley SL2 . . . . .187 D6
Hedgerow SL9 . . . . .177 E4
Hedgerows The MK4 . . . . .46 E4
Hedges Ct MK5 . . . . .46 B6
Hedingham St MK5 . . . . . .46 A5
Hedley Cl HP22 . . . . .118 A4
Hedley Rd HP10 . . . . .185 B8
Hedley View HP10 . . . . . .174 D1
Hedsor Hill SL8 . . . . .185 C1
Hedsor La Hedsor HP10 . .185 F2
　Taplow SL6 . . . . .186 A2
Hedsor Rd SL8 . . . . .185 B2
Hedsor View Cotts SL8 . . .195 F7
Heelands Fst Sch MK13 . . .34 C4
Heights The SL7 . . . . .194 B8
Hele Ct MK7 . . . . .48 B3
Helen Cotts SL4 . . . . .209 D5
Helena Rd SL4 . . . . .210 D5
Helford Cl HP21 . . . . .115 D4
Helford Pl MK6 . . . . .35 A1
Heligan Pl MK4 . . . . .45 C1
Hellfire Caves* HP14 . . . .160 F2
Hellyer Way SL8 . . . . .185 C3
Helmsley Rise MK4 . . . . . .45 E1
Helston La SL4 . . . . .210 B6
Helston Pl MK6 . . . . .34 F1
Hemel Hempstead Rd
　HP4 . . . . .107 F1
Hemingway Cl MK16 . . . . .21 F5
Hemingway Rd HP19 . . . . .100 F2
Hemming Way SL2 . . . . . .198 B2
Hemmings The HP4 . . . . .134 E3
Hemp Hill HP19 . . . . .115 A8
Hemp La HP23 . . . . .119 C1
Hempson Ave SL3 . . . . . .206 C3
Hempstead Rd HP3 . . . . .146 B5
Hemsdale SL6 . . . . .195 B1
Hemwood Rd SL4 . . . . . . .209 A4
Hencroft Mews 14 SL1 . . .205 F4
Hencroft St N SL1 . . . . . .205 F4
Hencroft St S SL1 . . . . . .205 F3
Henders MK11 . . . . .32 E5
Hendon Way TW19 . . . . . .213 D1
Hendons Way SL6 . . . . . .203 B1
Hendrix Dr MK8 . . . . .45 D7
Hengistbury La SL6 . . . . . .46 A1
Henley Coll The RG9 . . . . .191 E1
Henley Coll The (Rotherham
　Bldgs) RG9 . . . . .191 F1
Henley Lodge 12 SL6 . . . .202 F6
Henley Rd Hurley SL6 . . . .193 D3
　Maidenhead SL6,SL7 . . . . .194 B8
　Marlow SL7 . . . . .194 B8
　Slough SL1 . . . . .204 F7
Henley-on-Thames Sta
　RG9 . . . . .191 E1
Hennerton Way HP13 . . . .173 F6
Henrietta Rd OX9 . . . . . . .126 A1
Henry III Twr 17 SL4 . . . . .210 D6
Henry Rd Aylesbury HP20 .116 B8
　Slough SL1 . . . . .205 D4
Henry St HP23 . . . . .119 A3
Hensman Gate MK10 . . . . .35 F2
Henson Cl MK43 . . . . .24 E3
Henton Mews 5 HP19 . . . .115 A8
Hepleswell MK8 . . . . .33 E1
Hepplewhite Cl HP13 . . . .173 B6
Herbert Rd HP13 . . . . . . .174 A7
Herberts Hole
　Chesham HP5 . . . . .143 C1
　South Heath HP5,HP16 . . .142 F1
Hercies Rd UB10 . . . . . . .201 F5
Herd's Hill HP18 . . . . .64 A4
Herdman Cl MK12 . . . . . . .33 B5
Hereford Ho HP13 . . . . . .173 F8
Hereford Way HP19 . . . . .101 A3
Heritage Cl UB8 . . . . .201 C1
Heritage Gate SL9 . . . . . .188 E7
Heritage House Sch
　HP5 . . . . .144 D1
Heritage Wlk WD3 . . . . . .167 C4
Hermitage Cl SL3 . . . . . . .206 C3
Hermitage La SL4 . . . . . . .210 A4
Hermitage Prim Sch
　UB8 . . . . .201 D5
Hermitage The
　Great Missenden HP16 . . .152 A7
　Uxbridge UB8 . . . . .201 D6
Heron Cl Aylesbury HP20 . .116 C8
　Uxbridge UB8 . . . . .201 D6
Heron Dr SL3 . . . . .207 B2
Heron Lodge MK14 . . . . . .34 C6
Herons Elm HP4 . . . . .134 E7
Herons Pl
　Maidenhead SL6 . . . . . . .196 C3
　Marlow SL7 . . . . .183 E3
Heronsfield Ho WD3 . . . . .167 B3

Heronsgate Fst Sch MK7 . .48 B5
Heronsgate Mid Sch
　MK7 . . . . .48 B5
Heronsgate Rd WD3 . . . . .167 B3
Herries Sch SL6 . . . . .195 B3
Herriot Cl MK3 . . . . .22 A5
Herschel Gram Sch SL1 . .205 C7
Herschel St SL1 . . . . .205 F4
Herston Cl HP21 . . . . .116 B5
Hertford Pl MK3 . . . . .46 F2
Hervines Cl SL6 . . . . .154 C2
Hervines Rd HP6 . . . . . . .154 C2
Hesketh Rd NN12 . . . . . . .18 E6
Het's Orch HP27 . . . . .149 E5
Hetherington Cl SL2 . . . . .197 F2
Hetherington Way UB10 . .201 E8
Hetton Cl MK13 . . . . .34 C4
Heusden Way SL9 . . . . . .188 F3
Hever Cl Maidenhead SL6 .202 C6
　Pitstone LU7 . . . . .105 D2
Hewgate Ct RG9 . . . . . . .191 E1
Hexham Gdns MK3 . . . . . .57 D6
Heydon Cl MK13 . . . . .34 A7
Heynes Gn SL6 . . . . .202 B3
Heythrop Dr UB10 . . . . . . .201 F8
Heywood Ave SL6 . . . . . . .202 A1
Heywood Court Cl SL6 . . .202 A2
Heywood Gdns SL6 . . . . .202 A1
Hibbert Rd SL6 . . . . .203 B8
Hibbert's Alley 16 SL4 . . . .210 D6
Hibberts Way SL6 . . . . . .188 E8
Hickman St HP19 . . . . . . .114 F8
Hickmans Cl MK18 . . . . . .51 B6
Hickox Ct HP10 . . . . .185 F7
Hicks Farm Rise HP13 . . .173 F7
Hidcote Dr MK4 . . . . .45 F1
Hide The MK6 . . . . .47 C6
Higgs Ct MK5 . . . . .46 A8
High Ash CE Prim Sch
　MK17 . . . . .59 D2
High Beeches
　Gerrards Cross SL9 . . . . .188 D2
　High Wycombe HP12 . . . . .172 C6
High Beeches Cl SL7 . . . .183 C7
High Bois La HP6 . . . . . . .154 D4
High Coppice HP7 . . . . . .165 C4
High Halden MK7 . . . . . . .48 B8
High Heavens Wood
　SL7 . . . . .183 C8
High Land Ct HP18 . . . . . .96 A1
High March Sch HP9 . . . .175 D4
High Mdw SL6 . . . . .196 C3
High Moors HP22 . . . . . . .131 B3
High Park Dr MK12 . . . . . .33 A6
High Rd
　Cookham Rise SL6 . . . . . .195 E2
　Soulbury LU7 . . . . .69 E2
　Uxbridge UB8 . . . . .208 C4
High St Amersham HP7 . . .165 A7
　Aylesbury HP20 . . . . .115 D4
　Berkhamsted,Berkhamsted
　　HP4 . . . . .134 E6
　Berkhamsted,Northchurch
　　HP4 . . . . .134 C4
　Bovingdon HP3 . . . . .146 A4
　Bray SL6 . . . . .203 C4
　Brill HP18 . . . . .110 A8
　Buckingham MK18 . . . . . . .41 D1
　Burcott LU7 . . . . .79 D4
　Burnham SL1 . . . . .197 C2
　Chalfont St Giles HP8 . . . .177 C8
　Chalfont St Peter SL9 . . . .177 C2
　Chalvey SL1 . . . . .205 D3
　Cheddington LU7 . . . . . . .105 A7
　Chesham HP5 . . . . .154 B8
　Chinnor OX39 . . . . .147 D7
　Chinnor,Kingston Blount
　　OX39 . . . . .147 A4
　Colnbrook SL3 . . . . .212 C7
　Cookham SL6 . . . . .196 B7
　Cranfield MK43 . . . . .25 B1
　Cranfield MK43 . . . . .37 F8
　Cublington LU7 . . . . .78 B1
　Datchet SL3 . . . . .211 B6
　Deanshanger MK19 . . . . . .31 E4
　Dinton HP17 . . . . .113 E2
　Eaton Bray LU6 . . . . .92 E6
　Edlesborough LU6 . . . . . . .92 E3
　Emberton MK46 . . . . .13 E7
　Eton SL4 . . . . .210 D8
　Great Horwood MK17 . . . . .55 A3
　Great Missenden HP16 . . .152 A7
　Haddenham HP17 . . . . . .126 F6
　Hanslope MK19 . . . . .11 A2
　Harmondsworth UB7 . . . . .213 D8
　Harrold MK43 . . . . .3 F6
　Haversham MK19 . . . . . . .21 A3
　High Wycombe HP11 . . . . .173 B6
　High Wycombe,Downley
　　HP13 . . . . .161 D3
　Iver SL0 . . . . .207 D3
　Ivinghoe LU7 . . . . .105 E5
　Lane End HP14 . . . . .171 B4
　Lavendon MK46 . . . . .7 E8
　Leighton Buzzard LU7 . . . . .80 F6
　Lewknor OX49 . . . . .157 B8
　Long Crendon HP18 . . . . .125 D6
　Ludgershall HP18 . . . . . . .96 B8
　Maidenhead SL6 . . . . . . .202 F7
　Marlow SL7 . . . . .183 E1
　Milton Keynes MK2 . . . . . .47 E1
　Milton Keynes, New Bradwell
　　MK13 . . . . .34 A7
　Milton Keynes,Great Linford
　　MK14 . . . . .21 E1
　Milton Keynes,Stony Stratford
　　MK11 . . . . .32 D6
　Nash MK17 . . . . .44 C1

High St continued
　Newport Pagnell MK16 . . . .22 D4
　North Crawley MK16 . . . . .24 B6
　North Marston MK18 . . . . .76 A2
　Olney MK46 . . . . .6 F3
　Paulerspury NN12 . . . . . . .17 C8
　Potterspury NN12 . . . . . . .18 D3
　Prestwood HP16 . . . . . . .151 E6
　Princes Risborough HP27 .139 B3
　Sherington MK16 . . . . .13 F2
　Slough SL3 . . . . .207 A2
　Slough,Upton SL1 . . . . . .205 F4
　Stanwell TW19 . . . . .213 D1
　Stoke Goldington MK16 . . .12 B6
　Syresham NN13 . . . . .27 B7
　Taplow SL6 . . . . .196 E1
　Thame OX9 . . . . .125 E1
　Thornborough MK18 . . . . .54 A8
　Tring HP23 . . . . .119 A3
　Turvey MK43 . . . . .8 E5
　Uxbridge UB8 . . . . .201 D5
　Uxbridge,Cowley UB8 . . . .201 C1
　Waddesdon HP18 . . . . . . .99 A6
　Weedon HP22 . . . . .87 C1
　Wendover HP22 . . . . .131 B4
　West Drayton UB7 . . . . . .208 E6
　West Wycombe HP14 . . . .160 F2
　Westcott HP18 . . . . .98 B7
　Weston Underwood MK46 . .6 B5
　Whaddon MK17 . . . . .45 B1
　Whitchurch HP22 . . . . . . .87 A6
　Windsor SL4 . . . . .210 D6
　Wing LU7 . . . . .79 E2
　Winslow MK18 . . . . .65 F4
　Woburn Sands MK17 . . . . .49 B8
　Wraysbury TW19 . . . . . . .211 F1
　Yardley Gobion NN12 . . . . .18 F6
　Yardley Hastings NN7 . . . . .1 B6
High St N LU7 . . . . .68 D2
High St S Olney MK46 . . . . .6 F3
　Stewkley LU7 . . . . .78 E8
High St The MK8 . . . . .33 E1
High Town Rd SL6 . . . . . .202 F7
High Trees MK6 . . . . .47 B8
High View
　Chalfont St Giles HP8 . . . .177 D8
　Deanshanger MK19 . . . . . .31 E5
High View Cl SL7 . . . . . . .183 C8
High Wycombe CE Comb Sch
　HP11 . . . . .173 A6
High Wycombe Sta
　HP13 . . . . .173 B7
Higham Cross Rd MK19 . . .10 E4
Higham Mead HP5 . . . . . .144 C1
Higham Rd HP5 . . . . .144 C1
Highbridge Ind Est UB8 . . .201 C5
Highbridge Rd HP21 . . . . .115 E8
Highbridge Wlk 4
　HP21 . . . . .115 E8
Highbury La MK9 . . . . .35 B3
Highcrest Com Sch
　HP13 . . . . .173 E7
Highcroft Cl NN12 . . . . . . .18 E6
Highfield
　Chalfont St Giles HP8 . . . .177 D8
　Long Crendon HP18 . . . . .125 D7
Highfield Ave HP12 . . . . . .172 B5
Highfield Cl
　Amersham HP6 . . . . .154 D2
　Milton Keynes MK3 . . . . . .47 B2
　Newport Pagnell MK16 . . . .22 E4
Highfield Ct
　Farnham Royal SL2 . . . . .198 B4
　Hazelmere HP15 . . . . . . .163 A3
Highfield Dr UB10 . . . . . . .190 F4
Highfield La SL6 . . . . .202 A4
Highfield Pk SL7 . . . . .183 B1
Highfield Rd
　Berkhamsted HP4 . . . . . .135 A4
　Bourne End SL8 . . . . . . .185 B4
　Chesham HP5 . . . . .144 B2
　Flackwell Heath HP10 . . . .185 A8
　Maidenhead SL6 . . . . . . .202 B8
　Princes Risborough HP27 .139 C4
　Tring HP23 . . . . .118 E3
　Wigginton HP23 . . . . .119 D1
　Windsor SL4 . . . . .209 F4
　Winslow MK18 . . . . .65 F5
Highfield Sch SL6 . . . . . . .202 E7
Highfield Way
　Hazelmere HP15 . . . . . . .163 A3
　Yardley Hastings NN7 . . . . .1 B6
Highgate Mews 2
　HP19 . . . . .100 F1
Highgate Over MK7 . . . . . .48 B6
Highgrove Hill MK8 . . . . . .45 D8
Highgrove Pk SL6 . . . . . . .202 E8
Highland Cl MK3 . . . . .46 F3
Highland Rd HP5 . . . . . . .165 D8
Highland View Cvn Pk
　UB7 . . . . .208 C2
Highlands
　Flackwell Heath HP10 . . . .185 B7
　High Wycombe HP13 . . . . .174 A5
Highlands Cl SL9 . . . . . . .177 F3
Highlands End HP7 . . . . . .177 F3
Highlands La SL9 . . . . . . .177 F3
Highlands Rd
　Buckingham MK18 . . . . . . .41 E2
　Seer Green HP9 . . . . . . .176 C5
Highlands The SL2 . . . . . .198 C7
Highlea Ave HP10 . . . . . . .185 A8
Highley Gr MK10 . . . . .36 B3
Highmoor HP7 . . . . .165 D8
Highmore Cotts HP7 . . . . .152 F3

232 Hig – Hut

Highmore Croft MK8 ....45 D6
Highover Pk HP7 ......165 D7
Highveer Croft MK4 .....46 B1
Highway MK17 ....68 C6
Highway Ave SL6 ......202 A6
Highway Ct
Beaconsfield HP9 ....175 D3
Chesham HP5 ....144 D1
Highway Rd SL6 ....202 B6
Highway The HP9 ......175 D2
Highwood Ave HP12 ...172 B5
Highwood Bottom
HP27 ....150 A5
Highwood Cres HP12 ...172 B6
Highwoods Cl SL7 ......183 C7
Highwoods Dr SL7 ......183 C7
Highworth Cl HP13 .....162 E1
Highworth Comb Sch
HP13 ....162 E1
Hikers Way HP18 ....125 F4
Hilbre Ct MK4 ....45 F1
Hilbury Cl HP6 ....154 C3
Hilda Wharf HP20 ......115 F8
Hildreth Rd HP16 ......151 C5
Hilgrove Ho SL6 ....195 D1
Hiljon Cres SL9 ....177 E2
Hill Ave Amersham HP6 ..154 C1
Hazelmere HP15 ....163 B5
Hill Cl HP10 ....185 F7
Hill Cotts HP18 ....97 E1
Hill Farm MK18 ....76 A2
Hill Farm App HP10 ....185 F7
Hill Farm Ct OX39 .....147 D6
Hill Farm La
Chalfont St Giles HP8 ....166 A1
Little Horwood MK17 ......55 E2
Hill Farm Rd
Chalfont St Peter SL9 ....177 E3
Chesham HP5 ....154 D5
Marlow Bottom SL7 ......183 E5
Taplow SL6 ....196 E2
Hill Farm Way HP15 ....163 B2
Hill Gr SL9 ....177 E3
Hill Ho SL6 ....196 D1
Hill House Cl SL9 ......177 E3
Hill Mdw HP7 ....164 F4
Hill Mead HP4 ....135 A3
Hill Pl SL2 ....198 B5
Hill Rd Chinnor OX39 ....147 D5
Christmas Common OX49 .168 A8
Lewknor OX49 ....157 A7
Lewknor OX49 ....157 C6
Hill Rise SL9 ....177 D1
Hill Rise Cres SL9 ......177 E1
Hill Side LU7 ....104 F7
Hill St HP13 ....174 A5
Hill The Syresham NN13 ...27 B8
Winchmore Hill HP7 ....164 C3
Hill Top Dr SL7 ....183 B2
Hill Top La OX39 ......147 F4
Hill View
Berkhamsted HP4 ....135 A6
Great Kimble HP17 ....129 D1
Hedgerley SL2 ....187 D3
Newport Pagnell MK16 ....22 A3
Oakley HP18 ....109 D5
Hill View Rd TW19 .....211 D1
Hill Waye SL9 ....188 F4
Hillary Cl Aylesbury HP21 116 A5
High Wycombe HP13 .....173 E6
Hillary Rd
High Wycombe HP13 .....173 E6
Slough SL3 ....206 E4
Hillbeck Gr MK10 ....35 E3
Hillbottom Rd HP12 ....172 B7
Hillcrest MK43 ....25 C2
Hillcrest Ave SL6 ......195 E6
Hillcrest Cl MK5 ....46 B6
Hillcrest Ct HP6 ....154 C1
Hillcrest Rise MK18 .....52 E6
Hillcrest Way MK18 .....52 E5
Hillcrest Waye SL9 .....188 F5
Hillcroft Rd
Chesham HP5 ....144 D2
Tylers Green HP10 ....163 C1
Hillersdon SL2 ....206 B8
Hillersdon Chase MK17 ...69 D8
Hillesden Hamlet MK18 ...51 F1
Hillesden Way MK18 .....41 E1
Hillfield Cl HP13 ......161 E2
Hillfield Rd SL9 ....177 E3
Hillfield Sq SL9 ....177 E3
Hilliard Dr MK13 ....34 A3
Hilliards Rd UB8 ......208 D7
Hillier Rd HP21 ....115 D3
Hillingdon Hill UB10 ...201 E2
Hillingdon Hospl UB8 ..208 F8
Hillingdon Rd UB10 ....201 E3
Hillingdon Tuition Ctr
UB7 ....208 E5
Hillington Cl HP19 .....115 B7
Hillman Cl UB8 ....201 E7
Hillmead Ct SL6 ....203 F8
Hillrise SL3 ....212 A8
Hills Cl MK14 ....34 E7
Hills La SL6 ....195 D7
Hillside Chesham HP5 ...144 A3
Gawcott MK18 ....51 F4
High Wycombe HP13 ....173 D7
Maidenhead SL6 ....202 D5
Slough SL1 ....205 E4
South Harefield UB9 .....190 C6
Tingewick MK18 ....51 B6
Hillside Cl
Chalfont St Giles HP8 ....177 B7
Hillside Cl *continued*
Chalfont St Peter SL9 ....177 E4
Upper Arncott OX25 ....94 E7
Hillside Cotts HP18 ....112 F2
Hillside Ct SL0 ....208 B4
Hillside Ctr HP11 ......172 F7
Hillside Gdns
Amersham HP7 ....165 E7
Berkhamsted HP4 ....135 D3
High Wycombe HP13 ....173 D7
Hillside Rd
Chorleywood WD3 ....167 C4
Marlow SL7 ....183 E4
Tylers Green HP10 ....163 A2
Hilltop HP18 ....125 D5
Hilltop Ave MK18 ....41 E2
Hilltop Fst Sch SL4 ....209 E4
Hilltop Rd HP4 ....135 C3
Hillview Saunderton HP14 149 C1
Sherington MK16 ....14 A1
Hillview Rd HP13 ......173 D8
Hillway Amersham HP7 ..165 B6
Woburn Sands MK17 ....49 A6
Hillwerke OX39 ....147 C6
Hillyer Ct MK6 ....35 C1
Hilperton Rd 3 SL1 .....205 E4
Hilton Ave HP20 ....101 E2
Hilton Cl UB8 ....201 B3
Himley Gn LU7 ....80 D6
Hindemith Gdns MK7 ....48 D5
Hindhay La SL6 ....195 B3
Hindhead Knoll MK7 ....48 B6
Hinds Way HP21 ....115 B6
Hinkley Cl UB9 ....190 C7
Hinksey Cl SL3 ....207 B3
Hinton Cl HP13 ....162 A1
Hinton Ct MK3 ....46 F1
Hinton Rd Slough SL1 ...204 E6
Uxbridge UB8 ....201 C4
Hipwell Ct MK46 ....6 F3
Hitcham Grange SL6 ...196 E1
Hitcham Ho SL1 ....197 A1
Hitcham La SL6,SL1 ....196 F2
Hitcham Rd SL1,SL6 ....204 A8
Hither Mdw SL9 ....177 E1
Hithercroft Rd HP13 ...161 E1
Hithermoor Rd TW19 ..213 A2
Hiving's Hill HP5 ......144 A2
Hivings Pk HP5 ....144 B4
HM Prison (Bullingdon)
OX25,HP18 ....95 A7
HM Prison (The Mount)
HP3 ....145 F4
HM Young Offender Inst
(Finnamore Wood Camp)
SL7 ....182 D7
HM Young Offender Inst
(Grendon) HP18 ....73 B1
Hoathly Mews MK7 ......48 B8
Hobart Cl HP13 ....162 E1
Hobart Cotts HP16 .....150 D8
Hobart Cres MK15 ....35 B7
Hobart Ct SL7 ....184 A3
Hobart Rd HP13 ....162 D1
Hobarts Dr UB9 ....189 F5
Hobbis Dr SL6 ....202 A6
Hobbs Rd HP14 ....171 C4
Hobbshill Rd HP16 .....152 B6
Hobsons Wlk HP23 .....118 F5
Hockett La SL6 ....195 A6
Hockley La SL2 ....199 B4
Hockliffe Brae MK7 .....48 C5
Hodder La MK4 ....46 C2
Hodds Wood Rd HP5 ...154 C6
Hodge Lea La MK12 ......33 D4
Hodgemoor View HP8 ...177 A7
Hodgemore Ct MK14 .....21 F2
Hodges Mews HP12 ....172 C6
Hoe Mdw HP9 ....175 C4
Hog Hall La HP4 ....107 A5
Hog La Ashley Green HP5 144 D8
Berkhamsted HP5 ....134 C2
Hogarth Cl SL1 ....204 E6
Hogarths Ct 9 MK8 ......33 F1
Hogback Wood Rd HP9 .175 B4
Hogfair La SL1 ....197 C1
Hogg La HP15 ....163 D6
Hogpits Bottom HP3 ...156 B7
Hogshaw Rd MK18 ....75 E6
Hogtrough La HP22 ....131 D2
Holborn Cres MK4 ....57 A8
Holdom Ave MK1 ....47 D2
Holes La MK46 ....6 F4
Holiday La MK19 ....10 F4
Holland Cl Chinnor OX39 147 D7
Wendover HP22 ....131 B4
Holland Rd
Aylesbury HP19 ....101 B2
Marlow SL7 ....183 F3
Holland Way MK16 ......22 C3
Hollandridge La OX49,
RG9 ....168 D4
Holliday Cl MK8 ....45 E7
Holliday St HP4 ....135 D4
Hollies Ct LU7 ....80 E7
Hollies The
Beaconsfield HP9 ....175 E3
Bovingdon HP3 ....146 A2
Tring HP23 ....119 D1
Hollin La MK12 ....33 E4
Hollingdon Depot LU7 ....69 D3
Hollingdon Rd LU7 ......69 C3
Hollington HP18 ....125 B7
Hollinwell Cl 3 MK4 ....46 D1
Hollis Rd HP13 ....173 F8
Hollister Chase MK5 ....46 B4
Hollow Hill End MK18 ....75 F7
Hollow Hill La SL0 ....207 C5
Hollow Rise HP13 ......162 B1
Hollow Way HP5 ....143 E1
Hollow Way La HP5,HP6 154 E4
Hollow Wood MK46 ....6 E3
Holloway Cl UB7 ....208 E1
Holloway Dr MK18 ......41 E2
Holloway La
Chenies WD3 ....156 C2
Turville Heath RG9 ......169 C4
West Drayton UB7 ....208 F1
Holloway The
Monks Risborough HP27 ..139 D5
Tring HP22,HP23 ....118 C4
Holly Cl
Farnham Common SL2 ...198 C8
Milton Keynes MK8 ....45 E6
Holly Cres SL4 ....209 D5
Holly Dr Aylesbury HP21 .115 E6
Berkhamsted HP4 ....135 D3
Maidenhead SL6 ....202 F8
Windsor SL4 ....210 E2
Holly End HP14 ....161 C8
Holly Gdns UB7 ....208 F4
Holly Green La HP27 ...138 A3
Holly Hedges La HP3 ...156 C8
Holly Pl HP11 ....174 A3
Holly Tree La HP18 ....112 F3
Holly Wlk MK17 ....49 B2
Hollyberry Gr HP15 ....163 C7
Hollybush Cnr SL2 ....187 C2
Hollybush Hill SL2 ....199 B5
Hollybush La
Amersham HP6 ....154 D3
Cookham Dean SL6 ......195 B6
Denham UB9 ....200 E8
Iver SL0,SL3 ....207 B7
Hollybush Rd HP5 .....144 A4
Hollybush Row HP23 ...133 D8
Hollyfield HP23 ....119 C5
Hollyfield Cl HP23 ....119 C5
Hollytree Cl Botley HP5 .155 B8
Chalfont St Peter SL9 ....177 E5
Holm Gate MK5 ....46 A8
Holman St HP19 ....101 C2
Holmanleaze SL6 ......203 A8
Holmedale SL2 ....206 C6
Holmer Green Fst Sch
HP15 ....163 B7
Holmer Green Jun Sch
HP15 ....163 D7
Holmer Green Rd HP15 .163 A4
Holmer Green Senior Sch
HP15 ....163 B7
Holmer Pl HP15 ....163 C7
Holmers Ct HP12 ......172 B3
Holmers Farm Way
HP12 ....172 C3
Holmers La HP12 ......172 C3
Holmewood MK4 ....46 E4
Holmfield Cl MK6 ....47 D5
Holmlea Rd SL3 ....211 D6
Holmlea Wlk SL3 ......211 C6
Holmoak Wlk HP15 .....163 B3
Holmsdale Cl SL0 .....207 F7
Holmwood Cl SL6 .....202 B5
Holmwood Fst Sch MK8 ...33 F1
Holne Chase Comb Sch
MK3 ....58 A7
Holst Cres MK7 ....48 D4
Holt Gr MK5 ....46 A8
Holt The MK18 ....52 E7
Holton Hill MK4 ....46 C2
Holton Rd MK18 ....41 D2
Holts Gn MK17 ....59 C1
Holtspur Ave HP10 ....185 F7
Holtspur Cl HP9 ......186 A8
Holtspur Ct HP9 ......186 A8
Holtspur La HP10 .....185 F6
Holtspur Par HP9 .....186 A8
Holtspur Sch HP9 .....175 A1
Holtspur Top La HP9 ...175 A2
Holtspur Way HP9 .....175 A1
Holy Family RC Prim Sch
SL3 ....206 F1
Holy Thorn La MK5 .....46 A5
Holy Trinity CE Prim Sch
SL6 ....196 B7
Holy Trinity CE Sch SL7 183 D3
Holyhead Cres MK3 .....57 C8
Holyhead Mews SL1 ...204 D7
Holyport Rd SL6 ......203 B1
Holyrood MK8 ....45 E8
Holywell CE Mid Sch
MK43 ....25 B1
Holywell Gdns HP13 ...173 E7
Holywell Pl MK6 ....35 C2
Holywell Rd MK43 ....25 C1
Home Cl
Milton Keynes MK3 ....47 B2
Shabbington HP18 ....124 D3
Weston Turville HP22 .....116 F2
Home Ct MK10 ....36 A3
Home Farm
Newton Longville MK17 ...57 D4
Tring HP23 ....118 F2
Home Farm Ct
Bovingdon HP3 ....145 F1
Emberton MK46 ....13 E8
Home Farm La MK17 ....59 D2
Home Farm Rd HP4 ....134 D7
Home Farm Way SL3 ...199 C4
Home Field
Aylesbury HP19 ....115 A7
Bow Brickhill MK17 ....48 B3
Home Mdw SL2 ....198 C3
Home Meadow Dr HP10 185 B7
Home Way WD3 ....167 F1
Home Wood SL7 ....193 F6
Homefarm Ct HP8 .....177 A7
Homefield HP3 ....146 B3
Homefield Cl HP14 ....158 E4
Homefield Rd WD3 ....167 D5
Homeground MK18 ......52 E6
Homelands Gdns HP15 .162 D8
Homelands Way RG9 ...191 D1
Homer Fst Sch SL4 ....209 D6
Homeridings Ho MK13 ....34 B4
Homers Rd SL4 ....209 D6
Homeside Cl SL6 ......195 E2
Homestall MK18 ....52 D6
Homestall Cl MK5 ....46 A7
Homestead Cl HP17 ....114 A4
Homestead Pl 14 HP19 .115 A8
Homestead Rd SL6 ....202 D4
Homestead The
Great Kingshill HP15 ....151 D1
High Wycombe HP12 ....172 D3
Milton Keynes MK5 ....46 A6
Thame OX9 ....125 E1
Homestead Way NN12 ....18 E3
Homeward Ct MK5 ......46 B7
Homewood SL3 ....206 D7
Homewood Ct WD3 ....167 F5
Honey Banks HP22 .....131 C4
Honey Hill Emberton MK46 13 F7
Uxbridge UB10 ....201 F5
Honey Hill Dr MK19 .....31 E5
Honey La SL6 ....193 E2
Honey Way HP14 ......161 B8
Honeycroft Hill UB10 ...201 E5
Honeypot Cl MK13 ......34 B4
Honeysuckle Cl SL0 ....207 C7
Honeysuckle Ct SL3 ....212 C7
Honeysuckle Field HP5 .144 C2
Honeysuckle Rd HP15 ..162 F7
Honeywick La LU6 ......92 E8
Honiton Ct MK7 ....48 C7
Honor End La HP16 ....151 A7
Honor Rd HP16 ....151 D6
Honorwood Cl HP16 ...151 B6
Honour Cl HP20 ....102 A2
Honours Mead HP3 ....146 A4
Hoods Farm Cl HP22 ...102 C4
Hooke The MK15 ....35 D7
Hooper Gate MK15 .....35 C7
Hop Gdns RG9 ....191 D2
Hopcraft Cl OX25 ....94 E7
Hope Brook Cotts LU7 ...91 F2
Hopkins Cl MK10 ....36 A2
Hopkins Ct HP20 ......101 F2
Hoppers Mdw MK5 ......46 A8
Hoppers Way HP15 ....162 D8
Hopton Gr MK16 ....22 F3
Hopton Rd OX9 ....126 A1
Hordern Cl HP17 ......126 F6
Horn La MK11 ....32 D5
Horn St MK18 ....65 F4
Hornbeam MK16 ....22 A3
Hornbeam Cl HP12 ....172 B4
Hornbeam Gdns 8 SL1 .206 A3
Hornbeam Wlk HP15 ...163 A3
Hornbill Cl UB8 ....208 D7
Hornby Chase MK4 .....46 B2
Horners Croft MK12 .....33 C5
Hornhill Rd WD3 ......178 D5
Horns La
High Wycombe HP12 .....172 A3
Princes Risborough HP27 .139 B3
Horse Hill HP5 ....155 D7
Horsebuck La HP23 ....133 E3
Horsefair Gn MK11 ......32 D5
Horseguards Dr SL6 ...203 B7
Horsemoor Cl SL3 .....207 A2
Horsemoor La HP7 .....164 C2
Horsenden La HP27 ....138 F2
Horsenden Rd HP13 ...173 F5
Horsepond MK17 ....59 C2
Horsepool La MK17 .....49 F4
Horseshoe Cl LU7 .....105 A7
Horseshoe Cloisters 3
SL4 ....210 D6
Horseshoe Cres HP9 ...175 F1
Horseshoe Hill SL1 ....197 C8
Horseshoe Rd HP14 ...159 C7
Horsetone Bglws HP17 .129 D2
Horsham Reach SL6 ...196 C2
Horsleys WD3 ....178 D5
Horton Bridge Rd UB7 .208 F5
Horton Cl
Aylesbury HP19 ....115 A7
Maidenhead SL6 ....196 C1
West Drayton UB7 ....208 F5
Horton Depot SL3 .....212 C4
Horton Gate MK14 ......21 F2
Horton Gdns SL3 ......211 F4
Horton Grange SL6 ....196 C1
Horton Ind Pk UB7 ....208 F5
Horton Par UB7 ....208 E5
Horton Rd Datchet SL3 ..211 D6
Horton SL3 ....212 A6
Ivinghoe LU7 ....91 A2
Slapton LU7 ....91 C6
Stanwell TW19 ....213 A2
Stanwell TW19 ....213 B1
West Drayton UB7 ....208 F5
Poyle SL3 ....212 E4
Horton Road Ind Est
UB7 ....208 F5
Horton Trad Est SL3 ...212 B4
Hortonsfield Rd NN12 ...18 F5
Horwood Ct MK1 ....47 D2
Hospital Circular Rd
HP22 ....131 D6
Hospital Hill HP5 ......154 C7
Hospital Rdbt MK6 ......47 B6
Hotch Croft MK43 ....25 C3
Hotley Bottom La HP16 .151 C8
Houghton Ct 4 MK8 .....45 F8
Housman Cl MK16 ....22 A5
Houston Ct 6 SL4 .....210 C5
How's Cl UB8 ....201 C4
How's Rd UB8 ....201 C4
Howard Agne Cl HP3 ...146 A4
Howard Ave
Aylesbury HP21 ....116 B6
Slough SL2 ....205 E8
Howard Cres HP9 .....176 D5
Howard Ct 1 SL8 ......185 A3
Howard Ind Est HP5 ...144 C2
Howard Mews SL3 .....212 B8
Howard Rd Chesham HP5 144 B3
Seer Green HP9 ....176 D5
Howard Way MK16 ......23 A3
Howards Thicket SL9 ...188 C2
Howards Wood Dr SL9 .188 D2
Howarth Rd SL6 ......203 A6
Howe Ct MK10 ....36 A3
Howe Dr HP9 ....175 E5
Howe Hill La HP15 ....163 B8
Howe Park Fst Sch MK4 .46 B1
Howe Rock Pl MK4 ......46 B1
Howell Hill Cl LU7 ......90 D5
Howitt Dr MK13 ....34 B8
Howland Pl MK17 ....60 F7
Howletts Cl HP19 .....115 A7
Hoylake Cl
Milton Keynes MK3 ....57 D7
Slough SL1 ....204 E4
Hoyton Gate MK8 ....45 D6
HRH Princess Christians
Hospl SL4 ....210 D5
Hubbard Cl MK18 ....41 F1
Hubbards Ct WD3 .....167 D4
Hubbards Rd WD3 .....167 D4
Hubert Day Cl HP9 ....175 D3
Hubert Rd SL3 ....206 D3
Huckleberry Cl MK7 .....48 B6
Hudnall La HP4 ....121 E7
Hudson La MK8 ....45 D7
Hudsons Ave UB9 .....189 F6
Hugh Park Cl MK5 ......46 C8
Hughenden Ave HP13 ..173 A8
Hughenden Cl SL6 ....202 C6
Hughenden Ct UB8 ....201 C1
Hughenden Gn HP21 ...115 E4
Hughenden Inf Sch
HP14 ....162 A7
Hughenden Manor★
HP14 ....162 A3
Hughenden Rd
High Wycombe HP13 .....162 B1
Slough SL1 ....205 D7
Hughenden View HP13 .173 B8
Hulbert End HP21 .....116 D5
Hulcombe Wlk HP20 ...101 E2
Hull Cl Aylesbury HP21 ..115 E6
Slough SL1 ....205 C4
Hulton Dr MK46 ....13 F8
Humber Cl UB7 ....208 D5
Humber Dr HP21 ......115 C5
Humber Way
Milton Keynes MK3 ....46 E1
Slough SL3 ....207 A2
Humphrey Talbot Ave
LU6 ....107 F7
Humphries Cl HP22 .....88 D5
Hundred Acres La HP7 .165 D8
Hungerford Ave SL2 ...205 E8
Hungerford Dr SL6 ....195 E3
Hungerford Ho 1 MK4 ...46 D1
Hunsdon Cl MK14 ....34 D6
Hunsford Lodge SL4 ...210 A4
Hunstanton Cl SL3 ....212 C7
Hunstanton Way MK3 ...57 D8
Hunt Rd HP13 ....173 E6
Hunt's La SL6 ....196 E3
Hunter Ct SL1 ....204 C8
Hunter Dr MK2 ....58 C6
Hunter St MK18 ....52 C8
Huntercombe Cl SL1 ...204 C7
Huntercombe La N SL6 .204 C7
Huntercombe La S SL6 .204 C6
Huntercombe Manor Hospl
SL6 ....204 C6
Huntercombe Spur SL6 204 C6
Hunters Cl
Bovingdon HP3 ....146 A2
Chesham HP5 ....144 A1
Tring HP23 ....119 B5
Hunters Hill HP13 .....173 F5
Hunters Mews SL4 ....210 C6
Hunters Pk HP4 ....135 E5
Hunters Point OX39 ...147 C6
Hunters Reach MK13 ....34 A3
Hunters Way SL1 .....204 E4
Huntingbrooke 6 MK8 ...45 F8
Huntingdon Cres MK3 ...57 D6
Huntingdon Pl SL3 ....207 B3
Huntley Cl HP13 ......162 C2
Huntley Cres MK9 ......35 A3
Hunts Hill La HP14 ....161 E5
Huntsman Gr MK14 ......22 A2
Huntsmans Cl HP4 ....107 C5
Huntswood La SL6,SL1 .196 F4
Hurley Croft MK10 ......36 B1
Hurley High St SL6 ....193 F4
Hurley La SL7 ....194 B3
Hurlstone Gr MK4 ......46 D3
Hurricane Way SL3 ....207 B1
Hurst Rd SL1 ....204 D8
Hurstfield Dr SL6 .....204 B7
Hurstleigh WD3 ....167 C4
Hurworth Ave SL3 .....206 C3
Hutchings Cl MK5 ....46 A8

Hutchings Rd HP9 ....175 D5
Hutton Ave MK6 ....34 F1
Hutton Ct MK17 ....49 B5
Hutton Way MK17 ....49 B5
Huxley Cl
  Newport Pagnell MK16 ......21 F4
  Uxbridge UB8 ....201 D1
Huxtable Gdns SL8 ....203 E1
Hyacinth Dr UB10 ....201 E5
Hychenden Cl HP14 ....161 E6
Hyde Cl MK16 ....22 C2
Hyde Gn
  Beaconsfield HP9 ....175 F3
  Marlow SL7 ....183 F1
Hyde Heath Inf Sch
  HP6 ....153 C5
Hyde Heath Rd HP6,
  HP10 ....153 A6
Hyde La Bovingdon HP3 .146 A3
  South Heath HP16 ....152 A4
Hyde Mdws HP3 ....146 A4
Hyde The HP22 ....116 F2
Hyland Ho 9 SL8 ....185 B3
Hylle Cl SL4 ....209 E6
Hylton Rd HP12 ....172 C7
Hyrons Cl MK14 ....154 E1
Hyrons Cl HP6 ....154 E1
Hyrons La HP6 ....154 D1
Hythe The MK8 ....33 C7

I

Ibotson Ct SL3 ....212 E6
Ibstone Ave MK13 ....34 D4
Ibstone CE Inf Sch
  HP14 ....169 D6
Ibstone Rd HP14 ....158 C3
Ickford Comb Sch HP18 124 A3
Ickford Rd
  Shabbington HP18 ....124 C2
  Worminghall HP18 ....123 E6
Icknield Cl Chinnor OX39 .147 A4
  Wendover HP22 ....131 C5
Icknield Cotts HP17 ....129 F2
Icknield Gn HP23 ....119 A6
Icknield Way
  Dunstable LU6 ....93 C4
  Tring HP23 ....118 E4
Icknield Way Farm Cotts
  LU6 ....93 C3
Ideal Ho 3 HP20 ....115 E8
Iffley Ct UB8 ....201 D5
Ilchester Cl SL6 ....202 C5
Ilex Cl HP15 ....163 B3
Ilex Ct HP4 ....135 B4
Illingworth SL4 ....209 E4
Illingworth Pl MK6 ....46 F8
Imperial Ct
  Henley-on-T RG9 ....191 E1
  Loudwater HP10 ....174 C2
  Windsor SL4 ....210 A4
Imperial Rd SL4 ....210 A5
In The Ray SL6 ....203 B8
Independent Bsns Pk
  HP14 ....158 C5
India Rd SL1 ....206 B4
Ingleglen SL2 ....198 B7
Ingleside SL3 ....212 F6
Ingleton Cl MK13 ....34 C4
Ingram Ave HP21 ....116 C5
Inkerman Dr HP15 ....163 B5
Inkerman Rd SL4 ....204 F2
Inkerman Terr HP5 ....154 C6
Inn Farm Ct MK16 ....22 D7
Innes Ct MK8 ....45 E4
Innholder St MK14 ....34 F6
Innings Gate RG9 ....170 D4
Inniscrown Ho SL3 ....211 B7
Institute Rd Marlow SL7 .183 E1
  Taplow SL6 ....203 F7
Intalbury Ave HP19 ....101 A2
Inverness Cl MK3 ....46 F4
Inwood Cl SL6 ....195 B6
Iona Cres SL1 ....204 E5
Ipswich Rd SL1 ....205 A4
Ireland Cl MK7 ....48 D4
Ireton Cl OX9 ....125 F1
Iris Cl HP21 ....115 D3
Iris Ct HP20 ....116 B8
Ironmonger Ct MK14 ....34 F6
Irvine Dr HP22 ....116 A2
Irvine Ho SL4 ....209 E5
Irving Cres LU7 ....105 A8
Irving Dale MK7 ....48 E5
Isaacson Dr MK7 ....48 E2
Isambard Cl UB8 ....201 D1
Isis Cl HP21 ....115 D3
Isis Way SL8 ....185 B4
Isis Wlk MK3 ....46 E1
Island Ho UB7 ....213 B6
Island The MK18 ....63 D2
Isle Of Wight La LU6 ....93 F4
Islet Park Dr SL6 ....196 C3
Islet Park Ho SL6 ....196 C3
Islet Pk SL6 ....196 C3
Islet Rd SL6 ....196 C3
Isling Brook MK5 ....46 B3
Ivanhoe Cl UB8 ....208 D8
Iver Ct MK18 ....52 C7
Iver Heath Inf Sch SL0 .200 D2
Iver Heath Jun Sch SL0 200 D3
Iver La SL0 ....208 A8
Iver Lodge SL0 ....207 F7
Iver Sta SL0 ....207 F4
Iver Village Inf Sch SL0 .207 F7
Iver Village Jun Sch The
  SL0 ....207 E7

Iverdale Cl SL0 ....207 C6
Ives Rd SL3 ....207 A3
Ivester Ct LU7 ....80 E6
Ivinghoe Way HP20 ....101 F1
Ivinghoe Way LU6 ....92 E1
Ivinghoe YH ★ LU7 ....105 E5
Ivins Rd HP9 ....175 A1
Ivy Cl Longwick HP27 ....138 E5
  Newport Pagnell MK16 ....22 E4
Ivy Cotts HP8 ....177 B8
Ivy Cres SL1 ....204 F6
Ivy House La HP4 ....135 C4
Ivy La Bierton HP22 ....102 D1
  Burcott LU7 ....79 D4
  Great Brickhill MK17 ....70 C8
  Newton Longville MK17 ....57 C3
  Stewkley LU7 ....68 E1
Ivy Pl HP14 ....171 C5
Ivybridge Cl UB8 ....201 E2
Ivyhill Ct HP27 ....139 B3

J

Jack's La MK43 ....8 E5
Jacks Cl MK46 ....7 E7
Jackson Cl UB10 ....201 E6
Jackson St HP15 ....163 A3
Jackson Ind Est SL8 ....185 B2
Jackson Rd
  Aylesbury HP19 ....101 A3
  Uxbridge UB10 ....201 E5
Jacksons Cl LU6 ....92 E4
Jacob Cl SL4 ....209 D6
Jacobs Cl MK14 ....34 D7
Jakeman Way HP21 ....115 B6
Jakes Rd SL6 ....203 A8
Jamaica MK6 ....47 A6
James Cl
  Hazelmere HP15 ....163 A6
  Marlow SL7 ....183 F4
James Elliman Sch SL2 205 E6
James Martin Cl UB9 ....190 A5
James Rd HP14 ....171 B4
James St SL4 ....210 D6
James Way MK1 ....47 B1
Jane Cl HP21 ....116 A4
Jansel Sq HP21 ....116 B6
Japonica La MK15 ....35 C5
Jardine Cotts SL2 ....199 A8
Jarman Ct MK18 ....52 F8
Jarratt Ho SL4 ....210 A4
Jarry Ct SL7 ....183 F3
Jarvis Cl HP21 ....116 A4
Jasmine Cl HP21 ....116 A4
Jasmine Cres HP27 ....139 B3
Jasmine Wlk HP5 ....144 A1
Jason Ho HP12 ....172 E4
Jasons Hill HP5 ....145 B2
Jeeves Ct MK6 ....47 C7
Jefferies Rd HP17 ....114 B5
Jefferson Cl SL3 ....207 A2
Jeffrey Wlk HP19 ....115 A7
Jeffries Ct SL8 ....185 B2
Jellicoe Cl SL1 ....205 B4
Jenkins Cl MK5 ....45 F5
Jenkins La HP22 ....89 C3
Jenkins La HP23 ....132 E3
Jenna Way MK16 ....23 A3
Jenner Rd HP21 ....115 E5
Jennery La HP9 ....197 C2
Jennings MK14 ....34 C7
Jennings Field HP10 ....185 C7
Jennings Wharf SL4 ....210 D7
Jerome Cl SL7 ....183 F4
Jersey Rd MK12 ....33 C6
Jesse's La HP18 ....125 D6
Jesus Hospl (almshos)
  SL6 ....203 C3
Job's La SL6 ....195 B8
John Colet Sch HP22 ....131 C5
John Hall Way HP12 ....172 D3
John Hampden Gram Sch
  HP11 ....172 F4
John Hampden Sch The
  HP22 ....131 B5
John Hampden Way
  HP16 ....151 B7
John Hellins Prim Sch
  NN12 ....18 D3
John Taylor Ct SL1 ....205 C5
John Watson Sch OX33 .122 A3
Johns La HP5 ....134 E1
Johnson Rd HP14 ....171 B5
Johnsons Field MK46 ....6 E4
Johnston Pl MK6 ....46 E4
Joiner's Cl Botley HP5 .145 B1
  Chalfont St Peter SL9 ....177 F3
Joiner's La SL9 ....177 E3
Joiners Way
  Chalfont St Peter SL9 ....177 E3
  Lavendon MK46 ....7 E4
Jonathan Ct SL6 ....202 E7
Jonathans La MK6 ....47 A6
Jonathans Ct MK6 ....47 A6
Jones Way SL2 ....187 C2
Joplin Ct MK8 ....45 F7
Jordans La HP9 ....176 F3
Jordans Sch HP9 ....176 F4
Joules Ct MK5 ....46 C4
Jourdelay's Pas SL4 ....210 D8
Journeys End SL2 ....205 E3
Jubilee Cotts MK18 ....64 F3
Jubilee Rd
  High Wycombe HP11 ....172 E7

Jubilee Rd continued
  High Wycombe, Downley
  HP13 ....161 E2
  Stokenchurch HP14 ....158 F3
Jubilee Terr MK11 ....32 E5
Jubilee Way SL3 ....211 C7
Judge's La LU7 ....80 E7
Juniper Pl HP15 ....163 B3
Juniper Ct
  Flackwell Heath HP10 .185 C7
  Slough SL1 ....206 B8
Juniper Dr
  High Wycombe HP12 ....172 C5
  Maidenhead SL6 ....203 B8
Juniper Gdns MK7 ....48 B7
Juniper La HP19 ....101 C2
Juniper Rd SL7 ....183 D5
Jupiter Hts MK18 ....201 F4
Juson's Glebe HP22 ....131 C5
Jutland Ho SL4 ....209 D7

K

Kalman Gdns MK7 ....48 C5
Kaplan Cl MK5 ....46 B5
Karenza HP21 ....158 E5
Katherine Cl
  Tylers Green HP10 ....174 C8
  Walton MK7 ....48 A4
Katrine Pl MK2 ....58 D5
Kay Cl HP23 ....119 A5
Kaybridge Cl 1 HP13 ....173 F5
Kaywood Cl SL3 ....206 C3
Keach Cl MK18 ....66 A5
Keasden Ct MK4 ....46 B2
Keaton Cl MK8 ....45 D7
Keats Cl Aylesbury HP21 .115 F6
  High Wycombe HP11 ....172 F6
  Newport Pagnell MK16 ...22 A4
Keats La SL4 ....210 C8
Keats Way
  Milton Keynes MK3 ....57 F7
  West Drayton UB7 ....208 F3
Keble Cl HP19 ....115 B8
Keble Rd SL6 ....202 E8
Keel Dr SL1 ....205 C4
Keeler Cl SL4 ....209 C6
Keen Cl HP19 ....115 A8
Keen's Cl HP13 ....162 E1
Keens La OX39 ....147 D6
Keensacre SL0 ....200 D3
Keep Hill Dr HP11 ....173 D6
Keep Hill Rd HP11 ....173 D5
Keepers Cl LU7 ....105 A7
Keepers Farm Cl SL4 ....209 E5
Keepers La HP6,HP27 ....153 C3
Keinches La MK18 ....87 A6
Keith Park Rd UB10 ....201 E6
Kellan Dr MK6 ....35 A1
Keller Ct MK11 ....33 B2
Kelpatrick Rd SL1 ....204 D7
Kelsey Ct
  Maidenhead SL6 ....202 D3
  Milton Keynes MK4 ....56 F8
Kelso Cl MK3 ....57 D6
Kelvin Ct HP13 ....172 F8
Kelvin Dr MK5 ....46 D4
Kemble St MK15 ....35 B6
Kempe Cl SL3 ....207 C2
Kempson Ct HP21 ....101 B1
Kempton Gdns MK3 ....57 D6
Kemsley Chase SL2 ....198 D4
Kenchester MK13 ....33 F5
Kendal Cl
  Aylesbury HP21 ....116 B6
  Slough SL1 ....206 A6
Kendal Dr SL2 ....206 A6
Kendal Gdns LU7 ....80 C7
Kendall Pl
  Maidenhead SL6 ....202 C4
  Milton Keynes MK5 ....45 C5
Kendalls Cl HP13 ....173 F6
Kendrick Rd SL3 ....206 B3
Kenilworth Cl SL1 ....205 F3
Kenilworth Dr
  Aylesbury HP19 ....101 D2
  Milton Keynes MK3 ....57 F7
Kennally Cl HP21 ....116 A7
Kennally Cl 11 SL4 ....209 C5
Kennally Pl 12 SL4 ....209 C5
Kennally Row 13 SL4 ....209 C5
Kennally Wlk 14 SL4 ....209 C5
Kennedy Ave HP11 ....173 B4
Kennedy Cl
  Farnham Common SL2 .198 C6
  Maidenhead SL6 ....202 C6
  Marlow SL7 ....183 E3
Kennedy Ho SL1 ....204 D5
Kennel La SL6 ....195 C7
Kennels Dr
  Paulerspury NN12 ....17 D3
  Pottersbury NN12 ....18 A3
Kennet Cl
  Aylesbury HP21 ....115 C4
  High Wycombe HP13 ....162 D2
Kennet Dr MK3 ....57 E8
Kennet Pl MK3 ....57 F8
Kennett Cl
  Bourne End SL8 ....185 B4
  Maidenhead SL6 ....202 F7
Kennett Rd SL3 ....207 B3
Kennington Cl MK16 ....22 C3
Kennish Cl MK13 ....65 F4
Kensington Dr
  Great Holm MK8 ....46 A8

Kensington Dr continued
  Milton Keynes MK6 ....33 F1
Kensington Path 3
  HP19 ....100 F1
Kensington Pl MK46 ....6 F5
Kent Ave SL1 ....205 C8
Kent Cl UB8 ....201 C6
Kent Ho MK3 ....46 F7
Kent Lodge 6 SL6 ....202 F6
Kent Way SL6 ....195 C6
Kentmere Rd HP21 ....116 B7
Kenton Cl SL7 ....183 E2
Kenton Ct HP19 ....101 C2
Kenton's La SL4 ....209 C5
Kents Hill Fst Sch MK7 ...48 A7
Kents Hill Rdbt MK10 ....47 E8
Kents Rd MK4 ....34 D8
Kenway Dr HP7 ....166 B8
Kenwell Ct MK15 ....35 C3
Kenwood Cl SL6 ....202 A7
Kenwood Dr WD3 ....178 F8
Kenwood Gate MK6 ....35 B2
Keppel Ave MK19 ....20 D2
Keppel St SL4 ....210 D5
Kepwick MK8 ....33 E1
Kercroft MK8 ....33 E2
Kernow Cres MK6 ....35 A1
Kerria Pl MK3 ....47 A3
Kerry Cl HP19 ....101 A3
Kersey MK14 ....34 C8
Kesters Rd HP5 ....154 D7
Kestrel Cl
  2 Berkhamsted HP4 ....135 C3
  High Wycombe HP13 ....161 C1
Kestrel Dr HP15 ....163 B5
Kestrel Path SL2 ....197 E1
Kestrel Way
  Aylesbury HP19 ....101 E4
  Buckingham MK18 ....52 F7
Keswick Ct SL6 ....205 F6
Keswick Rd MK19 ....11 B2
Ketchmere Cl MK18 ....125 C6
Ketelbey Nook MK7 ....48 E8
Ketton Cl MK15 ....35 D7
Kew Ct MK8 ....33 F1
Kew Gr HP11 ....173 B4
Kew Pl HP11 ....173 B4
Keyes Way MK18 ....41 E2
Keynes Cl MK16 ....22 E4
Keys Pl SL6 ....202 F6
Khasiaberry MK7 ....48 B5
Kidd Cl MK8 ....45 E6
Kidderminster Rd SL2 ...198 A2
Kidderminster Wlk MK10 .36 B2
Kidwells Cl SL6 ....202 F8
Kidwells Park Dr SL6 ....202 F7
Kildonan Pl MK12 ....33 D4
Kilfillan Gdns HP4 ....135 A4
Kilfillan Pk HP4 ....135 A3
Kilgour Ct 2 LU7 ....80 F7
Kilkenny Ho MK4 ....45 E2
Killarney Dr SL6 ....202 E7
Killerton Cl MK4 ....45 F2
Kiln Ave HP6 ....155 C1
Kiln Cl Calvert MK18,OX27 .73 D5
  Prestwood HP16 ....151 C7
Kiln Croft Cl SL7 ....184 A3
Kiln Ct HP9 ....186 B8
Kiln Farm Ind Est MK11 .33 A3
Kiln Farm Rdbt MK11 ....33 A3
Kiln Fields SL6 ....185 E1
Kiln La Botley HP5 ....155 C8
  Cores End SL8,HP10 ....185 D3
  Hedgerley SL2 ....187 D3
  Lacey Green HP27 ....149 F5
Kiln Pl MK15 ....195 A3
Kiln Pond La MK15 ....161 D3
Kiln Rd Hastoe HP23 ....133 B6
  Prestwood HP16 ....151 B7
Kiln The HP5 ....144 C1
Kilner Rd HP21 ....115 E5
Kilnwood HP14 ....150 B1
Kilpin Gn MK16 ....24 B6
Kilwinning Dr MK10 ....35 F1
Kimbells Pk HP18 ....124 D2
Kimber Cl SL4 ....210 A4
Kimber's La SL6 ....202 E3
Kimberley Cl SL6 ....206 F2
Kimbers Dr SL1 ....197 C2
Kimble Ct HP22 ....129 E3
Kimble Park Cvn Site
  HP17 ....129 E3
Kimble Park Rd HP17 ....129 E3
Kimblewick Rd HP17 ....129 C5
Kimbolton Ct MK14 ....35 A8
Kincardine Dr MK3 ....46 F3
Kindermann Ct MK5 ....46 B5
Kindleton MK14 ....34 F8
Kinellan Ct HP9 ....175 D3
King Charles Cl HP21 ....116 A7
King Edward Ave HP21 .116 A7
King Edward Ct 5 SL4 .210 D6
King Edward St
  Milton Keynes MK13 ....33 F7
  Slough SL1 ....205 D4
King Edward VII Ave
  SL4 ....210 E8
King Edward VII Hospl
  SL4 ....210 C4
King George Cres MK11 .32 E6
King George V Rd HP6 .154 F1
King John's Cl TW19 ....211 C2
King John's Pal SL4 ....212 C5
King St Chesham HP5 ....154 B7
  Maidenhead SL6 ....202 F6
  Maidenhead SL6 ....202 F7
  Milton Keynes MK11 ....32 E6
  Piddington HP14 ....160 C1

King St continued
  Tring HP23 ....119 A3
King Stable St SL4 ....210 D7
King's Cross HP18 ....113 A1
King's Gr SL6 ....202 E6
King's La
  Great Missenden HP16 .141 C2
  Lee Common HP16,HP22 141 F7
  South Heath HP16 ....152 E8
King's Rd Aylesbury HP21 115 F8
  Henley-on-T RG9 ....191 D2
  High Wycombe HP11 ....173 F4
  Loudwater HP11 ....174 A4
  Slough SL1 ....205 E3
  Uxbridge UB8 ....201 D3
King's Rd Windsor SL4 ....210 D3
  Windsor SL4 ....210 D5
King's Road Ho SL4 ....210 D5
King's Terr SL3 ....212 B8
King's Wood Sch HP13 .173 F8
Kingfisher HP19 ....101 E4
Kingfisher Ct
  3 High Wycombe HP11 .173 A6
  Slough SL2 ....198 B1
Kingfisher Ctr The MK16 .22 C3
Kingfisher Ho
  Loudwater HP11 ....174 A4
  Marlow SL7 ....183 F2
Kingfisher Pl HP11 ....174 A4
Kingfisher Rd MK18 ....52 F7
Kinghorn La SL6 ....195 D3
Kinghorn Pk SL6 ....195 D3
Kings Chase SL6 ....202 F6
Kings Cl
  Beaconsfield HP9 ....186 A8
  Chalfont St Giles HP8 .177 D8
  Henley-on-T RG9 ....191 D2
  Westcott HP18 ....98 C6
  Worminghall HP18 ....123 D5
Kings Ct HP4 ....135 D5
Kings Farm Rd WD3 ....167 D3
Kings Hall Par HP22 ....131 D5
Kings La SL6 ....195 B8
Kings Lodge
  Amersham HP6 ....154 D1
  Finmere MK18 ....50 D6
Kings Mdw HP22 ....102 C4
Kings Mead LU6 ....92 E3
Kings Oak Cl HP27 ....139 C5
Kings Rd
  Berkhamsted HP4 ....135 B3
  Chalfont St Giles HP8 .177 D8
  Henley-On-T RG9 ....191 D2
  West Drayton UB7 ....208 F4
Kings Ride HP10 ....163 D4
Kings Sq HP11 ....173 F4
Kings St LU7 ....78 E7
Kings Wlk RG9 ....191 D2
Kings Wood SL7 ....193 D7
Kingsash Rd HP19 ....114 D2
Kingsbridge MK4 ....46 D2
Kingsbrook Sch MK19 ....31 E4
Kingsbury HP20 ....115 D8
Kingsbury Dr SL4 ....211 D1
Kingscote Sch SL3 ....188 E8
Kingsdale Rd HP4 ....135 A3
Kingsey Rd OX9 ....126 D1
Kingsfield SL4 ....209 D6
Kingsfold MK13 ....34 B7
Kingsgate HP19 ....115 B8
Kingshill Dr MK19 ....31 E5
Kingshill Rd HP13,HP15 .162 D3
Kingshill Way HP4 ....135 D2
Kingsland Rd HP21 ....116 A4
Kingsley Cl MK16 ....21 F4
Kingsley Cres HP11 ....172 F6
Kingsley Dr SL7 ....183 C6
Kingsley Path SL2 ....197 D1
Kingsley Wlk HP19 ....114 A4
Kingsmead HP27 ....139 B6
Kingsmead SL1 ....205 C5
Kingsmead Office Campus
  HP11 ....174 B3
Kingsmead Rd HP11 ....174 B3
Kingsmead Rdbt MK4 ....56 F8
Kingsoe Leys MK10 ....36 A2
Kingston Ave
  Milton Keynes MK11 ....32 E5
  West Drayton UB7 ....208 F6
Kingston Hill OX39,HP14 158 B8
Kingston La
  Uxbridge UB8 ....201 E2
  West Drayton UB7 ....208 F4
Kingston Rd HP13 ....162 D2
Kingston Rdbt MK10 ....36 D1
Kingsway
  Farnham Common SL2 .198 C6
  Gerrards Cross SL9 ....188 E8
  Iver SL0 ....207 E7
  5 Slough SL3 ....206 C3
Kingsway Ho 6 SL6 ....202 F7
Kingswood Ave HP10 ....174 B8
Kingswood Creek TW19 174 D2
Kingswood Cl SL6 ....202 F5
Kingswood Ho SL2 ....205 C8
Kingswood La
  Kingswood HP18 ....83 B2
  Ludgershall HP18 ....96 F6
Kingswood Par SL7 ....183 D5
Kingswood Pl HP13 ....162 E1
Kingswood Rd HP10 ....163 A1
Kingswood View HP13 .162 E1
Kinloch Pl MK14 ....58 E5
Kinnaird Cl SL1 ....204 C7
Kinnear Cl MK8 ....45 E7

Kinross Dr MK3 ....46 E2
Kinson Gn HP20 ....101 F3
Kipling Ct SL4 ....210 D5
Kipling Dr MK16 ....21 F4
Kipling Rd MK3 ....58 A7
Kippell Hill MK46 ....6 F5
Kirby Est UB7 ....208 D6
Kirby Way UB8 ....201 F1
Kirke Cl MK5 ....46 A5
Kirkeby Cl MK14 ....34 D6
Kirkham Ct MK5 ....46 C8
Kirkstall Pl MK6 ....46 D8
Kirkwall Spur SL1,SL2 ....205 E8
Kirkwood Gr MK5 ....45 D5
Kirtle Rd HP5 ....144 C1
Kirtlington MK15 ....35 B5
Kitchener Cl MK46 ....7 A3
Kitchener Rd HP11 ....172 E4
Kite Field HP4 ....134 E7
Kite Hill MK6 ....47 B8
Kite Wood Rd HP10 ....163 B1
Kitelee Cl MK19 ....11 A3
Kitsbury Ct HP4 ....135 B4
Kitsbury Rd MK4 ....135 B4
Kitsbury Terr HP4 ....135 B4
Kittiwake HP19 ....101 E4
Klee Cl HP22 ....85 A5
Klondyke SL7 ....183 D2
Knapp Gate MK5 ....45 F7
Knaresborough Ct MK3 ....57 D7
Knaves Beech HP10 ....174 D1
Knaves Beech Bsns Ctr
  HP10 ....174 D1
Knaves Beech Ind Est
  HP10 ....174 C1
Knaves Beech Way
  HP10 ....174 C1
Knaves Hill LU7 ....80 D5
Knaves Hollow HP10 ....174 D1
Knebworth Gate MK14 ....22 A1
Knighton-Way La HP5 ....201 B6
Knights Cl Eaton Bray LU6 ....92 E5
  Great Brickhill MK17 ....59 D1
  Windsor SL4 ....209 D6
Knights Ct LU6 ....92 E5
Knights Gn WD3 ....167 E6
Knights Hill HP12 ....172 E6
Knights Pl 5 SL4 ....210 C5
Knights Templar Way
  HP11 ....173 B4
Knightsbridge Ct SL3 ....207 A2
Knoll Cl MK16 ....13 F2
Knoll The
  Aspley Heath MK17 ....49 A1
  Sherington MK16 ....13 F2
Knolls Cl HP22 ....89 B3
Knolls View LU6 ....92 B5
Knottocks Cl HP9 ....175 D5
Knottocks Dr HP9 ....175 D5
Knottocks End HP9 ....175 D5
Knowl Gate MK5 ....46 C7
Knowland Way UB9 ....189 F5
Knowles Cl UB7 ....208 E5
Knowles Fst Sch MK2 ....58 D8
Knowles Gn MK2 ....58 C8
Knowles Mid Sch MK2 ....58 D8
Knowlhill Rdbt MK5 ....46 F6
Knowsley Cl SL6 ....195 A1
Knox Bridge MK7 ....48 B8
Kola Ho SL2 ....206 B6
Kop Hill Rd HP27 ....139 D3
Kramer Ct MK8 ....45 D6
Krohn Cl MK18 ....52 F8
Krypton Cl MK5 ....46 C6
Kynaston Ave HP21 ....115 E4
Kynaston Sch HP21 ....115 E3

L

La Roche Cl 4 SL3 ....206 C3
Laburnham Cotts LU7 ....69 E3
Laburnham Rd SL6 ....202 E6
Laburnum Ave UB7 ....208 F6
Laburnum Cl SL7 ....183 E4
Laburnum Gr
  Milton Keynes MK2 ....58 E7
  Slough SL3 ....212 B8
Laburnum Rd HP12 ....172 C5
Lace Mews MK46 ....7 A4
Lacemakers
  Chinnor OX39 ....147 C6
  Long Crendon HP18 ....125 C2
Lacey Dr HP14 ....161 C2
Laceys Dr HP15 ....163 B5
Lacy Dr MK15 ....35 A8
Ladbroke Cl HP20 ....101 E2
Ladbrooke Rd SL1 ....205 D3
Lady Cooper Ct HP4 ....135 E6
Lady Verney Cl HP14 ....173 B8
Lady Yorke Pk SL0 ....200 D6
Ladybridge Terr MK43 ....8 E5
Ladymead Cl MK17 ....56 B8
Ladymeadow Ct MK10 ....35 E3
Ladysmith Rd LU7 ....105 C5
Ladywalk WD3 ....178 E6
Laggan Ct MK2 ....58 D4
Laggan Rd SL6 ....195 F1
Laggan Sq SL6 ....195 F1
Lagger Cl HP8 ....177 B7
Lagger The HP8 ....177 B7
Lagley Ho HP4 ....135 A5
Lagonda Cl MK16 ....22 E4

Laidon Cl MK2 ....58 D4
Lake Ave SL1 ....205 D6
Lake Cl MK18 ....66 B6
Lake End Ct SL6 ....204 A7
Lake End Rd SL4,SL6 ....204 B5
Lake View SL6 ....196 A1
Laker Ct MK6 ....46 E7
Lakes Cotts LU7 ....90 C8
Lakes La
  Beaconsfield HP9 ....186 F8
  Newport Pagnell MK16 ....22 B5
Lakes The SL7 ....194 A6
Lakeside Aylesbury HP19 ....101 E4
  Maidenhead SL6 ....196 B1
  Tring HP23 ....119 A5
Lakeside Dr SL2 ....198 F4
Lakeside Est SL3 ....212 F7
Lakeside Rd SL3 ....212 F7
Lamb Cl MK16 ....22 A4
Lamb La MK7 ....48 C7
Lambe Rd HP22 ....131 C5
Lamberhurst HP7 ....48 B8
Lambert Ave SL3 ....206 E3
Lambert Wlk OX9 ....125 F1
Lamberts Croft MK12 ....33 C5
Lambourn Ct MK4 ....46 D2
Lambourne Ave HP21 ....115 D3
Lambourne Ct
  Maidenhead SL6 ....203 C8
  Uxbridge UB8 ....201 B4
Lambourne Dr SL6 ....202 C3
Lambridge La RG9 ....191 C3
Lambridge Wood Rd
  RG9 ....191 B4
Lambscroft Way SL9 ....177 E1
Lambton Ho SL4 ....210 A4
Lambtons Way MK18 ....66 B5
Lamesley Ho SL6 ....202 E6
Lammas MK6 ....47 A5
Lammas Ave SL4 ....210 D5
Lammas Ct SL4 ....210 D5
Lammas La HP18 ....112 B2
Lammas Path HP18 ....112 B2
Lammas Rd
  Cheddington LU7 ....105 A7
  Slough SL1 ....204 D8
Lammas Way
  Lane End HP14 ....171 A4
  Loudwater HP10 ....174 A4
Lampitts Cross MK6 ....47 B6
Lamport Ct MK8 ....46 A8
Lamva Ct MK11 ....32 F5
Lanark Ho MK3 ....46 F1
Lancaster Ave SL2 ....198 C1
Lancaster Cl TW19 ....213 E1
Lancaster Ct HP12 ....172 D4
Lancaster Dr HP3 ....145 F4
Lancaster Gate MK3 ....57 E7
Lancaster Rd
  Aylesbury HP21 ....116 B6
  High Wycombe HP12 ....172 E4
  Maidenhead SL6 ....202 B8
  Uxbridge UB8 ....201 D5
Lancaster Ride HP10 ....174 B8
Lancastria Mews SL6 ....202 D7
Lance Way HP13 ....174 A6
Lancelot Cl SL1 ....205 A4
Lanchester Rd MK43 ....24 D2
Lancot Ave LU6 ....93 F8
Lancot Dr LU6 ....93 F8
Lancot Lower Sch LU6 ....93 E8
Lancot Pl LU6 ....93 E8
Lancotbury Cl LU6 ....93 C7
Lancresse Ct UB8 ....201 D6
Lander Rd HP19 ....100 F3
Landon Ct HP21 ....115 F7
Landrace Ct MK5 ....45 F3
Lands End Gr MK4 ....56 F8
Lands The LU7 ....79 F3
Landsborough Gate
  MK15 ....35 C7
Lane End Ho MK4 ....134 F4
Lane End Ind Est HP14 ....171 B4
Lane End Rd HP12 ....172 B6
Lane The
  Grafton Regis NN12 ....9 D2
  Mursley MK17 ....67 D6
Lane Wood Cl HP7 ....165 F8
Lanercost Cres MK10 ....36 B1
Lanfranc Gdns MK15 ....35 B7
Langcliffe Dr MK13 ....34 C5
Langdale Cl
  Maidenhead SL6 ....203 A6
  Milton Keynes MK2 ....58 D4
Langdale Ho HP11 ....174 A4
Langdale Lodge HP10 ....174 C2
Langdon Ave HP21 ....116 B5
Langdon St HP23 ....119 A3
Langerstone La MK4 ....46 B1
Langford Pl MK7 ....48 A3
Langland Comb Sch MK6 47 C6
Langland Ho MK6 ....47 C6
Langland Rd MK6 ....47 C6
Langlands MK6 ....47 C6
Langley Broom SL3 ....206 F1
Langley Bsns Ctr SL3 ....207 A4
Langley Bsns Pk SL3 ....207 A4
Langley Cl MK18 ....65 E4
Langley Cnr SL3 ....199 F6
Langley Gram Sch SL3 ....206 F2
Langley Manor Sch The
  SL3 ....206 E5
Langley Park Ctry Pk★
  SL0,SL3 ....200 A1
Langley Park Rd SL3 ....207 B6
Langley Rd SL3 ....206 E3
Langley Sta SL3 ....207 A4
Langley Way SL7 ....183 C2

Langleywood Sch SL3 ....206 E3
Langmuir Ct MK5 ....46 C4
Langney Gn MK4 ....57 A8
Langport Cres MK5 ....45 D5
Langston Ct HP12 ....172 C8
Langstone Ct HP20 ....101 F3
Langstone Ct 11 HP20 ....101 F3
Langton Cl
  Maidenhead SL6 ....202 D8
  Slough SL1 ....204 D5
Langton Dr MK8 ....33 E3
Langton's Mdw SL2 ....198 C6
Lanner Wlk MK6 ....47 B8
Lanrick Copse HP4 ....135 E5
Lansdell Ave HP12 ....172 B3
Lansdown Rd SL9 ....177 D2
Lansdowne Ave SL1 ....205 E5
Lansdowne Ct
  Maidenhead SL6 ....203 C7
  Slough SL1 ....205 E5
Lansdowne Rd
  Aylesbury HP20 ....101 D2
  Chesham HP5 ....144 C2
Lansdowne Way HP11 ....172 E3
Lantern Way UB7 ....208 E4
Lanterns Wlk SL6 ....203 B7
Lanthorn MK14 ....34 E6
Lappetts La HP16 ....152 E8
Larch Cl Aylesbury HP20 ....102 A2
  Slough SL2 ....205 B8
  Tylers Green HP10 ....163 C2
Larch Gr MK2 ....58 E7
Larch Rise HP4 ....135 A5
Larches The
  Berkhamsted HP4 ....134 D5
  Holmer Green HP15 ....163 D7
  Little Chalfont HP6 ....155 B1
Larchfield Prim Sch
  SL6 ....202 E4
Larchfield Rd SL6 ....202 E5
Larchlands The HP10 ....163 D1
Larchmoor Pk SL2 ....199 A7
Larchwood HP16 ....152 B4
Lark Cl MK8 ....52 E7
Lark Rise HP15 ....163 B5
Lark Vale HP19 ....101 E3
Larkfield SL6 ....203 B1
Larkfield Cl HP13 ....162 F1
Larkin Cl MK16 ....22 A5
Larkings La SL2 ....199 B4
Larks Rise HP5 ....154 D6
Larkspur Ave MK14 ....34 E5
Larkspur Way HP15 ....162 F6
Larwood Pl MK6 ....34 F1
Lasborough Rd MK10 ....36 C1
Lascelles Rd OX9 ....125 F1
Lascelles Ho 8 SL1 ....206 A4
Lascelles Rd SL3 ....206 B3
Laser Cl MK5 ....46 C6
Lashlake Rd OX9 ....125 F1
Lassell Gdns SL6 ....203 B7
Lastingham Gr MK4 ....46 B2
Latchmoor Ave SL9 ....188 D7
Latchmoor Gr SL9 ....188 D7
Latchmoor Way SL9 ....188 D7
Latimer Latimer HP5 ....155 E2
  Milton Keynes MK11 ....32 E4
Latimer Cl MK4 ....166 C8
Latimer Ct HP20 ....116 A8
Latimer Rd Chesham HP5 154 E5
  Little Chalfont HP5 ....155 C2
Latimer Way HP9 ....175 C6
Laud's Cl RG9 ....191 C1
Launceston WD3 ....167 B3
Launceston St MK5 ....46 B6
Launde 1 MK10 ....36 A1
Laurance Ct 2 SL7 ....183 D2
Laurel Ave SL4 ....206 A4
Laurel Bank HP3 ....146 F8
Laurel Cl
  Milton Keynes MK8 ....45 D7
  Poyle SL3 ....212 E7
  Prestwood HP16 ....151 B7
  Speen HP27 ....150 C8
Laurel Ct Amersham HP6 154 C3
  Iver Heath SL0 ....200 D5
Laurel Dr
  Loudwater HP11 ....174 B3
  Walter's Ash HP14 ....161 D7
Laurel La UB7 ....208 E2
Laurel Rd SL9 ....177 D2
Laurel Way 4 HP21 ....115 B5
Laurels Rd SL0 ....200 D3
Laurels The
  High Wycombe HP12 ....172 C4
  Milton Keynes MK1 ....47 D1
Lautrec Way HP19 ....100 F2
Lautree Gdns SL6 ....195 E7
Lavender Cl HP21 ....115 B5
Lavender Gr MK7 ....48 A5
Lavender Rd UB8 ....208 F8
Lavender Way HP15 ....162 F7
Lavender Wlk HP21 ....115 B6
Lavendon Comb Sch MK46 7 B8
Lavendon Rd MK46 ....7 A5
Lavric Rd HP21 ....115 C6
Lawford Ave WD3 ....167 C3
Lawford Cl WD3 ....167 C3
Lawkland SL2 ....198 C2
Lawn Ave UB7 ....208 D4
Lawn Cl MK18 ....65 E4
Lawn Ct SL1 ....211 C7
Lawn Farm Bsns Ctr
  HP18 ....83 D4
Lawn Hill HP18 ....73 A2
Lawn House La HP18 ....72 F1
Lawn Rd UB8 ....201 C5
Lawn The SL3 ....211 C6
Lawns The Brill HP18 ....96 B1

Lawns The continued
  Tylers Green HP10 ....163 B2
Lawnsmead Gdns MK16 ....22 D5
Lawrence Cl HP20 ....102 A2
Lawrence Ct SL4 ....210 C5
Lawrence Gr HP16 ....151 D5
Lawrence Way SL1 ....204 D8
Lawrence Wlk MK16 ....21 F5
Laws Cl MK43 ....8 E6
Lawson Pl MK5 ....46 B5
Lawsone Rise HP13 ....162 B1
Laxton Gn SL6 ....202 C3
Lay Rd HP19 ....101 B2
Layburn Cres SL3 ....212 B8
Layter's Ave SL9 ....177 C1
Layter's Ave S SL9 ....177 C1
Layter's Cl SL9 ....177 C1
Layter's End SL9 ....177 C1
Layters Green La SL9 ....177 B1
Layters Way SL9 ....188 D6
Lea Cl SL7 ....183 D6
Lea Ct HP7 ....165 F8
Lea Inf Sch SL2 ....206 B6
Lea Jun Sch SL2 ....206 B6
Lea La HP18 ....125 F4
Leaberry MK13 ....34 A8
Leach Rd HP21 ....115 C7
Leachcroft SL9 ....177 B2
Leaches Farm Bsns Ctr
  HP18 ....81 F4
Leacroft Cl HP21 ....208 E6
Leacroft Rd SL0 ....207 E7
Leadenhall Rdbt MK6 ....46 F7
Leaders Cl HP22 ....89 B3
Leafield Rise MK8 ....33 D2
Leafy La HP23 ....118 E1
Leaholme Gdns SL1 ....204 D8
Leapingwell La MK18 ....66 B5
Leary Cres MK16 ....22 E4
Leas Cl HP13 ....173 F8
Leas Dr SL0 ....207 E7
Leaside MK16 ....12 B6
Leasowe Pl MK13 ....34 C3
Leather La HP16 ....142 A3
Leaver Rd RG9 ....191 C1
Leckhampstead HP18 ....48 A2
Leckhampstead Rd MK19 ....31 A3
Ledborough Gate HP9 ....175 E4
Ledborough La HP9 ....175 E4
Ledborough Wood HP9 ....175 E4
Ledburn LU7 ....90 C8
Ledburn Gr LU7 ....80 E6
Ledbury MK14 ....21 E1
Ledeview Ct HP11 ....174 A4
Ledger's Rd SL1 ....205 D4
Lee Common CE Sch
  HP16 ....142 D5
Lee Cotts
  Buckmoorend HP17 ....140 D6
  Lacey Green HP27 ....149 A4
Lee Cres HP17 ....114 D5
Lee Ct 7 HP12 ....172 E7
Lee Farm Cl HP5 ....145 A1
Lee Ho 2 MK2 ....58 C8
Lee La SL6 ....194 F1
Lee Rd Aylesbury HP21 ....115 D6
  Quainton HP22 ....84 F5
  Saunderton HP27 ....148 F6
Leeches Way LU7 ....105 A7
Leeds Rd SL1 ....205 E6
Lees Cl SL6 ....202 B5
Lees Gdns SL6 ....202 B5
Lees Wlk SL7 ....183 C2
Leeson Gdns SL4 ....204 E2
Legoland Windsor★
  SL4 ....209 D2
Leicester Ct RG9 ....191 D3
Leigh Hill MK4 ....46 D2
Leigh Pk SL3 ....211 B7
Leigh Rd SL1 ....205 B6
Leigh Sq SL4 ....209 D5
Leigh St HP11 ....172 F7
Leighton Buzzard Sta
  LU7 ....80 E7
Leighton Gdns SL6 ....196 B1
Leighton Ho 7 SL3 ....183 E2
Leighton Mid Sch LU7 ....80 F6
Leighton Rd
  Edlesborough LU6 ....92 D4
  Leighton Buzzard LU7 ....80 F7
  Soulbury LU7 ....70 B1
  Stoke Hammond MK17 ....69 E7
  Wing LU7 ....80 A3
  Wingrave HP22 ....89 C3
Leighton St MK17 ....60 E6
Leiston Spur SL1 ....205 E7
Leisure Plaza★ MK9 ....46 C8
Leith Cl SL1 ....206 A5
Leith Rd HP19 ....115 A8
Lembrook Wlk HP21 ....115 C6
Lenborough Cl MK18 ....52 C7
Lenborough Ct MK15 ....35 C2
Lenborough Rd MK18 ....52 C7
Lennon Dr MK8 ....45 E7
Lennox Rd MK2 ....58 D7
Lent Gn SL1 ....197 B1
Lent Green La SL1 ....197 B1
Lent Rise Comb Sch
  SL1 ....204 B8
Lent Rise Rd SL1 ....204 B8
Lenthall Cl MK14 ....34 A5
Leominster Gate 4
  MK10 ....36 A1
Leon Ave MK2 ....58 D8
Leon Sch & Sports Coll
  MK2 ....58 C5
Leonards Cl HP18 ....72 F2
Leonardslee MK4 ....45 F2

Leopard Dr MK15 ....35 A7
Leopold Mall 5 SL1 ....205 F4
Leopold Rd LU7 ....80 D7
Lerwick Dr SL1 ....205 E8
Leslie Dunne Ho SL4 ....209 E5
Lester Cl MK7 ....48 C7
Lester Gr HP15 ....163 A4
Lesters Rd SL6 ....195 D6
Letchfield HP5 ....155 B8
Letter Box La HP27 ....139 D7
Leven Cl
  Leighton Buzzard LU7 ....80 B7
  Milton Keynes MK2 ....58 D5
Levens Hall Dr MK4 ....45 F1
Leverkus Ct OX39 ....147 C6
Leverkus Ho OX39 ....147 C6
Levings Cl HP19 ....101 A3
Lewens Croft MK16 ....16 A3
Lewes Cl SL1 ....205 C4
Lewes Ho MK3 ....57 D7
Lewins Farm Ct SL1 ....204 F6
Lewins Rd SL9 ....188 D8
Lewins Way SL1 ....204 F6
Lewins Yd HP5 ....154 B8
Lewis Cl MK16 ....21 F5
Lewis La SL9 ....177 E2
Lewknor CE Prim Sch
  OX49 ....157 B8
Lewknor Cl OX49 ....157 A7
Lexham Gdns HP6 ....154 C2
Lexington Ave SL6 ....202 D5
Ley Field Rd HP21 ....115 E6
Ley Hill Sch HP5 ....145 B1
Leybourne Gdns OX39 ....147 C7
Leyburne Cl LU7 ....90 C8
Leyland Pl 3 MK6 ....34 E1
Leylands La TW19 ....213 A2
Leys Ct MK5 ....46 B8
Leys La MK18 ....62 B8
Leys Rd MK5 ....46 B8
Leys The Amersham HP6 ....154 B4
  Buckingham MK18 ....41 F3
  Halton HP22 ....117 C1
  Tring HP23 ....119 B4
  Woburn Sands MK17 ....49 B4
  Yardley Hastings NN7 ....1 A6
Leys View MK16 ....13 F1
Leywood HP7 ....165 E7
Libra Ho HP10 ....185 A8
Lichfield Down MK7 ....48 B5
Lichfield Ho HP21 ....115 F6
Lidcote LU7 ....78 A5
Liddall Way UB7 ....208 F5
Liddell SL4 ....209 C4
Liddell Pl SL4 ....209 C4
Liddell Sq 14 SL4 ....209 C5
Liddell Way SL4 ....209 C4
Liffre Dr HP22 ....131 B6
Lightfoot Ct MK7 ....47 F5
Lightlands La SL6 ....195 F5
Ligo Ave HP22 ....116 C2
Lilac Cl MK17 ....57 C3
Lilac Ct SL2 ....197 F2
Lilac Pl UB7 ....208 F6
Lilies The HP22 ....87 C1
Lilleshall Ave MK10 ....35 F1
Lilley Way SL1 ....204 E5
Lillibrooke Cres SL6 ....202 A3
Lilly Hill MK46 ....6 F5
Lillyfee Farm La HP16 ....186 B5
Lily Bottom La HP27 ....150 A7
Lily Dr UB7 ....208 D2
Lily's Wlk HP11 ....173 A6
Limbaud Cl MK7 ....48 A5
Lime Ave
  Buckingham MK18 ....52 F7
  High Wycombe HP11 ....173 D5
  West Drayton UB7 ....208 F6
  Windsor SL4 ....209 C6
Lime Cl Hazelmere HP15 ....163 A3
  Newport Pagnell MK16 ....22 B3
Lime Gr Chinnor OX39 ....147 D6
  Leighton Buzzard LU7 ....80 E8
  Woburn Sands MK17 ....49 B4
Lime Rd
  Princes Risborough HP27 ....139 B3
  Yardley Gobion NN12 ....18 E6
Lime St MK46 ....6 F3
Lime Tree Cl HP15 ....162 D8
Lime Tree Wlk HP7 ....165 F8
Lime Wlk
  Maidenhead SL6 ....202 A8
  New Denham UB9 ....201 C7
Limerick La MK9 ....35 B3
Limes Ave HP21 ....116 B7
Limes The
  Amersham HP6 ....154 B3
  Milton Keynes MK11 ....32 E5
  Milton Keynes,Fenny Stratford
  MK2 ....58 E8
  Stoke Mandeville HP22 ....116 B2
  Windsor SL4 ....209 C6
Limes Way HP18 ....124 D2
Limit Home Pk HP4 ....134 D7
Limmer La HP12 ....172 B3
Limmers Mead HP15 ....162 D8
Linceslade Gr MK5 ....34 B1
Linchfield HP13 ....173 E7
Linchfield Rd SL3 ....211 C6
Lincoln MK14 ....34 C8
Lincoln Cl HP21 ....116 B2
Lincoln Ct
  Berkhamsted HP4 ....135 B4
  3 Slough SL1 ....205 E3
Lincoln Hatch La SL1 ....197 C1
Lincoln Ho HP10 ....185 D3
Lincoln Park Bsns Ctr
  HP12 ....172 D6

Lincoln Pk
Amersham HP7 . . . . .165 E8
Brackley NN13 . . . . .38 A5
Lincoln Rd
Chalfont St Peter SL9 . . .177 E2
High Wycombe HP12 . . .172 E5
Maidenhead SL6 . . . . . . .202 B8
Lincoln Way SL1 . . . . . . .204 D6
Lincolns The HP16 . . . . . .152 A3
Lincolnshire Cl MK3 . . . . .46 E1
Lincombe Slade LU7 . . . . .80 E8
Lincroft MK43 . . . . .25 B1
Linden SL3 . . . . .207 B1
Linden Ave SL6 . . . . .195 D1
Linden Cl HP12 . . . . .172 D6
Linden Dr
Chalfont St Peter SL9 . . .177 E1
Farnham Royal SL2 . . . . .198 C4
Linden End HP21 . . . . . . .115 F6
Linden Gr MK14 . . . . .34 F8
Linden Lea HP22 . . . . . . .131 B6
Linden Way HP17 . . . . . .128 B2
Linden Wlk HP15 . . . . . . .163 B3
Lindens The HP5 . . . . . . .146 F8
Lindisfarne Dr MK10 . . . . .36 A1
Lindo Cl HP5 . . . . .144 B1
Lindores Croft MK10 . . . . .36 B1
Lindsay Ave HP12 . . . . . .172 E7
Lindsay Cl TW19 . . . . . . .213 D2
Lindsey Rd UB9 . . . . .190 A1
Lines Hill HP22 . . . . .88 B3
Lines Rd HP14 . . . . .171 B5
Lines The HP14 . . . . .88 C4
Linfields HP7 . . . . .166 C7
Linford Ave MK16 . . . . . . .22 A4
Linford Day Hospl MK16 . .33 C5
Linford La
Milton Keynes,Willen MK15 .35 D7
Milton Keynes,Woolstone
MK15 . . . . .35 C3
Linford Lakes (Nature
Reserve)★ MK14 . . . . . . .21 D3
Lingfield MK12 . . . . .33 E4
Lingfield HP13 . . . . .174 A5
Lingholm Cl SL6 . . . . .202 C6
Linington Ave HP5 . . . . . .145 A1
Link Cl HP12 . . . . .172 D6
Link Rd Datchet SL3 . . . .211 C6
Great Missenden HP16 . .152 A7
High Wycombe HP12 . . .172 D6
Link The Hazelmere HP15 163 A5
Slough SL2 . . . . .206 B7
Link Way UB9 . . . . .190 A5
Links App HP10 . . . . .185 B8
Links Rd HP10 . . . . .185 C8
Links Way HP10 . . . . .185 B8
Linkswood Rd SL1 . . . . . .197 C3
Linnet HP18 . . . . .98 C5
Linnet Dr HP12 . . . . .172 B3
Linney Ct MK4 . . . . .46 A1
Linslade Lower Sch LU7 . .80 D7
Linslade Mid Sch LU7 . . . .80 E5
Linslade Rd LU7 . . . . .70 F4
Lintlaw Pl MK3 . . . . .47 A3
Linton Cl MK13 . . . . .34 C4
Lintott Ct TW19 . . . . .213 D1
Linx The MK3 . . . . .47 A2
Lionel Ave HP22 . . . . .131 A6
Lionel Cl HP22 . . . . .131 A5
Lipscomb La MK5 . . . . . . .46 A7
Lipscombe Dr HP8 . . . . . . .41 E1
Lisburn Path 1 HP20 . . .101 F2
Lisle Rd HP13 . . . . .162 A1
Lisleys Field HP15 . . . . . .162 D7
Lismore Pk SL2 . . . . .205 F7
Lissel Rd MK6 . . . . .203 A6
Lister Ct SL1 . . . . .204 E6
Liston Ct 7 SL7 . . . . .183 D2
Liston Ho 9 SL7 . . . . . . .183 E2
Liston Rd SL7 . . . . .183 D2
Litcham Spur SL1 . . . . . . .205 D7
Little Balmer MK18 . . . . . .52 E6
Little Benty UB7 . . . . .208 D1
Little Boltons 13 SL7 . . .183 E4
Little Bridge Rd HP4 . . . .135 D4
Little Britain HP18 . . . . . . .99 D5
Little Buntings SL4 . . . . . .209 F4
Little Chalfont Comb Sch
HP6 . . . . .166 E8
Little Chartridge Ct
HP5 . . . . .144 A1
Little Cl Aylesbury HP20 . .101 D1
Flackwell Heath HP10 . . .185 B6
High Wycombe HP12 . . .172 E3
Little Dunmow MK10 . . . . .36 A1
Little Gaddesden CE Prim
Sch HP4 . . . . .121 C8
Little Gaddesden Ho
HP4 . . . . .121 E5
Little Greencroft HP5 . . . .144 A1
Little Habton 3 MK4 . . . . .46 B2
Little Ham La HP27 . . . . . .139 B5
Little Hame HP21 . . . . .35 F3
Little Hampden Cl HP22 131 A4
Little Hill WD3 . . . . .167 C3
Little Hivings HP5 . . . . . . .144 A4
Little Hollis HP16 . . . . . . .151 E7
Little Hoo HP23 . . . . .118 F4
Little Horwood Manor
MK17 . . . . .55 E4
Little Horwood Rd MK17 .55 C5
Little Hundridge La
HP16 . . . . .153 A8
Little Kimble Sta HP17 . . .175 F1
Little Kingshill Comb Sch
HP16 . . . . .152 B2

Little La
Lacey Green HP27 . . . . .149 C4
Yardley Hastings NN7 . . . . .1 A7
Little Linford La MK16,
MK19 . . . . .21 E4
Little London
Deanshanger MK19 . . . . . .31 E4
Whitchurch HP22 . . . . . . .87 A5
Little London Gn HP18 .109 F5
Little Marlow CE Sch
SL7 . . . . .184 C5
Little Marlow Rd SL7 . . .183 E3
Little Marsh OX27 . . . . . . .72 A3
Little Mdw MK5 . . . . .46 C7
Little Missenden CE Sch
HP7 . . . . .153 A2
Little Mollards HP22 . . . . .89 A3
Little Orchard Cl HP27 . .138 E5
Little Orchs HP20 . . . . . . .101 F3
Little Pk Bovingdon HP3 .146 A3
Princes Risborough HP27 .139 C3
Little Reeves Ave HP7 . . .165 F8
Little Shardeloes HP7 . . .165 A8
Little Spinney MK43 . . . . .25 C3
Little Spring HP5 . . . . . . .144 B3
Little Spring Sch HP5 . . .144 B3
Little Stanton NN7 . . . . .1 B6
Little Stanton MK14 . . . . . .34 D8
Little Stocking MK5 . . . . . .46 A3
Little Sutton La SL3 . . . . .207 C1
Little Tring Rd HP23 . . . . .118 F6
Little Twye HP23 . . . . .132 E3
Little Twye Rd HP23 . . . . .132 E3
Little Windmill Hill
WD4 . . . . .156 F7
Little Wood HP14 . . . . . . .158 E5
Little Woodlands SL4 . . . .209 F4
Littlebrook Ave SL2 . . . . .204 E8
Littlecote MK8 . . . . .34 A1
Littledown Rd SL1 . . . . . .205 F5
Littledown Sch SL1 . . . . .205 F6
Littlefield Ct UB7 . . . . . . .213 D7
Littlemere MK8 . . . . .33 D1
Littleport Spur SL1 . . . . . .205 E7
Littleworth LU7 . . . . .79 E3
Littleworth Rd
Hedgerley SL1 . . . . .186 C1
High Wycombe HP13 . . .161 E2
Litton Ct HP10 . . . . .174 C2
Liverpool Rd SL1 . . . . . . .205 B7
Liverpool Victoria Ho 3
HP13 . . . . .173 B7
Livesey Hill MK5 . . . . .46 B5
Livingstone Dr MK15 . . . . .35 C5
Llanbury Cl SL9 . . . . .177 E3
Lloyds MK6 . . . . .47 A7
Loakes Ho HP11 . . . . .173 A6
Loakes Rd HP11 . . . . .173 A6
Lochinvar Cl SL1 . . . . . . .205 B4
Lochnell Rd HP4 . . . . .134 F6
Lochy Dr LU7 . . . . .80 C7
Lock Ave SL6 . . . . .196 C2
Lock Bridge Rd SL8 . . . . .185 A3
Lock La Cosgrove MK19 . . .19 E2
Maidenhead SL6 . . . . . . .202 C4
Lock Mead SL6 . . . . .196 C2
Lock Path SL4 . . . . .209 D8
Lock Rd SL7 . . . . .183 F1
Lock View La MK1 . . . . . . .47 E1
Lockbridge Ct SL6 . . . . . .203 C8
Locke Cl HP19 . . . . .101 A2
Locke Gdns SL3 . . . . .206 C4
Locke Rd MK2 . . . . .58 C8
Lockets Cl SL4 . . . . .209 D6
Locksley Ct 4 SL1 . . . . . .205 E3
Lockton Ct MK4 . . . . .46 B3
Lockview Cotts MK1 . . . . .47 E1
Lodden Cl HP21 . . . . .115 D3
Loddon Ct SL8 . . . . .202 D8
Loddon Rd SL8 . . . . .185 A4
Loddon Spur SL1 . . . . . . .205 E7
Lodge Cl
Cheddington LU7 . . . . . .105 A7
Marlow SL7 . . . . .183 E1
Padbury MK18 . . . . .53 C2
Slough SL1 . . . . .205 C4
Uxbridge UB8 . . . . .201 C1
Lodge Farm Bsns Ctr
MK19 . . . . .20 C3
Lodge Farm Cl HP22 . . . .116 E2
Lodge Farm Cl MK19 . . . . .19 F6
Lodge Gate MK14 . . . . . . .34 E7
Lodge La
Prestwood HP16 . . . . . . .151 D5
Stoke Hammond MK17 . . .69 D4
Lodge Park Terr MK16 . . . .22 C4
Lodge Rd MK43 . . . . .37 F8
Lodge The
Aylesbury HP19 . . . . . . .115 A7
Slough SL2 . . . . .206 A3
Lodgings of the Military
Knights 4 SL4 . . . . . . .210 D6
Lodore Gn UB10 . . . . .190 A5
Logan Rock MK4 . . . . .57 B8
Lollards Cl HP6 . . . . .154 C7
Lombardy Dr HP4 . . . . . . .135 D3
Lomond Dr
Leighton Buzzard LU7 . . . .80 C7
Milton Keynes MK2 . . . . . .58 D4
London Central High Sch
HP11 . . . . .173 B4
London End
Beaconsfield HP9 . . . . . .175 F1
Newton Longville MK17 . . .57 D4
Woburn MK17 . . . . .60 F6
London End La MK17 . . . . .48 D1

London Ho MK11 . . . . .32 D5
London Rd
Aston Clinton HP22 . . . . .117 E4
Beaconsfield HP9 . . . . . .187 B8
Berkhamsted HP4 . . . . . .135 E3
Buckingham MK18 . . . . . .52 E6
Chalfont St Giles HP8 . . .177 C7
Datchet SL3 . . . . .211 C7
Felden HP3 . . . . .146 F8
High Wycombe HP11 . . . .173 E5
Little Kingshill HP16 . . . .152 B5
Loughton MK5 . . . . .46 B7
Milton Common OX9 . . . .136 B3
Milton Keynes MK16 . . . . .36 B5
Milton Keynes,Stony Stratford
MK11 . . . . .32 E4
Newport Pagnell MK16 . . .22 F3
Old Stratford MK19 . . . . . .32 C7
Slough,Brands Hill SL3 . .212 B8
Slough,Langley SL3 . . . . .206 D2
Tring HP23 . . . . .119 C3
Wendover HP22 . . . . .141 D6
Wheatley OX33 . . . . .122 B1
Slough SL3 . . . . .212 B8
London Rd E HP7 . . . . . . .165 E6
London Rd W HP7 . . . . . . .165 C7
Londrina Ct 9 HP4 . . . . .135 D4
Londrina Terr 10 HP4 . . .135 D4
Long Ayres MK7 . . . . .48 A3
Long Cl SL2 . . . . .198 B5
Long Close Prep Sch
SL3 . . . . .206 A2
Long Crendon Ind Est
HP18 . . . . .125 E5
Long Crendon Rd HP18 124 D3
Long Crendon Sch
HP18 . . . . .125 C7
Long Croft Rd WD3 . . . . .178 D5
Long Dr SL1 . . . . .197 C2
Long Furlong
Haddenham HP17 . . . . . .126 F3
Stone HP17 . . . . .114 B5
Long Furlong Dr SL2 . . . .197 E1
Long Gr HP9 . . . . .176 C4
Long Hale LU7 . . . . .105 C4
Long Hedge LU7 . . . . .105 C4
Long Hide HP27 . . . . .139 C4
Long La Bovingdon HP3 . .155 F8
Cookham Rise SL6 . . . . .195 D5
Heronsgate WD3 . . . . . .167 A4
Olney MK46 . . . . .6 F4
Rickmansworth WD3 . . . .167 F1
Stanwell TW19 . . . . .213 F1
Long Ley LU7 . . . . .105 A4
Long Leys HP15 . . . . .115 A8
Long Lional HP20 . . . . . . .115 D8
Long Marston CE Prim Sch
HP23 . . . . .104 B4
Long Marston La LU7 . . . .104 E3
Long Marston Rd LU7 . . .104 F2
Long Massey MK46 . . . . . . .6 C3
Long Mdw
Aylesbury HP21 . . . . . . .116 B6
Chesham HP5 . . . . .144 C3
Long Meadow Cl HP27 . .139 C5
Long Meadow Sch MK5 . .45 F3
Long Orchard Dr HP10 . .174 C8
Long Park Cl HP6 . . . . . . .154 C3
Long Park Way HP6 . . . . .154 C3
Long Pk HP6 . . . . .154 C3
Long Plough HP22 . . . . . .117 D5
Long Readings La SL2 . . .198 B2
Long Ride HP27 . . . . .139 C3
Long Row
Leckhampstead MK18 . . . .30 C1
Prestwood HP16 . . . . . . .151 D6
Long View HP5 . . . . .135 A6
Long Wall HP17 . . . . .126 F5
Long Wlk HP8 . . . . .176 F4
Long Wood Dr HP9 . . . . .176 F4
Longbottom La HP9 . . . . .176 C3
Longbourn SL4 . . . . .210 A4
Longbridge Cl HP23 . . . . .119 A6
Longbridge Way UB8 . . . .201 D3
Longcroft HP22 . . . . .117 F5
Longcroft Ave HP22 . . . . .131 D6
Longcroft La
Bovingdon HP3 . . . . .146 D5
Paulerspury NN12 . . . . . . .17 C8
Longcross MK15 . . . . .35 A4
Longdown Hill HP27 . . . . .139 F5
Longdown Mews HP19 . . .114 F2
Longfellow Dr MK16 . . . . .22 A4
Longfield Hedgerley SL2 . .187 D1
Little Kingshill HP16 . . . .152 B4
Longfield Gdns HP23 . . . .118 E3
Longfield Rd
Chesham HP5 . . . . .143 F2
Tring HP23 . . . . .118 F3
Longford Rdbt UB7 . . . . . .213 B6
Longhedge MK7 . . . . .48 A2
Longland Way HP12 . . . . .172 D5
Longlands Ct MK16 . . . . . .66 A5
Longlands Wlk MK18 . . . . .66 A5
Longleat Ct 7 MK8 . . . . . .33 F1
Longleat Gdns SL6 . . . . .202 D6
Longlees WD3 . . . . .178 D5
Longmead SL4 . . . . .209 E6
Longmead La SL1 . . . . . . .197 D5
Longmead Prim Sch
UB7 . . . . .208 E2
Longmire MK46 . . . . .7 F4
Longmore WD3 . . . . .178 F6
Longpeak Cl MK4 . . . . .46 B1

Longridge Scout Boating
Activity Ctr SL7 . . . . . . .194 F8
Longstone Rd SL0 . . . . . . .200 C4
Longview HP9 . . . . .185 F8
Longville MK12 . . . . .33 B7
Longwick CE Comb Sch
HP27 . . . . .138 D6
Longwick Rd
Longwick HP27 . . . . .138 F6
Monks Risborough HP27 .139 A5
Longwood Ave SL3 . . . . . .207 B1
Longwood La HP7 . . . . . . .165 D6
Longworth Dr SL6 . . . . . . .196 C1
Lonsdale Cl SL6 . . . . .196 A1
Lonsdale Way SL6 . . . . . . .203 C1
Look Ahead SL1 . . . . .205 E4
Loose Path HP19 . . . . . . .114 F8
Loosen Dr SL6 . . . . .202 A3
Loosley Hill HP27 . . . . . . .149 C5
Lord Grey Sch HP27 . . . . .149 A1
Lord Knyvett Cl TW19 . . .213 D1
Lord Knyvetts Ct 12
TW19 . . . . .213 E1
Lord Mayors Dr SL2 . . . . .198 A4
Lord Raglan Ho SL4 . . . . .210 C4
Lords Cl MK2 . . . . .47 C1
Lords Mead LU6 . . . . .92 E6
Lords Mill Ct HP5 . . . . . . .154 C7
Lords Terr LU6 . . . . .92 E6
Lordsmead MK43 . . . . .25 C2
Loriner Pl MK14 . . . . .35 A6
Loring Rd
Berkhamsted HP4 . . . . . .135 C3
Dunstable LU6 . . . . .93 F8
Windsor SL4 . . . . .209 F6
Lorne Cl SL1 . . . . .205 C3
Lorraine Cl HP13 . . . . . . .173 E8
Loseley Ct MK8 . . . . .33 F1
Losfield Rd SL4 . . . . .209 E6
Lossie Dr SL1 . . . . .207 B6
Lothersdale MK13 . . . . . . .34 B5
Lothian Cl MK3 . . . . .46 E2
Lott Mdw HP21 . . . . .115 B5
Lott Wlk HP21 . . . . .115 D3
Louches La HP14 . . . . . . .161 B6
Loudhams Rd HP7 . . . . . .166 C8
Loudhams Wood La
HP8 . . . . .166 D7
Loudwater Comb Sch
HP11 . . . . .174 B2
Loughton Manor First Sch
MK5 . . . . .46 A8
Loughton Middle Sch
MK5 . . . . .46 A7
Loughton Rd MK13 . . . . . . .34 A3
Loughton Rdbt MK8 . . . . . .45 E8
Louisa Cotts 10 HP23 . . .119 A3
Louise Wlk HP3 . . . . .146 A3
Lovat Mid Sch MK16 . . . . .22 D3
Lovat St MK16 . . . . .22 D4
Lovatt Dr MK3 . . . . .57 E8
Love Green La SL0 . . . . . .207 E8
Love Hill La SL3 . . . . .207 A6
Love La SL0 . . . . .207 D7
Love Row MK17 . . . . .68 D6
Lovegrove Dr SL2 . . . . . . .197 F1
Lovejoy La SL4 . . . . .209 D5
Lovel End SL9 . . . . .177 C3
Lovel Mead SL9 . . . . .177 C3
Lovel Rd SL9 . . . . .177 C2
Lovelace Cl SL4 . . . . .193 F4
Lovett Gdns SL6 . . . . .196 C3
Lovett Rd UB9 . . . . .190 C8
Lovetts End LU7 . . . . .78 E8
Lovibonds Ave UB7 . . . . .208 F7
Lowbrook Cl HP21 . . . . . .116 A4
Lowbrook Dr SL6 . . . . . . .202 A3
Lowbrook Prim Sch
SL6 . . . . .202 A3
Lowdell Cl UB7 . . . . .208 E7
Lowdon Dr HP11 . . . . .173 D4
Lower Ascott LU7 . . . . .79 F1
Lower Boynton Rd SL6 . . .202 E6
Lower Britwell Rd SL2 . . .197 C6
Lower Church St
Cuddington HP18 . . . . . .112 F3
Stokenchurch HP14 . . . . .158 E5
Lower Cippenham La
SL1 . . . . .204 F6
Lower Cl HP18 . . . . .124 D3
Lower Cookham Rd SL6 196 C3
Lower Dr HP9 . . . . .175 D5
Lower Eighth St MK9 . . . . .34 E2
Lower End Ashendon HP18 97 E1
Lower End MK18 . . . . .53 F8
Newton Longville MK17 . . .57 C3
Piddington OX25 . . . . .95 E8
Wingrave HP22 . . . . .89 B2
Lower End Rd MK17 . . . . . .57 A6
Lower Farm Cl HP18 . . . . .124 D3
Lower Farm Gate HP17 . .114 A4
Lower Fourth St MK9 . . . . .34 D1
Lower Furney Cl HP13 . . .173 D8
Lower Gn
Cuddington HP18 . . . . . .112 F3
Westcott HP18 . . . . .98 C7
Weston Turville HP22 . . . .117 A3
Lower Green La HP22 . . . .112 C2
Lower Hammersley La
HP13 . . . . .174 B4
Lower Icknield Way
Chinnor OX39 . . . . .147 D8
Great Kimble HP17 . . . . .129 D1
Marsworth HP23 . . . . . . .105 A3
Monks Risborough HP27 .139 B8
Pitch Green HP27 . . . . . .138 C3
Wilstone HP22,HP23 . . . .118 C7

Lower Kings Rd HP4 . . . . .135 C5
Lower Lees Rd SL2 . . . . . .198 B2
Lower Lodge La HP15 . . . .163 A5
Lower Mead SL0 . . . . .200 D2
Lower Mount Farm SL6 195 D5
Lower Ninth St MK9 . . . . . .34 E2
Lower Pound La SL7 . . . . .194 D8
Lower Rd
Aylesbury HP21,HP22 . . .115 F3
Blackthorn OX25 . . . . .81 A4
Chinnor OX39 . . . . .147 C7
Chorleywood WD3 . . . . . .167 D5
Cookham Rise SL6 . . . . .195 E7
Denham UB9 . . . . .189 D4
Gerrards Cross SL9 . . . . .188 F7
Hardwick HP22 . . . . .87 B3
Lacey Green HP27 . . . . . .149 D6
Lower Ridge SL8 . . . . .185 B4
Lower Riding HP9 . . . . . . .175 B2
Lower Second St MK9 . . . .34 D1
Lower St Pury End NN12 . .17 A7
Quainton HP22 . . . . .85 A5
Lower Stonehayes MK14 . .34 F7
Lower Tenth St MK9 . . . . . .34 E2
Lower Third St MK9 . . . . . .34 D3
Lower Twelfth St MK9 . . . .34 F3
Lower Ventnor Cotts
SL6 . . . . .195 C8
Lower Ward SL4 . . . . .210 D7
Lower Way
Great Brickhill MK17 . . . . .59 C1
Padbury MK18 . . . . .53 C2
Lower Weald MK19 . . . . . . .32 E2
Lower Wharf MK18 . . . . . . .41 E1
Lowes Cl HP14 . . . . .158 C5
Lowestoft Dr SL1 . . . . . . .204 D7
Lowfield Cl HP15 . . . . .163 B3
Lowfield Way HP15 . . . . . .163 B3
Lowick Pl 4 MK4 . . . . .46 B2
Lowland Rd MK5 . . . . .57 C8
Lowlands Cres HP15 . . . . .151 C3
Lowlands Rd TW19 . . . . . .213 D2
Lowman Way HP21 . . . . . .115 D4
Lowndes Ave HP5 . . . . . . .144 B1
Lowndes Gr MK5 . . . . .45 F7
Lowndes Way SL6 . . . . . . .66 A5
Lownes Path HP19 . . . . . .114 F8
Loxbeare Dr MK4 . . . . .46 C4
Loxboro Hill HP14 . . . . . . .160 D4
Loxley Rd HP4 . . . . .134 F6
Loxwood Cl HP3 . . . . .146 B3
Loyne Cl LU7 . . . . .80 C8
Lucas Pl MK6 . . . . .47 D8
Lucas Rd HP13 . . . . .173 C7
Luccombe MK4 . . . . .46 D3
Lucky La or Cock La
HP20 . . . . .101 D1
Lucy La MK5 . . . . .46 B8
Ludgate Milton Keynes MK6 46 E7
Tring HP23 . . . . .118 F4
Ludgershall Rd OX25 . . . . .95 E7
Ludlow Dr OX9 . . . . .126 A1
Ludlow Ho SL6 . . . . .202 E6
Ludlow Mews HP11 . . . . . .174 A4
Ludlow Pl HP20 . . . . .116 B8
Ludlow Rd SL6 . . . . .202 E6
Luff Cl SL4 . . . . .209 E4
Lufford Pk MK14 . . . . .34 F8
Luke Pl MK10 . . . . .35 F3
Luker Ave RG9 . . . . .191 D3
Lukes La HP23 . . . . .104 D3
Lukes Lea HP23 . . . . .105 A1
Lullingstone Dr MK13 . . . . .33 F5
Lumber La NN12 . . . . .17 B7
Lundholme MK13 . . . . .34 B5
Lundy Ct SL1 . . . . .204 E6
Lupin Cl UB7 . . . . .208 D1
Lupin Ct HP21 . . . . .115 B5
Lupin Wlk HP21 . . . . .115 B5
Lutman La SL6 . . . . .195 F2
Luttlemarsh MK7 . . . . .48 A5
Lutyens Gr MK7 . . . . .48 C5
Luxborough Gr MK4 . . . . . .46 C4
Lychgate Cotts HP3 . . . . .146 B4
Lycrome La HP5 . . . . .144 D3
Lycrome Rd HP5 . . . . .144 E3
Lyde End HP27 . . . . .138 B1
Lydford Ave SL2 . . . . .205 D8
Lydiard MK8 . . . . .33 E1
Lydiard HP21 . . . . .116 A4
Lydsey Cl SL2 . . . . .198 A2
Lye Green Cotts HP5 . . . .144 E3
Lye Green Rd HP5 . . . . . .144 E2
Lye The HP4 . . . . .121 D6
Lyell Pl E SL4 . . . . .209 C4
Lyell Pl W SL4 . . . . .209 C4
Lyell Rd SL4 . . . . .209 C4
Lyell Wlk E SL4 . . . . .209 C4
Lyell Wlk W SL4 . . . . .209 C4
Lyme Ave HP4 . . . . .134 D7
Lynch Cl UB8 . . . . .201 C5
Lynch Hill Comb Sch
SL2 . . . . .197 F2
Lynch Hill La SL2 . . . . . . .197 E2
Lynch The UB8 . . . . .201 C5
Lyndhurst Ave SL6 . . . . . .195 E6
Lyndhurst Cl HP13 . . . . . .161 D1
Lyndhurst Rd HP5 . . . . . . .144 B2
Lyndon Cl HP16 . . . . .151 C7
Lyndon Gdns HP13 . . . . . .173 E8
Lyndwood Dr SL4 . . . . . . .211 A1
Lyndwood Par SL4 . . . . . .211 A2
Lyneham Gdns SL6 . . . . . .195 B1
Lynher Cl HP21 . . . . .115 C4

Lynmouth Cres MK4 ....46 D4
Lynott Cl MK8 ....45 E6
Lynton Gn SL6 ....202 E7
Lynwood Ave SL3 ....206 D3
Lynwood Rd HP21 ....116 A5
Lyon Rd MK1 ....47 B2
Lysander Cl HP3 ....146 A4
Lysander Mead SL6 ....203 C8

M

Macdonald Cl HP6 ....154 D4
Mackenzie Mall 3 SL1 ....205 F4
Mackenzie St 2 SL1 ....205 F4
Maconi Croft MK5 ....46 C5
Madeira Wlk SL4 ....210 D6
Madeley Cl HP6 ....154 D3
Madeley Rd HP21 ....115 E6
Magdalen Cl
  Milton Keynes MK11 ....32 D6
  Syresham NN13 ....27 C8
Magdalen Ho MK11 ....32 D6
Magenta Cl MK2 ....58 D6
Magnolia Dene HP15 ....162 F2
Magnolia Gdns SL3 ....206 C3
Magnolia St UB7 ....208 D2
Magnolia Way HP10 ....185 E7
Magpie Cl
  Flackwell Heath HP10 ....174 A1
  Milton Keynes MK5 ....46 B4
Magpie La Coleshill HP7 ....165 A1
  Flackwell Heath HP10 ....174 A1
  Loudwater HP13 ....174 B3
Magpie Way Slough SL2 ....197 F1
  Winslow MK18 ....66 B6
Mahler Cl MK7 ....48 C5
Mahoney Ct HP11 ....172 F8
Maidenhead Ave MK13 ....34 C3
Maidenhead Coll for Girls
  SL6 ....202 E7
Maidenhead Court Pk
  SL6 ....196 B3
Maidenhead Rd
  Cookham Rise SL6 ....195 F6
  Windsor SL4 ....209 E7
Maidenhead Sta SL6 ....202 F6
Maids Moreton CE Sch
  MK18 ....41 E3
Maidstone Rd MK10 ....36 C2
Main Dr
  Gerrards Cross SL9 ....188 C6
  Iver SL0 ....207 E3
  Pottersbury NN12 ....18 B2
Main Par WD3 ....167 C5
Main Rd Astwood MK16 ....16 B3
  Drayton Parslow MK17 ....68 B5
  Lacey Green HP27 ....149 E5
  Syresham NN13 ....27 C7
  Upper Winchendon HP18 ....99 A1
  Walter's Ash HP14 ....161 C7
Main Rd N HP4 ....107 A6
Main Rd S HP4 ....107 D4
Main St Adstock MK18 ....53 F1
  Akeley MK18 ....41 F8
  Ashendon HP18 ....97 F1
  Beachampton MK19 ....44 A6
  Buckingham MK18 ....41 F3
  Chackmore MK18 ....41 B4
  Charndon OX27 ....72 E5
  Cosgrove MK19 ....19 E2
  Gawcott MK18 ....51 F4
  Grendon Underwood HP18 ....83 B5
  Mursley MK17 ....67 D6
  Padbury MK18 ....53 B1
  Poundon OX27 ....71 F7
  Preston Bissett MK18 ....62 B8
  Shalstone MK18 ....39 E6
  Tingewick MK18 ....51 B6
  Turweston NN13 ....38 C8
  Twyford MK18 ....62 C1
  Westbury NN13 ....39 A4
  Weston Turville HP22 ....116 E2
Maitland Dr HP13 ....173 B8
Maitland Rd HP22 ....131 D7
Major's Farm Rd
  Datchet SL3 ....211 E8
  Slough SL3 ....212 A8
Malbons Ct MK6 ....46 E7
Malborough Ho HP4 ....135 A3
Malborough Way NN12 ....18 F5
Malcolm Rd UB10 ....201 E4
Malden Cl HP6 ....154 F1
Malders La SL6 ....195 C3
Malet Cl HP14 ....158 F5
Malins Gate MK14 ....34 E8
Malkin Dr HP9 ....175 C3
Mallard Cl HP21 ....101 E4
Mallard Croft HP17 ....127 A7
Mallard Dr
  Buckingham MK18 ....52 B8
  Slough SL3 ....204 F6
Mallard Ho HP11 ....173 C6
Mallets End HP22 ....85 B4
Malletts Cl MK11 ....32 E5
Mallow Gate MK14 ....34 E4
Mallow Pk SL6 ....195 C1
Malpas Rd SL2 ....206 B6
Malt La NN13 ....27 C8
Malthouse Flats RG9 ....192 D6
Malthouse Sq
  Beaconsfield HP9 ....186 F8
  Princes Risborough HP27 ....139 B4

Malthouse Way 2 SL7 ....183 D1
Malting Cl MK16 ....12 B6
Malting La Aldbury HP23 ....120 D5
  Dagnall HP4 ....107 C5
Maltings Cl
  Cranfield MK43 ....25 A1
  Stewkley LU7 ....78 E8
Maltings Field MK19 ....19 F5
Maltings The
  Chackmore MK18 ....41 B4
  Olney MK46 ....7 A3
  Tingewick MK18 ....51 B6
Maltmans Green Sch
  SL9 ....188 C8
Maltmans La SL9 ....188 C8
Malton Ave SL1 ....205 B6
Malton Cl MK10 ....35 F1
Malvern Cl HP13 ....172 E8
Malvern Ct SL3 ....212 A7
Malvern Dr
  Leighton Buzzard LU7 ....80 C8
  Milton Keynes MK11 ....33 A4
Malvern Rd
  Aylesbury HP20 ....116 C8
  Maidenhead SL6 ....195 D1
Malyns Cl OX39 ....147 C7
Manchester Terr HP14 ....171 B4
Mandela Ct UB8 ....208 C7
Mandelyns HP4 ....134 E7
Mandeville Dr MK10 ....36 C2
Mandeville Mews HP21 ....115 E4
Mandeville Rd
  Aylesbury HP21 ....115 E5
  Prestwood HP16 ....151 B7
Mandeville Upper Sch
  HP21 ....115 D4
Manifold Cl SL2 ....198 A2
Manifold La MK4,MK5 ....46 B3
Manor Cl
  Berkhamsted HP4 ....135 C4
  Bledlow HP27 ....138 B1
  Cosgrove MK19 ....19 E2
  Hanslope MK19 ....11 A2
  Milton Keynes MK10 ....35 F3
  Prestwood HP16 ....151 D4
  Salford MK17 ....37 D3
  Stoke Hammond MK17 ....69 E7
  Tylers Green HP10 ....163 A2
Manor Cotts
  Chorleywood WD3 ....167 B3
  Milton Keynes MK12 ....33 B7
Manor Court Yd
  High Wycombe HP13 ....162 A1
  Waterperry OX33 ....123 B2
Manor Cres
  Seer Green HP9 ....176 D5
  Wendover HP22 ....131 C5
Manor Ct Emberton MK46 ....13 F8
  Leighton Buzzard LU7 ....70 E2
  Marlow SL7 ....183 C3
  Slough,Cippenham SL1 ....204 F5
  6 Slough,Upton Park SL1 ....205 F3
  Twyford MK18 ....62 C1
Manor Ctyd
  Haddenham HP17 ....127 D4
  Sherington MK16 ....13 F1
Manor Dr Amersham HP6 ....154 B3
  Aylesbury MK20 ....101 F2
  Haversham MK19 ....20 E2
  Stewkley LU7 ....78 E8
Manor Farm Cl
  Soulbury LU7 ....69 E2
  Stone HP17 ....114 C5
  Weston Turville HP22 ....116 E2
  Windsor SL4 ....209 F4
Manor Farm Comm Inf Sch
  HP15 ....163 B2
Manor Farm Comm Jun Sch
  HP15 ....163 B2
Manor Farm Cotts SL4 ....211 A2
Manor Farm Ct HP22 ....87 B2
Manor Farm Ctyd HP22 ....102 D8
Manor Farm Ho SL4 ....209 F4
Manor Farm La LU7 ....90 C8
Manor Farm Way HP9 ....176 D4
Manor Gdns
  Grendon Underwood HP18 ....83 A6
  High Wycombe HP13 ....162 A1
  Maids Moreton MK18 ....41 E2
  Wooburn Green HP10 ....185 E5
Manor Ho Brill HP18 ....110 A8
  Hambleden RG9 ....181 D2
Manor House Cl HP20 ....101 F1
Manor House Hospl
  HP20 ....101 F1
Manor House La SL3 ....211 B6
Manor La
  Gerrards Cross SL9 ....188 D4
  Maidenhead SL6 ....202 E4
Manor Park Ave HP27 ....139 A3
Manor Pk MK18 ....41 F4
Manor Pound Rd LU7 ....105 A7
Manor Rd Akeley MK18 ....41 F7
  Aylesbury HP20 ....101 E1
  Cheddington LU7 ....104 F7
  Chesham HP5 ....144 C2
  Emmington OX9 ....137 B6
  Maidenhead SL6 ....202 E4
  Milton Keynes,Bletchley
    MK2 ....58 E8
  Milton Keynes,Wolverton
    MK12 ....33 B7
  Newport Pagnell MK16 ....22 A4
  Newton Longville MK17 ....57 D3
  Oakley HP18 ....109 D5
  Oving HP22 ....86 C7
  Princes Risborough HP27 ....139 A2

Manor Rd continued
  Rowsham HP22 ....102 D8
  Seer Green HP9 ....176 D5
  Tring HP23 ....119 A5
  Tylers Green HP10 ....163 A2
  Wendover HP22 ....131 C5
  Windsor SL4 ....209 E5
Manor St
  Berkhamsted HP4 ....135 D4
  Buckingham MK18 ....52 C8
Manor View HP15 ....163 B2
Manor View Ho HP13 ....161 E2
Manor Way
  Chesham HP5 ....144 D1
  Coleshill HP7 ....164 F3
  Yardley Gobion NN12 ....18 E6
Manor Waye UB8 ....201 D4
Manorfields Rd MK19 ....32 B6
Mansard Cl 8 HP23 ....119 A3
Manse Rd MK11 ....32 D6
Mansel Cl Cosgrove MK19 ....19 E2
  Slough SL2 ....206 B8
Mansell Cl
  Milton Keynes MK5 ....46 A6
  Windsor SL4 ....209 E6
Manshead CE Inf Sch MK11 ....32 F5
Mansion Dr HP23 ....119 B3
Mansion Hill HP22 ....131 E8
Mansion La Harrold MK43 ....3 F1
  Iver SL0 ....207 C6
Mansion The HP4 ....135 E6
Manton Rd LU6 ....93 D5
Maple Ave UB7 ....208 F5
Maple Cl
  Hazelmere HP15 ....163 A3
  High Wycombe HP12 ....172 C5
  Maidenhead SL6 ....202 C5
Maple Cres SL2 ....206 B6
Maple Ct
  Gerrards Cross SL9 ....188 F6
  Marlow SL7 ....183 E3
  Windsor SL4 ....210 C4
Maple Gr
  Milton Keynes MK2 ....58 E8
  Woburn Sands MK17 ....49 B4
Maple Leys MK18 ....63 E3
Maple Lodge Cl WD3 ....178 B6
Maple Pl UB7 ....208 F5
Maple Rise SL7 ....183 E3
Mapledean MK12 ....33 E4
Mapledurham MK7 ....48 B3
Mapledurham Wlk SL6 ....195 C3
Maplefield La HP8 ....166 B6
Maples The
  5 Bourne End SL8 ....185 B3
  Wendover HP22 ....131 C5
Maplewood Gdns HP9 ....175 B1
Maplewood Sch HP13 ....161 D3
Maplin Pk SL3 ....207 B4
Mapperton Cl MK4 ....45 F1
Mapridge Green La
  HP16 ....141 D1
Mara Pl MK9 ....35 A3
Marand Ct HP21 ....115 F8
Marbeck Cl SL4 ....209 D6
March Edge MK18 ....41 E1
March Mdw MK7 ....48 D7
March Pl HP19 ....115 B8
Marchant Cl SL7 ....184 A3
Marches The SL4 ....205 D2
Marcia Ct SL1 ....204 F5
Marcourt Rd HP14 ....158 F3
Mardle Rd LU7 ....80 E6
Mare Leys MK18 ....52 F8
Maree Cl
  Leighton Buzzard LU7 ....80 C7
  Milton Keynes MK2 ....58 C5
Marefield Rd SL7 ....183 D2
Marescroft Rd SL2 ....197 E1
Margaret Ct HP13 ....173 C6
Margaret Powell Sq MK9 ....34 F3
Margaret Smythe Ho
  SL9 ....188 F5
Marie Cl OX27 ....71 F7
Marigold Pl MK14 ....34 E4
Marigold Wlk HP15 ....162 F6
Marina Dr Dunstable LU6 ....93 E7
  Milton Keynes MK12 ....33 D6
Marina Rdbt MK6 ....47 C7
Marina Way Iver SL0 ....208 A6
  Slough SL1 ....204 D6
Marish Ct SL3 ....207 A3
Marish La UB9 ....189 D7
Marish Prim Sch SL3 ....207 A3
Marish Wharf Ind Est
  SL3 ....206 A4
Marjoram Pl MK14 ....34 E4
Mark Dr SL9 ....177 E6
Markenfield Pl MK4 ....45 E1
Market Hill
  Buckingham MK18 ....41 D1
  Milton Keynes MK6 ....47 B8
  Whitchurch HP22 ....86 F6
Market Ho 5 SL9 ....177 D2
Market La SL3 ....207 C3
Market Par HP15 ....163 A4
Market Pl
  Chalfont St Peter SL9 ....177 D2
  Colnbrook SL3 ....212 D2
  Henley-on-T RG9 ....191 D2
  Olney MK46 ....6 F3
Market Place Mews 5
  RG9 ....191 D2

Market Sq
  Amersham HP7 ....165 B7
  Aylesbury HP20 ....115 D8
  Buckingham MK18 ....41 D1
  Chesham HP5 ....154 B8
  Hanslope MK19 ....11 A2
  Marlow SL7 ....183 D2
  Milton Keynes MK13 ....32 D5
  Princes Risborough HP27 ....139 B3
  Uxbridge UB8 ....201 C5
  Winslow MK18 ....65 F4
Market St
  19 Aylesbury HP20 ....115 D8
  Maidenhead SL6 ....202 F7
  9 Windsor SL4 ....210 D6
Markham Cl HP19 ....115 A7
Markhams MK18 ....52 D8
Marks Orch MK18 ....75 F7
Marlborough Cl SL6 ....202 A6
Marlborough Gate MK9 ....34 F3
Marlborough Ho 5 SL6 ....202 F6
Marlborough Rd
  Aylesbury HP21 ....115 E4
  Maidenhead SL6 ....202 A6
  Slough SL3 ....206 D2
Marlborough St
  Milton Keynes,Neath Hill
    MK14 ....34 E6
  Milton Keynes,Tinkers Bridge
    MK6 ....47 D6
Marlborough Trad Est
  HP11 ....172 F7
Marley Gr MK8 ....45 E7
Marlin Cl HP4 ....134 F5
Marlin Copse HP4 ....135 A3
Marlin Ct SL1 ....183 D1
Marlin Hill HP23 ....133 A8
Marlins Cl WD3 ....167 F7
Marlins End HP4 ....134 F3
Marlow Bottom SL7 ....183 D6
Marlow Bridge La SL7 ....194 E8
Marlow CE Inf Sch SL7 ....183 D3
Marlow Com Hospl SL7 ....183 F2
Marlow Comm SL7 ....182 F3
Marlow Dr MK16 ....22 A4
Marlow Hill HP11 ....173 A5
Marlow Ho 1 SL7 ....183 D2
Marlow Lodge 13 SL6 ....202 F6
Marlow Mill SL7 ....183 E1
Marlow Rd Bisham SL7 ....194 E7
  Henley-on-T RG9 ....191 E3
  High Wycombe HP11 ....172 E4
  Lane End HP14,SL7 ....171 E2
  Little Marlow SL7 ....184 C5
  Maidenhead SL6 ....202 F7
Marlow Sta SL7 ....183 F2
Marquis Ct MK17 ....60 F7
Marram Cl MK6 ....47 A5
Marriott Terr WD3 ....167 F5
Marriott's Cl HP17 ....126 F6
Marriott's La HP17 ....126 F6
Marriott's Way HP17 ....126 F6
Marriotts Ave HP16 ....142 E1
Marrod's Bottom HP7 ....175 C8
Marron La MK12 ....33 C5
Marroway HP22 ....116 D2
Marsh Ct HP11 ....173 F4
Marsh Dr MK14 ....21 E1
Marsh End Rd MK16 ....22 C8
Marsh Gibbon CE Inf Sch
  OX27 ....71 F3
Marsh Gibbon Rd HP18 ....82 E8
Marsh La
  Stoke Mandeville HP22 ....129 F8
  Taplow SL6 ....203 E4
Marsh Rd
  Great Kimble HP22 ....129 D4
  Shabbington HP18 ....124 D3
Marsh Sch HP11 ....173 F4
Marshall Court Ind Pk
  MK1 ....47 B1
Marshalls La MK15 ....35 C2
Marshalls Lea HP22 ....102 C3
Marsham Ct HP21 ....116 A4
Marsham La SL9 ....188 D5
Marsham Lodge SL9 ....188 E5
Marsham Way SL9 ....188 E5
Marshaw Pl 3 MK4 ....46 C2
Marshcroft La HP23 ....119 D6
Marshfield SL3 ....211 C6
Marshgate Trad Est
  SL6 ....204 A7
Marshment Cl HP20 ....117 D5
Marshworth MK6 ....47 D6
Marston Ct HP5 ....144 A4
Marston Ct HP23 ....104 B4
Marston Hill
  Granborough MK18 ....75 F6
  Thame OX9 ....126 A1
Marstonfields Rd MK18 ....76 B2
Marsworth CE Inf Sch
  HP23 ....105 A2
Marsworth Rd LU7 ....105 D4
Marsworth Reservoir (Nature
  Reserve)* HP23 ....119 A8
Martell Ct MK7 ....48 A3
Martin Cl
  Buckingham MK18 ....52 F7
  Milton Keynes MK14 ....34 E6
  Uxbridge UB10 ....201 E3
  Windsor SL4 ....209 D6

Martin Dell Cotts HP16 ....142 E4
Martin Rd
  Maidenhead SL6 ....202 F8
  Slough SL1 ....205 E3
Martin's Plain SL2 ....198 F3
Martindale SL0 ....200 D1
Martingale Pl MK14 ....34 F5
Martins Dr The LU7 ....80 F8
Martinsend La HP16 ....151 E7
Martyrs Ct HP7 ....165 C8
Marunden Gn SL2 ....197 F2
Marwood Cl MK4 ....46 D3
Mary Cross Cl HP23 ....119 D1
Mary MacManus Dr
  MK18 ....41 D1
Mary Morgan Ct SL2 ....205 D8
Mary Towerton Sch The
  HP14 ....159 D3
Marygold Wlk HP6 ....166 C8
Maryland Coll MK17 ....60 E6
Maryland Rd MK15 ....35 B8
Maryot Cl MK16 ....13 F2
Marys Mead HP15 ....163 A5
Maryside SL3 ....206 E4
Mascoll Path SL2 ....197 F2
Masefield Cl
  Chesham HP5 ....144 B3
  Newport Pagnell MK16 ....22 A4
Masefield Gr MK3 ....58 A7
Maslin Dr MK6 ....47 B5
Mason MK14 ....34 C8
Mason's Ct
  Aylesbury HP19 ....115 B7
  Slough SL1 ....204 E6
Masons Cl HP16 ....151 C5
Masons Ct HP5 ....144 C1
Masons Rd SL1 ....204 E6
Masons Yd HP4 ....135 D4
Massie Cl MK15 ....35 B6
Mathiesen Rd MK13 ....34 A6
Mathisen Way SL3 ....212 C6
Matilda Gdns MK5 ....46 B5
Matlock Rd HP20 ....101 F2
Matson Dr RG9 ....191 F2
Matthew Ct MK5 ....46 B6
Matthews Cl 12 HP20 ....101 F2
Maud Jane's Cl LU7 ....105 E5
Maude Cl HP9 ....176 A1
Maude Rd HP9 ....176 A1
Maudsley Cl MK5 ....46 C6
Maudsley Ho SL6 ....203 A7
Mauduit Cl MK19 ....11 A3
Maulden Gdns MK14 ....35 A8
Maurice Mount HP15 ....162 F5
Mavoncliff Dr MK4 ....57 A8
Maxham MK5 ....46 A3
Maxwell Ct SL1 ....197 C1
Maxwell Dr HP15 ....163 B5
Maxwell Pl HP9 ....175 E3
Maxwell Rd
  Beaconsfield HP9 ....175 E3
  West Drayton UB7 ....208 F2
May Cl LU6 ....92 E6
May Rd MK43 ....8 E6
May Tree Cl SL7 ....183 C6
Maybach Cts MK5 ....46 B5
Maybrook Gdns HP13 ....173 C8
Maybury Cl SL1 ....204 D7
Maybush Gdns HP16 ....151 C6
Maybush Wlk MK46 ....6 E5
Mayditch Pl MK13 ....34 A3
Mayer Gdns MK5 ....46 C5
Mayfield Cvn Pk UB7 ....208 C3
Mayfield Dr SL4 ....210 A4
Mayfield Rd HP10 ....185 E6
Mayflower Ct HP17 ....114 F5
Mayflower Way
  Beaconsfield HP9 ....186 A8
  Farnham Common SL2 ....198 C3
Maygoods Cl UB8 ....208 D8
Maygoods Gn UB8 ....208 D8
Maygoods La UB8 ....208 D8
Maygoods View UB8 ....208 C8
Mayhall Farm HP6 ....154 A4
Mayhall La HP6 ....154 B4
Mayhew Cres HP13 ....173 D8
Maylands Dr UB8 ....201 D6
Maynard Cl MK13 ....34 A3
Maynard Ct SL4 ....210 A6
Mayorfield Ho 1 SL7 ....183 D2
Maypole Rd SL6 ....204 A8
Mays Way NN12 ....18 D3
McAuliffe Dr SL1,SL2 ....197 F8
McConnell Dr MK12 ....33 E6
McDougall Rd 8 HP4 ....135 D4
McEwen Ride HP22 ....117 D1
McKay Trad Est SL3 ....212 C6
McKenzie Cl MK18 ....52 D8
McLellan Pl HP12 ....172 D5
McLernon Way MK18 ....66 A5
Mead Acre HP27 ....139 B5
Mead Ave SL3 ....207 B4
Mead Cl Denham UB9 ....190 A2
  7 Marlow SL7 ....183 F3
  Monks Risborough HP27 ....139 B6
  Slough SL3 ....207 B4
Mead Haze SL6 ....196 C2
Mead Ho SL0 ....200 D2
Mead Pk HP15 ....163 C7
Mead Platt HP14 ....158 D5
Mead Rd UB8 ....201 D5
Mead St HP13 ....174 A4
Mead The
  Beaconsfield HP9 ....175 E2
  Soulbury LU7 ....69 E3
Mead Way
  High Wycombe HP11 ....173 F4
  Slough SL1 ....204 D8

Mead Wlk SL3 . . . . .207 B4
Meades La HP5 . . . . .154 B7
Meadfield Ave SL3 . . . . . . .207 A3
Meadfield Rd SL3 . . . . .207 B3
Meadfurlong Mid Sch
MK6 . . . . .34 F1
Meadow Bank 6 SL8 . . . .185 B3
Meadow Cl
Aylesbury HP20 . . . . .102 A1
Chesham HP5 . . . . .144 A4
Cublington LU7 . . . . .78 C1
High Wycombe HP11 . . . . . .173 F4
Marlow SL7 . . . . .183 F1
Oakley HP18 . . . . .109 D4
Old Windsor SL4 . . . . .211 B2
Tring HP23 . . . . .119 A4
Meadow Cotts
Beaconsfield HP9 . . . . .175 E1
Little Kingshill HP16 . . . . . . .152 B3
Stone HP17 . . . . .114 D3
Meadow Ct MK46 . . . . .5 D2
Meadow Dr
Amersham HP6 . . . . .154 E2
Longwick HP27 . . . . .138 D6
Meadow Gate
Padbury MK18 . . . . .53 B2
Prestwood HP16 . . . . .151 C3
Meadow Gdns MK18 . . . . . .52 E6
Meadow High Sch UB8 .208 E8
Meadow La
Beaconsfield HP9 . . . . .175 F2
Eton SL4 . . . . .210 C7
Long Crendon HP18 . . . . . .125 E4
Milton Keynes MK10 . . . . . . .36 A3
Pitstone LU7 . . . . .105 E3
South Heath HP16 . . . . . . .152 E8
Meadow Pk HP22 . . . . . . .116 C2
Meadow Rd
Berkhamsted HP4 . . . . .135 B6
Chinnor OX39 . . . . .147 D6
Henley-on-T RG9 . . . . .191 E1
Slough SL3 . . . . .206 E3
Meadow Rise HP27 . . . . . .149 E5
Meadow Row MK18 . . . . . . .41 D1
Meadow View
Aspley Guise MK17 . . . . . . .49 D6
Chalfont St Giles HP8 . . . . .177 A7
Long Crendon HP18 . . . . . .125 E4
Marlow Bottom SL7 . . . . . . .183 E6
Potterspury NN12 . . . . .18 D3
Stanwell TW19 . . . . .213 A2
Uxbridge UB8 . . . . .208 C8
Meadow Way
Aylesbury HP20 . . . . .102 A1
Dorney SL6 . . . . .203 F4
Felden HP3 . . . . .146 F7
Hyde Heath HP6 . . . . .153 C4
Old Windsor SL4 . . . . .211 B1
Thame OX9 . . . . .125 F1
Wing LU7 . . . . .79 E3
Meadow Wlk
Bourne End SL8 . . . . .185 A5
Buckingham MK18 . . . . .41 D1
Tylers Green HP10 . . . . . . .163 C1
Meadoway
Steeple Claydon MK18 . . . . .63 E3
Stone HP17 . . . . .114 F5
Meadowbank Cl
Bovingdon HP3 . . . . .146 B3
Long Crendon HP18 . . . . . .125 C2
Meadowbrook HP23 . . . . . .119 B6
Meadowbrook Cl SL3 . . . . .212 F6
Meadowcott La HP7 . . . . . .164 F3
Meadowcroft
Aylesbury HP19 . . . . .101 B3
Berkhamsted HP4 . . . . .134 D7
Chalfont St Peter SL9 . . . . .177 D1
Meadowlea Cl UB7 . . . . . . .213 D8
Meadows Hth Sch HP10 185 E7
Meadows The
Amersham HP7 . . . . .154 E1
Flackwell Heath HP10 . . . . .185 B8
Old Stratford MK19 . . . . . . .32 B6
Whitchurch HP22 . . . . .86 F7
Meadowside HP9 . . . . .176 F4
Meadowsweet MK7 . . . . . . .48 B5
Meadowview TW19 . . . . . . .212 F4
Meads Cl MK13 . . . . .34 B8
Meads The
Berkhamsted HP4 . . . . .134 F6
Eaton Bray LU6 . . . . .92 E5
Stoke Poges SL2 . . . . .199 A2
Tring HP23 . . . . .119 B4
Uxbridge UB8 . . . . .201 E1
4 Windsor SL4 . . . . .210 A5
Meadway
Berkhamsted HP4 . . . . .135 E5
Buckingham MK18 . . . . .52 D6
Dunstable LU6 . . . . .93 F7
Oving HP22 . . . . .76 E1
Meadway Ct LU6 . . . . .93 F7
Meadway Pk SL9 . . . . .188 D3
Meadway The MK5 . . . . . . .46 A7
Meare Est HP10 . . . . .185 E8
Meavy Cl HP13 . . . . .174 B3
Medale Rd MK6 . . . . .47 B5
Medallion Pl MK6 . . . . .203 B7
Medbourne Rdbt MK8 . . . . .45 E6
Medeswell MK4 . . . . .46 E3
Medhurst MK8 . . . . .33 E2
Medland MK6 . . . . .47 D7
Medley Cl LU6 . . . . .92 F5
Medman Cl SL2 . . . . .201 C3
Medway Cl MK16 . . . . .22 E3
Meeting Oak La MK18 . . . . .66 B5
Megdale Pl HP20 . . . . .101 D2
Melbourne Ave SL1 . . . . . .205 C7
Melbourne Cl HP21 . . . . . .115 E5

Melbourne Rd HP13 . . . . . .173 F6
Melbourne Terr MK13 . . . . .34 A7
Melford Gn HP19 . . . . .101 C3
Melfort Dr
Leighton Buzzard LU7 . . . . . .80 B6
Milton Keynes MK2 . . . . . . .58 D4
Melick Rd MK6 . . . . .47 B4
Melissa Ct HP13 . . . . .173 D6
Mellish Ct MK3 . . . . .47 A1
Mellstock Rd HP21 . . . . . . .115 F5
Melrose Ave MK3 . . . . .47 A3
Melrose Ct HP13 . . . . .162 B1
Melrose Wlk HP21 . . . . . . .115 F5
Melton MK14 . . . . .34 C8
Melton Ct Dunstable LU6 . . . .93 F7
Maidenhead SL6 . . . . .202 F6
Mendelssohn Gr MK7 . . . . .48 C4
Mendip Cl SL3 . . . . .207 A1
Mendip Way HP13 . . . . . . .172 F8
Mendy St HP11 . . . . .173 A7
Menmarsh Rd HP18 . . . . . .123 E6
Menteith Cl MK2 . . . . .58 C5
Mentmore ★ LU7 . . . . .90 C4
Mentmore Cl HP12 . . . . . . .172 B6
Mentmore Cross Rds
LU7 . . . . .89 F6
Mentmore Ct
Mentmore LU7 . . . . .90 D5
2 Milton Keynes MK8 . . . . .45 E4
Mentmore Gdns LU7 . . . . . .80 E5
Mentmore Gn HP21 . . . . . .115 E4
Mentmore Rd
Cheddington LU7 . . . . .104 F8
High Wycombe HP12 . . . . . .172 B6
Leighton Buzzard LU7 . . . . . .80 E5
Mentmore View HP23 . . . . .118 F5
Mentone Ave HP7 . . . . .49 D4
Menzies Ct MK5 . . . . .46 B4
Mercer Wlk UB8 . . . . .201 C5
Mercers Dr MK13 . . . . .34 B6
Mercers Mdw HP22 . . . . . .131 B6
Merchant La
Cranfield MK43 . . . . .25 A1
Cranfield, Wharley End
MK43 . . . . .24 F2
Merchant Pl MK10 . . . . .35 E3
Mercia Rd SL6 . . . . .202 C4
Mercian Way SL1 . . . . .204 D5
Mercury Gr MK8 . . . . .45 E7
Mercury Pk The HP10 . . . . .185 E2
Mere Cl SL7 . . . . .183 F2
Mere La MK18 . . . . .50 E6
Mere Pk SL7 . . . . .183 F2
Mere Rd Finmere MK18 . . . .50 D6
Slough SL3 . . . . .205 F3
Merebrook First Sch
MK4 . . . . .46 C3
Meredith Dr HP19 . . . . . . .100 F4
Meriland Ct MK2 . . . . .58 E4
Merlebank HP5 . . . . .154 C7
Merlewood Cl HP11 . . . . . .173 A4
Merlewood Dr MK5 . . . . . . .45 F4
Merlin Cl SL3 . . . . .212 B8
Merlin Ct SL6 . . . . .202 B8
Merlin Ctr HP19 . . . . .101 C1
Merlin Ctr The HP19 . . . . . .172 E5
Merlin Wlk MK6 . . . . .47 B8
Merling Croft HP4 . . . . .134 E7
Merrydown HP13 . . . . .161 B1
Merryfields UB8 . . . . .201 D3
Mersey Cl MK3 . . . . .46 E1
Mersey Way MK3 . . . . .46 E1
Merthen Gr MK4 . . . . .57 B8
Merton Cl SL6 . . . . .202 C3
Merton Ct SL1 . . . . .206 A3
Merton Dr MK6 . . . . .47 A4
Merton Rd
Princes Risborough HP27 . . .139 B2
Slough SL1 . . . . .206 B2
Merwin Way SL4 . . . . .209 D4
Meryton Ho SL4 . . . . .210 A4
Messenger Ct HP21 . . . . . .116 A6
Metcalfe Gr MK14 . . . . .22 B2
Mews Cotts HP15 . . . . .162 D7
Mews Gamnel HP23 . . . . . .119 B6
Mews The HP6 . . . . .154 D3
Michael Cl SL6 . . . . .202 C5
Michaels Mews 6
HP19 . . . . .115 A8
Michigan Dr
Milton Keynes MK15 . . . . . . .35 C8
Newport Pagnell MK15 . . . . .22 C1
Micholls Ave SL9 . . . . .177 E5
Micklefield Rd HP13 . . . . . .174 A7
Mickleton MK15 . . . . .35 A6
Mid Cross La SL9 . . . . .177 F5
Midas Ind Est UB8 . . . . . . .201 B3
Midcot Way HP4 . . . . .134 F6
Midcroft SL2 . . . . .198 B1
Middle Cl HP6 . . . . .154 C7
Middle Cres UB9 . . . . .189 D4
Middle Dr HP9 . . . . .175 D5
Middle Field HP22 . . . . . . .116 F3
Middle Gn SL3 . . . . .206 E6
Middle La HP21 . . . . .146 A1
Middle Mdw HP8 . . . . .177 C7
Middle Rd
Aylesbury HP21 . . . . .116 B7
Berkhamsted HP4 . . . . .135 B4
Denham UB9 . . . . .189 D4
Middle Slade MK18 . . . . . . .52 D6
Middle Way OX33 . . . . .147 B6
Middle Weald MK19 . . . . . . .32 E2
Middle Wlk SL1 . . . . .197 C2
Middlebrook Rd HP13 . . . . .161 E1
Middlefield Cl MK18 . . . . . . .41 F1
Middlegreen Rd SL3 . . . . . .206 D5

Middlegreen Trad Est
SL3 . . . . .206 D4
Middlesex Dr MK3 . . . . .46 F1
Middleton MK14 . . . . .34 E7
Middleton Prim Sch
MK10 . . . . .35 E3
Middleway The HP12 . . . . . .172 C6
Midhurst MK11 . . . . .33 A6
Midland Rd MK46 . . . . .7 A5
Midshires Bsns Pk
HP19 . . . . .101 A1
Midsumer Ct HP15 . . . . . . .163 A3
Midsummer Arc MK9 . . . . . .34 E3
Midsummer Bvd MK9 . . . . . .34 E3
Midsummer Dr HP18 . . . . . .82 F6
Midsummer Pl MK9 . . . . . . .34 E3
Midsummer Rdbt MK9 . . . . .34 E3
Miersfield HP11 . . . . .172 D3
Mikern Cl MK2 . . . . .58 C8
Milburn Ave MK6 . . . . .46 E8
Milburn Dr UB7 . . . . .208 E6
Mildenhall Rd SL1 . . . . .205 E7
Mile Elm SL7 . . . . .184 A3
Milebush LU7 . . . . .80 C8
Milecastle MK13 . . . . .34 A5
Miles Cl Aylesbury HP21 . . . .116 A7
Milton Keynes MK14 . . . . . . .22 A7
Miles Ct HP22 . . . . .102 B3
Miles End HP21 . . . . .115 B6
Milesmere MK8 . . . . .33 D1
Milestone Cl HP14 . . . . . . .158 E5
Milfoil Ave MK14 . . . . .34 E4
Milford Ave HP11 . . . . .32 E4
Milford Ct 4 SL1 . . . . .206 A4
Milk Hall Barns HP5 . . . . . .154 F5
Mill Ave UB8 . . . . .201 C3
Mill Bridge Pl UB8 . . . . . . .201 C3
Mill Cl Chesham HP5 . . . . . .154 E5
West Drayton UB7 . . . . . . .208 D3
Wingrave HP22 . . . . .89 A3
Mill Cnr HP18 . . . . .83 A8
Mill Cotts HP18 . . . . .185 D4
Mill Ct Horton SL3 . . . . . . .212 C3
Milton Keynes MK12 . . . . . . .33 A5
Waddesdon HP18 . . . . .99 A7
West Drayton UB7 . . . . . . .208 D3
Mill End Cl
Edlesborough LU6 . . . . .92 F4
Prestwood HP16 . . . . .151 B5
Mill End Rd HP12 . . . . .172 C6
Mill Gdns HP23 . . . . .119 B4
Mill Gn MK43 . . . . .8 D5
Mill Ho Buckingham MK18 . . .52 C8
West Drayton UB7 . . . . . . .208 D3
Mill La Amersham HP7 . . . . .165 A8
Aspley Guise MK17 . . . . . . .49 C5
Beaconsfield HP9 . . . . .175 E1
Brackley NN13 . . . . .38 A6
Buckingham MK18 . . . . .52 C8
Chalfont St Giles HP8 . . . . .166 B1
Chinnor OX39 . . . . .147 B7
Cookham SL6 . . . . .196 C2
Gerrards Cross SL9 . . . . . . .188 F5
Great Brickhill MK17 . . . . . . .58 F2
Horton SL3 . . . . .212 C4
Horton-cum-S OX33 . . . . . .108 A6
Hulcote MK17 . . . . .37 E1
Hurley SL6 . . . . .193 F4
Milton Keynes,Bradville
MK13 . . . . .34 A7
Milton Keynes,Stony Stratford
MK11 . . . . .32 C5
Milton Keynes,Woolstone
MK15 . . . . .35 C3
Monks Risborough HP27 . . .139 B6
Salford MK17 . . . . .37 C3
South Heath HP16 . . . . . . .152 C7
Stokenchurch HP14 . . . . . . .158 C5
Taplow SL6 . . . . .203 C8
Thame OX9 . . . . .126 B3
Turvey MK43 . . . . .8 D5
Twyford MK18 . . . . .62 C1
Upper Arncott OX25 . . . . . . .94 E7
Westbury NN13 . . . . .39 A4
Weston Turville HP22 . . . . . .117 A4
Windsor SL4 . . . . .210 A7
Wingrave HP22 . . . . .89 C2
Mill Lane Com Prim Sch
OX39 . . . . .147 B7
Mill Mdw HP19 . . . . .115 B8
Mill Mead HP22 . . . . .131 B5
Mill Pl SL3 . . . . .211 D5
Mill Place Car Pk SL3 . . . . .211 C5
Mill Rd Cranfield MK43 . . . . .25 C2
2 Leighton Buzzard LU7 . . . .80 F8
Marlow SL7 . . . . .183 E1
Milton Keynes MK2 . . . . . . .58 E7
Oakley HP18 . . . . .109 D4
Slapton LU7 . . . . .91 D7
Stokenchurch HP14 . . . . . . .158 C5
West Drayton UB7 . . . . . . .208 D3
Whitfield NN13 . . . . .26 E3
Mill Sq MK12 . . . . .33 A5
Mill St Aylesbury HP20 . . . . .101 E1
Berkhamsted HP4 . . . . .135 C4
Colnbrook SL3 . . . . .212 D7
High Wycombe HP11 . . . . . .172 F7
Newport Pagnell MK16 . . . . .22 D5
Slough SL2 . . . . .205 F5
Mill Stream Cl HP27 . . . . . .139 A2
Mill Terr MK12 . . . . .33 A6
Mill The
Milton Keynes MK12 . . . . . . .32 E2
Wooburn Green HP10 . . . . .185 E8
Mill Twr MK12 . . . . .92 E6
Mill View Rd HP23 . . . . . . .118 F4
Mill W SL2 . . . . .205 F5

Mill Way
Aspley Guise MK17 . . . . . . .49 D5
Aylesbury HP20 . . . . .115 C8
Rickmansworth WD3 . . . . . .167 F1
Millards Cl MK43 . . . . .25 C2
Millards Pl MK43 . . . . .25 C2
Millbank
Leighton Buzzard LU7 . . . . . .80 F8
Marlow SL7 . . . . .183 F1
Millbank Pl MK7 . . . . .48 B8
Millboard Rd SL8 . . . . .185 B3
Millbrook Cl HP12 . . . . .172 D8
Millbrook Comb Sch
HP12 . . . . .172 D8
Millbrook Way SL3 . . . . . . .212 C5
Milldun Way HP12 . . . . . . .172 D6
Millennium Cl UB8 . . . . . . .201 C3
Millennium Point HP19 . . . .101 A1
Miller Pl MK9 . . . . .188 D6
Miller's La SL4 . . . . .211 A1
Millers Cl HP18 . . . . .82 F6
Millers Turn OX39 . . . . .147 B6
Millers Way
Aylesbury HP19 . . . . .115 A8
Milton Keynes MK12 . . . . . . .33 D5
Millfield HP4 . . . . .135 D5
Millfield Ave OX27 . . . . .71 F3
Millfield Cl Cranfield MK43 . . .25 B2
Marsh Gibbon OX27 . . . . . . .71 F3
Millfields HP5 . . . . .154 C6
Millhayes MK14 . . . . .34 F8
Millholm Rise MK6 . . . . . . .47 E5
Milliners The 1 HP20 . . . . .101 C1
Millington Gate MK15 . . . . . .35 D7
Millshot Dr HP7 . . . . .165 D7
Millside SL8 . . . . .185 C3
Millstream HP22 . . . . .116 F2
Millstream La SL1 . . . . .204 E5
Millstream Way
Leighton Buzzard LU7 . . . . . .80 F7
Wooburn Green HP10 . . . . .185 E8
Milner Rd SL1 . . . . .204 A8
Milton Ave SL9 . . . . .188 D8
Milton Cl
Henley-on-T RG9 . . . . .191 D2
Horton SL3 . . . . .212 A4
Milton Dr MK16 . . . . .22 E4
Milton Fields HP8 . . . . .177 B7
Milton Gdns HP27 . . . . . . .139 A2
Milton Gr MK3 . . . . .57 F7
Milton Hill HP27 . . . . .177 B7
Milton Keynes Central Sta
MK9 . . . . .34 C1
Milton Keynes Coll MK6 . .46 F7
Milton Keynes Coll (Bletchley
Ctr) MK3 . . . . .58 B8
Milton Keynes Coll
(Wolverton Ctr) MK12 . .33 B6
Milton Keynes General Hospl
MK6 . . . . .47 B7
Milton Keynes Materials
Recycling Factory ★
MK12 . . . . .33 C8
Milton Keynes Mus ★
MK12 . . . . .33 D5
Milton Keynes Prep Sch
MK3 . . . . .57 D8
Milton Lawns HP6 . . . . . . .154 D3
Milton Rd
Aston Clinton HP22 . . . . . . .117 F5
Aylesbury HP21 . . . . .115 F6
Chesham HP5 . . . . .144 B2
Milton Keynes,Broughton
MK10 . . . . .36 B3
Milton Keynes,Willen MK15 . .35 D7
Slough SL2 . . . . .198 D1
Walton MK7 . . . . .47 F6
Milton Way UB7 . . . . .208 F2
Milton's Cottage (Mus) ★
HP8 . . . . .177 B7
Milverton Cl SL6 . . . . .202 B3
Mimosa Ct HP21 . . . . .115 B6
Mina Ave SL3 . . . . .206 D4
Mineral La HP5 . . . . .154 C7
Minerva Cl TW19 . . . . .213 A2
Minerva Gdns MK7 . . . . . . .48 C7
Minerva Way HP9 . . . . .176 A1
Mines Cl HP13 . . . . .161 D3
Ministry Wharf HP14 . . . . . .149 C1
Minniecroft Rd SL1 . . . . . . .197 B2
Minorca Gr MK5 . . . . .46 A4
Minshull Ct MK18 . . . . .41 D1
Minster Way SL3 . . . . .206 F4
Minstrel Ct MK13 . . . . .34 B7
Minton Cl MK14 . . . . .22 A1
Minton Rise SL6 . . . . .204 B7
Mirador Cres SL2 . . . . .206 B6
Mirrie La UB9 . . . . .189 C6
Misbourne Ave
Chalfont St Peter SL9 . . . . .177 E5
High Wycombe HP13 . . . . . .173 F6
Misbourne Cl
Aylesbury HP21 . . . . .115 D3
Chalfont St Peter SL9 . . . . .177 E5
Misbourne Ct SL3 . . . . . . .207 A2
Misbourne Dr HP16 . . . . . .152 B6
Misbourne Ho HP8 . . . . . . .166 C1
Misbourne Mdws UB9 . . . . .189 D3
Misbourne Sch The
HP16 . . . . .152 B6
Misbourne Vale SL9 . . . . . .177 C5
Miss Joans Ride HP4 . . . . . .107 D7
Missenden Abbey Adult Ed
Coll HP16 . . . . .152 B6
Missenden Cl SL1 . . . . .65 F4
Missenden Gdns SL1 . . . . . .204 D5
Missenden Rd
Chesham HP5 . . . . .154 A7

Mea – Moo 237

Missenden Rd continued
Ellesborough HP17 . . . . . . .130 C2
Great Kingshill HP15 . . . . . .151 D2
Winslow HP18 . . . . .65 F4
Miswell La HP23 . . . . .118 F3
Mitcham Pl MK13 . . . . .34 D3
Mitcham Wlk HP19 . . . . . . .101 A2
Mitchell Cl
Bovingdon HP3 . . . . .145 F4
Slough SL1 . . . . .205 A4
Mitchell Rd MK43 . . . . .24 E2
Mitchell Wlk HP6 . . . . .154 E1
Mithras Gdns MK7 . . . . . . .48 C6
Mitre Cl SL6 . . . . .52 C7
Mitre St MK18 . . . . .52 C7
Moat Cl Prestwood HP16 . . .151 C6
Wendover HP22 . . . . .131 B6
Moat Dr Prestwood HP16 . . .151 C7
Slough SL2 . . . . .206 C8
Moat End HP22 . . . . .102 B4
Moat House The MK18 . . . . .52 D8
Moat La
Aston Abbotts HP22 . . . . . . .88 D4
Marsh Gibbon OX27 . . . . . . .71 F2
Prestwood HP16 . . . . .151 C7
Wingrave HP22 . . . . .89 B2
Moat Pl UB9 . . . . .201 B8
Mobwell Terr 3 HP16 . . . . .152 A8
Model Row HP16 . . . . .117 F6
Moeran Cl MK7 . . . . .48 C5
Moffy Hill SL6 . . . . .195 E2
Mole Run HP13 . . . . .161 C1
Molyneaux Ave HP3 . . . . . .145 C4
Molyns Ho RG9 . . . . .191 E3
Molyns Mews SL1 . . . . . . .204 E5
Monellan Cres MK7 . . . . . . .48 A3
Monellan Gr MK7 . . . . .48 A2
Monet Pl HP19 . . . . .100 E2
Money La UB7 . . . . .208 D3
Monkey Island La SL6 . . . . .203 E2
Monks Hollow SL7 . . . . . . .183 C5
Monks Path 9 HP19 . . . . . .115 A8
Monks Rd SL4 . . . . .209 D5
Monks Risborough CE Prim
Sch HP27 . . . . .139 D5
Monks Risborough Sta
HP27 . . . . .139 B6
Monks Way
Harmondsworth UB7 . . . . . .213 E8
Milton Keynes MK12,MK13,
MK14,MK15 . . . . .34 C6
Monksfield Way SL2 . . . . . .198 A2
Monkston Comb Sch
MK10 . . . . .36 B1
Monkston Rdbt MK10 . . . . . .36 B2
Monkswood Ct 11 SL7 . . . .183 E2
Monkton Way HP27 . . . . . .150 C5
Monmouth Cl HP19 . . . . . .101 A2
Monmouth Rd MK4 . . . . . . .45 E1
Monro Ave MK8 . . . . .45 E7
Montabaur Rd NN13 . . . . . .38 A7
Montagu Dr MK6 . . . . .47 B8
Montagu Rd SL3 . . . . .211 B6
Montague Rd
Aylesbury HP21 . . . . .115 D7
Berkhamsted HP4 . . . . .135 B4
Slough SL1 . . . . .205 F6
Uxbridge UB8 . . . . .201 D5
Montem La SL1 . . . . .205 D4
Montem Prim Sch SL1 . . . .205 B4
Montfort Mews HP15 . . . . .162 E2
Montgomerie Cl MK15 . . . . .35 A6
Montgomery Cres MK15 . . . .35 B7
Montgomery Pl SL2 . . . . . .206 C7
Montpellier Ct SL4 . . . . . . .210 C5
Montrose Ave
Datchet SL3 . . . . .211 C7
Slough SL1 . . . . .205 B7
Montrose Dr SL6 . . . . .202 A6
Montrose Way SL3 . . . . . . .211 C7
Monument La SL9 . . . . .177 E5
Monycrower Dr SL6 . . . . . .202 E2
Moon St MK12 . . . . .33 D5
Moor End Eaton Bray LU6 . . .92 F5
Frieth RG9 . . . . .171 A1
Maidenhead SL6 . . . . .203 C1
Moor End Cl LU6 . . . . .92 F4
Moor End La LU6 . . . . .92 F5
Moor Furlong SL1 . . . . .204 E5
Moor La
Harmondsworth UB7 . . . . . .213 C8
High Wycombe HP13 . . . . . .161 D3
Maidenhead SL6 . . . . .195 F1
Sarratt WD3 . . . . .156 E3
Moor Pk
Milton Keynes MK3 . . . . . . .57 D8
Wendover HP22 . . . . .131 B7
Moor Rd HP5 . . . . .154 C6
Moor The SL7 . . . . .184 C4
Moor's Farm Cotts HP5 145 B4
Moorbridge Rd SL6 . . . . . . .203 A7
Moorcroft Sch UB8 . . . . . . .208 F7
Moore Cl SL1 . . . . .205 B4
Moore Rd HP4 . . . . .134 F6
Moorend La Thame OX9 . . . .125 F1
Thame OX9 . . . . .126 A2
Moorend Rd NN12 . . . . . . .18 E6
Moores Hill MK46 . . . . .6 F5
Moores La SL4 . . . . .204 F1
Moorfield MK17 . . . . .57 D3
Moorfield Rd
Denham Green UB9 . . . . . .190 A5
Uxbridge UB8 . . . . .208 D5
Moorfield Terr SL6 . . . . . . .203 A8
Moorfoot MK11 . . . . .33 A4

Moorgate MK6 .....46 F7
Moorhall Rd UB9 .....190 B6
Moorhen Ct 2 HP20 .....101 E3
Moorhen Way MK18 .....52 E8
Moorhills Cres LU7 .....79 F3
Moorhills Rd LU7 .....79 F3
Moorings The
 Buckingham MK18 .....52 C8
 Windsor SL4 .....210 A7
Moorland Fst Sch MK6 .....47 B5
Moorland Rd UB7 .....213 C8
Moorlands LU7 .....79 E3
Moorlands Rd LU7 .....79 F3
Moors Cl MK19 .....31 E5
Moorside HP10 .....185 E8
Moorside Cl SL6 .....195 F1
Moorstown Ct 7 SL1 .....205 E4
Mop End La HP7 .....164 B7
Morar Cl LU7 .....80 C7
Moray Dr SL2 .....206 A3
Moray Pl MK3 .....46 F2
Mordaunt Cl MK43 .....8 E6
Mordaunts St SL3 .....35 C2
More Ave HP21 .....115 D7
Moreau Wlk SL3 .....206 E7
Morebath Gr MK4 .....46 C4
Morefields HP23 .....119 A6
Moreland Ave SL3 .....212 C7
Moreland Cl SL3 .....212 C7
Moreland Dr SL9 .....188 F4
Morello Dr SL3 .....206 F5
Moreton Dr MK18 .....41 E2
Moreton La HP17 .....115 A1
Moreton Rd MK18 .....41 D2
Moreton Way SL1 .....204 D5
Morland Dr MK8 .....45 D6
Morley Cl SL3 .....206 F4
Morley Cres MK7 .....48 D4
Morrell Cl MK5 .....46 B5
Morrice Cl SL3 .....207 A2
Morris Cl SL9 .....177 F2
Morris Ct
 Aylesbury HP21 .....115 D4
 Windsor SL4 .....209 E6
Morris Wlk MK16 .....22 A4
Morrison Ct MK8 .....45 E6
Mortain Cl MK7 .....48 B3
Mortain Dr HP4 .....134 F6
Morten Gdns UB9 .....190 A4
Mortens Wood HP7 .....165 E7
Mortimer Hill HP23 .....119 B4
Mortimer Rd SL3 .....206 D3
Mortimer Rise HP23 .....119 B4
Morton Cl
 North Marston MK18 .....76 B2
 Pitstone LU7 .....105 C4
 Uxbridge UB8 .....201 F1
Morton Dr SL1 .....197 E8
Morton King Cl HP18 .....124 D3
Moseley Rd HP14 .....161 C7
Moses Plat La HP27 .....150 B5
Moss Cl HP9 .....176 D4
Mossdale MK13 .....34 F6
Mossway HP9 .....175 C5
Mossy Vale SL6 .....195 D1
Moundsfield Way SL1 .....204 E4
Mount Ave MK1 .....47 E3
Mount Cl
 Aston Clinton HP22 .....117 F4
 Farnham Common SL2 .....198 C8
 High Wycombe HP12 .....172 E6
Mount Farm Ind Est MK1 47 D4
Mount Farm Rdbt MK1 .....47 D4
Mount Hill La SL9 .....188 B2
Mount La UB9 .....189 D2
Mount Nugent HP5 .....144 A4
Mount Pleasant
 Aspley Guise MK17 .....49 F4
 Aylesbury HP19 .....101 D1
 Lane End HP14 .....171 B5
 Milton Keynes MK6 .....47 E4
 Soulbury LU7 .....69 E3
 Steeple Claydon MK18 .....63 F2
 Stoke Goldington MK16 .....12 B7
 Stoke Hammond MK17 .....69 E7
 Whitchurch HP22 .....86 F7
 Yardley Gobion NN12 .....18 F6
Mount Pleasant Cl MK18 52 C7
Mount Pleasant Cotts 2
 SL8 .....185 B3
Mount St HP20 .....115 D8
Mount The
 Aspley Guise MK17 .....49 D4
 Milton Keynes MK6 .....47 E4
Mount View RG9 .....191 D2
Mount View Ct 4 RG9 .....191 D2
Mount Way HP27 .....139 A3
Mountain Ash SL7 .....183 D6
Mountbatten Cl 7 SL1 .....206 A3
Mountbatten Sq 8 SL4 .....210 C6
Mounthill Ave MK19 .....32 B7
Mountsfield Ct
 Newport Pagnell MK16 .....22 C3
 Stanwell TW19 .....213 A2
Mow Mead MK46 .....6 F5
Mowbray Dr LU7 .....80 C7
Mowbray Rd HP20 .....101 D2
Mowhills MK43 .....3 F6
Moyleen Rise SL7 .....183 C1
Mozart Cl MK7 .....48 C4
Muddiford La MK4 .....46 D4
Muirfield Dr MK3 .....46 D1
Mulberry Ave SL4 .....210 F5

Mulberry Cl
 Amersham HP7 .....165 F8
 High Wycombe HP12 .....172 C5
 Tring HP23 .....119 A5
Mulberry Ct HP15 .....163 D7
Mulberry Dr SL3 .....206 E1
Mulberry Wlk SL6 .....202 C8
Mullen Ave MK14 .....34 F4
Mullins Way HP19 .....100 E2
Mullion Pl MK6 .....35 A1
Mumfords La SL9 .....188 A7
Munces Rd SL7 .....183 D6
Munday's Farm HP21 .....116 B7
Mundaydean La SL7 .....183 B4
Mundesley Spur SL1 .....205 E7
Murcott Rd OX6 .....94 D6
Murray Rd HP4 .....135 C6
Murrey Cl MK5 .....46 C5
Murrin Rd SL6 .....202 C8
Mursley CE Sch MK17 .....67 D6
Mursley Ct MK11 .....32 F5
Mursley Rd
 Little Horwood MK17 .....55 E2
 Swanbourne MK17 .....67 B3
Mus of Eton Life The★
 SL4 .....210 D8
Museum Ct 9 HP23 .....119 A3
Musgrave Rd OX39 .....147 D7
Musgrave Wlk HP14 .....158 F5
Musgrove Pl MK5 .....45 F6
Myddleton Dr UB8 .....201 C4
Mylne Cl HP13 .....172 F4
Mynchen Cl HP9 .....175 D6
Mynchen End HP9 .....175 D6
Mynchen Rd HP9 .....175 D6
Myrke The SL3 .....205 F2
Myrtle Bank MK12 .....33 E5
Myrtle Cl Poyle SL3 .....212 E5
 Uxbridge UB8 .....208 F8
 West Drayton UB7 .....208 F8
Myrtle Cres SL2 .....205 F5

N

Nag's Head La HP16 .....152 A4
Nailzee Cl SL9 .....188 E4
Nairdwood Cl HP16 .....151 E4
Nairdwood La HP16 .....151 D5
Nairdwood Way HP16 .....151 E4
Nairn Cl MK3 .....46 E2
Naisby Dr MK17 .....59 C1
Nalders Rd HP5 .....144 D2
Nan Aires HP22 .....89 A3
Nancy Hall Ct HP12 .....172 D3
Naphill & Walters Ash Sch
 HP14 .....150 B1
Naphill Pl MK13 .....34 C3
Napier Cl UB7 .....208 F3
Napier Rd
 Aylesbury HP19 .....114 F8
 Harmondsworth TW6 .....213 D6
 Maidenhead SL6 .....202 B6
Napier St MK2 .....58 D8
Nappin Cl HP19 .....101 A3
Nappins Cl HP18 .....125 D5
Narbeth Dr HP20 .....116 B8
Narcot La
 Chalfont St Giles HP8 .....177 B5
 Chalfont St Peter HP8 .....177 B5
Narcot Rd HP8 .....177 A7
Narcot Way HP8 .....177 B6
Narrow La HP13 .....161 E3
Narrow Path MK17 .....49 B3
Naseby Cl
 Newport Pagnell MK16 .....22 A3
 Thame OX9 .....126 B1
Naseby Ct
 Buckingham MK18 .....41 E2
 Milton Keynes MK13 .....34 B6
Nash Cl HP21 .....116 A4
Nash Croft MK4 .....57 B8
Nash Lee End HP22 .....130 F6
Nash Lee La HP22 .....130 E6
Nash Lee Rd
 Nash Lee HP22 .....130 D6
 World's End HP22 .....130 D7
Nash Pl HP10 .....163 B1
Nash Rd
 Great Horwood MK17 .....55 A4
 Slough SL3 .....207 A3
 Thornborough MK18 .....54 B8
 Whaddon MK17 .....45 A1
Nashdom SL1 .....196 F5
Nashdom La SL1 .....197 B6
Nashleigh Hill HP5 .....144 D3
Nashleigh Ho HP5 .....144 D3
Nashs Farm HP22 .....88 D4
Nathanial Cl MK5 .....46 B5
Nathaniel Wlk HP23 .....119 A5
National Badminton Ctr
 MK8 .....34 A1
National Bowl The★
 MK6 .....46 E5
National Film & Television
 Sch HP9 .....175 E1
National Hockey Stad
 MK9 .....34 C1
Natwoke Cl HP16 .....175 D5
Neal Cl SL9 .....189 B3
Neale Cl HP12 .....172 D3
Neapland MK6 .....47 B5
Near Town MK46 .....7 A4
Near Town Gdns MK46 .....7 A3
Nearton End MK17 .....67 A3
Neath Cres MK3 .....47 A2
Neath Hill Rdbt MK15 .....35 A6
Needham Cl SL4 .....209 E6

Needham Ct 4 HP11 .....172 F7
Neild Way WD3 .....167 F2
Neilson Ct MK7 .....48 C5
Nelson Cl
 High Wycombe HP13 .....173 F5
 Milton Keynes MK8 .....45 E6
 Slough SL3 .....206 D2
 Winchmore Hill HP7 .....164 C3
Nelson Ct MK18 .....52 C8
Nelson Rd Dagnall HP4 .....107 C5
 Harmondsworth TW6 .....213 F6
 Windsor SL4 .....209 F4
Nelson St MK18 .....52 C8
Nelson Terr HP20 .....115 D8
Nene Ct Aylesbury HP21 .....115 C4
 Newport Pagnell MK16 .....22 D3
Nene Dr MK3 .....57 E8
Neptune Way SL1 .....204 E4
Ness Way MK2 .....58 D5
Nether Cl NN13 .....38 A7
Nether Gr MK5 .....46 B3
Nether Winchendon Ho★
 HP18 .....112 E5
Netherby Cl HP23 .....119 C6
Nethercote La OX49 .....157 A8
Netherfield Rdbt MK6 .....47 C7
Netherwood Rd HP9 .....175 D5
Netley Cl MK8 .....36 A1
Nettlecombe MK4 .....46 C3
Nettleden Rd HP4 .....121 E4
Nettleton Rd UB10 .....201 F8
Neve Ho SL6 .....202 F8
Nevill Cl MK19 .....11 B2
Neville Cl SL2 .....198 F6
Neville Ct SL1 .....197 C2
Nevis Cl LU7 .....80 C7
Nevis Gr MK2 .....58 E4
New Bradwell Comb Sch
 MK13 .....33 F7
New Chapter Comb sch
 MK6 .....47 A5
New Chilterns HP7 .....165 E8
New Cl RG9 .....192 A8
New Coll SL1 .....51 F8
New College Ct MK18 .....41 B4
New Cotts RG9 .....180 C1
New Ct
 High Wycombe HP13 .....173 C6
 Marlow SL7 .....183 D2
New Dr HP13 .....173 E8
New Garden Dr UB7 .....208 E4
New Hall Cl HP3 .....146 A4
New Horton Manor SL3 212 A4
New Inn La SL1 .....51 F4
New Mdw HP21 .....116 C7
New Mill Terr HP23 .....119 B6
New Par
 Chorleywood WD3 .....167 C5
 West Drayton UB7 .....208 E5
New Peachey La UB8 .....208 D8
New Pond Rd HP15 .....163 C7
New Provident Pl 5
 HP4 .....135 D4
New Rd Amersham HP6 .....154 E2
 Aston Clinton HP22 .....117 E5
 Berkhamsted HP4 .....135 D6
 Berkhamsted,Northchurch
 HP4 .....134 F7
 Bolter End HP14 .....170 F6
 Bourne End SL8 .....185 B4
 Castlethorpe MK19 .....19 F5
 Chipperfield WD4 .....146 F1
 Coleshill HP7 .....164 F4
 Cookham Rise SL6 .....195 F7
 Datchet SL3 .....211 D6
 Dinton HP17 .....113 E2
 Drayton Parslow MK17 .....68 C5
 Great Kingshill HP15 .....162 D8
 Harrold MK43 .....3 E6
 High Wycombe HP12 .....172 C5
 Hurley SL6 .....193 F3
 Leighton Buzzard LU7 .....80 E7
 Little Chalfont HP8 .....166 F6
 Little Kingshill HP16 .....152 B4
 Marlow Bottom SL7 .....183 D6
 Naphill HP14 .....150 A2
 Prestwood HP16 .....151 D6
 Princes Risborough HP27 .....139 C3
 Sarratt HP8 .....156 F1
 Slough SL3 .....207 A3
 Stokenchurch HP14 .....158 F4
 Tring HP23 .....119 B6
 Tylers Green HP10 .....163 C1
 Weedon HP22 .....101 B8
 Weston Turville HP22 .....116 E5
 Wilstone HP23 .....118 D8
New Road Cl HP12 .....172 C6
New Road Gdns HP12 .....172 C6
New Row Hoggeston MK18 77 B7
 Lavendon MK46 .....7 E8
New Sq SL1 .....205 F4
New St Aylesbury HP20 .....101 D1
 Berkhamsted HP4 .....135 D4
 Cheddington LU7 .....104 F7
 Henley-on-T RG9 .....191 E2
 Milton Keynes MK11 .....32 D5
 Tingewick MK18 .....51 B6
 Waddesdon HP18 .....99 A7
New Windsor St UB8 .....201 C4
New Zealand Cotts HP22 88 E4
New Zealand Gdns LU7 .....79 E2
Newark Ct MK7 .....48 A3
Newbarn La HP9 .....176 E6
Newberry Cres SL4 .....209 D5
Newbery Way SL1 .....205 D4
Newbolt Cl
 Newport Pagnell MK16 .....21 F5
 Paulerspury NN12 .....17 B8

Newbridge Oval MK4 .....46 B3
Newbury Ct MK3 .....57 D6
Newbury Dr SL6 .....203 B6
Newbury Rd MK7 .....213 F6
Newby Pl MK4 .....46 B2
Newchurch Rd SL2 .....204 F8
Newcombe Rise UB7 .....208 E7
Newcourt UB8 .....208 C8
Newcroft Cl UB8 .....208 F8
Newell Cl HP21 .....116 A6
Newells Hedge LU7 .....105 D5
Newfield Gdns SL7 .....183 F3
Newfield Rd SL7 .....183 F3
Newfield Way SL7 .....183 F2
Newground Rd HP23 .....120 B3
Newhaven Spur SL2 .....198 B1
Newhouse Rd HP3 .....146 A4
Newland Ho UB8 .....201 C4
Newlands Dr
 Maidenhead SL6 .....202 A7
 Poyle SL3 .....212 A4
Newlands Girls Sch SL6 202 A7
Newlyn Pl MK6 .....35 A2
Newmans Cl MK13 .....21 E1
Newmans Ctyd MK17 .....68 C6
Newmarket St MK10 .....36 C2
Newmer Pl MK12 .....172 B3
Newport Pagnell Rd
 MK43 .....16 C4
Newport Rd
 Astwood MK16 .....15 C2
 Emberton MK46 .....13 F6
 Hanslope MK19 .....11 B2
 Milton Keynes MK10 .....36 D1
 Milton Keynes,New Bradwell
 MK13 .....34 A8
 Milton Keynes,Oakgrove
 MK15 .....35 C5
 Milton Keynes,Willen MK15 .....35 D7
 Milton Keynes,Woughton on t G
 MK6 .....35 D1
 Moulsoe MK16 .....36 C7
 Slough SL2 .....197 E1
 Wavendon MK17 .....48 E7
 Woburn MK17 .....60 D8
 Woughton On T G MK6 .....47 D8
 Woughton Park MK6 .....47 D6
Newquay Cl MK4 .....46 B2
Newton Blossomville CE Fst
 Sch MK43 .....8 B4
Newton Cl SL3 .....206 F4
Newton Ct SL4 .....211 A1
Newton Longville CE Comb
 Sch MK17 .....57 D3
Newton Rd
 Drayton Parslow MK17 .....68 C5
 Milton Keynes MK3 .....57 E6
 Stoke Hammond MK17 .....69 D8
 Turvey MK43 .....8 E5
Newton Side Orch SL4 211 A1
Newton St MK46 .....7 A4
Newtonside SL4 .....211 A1
Newtown Inf Sch HP5 .....144 C2
Newtown Pk Marlow SL7 183 F3
 New Denham UB9 .....201 B6
Newville HP22 .....87 C1
Newyears Green La
 UB9 .....190 F5
Neyland Dr HP19 .....101 D3
Nicholas Gdns
 High Wycombe HP13 .....173 D8
 Slough SL1 .....204 E5
Nicholas Mead MK14 .....34 F8
Nicholas Winton Ct SL6 203 A8
Nicholls SL4 .....209 C4
Nicholls Wlk SL4 .....209 C4
Nicholson Gr MK8 .....45 E6
Nicholsons La SL6 .....202 F7
Nicholsons Shopping Ctr 2
 SL6 .....202 F7
Nickson Ct HP15 .....163 A3
Nicol Cl SL9 .....177 C2
Nicol End SL9 .....177 C2
Nicol Rd SL9 .....177 C2
Nielson Ct MK7 .....48 D5
Nigel Ct NN13 .....38 A5
Nightingale Cl
 Hazlemere HP15 .....163 B5
 Steeple Claydon MK18 .....63 E3
Nightingale Cres MK13 .....34 A7
Nightingale Ct
 1 High Wycombe HP13 .....173 B7
 6 Slough SL1 .....206 A3
Nightingale Ho HP21 .....174 A4
Nightingale La SL6 .....195 D3
Nightingale Lodge HP4 .....135 B4
Nightingale Pk SL2 .....197 F5
Nightingale Pl
 Buckingham MK18 .....41 E1
 Cookham Rise SL6 .....195 F7
Nightingale Rd
 Aylesbury HP21 .....115 E6
 2 Chesham HP5 .....144 B2
 Wendover HP22 .....131 B5
Nightingale Way SL4 .....189 F5
Nightingale Wlk SL4 .....210 C4
Nightingales Cnr HP7 .....166 C7
Nightingales Cl HP8 .....166 C7
Nightingales La HP8 .....166 C7
Nijinsky Ho UB8 .....201 D3
Nine Acres SL1 .....204 F5
Nine Elms Ave UB8 .....208 D8
Nine Elms Cl UB8 .....208 D8
Nine Stiles Cl UB9 .....201 B6
Ninnings Rd SL9 .....177 E3
Ninnings Way SL9 .....177 E3
Niplands Cotts HP10 .....185 D2

Nixey Cl SL1 .....206 A4
Nixons Cl MK6 .....46 E6
Noble Cl MK15 .....35 A7
Noble Ct SL2 .....205 F5
Noon Layer Dr MK10 .....35 E3
Norbrek MK8 .....33 E2
Norden Cl SL6 .....202 C4
Norden Mdws SL6 .....202 C5
Norden Rd SL6 .....202 C5
Norelands Dr SL1 .....197 C3
Norfolk Ave SL1 .....205 C8
Norfolk Ho 6 MK3 .....46 F1
Norfolk Park Cotts SL6 .....202 F8
Norfolk Rd
 Maidenhead SL6 .....202 F8
 Turvey MK43 .....8 E1
 Uxbridge UB8 .....201 D6
Norfolk Terr HP20 .....101 E1
Norgrove Pk SL9 .....188 E7
Norjo-An Villas HP5 .....154 C6
Norland Dr HP10 .....185 C8
Norman Ave RG9 .....191 E1
Norman Cres MK10 .....35 E3
Norman Way LU6 .....93 E8
Normandy Dr HP4 .....135 B6
Normandy Way MK3 .....46 E8
Normans Cl UB8 .....208 F8
Normans Ct 5 HP13 .....173 F6
Normans The SL2 .....206 B7
Normanstead RG9 .....191 D1
Normill Terr HP22 .....117 A6
Norreys Dr SL6 .....202 D4
Norris Ho SL6 .....202 E7
Norris Rd OX6 .....94 E8
North Burnham Cl SL1 .....197 B3
North Cl
 Drayton Parslow MK17 .....68 C5
 Medmenham SL7 .....193 D7
 Windsor SL4 .....209 F6
North Common Rd UB8 201 D7
North Cotts SL3 .....198 C2
North Crawley CE Fst Sch
 MK16 .....24 B6
North Crawley Rd MK16 .....23 C4
North Croft MK18 .....66 A4
North Dr Aylesbury HP21 .....115 E5
 Beaconsfield HP9 .....186 B8
 High Wycombe HP13 .....173 E8
North Eastern Rd HP19 .....101 C2
North Eighth St MK9 .....34 E3
North Elder Rdbt MK9 .....34 D2
North Eleventh St MK9 .....34 E3
North End Rd
 Quainton HP22 .....85 A5
 Steeple Claydon MK18 .....63 D3
North Fifth St MK9 .....34 E3
North Fourteenth St MK9 34 F4
North Fourth St MK9 .....34 D2
North Gate MK2 .....47 C1
North Gn
 3 Maidenhead SL6 .....195 F1
 Slough SL1 .....205 E6
North Grafton Rdbt
 MK13 .....34 C2
North Hill Dadford MK18 .....28 D2
 Sarratt WD3 .....167 E8
North Hills HP18 .....96 A1
North La MK7 .....47 C7
North Lee La
 North Lee HP22 .....130 A6
 Stoke Mandeville HP22 .....129 F7
North Links Rd HP18 .....96 A1
North Marston CE Comb Sch
 MK18 .....76 B2
North Marston La HP22 .....86 E7
North Mill Rd HP27 .....138 C3
North Ninth St MK9 .....34 E3
North Orbital Rd
 Denham Green UB9 .....189 F4
 Rickmansworth WD3 .....178 E7
North Overgate Rdbt
 MK15 .....35 B5
North Pk
 Gerrards Cross SL9 .....188 E8
 Iver SL0 .....207 D3
North Rd Amersham HP6 .....154 C3
 Berkhamsted HP4 .....135 B4
 Chorleywood WD3 .....167 D4
 Cryers Hill HP15 .....162 D5
 Maidenhead SL6 .....202 F7
 West Drayton UB7 .....208 F3
North Ridge MK6 .....35 B1
North Row Fulmer SL3 .....199 E8
 Milton Keynes MK9 .....34 C2
 Milton Keynes MK9 .....34 E3
North Saxon Rdbt MK14 .....34 D3
North Secklow Rdbt
 MK14 .....34 E3
North Second St MK9 .....34 C2
North Seventh St MK9 .....34 D2
North Sixth St MK9 .....34 D2
North Skeldon Rdbt MK9 35 A4
North Sq MK16 .....22 D5
North St
 Castlethorpe MK19 .....19 F5
 Milton Keynes,Bradville
 MK13 .....34 A7
 Milton Keynes,Fenny Stratford
 MK2 .....47 C1
 Thame OX9 .....125 F1
North Star La SL6 .....202 C6
North Tenth St MK9 .....34 E3
North Terr SL4 .....210 E7
North Third St MK9 .....34 C2
North Thirteenth St MK9 .....34 F3

North Town Cl 1 SL6 ... 195 F1
North Town Mead 4 SL6 ... 195 F1
North Town Moor SL6 ... 195 F1
North Town Rd SL6 ... 195 F1
North Twelfth St MK9 ... 34 F3
North View HP22 ... 87 B3
North Way
Deanshanger NN12 ... 31 E5
Potterspury NN12 ... 18 E2
Uxbridge UB10 ... 201 E5
North Witan Rdbt MK13 ... 34 D2
Northall Cl LU6 ... 92 D6
Northall Rd LU6 ... 92 D6
Northampton Ave SL1 ... 205 C7
Northampton Rd
Brackley NN13 ... 26 A1
Cosgrove MK19 ... 19 C1
Cosgrove MK19 ... 32 C8
Grafton Regis NN12 ... 9 C3
Lathbury MK16 ... 22 D6
Lavendon MK46 ... 7 F8
Yardley Hastings NN7 ... 1 A6
Northborough Rd SL2 ... 198 B1
Northbridge Rd HP4 ... 135 A6
Northchurch La HP5 ... 134 D2
Northchurch St Mary's CE Fst Sch HP4 ... 134 E6
Northcliffe LU6 ... 92 E6
Northcroft
Milton Keynes MK5 ... 46 C6
Slough SL2 ... 198 B1
Weedon HP22 ... 87 C1
Wooburn Green HP10 ... 185 F6
Northdean 5 SL6 ... 195 F1
Northdown Rd SL9 ... 177 E4
Northend MK46 ... 5 E3
Northend Cl HP10 ... 185 C7
Northend Ct MK18 ... 41 D1
Northend Sq MK18 ... 41 D1
Northend Workshops RG9 ... 168 E5
Northern Hts SL8 ... 185 B5
Northern Perimeter Rd (W) TW6 ... 213 D6
Northern Rd
Aylesbury HP19 ... 101 C2
Slough SL2 ... 198 D1
Northern Woods HP10 ... 185 C7
Northfield Ct HP9 ... 191 D3
Northfield Dr MK15 ... 35 F5
Northfield End RG9 ... 191 D3
Northfield Rd
Aylesbury HP20 ... 116 B8
Eton Wick SL4 ... 204 F2
Maidenhead SL6 ... 195 F1
Princes Risborough HP27 ... 139 C4
Tring HP23 ... 119 F7
Northfield Rdbt MK10 ... 36 A5
Northlands Rd MK18 ... 53 F1
Northleigh MK4 ... 46 D2
Northmead Rd SL2 ... 204 F8
Northmill HP27 ... 138 F3
Northolt Rd TW6 ... 213 E6
Northumberland Ave HP21 ... 116 B6
Northumberland Cl TW19 ... 213 E1
Northumbria Rd SL6 ... 202 B4
Northwich MK6 ... 47 D7
Northwood Rd TW6 ... 213 D6
Nortoft Rd SL9 ... 177 F5
Norton Leys MK7 ... 48 C7
Norton Rd UB8 ... 201 D2
Norton's Pl MK18 ... 52 C8
Nortons The MK7 ... 48 B3
Norvic Rd HP23 ... 105 A1
Norway Dr SL2 ... 206 B8
Norwich Ho
High Wycombe HP13 ... 173 F8
Maidenhead SL6 ... 202 E8
Norwood Cl HP20 ... 101 F2
Norwood Ct 4 HP7 ... 165 B7
Norwood La
Newport Pagnell MK16 ... 22 C3
Uxbridge SL0 ... 200 D1
Norwood Rd HP10 ... 174 B2
Notley Farm HP18 ... 126 A7
Nottingham Gr MK3 ... 46 E2
Nottingham Ho 3 HP13 ... 173 F7
Nottingham Rd WD3 ... 167 C1
Nova Lodge MK4 ... 46 B2
Novello Croft MK7 ... 48 D4
Nugent Ct Chesham HP5 ... 144 A3
Marlow SL7 ... 183 F3
Nuneham Gr MK4 ... 45 F3
Nup End Cl HP22 ... 89 B3
Nup End La HP22 ... 89 B3
Nurseries The LU6 ... 92 E6
Nursery Cl
Amersham HP7 ... 165 E8
Aylesbury HP21 ... 115 C5
Tylers Green HP10 ... 174 C8
Nursery Ct HP12 ... 172 D6
Nursery Dr HP14 ... 171 B5
Nursery Gdns
Milton Keynes MK13 ... 34 A4
Tring HP23 ... 119 B4
Nursery La Slough SL3 ... 206 D5
Tylers Green HP10 ... 174 C8
Nursery Pl SL4 ... 211 B1
Nursery Rd SL6 ... 204 B7
Nursery Way TW19 ... 211 D1
Nursery Waye UB8 ... 201 D4
Nursery Wlk SL7 ... 183 B1
Nutfield La HP11 ... 172 F8
Nuthatch 10 HP19 ... 101 F3
Nutkin Wlk UB10 ... 201 E5
Nutkins Way HP5 ... 144 C2
Nutmeg Cl MK7 ... 48 B5
Nye Way HP3 ... 146 A3

O

O'Grady Way HP19 ... 101 A3
O'Neill Rd MK8 ... 45 D6
Oak Barn Cl MK43 ... 25 A1
Oak Cres HP12 ... 172 C4
Oak Ct MK9 ... 34 E2
Oak Dr HP4 ... 135 D3
Oak End Dr SL0 ... 200 C3
Oak End Way
Chinnor OX39 ... 147 D5
Gerrards Cross SL9 ... 188 F6
Oak Farm Rare Breeds Pk★ HP22 ... 116 D8
Oak Field HP5 ... 144 B1
Oak Gn HP21 ... 115 C7
Oak Green Sch HP21 ... 115 C7
Oak La
Buckland Common HP23 ... 133 A2
Windsor SL4 ... 210 A6
Oak Lawn HP23 ... 119 A3
Oak Rd HP27 ... 139 C3
Oak St HP11 ... 173 C4
Oak Stubbs La SL6 ... 203 F4
Oak Tree Ave SL7 ... 183 D3
Oak Tree Cl SL7 ... 183 D3
Oak Tree Cotts HP18 ... 83 B5
Oak Tree Dr
Lane End HP14 ... 171 C5
Slough SL3 ... 207 B1
Oak Tree Rd SL7 ... 183 D4
Oak View HP15 ... 162 D8
Oakdene HP9 ... 175 E3
Oakdown Cres MK46 ... 6 F3
Oaken Gr SL6 ... 195 C1
Oaken Head MK4 ... 46 C2
Oakengrove HP16 ... 151 C5
Oakengrove Cl HP15 ... 163 C6
Oakengrove La HP15 ... 163 B3
Oakengrove Rd HP15 ... 163 A3
Oakeshott Ave HP14 ... 161 D6
Oakfield WD3 ... 167 F2
Oakfield Ave SL1 ... 205 B5
Oakfield Cl HP6 ... 154 C2
Oakfield Cnr HP6 ... 154 C2
Oakfield Fst Sch SL4 ... 210 B5
Oakfield Rd
Aylesbury HP20 ... 116 A8
Bourne End SL8 ... 185 A3
Oakgrove Rdbt MK10 ... 35 F2
Oakham Rise MK4 ... 45 E1
Oakhill Cl
Maple Cross WD3 ... 178 E6
Milton Keynes MK5 ... 45 E6
Oakhill Rd
Maple Cross WD3 ... 178 D6
Milton Keynes,Hazeley MK5 ... 45 D5
Milton Keynes,Shenley Church End MK5 ... 45 F6
Oakhill Rdbt MK5 ... 45 D5
Oakhurst SL6 ... 196 B4
Oakington Ave HP6 ... 166 E8
Oakland Way HP10 ... 174 A1
Oaklands HP4 ... 135 A4
Oaklands Ct HP6 ... 154 C1
Oakley HP10 ... 185 F7
Oakley CE Comb Sch HP18 ... 109 D4
Oakley Cres SL1 ... 205 E6
Oakley Gdns MK15 ... 35 B5
Oakley Green Rd SL4 ... 209 B5
Oakley La OX39 ... 147 B6
Oakley Rd Brill HP18 ... 110 A8
Chinnor OX39 ... 147 C6
Horton-cum-S OX33 ... 108 C5
Oakridge MK4 ... 46 E4
Oakridge Ct HP12 ... 172 D6
Oakridge Pl SL2 ... 198 C8
Oakridge Rd HP11 ... 172 E7
Oakridge Sch HP11 ... 172 E7
Oaks Rd TW19 ... 213 D2
Oaks The HP4 ... 135 A4
Oakside UB9 ... 201 B6
Oaktree Cl HP10 ... 163 B2
Oaktree Ct MK15 ... 35 C7
Oakview HP6 ... 153 D4
Oakway Amersham HP6 ... 154 B4
Winslow MK18 ... 66 A4
Oakwell Cl LU6 ... 93 F7
Oakwood
Berkhamsted HP4 ... 134 F3
Flackwell Heath HP10 ... 174 A2
Oakwood Dr MK2 ... 58 E7
Oat Cl HP21 ... 115 C3
Oatlands Dr SL1 ... 205 D7
Oban Ct SL1 ... 205 D4
Ockwells Rd SL6 ... 202 C2
Octagon Arc 10 HP11 ... 173 A7
Octagon Par 6 HP11 ... 173 A7
Octavian Dr MK13 ... 33 F5
Octavian Way NN13 ... 38 A7
Oddley La HP27 ... 148 D8
Odds Farm Est HP10 ... 186 B4
Odds Farm Pk★ HP10 ... 186 B4
Oddy Hill Tring HP23 ... 119 C3
Wigginton HP23 ... 119 C2
Odell Cl MK6 ... 47 C8
Odencroft Rd SL2 ... 198 A2
Odney La SL6 ... 196 B7
Offas La MK18 ... 66 B5
Ogilvie Rd HP12 ... 172 E7
Okeford Cl HP23 ... 118 F4
Okeford Dr HP23 ... 118 F4
Okeley La HP23 ... 118 E3
Old Airfield Ind Est HP23 ... 104 D6
Old Amersham Rd SL9 ... 189 B3
Old Bakery Ct SL0 ... 207 F7
Old Bakery The
Aston Abbotts HP22 ... 88 D5
Lane End HP14 ... 171 B4
Old Barn Cl MK18 ... 52 A4
Old Bix Rd RG9 ... 191 A6
Old Brewery Cl HP21 ... 115 E7
Old Burrs HP21 ... 115 D3
Old Chapel Cl HP17 ... 129 E3
Old Coach Dr HP11 ... 174 A4
Old Court Cl SL6 ... 202 B3
Old Dashwood Hill HP14 ... 159 F2
Old Dean HP3 ... 146 A4
Old End MK18 ... 53 B2
Old English Cl MK17 ... 44 C1
Old Farm LU7 ... 105 D4
Old Farm Cl
Beaconsfield HP9 ... 175 C5
Slapton LU7 ... 91 A3
Worminghall HP18 ... 123 E5
Old Farm Rd
High Wycombe HP13 ... 161 E2
West Drayton UB7 ... 208 D4
Old Ferry Dr TW19 ... 211 D1
Old Field Cl HP6 ... 166 E8
Old Fishery La HP1 ... 146 F8
Old Fives Ct SL1 ... 197 C2
Old Forge Cl
Maidenhead SL6 ... 203 A3
Tingewick MK18 ... 51 B6
Old Forge Gdns HP22 ... 102 B4
Old Forge Rd HP10 ... 174 C2
Old Forge The HP23 ... 104 B4
Old Gaol Mus★ MK18 ... 41 D1
Old Garden Ctr The HP27 ... 139 B3
Old Groveway MK6 ... 47 D5
Old Hardenwaye HP13 ... 162 E1
Old Heatherdene Cotts HP15 ... 162 D8
Old Horns La SL7 ... 172 A3
Old House Ct SL3 ... 206 D7
Old Kiln Rd
Flackwell Heath HP10 ... 185 A8
Tylers Green HP10 ... 163 C2
Old Linslade Rd LU7 ... 70 E3
Old Lodge Dr HP9 ... 175 E1
Old Luxters Farm Brewery★ RG9 ... 180 F7
Old Maltings The
Buckingham MK18 ... 52 C7
Thame OX9 ... 125 E1
Old Manor Cl
Askett HP27 ... 139 C7
Whaddon MK17 ... 45 B1
Old Manor Ct LU7 ... 78 E8
Old Marsh La SL6 ... 203 F4
Old Mead SL9 ... 177 E4
Old Meadow Cl HP4 ... 135 A2
Old Mews The MK46 ... 6 F4
Old Mill Cl HP17 ... 127 A6
Old Mill Furlong MK18 ... 66 A5
Old Mill Gdns 12 HP4 ... 135 D4
Old Mill La
Maidenhead SL6 ... 203 D4
Uxbridge UB8 ... 208 B8
Old Mill Pl TW19 ... 212 B1
Old Mill Rd UB9 ... 190 A1
Old Moor La HP10 ... 185 E8
Old Nursery Ct SL2 ... 187 C2
Old Oak Gdns HP4 ... 134 E7
Old Orch OX39 ... 137 E2
Old Orchard Mews 1 HP4 ... 135 C4
Old Orchards HP22 ... 102 A3
Old Oxford Rd HP14 ... 160 C1
Old Palace Ct SL3 ... 212 D6
Old Papermill Cl HP10 ... 185 E8
Old Plough Cl HP18 ... 112 B2
Old Post Office La 11 SL6 ... 202 F7
Old Rd LU7 ... 80 E7
Old Rectory La UB9 ... 189 E4
Old Risborough Rd HP22 ... 130 A8
Old Sax La HP5 ... 143 D4
Old School Cl
Halton HP22 ... 117 C1
Stokenchurch HP14 ... 158 E4
Old School Cotts HP5 ... 145 D5
Old School Ct
Buckingham MK18 ... 52 C8
Eaton Bray LU6 ... 92 E6
Old School La MK17 ... 69 E8
Old School La The MK18 ... 63 D3
Old School Rd UB8 ... 201 F1
Old School The HP10 ... 185 D4
Old Shire La WD3 ... 167 B3
Old Slade La SL0 ... 207 F2
Old Springfields MK18 ... 53 C2
Old Stable Yd MK19 ... 32 C7
Old Stable Yd The MK18 ... 65 F4
Old Station Cl MK18 ... 66 A5
Old Station La TW19 ... 212 A1
Old Station Way HP10 ... 185 E5
Old Stoke Rd HP21 ... 115 D6
Old Stratford Prim Sch MK19 ... 32 B6
Old Tan Yard Cl MK18 ... 65 F4
Old Town NN13 ... 38 A7
Old Town Cl HP9 ... 175 E1
Old Town Farm HP16 ... 152 A7
Old Uxbridge Rd WD3 ... 178 E3
Old Vicarage Way HP10 ... 185 D4
Old Watery La HP10 ... 185 E8
Old Windmill Way HP18 ... 125 C7
Old Wolverton Rd MK12 ... 33 C8
Oldacres SL6 ... 203 B7
Oldbrook Bvd MK6 ... 46 E8
Oldbrook Fst Sch MK6 ... 46 E8
Oldbury Gr HP9 ... 175 D5
Oldcastle Croft MK4 ... 46 A1
Olde Bell Cl MK17 ... 69 E7
Olde Bell La MK5 ... 46 A7
Oldershaw Mews SL6 ... 202 B8
Oldfield Prim Sch SL6 ... 203 B6
Oldfield Rd SL6 ... 203 B7
Oldfield Road Ind Est SL6 ... 203 B7
Oldhams Mdw 9 HP20 ... 101 F2
Oldhouse Cl HP11 ... 172 E3
Oldway La SL1 ... 204 D5
Oliffe Cl HP20 ... 101 D3
Oliffe Way HP20 ... 101 D3
Oliver Rd MK2 ... 58 C8
Oliver's Paddock SL7 ... 183 D5
Olivia Dr SL3 ... 206 F1
Olivier Way HP20 ... 116 A8
Olleberrie La WD4 ... 156 D7
Olney Fst Sch MK46 ... 6 E3
Olney Mid Sch MK46 ... 6 F5
Olney Rd Emberton MK46 ... 13 F8
Lavendon MK46 ... 7 E7
Olson Cotts HP14 ... 158 F4
Olympic Ho UB8 ... 201 F1
One Pin La SL2 ... 187 D1
One Tree La HP9 ... 175 E3
Onslow Ct MK7 ... 48 A4
Onslow Dr OX9 ... 126 B1
Onslow Gdns HP13 ... 173 E7
Onslow Mills UB7 ... 208 D6
Opal Ct SL3 ... 199 C1
Opal Dr MK15 ... 35 F4
Open University (Walton Hall) The MK7 ... 47 F7
Opendale Rd SL1 ... 204 B8
Oram Ct 3 SL7 ... 183 D2
Orbell Ct HP27 ... 139 B3
Orbison Ct MK8 ... 45 D7
Orchard Ave
Berkhamsted HP4 ... 135 A4
Slough SL1 ... 204 D8
Windsor SL4 ... 210 A6
Orchard Bglws SL2 ... 197 F5
Orchard Cl
15 Aylesbury HP20 ... 101 F3
Beaconsfield HP9 ... 175 D3
Chorleywood WD3 ... 167 D5
Cranfield MK43 ... 25 A1
Hughenden Valley HP14 ... 162 A7
Longwick HP27 ... 138 D7
Maidenhead SL6 ... 203 A3
Milton Keynes MK3 ... 57 F7
New Denham UB9 ... 201 B6
Newton Longville MK17 ... 57 C3
Oakley HP18 ... 109 D4
Stoke Mandeville HP22 ... 116 B1
Waddesdon HP18 ... 99 A7
Wendover HP22 ... 131 A5
Wingrave HP22 ... 89 B3
Yardley Gobion NN12 ... 18 F6
Orchard Ct
Aylesbury HP21 ... 115 F6
Bovingdon HP3 ... 146 A4
Harmondsworth TW6 ... 213 C7
Seer Green HP9 ... 176 C5
Orchard Dene MK18 ... 41 D1
Orchard Dr
Aston Clinton HP22 ... 117 E4
Chorleywood WD3 ... 167 D5
Hazelmere HP15 ... 163 A3
Leighton Buzzard LU7 ... 80 D6
Uxbridge UB8 ... 201 D1
Wooburn HP10 ... 185 D4
Orchard End
Edlesborough LU6 ... 92 E4
Hazelmere HP15 ... 163 B6
Orchard End Ave HP7 ... 165 F8
Orchard Gate SL2 ... 198 C7
Orchard Gr
Chalfont St Peter SL9 ... 177 C2
Flackwell Heath HP10 ... 185 B7
Maidenhead SL6 ... 202 C7
Orchard Ho
8 Bourne End SL8 ... 185 A4
Milton Keynes MK12 ... 33 D6
Orchard La
Amersham HP6 ... 154 D1
Harrold MK43 ... 3 F7
Prestwood HP16 ... 151 C6
Stewkley LU7 ... 78 E7
Orchard Leigh Villas HP5 ... 145 A4
Orchard Lodge SL1 ... 204 E5
Orchard Mews HP9 ... 176 D4
Orchard Mill SL8 ... 185 B1
Orchard Pk HP15 ... 163 C6
Orchard Pl
Monks Risborough HP27 ... 139 C5
Uxbridge UB8 ... 201 D5
Westbury NN13 ... 39 A4
Orchard Rd
Beaconsfield HP9 ... 175 F1
Chalfont St Giles HP8 ... 177 C8
Loudwater HP13 ... 174 A4
Old Windsor SL4 ... 211 B1
Seer Green HP9 ... 176 C5
Orchard Rise MK46 ... 6 F3
Orchard Row HP14 ... 171 A7
Orchard The
Aston Clinton HP22 ... 117 E5
Orchard The *continued*
Flackwell Heath HP10 ... 185 B7
Halton HP22 ... 131 C8
Hazelmere HP15 ... 163 A6
Hillesden MK18 ... 63 A7
Marlow SL7 ... 183 E3
Potterspury NN12 ... 18 C3
Walter's Ash HP14 ... 161 E6
Orchard View
Hillesden MK18 ... 63 B7
Uxbridge UB8 ... 201 D1
Orchard Way
Aylesbury HP20 ... 101 F2
Bovingdon HP3 ... 146 A3
Chinnor OX39 ... 147 C5
Cranfield MK43 ... 25 A1
East Claydon MK18 ... 74 E6
Eaton Bray LU6 ... 92 F5
Holmer Green HP15 ... 163 C6
North Crawley MK16 ... 24 A6
Pitstone LU7 ... 105 E4
Slough SL3 ... 206 F5
Stoke Goldington MK16 ... 12 B7
Wing LU7 ... 79 E2
Orchard Waye UB8 ... 201 D3
Orchard Wlk MK46 ... 7 F7
Orchards The
Eaton Bray LU6 ... 92 E7
Little Kingshill HP16 ... 152 A2
Slough SL3 ... 206 F5
Tring HP23 ... 118 F3
Orchardville SL1 ... 197 B1
Orchehill Ave SL9 ... 188 D7
Orchehill Ct SL9 ... 188 E6
Orchehill Rise SL9 ... 188 E6
Oregano Cl UB7 ... 208 F6
Orford Ct MK5 ... 46 B6
Oriel Cl MK12 ... 33 B6
Oriel Cotts MK18 ... 63 D2
Orkney Cl
Milton Keynes MK3 ... 46 F2
Stewkley LU7 ... 78 E8
Orkney Ct SL6 ... 196 E5
Ormesby Cl HP21 ... 116 A5
Ormond Rd OX9 ... 126 A1
Ormonde MK14 ... 34 D7
Ormsgill Ct MK13 ... 34 B5
Orne Gdns MK15 ... 35 A7
Orpington Gr MK5 ... 46 B4
Ortensia Dr MK7 ... 48 C7
Orwell Cl Aylesbury HP21 ... 115 D4
Newport Pagnell MK16 ... 21 F5
Windsor SL4 ... 210 D4
Orwell Dr HP21 ... 115 D4
Osborn Rd UB8 ... 201 C5
Osborn's Ct MK46 ... 6 F3
Osborne Ct SL4 ... 210 C5
Osborne Mews SL4 ... 210 C5
Osborne Rd SL4 ... 210 D4
Osborne St
Milton Keynes MK2 ... 58 C7
Slough SL1 ... 205 F4
Osborne Way HP23 ... 119 D1
Osbourne St MK12 ... 33 D6
Osier La MK5 ... 46 B4
Osier Way
Aylesbury HP20 ... 115 F8
Buckingham MK18 ... 52 C6
Osmington Pl HP23 ... 118 F4
Osney Rd SL6 ... 195 E2
Osprey Cl
Milton Keynes MK6 ... 47 B8
West Drayton UB7 ... 208 E4
Osprey The HP19 ... 101 E4
Osprey Wlk
Aylesbury HP19 ... 101 E4
Buckingham MK18 ... 52 F7
Osterley Cl MK16 ... 22 C3
Ostler Gate SL6 ... 195 C1
Ostlers Ct HP11 ... 174 A4
Ostlers La MK11 ... 32 D6
Otter Cl MK3 ... 46 D1
Otterburn Cres MK5 ... 45 D5
Otterfield Rd UB7 ... 208 E6
Otters Brook MK18 ... 52 E7
Otway Cl HP21 ... 115 E3
Oulton Cl HP21 ... 116 A5
Our Lady of Peace RC Inf Sch SL1 ... 204 C8
Our Lady of Peace RC Jun Sch SL1 ... 204 C8
Our Lady's RC Prim Sch HP6 ... 154 B4
Ousebank St MK16 ... 22 D5
Ousebank Way MK11 ... 32 D5
Ousedale Sch MK16 ... 22 B3
Ouseley Rd TW19 ... 211 D1
Outfield Rd SL9 ... 177 D3
Outlook Dr HP8 ... 177 D7
Ouzel Cl MK3 ... 46 E1
Oval The MK6 ... 46 E7
Oval Way SL9 ... 188 E7
Over Hampden HP16 ... 151 C7
Over The Misbourne UB9 ... 189 B5
Over The Misbourne Rd UB9 ... 189 C5
Overdale Rd HP5 ... 144 B3
Overdales HP15 ... 162 F3
Overend Cl MK13 ... 34 A4
Overgate MK6,MK9,MK14 ... 35 B4
Overhills MK46 ... 6 E4
Overn Ave MK18 ... 41 C1
Overn Cl MK18 ... 41 D1
Overn Cres MK18 ... 41 C1

240 Ove – Pie

Overshot Ho HP10 ....174 C2
Oversley Ct MK14 ......22 A1
Overstone Cl LU7 ......79 E2
Overstone Comb Sch
  LU7 ....79 E2
Overstrand HP22 ......117 E5
Overstreet MK15 ......35 A6
Overton Dr OX9 ......126 B1
Oville Ct MK5 ....46 B5
Oving Rd HP22 ....86 E7
Ovitts Cl MK18 ....66 A5
Owen Cl 4 SL3 ......206 F1
Owl 5 HP19 ....101 F3
Owlsears Cl HP9 ......175 D4
Oxendon Ct LU7 ....70 F1
Oxfield Cl HP4 ....135 A3
Oxfield Park Dr MK19 ...32 C7
Oxford & Cherwell Coll
  OX9 ....125 E1
Oxford Ave Burnham SL1 ..197 B3
  Slough SL1 ....204 F8
Oxford Gdns UB9 ......190 A1
Oxford Rd
  Aylesbury HP17,HP21 ..115 B7
  Denham UB9 ....189 D2
  Gerrards Cross SL9 ...188 D5
  High Wycombe HP11 ...173 A7
  Marlow SL7 ....183 D2
  Oakley HP18 ....109 D5
  Piddington HP14 ......160 D1
  Stokenchurch HP14 ...158 A5
  Stone HP17 ....114 C5
  Thame OX9 ....125 E1
  Uxbridge SL8,UB9 ....201 B6
  Windsor SL4 ....210 A6
Oxford Rd E SL4 ......210 C6
Oxford St
  5 High Wycombe HP11 .173 A7
  Lee Common HP16 .....142 D5
  Milton Keynes,Fenny Stratford
  MK2 ....58 C8
  Milton Keynes,Stony Stratford
  MK11 ....32 D5
  Milton Keynes,Wolverton
  MK12 ....33 D6
Oxhouse Ct MK5 ....46 A3
Oxley Park Rdbt MK5 ...45 F3
Oxleys MK46 ....6 E4
Oxman La MK12 ....33 A5
Oxwich Gr MK4 ....57 B8

P

Pack & Prime La RG9 ..191 C2
Packet Boat La UB8 ....208 C7
Packhorse Rd SL9 ....188 E6
Padbury CE Sch MK18 ..53 C2
Padbury Oaks LU7 ....213 B6
Padcroft Rd UB7 ......208 D5
Paddock Cl
  Maidenhead SL6 ......202 A2
  Milton Keynes MK14 ...34 E8
Paddock Cotts SL6 ....202 A2
Paddock The
  Aylesbury HP21 ......116 C7
  Chalfont St Peter SL9 ..177 C5
  Datchet SL3 ....211 B6
  Emberton MK46 ....13 F8
  Maidenhead SL6 ......195 C2
  Maids Moreton MK18 ..41 E4
Paddock Way MK2 ......47 D1
Paddocks End HP9 ....176 C4
Paddocks Hospl The
  HP27 ....139 C4
Paddocks The
  Chorleywood WD3 ....167 F5
  Flackwell Heath HP10 ..185 B8
  Haddenham HP17 ......127 A5
  High Wycombe HP12 ..172 B3
  Leighton Buzzard LU7 ..80 F8
  Prestwood HP16 ......151 C5
  Steeple Claydon MK18 ..63 E3
  Wendover HP22 ......131 B5
Padstow Ave MK6 ......34 F1
Padstow Cl
  Aylesbury HP20 ......101 F1
  Slough SL3 ....206 E3
Page Hill Ave MK18 ....41 E1
Pages Croft HP4 ......135 A6
Pages La UB8 ....201 C6
Pages Wharf SL6 ......203 C8
Paget Cl SL7 ....183 F4
Paget Ct UB7 ....208 E4
Paget Dr SL6 ....202 A4
Paget Rd SL3 ....206 F2
Pagg's Ct MK16 ....22 D4
Pagoda Rdbt MK15 .....35 C5
Pagoda The SL6 ......196 B1
Paines Orch LU7 ......105 A8
Pakenham Cl HP19 ....114 F8
Palace Cl SL1 ....204 F5
Palace Sq MK6 ....46 F7
Palliser Rd HP8 ......177 B6
Palmer Ave
  Aylesbury HP19 ......115 C8
  Upper Arncott OX25 ...94 F8
Palmer's Moor La SL0 .201 A1
Palmers Cl SL6 ......202 A3
Palmers Moor MK18 ...54 A8
Palmers Rd MK46 ......7 A3
Palmerston Ave SL3 ..206 B3
Panleigh Cotts HP14 ..171 B3
Pannier Pl MK14 ......35 A5

Panters Cl MK17 ......44 C1
Pantile Row SL3 ......207 A2
Pantile Wlk UB8 ......201 C5
Paprika Ct MK7 ....48 B5
Parade Ct 7 SL8 ....185 A4
Parade The
  Bourne End SL8 ......185 A3
  Farnham Common SL2 ..198 C6
  High Wycombe HP11 ..172 F6
  Uxbridge UB8 ....208 C8
  Windsor SL4 ....209 D6
Paradise MK17 ....57 D4
Paradise Mews RG9 ..191 D2
Paradise Rd RG9 ......191 C1
Parchment Cl HP6 ....154 E2
Parish La SL2 ....187 C1
Parish Piece HP15 ....163 C7
Park Ave
  Newport Pagnell MK16 .22 B4
  Totternhoe LU6 ....93 B8
  Wraysbury TW19 .....211 D3
Park Cl Cosgrove MK19 .19 F2
  Dunton MK18 ....77 E5
  Lane End HP14 ....171 C5
  Windsor SL4 ....210 D5
Park Cnr SL4 ....209 E4
Park Ct UB8 ....201 D4
Park Farm Rd HP12 ...161 B1
Park Farm Way HP14 ..171 C5
Park Gate LU7 ....79 E1
Park Gdns MK3 ....47 A1
Park Gr HP8 ....166 D6
Park Hill OX33 ......122 B1
Park Ho
  Berkhamsted HP4 ....135 B5
  Gerrards Cross SL9 ...188 E7
  Maidenhead SL6 ......202 E6
Park House Dr MK5 ....45 F6
Park La Beaconsfield HP9 .175 F1
  Burnham SL1 ....197 E4
  Eaton Bray LU6 ....92 D6
  Hazlemere HP15 ......163 A4
  Horton SL3 ....212 A4
  Lane End HP14 ......171 D5
  Maidensgrove RG9 ...179 D6
  Paulerspury NN12 .....17 B7
  Slough SL3 ....206 B3
  Stokenchurch HP14 ..158 E6
Park Lane Ct HP14 ...158 E5
Park Lawn SL2 ....198 C2
Park Mdw HP27 ......139 A3
Park Par SL2 ....198 C3
Park Parade Ctr The
  HP15 ....163 A5
Park Pl Amersham HP6 .154 F1
  Seer Green HP9 ......176 D5
Park Rd Amersham HP6 .154 F2
  Chesham HP5 ....154 B8
  Farnham Royal SL2 ...198 E3
  Granborough MK18 ....75 F6
  Grendon Underwood HP18 .82 F8
  Hanslope MK19 ....11 B1
  Hartwell NN7 ....10 C8
  Henley-on-T RG9 .....191 E1
  Milton Keynes MK11 ...32 D5
  Sherington MK16 ......14 A2
  Stanwell TW19 ......213 C1
  Tring HP23 ....118 F2
  Uxbridge UB8 ....201 E6
  Winslow MK18 ....65 F5
Park Rd E UB10 ......201 D3
Park Rd S MK18 ......65 F4
Park Rise HP4 ....134 E6
Park St Aylesbury HP20 .115 F8
  Berkhamsted HP4 ....135 B5
  High Wycombe HP11 ..173 D6
  Maidenhead SL6 ......202 F7
  Poyle SL3 ....212 D6
  Princes Risborough HP27 .139 B3
  Slough SL1 ....205 F4
  Tring HP23 ....119 A3
  Windsor SL4 ....210 D6
  Woburn MK17 ....60 F7
Park Street Ind Est
  HP20 ....115 F8
Park View
  Newport Pagnell MK16 .22 D4
  West Drayton UB7 ....208 E6
Park View Ct
  Berkhamsted HP4 ....135 B4
  High Wycombe HP12 ..172 D8
  4 Leighton Buzzard LU7 .80 E7
Park View Rd
  Berkhamsted HP4 ....135 B4
  Uxbridge UB8 ....208 F7
Parker Cl MK13 ....34 A6
Parker Knoll Way HP13 .173 A7
Parker Wlk HP19 ......101 D3
Parkfield WD3 ....167 F5
Parkgate SL7 ....197 C1
Parkhouse Bsns Ctr
  HP12 ....172 E8
Parkland Ave SL3 ....206 D2
Parklands MK11 ....21 D1
Parkminster MK10 .....36 A1
Parkside
  Gerrards Cross SL9 ...188 F7
  Henley-on-T RG9 .....191 C2
  Maidenhead SL6 ......195 D1
  Milton Keynes MK4 ...46 E3
  Naphill HP14 ....150 B1
Parkside Wlk SL1 ....206 A3
Parkstone Lodge SL3 .206 A3
Parkview
  Flackwell Heath HP10 .185 B7
  Maidenhead SL6 ......202 E4

Parkview Chase SL1 ...204 E7
Parkway
  Bow Brickhill MK17 ....48 D2
  Marlow SL7 ....184 A3
  Woburn Sands MK17 ...49 A6
Parkway The SL0 ......200 C4
Parkwood HP14 ......150 A2
Parlaunt Park Prim Sch
  SL3 ....207 B3
Parlaunt Rd SL3 ......207 B2
Parliament Cl HP16 ...151 B7
Parliament La SL6,SL1 .196 F5
Parliament Rd OX9 ...125 F1
Parmiter Rd HP19 ....115 B8
Parmoor La RG9 ......170 E1
Parneleys MK10 ....35 F2
Parrot Cl HP21 ......115 B6
Parrock La MK10 ......36 A3
Parrott's La HP23 ....133 A6
Parrs Rd HP14 ......158 E4
Parry Cotts SL4 ......177 E6
Parry Gn S SL3 ......207 A2
Parry Green N SL3 ...206 F2
Parsley Cl
  Aston Clinton HP22 ...117 C5
  Walton MK7 ....48 B5
Parslow Cl HP21 ....115 D3
Parslow Ct HP21 ....115 D3
Parson Cl MK18 ......65 F4
Parson's Fee HP20 ...115 D8
Parson's Wood La SL2 .198 D5
Parsonage Cl
  High Wycombe HP13 ..173 C6
  Tring HP23 ....119 A4
Parsonage Ct 1 HP23 .119 A3
Parsonage Farm HP22 .89 B3
Parsonage Gdns SL7 .183 E1
Parsonage La
  Farnham Common SL2 .198 D5
  Windsor SL4 ....210 A6
Parsonage Pl HP7 ...165 C8
Parsonage Rd HP8 ...177 B7
Parsons Cl LU7 ......78 E8
Parsons Cres MK5 ....46 C5
Parsons La HP22 .....102 B3
Parsons Rd SL3 ......206 F1
Parsons Wlk HP15 ...163 C6
Parton Rd HP22 ......131 A5
Parton Rd HP20 ......116 B3
Partridge Cl
  Buckingham MK18 .....52 F7
  Chesham HP5 ....144 E3
Partridge Mead SL6 ..195 E3
Partridge Piece MK43 ..25 C3
Partridge Way
  7 Aylesbury HP19 ....101 F3
  High Wycombe HP13 ..161 C2
Pascal Dr MK5 ....45 E5
Pascomb Rd LU6 ......93 F8
Passalewe La MK7 ....48 D7
Passmore MK6 ....47 A8
Pastern Pl MK14 ......35 A5
Pastures The
  Aylesbury HP20 ......102 B2
  Edlesborough LU6 .....92 F3
  High Wycombe HP13 ..161 E1
Patch Cl SL6 ....201 F4
Patches Field SL7 ...183 E5
Pateman St SL6 ......195 F1
Paterson Rd HP21 ...115 C6
Patricia Cl SL1 ......204 E6
Patrick Haugh Rd OX25 .94 F7
Patrick Way HP21 ....116 A4
Patricks La MK17 .....31 F4
Patrington Cl UB8 ...201 C2
Patriot Dr MK13 ......34 B2
Patrons Dr UB9 ......189 F5
Patterson Ct HP10 ...185 E7
Patterson Rd HP5 ....144 B3
Pattison La MK15 .....35 C3
Paul's Row HP11 ....173 B6
Paulerspury CE Prim Sch
  NN12 ....17 B8
Pauls Hill HP10 ......174 F6
Pavers Ct HP21 ......115 D3
Pavilion Cl HP20 ....116 A8
Pavilion Way HP6 ...166 C8
Pavilions The UB8 ...201 C5
Paxton Ave SL1 ......205 C3
Paxton Cl MK46 ......6 F3
Paxton Cres MK5 ....46 B5
Paxton Rd HP4 ......135 D4
Paynes Ct MK18 ......41 D1
Paynes Dr MK5 ......46 A8
Paynes Field Cl HP4 .134 D7
Payton Hos SL6 ......195 E6
Pea La HP4 ....134 D7
Peace La SL6 ....195 F6
Peace Rd SLO,SL3 ...200 A3
Peachey Cl UB8 ......208 D7
Peachey La UB8 .....208 D8
Peacock Hay MK4 ....46 C2
Peacock Rd SL7 .....184 A3
Peacocks Cl HP4 ....134 F6
Pear Tree Ave UB7 ..208 F7
Pear Tree Cl
  Amersham HP7 ......165 F8
  Seer Green HP9 ......176 C4
Pear Tree Ct HP15 ...163 C6
Pearce Cl
  Aylesbury HP21 ......115 C4
  Maidenhead SL6 .....195 F1
Pearce Dr SL6 ......195 F1
Pearce Rd Chesham HP5 .144 B2
  Maidenhead SL6 .....195 F1
Pearce's Orch RG9 ..191 D3

Pearl Gdns SL1 ......205 B5
Pearse Gr MK7 ....48 A4
Pearson Cl HP19 .....115 B6
Peartree Cl SL1 ......204 F5
Peartrees UB7 ......208 D6
Peascod Pl 12 SL4 ..210 D6
Peascod St SL4 ......210 D6
Peascroft HP13 ......125 D6
Peatey Ct HP13 ......173 D6
Pebble Brook Sch HP21 115 C7
Pebble La
  Aylesbury HP20 ......115 C8
  Brackley NN13 ....38 A7
Pebblemoor LU6 ......92 F3
Peckover Ct 8 MK8 ..33 F1
Pecks Farm HP22 ...102 C4
Peddle Ct HP11 ......172 F7
Pednor Bottom HP5 ..143 B3
Pednor Rd HP5 ......143 E2
Pednormead End HP5 .154 E2
Peebles Pl MK3 ......46 F3
Peel Cl SL4 ....210 B4
Peel Ct
  Monks Risborough HP27 .139 B4
  Slough SL1 ....205 B8
Peel Rd MK13 ....33 C6
Peel Way UB8 ....208 C6
Peerless Dr UB9 ....190 C7
Peers Dr MK17 ......49 E3
Peers La MK5 ....46 B6
Peggs La HP22 ......117 F5
Pelham Ct SL6 ......202 E7
Pelham Pl MK14 ......34 F5
Pelham Rd OX9 ......126 B1
Pelton Ct MK5 ....46 C5
Pemberley Lodge SL4 .210 A4
Pemberton Cl HP21 ..115 F5
Pemberton Rd SL2 ..197 E1
Pembridge Chase 4
  HP3 ....146 A3
Pembridge Cl 3 HP3 .146 A3
Pembridge Gr MK4 ...45 E1
Pembridge Rd HP3 ...146 A3
Pembroke Ho
  2 Milton Keynes MK3 .46 E1
  Olney MK46 ....6 F3
Pembroke Rd HP20 ..101 F1
Pencarrow Pl MK6 ....35 A1
Pendeen Ct SL1 ......205 A5
Pendennis Ct MK4 ...57 A8
Pendles Paddocks HP14 158 F2
Pendrill Ho 2 HP12 ..172 E7
Penfold HP22 ....116 F2
Penfold Cotts HP15 ..163 D7
Penfold La
  Holmer Green HP15 ..163 E8
  Hyde Heath HP7,HP15 .152 F1
Pengelly Ct MK6 ......35 A1
Penhale Cl MK4 ......57 B8
Penhow Rise MK4 ....45 E1
Penina Ct MK3 ......46 D1
Penington Rd HP9 ...186 B8
Penlee Rise MK4 ....57 B8
Penley Ct OX39 ......147 B6
Penling Cl SL6 ......195 E6
Penmon Cl MK10 .....35 F1
Penmoor Cl HP12 ....172 C8
Penn Ave HP5 ......144 A1
Penn Bottom HP10 ...163 E1
Penn Cl
  Chorleywood WD3 ...167 D3
  Uxbridge UB8 ....201 D1
Penn Ct 14 Marlow SL7 .183 E2
  Tylers Green HP10 ...174 B8
Penn Dr UB9 ....189 F5
Penn Gaskell La SL9 .177 D1
Penn Gn HP9 ....175 D4
Penn Haven SL9 .....188 F6
Penn Mdw SL2 ......198 F4
Penn Rd Aylesbury HP21 .115 D7
  Beaconsfield HP9 ....175 D5
  Chalfont St Peter SL9 .177 D2
  Datchet SL3 ....211 D6
  Hazlemere HP15 .....163 B3
  Milton Keynes MK2 ...58 E8
  Slough SL2 ....198 D1
Penn Sch HP10 ......174 D7
Penn Street Works Ind Est
  HP7 ....164 A4
Penn Way WD3 ......167 D3
Penn Wood View HP7 .164 A4
Pennefather Ct 7 HP21 115 E7
Pennine Rd SL2 ......205 A8
Pennings The HP22 ..131 B5
Pennington Pl OX9 ..126 B1
Pennington Rd
  Chalfont St Peter SL9 .177 D3
  High Wycombe HP13 .173 B6
Penningtons The HP6 .154 E2
Pennycress Way MK16 .21 F4
Pennycuik MK17 ......59 C1
Pennylets Gn SL2 ...199 A5
Pennyroyal MK7 ......48 B7
Penrith Cl UB8 ......201 D5
Penrith Way HP21 ...116 B7
Penryn Ave MK6 ......35 A2
Penshurst Cl SL9 ...177 D1
Penshurst Rd SL6 ...202 D5
Pentewan Gate MK6 ..34 F2
Pentland Rd
  Aylesbury HP21 ......115 C6
  Slough SL2 ....205 A8
Pentlands MK11 ......32 F4
Pentlands HP13 ......174 A4
Pentlands The HP13 .174 A4
Penwith Fst Sch MK6 .34 F1

Penwood Ct SL6 ......202 B7
Penwood La SL7 ......183 C1
Penyston Rd SL6 ....202 C7
Penzance Spur SL2 ..198 B1
Peplar Way SL1 ......197 B2
Peplow Cl UB7 ......208 D5
Peppard Mdw HP16 ..151 D5
Pepper Hill Fst Sch
  MK13 ....34 A7
Peppett's Gn HP5 ....143 D8
Peppiatts The LU6 ....92 B5
Pepys Cl SL3 ....212 B8
Pepys Dr HP16 ......151 C6
Perch Cl SL7 ....194 C8
Perch Mdws HP22 ...131 B8
Percheron Pl MK14 ..34 F5
Percy Bush Rd UB7 ..208 F3
Percy Pl SL3 ....211 B6
Percy Terr HP8 ......177 A7
Peregrine HP19 ......101 E3
Peregrine Bsns Pk
  HP13 ....174 A5
Peregrine Cl MK6 ....47 B8
Perivale MK10 ....35 C1
Perks La HP16 ......151 C3
Permayne MK13 ......34 A7
Perracombe MK4 .....46 E3
Perran Ave MK6 ......35 A1
Perrin Springs La RG9 .170 F1
Perry Hill HP18 ......73 A3
Perry Ho SL1 ....197 B2
Perry La Bledlow HP27 .138 C2
  Sherington MK16 .....14 A2
Perry Mead LU6 ......92 E6
Perry St HP22 ......131 A5
Perrycroft SL4 ......209 F4
Perryfields Way SL1 .197 B1
Perryman Way SL2 ..197 C2
Perrys The HP22 .....116 C3
Pershore Croft 1 MK10 .36 A1
Perth Ave SL1 ......205 B7
Perth Cl MK3 ....46 F2
Perth Rd HP13 ......173 D8
Perth Trad Est SL1 ..205 B8
Peter's Cl 1 HP16 ...151 C6
Peter's Pl HP4 ......134 E6
Peterborough Ave 2
  HP13 ....173 C7
Peterborough Gate
  MK15 ....35 C6
Peterhead Mews SL3 .207 A1
Peterhill Cl SL9 ......177 E5
Peterley Ave HP15,HP16 151 E3
Peterley La HP16 ....151 E3
Peters La HP27 ......139 E4
Petersfield HP22 ....116 C3
Petersfield Ave SL2 ..206 A5
Petersham Cl MK16 ..22 C2
Pettifer Way HP17 ...172 D6
Pettingrew Cl MK7 ..48 B6
Petty Cross SL1 ......204 E7
Petworth MK8 ....33 E1
Petworth Ct SL4 ....210 B6
Petworth Ho 2 MK8 .33 F1
Pevensey Cl
  Aylesbury HP21 ......116 B5
  Milton Keynes MK3 ...57 E7
Pevensey Rd SL2 ....205 A8
Peverel Dr MK1 ......47 B3
Peveril Cl HP21 ......116 B5
Pevers La MK46 ......6 A1
Pheasant Cl
  Berkhamsted HP4 ...135 C3
  Tring HP23 ....119 B6
Pheasant Dr HP13 ...161 C1
Pheasant Hill HP8 ...177 C8
Pheasant Rise HP5 ..154 D6
Pheasant Wlk SL9 ...177 E6
Pheasants Croft SL6 .202 A4
Pheasants Dr HP15 ..163 B5
Pheasants Ridge SL7 .183 C7
Philbye Mews SL1 ...204 F4
Philip Cotts SL8 .....185 C3
Philip Dr HP10 ......185 C7
Philip Rd HP13 ......173 D7
Philips Rd HP19 ....115 A8
Philipshill Wood Nature
  Reserve* WD3 ......167 A2
Phillimore Cl MK15 ..35 B7
Phillip Ct MK5 ......46 B6
Philpots Cl UB7 .....208 D6
Philps Cl HP14 ......171 C4
Phipps Cl
  Aylesbury HP20 ......102 A2
  Maidenhead SL6 .....202 A2
Phipps Rd SL1 ......204 E8
Phoebe La MK17 .....48 E6
Phoebe's Orch MK17 .69 E7
Phoenix Bsns Ctr 3
  HP5 ....144 B1
Phoenix Ct SL6 ......202 D4
Phoenix Dr MK6 ......46 C6
Phoenix Ho 7 HP19 .115 A8
Phygtle The SL9 ....177 E4
Phyllis Court Dr RG9 .191 E3
Picasso Pl HP12 ....100 F2
Pickering Dr MK4 ...46 B2
Pickford Dr SL3 ....207 A5
Pickins Piece SL3 ...212 A5
Pickwick Terr SL2 ...206 B6
Picton St MK4 ....45 E1
Picts La HP27 ....139 A2
Piddington La HP14 .171 B8
Piddington Rd HP14 ..96 A8
Pield Heath House Sch
  UB8 ....201 F1
Pield Heath Rd UB8 .201 F1

Pierson Rd SL4 209 D6
Pigeon Farm Rd HP14 158 E5
Piggott's Hill HP14 150 E1
Piggotts End 6 HP7 165 B7
Piggotts Orch HP7 165 B7
Pightle Cres MK18 41 D2
Pightle The
Buckingham MK18 41 D1
Maids Moreton MK18 41 F4
Oving HP22 86 D7
Pitstone LU7 105 D3
Pigott Dr MK5 46 A5
Pigott Orch HP22 85 A5
Pike Cl Marlow SL7 194 C8
Uxbridge UB10 201 F4
Pike Cnr HP21 116 C5
Pilch La MK17 54 D4
Pilgrim St MK15 35 A4
Pilgrims Cl HP27 139 B5
Pilot Trad Est HP12 172 E8
Pimms Cl HP13 174 A6
Pimms Gr HP13 174 A5
Pimpernel Gr MK7 48 B6
Pinchfield WD3 178 D5
Pinders Croft MK12 33 B5
Pine Chase HP12 172 B3
Pine Cl Berkhamsted HP4 135 B4
Hazelmere HP15 163 B3
Maidenhead SL6 202 B7
Pine Crest Mews LU7 80 E6
Pine Ct HP5 154 C8
Pine Gr MK17 49 A4
Pine Hill HP15 162 F3
Pine Rd LU6 106 F8
Pine Trees Dr UB10 201 E8
Pine Wlk
Berkhamsted HP4 134 D7
Hazelmere HP15 163 B3
Pineapple Rd HP7 165 F8
Pinecroft SL7 183 D4
Pineham Rdbt MK15 35 E5
Pinels Way HP11 172 E3
Piner Cotts SL4 209 E4
Pines Cl Amersham HP6 154 B2
Little Kingshill HP16 152 B4
Pines The Felden HP3 146 F7
Slough SL3 206 F5
Tylers Green HP10 163 B1
Pinetree Cl SL9 177 C3
Pinewood Ave UB8 208 F7
Pinewood Cl
Gerrards Cross SL9 188 E4
Iver Heath SL0 200 C5
Pinewood Dr MK2 58 E7
Pinewood Film Studios
SL0 200 B5
Pinewood Gn SL0 200 C5
Pinewood Mews TW19 213 D1
Pinewood Rd
High Wycombe HP12 172 C7
Iver Heath SL0 200 B4
Pinfold MK7 48 B6
Pinfold Yd MK18 51 B6
Pinglestone Cl UB7 213 E7
Pinions Rd HP13 173 E5
Pink Hill HP27 149 E8
Pink La SL1 197 B3
Pink Rd HP27 149 E7
Pinkard Ct MK6 47 C8
Pinkneys Dr SL6 195 A1
Pinkneys Rd SL6 202 A8
Pinks Cl MK5 46 C8
Pinkworthy MK4 46 D4
Pinn Cl UB8 208 D7
Pinstone Way SL9 189 B2
Pintail Cl HP19 101 E4
Pipard MK14 34 E7
Pipers Cl SL1 197 C2
Pipers Corner Sch
HP15 162 B7
Pipers Croft LU6 93 F7
Pipers Ct SL1 197 C2
Pipers La HP15 162 C8
Pipers Wood Cotts HP7 153 C2
Pipit Gdns 7 HP19 101 E4
Pipit Wlk 6 HP19 101 E4
Pippin Cl MK16 22 B3
Pippins Cl UB7 208 D3
Pippins Sch SL3 212 F6
Pippins The SL3 206 F5
Pipston Gn MK7 48 B7
Pistone Windmill* LU7 105 F4
Pitch Pond Cl HP9 175 C5
Pitch The HP14 159 D3
Pitchcott Rd HP22 86 B6
Pitcher La MK5 46 B8
Pitcher Wlk HP19 115 A7
Pitchford Ave MK18 41 E2
Pitchford Wlk MK18 41 F1
Pitfield MK11 33 B3
Pitstone Common Forest
Trails* HP4 120 E7
Pitstone Green Farm Mus*
LU7 105 D4
Pitt Gn MK18 41 F1
Pitters Piece HP18 125 B7
Pitts Rd SL1 205 C5
Place Farm Ho HP27 139 B6
Place Farm Way HP27 139 B5
Plackett Way SL1 204 D5
Plaines Cl SL1 204 F5
Plaiters Cl HP23 119 B4
Plantain Ct MK7 48 B6
Plantation Pl MK5 46 A4
Plantation Rd
Amersham HP6 154 E2
High Wycombe HP13 174 A7
Leighton Buzzard LU7 70 F3
Plantation Way HP6 154 E2
Platt The HP7 165 B7
Playing Field Rd NN13 39 A4
Pleasant Cotts SL0 200 B2
Pleasant Pl WD3 178 E3
Pleasaunce The HP22 117 E5
Pleshey Cl MK5 46 B6
Plested Ct HP22 116 C2
Plomer Green Ave
HP13 161 D2
Plomer Green La HP13 161 D3
Plomer Hill HP13 161 D1
Plough Cl HP21 115 E3
Plough La Sarratt WD4 156 F6
Wexham Street SL2 199 B4
Ploughlees La SL1 205 E6
Ploughley Rd OX25 94 E8
Plover Cl
1 Berkhamsted HP4 135 C3
Buckingham MK18 52 E7
Newport Pagnell MK16 22 F3
Plover The 4 HP19 101 E4
Plover Wlk 3 HP19 101 E4
Plowman Cl MK12 33 B5
Plum Park La NN12 17 D8
Plumer Rd HP11 172 E7
Plumstead Ave MK13 34 D3
Pluto Cl SL1 204 E4
Plym Cl HP21 115 C5
Plymouth Gr MK4 46 B1
Plymouth Rd SL1 204 E8
Pocketts Yd SL6 196 B7
Pocock Ave UB7 208 F3
Pococks La SL4 205 E1
Poets Chase HP21 115 F6
Points The SL6 202 B3
Poles Hill Chesham HP5 144 A2
Sarratt WD4 156 E6
Police Hos SL9 189 B3
Polidoris La HP15 163 C7
Polish Ave HP22 131 E8
Pollard Ave UB9 189 F5
Pollard Cl SL4 211 B2
Pollards WD3 178 D5
Pollys Yd MK14 22 D5
Pollywick Rd HP23 119 D1
Polmartin Ct MK6 35 A1
Polruan Pl
Fishermead MK6 47 A8
Milton Keynes MK6 35 A1
Polygon Bsns Ctr SL3 212 F5
Pomander Cres MK7 48 B7
Pomeroy Cl HP7 165 D7
Pond App HP15 163 C7
Pond Cl
Newton Longville MK17 57 C2
Tring HP23 119 A4
Winchmore Hill HP7 164 C3
Pond Cotts HP14 171 B4
Pond La
Chalfont St Peter SL9 177 C2
Little Gaddesden HP4 121 E7
Pond Park Rd HP5 144 B2
Ponderosa Cvn Site
TW19 212 F3
Pondgate MK7 48 B8
Pondwicks HP7 165 B8
Pool La SL1 205 E6
Poolmans Rd SL4 209 D4
Pope Ct HP23 118 F3
Pope Way HP21 115 E4
Popes Acre HP17 126 F5
Popes Cl Amersham HP6 154 F2
Colnbrook SL3 212 C7
Popes La SL6 195 C7
Poplar Ave
Amersham HP7 165 F8
West Drayton UB7 208 F6
Poplar Cl Aylesbury HP20 102 A2
Chesham HP5 144 C3
Milton Keynes MK6 47 E5
Poyle SL3 212 E6
Poplar Ho SL3 206 F1
Poplar Rd
Aylesbury HP20 102 A2
New Denham UB9 201 C6
Wooburn Green HP10 185 E7
Poplars Cl HP17 114 C5
Poplars Gr SL6 196 B2
Poplars Rd MK18 52 D8
Poplars The HP22 131 C5
Poppy Rd HP27 139 A2
Porlock La MK4 46 C4
Port Field Farm MK16 21 F5
Portal Cl UB10 201 F5
Portal Rd HP22 131 D6
Portchester Ct 1 MK8 33 F1
Porter's Cl MK19 31 E4
Porters Way UB7 208 F4
Portfield Cl MK18 52 E8
Portfield Way MK18 52 E8
Portfields Comb Sch
MK16 22 A5
Portfields Rd MK16 22 B4
Porthcawl Gn MK3 57 C8
Porthleven Pl MK6 35 A2
Porthmellin Cl MK4 57 B8
Portishead Dr MK4 56 F8
Portland Bsns Ctr SL3 211 B6
Portland Cl SL2 197 D1
Portland Dr MK15 35 C7
Portland Gdns SL7 183 D1
Portland Ho HP13 173 D8
Portland Pk SL9 188 D5
Portlands Alley SL7 183 D1
Portlands Mews 1 SL7 183 D1
Portlock Rd SL6 202 C7
Portmarnock Cl MK3 57 D8
Portnall Pl MK43 25 B2
Portobello Cl HP5 144 A2
Portobello Cotts
Lacey Green HP27 149 E5
Lewknor OX49 157 C2
Portrush Cl MK3 57 D8
Portsmouth Ct SL1 205 E6
Portway
Milton Keynes,Bradwell Common
MK5,MK9,MK13,MK14,
MK15 34 D2
Milton Keynes,Shenley Church End
MK8,MK5 45 F6
North Marston MK18 76 B1
Stone HP17 114 E4
Portway Dr HP12 161 B1
Portway Rd Stone HP17 114 E4
Twyford MK18 62 D1
Portway Rdbt MK5 34 B1
Post Mdw SL0 200 D2
Post Office Cotts SL2 199 A5
Post Office La
Beaconsfield HP9 175 D3
Slough SL3 206 D7
Whitchurch HP22 87 A6
Posting Ho HP23 120 A5
Potash La HP23 104 A5
Potkiln La HP9 176 D1
Potter Row HP16 142 C1
Potters Cl HP16 151 B7
Potters Cross SL0 200 E2
Potters Cross Cres
HP15 162 E2
Potters Glen MK18 53 B1
Potters La MK11 33 B4
Potterspury Lodge Sch
NN12 18 B6
Pottery Cl HP19 115 A7
Pottery Ct HP19 115 A7
Potts Pl 8 SL7 183 D2
Poulcott TW19 211 E1
Pound Cl
Steeple Claydon MK18 63 D3
Wicken MK19 31 A4
Pound Cres SL7 183 C1
Pound Hill MK17 59 C1
Pound La Heath End HP5 134 A1
Little Marlow SL7 184 C4
Marlow SL7 183 D1
North Crawley MK16 24 B7
Preston Bissett MK18 51 C1
Pound St HP22 131 B4
Pound The Cookham SL6 196 A7
Cookham Rise SL6 195 F7
Slough SL1 197 D1
Syresham NN13 27 B7
Poundfield La SL6 195 F7
Poundfield Rd NN12 18 E2
Pounds Cl MK43 25 B1
Powell Haven MK10 35 E3
Powis Cl SL6 202 B4
Powis La MK4 45 F2
Powney Rd SL6 202 C7
Poyle 14 Trad Est SL3 212 E4
Poyle La SL1 197 B3
Poyle New Cotts SL3 212 F5
Poyle Pk SL3 212 E4
Poyle Rd SL3 212 E5
Poyle Tech Ctr The SL3 212 E5
Poynings The SL0 207 F2
Pratt Ho HP6 154 F1
Prebendal Ave HP21 115 D7
Prebendal Cl 11 HP20 115 D8
Prebendal Ct 1 HP20 115 D8
Precedent Dr MK13 34 B3
Precincts The SL1 197 C1
Prentice Gr MK5 46 B3
Prescott Rd SL3 212 E5
Prescotts The UB9 189 F3
Presley Way MK8 45 E7
Press Rd UB8 201 D6
Preston Ct MK15 35 B7
Preston Hill HP5 144 D2
Preston Rd SL2 206 C6
Prestwick Cl MK3 57 D7
Prestwold Ho HP19 115 A7
Prestwold Way HP19 115 A7
Prestwood SL2 206 B7
Prestwood Cl HP12 172 D8
Prestwood Inf Sch
HP16 151 C7
Prestwood Jun Sch
HP16 151 C6
Prestwood Lodge Sch
HP16 151 D5
Prestwood Pl HP16 151 C6
Pretoria Rd HP13 173 C8
Priestend OX9 125 E1
Priestland Gdns HP4 135 E6
Priestley Ct HP13 173 D6
Priests Paddock HP9 175 B5
Primatt Cres MK5 46 B6
Primrose Cotts HP14 150 E1
Primrose Ct HP21 115 B6
Primrose Dr
Aylesbury HP21 115 B5
West Drayton UB7 208 D2
Primrose Gn HP15 162 F6
Primrose Hill HP15 162 F7
Primrose Lea SL7 183 D2
Primrose Rd MK13 34 A4
Primrose Terr HP18 110 A8
Primrose Way MK18 52 C7
Prince Albert's Wlk
SL3,SL4 211 B5
Prince Andrew Cl SL6 203 B8
Prince Andrew Rd SL6 196 B1
Prince Consort Cotts
SL4 210 D5
Prince Consort's Dr SL4 210 B2
Prince Edward St HP4 135 C4
Prince Philip Ave MK43 24 D2
Prince's La HP16 142 D5
Prince's Rd HP21 115 E8
Princes Cl
Berkhamsted HP4 135 A6
Chilton HP18 111 B3
Eton Wick SL4 204 F1
Princes Ct
Bourne End SL8 185 C3
Leighton Buzzard LU7 80 F8
Princes Gate HP13 173 D6
Princes Gdns HP27 139 B3
Princes Pl HP27 139 B2
Princes Rd SL8 185 C3
Princes Risborough Prim Sch
HP27 139 B5
Princes Risborough Sch
HP27 139 C2
Princes Risborough Sta
HP27 138 F2
Princes St
Piddington HP14 160 B1
2 Slough SL1 206 B4
Princes Terr SL8 185 C3
Princes Way MK2 58 C8
Princes Way Rdbt MK2 58 B8
Princess Ave SL4 210 B4
Princess Margaret Hospl The
SL4 210 D5
Princess St SL6 202 F6
Printers End HP19 101 B1
Prior Gr HP5 144 C1
Priors Cl Maidenhead SL6 203 B2
5 Slough SL1 206 A3
Priors Pk MK4 46 D2
Priors Rd SL4 209 D4
Priors Way SL6 203 B2
Priors Way Ind Est SL6 203 B2
Priory Ave
High Wycombe HP13 173 B7
South Harefield UB9 190 C7
Priory Cl Aylesbury HP19 101 C2
Denham UB9 190 A1
Horton-cum-S OX33 108 B5
Newport Pagnell MK16 22 E4
South Harefield UB9 190 C7
Priory Common Fst Sch
MK13 34 B4
Priory Cotts UB9 190 C7
Priory Cres HP19 101 C2
Priory Ct 2 HP4 135 C4
Priory Farm Cotts OX27 71 E2
Priory Gdns
Berkhamsted HP4 135 C4
South Harefield UB9 190 C7
Priory Rd
Gerrards Cross SL9 188 D8
High Wycombe HP13 173 B7
Slough SL1 204 C8
Priory Sch SL1 204 D8
Priory St MK16 22 E4
Priory Way Datchet SL3 211 B7
Gerrards Cross SL9 188 D8
Harmondsworth UB7 213 E8
Pritchard Ct MK14 34 E8
Proctor Rise MK8 45 D6
Progress Bsns Ctr SL1 204 D7
Progress Rd HP12 172 B7
Promenade SL4 210 C7
Prospect Cl MK17 68 D6
Prospect Cotts HP14 161 D6
Prospect Ct
Lane End HP14 171 B5
Yardley Gobion NN12 18 F6
Prospect Pl
Castlethorpe MK19 19 F5
Hurley SL6 193 F3
3 Windsor SL4 210 D4
Wing LU7 79 E2
Prospect Rd Marlow SL7 183 D2
Milton Keynes MK11 32 C5
Protheroe Field MK7 48 D4
Providence Pl
9 Maidenhead SL6 202 F7
Milton Keynes MK13 34 A4
Providence Rd UB7 208 F5
Prudential Bldgs 1 SL1 205 F4
Pudseys Cl SL6 195 B6
Puers Field HP9 176 E4
Puers La HP9 176 E4
Puffin Way HP19 101 F3
Pulborough Cl MK3 46 D1
Pulford Rd LU7 80 F6
Pullfields HP5 144 A1
Pulpit Cl HP5 144 A2
Pulpit La HP22 76 D1
Pump La N SL7 183 F6
Pump La S SL7 184 A4
Pump Mdw HP16 152 A8
Pumpkin Hill SL1 197 E6
Pumpus Gn MK18 66 A4
Punch Bowl La HP5 154 C7
Purbeck MK13 34 C6
Purbeck Cl HP21 116 B5
Purcel Dr MK16 22 C3
Purse La MK16 11 F8
Pursers Ct SL1 205 E7
Pursell Cl SL6 202 A3
Pursell Pl HP27 139 B5
Pursells Mdw HP14 161 C7
Purton Ct SL2 198 C5
Purton La SL2 198 C5
Pury Rd Alderton NN12 9 A2
Paulerspury NN12 17 D8
Pusey Way HP14 171 C5
Putlowes Dr HP18 100 C3
Putman Ho MK5 46 C5
Putman Pl RG9 191 E1
Putnams Dr HP22 117 D5
Puttenham Ct HP23 103 F2
Puxley Rd MK19 31 D5
Pyebush La HP9 187 A8
Pyghtle The Olney MK46 6 F3
Turvey MK43 8 E6
Pyghtles The HP22 85 B5
Pyke Hayes MK8 33 D3
Pym Wlk OX9 125 F1
Pymcombe Cl HP27 139 B5
Pynefield Ho WD3 167 F2
Pyxe Ct MK7 48 A4

Q

Quadrangle The HP13 173 E7
Quadrans Cl MK15 35 A7
Quadrant The
High Wycombe HP13 162 E1
Maidenhead SL6 203 A6
Quainton CE Comb Sch
HP22 85 A5
Quainton Rd
North Marston MK18 76 A2
Waddesdon HP18 99 A7
Quainton Road Sta*
HP22 84 F2
Quaker's Mead HP22 116 F3
Quakers Mede HP17 127 A6
Quantock Cl SL3 207 A1
Quantock Cres MK4 46 D2
Quarrendon Ave HP19 101 B2
Quarrendon Rd HP7 165 E7
Quarrendon Upper Sch
HP19 101 C2
Quarry Cl HP18 125 C7
Quarry Ct LU7 105 D2
Quarry Green Cl MK19 31 B3
Quarry Rd LU7 105 D2
Quarry Wood Rd SL6,
SL7 195 A8
Quarrydale Dr SL7 183 F2
Quaves Rd SL3 206 C3
Quebec Rd HP13 173 E6
Queen Alexandra Rd
HP11 173 A6
Queen Anne Royal Free CE
Fst Sch The SL4 210 D4
Queen Anne St MK13 33 F7
Queen Anne's Ct 10 SL4 210 C6
Queen Anne's Rd SL4 210 C3
Queen Catherine Rd
MK18 63 E2
Queen Charlotte St 10
SL4 210 D6
Queen Cl RG9 191 E1
Queen Eleanor Combined
Sch MK11 32 F4
Queen Eleanor St MK11 32 E6
Queen Elizabeth's Wlk
SL4 210 F5
Queen Mother's Dr UB9 189 F5
Queen Sq 8 HP11 173 A7
Queen St Aylesbury HP20 116 A8
Henley-on-T RG9 191 E1
High Wycombe HP13 173 C7
Leighton Buzzard LU7 80 F8
Maidenhead SL6 202 F7
Milton Keynes MK11 32 E6
Piddington HP14 160 B1
Pitstone LU7 105 D4
Tring HP23 119 A3
Waddesdon HP18 98 F6
Queen Victoria Rd
HP11 173 B6
Queen Victoria's Wlk
SL4 210 F6
Queen's Acre SL4 210 D3
Queen's Cl SL4 211 A2
Queen's Ct SL1 205 F6
Queen's Dr SL3 199 F4
Queen's Dr The WD3 167 F2
Queen's Gate SL4 210 D3
Queen's La 12 SL6 202 F7
Queen's Pk HP21 115 F8
Queen's Rd Datchet SL3 211 B7
Marlow SL7 183 D2
Uxbridge UB8 201 C2
Windsor SL4 210 C5
Queen's Terr 5 SL4 210 D4
Queens Acre
High Wycombe HP13 173 D6
Windsor SL4 210 D3
Queens Acre Ho 6 SL4 210 D4
Queens Ave MK16 22 C4
Queens Cl OX9 125 F2
Queens Ct HP13 173 C6
Queens Mead HP21 116 C7
Queens Rd
Berkhamsted HP4 135 A5
1 Chesham HP5 144 C1
Eton Wick SL4 204 F1
High Wycombe HP13 173 C6
Princes Risborough HP27 139 C4
Slough SL1 205 F6
West Drayton UB7 208 F4
Queensbury La MK10 35 E1
Queensgate HP19 115 A8
Queensmead SL3 211 B6
Queensmead Ho HP10 174 C2

Queensmead Rd HP10 ....174 C2
Queensmere SL1 ......205 F4
Queensmere Rd SL1 ...205 F4
Queensway Bletchley MK2 .58 C8
　Hazelmere HP15 ....163 A4
　Maidenhead SL6 ....195 A4
　Milton Keynes MK2 .....58 D8
Queensway The SL9 ....188 D7
Quickberry Pl HP7 .....165 C8
Quickley La WD3 ....167 C3
Quickley Rise WD3 .....167 B3
Quickly Brow WD3 .....167 B3
Quill Hall La HP6 ......154 F2
Quilter Mdw MK7 ....48 D5
Quilters Way HP22 .....130 D8
Quinbrookes SL2 ....206 C2
Quince Cl MK7 ....48 B5
Quinton Dr MK13 ....34 B3
Quoiting Sq SL7 ....183 D2
Quoitings Dr SL7 ......183 C2
Quoitings Gdns SL7 ....183 C2

R

Raans Rd HP6 ....154 F1
Rabans Cl HP19 ....100 F1
Rabans La HP19 ....100 F1
Rabbs Mill Ho UB8 ....201 D3
Rabbsfarm Prim Sch
　UB7 ....208 E6
Rachels Way HP5 ......154 D5
Rackstraw Gr MK7 ......48 D5
Radcliffe Sch The MK12 .33 B6
Radcliffe St MK12 ......33 D6
Radclive Rd MK18 ......51 F7
Radcot Ave SL3 ....207 B3
Radcot Cl SL6 ....195 E3
Radcote Lodge MK8 .....33 E1
Radian Ct MK5 ....46 C7
Radman Gr MK13 ....33 B5
Radnage CE Inf Sch
　HP14 ....159 D6
Radnage Common Rd
　HP14 ....159 D5
Radnage La HP14 ......148 C2
Radnor Cl RG9 ....191 E2
Radnor End HP20 ......101 E2
Radnor Way SL3 ....206 E2
Radworthy MK4 ....46 C3
Raeside Cl HP9 ....176 C5
Raglan Ct MK5 ....45 E1
Ragmans Cl SL7 ....183 C8
Ragmans La HP10,SL7 .172 D1
Ragnall's La OX33 ....108 A6
Ragstone Rd SL1 ......205 E3
Ragstones HP10 ....174 A1
Railway Cotts
　Steeple Claydon MK18 ..64 A1
　Wigginton MK23 ......119 F5
Railway St ❷ HP7 ....115 E8
Railway Terr SL2 .....205 F5
Rainborough Gdns
　HP20 ....101 E2
Rainbow Rd HP6 ....46 F7
Rainbow Ind Est UB7 ..208 D6
Rainsborough MK14 ....35 A8
Rainsborough Chase
　SL6 ....202 B3
Rake Way HP21 ....115 D3
Raleigh Cl SL1 ....205 A5
Ralphs Retreat HP15 ..162 F4
Ralston Ct ❷ SL4 ....210 D6
Ram Alley MK16 ....12 B6
Rambler Cl SL6 ....204 B7
Rambler La SL3 ....206 C3
Ramsay Cl MK13 ....34 B3
Ramsay View HP15 ....163 A3
Ramscote La HP5 .....143 F7
Ramsey Ct SL2 ....197 D1
Ramsgill Ct MK13 .....34 C5
Ramsons Ave MK14 ....34 E4
Ramsthorn Gr MK7 .....48 B6
Ramworth Way HP21 ..116 A6
Randall Cl SL3 ......206 F1
Randall Ct SL4 ......211 A1
Randolph Cl MK13 .....34 A6
Randolph Rd SL3 .....206 A3
Ranelagh Gdns MK16 ..22 C2
Rangers Ct MK8 ....33 F1
Rannal Dr OX39 .....147 C6
Rannoch Cl MK2 ......58 D5
Rannock Gdns LU7 ....80 C7
Ranston Cl UB9 ......189 F5
Rashleigh Pl MK6 .....46 E7
Ratcliffe Cl UB8 .....201 D2
Rathbone Pl MK8 ......45 E7
Ravel Ct MK7 ....48 D6
Raven Cl ❸ HP19 ....101 F3
Raven Cres HP18 .....98 C6
Raven Rd HP14 ....158 F4
Ravens Ct
　Berkhamsted HP4 .....135 E6
　High Wycombe HP13 ..161 E3
　Long Marston HP23 ..104 B4
Ravens Field SL3 ....206 D4
Ravens La HP4 ....135 D4
Ravens Wharf HP4 ....135 D4
Ravensbourne Pl MK6 ..46 E7
Ravensbourne Rd HP21 115 D4
Ravenscar Ct MK4 ....46 C2
Ravenscourt SL7 .....183 D2
Ravenscroft Rd RG9 ..191 D2
Ravensglass Croft MK10 .36 B3
Ravenshoe Cl SL8 ....185 A3

Ravensmead
　Chalfont St Peter SL9 ..177 F5
　Chinnor OX39 ....147 C6
Ravenstone Mill Rd
　MK46 ....12 E7
Ravensworth Rd SL2 ..198 A2
Ravigill Pl MK12 .....33 D4
Rawcliffe Ho SL6 ....203 A6
Rawlings La HP9 .....176 D7
Rawlins Rd MK13 .....34 A4
Ray Dr SL6 ....203 B8
Ray Ho ❺ SL8 ....185 A4
Ray Lea Cl SL6 ......203 B8
Ray Lea Rd SL6 ......203 B8
Ray Lodge SL6 ....203 B7
Ray Lodge Mews SL6 .203 B7
Ray Mdw SL6 ....196 A1
Ray Mead Ct SL6 ....196 C1
Ray Mead Rd SL6 ....203 C8
Ray Mill Rd E SL6 ...196 B1
Ray Mill Rd W SL6 ..203 A8
Ray Park Ave SL6 ...203 B8
Ray Park La SL6 ....203 B7
Ray Park Rd SL6 ....203 B8
Ray St SL6 ....203 B7
Ray's Hill HP5 ......133 C2
Rayfield SL6 ....203 B8
Raylands Mead SL9 ..188 C6
Rayleigh Cl MK5 .....46 B6
Raylens HP12 ....172 B5
Raymond Cl SL3 .....212 E6
Raymond Rd
　Maidenhead SL6 .....202 D7
　Slough SL3 ....207 A3
Rayners Way HP10 ..174 B3
Rayners Cl Colnbrook SL3 212 C7
　Loudwater HP10 ....174 C3
Rayners La MK9 .....35 E1
Rays Ave SL4 ....209 F7
Rays La HP10 ......163 C4
Razzaq Pl HP12 ....172 E7
Read Dr HP22 ......102 C4
Read Ho HP19 ......115 A4
Reade Ct SL2 ......198 C6
Reading Cl HP19 ....101 A3
Reading Rd RG9 ....191 E1
Readings The WD3 ..167 F6
Reads La LU7 ......78 D1
Recreation Rd HP13 .173 C7
Rectory Ave HP13 ..173 C7
Rectory Cl
　Farnham Royal SL2 .198 C2
　Marsh Gibbon OX27 ..71 F3
　Slapton LU7 ....91 D6
　Windsor SL4 ......210 A6
Rectory Ct
　❷ Amersham HP7 ...165 B7
　❸ High Wycombe HP13 173 F5
　Lewknor OX49 .....157 B8
　West Drayton UB7 .208 E4
Rectory Dr HP18 ....99 A6
Rectory Fields MK15 .35 D3
Rectory Gdns HP8 ..177 B7
Rectory Hill HP7 ...165 B8
Rectory La
　Amersham HP7 .....165 B7
　Berkhamsted HP4 ..135 C4
　Bix RG9 ....179 D1
　Yardley Hastings NN7 ..1 A7
Rectory Mdw OX39 ..147 D6
Rectory Orch MK46 ..7 F8
Rectory Rd SL6 ....196 E1
Rectory Terr SL2 ..198 C3
Red Cottage HP23 ..119 D1
Red Cottage Mews ❻
　SL3 ....206 C3
Red Ct SL1 ....205 E5
Red House Cl
　Beaconsfield HP9 ..175 B4
　Newton Longville MK17 .57 D4
Red Leaf Cl SL3 ...206 F5
Red Leys UB10 ....201 E5
Red Lion Cl MK43 ..25 B1
Red Lion Cotts SL2 .199 B1
Red Lion Dr HP14 ..158 D5
Red Lion St HP5 ...154 B7
Red Lion Way HP10 .185 E6
Red Lodge Gdns HP4 .135 A3
Red Roofs SL6 .....203 C7
Red Wing HP20 ....101 E3
Redbourne Ct MK11 ..32 F5
Redbridge MK14 ....34 D7
Redcliffe Wlk HP19 .101 B2
Redcote Manor MK7 .48 A4
Redding Dr HP6 ....154 A2
Redding Gr MK8 ....45 E6
Reddings Cl HP22 ..131 B6
Reddington Dr SL3 .206 E2
Redfern Ct UB8 ....201 C4
Redfield St SL4 ...209 D6
Redford Way UB8 ..201 D5
Redgrave Pl SL7 ..183 F3
Redhill UB9 ....189 D2
Redhouse Cl HP11 .172 E3
Redhuish Cl MK4 ..46 D3
Redland Cl MK18 ..63 D2
Redland Dr MK5 ...46 C7
Redland Way HP21 .116 A5
Redman Rd HP12 ..172 B3
Redpitch Pk HP10 .185 F6
Rediriff Cl SL6 ...202 D6
Redshaw Cl MK18 ..41 E1
Redshots Cl SL7 ..183 E4
Redvers Gate MK5 ..35 B7
Redway Sch The MK6 .47 C6
Redwood SL1 ......197 B3

Redwood Cl
　Hazelmere HP15 .....163 B3
　Wing LU7 ....79 E2
Redwood Dr
　Aylesbury HP21 .....115 E7
　Wing LU7 ....79 E2
Redwood Gate MK5 ...46 C4
Redwood Gdns SL1 ..205 D6
Redwood Glade LU7 ..70 F3
Redwood Pl HP9 ....175 D1
Redwoods The SL4 ..210 D4
Reed Cl SL0 ....207 E2
Reeves Croft MK12 ..33 C4
Reform Rd SL6 .....203 B2
Regal Ct Maidenhead SL6 203 B2
　⓮ Tring HP23 ......119 A3
Regency Ct HP21 ..116 B7
Regent Ct
　❸ Maidenhead SL6 .202 F7
　Slough SL1 ....205 E7
　Windsor SL4 ......210 D5
Regent Ho HP27 ...139 B4
Regent Rd HP21 ...116 B7
Regent St MK2 ....58 C8
Regents Hall MK11 .32 E5
Regents Pl SL6 ...202 D6
Regius Ct HP10 ...174 D8
Reid Ave SL6 .....202 E5
Reliance La MK9 ..35 B3
Rembrandt End HP19 .100 F2
Remenham Church La
　RG9 ....192 A4
Remenham La
　Remenham RG9 ....192 B5
　Remenham Hill RG9 .191 F3
Remenham Row RG9 .191 F3
Remenham Terr RG9 .192 C2
Remus Gate NN13 ..38 A6
Rendlesham MK5 ..35 C3
Rendlesham Way WD3 .167 C3
Renfrew Way MK3 .46 F3
Rennie Cl HP13 ..161 F1
Repton Cl SL6 ...202 C3
Repton Pl HP7 ...166 A8
Retreat La HP14 .148 D2
Retreat The
　Little Chalfont HP6 ..166 E8
　Milton Keynes MK4 ..45 E1
　Princes Risborough HP27 139 B4
Revel Rd HP10 ..185 D8
Revesby Cl SL6 .202 D3
Reyners Gn HP16 .152 B4
Reynold Dr HP20 .102 A2
Reynolds Cl
　Cranfield MK43 ....24 E2
　High Wycombe HP13 .173 E8
Reynolds Pl MK8 ..45 D6
Reynolds Rd HP9 .175 D3
Reynolds Wlk HP5 .144 A4
Rhodes Pl MK6 ...46 E7
Rhondda Cl MK1 ..47 E1
Rhoscolyn Dr MK3 .57 C8
Rhuddlan Cl MK5 ..45 F7
Rhymer Ct MK19 ..10 F4
Ribble Cl MK16 ..22 D4
Ribble Cres MK3 ..57 D8
Ribstone Rd SL6 .202 B3
Ricardo Rd SL4 ..211 B1
Richard Gdns HP13 .173 B8
Richards Way SL1 .204 F5
Richardson Pl ❷ MK6 .34 E1
Richborough MK13 .34 A6
Richings Way SL0 .207 F3
Richmond Cl
　Amersham HP6 ....154 F1
　Milton Keynes MK3 .46 D1
Richmond Cres SL1 .206 A5
Richmond Ct HP13 .173 C7
Richmond Rd HP20 .116 C7
Richmond Way MK16 .22 D3
Rick Yd The MK16 .13 F1
Rickard Cl
　Aylesbury HP21 ....115 D3
　West Drayton UB7 .208 D3
Rickford's Hill HP20 .115 D8
Rickley La MK3 ..58 A8
Rickley Mid Sch MK3 .57 F8
Rickman Wlk HP19 .115 A7
Rickman's La SL2 .198 E6
Rickmansworth La SL9 .177 F5
Rickmansworth Rd
　Amersham HP6 ....154 C2
　Chorleywood WD3 .167 F6
Rickyard
　Milton Keynes MK13 .34 A4
　Whitchurch HP22 ..87 A7
Rickyard Gr HP18 .83 B5
Rickyard The MK46 .7 C3
Ride The LU6 ....93 B6
Riders Way OX39 .147 C6
Ridge Cl Aylesbury HP21 .115 D3
　Lane End HP14 ...171 A4
Ridge Ct SL4 ....210 C4
Ridge Side HP14 .160 A8
Ridge View HP23 .119 C5
Ridge Way
　High Wycombe HP13 .162 C1
　Iver SL0 ....207 F6
　Long Crendon HP18 .125 F4
Ridgebank SL1 ..204 F6
Ridgemount End SL9 .177 E5
Ridgeway
　Berkhamsted HP4 .134 F4
　Milton Keynes,Stony Stratford
　MK11 ....32 F4
　Milton Keynes,Wolverton Mill
　MK12 ....33 A5

Ridgeway continued
　Wing LU7 ....79 E3
Ridgeway Cl
　Chesham HP5 .....144 B3
　Marlow SL7 ......183 E4
Ridgeway Cotts MK17 .37 F3
Ridgeway Ct ❸ HP20 .101 E1
Ridgeway Meads HP7 .138 B2
Ridgeway Rd HP5 .144 B3
Ridgeway The
　Amersham HP7 ...165 E7
　Gerrards Cross SL9 .188 D8
　Marlow SL7 ......183 E4
Ridgeway Trad Est The
　SL0 ....207 E6
Ridgewood RG9 ..181 C1
Ridgmont HP5 ....31 E5
Ridgmont Cl MK19 .31 E5
Ridgway MK17 ...49 B6
Riding Court Rd SL3 .211 C8
Riding Ct SL3 ...211 C8
Riding La HP9,HP10 .174 F3
Riding The MK19 .31 E5
Ridings Cotts HP15 .163 D6
Ridings The
　Amersham HP6 ...154 D4
　Iver SL0 ....207 F2
　Latimer HP5 ....155 D3
　Maidenhead SL6 .202 A7
Ridings Way LU7 .78 B1
Rigby Lodge SL1 .205 E4
Rignall Rd HP16 .151 E8
Riley Cl HP20 ...115 C8
Riley Rd SL7 ...183 D2
Rillington Gdns MK4 .46 B3
Rimmington Way HP19 .101 B1
Rimsdale Ct MK2 .58 D3
Ring Rd HP10 ...173 F2
Ring Rd E MK7 ..47 F7
Ring Rd N MK7 ..47 F7
Ring Rd W MK7 ..47 E7
Ringshall Dr HP4 .121 C8
Ringshall Rd HP4 .107 B3
Ringstead Way HP21 .116 A5
Ripley Cl
　High Wycombe HP13 .173 A8
　Milton Keynes MK4 ..45 E1
　Slough SL3 ......206 E2
Ripon Ho HP21 ..115 F6
Ripon St ❼ HP20 .101 D1
Risborough Rd
　Great Kimble HP17,HP27 139 E8
　Maidenhead SL6 .202 E8
　Stoke Mandeville HP17 .130 B2
Rise Hag Hill SL6 .204 A7
Rise The Amersham HP7 165 C8
　Gawcott MK18 ....51 F4
　Hazelmere HP15 .163 A5
　Loudwater HP11 .174 B4
　Uxbridge UB10 .201 F3
Riseley Rd SL6 ..202 D7
Risings The HP13 .162 B1
River & Rowing Mus *
　RG9 ....191 F1
River Cl MK16 ...22 D4
River Ct SL6 ....203 C6
River Gdns SL6 .203 D4
River Park Ind Est HP4 .135 A5
River Rd SL6 ...203 C6
River Side MK16 .22 D4
River St SL4 ....210 D7
River View HP10 .185 B7
River Wlk UB9 ..201 C1
Riverbank Point SL6 .201 C6
Riverbank The SL4 .210 D7
Rivercrest Rd MK19 .32 B6
Rivermead Ct SL7 .194 E8
Riverpark Dr SL7 .183 F1
Rivers Edge HP11 .174 A3
Rivers Fst Sch MK3 .46 E1
Riversdale SL8 ..185 B1
Riversdale Cotts SL8 .185 A1
Riversdale Cotts SL8 .185 A1
Riverside SL7 ..183 D1
Riverside Bsns Ctr
　HP11 ....172 F7
Riverside Cotts
　West Drayton UB7 .208 D1
　Wooburn Green HP10 .185 E8
Riverside Cvn Pk UB7 .208 C3
Riverside Fst Sch MK16 .22 E3
Riverside Gdns HP4 .135 A5
Riverside Mews MK18 .52 D8
Riverside Pk SL3 .212 E5
Riverside Pl MK13 .213 E1
Riverside Rd TW19 .213 E1
Riverside Way SL1 .201 B4
Riverside Wlk SL4 .210 D7
Riverswood Gdns HP11 .174 B3
Riverway SL4 ...210 C7
Riverwood Ave SL1 .184 A1
Riverwoods Dr SL7 .184 A1
Rivets Cl HP21 ..115 E6
Rivetts Cl MK46 ..6 E1
Rixband Cl MK7 .48 B4
Rixman Cl SL6 ..202 D5
Rixon Cl SL3 ...206 E7
Rixons Mdw HP19 .115 B7
Roade Hill NN7 ..9 F8
Robert Rd SL2 ..187 D2
Robert's Dr HP19 .101 D2
Roberts Cl
　Deanshanger MK19 ..31 E4
　Stanwell TW19 ..213 C1
　West Drayton UB7 .208 E5
Roberts La SL9 ..178 B5
Roberts Rd
　Haddenham HP17 ...127 B6

Roberts Rd continued
　High Wycombe HP13 ...173 B8
Roberts Ride HP15 ..163 A5
Roberts Way HP21 ..115 B6
Roberts Wood Dr SL9 .177 F5
Robertson Cl MK5 ...45 F7
Robertson Cnr LU6 ..93 F4
Robertson Rd ❻ HP4 .135 D4
Robertswood Comb Sch
　SL9 ....177 F3
Robeson Pl MK8 ...45 E8
Robin Cl Aylesbury HP19 .101 F3
　Buckingham MK18 ..52 F7
　Great Kingshill HP15 .151 D1
Robin Hill HP4 ...135 C3
Robin Ho HP11 ..174 A4
Robin Hood Cl SL1 .204 F5
Robin Par ❷ SL2 .198 C7
Robin Willis Way SL4 .211 A1
Robins Cl
　High Wycombe HP12 .172 D3
　Uxbridge UB8 ...208 C8
Robins Hill MK6 ..47 A6
Robins Orch SL9 .177 E4
Robins Platt OX39 .147 B6
Robinson Ct HP19 .100 F3
Robinson Ct SL6 .202 E4
Robinson Rd HP13 .174 B4
Robinswood Cl
　Beaconsfield HP9 ..175 C5
　Leighton Buzzard LU7 .70 F2
Robinwood Gr UB8 .201 F1
Robson Cl SL9 ...177 E5
Robson Ct ❹ HP16 .152 A8
Roche Gdns MK3 ..58 A8
Rochester Ct MK5 ..46 A5
Rochester Mews LU7 .80 E6
Rochester Pl HP19 .115 B8
Rochford Way SL6 .204 A7
Rochfords MK6 ...46 F6
Rochfords Gdns SL2 .206 C5
Rock Cl LU7 ......80 D6
Rock La LU7 .....80 D7
Rockall Ct SL3 ..207 B3
Rockingham Cl
　Pitstone LU7 .....105 D3
　Uxbridge UB8 ...201 C4
Rockingham Dr MK14 .34 E6
Rockingham Par UB8 .201 C5
Rockingham Pl HP9 .175 F1
Rockingham Rd UB8 .201 C4
Rockingham Wharf UB8 201 B4
Rocklane Farm LU7 .79 F7
Rockleigh Ct ❸ LU7 .80 E7
Rockspray Gr MK7 .48 B5
Rodney Way SL3 ..212 E6
Rodwell Gdns MK7 .48 D4
Rodwell Yd ❸ HP23 .119 A3
Roebuck Ave HP13 .173 F6
Roebuck Gn SL1 ..204 E5
Roebuck Way MK5 ..46 C6
Roeburn Cres MK4 ..46 C1
Rogers Croft MK6 ..47 D7
Rogers La SL2 ...198 F4
Roker Park Ave UB10 .201 E8
Rokesby Rd SL2 ..197 F2
Rolfe Cl HP9 ....175 E1
Rolvenden Gr MK7 .48 B7
Roman Lea SL6 ..195 F7
Roman Pl SL6 ...202 C6
Roman Way
　Aylesbury HP19 ...115 B8
　Bourne End SL8 ..185 B4
　Brackley NN13 ...38 A7
Romans Field Sch MK3 .46 E1
Romar Ct MK1 ...47 C2
Romney Ct ⓫ LU7 .183 F3
Romney Lock Rd SL4 .210 D7
Romney Rd HP21 ..115 C4
Romsey Cl SL3 ...206 F3
Romsey Dr SL2 ...187 D1
Romsey Way HP11 .173 B4
Romulus Way NN13 .38 A6
Ronald Rd HP9 ..175 F2
Ronaldsay Spur SL1 .205 E8
Rook Rd HP10 ...185 D4
Rook Tree Farm Ind Est
　MK17 ....37 F3
Rook Wood Way HP16 .152 B5
Rookery Cl SL7 ..183 D2
Rookery Mdw HP15 .163 C7
Rookery Way MK18 .63 F3
Rooks Terr UB7 ..208 E4
Rooksley Rdbt MK13 .34 B3
Ropa Ct ❻ LU7 ..80 F7
Rosamund's Cotts HP18 .83 B2
Rosary The HP15 .163 C7
Rose Ave Aylesbury HP19 101 C2
　Hazelmere HP15 .163 B2
Rose Bsns Est SL7 .183 C5
Rose Cnr HP14 ..158 E5
Rose Cotts SL6 ..202 C5
Rose Ct Amersham HP6 .154 C2
　Chesham HP5 ....154 D6
　Eaton Bray LU6 ..92 D6
　Olney MK46 ......6 F3
Rose Dr HP5 ....154 D7
Rose Hill SL1 ...197 A5
Rose La RG9 ...193 A1
Rose Terr HP18 ..99 A6
Rose Wlk SL2 ...205 B8
Roseary Cl LU7 ..208 D2
Rosebank Cl SL6 .195 E7
Rosebank Cotts HP10 .174 B3
Rosebarn La HP23 .104 D1
Rosebay Cl MK7 ..48 B5

Rosebery Ave
High Wycombe HP13 ....173 E5
Leighton Buzzard LU7 .....80 E7
Rosebery Cl MK18 ....77 B7
Rosebery Ct 4 LU7 ......80 F7
Rosebery Mews LU7 .....90 D4
Rosebery Rd HP22 ......117 F5
Rosebery Way HP23 .....119 B5
Rosehill HP4 ....135 B4
Rosehill Cres MK18 ......62 D1
Rosehill Ct SL1 ....206 A3
Roseleigh Cl SL6 ....202 A7
Rosemary Cl HP12 ......161 B1
Rosemary Ct
High Wycombe HP12 ....161 B1
Walton MK7 ....48 A5
Rosemary La HP17 ......127 A7
Rosemead HP22 ....117 E1
Rosemoor Mews HP19 ...114 F8
Rosemullion Ave MK4 ....57 B8
Rosery The 5 SL8 ......185 A3
Roses Cl LU7 ....78 B1
Roses La SL4 ....209 D5
Rosetree Cl HP16 ....151 C6
Rosewood Gdns HP12 ...172 C4
Rosewood Way SL2 .....198 C7
Rosken Gr SL2 ....198 B3
Roslyn Ct MK15 ....35 D7
Ross Rd
Aston Abbotts HP22 ......88 D5
Maidenhead SL6 ....202 E4
Ross Way MK3 ....46 F2
Rossal Pl MK12 ....33 D4
Rossendale MK14 ....34 D7
Rossetti Pl HP15 ....163 C7
Rossini Pl MK7 ....48 D5
Rossiter Cl SL3 ....206 E2
Rossway La HP4 ....134 A7
Rostrevor Gdns SL0 ....200 D3
Rothersthorpe MK14 .....35 A8
Rothesay Cl HP20 ......101 E1
Rothesay Ct HP4 ....135 A4
Rothschild Ave HP22 ....117 E5
Rothschild Rd
Leighton Buzzard LU7 .....80 F8
Wing LU7 ....79 E2
Rotten Row MK17 ....59 C2
Roughwood La HP8 .....166 E3
Round Hill HP17 ....114 D5
Round Wood Rd HP6 ....154 F2
Roundhead Dr OX9 .....125 F1
Roundheads End HP9 ...175 B4
Roundhill Ct HP17 ......126 E8
Roundlands HP27 ....149 E5
Roundwood Rd HP12 ....172 C7
Rouse Ct SL9 ....188 F6
Routs Gn HP14 ....148 D2
Roveley Ct MK11 ....32 F5
Row The Cholesbury HP5 .133 D2
Cold Brayfield MK46 ....8 B6
Lane End HP14 ....171 B4
Newton Blossomville MK43 ..8 B3
Winchmore Hill HP7 .....164 C3
Rowan Ave HP13 ....173 D8
Rowan Cl Aylesbury HP21 115 E4
Beaconsfield HP9 ......175 B1
Hazlemere HP15 ....163 A3
Rowan Dr MK19 ....20 D2
Rowan Gdns SL0 ....200 C3
Rowan Ho 1 SL8 ....185 A4
Rowan Pl HP6 ....154 F1
Rowan Rd UB7 ....208 E2
Rowan Way SL2 ....205 B8
Rowan Wlk HP5 ....144 B1
Rowanhurst Dr SL2 ....198 C7
Rowans The SL9 ....188 D8
Rowborough Rd HP22 ..131 D7
Rowland Cl SL4 ....209 D4
Rowland Ho HP9 ....175 F1
Rowland Way HP19 .....115 B7
Rowlands Cl MK2 ....58 E8
Rowle Cl MK14 ....34 E7
Rowley Furrows LU7 .....80 D8
Rowley La SL3 ....199 D4
Rowlheys Pl UB7 ....208 E3
Rowliff Rd HP12 ....172 C6
Rowsham Dell MK14 .....21 F2
Rowsham Rd HP22 .....102 C5
Rowton Heath MK5 ......45 C5
Roxburgh Way MK3 ......46 F3
Roxhill Rd MK43 ....25 F3
Roxwell Cl SL1 ....204 E5
Roxwell Path 5 HP20 ..101 F2
Royal Buckinghamshire
Hospl HP19 ....101 D1
Royal Cl UB7,UB8 ......208 F7
Royal Cotts
Cookham Dean SL6 .....195 C4
Winchmore Hill HP7 ....164 C4
Royal Ct HP23 ....120 A5
Royal Free Ct 13 SL4 ..210 D6
Royal Gram Sch The
HP13 ....162 C1
Royal La UB8 ....201 F1
Royal Latin Sch MK18 ....52 D7
Royal Mans RG9 ....191 E1
Royal Mead HP17 ......130 C5
Royal Windsor Race Course
SL4 ....209 E7
Royce Cl LU6 ....93 F7
Royce Rd MK43 ....24 D3
Royle Cl SL9 ....177 F3
Royston Way SL1 ......204 D8
Rubbra Cl MK7 ....48 C5
Rubens Cl HP19 ....100 F2
Ruby Cl SL1 ....205 A4
Ruckles Way HP7 ......165 C7

Rudchesters MK13 ....33 F5
Rudd's La HP17 ....127 A7
Ruddlesway SL4 ....209 D6
Rudds Cl MK18 ....66 A5
Rudsworth Cl SL3 ......212 D7
Ruffle Cl UB7 ....208 E4
Rugby Rise HP11 ....174 A3
Rugwood Rd HP10 .....173 F2
Rumptons Paddock HP18 82 F6
Run Furrow HP17 ......127 A7
Runford Ct MK5 ....46 C5
Runnymede MK14 ....21 F2
Runrig Hill HP6 ....154 E4
Rupert Ave HP12 ......172 E4
Rupert Ct RG9 ....191 E3
Rupert House Sch RG9 .191 E3
Rupert Way OX9 ....126 A1
Rupert's La 191 E3
Ruscombe Gdns SL3 ...211 A7
Ruscote HP4 ....135 A4
Rushall Rd OX9 ....126 A1
Rushbeds Wood Nature
Reserve★ HP18 ....96 D4
Rushbrooke Cl HP13 ...162 F2
Rushburn HP10 ....185 F6
Rushendon Furlong
LU7 ....105 E5
Rushes Mead UB8 .....201 C4
Rushes The
Maidenhead SL6 ....203 C6
Marlow SL7 ....194 C8
Rushfields Cl MK4 ....45 F1
Rushington Ave SL6 ...202 F5
Rushleys Cl MK5 ....46 A8
Rushmere Cl MK17 ......48 D2
Rushmere La HP5 .....145 B3
Rushmere Ret Pk MK1 ..47 D2
Rushmoor Ave HP15 ...163 B8
Rushton Ct 5 MK8 ......45 F8
Ruskin Ct MK16 ....22 C3
Ruskin Way HP20 ......101 D2
Rusland Cir MK4 ....46 C2
Russel Ct HP14 ....161 C1
Russell Ave HP21 .....115 C6
Russell Cl
Little Chalfont HP6 ....166 D8
Tylers Green HP10 ....163 B1
Russell Ct
Aylesbury HP21 ....115 E6
Chesham HP5 ....144 D2
Maidenhead SL6 ......202 F7
Wendover HP22 ....131 B5
Russell Dr TW19 ......213 D1
Russell Fst Sch MK11 ....32 D5
Russell Ho 4 SL8 .....185 A4
Russell Sch The WD3 ..167 B5
Russell St
Milton Keynes MK11 .....32 D5
Windsor SL4 ....210 D6
Woburn Sands MK17 ....49 B4
Russet Cl TW19 ....212 F1
Russet Rd SL6 ....202 C3
Russets The SL9 ......177 D1
Russett Hill SL9 ....188 E8
Russwell La MK17 ....59 C6
Rustics Cl MK18 ....73 B5
Rustlings Gate HP14 ..171 C6
Rutherford Cl
Uxbridge UB8 ....201 F1
Windsor SL4 ....209 F6
Rutherford Gate MK5 ...46 C5
Rutherford Rd HP21 ...115 E4
Ruthven Cl MK2 ....58 C4
Rutland Ave
High Wycombe HP12 ...172 D6
Slough SL1 ....205 C8
Rutland Ct 2 HP11 ....173 A6
Rutland Gate SL6 .....202 C6
Rutland Ho 3 MK3 ......46 F1
Rutland Pl SL6 ....202 C6
Rutland Rd SL6 ....202 D6
Rutland St HP11 ......173 A6
Ryans Mount SL7 .....183 C6
Rycote La MK4 ....136 D5
Rycote Lane Ind Est
OX9 ....136 C4
Rycroft Milton Keynes MK4 .46 E3
Windsor SL4 ....209 F4
Rydal Way
High Wycombe HP12 ...172 B6
Milton Keynes MK2 .....58 D5
Ryder Cl HP3 ....146 A4
Ryding The MK5 ....46 A4
Rydings SL4 ....209 F4
Rye Cl Aylesbury HP21 ..115 D4
Maidenhead SL6 ......202 A4
Rye Ct 9 SL1 ....206 A4
Rye View HP13 ....173 C7
Ryecote Chapel★ OX9 .136 D6
Ryecroft Rd HP5 ......154 A7
Ryefield Terr SL3 .....212 D7
Ryeland MK11 ....32 E6
Ryeland Cl HP17 ......130 C4
Ryemead Way HP11 ...173 F4
Rylstone Cl
Maidenhead SL6 ......202 A3
Milton Keynes MK13 ....34 B3
Ryman Ct WD3 ....167 C3
Rymill Cl HP3 ....146 A4
Ryton Pl MK4 ....46 C3
Ryvers End SL3 ....206 F3
Ryvers Prim Sch SL3 ..206 D3
Ryvers Rd SL3 ....206 F3

S

Sabina Cl HP12 ....172 E6
Sacred Heart RC Prim Sch
The RG9 ....191 D1
Saddington MK6 ....47 D6
Saddlers Pl MK14 ....35 A5
Sadleirs Gn MK17 ....49 B5
Sadlers Mews SL6 .....203 B7
Saffron Cl SL3 ....211 B6
Saffron Ct HP13 ......173 C6
Saffron Rd HP13 ......173 C6
Saffron Rise LU6 ....92 E6
Saffron St MK2 ....58 D7
Saham Croft Cl MK18 ...65 E4
Sailing Club Rd SL8 ...185 A3
Saint-Cloud Way SL6 ..203 A7
St Abbs Cl MK4 ....56 F8
St Adrian's Cl SL6 ....202 B4
St Agnes Gate
Wendover HP22 ....131 A5
Wendover HP22 ....131 A5
St Aidan's Cl MK4 ......57 E6
St Alban's Rd MK18 .....65 F4
St Alban's St SL4 .....210 D6
St Albans Cl 7 SL4 ...210 D6
St Andrew's Ave SL4 ..209 F5
St Andrew's CE Fst Sch
MK14 ....34 E4
St Andrew's CE Prim Sch
Chinnor OX39 ....147 C7
Uxbridge UB8 ....201 D4
St Andrew's Cl
High Wycombe HP13 ...162 F1
Old Windsor SL4 ......211 A1
Wraysbury TW19 ......211 E1
St Andrew's Cres SL4 .209 F6
St Andrew's Rd
Chinnor OX39 ....147 C5
Milton Keynes MK3 .....57 E7
Uxbridge UB10 ....201 E5
St Andrews Cotts 1
SL4 ....210 A5
St Andrews Ct
Colnbrook SL3 ....212 D7
2 Slough SL1 ....205 E3
St Andrews Ho OX39 ..147 C6
St Andrews Way SL1 ..204 D6
St Andrews Way Ind Est
HP19 ....101 C1
St Ann's HP10 ....174 C2
St Ann's Ct HP10 .....174 C2
St Anne's Cl
Henley-on-T RG9 ......191 D1
Wendover HP22 ....131 D1
St Anne's Rd
Aylesbury HP19 ....115 B8
South Harefield UB9 ...190 C8
St Anthony's Cl HP19 ..115 B8
St Anthony's Ct HP9 ..186 C8
St Anthony's Pl MK4 ...57 B8
St Anthony's RC Prim Sch
UB7 ....208 D4
St Augustine's RC Prim Sch
HP11 ....173 A4
St Bartholomew's CE Sch
HP23 ....119 D1
St Bartholomews MK10 ..36 A1
St Bees MK10 ....36 B1
St Bernard's Convent Sch
SL3 ....206 C4
St Bernard's Prep Sch
SL1 ....206 B4
St Bernard's RC Sch
HP11 ....173 A4
St Bernards Ct HP13 ..173 C6
St Bernards Rd SL3 ...206 C5
St Birinus HP19 ....174 A2
St Botolphs 2 MK10 ...36 B1
St Brides Cl MK6 ....35 C2
St Catherine RC Prim Sch
UB7 ....208 D4
St Catherine's Ave MK3 .57 D6
St Catherine's Ct HP19 .115 B8
St Catherines Ct 3 SL4 .210 A5
St Chad's Rd SL6 .....202 B4
St Christopher Rd UB8 .208 D8
St Christopher's Cl
HP16 ....152 B3
St Christophers Ct WD3 167 D5
St Clement Cl UB8 ....208 D7
St Clement Danes Sch
WD3 ....167 D7
St Clement's Dr MK3 ...57 D6
St Columba's Cl SL6 ..202 A4
St David Cl UB8 ......208 D8
St David's Cl
Iver Heath SL0 ....200 D4
Maidenhead SL6 ......202 A4
St David's Ct NN13 .....38 A8
St David's Par SL0 ....200 D4
St David's Rd MK3 ......57 C6
St Dunstans MK6 ....47 A6
St Edmund Campion RC Prim
Sch UB8 ....202 B5
St Edmund's Cl HP19 ..115 B8
St Edmunds HP4 ......135 C3
St Edward's RC Fst Sch
SL4 ....210 A6
St Edward's RC Jun Sch
HP21 ....116 A7
St Edward's Royal Free
Ecumenical Mid Sch
SL4 ....210 A6
St Edwards Ct MK14 ....34 F7
St Elmo Cl SL2 ....198 D1
St Elmo Cres SL2 .....198 D1

St Ethelbert's RC Prim Sch
SL2 ....206 A2
St Faith's Cl MK17 ......57 D5
St Francis de Sales High Sch
HP23 ....118 F3
St Francis Rd
Beacon's Bottom HP14 .159 D3
Denham Green UB9 ...189 F5
St George's CE Inf Sch
HP7 ....165 E8
St George's Cl
High Wycombe HP13 ...173 D7
Windsor SL4 ....209 E6
St George's Dr UB10 ..190 A7
St George's Rd MK3 ....57 E6
St George's Sch SL4 ..210 D7
St Georges Cres SL1 ..204 D6
St Georges Cr HP12 ...172 D8
St Georges Ind Est HP7 165 F8
St Georges Lodge SL6 196 B7
St Georges Way 33 D7
St Giles Mews MK11 ....32 D6
St Giles St MK13 ....33 F7
St Govans Cl MK4 ......57 B8
St Helen Cl UB8 ....208 D8
St Helens Gr MK10 .....47 F8
St Hilda's Ct HP19 ....115 B8
St Hilda's Way HP10 ..174 A2
St Huberts Cl SL9 .....188 E4
St Huberts Cotts SL9 .188 E4
St Huberts La SL9 ....188 E4
St Hugh's Ave HP13 ...173 F6
St Hugh's Cl MK4 .....158 F4
St Hugh's Pl HP14 ....158 F4
St Ives Cres MK4 ....57 B8
St Ives Rd SL6 ....203 A7
St James CE Sch, Akeley
MK18 ....41 F8
St James MK16 ....11 A2
St James Ctyd 8 SL7 .183 E2
St James Pl SL1 ......204 C7
St James Rd MK13 .....33 F7
St James Way HP22 ..102 B3
St James Wlk SL0 ....207 E4
St John St MK16 ....22 D4
St John's Ave 174 B8
St John's CE Comb Sch
HP27 ....149 F4
St John's Cl UB8 .....201 D4
St John's Cres MK12 ...33 D5
St John's La MK19 ......31 B4
St John's Manor Ho
HP15 ....162 E2
St John's Rd
4 Aylesbury HP20 ...101 E1
Hazlemere HP15 .....162 F1
Milton Keynes MK3 .....57 E6
Uxbridge UB8 ....201 B4
St John's St HP20 ....101 E1
St John's Terr MK16 ...22 D4
St John's Well Ct MK5 .135 B5
St John's Well La HP4 .135 B5
St Johns Cl HP10 .....163 B1
St Johns Dr Stone HP17 114 B5
Windsor SL4 ....210 A5
St Johns La MK18 ....75 F2
St Johns Rd Slough SL2 197 D1
Tylers Green HP10 ....163 B1
Windsor SL4 ....210 A5
St Joseph's RC Comb Sch
SL9 ....188 C8
St Joseph's RC High Sch
SL2 ....206 A4
St Joseph's RC Inf Sch
HP21 ....116 A7
St Josephs Cl MK46 .....6 F4
St Josephs Mews HP5 175 F2
St Katherine's Way HP4 134 F7
St Laurence CE Jun Sch
UB8 ....208 D8
St Laurence Cl UB8 ...208 C8
St Laurence Rd MK18 ...65 F4
St Laurence Way SL1 .206 A3
St Lawrence Ct MK18 ..146 A4
St Lawrence View MK13 .34 A4
St Leger Ct MK14 ....34 E8
St Leger Dr MK14 ....34 E7
St Leonard's Ave 2 SL4 210 C5
St Leonard's Hill SL4 .209 E4
St Leonard's Rd
Oakley Green SL4 ....209 D1
Windsor SL4 ....210 C4
St Leonard's Way LU6 ..92 E1
St Leonards Rd HP6 ..154 E1
St Leonards Wlk SL0 ..207 F3
St Louis RC Comb Sch
HP20 ....101 F2
St Luke Cl UB8 ....208 D8
St Luke's CE Prim Sch
SL6 ....202 F8
St Luke's Rd
Maidenhead SL6 ......202 F8
Old Windsor SL4 ......211 A1
Uxbridge UB8 ....201 E5
St Margaret Ct MK2 ....58 C4
St Margaret's Cl
Berkhamsted HP4 .....135 D3
Iver Heath SL0 ....200 D3
Tylers Green HP10 ....174 C8
St Margaret's Ct SL0 ..200 D3
St Margaret's Gate SL0 200 D3
St Margaret's Rd SL6 ..202 A7
St Margarets Cl MK16 ..22 D4
St Margarets Gr HP15 .151 E3
St Margarets Cres SL6 .202 B7
St Mark's Hospl SL6 ..202 C5
St Mark's Pl SL4 ......210 C5

St Mark's Rd
Aylesbury HP21 ....115 C7
Henley-on-T RG9 ......191 E1
Maidenhead SL6 ......202 F8
Windsor SL4 ....210 C5
St Martin Cl UB8 ......208 D7
St Martin's Cl UB8 ....208 D3
St Martin's Rd UB7 ...208 D3
St Martin's St MK2 .....58 C8
St Mary & All Saints CE Prim
Sch HP9 ....175 D3
St Mary & St Giles CE Mid
Sch MK11 ....32 E6
St Mary Magdalene RC Comb
Sch MK12 ....33 A5
St Mary St
High Wycombe HP11 ...173 B6
Milton Keynes MK13 ....33 F7
St Mary's Ave
Berkhamsted HP4 .....134 D6
Milton Keynes MK3 .....57 E7
Milton Keynes,Stony Stratford
MK11 ....32 E6
St Mary's CE Comb Sch
HP7 ....165 A8
St Mary's CE Prim Sch
SL1 ....206 A3
St Mary's CE Sch HP19 115 A3
St Mary's Cl
Lee Common HP16 ....142 D5
Maidenhead SL6 ......203 A7
South Harefield UB9 ..190 B8
Wavendon MK17 ....48 B8
St Mary's Glebe LU6 ...92 E4
St Mary's RC Prim Sch
Maidenhead SL6 ......195 F2
Uxbridge UB8 ....201 C4
St Mary's Rd
Denham Green UB9 ...189 F5
Slough SL3 ....206 E4
South Harefield UB9 ..190 B8
St Mary's Row 7 HP20 115 D4
St Mary's Sch SL4 ....188 E2
St Mary's Sq 3 HP20 .115 D4
St Mary's Way
Chalfont St Peter SL9 .177 D1
Chesham HP5 ....154 B8
Leighton Buzzard LU7 ..80 C3
St Mary's Wlk 10 SL6 .202 F7
St Marys Cl
East Claydon MK18 .....74 F8
Mursley MK17 ....67 D6
St Marys Ct MK18 ......51 B2
St Marys Rd MK18 ......74 F7
St Matthew Cl UB8 ....208 D7
St Matthew's CE Prim Sch
UB7 ....208 E5
St Matthews Ct MK3 ....57 D6
St Michael's CE Comb Sch
LU7 ....68 C1
St Michael's Cl HP22 ..117 C1
St Michael's Ct Ashton NN7 9 F8
Slough SL3 ....197 D1
St Michael's Gn HP9 ..175 D3
St Michaels Cl
Edgcott HP18 ....72 F2
Halton HP22 ....131 C8
Stewkley LU7 ....68 E1
St Michaels Dr
Milton Keynes MK7 .....47 F6
Walton MK7 ....47 E7
St Michaels Way MK18 ..63 E2
St Monica's RC Comb Sch
MK14 ....34 C5
St Nicholas CE Comb Sch
SL6 ....196 E1
St Nicholas Cl
Cublington LU7 ....78 B1
Little Chalfont HP7 ...166 B1
Uxbridge UB8 ....208 D1
St Patrick's Cl SL6 ....202 B4
St Patrick's Way MK3 ...57 C6
St Paul Cl UB8 ....208 D8
St Paul's CE Comb Sch
HP10 ....185 D4
St Paul's Ct SL6 ......202 F6
St Paul's Rd MK3 ....57 E6
St Pauls Ave SL2 .....206 C4
St Pauls Cl MK11 ....32 D6
St Pauls RC Sch MK6 ...46 F7
St Pauls Yd MK16 ......22 D4
St Peter St SL7 ....183 E1
St Peter's Ave HP19 ..101 E4
St Peter's CE Comb Sch
SL1 ....197 B2
St Peter's CE Mid Sch
SL4 ....210 F1
St Peter's Cl
Burnham SL1 ....197 B1
Old Windsor SL4 ......211 A2
St Peter's Ct SL9 .....177 E2
St Peter's Gate NN13 ..38 A7
St Peter's RC Prim Sch
SL7 ....183 D3
St Peter's Rd
Brackley NN13 ....38 A8
Maidenhead SL6 ......195 D2
Uxbridge UB8 ....208 D8
St Peters Cl
Loudwater HP11 ......174 B1
Speen HP17 ....150 A4
St Peters Hill HP23 ...119 A4
St Peters Way
Chorleywood WD3 ....167 B5
Milton Keynes MK13 ...34 A8

St Pirans Sch SL6 . . . . .195 E1
St Rumbold's La MK18 . .52 C8
St Stephen's Rd UB7 . . .208 D5
St Stephens Dr MK15 . . . .35 B7
St Teresa's Cl HP27 . . . . .139 B4
St Teresa's Sch HP27 . . .139 B4
St Thomas Aquinas RC Comb
  Sch MK3 . . . . .57 E7
St Thomas Ct MK4 . . . . . .45 F1
St Thomas More RC Prim Sch
  HP4 . . . . .135 A4
St Thomas Wlk SL3 . . . . .212 D7
St Tiggywinkles Wildlife
  Hospl★ HP17 . . . . .127 A4
St Vincents MK17 . . . . . . .49 C4
Salcey Forest Trail (Rose
  Copse)★ NN7 . . . . .4 C2
Salden Cl
  Drayton Parslow MK17 . . . . .68 C6
  Milton Keynes MK5 . . . . . . .46 B6
Salford Rd MK18 . . . . .49 D7
Salisbury Ave SL2 . . . . . .205 C8
Salisbury Cl
  Amersham HP7 . . . . .165 E4
  Princes Risborough HP27 . .139 C3
Salisbury Ct SL6 . . . . .202 E5
Salisbury Gr MK14 . . . . . .21 F2
Salisbury Mews SL1 . . . . .198 C1
Salisbury Rd
  High Wycombe HP13 . . . . .162 D1
  Uxbridge UB8 . . . . .201 B3
Sallowsprings LU6 . . . . . . .93 F2
Salmons La HP16 . . . . . . .151 D6
Salop Rd MK3 . . . . .46 F2
Salt Hill Ave SL1 . . . . . . .205 C5
Salt Hill Cl UB8 . . . . .201 E7
Salt Hill Dr SL1 . . . . .205 C5
Salt Hill Mans SL1 . . . . . .205 C5
Salt Hill Way SL1 . . . . . . .205 D5
Saltash Cl HP13 . . . . .174 B4
Salter's Cl HP4 . . . . .134 F6
Salters Cl
  Ludgershall HP18 . . . . .96 C8
  Maidenhead SL6 . . . . .203 A4
Salters La HP18 . . . . .96 C8
Salters Mews MK14 . . . . . .34 F6
Salters Rd SL6 . . . . .203 B7
Salters Row HP10 . . . . . . .186 A4
Salton Link MK4 . . . . .46 B2
Saltwood Ave MK4 . . . . . .45 E1
Samphire Ct MK7 . . . . . . .48 A6
Sampsons Gn SL2 . . . . . . .197 F2
Sampsons Hill HP7 . . . . . .164 E2
Samuel Ct MK16 . . . . .22 F3
San Remo Rd MK17 . . . . . .49 D2
Sanctuary Rd HP15 . . . . . .163 B5
Sandage Rd HP14 . . . . . . .171 B5
Sandal Ct MK5 . . . . .46 A5
Sandbrier Cl MK7 . . . . . . .48 B6
Sandbrook La HP23 . . . . . .104 C1
Sandels Way HP9 . . . . . . .175 D4
Sandelswood End HP9 . . . .175 D5
Sanders La NN12 . . . . .18 D3
Sanderson Rd UB8 . . . . . .201 C6
Sandford Gdns HP11 . . . . .173 B4
Sandhill Rd MK18 . . . . . . .74 F8
Sandhill Way HP19 . . . . . .115 A8
Sandholme MK18 . . . . .63 E2
Sandhurst Dr MK18 . . . . . .52 C7
Sandisplatt Rd SL6 . . . . . .202 A6
Sandlers End SL2 . . . . . . .198 B1
Sandles The SL4 . . . . .205 B1
Sandleswood Cl HP9 . . . . .175 D4
Sandon Cl HP23 . . . . .118 F4
Sandown Ct
  [8] High Wycombe HP12 . . . .172 E7
  Milton Keynes MK3 . . . . . . .57 D8
Sandown Rd SL2 . . . . .204 F8
Sandpiper [1] HP19 . . . . . .101 E4
Sandpit Hill MK18 . . . . . . .50 F6
Sandpit Hill Cotts HP23 . .133 B2
Sandpit La HP10 . . . . .174 C7
Sandringham Ct
  [8] High Wycombe HP13 . . . .173 B7
  Newport Pagnell MK16 . . . . .22 B4
  Slough SL1 . . . . .204 D7
Sandringham Pl MK2 . . . . .58 C8
Sandringham Rd
  Maidenhead SL6 . . . . .195 E2
  Stanwell TW6 . . . . .213 E2
Sands Farm Dr SL1 . . . . . .197 C1
Sands Ind Est HP12 . . . . .172 B2
Sandstone Cl MK18 . . . . . .73 B5
Sandwell Ct MK8 . . . . .33 C2
Sandy Cl
  Buckingham MK18 . . . . .52 F8
  Milton Keynes MK14 . . . . . .34 D8
Sandy La
  Aspley Heath MK17 . . . . . . .49 B2
  Leighton Buzzard LU7 . . . . . .70 F3
  Long Crendon HP18 . . . . . .125 B6
Sandy Mead SL2 . . . . .203 C1
Sandy Rd MK18 . . . . .73 B5
Sandy Rise SL9 . . . . .177 E2
Sandycroft Rd HP6 . . . . . .155 C1
Sandygate Cl SL7 . . . . . . .183 D3
Sandygate Rd SL7 . . . . . . .183 D3
Sandywell Dr MK15 . . . . . .35 A6
Santen Gr MK2 . . . . .58 D4
Saracens' Wharf MK2 . . . . .47 E1
Sargeant Cl UB8 . . . . .201 D2
Sarum Complex UB8 . . . . .201 B3
Satis Ho SL3 . . . . .211 C7
Saunders Cl MK7 . . . . .48 D6

Saunders Ct [1] HP13 . . . .173 F6
Saunders End HP6 . . . . . .153 C5
Saunders Pl HP19 . . . . . . .115 A7
Saunders Rd UB10 . . . . . .201 F4
Saunders Wood Copse
  HP14 . . . . .158 F4
Saunderton Sta HP14 . . . .149 C1
Saunderton Vale HP14 . . . .149 C1
Savage Croft MK10 . . . . . .35 E3
Savay Cl UB9 . . . . .190 A4
Savay La UB9 . . . . .190 A4
Savernake Rd HP19 . . . . . .101 D3
Savill La MK4,MK5 . . . . . . .45 F2
Savill Way SL7 . . . . .183 F2
Savoy Cres MK9 . . . . .34 F3
Savoy Ct SL6 . . . . .195 F1
Sawley Ho [5] MK3 . . . . . . .46 F1
Sawmill Cotts SL3 . . . . . . .199 F2
Sawmill Rd HP27 . . . . . . .138 D7
Sawpit Hill HP15 . . . . . . .163 B5
Sawyer's Cl SL4 . . . . .209 E7
Sawyers Cl SL6 . . . . .202 A2
Sawyers Cres SL6 . . . . . . .202 A2
Saxeways Bsns Ctr HP5 . . .143 E3
Saxhorn Rd HP14 . . . . . . .171 C4
Saxon Cl
  Amersham HP6 . . . . .154 D1
  Dunstable LU6 . . . . .93 E8
  Slough SL3 . . . . .206 F4
  Uxbridge UB8 . . . . .208 E8
Saxon Ct
  High Wycombe HP12 . . . . .172 D8
  Stanwell TW19 . . . . .213 A2
Saxon Gate MK9 . . . . .34 E2
Saxon Gdns SL6 . . . . .196 D1
Saxon Lodge SL1 . . . . . . .204 F5
Saxon St
  Milton Keynes MK2 . . . . . . .58 C8
  Milton Keynes,Ashland MK1,
    MK6 . . . . .47 C4
  Milton Keynes,Heelands
    MK6,MK13,MK14 . . . . .34 C5
Saxon Way
  Harmondsworth UB7 . . . . . .213 C8
  Old Windsor SL4 . . . . .211 B1
Saxon Way Trad Ctr
  UB7 . . . . .213 C8
Saye & Sele Cl HP18 . . . . .82 F6
Sayers Gdns HP4 . . . . . . .135 A6
Sayward Cl HP5 . . . . .144 D1
Scafell Rd SL2 . . . . .204 F8
Scarborough Way SL1 . . . .205 B4
Scardale MK13 . . . . .34 C5
Scarlett Ave MK22 . . . . . .131 E6
Scatterdells La WD4 . . . . .146 F1
Scatterill Cl MK13 . . . . . . .34 A4
Scholars Way HP6 . . . . . . .154 F1
Scholars Wlk
  Chalfont St Peter SL9 . . . . .177 E4
  Slough SL3 . . . . .207 A4
School Cl Asheridge HP5 . .143 E5
  Cryers Hill HP15 . . . . .162 C6
  High Wycombe HP11 . . . . . .173 A4
  High Wycombe, Downley
    HP13 . . . . .161 D2
  Holmer Green HP15 . . . . . .163 C7
  Ickford HP18 . . . . .124 A3
School Dr MK17 . . . . .57 C3
School End
  Chetwode MK18 . . . . .61 D8
  Great Horwood MK18 . . . . . .55 A3
School Hill
  Charndon OX27 . . . . .73 A6
  North Marston MK18 . . . . . .76 B2
School Ho TW19 . . . . .213 C1
School La
  Amersham HP7 . . . . .165 A8
  Buckingham MK18 . . . . .52 C8
  Castlethorpe MK19 . . . . . . .19 F5
  Chalfont St Giles HP8 . . . . .177 B7
  Chalfont St Peter SL9 . . . . .177 D1
  Chearsley HP18 . . . . .112 B2
  Cookham SL6 . . . . .196 B7
  Cookham Dean SL6 . . . . . .195 B7
  Dinton HP17 . . . . .113 F2
  Eaton Bray LU6 . . . . .92 F6
  Little Marlow SL7 . . . . . . .184 C5
  Maidenhead SL6 . . . . .195 E1
  Medmenham SL7 . . . . .193 B6
  Milton Keynes MK5 . . . . . . .46 B8
  Oakley MK18 . . . . .109 D5
  Penn Street HP7 . . . . .164 B5
  Preston Bissett MK18 . . . . . .62 B8
  Seer Green HP9 . . . . .176 D4
  Shabbington HP18 . . . . . . .124 D3
  Sherington MK16 . . . . .14 A2
  Slough SL2 . . . . .205 F6
  Turville RG9 . . . . .169 F3
  Twyford MK18 . . . . .62 D2
  Upper Winchendon HP18 . . . .99 A1
  Waddesdon HP18 . . . . .99 A6
  Weston Turville HP22 . . . . .116 F1
  Wexham Street SL2 . . . . . .199 B5
  Yardley Gobion NN12 . . . . . .18 E6
School Rd
  Harmondsworth UB7 . . . . . .213 D8
  Tylers Green HP10 . . . . . . .174 D8
  Wooburn Green HP10 . . . . .185 E6
School St MK13 . . . . .33 F7
School The HP23 . . . . .118 C8
School Way HP11 . . . . . . .174 B2
Schorne La MK18 . . . . .76 B2
Schumann Cl MK7 . . . . . . .48 C4
Scotch Firs MK7 . . . . .48 C6
Scotlands Dr SL2 . . . . . . .198 B6
Scotney Gdns MK3 . . . . . . .57 E8
Scotsgrove Cotts OX9 . . . .126 A4
Scotsgrove Hill OX9 . . . . .126 A3
Scotswood Cl HP9 . . . . . . .175 D5

Scott Cl
  Farnham Common SL2 . . . . .198 C7
  West Drayton UB7 . . . . . . .208 F2
Scott Dr MK16 . . . . .22 A5
Scott End HP19 . . . . .100 F2
Scott Evans Ct MK18 . . . . .66 A5
Scotts Cl
  Marsh Gibbon OX27 . . . . . . .72 A3
  Stoke Hammond MK17 . . . . .69 E8
  Stoke Hammond MK17 . . . . .69 E8
Scotts Cnr NN13 . . . . .39 A4
Scotts Farm Cl MK18 . . . . .41 E4
Scotts La Adstock MK18 . . .53 F1
  Buckingham MK18 . . . . .41 E3
  Marsh Gibbon OX27 . . . . . . .71 E2
Scriven Cl MK15 . . . . .35 E7
Scriveners La NN12 . . . . . .17 A8
Scrubb's La HP14 . . . . . . .160 B7
Seabrooke Ct MK8 . . . . . . .45 D6
Seacourt SL3 . . . . .207 B2
Seaford Rd TW6 . . . . .213 D2
Seagrave Ct MK7 . . . . .48 A4
Seagrave Rd HP9 . . . . . . .175 C4
Sears The LU6 . . . . .92 B5
Seaton Dr HP21 . . . . .115 C4
Secklow Gate MK9 . . . . . . .34 F3
Second Ave MK1 . . . . .47 C2
Second Cres SL1 . . . . .205 C8
Second St HP11 . . . . .173 C4
Sedgemere MK8 . . . . .33 D2
Sedgemoor Dr OX9 . . . . . .126 A1
Sedgmoor Cl HP10 . . . . . .185 A7
Sedgmoor Gdns HP10 . . . .185 A8
Sedgmoor La HP10 . . . . . .185 B7
Sedgmoor Rd HP10 . . . . . .185 A8
Sedley Gr UB9 . . . . .190 C7
Sedrup La HP17 . . . . .114 F4
Seeleys Cl HP9 . . . . .175 D3
Seeleys Ct HP9 . . . . .175 D3
Seeleys La HP9 . . . . .175 D3
Seeleys Rd HP9 . . . . .175 C4
Seer Green & Jordans Sta
  HP9 . . . . .176 C3
Seer Green CE Comb Sch
  HP9 . . . . .176 C4
Seer Green La HP9 . . . . . .176 B3
Seer Mead HP9 . . . . .176 D4
Sefton Cl SL2 . . . . .198 F4
Sefton Paddock SL2 . . . . .199 A5
Sefton Park Cotts SL2 . . . .199 A4
Sefton Way UB8 . . . . .208 C2
Selbourne Ave MK3 . . . . . .57 F7
Selbourne Ho [10] SL8 . . . .185 A4
Selby Gr MK5 . . . . .46 B5
Selim Ct [4] SL1 . . . . .206 B4
Selkirk Ave HP19 . . . . . . .101 D2
Selkirk Gr MK3 . . . . .46 F2
Selwood Cl TW19 . . . . . . .213 C1
Selwood Gdns TW19 . . . . .213 C1
Selwood Way HP13 . . . . . .161 E2
Selworthy MK4 . . . . .46 D3
Selwyn Cl SL4 . . . . .209 E5
Selwyn Ct HP21 . . . . .116 B6
Selwyn Pl SL1 . . . . .204 F6
September Ct UB10 . . . . . .201 D3
Serjeants Gn MK14 . . . . . .34 F6
Serles Cl MK6 . . . . .47 A6
Sermed Ct SL2 . . . . .206 C5
Serpentine Ct MK2 . . . . . . .58 D5
Servite Ho SL6 . . . . .203 B8
Seven Acre Ho HP10 . . . . .174 C2
Seven Acres HP18 . . . . . . .125 B7
Seven Gables MK18 . . . . . .65 D6
Sevenhills Rd SL0 . . . . . . .200 C6
Severalls Ave HP5 . . . . . . .144 C2
Severn Cres SL3 . . . . .207 B1
Severn Dr MK16 . . . . .22 E4
Severn Ho HP13 . . . . .173 F7
Severn Way MK3 . . . . .57 D8
Sewell Cl HP19 . . . . .100 F2
Seymour Cl
  Flackwell Heath HP10 . . . . .173 F2
  Maidenhead SL6 . . . . .202 B3
Seymour Court La SL7 . . . .183 B5
Seymour Court Rd SL7 . . . .183 C4
Seymour Ct
  Berkhamsted HP4 . . . . .134 E6
  Tring HP23 . . . . .119 A4
Seymour Ho
  High Wycombe HP12 . . . . . .172 E4
  Slough SL3 . . . . .206 E4
Seymour Park Rd SL7 . . . .183 D3
Seymour Plain SL7 . . . . . .183 C5
Seymour Rd
  Berkhamsted HP4 . . . . .134 E6
  Chalfont St Giles HP8 . . . . .177 C6
  Slough SL1 . . . . .205 F6
Shackleton Ct [6] TW19 . . .213 E1
Shackleton Pl MK6 . . . . . . .34 E1
Shackleton Rd
  High Wycombe HP12 . . . . . .172 E5
  Slough SL1 . . . . .205 F6
Shaftesbury Cres MK3 . . . .47 A1
Shaftesbury Ct
  Maidenhead SL6 . . . . .202 E5
  [6] Slough SL1 . . . . .205 E4
  Winslow MK18 . . . . .65 F5
Shaftesbury Ho HP21 . . . . .116 C7
Shaftesbury St HP11 . . . . .172 F8
Shaggy Calf La SL2 . . . . . .206 A6
Shakespeare Cl MK16 . . . . .22 A5
Shakespeare Lodge SL1 . . .204 F5
Shakespeare Orch HP18 . . .82 F6
Shakespeare Way HP20 . . .116 A8
Shallowford Cl MK4 . . . . . .46 D4
Shamaa Ho [18] SL1 . . . . .205 F4
Shamrock Cl MK7 . . . . .48 B6

Shannon Ct
  Chesham HP5 . . . . .144 C1
  Milton Keynes MK14 . . . . . .35 A6
Shantock Hall La HP3 . . . .145 E1
Shantock La HP3 . . . . .145 E1
Shantung PI HP5 . . . . .154 C6
Shardeloes HP7 . . . . .164 D8
Sharkham St MK4 . . . . .46 B1
Sharman Row [8] SL3 . . . .206 F1
Sharman Wlk MK13 . . . . . .34 B3
Sharney Ave SL3 . . . . .207 B3
Sharp Cl HP21 . . . . .115 C5
Sharp's Cl HP17 . . . . .99 B6
Sharrow Vale HP12 . . . . . .172 E7
Shaw Cl Aylesbury HP20 . .116 A8
  Newport Pagnell MK16 . . . . .22 A5
Shaw Ct Aylesbury HP21 . .115 E3
  Old Windsor SL4 . . . . .211 A2
Shaw The SL6 . . . . .195 E6
Shawfield Ct UB7 . . . . . . .208 E3
Shaws Cl HP16 . . . . .151 D5
Shearmans MK11 . . . . .33 A4
Sheehy Way SL2 . . . . .206 B6
Sheelin Gr MK2 . . . . .58 D4
Sheep St MK18 . . . . .66 A4
Sheepcoat Cl MK5 . . . . . . .46 A5
Sheepcote Cl HP9 . . . . . . .175 C4
Sheepcote Dell Rd
  HP15 . . . . .163 E7
Sheepcote Gdns SL6 . . . . .195 C8
Sheepcote La HP10,SL1 . . .186 A2
Sheepcote Rd
  Eton Wick SL4 . . . . .205 A1
  Windsor SL4 . . . . .209 E5
Sheepfold La HP7 . . . . . . .165 D7
Sheephouse Rd SL6 . . . . . .196 B2
Sheeplane MK17 . . . . .60 C2
Sheepridge La SL7,SL8 . . .184 E2
Sheering Gr MK13 . . . . . . .34 B8
Sheerness Ct MK4 . . . . . . .57 A8
Sheerstock HP17 . . . . .126 E5
Sheerwater HP19 . . . . . . .101 E4
Sheet St SL4 . . . . .210 D6
Sheet Street Rd SL4 . . . . .210 C2
Sheffield Dr HP21 . . . . . . .115 E6
Sheffield Rd SL1 . . . . .205 C7
Shelburne Ct HP12 . . . . . .172 E4
Shelburne Rd HP12 . . . . . .172 E4
Sheldon Ct MK8 . . . . .33 F1
Sheldon Rd HP18 . . . . . . .124 A3
Shelduck Cl [3] HP20 . . . .101 E3
Shelley Cl
  Medmenham SL7 . . . . .193 D7
  Newport Pagnell MK16 . . . . .22 B4
  Slough SL3 . . . . .206 F1
  Wooburn Green HP10 . . . . .185 E8
Shelley Dr MK3 . . . . .46 F4
Shelley Rd Chesham HP5 . .144 B2
  High Wycombe HP11 . . . . . .172 F5
  [12] Marlow SL7 . . . . .183 F3
Shellfield Cl TW19 . . . . . .213 A2
Shelsmore MK14 . . . . .35 A8
Shelton Ct Slough SL3 . . . .206 C3
  Woburn Sands MK17 . . . . . .49 B4
Shenley Brook End Sch
  MK5 . . . . .46 A2
Shenley Rd
  Milton Keynes,Bletchley
    MK3 . . . . .46 E1
  Milton Keynes,Bletchley
    MK3 . . . . .57 F8
  Milton Keynes,Loughton
    MK5 . . . . .46 A7
  Whaddon MK17 . . . . .56 C8
Shenley Rdbt MK5 . . . . . . .46 A2
Shenston Ct [13] SL4 . . . .210 C6
Shenstone Dr SL1 . . . . . . .197 D1
Shenstone Hill HP4 . . . . . .135 E5
Shepherd Cl HP20 . . . . . . .102 A2
Shepherd's La WD3 . . . . . .167 E2
Shepherds MK11 . . . . .33 A4
Shepherds Cl
  Beaconsfield HP9 . . . . .175 F1
  Hurley SL6 . . . . .193 F3
  Uxbridge UB8 . . . . .201 C1
Shepherds Ct SL4 . . . . . . .209 E5
Shepherds Fold HP15 . . . .163 D8
Shepherds Gate HP16 . . . .152 A2
Shepherds La
  Beaconsfield HP9 . . . . .175 F1
  Hazlemere HP15 . . . . .162 F5
  Hurley SL6 . . . . .193 E4
Shepherds Row HP5 . . . . . .66 A4
Shepherds Way HP5 . . . . . .154 D6
Shepherdswell Fst Sch
  MK6 . . . . .35 B2
Sheppards Cl MK16 . . . . . .22 C4
Shepperds Cl MK18 . . . . . .76 A2
Shepperds Gn MK5 . . . . . . .45 F6
Shepperton Cl MK19 . . . . . .19 F5
Sheraton Dr HP13 . . . . . . .162 D1
Sheraton Ho WD3 . . . . . . .167 C5
Sherborne Cl SL3 . . . . . . .212 E6
Sherborne Ct SL6 . . . . . . .202 E5
Sherbourne Dr
  Bow Brickhill MK7 . . . . .48 B4
  Maidenhead SL6 . . . . .202 C5
  Windsor SL4 . . . . .209 F3
Sherbourne Wlk SL2 . . . . .198 C8
Shereway HP19 . . . . .115 B8
Shergold Way SL6 . . . . . . .195 F6
Sheridan Cl HP21 . . . . . . .115 D3
Sheridan Ct
  Maidenhead SL6 . . . . .203 B8
  Slough SL1 . . . . .204 E6
Sheriff Ct HP19 . . . . .115 B8
Sheringham Ct SL6 . . . . . .202 E7

Sherington CE Fst Sch
  MK16 . . . . .14 A2
Sherington Rd MK16 . . . . . .22 E7
Sherman Rd SL1 . . . . .205 E8
Shernfold MK7 . . . . .48 B7
Sherriff Cotts HP18 . . . . . .99 A7
Sherwood Cl SL3 . . . . .206 E3
Sherwood Ct
  Colnbrook SL3 . . . . .212 D7
  [10] Slough SL1 . . . . .206 F1
Sherwood Dr
  Maidenhead SL6 . . . . .202 A6
  Milton Keynes MK1,MK2,
    MK3 . . . . .47 B1
Shields Ct HP10 . . . . .163 B1
Shifford Cres SL6 . . . . . . .195 E3
Shilling Cl MK15 . . . . .35 A7
Shillingridge Pk SL7 . . . . .182 C5
Shinfield Cl MK18 . . . . . . .63 D2
Ship Hill SL1 . . . . .186 E4
Ship La LU7 . . . . .105 D3
Ship Rd LU7 . . . . .80 E6
Ship St HP11 . . . . .173 A7
Shiplake Ho SL8 . . . . .185 A4
Shipley Rd MK16 . . . . .22 B4
Shipman Ct MK15 . . . . .35 B7
Shipton MK18 . . . . .66 B3
Shipton Hill MK13 . . . . . . .34 B6
Shipton Rd UB10 . . . . .201 F8
Shire Ct MK14 . . . . .35 A5
Shire La
  Chalfont St Peter HP8,SL9 . .178 B6
  Cholesbury HP23 . . . . .133 B4
  Chorleywood WD3 . . . . . . .167 C4
  North Crawley MK16 . . . . . .24 E4
Shires Bsns Pk The
  NN13 . . . . .38 A6
Shires Rd NN13 . . . . .38 A6
Shirley Ave SL4 . . . . .209 F6
Shirley Moor MK7 . . . . . . .48 B8
Shirley Rd SL6 . . . . .202 C5
Shirwell Cres MK4 . . . . . . .46 D5
Shogmoor La RG9 . . . . . . .170 C1
Shootacre Cnr HP27 . . . . .149 A8
Shootacre La HP27 . . . . . .149 A8
Shootersway HP4 . . . . . . .134 E4
Shootersway La HP4 . . . . .134 F4
Shootersway Pk HP4 . . . . .134 F3
Shop La NN7 . . . . .1 B6
Shoppenhanger's Rd
  SL6 . . . . .202 E4
Shorediche Cl UB10 . . . . .190 F1
Shoreham Rd (E) TW6 . . . .213 E2
Shoreham Rd (W) TW6 . . .213 E2
Shoreham Rise SL2 . . . . . .197 D1
Short Ditch HP17 . . . . . . .127 A7
Short Hale LU7 . . . . .105 D3
Short Massey MK46 . . . . . . .6 E5
Short Rd TW6 . . . . .213 D1
Short St HP11 . . . . .172 F7
Shortborough Ave
  HP27 . . . . .139 B5
Shortfern SL2 . . . . .206 C7
Shortway Amersham HP6 . .154 D2
  Chesham HP5 . . . . .144 B2
Shotfield Rd HP14 . . . . . . .171 C4
Shothanger Way HP3 . . . . .146 D6
Shouler Cl MK5 . . . . .46 A5
Shrewsbury Ct MK3 . . . . . .36 A2
Shrimpton Cl HP9 . . . . . . .175 D6
Shrimpton Rd
  Beaconsfield HP9 . . . . .175 D6
  High Wycombe HP12 . . . . . .172 B3
Shropshire Ct MK3 . . . . . . .46 E1
Shrubbery Cl HP13 . . . . . .173 B8
Shrubbery Rd HP13 . . . . . .173 B8
Shrublands Ave HP4 . . . . .135 A4
Shrublands Rd HP4 . . . . . .135 A5
Shucklow Hill MK17 . . . . . .55 E3
Shugars Gn HP23 . . . . . . .119 B5
Shupp's La HP18 . . . . .112 B1
Shutlanger Rd NN12 . . . . . .9 A8
Shuttleworth Gr MK7 . . . . .48 D6
Sibleys Rise HP16 . . . . . . .152 D8
Side Rd UB9 . . . . .189 D4
Sidings Ind Est The
  NN13 . . . . .38 A4
Sidings The HP11 . . . . . . .174 B3
Sidlow Ct MK11 . . . . .32 F4
Sidney Cl UB8 . . . . .201 C5
Sidney Ho HP14 . . . . .171 C5
Sidney Rd SL4 . . . . .209 C4
Sidney Terr HP22 . . . . . . .131 B5
Silbury Arc MK9 . . . . .34 E3
Silbury Bvd MK9 . . . . .34 D2
Silbury Rdbt MK9 . . . . .34 C1
Silchester Ho SL6 . . . . . . .203 B8
Silchester House Sch
  SL6 . . . . .203 D7
Silco Dr SL6 . . . . .202 E6
Silicon Ct MK5 . . . . .46 C5
Silk Mill Way HP23 . . . . . .119 A5
Silk St HP18 . . . . .99 A6
Silkwood Ct SL1 . . . . .205 F6
Sillswood MK46 . . . . .6 E4
Silsden Cres HP8 . . . . .177 D7
Silver Birch Cl UB10 . . . . .201 E8
Silver Birch Cvn Site
  HP14 . . . . .150 B1
Silver Birch Dr HP27 . . . . .149 C5
Silver Cl SL6 . . . . .202 A5
Silver End MK46 . . . . .7 A3
Silver Hill HP8 . . . . .177 B8
Silver St
  [20] Aylesbury HP20 . . . . .115 D8
  Cublington LU7 . . . . .78 B1
  Milton Keynes MK11 . . . . . .32 D5

Silver St continued
Newport Pagnell MK16 . . . . . .22 D4
Silverbeck Way TW19 . . . . .213 A2
Silverbirches La MK17 . . . . .49 A2
Silverdale Cl
4 Aylesbury HP20 . . . . . . .101 D1
Tyler Green HP10 . . . . .163 A1
Silvermead HP18 . . . . .123 D5
Silverstone Mews SL6 . . . . .202 C4
Silverstone Motor Racing
Circuit* MK18 . . . . .28 F8
Silvertrees Dr SL6 . . . . . . .202 A5
Silverweed Ct MK7 . . . . . . .48 B5
Simatt Ho HP10 . . . . .174 C2
Simdims MK43 . . . . .25 A1
Simmons Cl SL3 . . . . .207 A2
Simmons Ct
Aylesbury HP21 . . . . .115 E4
High Wycombe HP12 . . . . . .172 E2
Simmons Rd RG9 . . . . .191 D3
Simmons Way
Lane End HP14 . . . . .171 C4
Thame OX9 . . . . .125 F1
Simms Croft MK10 . . . . . . .36 A2
Simnel MK6 . . . . .47 B6
Simon Dean HP3 . . . . .146 A4
Simon's Way MK18 . . . . . . .39 E7
Simons Lea MK18 . . . . .34 B4
Simonsbath MK4 . . . . .46 D2
Simpson Cl SL6 . . . . .203 B8
Simpson Comb Sch MK6 .47 D5
Simpson Dr MK6 . . . . .47 E5
Simpson Pl HP21 . . . . .115 F5
Simpson Rd MK1,MK2,
MK6 . . . . .47 E3
Simpson Rdbt MK6 . . . . . . .47 D5
Simpsons Way SL1 . . . . . . .205 E5
Sinclair Ct MK1 . . . . .47 B3
Sinclair Rd SL4 . . . . .210 C4
Singleborough La MK17 . . . .54 F3
Singleton Dr MK8 . . . . .45 D6
Singleton Way 8 HP19 . .115 A8
Singret Pl UB8 . . . . .201 C1
Sion Terr MK18 . . . . .51 B6
Sipson Rd UB7 . . . . .208 D3
Sipthorp Cl MK7 . . . . .48 C6
Sir Frank Markham Com Coll
MK6 . . . . .46 F7
Sir Frank Markham Com Sch
MK6 . . . . .47 A7
Sir Henry Floyd Gram Sch
HP21 . . . . .115 C7
Sir Henry Peakes Dr
SL2 . . . . .198 A6
Sir Peter's Way HP4 . . . . . .107 E6
Sir Sydney Camm Ho
SL4 . . . . .210 B6
Sir William Borlase's Gram
Sch SL7 . . . . .183 C1
Sir William Ramsay Sch
HP15 . . . . .163 A3
Sissinghurst Dr MK4 . . . . . .45 E2
Sitwell Cl MK16 . . . . .21 F5
Six Cotts MK18 . . . . .29 E5
Sixth St HP11 . . . . .173 C4
Sixty Acres Rd HP16 . . . . .151 C6
Skeats Wharf MK15 . . . . . . .35 A7
Skeldon Gate MK14 . . . . . . .35 A4
Skeldon Rdbt MK9 . . . . .35 A4
Skelton Cl HP9 . . . . .186 A8
Skene Cl MK2 . . . . .58 C7
Skerries Ct SL3 . . . . .207 A2
Skimmers Cl HP15 . . . . . . .163 C6
Skimmers End HP15 . . . . . .163 C6
Skimmers Field HP15 . . . . .163 C6
Skip La UB9 . . . . .190 E3
Skippon Way OX9 . . . . .125 F2
Skipton Cl MK15 . . . . .35 C6
Skittle Gn MK7 . . . . .138 A2
Skydmore Path SL2 . . . . . .197 F1
Skye Lodge SL1 . . . . .205 E5
Skylark Rd UB9 . . . . .189 C3
Skyport Dr UB7 . . . . .213 D7
Skyway 14 Trad Est SL3 . . . .212 F4
Slad La Lacey Green HP27 149 F3
Lacey Green HP27 . . . . . . .149 F4
Slade Hill
Aylesbury HP19 . . . . .115 A7
Mixbury NN13 . . . . .38 D1
Slade La MK11 . . . . .33 A4
Slade Oak La UB9 . . . . . . .189 C5
Slade Rd HP14 . . . . .158 E4
Slade The MK17 . . . . .57 D3
Slapton La LU6 . . . . .91 F6
Slated Row MK12 . . . . .33 B7
Slated Row Sch MK12 . . . . .33 A7
Slater St HP13 . . . . .173 C6
Slattenham Cl HP19 . . . . . .115 B7
Slave Hill HP17 . . . . .126 F5
Slayter Rd HP14 . . . . .171 C4
Slickett's La LU6 . . . . .92 F3
Slipe The LU7 . . . . .105 A7
Slough & Eton CE Sch
SL1 . . . . .205 D3
Slough Gram Sch SL2 . . . .206 B3
Slough Interchange Ind Est
SL2 . . . . .206 A4
Slough La HP14 . . . . .160 C6
Slough Mus* SL1 . . . . .206 A4
Slough Rd Datchet SL3 . . . .211 B8
Iver Heath SL0 . . . . .200 E3
Slough SL4 . . . . .205 E2
Slough Sta SL1 . . . . .205 F5
Slough Trad Est SL1 . . . . . .205 B7
Sly Cnr HP16 . . . . .142 E4
Smabridge Wlk MK15 . . . . . .35 D7
Small Cres MK18 . . . . .52 F8
Smalldean La HP27 . . . . . .149 E2

Smarden Bell MK7 . . . . . . .48 B8
Smeaton Cl
Aylesbury HP19 . . . . .101 A1
Blakelands MK14 . . . . .22 A2
Smewin Ct HP11 . . . . .172 E7
Smith Cl HP20 . . . . .116 B7
Smith Ctr The RG9 . . . . . . .191 B5
Smith's La
Waterperry Common OX33 122 F7
Windsor SL4 . . . . .209 A6
Smithergill Ct MK13 . . . . . . .34 C5
Smithfield End MK17 . . . . . .66 F4
Smithfield Rd MK13 . . . . . . .34 C5
Smithsons Pl MK9 . . . . .35 B3
Snaith Cres MK5 . . . . .46 B7
Snakeley Cl HP10 . . . . .174 C1
Snape Spur SL1 . . . . .205 E7
Snells La HP7 . . . . .166 C7
Snells Wood Ct HP7 . . . . . .166 C7
Snelshall St MK4 . . . . .56 F8
Snowball Hill SL6 . . . . .202 A1
Snowberry Cl MK12 . . . . . . .33 D5
Snowden Cl SL4 . . . . .209 D3
Snowdon Dr MK6 . . . . .46 D7
Snowdrop Way MK15 . . . . .162 F9
Snowhill Cotts HP5 . . . . . . .144 F7
Snowshill Cl MK14 . . . . .21 F2
Soames Ct MK46 . . . . .7 F7
Soane Wlk HP13 . . . . .173 A8
Soho Cres HP10 . . . . .185 D4
Soho Mills Ind Est
HP10 . . . . .185 D4
Sokeman Cl MK12 . . . . .33 A5
Solar Ct MK14 . . . . .21 E1
Solesbridge Cl WD3 . . . . . .167 F6
Solesbridge La WD3 . . . . . .167 F6
Somerford Cl SL6 . . . . .203 B8
Somerford Pl HP9 . . . . .175 D3
Somerlea SL6 . . . . .196 C3
Somers Lees 16 HP19 . . . . .115 A8
Somersby Cres SL6 . . . . . . .202 E3
Somerset MK3 . . . . .46 F1
Somerset Lodge 3 SL6 . . . .202 F6
Somerset Way SL0 . . . . . . .207 F4
Somerville Rd SL4 . . . . .205 C1
Somerville Way HP19 . . . . .115 B8
Sophie Gdns SL3 . . . . .206 D4
Sorensen Ct MK5 . . . . .45 E4
Sorrell Dr MK16 . . . . .21 F4
Soskin Dr MK14 . . . . .34 D6
Sospel Ct SL2 . . . . .198 C3
Soulbury Rd Burcott LU7 . .79 D4
Leighton Buzzard LU7 . . . . .80 D7
Stewkley LU7 . . . . .68 F1
South Bank NN13 . . . . .38 B7
South Bank Rd HP4 . . . . . .134 F6
South Cl
Medmenham SL7 . . . . .193 D7
Slough SL1 . . . . .204 D6
West Drayton UB7 . . . . . . .208 F3
South Common Rd UB8 . .201 E6
South Cottage Dr WD3 . .167 F4
South Cottage Gdns
WD3 . . . . .167 F4
South Dr
Beaconsfield HP9 . . . . .186 B8
High Wycombe HP13 . . . . . .173 D8
South Eighth St MK9 . . . . . .34 E1
South End Rd HP17 . . . . . .126 F5
South End La LU6 . . . . .92 B4
South Enmore Rd MK6 . . . . .35 B3
South Field Cl SL4 . . . . . . .204 C3
South Fifth St MK9 . . . . .34 E1
South Fourth St MK9 . . . . . .34 D1
South Gn SL1 . . . . .205 D4
South Hall MK18 . . . . .41 E3
South Hills HP18 . . . . .96 A1
South Ho MK1 . . . . .47 D3
South La LU7 . . . . .78 E7
South Lawne MK3 . . . . .57 F8
South Maundin HP14 . . . . . .162 A7
South Meadow La SL4 . . . .210 C8
South Ninth St MK9 . . . . . . .34 F2
South Overgate Rdbt
MK6 . . . . .35 B3
South Park Ave WD3 . . . . .167 F4
South Park Cres SL9 . . . . . .188 F7
South Park Ct SL9 . . . . .188 E6
South Park Dr SL9 . . . . .188 E7
South Park Gdns HP4 . . . . .135 B5
South Park View SL9 . . . . . .188 F7
South Path SL4 . . . . .210 C5
South Pk SL9 . . . . .188 F6
South Pl SL7 . . . . .188 F7
South Rd Amersham HP6 . .154 C3
Chorleywood WD3 . . . . . . .167 C4
Maidenhead SL6 . . . . .202 E6
West Drayton UB7 . . . . . . .208 F3
South Row Fulmer SL3 . . . . .199 E8
Milton Keynes MK9 . . . . . . .34 E1
Milton Keynes MK9 . . . . . . .34 D1
South Saxon Rdbt MK9 . . . . .34 F1
South Secklow Rdbt MK6 . . . .34 F2
South Second St MK9 . . . . . .34 D1
South Seventh St MK9 . . . . .34 E1
South Side SL9 . . . . .188 D8
South Sixth St MK9 . . . . . . .34 E1
South St
Castlethorpe MK19 . . . . . . .19 F5
Wendover HP22 . . . . .131 B4
South Tenth St MK9 . . . . . . .34 F2
South Terr
Milton Keynes MK2 . . . . . . .58 C8
Windsor SL4 . . . . .210 E6
South Vale NN7 . . . . .1 A5
South View
Cookham Rise SL6 . . . . . .195 E7

South View continued
Eton SL4 . . . . .205 B1
High Wycombe HP13 . . . . . .161 D2
Wooburn Green HP10 . . . . .185 D8
South View Rd SL9 . . . . . . .188 D7
South Way HP9 . . . . .186 A8
South Witan Rdbt MK6 . . . . .34 E1
Southampton Rd TW6 . . . . .213 F1
Southbourne 1 HP13 . . . . .173 C7
Southbourne Dr SL8 . . . . . .185 A3
Southbridge Gr MK7 . . . . . . .48 A7
Southcliffe Dr SL9 . . . . .177 E5
Southcote Way HP10 . . . . . .163 B1
Southcott Lower Sch
LU7 . . . . .80 D8
Southcott Village LU7 . . . . . .80 D6
Southcourt Ave LU7 . . . . . . .80 D6
Southcourt Ho LU7 . . . . .80 D7
Southcourt Rd LU7 . . . . .80 D7
Southcroft SL2 . . . . .198 B1
Southern Cotts TW19 . . . . .213 A2
Southern Perimeter Rd
TW6,TW19 . . . . .213 D2
Southern Rd
Aylesbury HP19 . . . . .101 C1
Thame OX9 . . . . .125 C1
Southern Way MK12 . . . . . . .33 D5
Southfield Cl MK15 . . . . .35 C7
Southfield Cotts HP17 . . . . .130 C3
Southfield Dr HP15 . . . . . . .163 A6
Southfield Gdns SL1 . . . . . .204 B8
Southfield Rd
Aylesbury HP20 . . . . .116 B8
Flackwell Heath HP10 . . . .174 A1
High Wycombe HP13 . . . . . .161 D1
Princes Risborough HP27 . .139 C1
Southgate Ho SL6 . . . . .202 F8
Southlands Rd UB9 . . . . . . .189 F1
Southlea Rd SL3,SL4 . . . . . .211 B5
Southview Rd SL7 . . . . .183 E4
Southwick Ct MK8 . . . . .45 F8
Southwold Cl HP21 . . . . . . .116 A6
Southwold Spur SL3 . . . . . .207 C4
Southwood Gdns SL6 . . . . .195 E5
Southwood Mid Sch
MK14 . . . . .34 C5
Southwood Rd SL6 . . . . . . .195 E5
Sovereign Beeches SL2 198 B6
Sovereign Cl MK18 . . . . .75 F7
Sovereign Ct
Aylesbury HP19 . . . . .101 D1
High Wycombe HP13 . . . . . .173 D6
Sovereign Dr MK15 . . . . . . .35 A7
Sovereign Hts SL3 . . . . . . .212 A8
Sovereign Lodge MK15 . . . .35 A7
Spa Cl HP18 . . . . .110 B8
Spackmans Way SL1 . . . . . .205 D3
Spade Oak Farm SL8 . . . . .184 E3
Spade Oak Mdw SL8 . . . . . .184 E4
Spark Way MK16 . . . . .21 F5
Sparrow Cl HP19 . . . . .101 F3
Sparrow Hall Bsns Pk
LU6 . . . . .92 D3
Sparrow Hall Farm LU6 . .92 D3
Sparsholt Cl 5 MK4 . . . . . . .46 C2
Spearing Rd HP12 . . . . .172 C7
Spearmast Ind Est HP12 172 B6
Spearmint Cl MK7 . . . . .48 B5
Specklands MK5 . . . . .46 A8
Speedbird Way UB7 . . . . . .213 B7
Speedwell Pl MK14 . . . . . . .34 C4
Speen CE Sch HP27 . . . . . .150 B4
Speen Rd HP14,HP16,
HP27 . . . . .150 D2
Speldhurst St MK7 . . . . .48 B7
Spencer MK14 . . . . .34 C8
Spencer Cl MK18 . . . . .201 C2
Spencer Gdns OX27 . . . . . .72 E5
Spencer Rd SL3 . . . . .206 F3
Spencer Villas SL1 . . . . . . .204 F5
Spencers Cl SL6 . . . . .202 D8
Spencers La SL6 . . . . .195 D8
Spencers Rd SL6 . . . . .202 D8
Spenlows Rd MK3 . . . . .47 A3
Spens SL6 . . . . .202 F8
Spenser Ho HP21 . . . . .115 F6
Spenser Rd HP21 . . . . .115 F6
Sperling Rd SL6 . . . . .195 F1
Spickett's La HP18 . . . . . . .113 A3
Spier's La OX27 . . . . .71 F2
Spiert The HP17 . . . . .114 D5
Spindle Ct HP15 . . . . .163 A3
Spindle Ct HP12 . . . . .172 E7
Spinfield La SL7 . . . . .183 B2
Spinfield La W SL7 . . . . . . .183 C1
Spinfield Mount SL7 . . . . . .183 B1
Spinfield Pk SL7 . . . . .183 C1
Spinfield Sch SL7 . . . . .183 B2
Spinners Wlk
Marlow SL7 . . . . .183 C1
Windsor SL4 . . . . .210 C6
Spinney SL1 . . . . .205 B5
Spinney Bglws LU7 . . . . . . .91 C6
Spinney Cl
Steeple Claydon MK18 . . . .63 E2
West Drayton UB7 . . . . . . .208 E6
Spinney Cotts OX33 . . . . . .123 B1
Spinney Cres LU6 . . . . .93 F6
Spinney Hill Rd MK46 . . . . . .6 E3
Spinney La MK17 . . . . .49 F4
Spinney The
Beaconsfield HP9 . . . . .175 E4
Berkhamsted HP4 . . . . .134 F3
Chesham HP5 . . . . .144 D2
Gerrards Cross SL9 . . . . . .188 D3
High Wycombe HP11 . . . . . .173 A4
Holmer Green HP15 . . . . . .163 D7

Spinney The continued
Milton Keynes MK13 . . . . . .34 A4
Winslow MK18 . . . . .66 A6
Spire View TW19 . . . . .213 C1
Spitfire Cl SL3 . . . . .207 A2
Spittal St SL7 . . . . .183 D2
Spoondell LU6 . . . . .93 F7
Spooney Moult MK13 . . . . . .33 C5
Sportsman Cl MK18 . . . . . . .63 D3
Spout La TW19 . . . . .213 A3
Spout La N TW19 . . . . .213 B3
Sprigs Holly La HP14 . . . . .159 B8
Spring Cl
High Wycombe HP13 . . . . . .173 F7
Latimer HP5 . . . . .155 D3
Maidenhead SL6 . . . . .195 F2
Spring Coppice HP14 . . . . .171 F5
Spring Coppice La
HP27 . . . . .150 D5
Spring Field Rd HP4 . . . . . .135 A6
Spring Gardens Rd
HP13 . . . . .173 E5
Spring Gdns
Bourne End SL8 . . . . .185 A4
Marlow SL7 . . . . .183 E3
Newport Pagnell MK16 . . . . .22 C4
Wooburn Green HP10 . . . . .185 D8
Spring Gr MK17 . . . . .49 B5
Spring Hill SL6 . . . . .202 E3
Spring Ho SL7 . . . . .183 E3
Spring La Alderton NN12 . . . .9 A2
Clifton Reynes MK46 . . . . . . .7 C3
Cookham Dean SL6 . . . . . .195 C5
Farnham Common SL2 . . . .198 C5
Flackwell Heath HP10 . . . .173 F3
Great Horwood MK17 . . . . . .55 A2
Olney MK46 . . . . .6 F3
Slough SL1 . . . . .204 F5
Spring Mdw HP18 . . . . .97 A1
Spring Valley Dr HP14 . . . . .162 A7
Springate Field SL3 . . . . . .206 E4
Springbank Ct MK16 . . . . . .12 B7
Springdale Cotts SL8 . . . . .185 B2
Springett Pl HP6 . . . . .154 F2
Springfield Bvd MK6 . . . . . . .35 B2
Springfield SL1 . . . . .206 A3
Springfield Cl
Aylesbury HP21 . . . . .115 C8
Chesham HP5 . . . . .154 C7
Windsor SL4 . . . . .210 B5
Springfield Ct
1 Leighton Buzzard LU7 . .80 E7
Maidenhead SL6 . . . . .203 B7
Milton Keynes MK6 . . . . . . .35 B2
Springfield Gdns
Chinnor OX39 . . . . .147 C5
Deanshanger MK19 . . . . . . .31 E4
Springfield Hollow
HP14 . . . . .158 E5
Springfield Mid Sch MK6 35 B2
Springfield Pk SL6 . . . . . . .203 C1
Springfield Rd
Chesham HP5 . . . . .154 C7
Dunstable LU6 . . . . .93 D5
Leighton Buzzard LU7 . . . . .80 E7
Olney MK46 . . . . .6 F4
Slough SL3 . . . . .212 B4
Stokenchurch HP14 . . . . . .158 F4
Windsor SL4 . . . . .210 B5
Springfield Rdbt MK6 . . . . . .35 A2
Springfield Way MK43 . . . . . .25 C2
Springfields
Amersham HP6 . . . . .154 C2
Padbury MK18 . . . . .53 C2
Tylers Green HP10 . . . . . . .163 C2
Springfields Cl MK18 . . . . . .53 C2
Springfields Sch MK18 . . . . .53 C1
Springhill (HM Prison)
HP18 . . . . .73 A1
Springhill Rd HP18 . . . . .83 A8
Springs Cl HP17 . . . . .130 B2
Springs La HP17 . . . . .130 B3
Springside 2 LU7 . . . . .80 E7
Springwater Mill HP11 . . . . .173 E4
Springwood HP27 . . . . .150 D4
Spruce Cl 7 SL1 . . . . .205 F3
Spruce Dene HP15 . . . . . . .162 F2
Spruce Rd HP19 . . . . .114 F8
Spur The SL1 . . . . .204 D8
Spurgrove La RG9 . . . . .170 E2
Spurlands End Rd HP15 . . .163 A8
Spurt St HP18 . . . . .112 F3
Square Close Cotts RG9 169 F3
Square The Akeley MK18 . . .41 F8
Aspley Guise MK17 . . . . . . .49 E4
Brill HP18 . . . . .110 A8
Great Missenden HP16 . . . .152 B7
Harmondsworth UB7 . . . . .213 B6
Long Crendon HP18 . . . . . .125 C6
Milton Keynes MK12 . . . . . .33 D6
Preston Bissett MK18 . . . . . .62 B2
Waddesdon HP18 . . . . .99 A6
Yardley Hastings NN7 . . . . . .1 A6
Squires Cl MK46 . . . . .7 A6
Squirrel La HP12 . . . . .172 C5
Squirrel Rd SL7 . . . . .183 D6
Squirrels Way MK18 . . . . . . .52 E7
Stable Cl MK15 . . . . .50 C7
Stable Cotts SL7 . . . . .194 C5
Stable La HP9 . . . . .176 C4
Stable Rd HP21 . . . . .131 E2
Stablebridge Rd HP22 . . . . .117 F3
Stables Ct SL7 . . . . .183 B1
Stables The MK19 . . . . .20 F3
Stacey Av MK12 . . . . .33 D6
Stacey Bushes Trad Ctr
MK12 . . . . .33 C6
Stacey Ho HP12 . . . . .172 E4

Stacey's Ct HP8 . . . . .177 C8
Staddle Stones HP27 . . . . .139 B4
Stafferton Way SL6 . . . . . . .203 A6
Stafford Ave SL2 . . . . .198 C5
Stafford Cl SL6 . . . . .204 B7
Stafford Gr MK5 . . . . .46 B6
Stafford Keep HP19 . . . . . . .115 A8
Stag Ct WD3 . . . . .167 C5
Stag La Berkhamsted HP4 135 B5
Chorleywood WD3 . . . . . . .167 C3
Great Kingshill HP15 . . . . .151 D1
Stagshaw Gr 5 MK4 . . . . . . .46 B2
Stainby Cl UB7 . . . . .208 E3
Stainton Dr MK13 . . . . .34 C4
Stamford Ave MK6 . . . . .35 B2
Stamford Rd SL6 . . . . .202 C6
Stanbridge Cl HP17 . . . . . . .127 A7
Stanbridge La HP17 . . . . . . .32 F5
Stanbridge Rd HP17 . . . . . .127 B6
Stanbrook Pl MK10 . . . . .36 A1
Standfield Cl HP19 . . . . .115 A8
Standing Way
Milton Keynes,Coldharbour
Spinney MK3,MK4 . . . . . . .46 E3
Milton Keynes,Kingston
MK10 . . . . .36 C1
Milton Keynes,Peartree Bridge
MK10,MK4,MK6 . . . . .47 C7
Milton Keynes,Snelshall East
MK4 . . . . .57 B7
Standring Pl HP20 . . . . .101 F2
Stanhope Cl HP22 . . . . .131 B2
Stanhope Heath TW19 . . . . .213 C1
Stanhope Rd
Aylesbury HP20 . . . . .116 A8
Slough SL1 . . . . .204 D7
Stanhope Way TW19 . . . . . .213 C1
Stanier Rise HP4 . . . . .134 F7
Stanier Sq 5 MK2 . . . . .58 C8
Stanley Ave HP5 . . . . .154 B8
Stanley Cl Marlow SL7 . . . . .183 F3
Uxbridge UB8 . . . . .201 D3
Stanley Cotts SL2 . . . . .205 F5
Stanley Ct MK46 . . . . .6 F5
Stanley Gdns HP23 . . . . . . .118 F3
Stanley Green E SL3 . . . . . .206 F2
Stanley Green W SL3 . . . . . .206 F2
Stanley Hill HP7 . . . . .165 E7
Stanley Hill Ave HP7 . . . . . .165 E8
Stanley Ho SL4 . . . . .211 A2
Stanley Pl HP12 . . . . .172 C5
Stanley Spencer Art Gall &
Mus* SL6 . . . . .196 B7
Stanmore Gdns MK16 . . . . . .22 B2
Stanstead Pl HP7 . . . . .165 C8
Stansted Rd TW6 . . . . .213 F1
Stanton Ave MK13 . . . . .34 A6
Stanton Gate MK14 . . . . . . .34 D8
Stanton Mid Sch MK13 . . . . .34 B7
Stanton Way SL3 . . . . .206 E2
Stanton Wood Rdbt
MK14 . . . . .34 D4
Stantonbury Campus
MK14 . . . . .34 C8
Stantonbury Cl MK13 . . . . . .34 A8
Stanway Cl MK15 . . . . .35 B6
Stanwell Cl TW19 . . . . .213 D1
Stanwell Fields CE Prim Sch
TW19 . . . . .213 D1
Stanwell Gdns TW19 . . . . . .213 D1
Stanwell Moor Rd TW6,
TW19,UB7 . . . . .213 B4
Stanwell Rd SL3 . . . . .212 C4
Stapeley Ct MK4 . . . . .45 F2
Staple Hall Rd MK1 . . . . . . .47 E1
Stapleton Cl SL7 . . . . .183 F4
Stars La HP17 . . . . .113 C2
Startins La SL6 . . . . .195 C8
Starveall Cl UB7 . . . . .208 F3
Starwood Ct 1 SL3 . . . . . . .206 C3
Staters Pound MK15 . . . . . . .35 A7
Statham Pl MK6 . . . . .46 F8
Station App
Amersham HP6 . . . . .154 C1
Chorleywood WD3 . . . . . . .167 D5
Denham UB9 . . . . .189 D4
Gerrards Cross SL9 . . . . . .188 E6
Great Missenden HP16 . . . .152 A7
Little Chalfont HP7 . . . . . . .166 D8
Maidenhead SL6 . . . . .202 F6
Marlow SL7 . . . . .183 E2
Wendover HP22 . . . . .131 B4
West Drayton UB7 . . . . . . .208 E5
Station Cotts
Denham UB9 . . . . .190 A4
Winslow MK18 . . . . .66 A5
Station Hill SL6 . . . . .195 F7
Station Par
Beaconsfield HP9 . . . . .175 D3
Cookham Rise SL8 . . . . . . .195 F6
Denham Green UB9 . . . . . .190 A4
Station Rd Aldbury HP23 . .120 B5
Amersham HP7 . . . . .165 C8
Beaconsfield HP9 . . . . .175 D3
Berkhamsted HP4 . . . . .135 D4
Blackthorn OX25 . . . . .81 A4
Bourne End SL8 . . . . .185 A3
Bow Brickhill MK17 . . . . . . .48 C2
Buckingham MK18 . . . . . . .52 E7
Castlethorpe MK19 . . . . . . .19 F5
Cheddington LU7 . . . . .91 A1
Chesham HP5 . . . . .154 C8
Chinnor OX39 . . . . .147 D5
Cookham Rise SL6 . . . . . .195 F7
Gerrards Cross SL9 . . . . . .188 E6

Station Rd continued
Haddenham HP17 . . . . . . .126 E5
Henley-on-T RG9 . . . . . . .191 E1
High Wycombe HP13 . . .173 C6
Ivinghoe LU7 . . . . .105 E5
Leighton Buzzard LU7 . . .80 E7
Little Kimble HP17 . . . . . .129 E2
Long Marston HP23 . . . . .104 B4
Loudwater HP10 . . . . . . .174 C2
Marlow SL7 . . . . .183 E1
Marsh Gibbon OX27 . . . . .71 F3
Mursley MK17 . . . . .67 B7
Newport Pagnell MK16 . . .22 C4
Padbury MK18 . . . . .53 B1
Princes Risborough HP27 .139 A2
Quainton HP22 . . . . .85 A4
Slough SL1 . . . . .204 E7
Slough,Langley SL3 . . . . .207 A4
Stoke Mandeville HP22 . .116 B2
Swanbourne MK17 . . . . . .67 A4
Taplow SL6 . . . . .203 F7
Tring HP23 . . . . .119 D4
Uxbridge UB8 . . . . .201 D1
West Drayton UB7 . . . . . .208 E4
Winslow MK18 . . . . .66 A5
Woburn Sands MK17 . . . .49 B5
Wraysbury TW19 . . . . . . .212 A1
Station Rd Ind Est MK18 .66 A5
Station Rise SL7 . . . . . . .183 E2
Station Sq MK9 . . . . .34 C1
Station Terr
Buckingham MK18 . . . . . . .52 C7
Milton Keynes MK14 . . . . .21 E2
Station Way HP20 . . . . . .115 D7
Staunton Ho MK17 . . . . . .60 F7
Staunton Rd SL2 . . . . . . .205 D8
Staveley Cl HP21 . . . . . . .116 C4
Stavordale 🛚 MK4 . . . . . .36 A1
Stayning La MK14 . . . . . . .34 F6
Steeple Cl MK4 . . . . .57 A8
Steeple Claydon Sch
MK18 . . . . .63 E3
Steinbeck Cres MK18 . . . .56 F7
Stephenson Cl
Aylesbury HP19 . . . . .115 B7
High Wycombe HP13 . . . .161 F1
Leighton Buzzard LU7 . . . .80 E7
Stephenson Ct 🛯 SL1 . . .205 F4
Stephenson Dr SL4 . . . . .210 B7
Stepnells HP23 . . . . .105 A1
Steppingstones LU6 . . . . .93 F8
Stevens Cl
Holmer Green HP15 . . . . .163 B7
Prestwood HP16 . . . . . . .151 D5
Stevens Field MK7 . . . . . .48 D6
Stevens Ho 🛚 HP7 . . . . .165 B7
Stevenson Rd SL2 . . . . . .187 D2
Stewart Ave SL1 . . . . . . .205 F8
Stewarts Dr SL2 . . . . . . .198 B7
Stewarts Way SL7 . . . . . .183 D7
Stewkley La MK17 . . . . . . .67 E4
Stewkley Rd
Cublington LU7 . . . . .78 C1
Hollingdon LU7 . . . . .69 C2
Wing LU7 . . . . .79 B3
Stile Mdw HP9 . . . . .175 E3
Stile Rd SL3 . . . . .206 D3
Stilebrook Rd MK46 . . . . . .6 F6
Stilwell Dr UB8 . . . . .201 F1
Stirling Ave HP20 . . . . . .101 E1
Stirling Cl
Milton Keynes MK15 . . . . .35 A6
Uxbridge UB8 . . . . .201 C2
Windsor SL4 . . . . .209 D5
Stirling Gr SL6 . . . . .202 A8
Stirling Ho
🛚 High Wycombe HP13 . . .173 F7
Milton Keynes MK3 . . . . . .57 D7
Stirling Rd
High Wycombe HP12 . . . .172 D5
Slough SL1 . . . . .205 A8
Stanwell TW6 . . . . .213 F1
Stock Field HP15 . . . . . .163 B3
Stock La MK17 . . . . .45 B1
Stockaway HP22 . . . . .87 C1
Stockdale MK13 . . . . .34 C5
Stockdales Rd SL4 . . . . .204 F2
Stocken Cl MK46 . . . . .6 E4
Stockgrove Ctry Pk★
LU7 . . . . .70 F7
Stockgrove Park Ho LU7 .70 F8
Stockhall Cres LU7 . . . . .68 D2
Stocking Green Cl MK19 .11 A3
Stocking La HP14 . . . . . .161 E7
Stocklake HP20 . . . . .101 E1
Stocklands Way HP16 . . .151 D5
Stockley Acad UB8 . . . . .208 F1
Stockleys La MK18 . . . . . .51 B6
Stockport Rd WD3 . . . . . .167 C2
Stocks Cl MK18 . . . . .65 F4
Stocks Rd HP23 . . . . . . .120 C1
Stocks The MK19 . . . . . . .19 E2
Stockwell HP17 . . . . .127 A6
Stockwell Furlong
HP17 . . . . .127 A6
Stockwell La
Longwick HP17 . . . . .139 A8
Wavendon MK17 . . . . .48 D7
Stockwells SL6 . . . . .196 D1
Stoke Bruerne CE Prim Sch
NN12 . . . . .9 A8
Stoke Common Rd SL2,
SL3 . . . . .199 B8
Stoke Court Dr SL2 . . . . .198 F4
Stoke Farm La HP21 . . . .115 E3

Stoke Gdns SL1 . . . . . . .205 F5
Stoke Gn SL2 . . . . .199 A1
Stoke Goldington CE Fst Sch
MK16 . . . . .12 B6
Stoke Ho 🛛 SL1 . . . . . . .205 F3
Stoke La MK17 . . . . .59 C1
Stoke Leys Sch HP21 . . .115 E3
Stoke Mandeville Comb Sch
HP22 . . . . .116 A1
Stoke Mandeville Hospl
HP21 . . . . .115 F4
Stoke Mandeville Sta
HP22 . . . . .116 B2
Stoke Park Ave SL2 . . . .198 C2
Stoke Poges La SL1 . . . .205 E7
Stoke Poges Sch
Stoke Poges SL2 . . . . . . .198 F5
Stoke Poges SL2 . . . . . . .199 B5
Stoke Rd Ashton NN7 . . . .9 E8
Aylesbury HP21 . . . . .115 E6
Leighton Buzzard LU7 . . . .70 D1
Milton Keynes MK2 . . . . . .58 E5
Newton Longville MK17 . . .57 F3
Slough SL2 . . . . .205 F7
Stoke View SL1 . . . . .205 F5
Stoke Wood SL2 . . . . . . .198 F8
Stokenchurch Cty Fst Sch
HP14 . . . . .158 D5
Stokenchurch Pl MK13 . . .34 C3
Stokenchurch Prim Sch
HP14 . . . . .158 E5
Stokes Croft
Haddenham HP17 . . . . . .127 A6
Haddenham HP17 . . . . . .127 A7
Stokes End HP17 . . . . . .127 A7
Stokes La HP17 . . . . .127 A7
Stokesay SL2 . . . . .205 F6
Stokesay Ct MK4 . . . . . . .45 E2
Stokesley Rise MK10 . . .185 E8
Stolford Rise MK4 . . . . . .46 B1
Stomp Rd SL1 . . . . .204 B8
Stompits Rd SL6 . . . . . . .203 C1
Stone CE Comb Sch
HP17 . . . . .114 D5
Stone Cl UB7 . . . . .208 F5
Stone Croft HP17 . . . . . .114 D5
Stone Ct MK46 . . . . .13 E8
Stone Hill MK4 . . . . .33 D1
Stone House La SL6 . . . .184 D1
Stone Pit Cl MK46 . . . . . . .6 E3
Stone View HP22 . . . . . . .86 D7
Stonebridge Field SL4 . .205 B1
Stonebridge Rd HP19 . . .101 B2
Stonebridge Rdbt MK13 . .33 E8
Stonechat HP19 . . . . . . .101 E3
Stonecroft HP6 . . . . .153 C4
Stonecroft Ave SL0 . . . .207 E7
Stonecrop Pl MK14 . . . . . .34 E4
Stonefield Pk SL6 . . . . . .202 C7
Stonefield Rd HP14 . . . .161 C8
Stonegate MK13 . . . . .34 A5
Stonehaven Rd HP19 . . .101 B2
Stoneleigh Ct MK4 . . . . . .45 E1
Stonepitts Pk HP18 . . . . .111 B3
Stones Row HP11 . . . . . .173 F4
Stones Way MK17 . . . . . . .68 C6
Stoney Cl HP4 . . . . .134 F6
Stoney Dean Sch HP7 . . .165 F8
Stoney Gr Chesham HP5 .144 C1
Chesham HP5 . . . . .144 D1
Stoney La
Berkhamsted HP1 . . . . . .146 B8
Bovingdon HP3 . . . . .146 C5
Chipperfield WD4 . . . . . .146 F1
Cholesbury HP5 . . . . .133 F1
East Burnham SL2 . . . . . .198 A4
Stoney Meade SL1 . . . . .205 B5
Stoney Ware SL7 . . . . . . .194 E8
Stoneycroft HP23 . . . . . .120 C5
Stoneyfield SL9 . . . . .188 C3
Stonor RG9 . . . . .179 F6
Stonor Ct MK8 . . . . .45 F8
Stonor Rd★ RG9 . . . . . .180 A7
Stony Hill NN12 . . . . .17 C8
Stony La
Little Chalfont HP6 . . . . .155 F1
Little Kingshill HP16 . . . .152 C3
Stony Stratford Nature
Reserve★ MK11,MK19 . . .32 D7
Stookslade HP22 . . . . . . .89 A3
Stopps Orch HP27 . . . . . .139 C5
Stork Cl 🛛 HP19 . . . . . . .101 F3
Stornaway Rd SL3 . . . . . .207 C2
Stotfold Ct MK11 . . . . . . .32 E4
Stour Cl Aylesbury HP21 .115 C4
Milton Keynes MK3 . . . . . .57 C4
Newport Pagnell MK16 . . .22 E3
Slough SL1 . . . . .205 B3
Stourhead Gate MK4 . . . .45 E2
Stovell Rd SL4 . . . . .210 B7
Stowe Ave MK18 . . . . .41 B3
Stowe Cl MK18 . . . . .41 C1
Stowe Ct MK14 . . . . .34 C8
Stowe Landscape Gdns★
MK18 . . . . .40 F7
Stowe Rd SL1 . . . . .204 E6
Stowe Rise MK18 . . . . . . .41 C1
Stowe Sch MK18 . . . . . . .40 F7
Stowe View MK18 . . . . . . .51 A7
Straight Bit HP10 . . . . . .185 B8
Straight Rd SL4 . . . . .211 B1
Strande La SL6 . . . . .195 F5
Strande Pk SL6 . . . . .195 F5
Strande View Wlk SL6 . . .195 F5
Strangers La MK18 . . . . . .51 A6
Strangford Dr MK2 . . . . . .58 C4
Stranraer Gdns SL1 . . . .205 E5

Stranraer Rd TW19 . . . .213 E1
Stranraer Way 🛯 TW6 . .213 E1
Stratfield Ct
Maidenhead SL6 . . . . . . .203 B8
Milton Keynes MK8 . . . . . .33 F1
Stratfield Rd SL1 . . . . . .206 A4
Stratford Arc MK11 . . . . .32 D6
Stratford Ave UB10 . . . .201 F3
Stratford Cl SL2 . . . . . . .197 D1
Stratford Dr
Aylesbury HP21 . . . . .115 B6
Wooburn HP10 . . . . .185 D4
Stratford Gdns SL6 . . . .202 C4
Stratford Rd
Buckingham MK18 . . . . . . .41 E1
Cosgrove MK19 . . . . .19 D1
Deanshanger MK19 . . . . . .31 F4
Maids Moreton MK18 . . . .42 C2
Milton Keynes MK12 . . . . .33 C7
Nash MK17 . . . . .44 C1
Old Stratford MK19 . . . . . .32 B5
Whaddon MK17 . . . . .45 A3
Stratfords Way HP17 . . .127 A6
Strathcona Cl HP10 . . . .185 C7
Strathcona Way HP10 . . .185 C7
Strathnaver Pl MK2 . . . . .33 D4
Stratton Chase Dr
Chalfont St Giles HP8 . . .177 B8
Chalfont St Peter HP8 . . .177 A8
Stratton Gn HP21 . . . . . .116 C4
Stratton Rd
Beaconsfield HP9 . . . . . . .175 B2
Princes Risborough HP27 .139 A3
Strauss Gr MK7 . . . . .48 C4
Strawberry Cl HP16 . . . .151 D5
Straws Hadley Ct HP22 . .89 B2
Streamside SL1 . . . . .204 F5
Streamside Wlk HP21 . . .115 C6
Streatham Pl MK13 . . . . . .34 C2
Stretton Cl HP10 . . . . . . .174 C8
Stretton Pl HP6 . . . . .154 F1
Stringers Cotts 🛙 SL9 . .177 D2
Stringfellow Cl MK43 . . . .24 E2
Stroma Ct SL1 . . . . .204 D6
Stroud Cl SL4 . . . . .209 D4
Strudwick Dr MK6 . . . . . . .46 F8
Stuart Ct
Milton Keynes MK2 . . . . . .47 D1
Windsor SL4 . . . . .209 F5
Stuart Cl HP6 . . . . .154 D1
Stuart Rd HP13 . . . . .173 C6
Stuart Way Thame OX9 . .126 A1
Windsor SL4 . . . . .209 F5
Stubble Hill HP19 . . . . . .115 A8
Stubbles La SL6 . . . . . . .195 B6
Stubbs End Cl HP6 . . . . .154 E3
Stubbs Field MK5 . . . . . . .46 A3
Stubbs Wood HP6 . . . . . .154 E3
Stuchbury Cl HP15 . . . . .163 A8
Studdridge Ct HP14 . . . .158 C4
Studham La HP4 . . . . . . .107 D4
Studland Cl HP21 . . . . . .116 B5
Studley Knapp MK7 . . . . .48 B7
Studridge La HP27 . . . . .150 B4
Sturges Cl MK7 . . . . .48 A5
Sturman Ho MK6 . . . . . . .154 C2
Stylecroft Rd HP8 . . . . . .177 D8
Styles Cl OX27 . . . . .71 E2
Styles Ct HP18 . . . . .99 A7
Sudgrove Ho MK15 . . . . . .35 A6
Suffield Rd HP11 . . . . . . .172 F6
Suffolk Cl
Milton Keynes MK3 . . . . . .46 F1
Slough SL1 . . . . .204 E7
Suffolk Ct
Maidenhead SL6 . . . . . . .202 F8
Marsh Gibbon OX27 . . . . .71 F3
Suffolk Ho HP10 . . . . . . .185 E6
Suffolk Rd SL6 . . . . .202 D4
Sulby Cl HP21 . . . . .115 C5
Sulgrave Cres HP23 . . . .119 C5
Sulgrave Ct 🛘 MK8 . . . . .45 F8
Sullivan Cres MK7 . . . . . .48 C5
Sultan Croft MK5 . . . . . . .46 A4
Sumburgh Way SL1 . . . .205 E8
Summerfield Comb Sch
MK13 . . . . .34 C5
Summergill Ct MK13 . . . . .34 C5
Summerhayes MK14 . . . . .34 F7
Summerhouse La UB7 . . .213 D8
Summerlea SL1 . . . . .205 B5
Summerleaze Rd SL6 . . .196 B1
Summerleys LU6 . . . . .92 E4
Summerleys Rd HP27 . . .138 F4
Summers Rd SL1 . . . . . .197 C2
Summerson Rd MK6 . . . . .46 F5
Summerson Rd
Bleak Hall MK6 . . . . .47 A5
Milton Keynes MK6 . . . . . .46 F5
Summit Ctr UB7 . . . . . . .213 D7
Sumner Ct MK5 . . . . .46 A8
Sun Cl SL4 . . . . .210 D8
Sun Cres HP18 . . . . .109 D5
Sun La SL6 . . . . .202 F7
Sun Pas 🛭 SL4 . . . . . . .210 D6
Sunbury Cl MK13 . . . . . . .34 A6
Sunbury Ct SL4 . . . . .210 D8
Sunbury Rd SL4 . . . . . . .210 D8
Sunderland Ct
Milton Keynes MK4 . . . . . .45 F1
🛘 Stanwell TW19 . . . . . .213 E1
Sunderland Rd SL6 . . . .202 B8
Sunningdale Cl HP12 . . .172 B5
Sunningdale Way MK3 . . .57 D8
Sunny Bank HP15 . . . . . .162 F6
Sunny Brook Cl HP22 . . .117 D6
Sunny Croft HP13 . . . . . .161 C2
Sunny View NN7 . . . . .1 B6

Sunnybank
Cheddington LU7 . . . . . . .104 F7
Marlow SL7 . . . . .183 D4
Sunnyhill Rd WD3 . . . . . .178 D4
Sunnymeads Sta TW19 . .211 E4
Sunnymede Ave HP5 . . . .144 E3
Sunnymede Cotts SL6 . . .196 B1
Sunnyside Cotts SL6 . . . .145 A5
Sunnyside Rd HP5 . . . . . .144 A5
Sunray Ave UB7 . . . . . . .208 D4
Sunridge Cl MK16 . . . . . . .22 C3
Sunrise Parkway MK14 . .34 E6
Sunset Cl MK2 . . . . .58 C7
Sunset Wlk MK9 . . . . .34 E2
Sunters End HP12 . . . . . .172 A7
Sunters Wood Cl HP12 . .172 B5
Surly Hall Wlk SL4 . . . . .209 F6
Surrey Ave SL2 . . . . .198 C1
Surrey Pl
Milton Keynes MK3 . . . . . .46 F2
Tring HP23 . . . . .119 A3
Surrey Rd MK3 . . . . .46 F2
Sussex Cl
Aylesbury HP19 . . . . .101 A3
Chalfont St Giles HP8 . . .177 B8
High Wycombe HP13 . . . .162 D1
Slough SL1 . . . . .206 B4
Sussex Ho SL2 . . . . .198 C6
Sussex Keep 🛧 SL1 . . . .206 B4
Sussex Lodge 🛧 SL6 . . .202 F6
Sussex Pl SL1 . . . . .206 B4
Sussex Rd MK3 . . . . .46 F1
Sussex Way SL0 . . . . . . .189 F6
Sutcliffe Ave MK6 . . . . . . .34 E1
Sutherland Gr MK3 . . . . . .46 F3
Sutherland Grange SL4 .209 D7
Sutherland Wlk HP21 . . .115 F5
Sutleye Ct MK5 . . . . .46 A5
Sutton Ave SL3 . . . . .206 C4
Sutton Cl Cookham SL6 . .196 B7
Maidenhead SL6 . . . . . . .202 C5
Tring HP23 . . . . .119 B6
Sutton Ct MK4 . . . . .46 C1
Sutton La Slough SL3 . . .207 B1
Slough SL3 . . . . .207 C2
Sutton Pl SL3 . . . . .212 B8
Sutton Rd SL6 . . . . .196 B6
Swabey Rd SL3 . . . . .207 A2
Swains Cl UB7 . . . . .208 E4
Swains La HP21 . . . . .174 B1
Swains Mkt HP10 . . . . . .174 A1
Swakeleys Dr UB10 . . . .201 F8
Swakeleys Rd UB10 . . . .201 E8
Swale Rd HP21 . . . . .115 C5
Swallow Cl MK18 . . . . . . .52 E7
Swallow Dr MK15 . . . . . .163 B5
Swallow Ho SL7 . . . . .184 A1
Swallow La
Aylesbury HP19 . . . . .114 F8
Stoke Mandeville HP22 . .116 A1
Swallow St Iver SL0 . . . .207 D8
Iver Heath SL0 . . . . .200 D1
Swallowdale SL0 . . . . . . .200 D2
Swallowfield MK8 . . . . . . .33 E1
Swallowfield Lower Sch
MK17 . . . . .49 B5
Swan Cl Aylesbury HP19 .101 E3
Blackthorn OX25 . . . . .81 A3
Buckingham MK18 . . . . . . .52 E7
Chesham HP5 . . . . .144 B4
Ivinghoe Aston LU7 . . . . . .92 A1
Whitchurch HP22 . . . . . . .87 B5
Swan Cotts HP17 . . . . . . .129 C1
Swan Ct
Chorleywood WD3 . . . . . .167 C5
Datchet SL3 . . . . .211 B6
Leighton Buzzard LU7 . . . .80 E6
Olney MK46 . . . . .7 A4
West Drayton UB7 . . . . . .208 D4
Swan Hill SL6 . . . . .112 F3
Swan Hill Cotts HP13 . . .112 F3
Swan La Lee Gate HP16 . .142 C8
Marsh Gibbon OX6 . . . . . .72 A3
Swan Mews HP22 . . . . . .131 B5
Swan Rd Iver SL0 . . . . . .207 F7
West Drayton UB7 . . . . . .208 D4
Swan Terr
Milton Keynes MK11 . . . . .32 D5
Windsor SL4 . . . . .210 A7
Swan Wharf Bsns Ctr
UB8 . . . . .201 C3
Swanbourne CE Sch
MK17 . . . . .67 A3
Swanbourne House Sch
MK17 . . . . .66 F3
Swanbourne Rd MK17 . . .67 D4
Swanbrook Ct SL6 . . . . .203 A7
Swann Rd HP22 . . . . .131 D8
Swansons LU6 . . . . .92 F3
Swanwick La MK10 . . . . . .36 B3
Swayne Rise MK10 . . . . . .36 A2
Sweetcroft La UB10 . . . .201 F6
Sweetlands Cnr MK7 . . . .48 B8
Swift Cl Aylesbury HP19 .101 F3
Newport Pagnell MK16 . . .22 A5
Swift Ho SL7 . . . . .184 A2
Swimbridge La MK4 . . . . .46 D4
Swinden Ct MK13 . . . . . . .34 B4
Swing Gate La HP4 . . . . .135 D2
Swing Gate Sch HP4 . . . .135 D3
Swinnerton Ho RG9 . . . .191 E3
Switchback Cl SL6 . . . . .195 D2
Switchback Rd SL6 . . . . .195 D3
Switchback Rd S SL6 . . .195 D3
Switchback The SL6 . . . .195 D2
Sycamore Ave MK2 . . . . .58 C4
Sycamore Cl
Amersham HP6 . . . . .154 D2

Sycamore Cl continued
🛙 Bourne End SL8 . . . . .185 B3
Buckingham MK18 . . . . . . .52 F7
Chalfont St Giles HP8 . . .177 A7
Long Crendon HP18 . . . .125 C6
Maidenhead SL6 . . . . . . .202 C3
Stewkley LU7 . . . . .68 D2
West Drayton UB7 . . . . . .208 F6
Sycamore Cnr HP6 . . . . .154 D2
Sycamore Ct
Aylesbury HP19 . . . . .101 D1
High Wycombe HP12 . . . .172 C4
Windsor SL4 . . . . .210 C4
Sycamore Dene HP5 . . . .144 D3
Sycamore Dr
Marlow Bottom SL7 . . . . .183 D5
Tring HP23 . . . . .119 B4
Sycamore Ho
Amersham HP6 . . . . .154 D2
Princes Risborough HP27 .139 B3
Sycamore Leys MK18 . . . .63 E3
Sycamore Pl HP6 . . . . . .154 C1
Sycamore Rd
Amersham HP6 . . . . .154 D2
Chalfont St Giles HP8 . . .177 A7
High Wycombe HP12 . . . .172 C4
Sycamore Rise
Berkhamsted HP4 . . . . . .135 D3
Chalfont St Giles HP8 . . .177 A7
Sycamore Way HP15 . . . .163 A3
Sycamore Wlk SL3 . . . . .206 E7
Sycamores The HP3 . . . .146 F8
Sydney Gr SL1 . . . . .205 C7
Sygnus Ct 🛘 SL6 . . . . . .202 F7
Syke Cluan SL0 . . . . .207 E4
Syke Ings SL0 . . . . .207 E4
Sykes Croft MK4 . . . . .46 C1
Sykes Rd SL1 . . . . .205 B8
Sylvana Cl UB10 . . . . . . .201 F4
Sylvester Rd SL6 . . . . . .195 E2
Sylvia Cl HP16 . . . . .152 B4
Symington Ct MK5 . . . . . .46 B5
Syon Gdns MK16 . . . . . . .22 C2
Syresham St James CE Prim
Sch NN13 . . . . .27 C7

T

Tabard Gdns MK16 . . . . . .22 C2
Tachbrook Rd UB8 . . . . .201 C3
Tacknell Dr MK5 . . . . .46 A4
Tacks La HP17 . . . . .126 F6
Tadmarton MK15 . . . . . . .35 A6
Tadmere MK8 . . . . .33 D1
Talbot Ave
High Wycombe HP13 . . . .161 D2
Slough SL3 . . . . .206 F4
Talbot Ct
Milton Keynes MK15 . . . . .35 C1
Windsor SL4 . . . . .210 B4
Talbot Pl SL3 . . . . .211 C6
Talbot Rd HP22 . . . . .117 E5
Talbots Dr SL6 . . . . .202 B6
Talbots Hyde MK46 . . . . . .6 E4
Tall Oaks HP6 . . . . .154 D2
Tall Pines LU7 . . . . .70 F2
Tall Trees SL3 . . . . .212 E6
Talland Ave MK6 . . . . .34 F1
Tallis La MK7 . . . . .48 C5
Tamar Cl Aylesbury HP21 .115 C4
Loudwater HP13 . . . . . . .174 B4
Tamar Ho
High Wycombe HP13 . . . .173 F7
Milton Keynes MK3 . . . . . .46 E1
Tamar Way SL3 . . . . .207 B2
Tamarisk Ct MK7 . . . . . . .48 B5
Tamarisk Way SL1 . . . . .205 B5
Tamworth Stubb MK7 . . . .48 A5
Tancred Rd HP13 . . . . . .162 A1
Tandra MK6 . . . . .47 B5
Tandys Cl MK43 . . . . .8 E5
Tanfield La MK10 . . . . . . .36 A3
Tangier Ct SL4 . . . . .210 D8
Tangier La SL4 . . . . .210 D8
Tank House Rd MK18 . . . .66 B6
Tanners Dr MK14 . . . . . . .22 A2
Tannery Rd HP13 . . . . . .174 A4
Tannery Road Ind Est
HP13 . . . . .174 A4
Tansman La MK7 . . . . . . .48 D5
Tanton Ho HP16 . . . . . . .151 F8
Tapestries Hall SL4 . . . .211 A2
Tapestries The SL4 . . . .211 A2
Taplin Way HP10 . . . . . . .163 C1
Taplow Common Rd
SL1 . . . . .197 A3
Taplow Rd SL6 . . . . .204 C3
Taplow Sta SL6 . . . . .203 F7
Tapping Rd HP14 . . . . . .171 C5
Taranis Cl MK7 . . . . .48 C7
Tarbay La SL4 . . . . .209 B5
Tarbert Cl MK2 . . . . .58 C5
Tarmac Way UB7 . . . . . . .213 B7
Tarnbrook Cl 🛚 MK4 . . . .46 B2
Tarragon Cl MK7 . . . . . . .48 A6
Task The MK46 . . . . .7 A4
Taskers Row LU6 . . . . . . .92 F4
Taskers Row Cotts LU6 . .92 F4
Tatchbrook Cl SL6 . . . . .203 A8
Tate Rd SL1 . . . . .177 F5
Tatling Gr MK7 . . . . .48 A6
Tattam Cl MK15 . . . . .35 C2
Tattams La MK17 . . . . . . .67 B3
Tattenhoe La MK3 . . . . . . .57 D8
Tattenhoe St MK5 . . . . . . .45 E4
Tattershall Cl MK5 . . . . . .46 A6
Tattlers Hill HP22 . . . . . . .89 B3

Taunton Deane MK4 ....46 D2
Taurus Cl MK18 ....63 D2
Tavelhurst MK8 ....33 E1
Taverner MK7 ....48 D5
Tavistock Cl
  Maidenhead SL6 ......202 A8
  Woburn Sands MK17 ...49 B6
Tavistock Mews HP12 ..172 E7
Tavistock Rd UB7 .....208 D5
Tavistock St MK2 .....47 D1
Tavistock Wlk HP20 ...101 E2
Tay Rd MK3 ....46 E1
Taylor Rd HP21 ....115 D5
Taylor's Ride LU7 .....70 F2
Taylors Cl SL7 ....183 E2
Taylors Ct SL6 ....202 B8
Taylors La
  Little Missenden HP7 ..153 A3
  St Leonards HP23 .....132 C3
  Stewkley LU7 ....78 E4
Taylors Mews MK14 ...34 F6
Taylors Rd HP5 ....144 D2
Taylors Turn HP13 ....161 D2
Taymouth Pl MK9 .....35 B3
Teal Ho HP11 ....173 C6
Teale Cl OX25 ....94 E7
Teasel Ave MK14 .....34 E5
Tedder Cl UB10 ......201 F5
Tedder Rd HP22 ......131 D5
Tees Rd HP21 ....115 C5
Tees Way MK3 ....46 D1
Teesdale Rd SL2 .....204 F8
Teign Cl MK16 ....22 D4
Teikyo Sch (UK) SL2 ..199 D5
Telford Dr HP19 ......100 F1
Telford Dr SL1 ......205 A4
Telford Way
  High Wycombe HP13 ..162 A1
  Milton Keynes MK14 ...22 B1
Telston Cl SL8 ......185 A5
Temperance Terr MK11 ..32 C6
Templars Pl [2] SL7 ..183 E1
Templars MK14 ......34 C7
Temple Cl
  Buckingham MK18 ....41 E2
  Milton Keynes MK3 ...57 D7
Temple End HP13 ....173 A8
Temple Gate HP13 ...173 A7
Temple Ho RG9 ......191 E3
Temple La SL7 ......194 D6
Temple Mill Cotts SL7 ..194 C5
Temple Mill Island SL7 ..194 C5
Temple Orch HP13 ....173 B7
Temple Pk SL6 ......193 F3
Temple Rd SL4 ......210 D5
Temple Sq [17] HP20 ..115 D8
Temple St
  Aylesbury HP20 ......115 D8
  Brill HP18 ....96 A1
  High Wycombe HP11 ...173 A4
Temple Way SL2 ....198 C7
Templecroft Terr HP14 ..114 A4
Templewood Gate SL2 ..198 E7
Templewood La SL2 ..198 E8
Tenby Gr MK4 ....45 D1
Tene Acres MK5 .....45 F6
Tennant Cl MK8 .....45 D6
Tennis La MK18 .....66 A3
Tennyson Dr MK16 ...22 A4
Tennyson Gr MK3 ....57 F7
Tennyson Rd
  Aylesbury HP21 ......115 F6
  High Wycombe HP11 ..173 A5
Tennyson Way SL2 ...197 E1
Tenterden Cres MK7 ..48 B7
Tenzing Dr HP13 .....173 E6
Terrace The
  Aspley Guise MK17 ...49 E5
  Bray SL6 ....203 A3
  [7] Tring HP23 ......119 A3
Terrent Ct SL4 ......210 A5
Terrick Row HP17 ....130 B5
Terrington Hill SL7 ...183 B2
Terry Dr HP19 ....101 C3
Terry Orch HP13 .....173 C8
Terry Pl UB8 ....208 C8
Terry Rd HP13 ....173 C8
Terry's La SL6 ......195 F8
Terryfield Rd HP13 ...173 E6
Testwood Rd SL4 ....209 D6
Tetherdown HP16 ....151 C5
Tewkesbury La MK10 ..35 F1
Tews End La NN12 ....17 B8
Thackeray End HP19 ..100 F2
Thame Ho [5] HP13 ...173 B7
Thame Rd
  Aylesbury HP21 ......115 D7
  Blackthorn OX25 .....81 A3
  Brill HP18 ....110 B7
  Chilton HP18 ....111 B3
  Chinnor OX39 ....147 B8
  Haddenham HP17 .....126 D5
  Long Crendon HP18,OX9 ..125 D4
  Longwick HP27 ......138 E6
  Piddington OX25 .....95 D6
Thame Rd S HP21 ....115 B8
Thame Valley Falconry & Conservation Ctr★
  SL7 ....184 A4
Thames SL4 ....210 D7
Thames Bank SL6 ...203 C7
Thames Cl
  Bourne End SL8 .....185 A4
  Milton Keynes MK3 ...57 E8
Thames Cres SL6 ....196 B2
Thames Dr MK16 ....22 E3
Thames Ho Datchet SL3 ..211 B6

Thames Ho continued
  Henley-on-T RG9 .....191 E3
Thames Ind Est SL7 ..183 F2
Thames Mead SL4 ...209 E6
Thames Rd SL3 .....207 B3
Thames Reach SL7 ..193 C6
Thames Side
  Henley-On-T RG9 ....191 E2
  Windsor SL4 ....210 D7
Thames St SL4 .....210 D7
Thames Valley Nuffield Hospl
  The SL3 ....199 C4
Thames Valley Univ (Slough Campus) SL1 ....205 E5
Thamesbourne Mews [3]
  SL8 ....185 A3
Thamesfield Gdns SL7 ..183 E1
Thane Ct MK14 .....34 C7
Thanestead Copse
  HP10 ....174 C2
Thanestead Ct HP10 ..174 C2
Thatcher Cl UB7 ....208 E4
Thatchers Dr SL6 ...202 A5
Theatre Wlk MK9 ...34 F3
Thellusson Way WD3 ..167 F2
Theydon Ave MK17 ..49 B4
Thicket The
  Tylers Green HP10 ...163 A1
  West Drayton UB7 ...208 E7
Third Ave Marlow SL7 ..183 F2
  Milton Keynes MK1 ...47 B2
Third Cres SL1 .....205 C8
Third St HP11 ......173 B4
Thirkleby Cl MK3 ...205 C5
Thirlby La MK5 .....46 A6
Thirlmere Ave
  Milton Keynes MK2 ...58 C6
  Slough SL1 ....204 C8
Thirsk Gdns MK3 ...57 C6
Thistle Ct HP21 ....185 A6
Thomas Bourne Ho [1]
  HP4 ....135 D4
Thomas Coram Sch The
  HP4 ....135 D2
Thomas Ct
  Berkhamsted HP4 ....134 C6
  Maidenhead SL6 .....202 A2
Thomas Dr MK16 ...22 A6
Thomas Harding Jun Sch
  HP5 ....154 B7
Thomas Hickman Sch
  HP19 ....101 A3
Thomas Rd HP10 ...185 D4
Thomas Valentine Ho
  HP8 ....177 A7
Thompkins La SL2 ..198 A5
Thompson Cl SL3 ...207 A2
Thompson Rd UB10 ..201 E5
Thompson St MK13 ..34 A7
Thomson Cl HP21 ...115 B6
Thomson Wlk HP21 ..115 B6
Thorn Dr SL3 ......206 E7
Thornaby Pl HP10 ...185 E8
Thornbank Cl TW19 ..213 A4
Thornborough Inf Sch
  MK18 ....54 A4
Thornborough Rd MK17 ..55 B8
Thornbridge Rd SL0 ..200 C4
Thorncliffe MK8 ....33 D1
Thorndike SL2 .....205 B8
Thorne Rd HP14 ....171 C4
Thorne Way
  Aston Clinton HP22 ..118 A4
  Aylesbury HP20 .....101 F2
Thorney Lane N SL0 ..207 F6
Thorney Lane S SL0 ..207 F5
Thorney Mill Rd SL0,
  UB7 ....208 B3
Thorneycroft La MK15 ..35 B5
Thornhill Cl HP7 ...165 B7
Thornhill Cl HP7 ...165 B7
Thornhill Rd UB10 ..201 F8
Thornlea Croft MK46 ..6 F3
Thornley Croft MK4 ..46 C2
Thorns Cl HP27 ....139 D5
Thorns La HP27 ....139 E5
Thornton Ave UB7 ..208 F3
Thornton Cl UB7 ...208 F3
Thornton Coll Convent of Jesus & Mary★ 43 C5
Thornton Cres MK2 ..131 A5
Thornton Rd MK17 ..44 A1
Thorntree Dr HP23 ..118 F4
Thorpe Cl HP21 ....116 A4
Thorpe House Sch SL8 ..185 B2
Thorpeness Croft MK4 ..56 F8
Thorwold Pl MK5 ...46 B6
Thrasher Rd HP21 ..115 D5
Three Close La HP4 ..135 C4
Three Gables MK7 ..175 E2
Three Households HP8 ..176 F6
Three Oaks Cl UB10 ..190 F1
Three Points La MK18 ..74 A1
Thresher Gr MK12 ...33 A5
Thrift La SL6 ......202 D1
Thrift View MK43 ...25 C2
Thrupp Cl MK19 ....20 A6
Thrush Cl
  [6] Aylesbury HP19 ...101 F3
  High Wycombe HP12 ..172 C4
Thurlby Way SL6 ...202 D3
Thurley Cotts SL2 ..199 B3
Thurne Cl MK13 ....22 E3
Thursby Rd MK15 ...35 D7
Thurston Rd SL1 ...205 E7
Thyme Cl MK16 ....21 F5
Tibbys La HP18 ....112 F3
Ticehurst Cl MK7 ...48 B7

Ticehurst Cl MK7 ...48 B7
Tichborne WD3 ....178 D5
Tickford Arc MK16 ..22 D4
Tickford St MK16 ...22 E4
Tidbury Cl MK17 ...49 A4
Tiddenfoot Waterside Pk★
  LU7 ....80 E4
Tierney St [3] SL7 ...183 E1
Tiffany Cl MK2 .....58 D6
Tilbrook Ind Est MK7 ..48 B3
Tilbrook Rdbt MK7 ..48 B2
Tilbury Wlk SL3 ....207 B3
Tilburywood Cl HP13 ..161 C2
Tilebarn Cl RG9 ....191 C1
Tilecotes Cl SL7 ...183 C2
Tilehouse Comb Sch
  UB9 ....189 F5
Tilehouse Gdns SL7 ..183 E1
Tilehouse La UB9 ...189 E6
Tilehouse Way UB9 ..189 F4
Tilers Rd MK11 ....33 B2
Tilling Cres HP13 ...174 A7
Tillman Ct MK7 ....33 C5
Tilstone Ave SL4 ..204 E2
Tilstone Cl SL4 ...204 E1
Tilsworth Rd HP9 ..175 C1
Timber La HP7 .....60 F7
Timber Way MK17 ..147 C6
Timberley La HP16 ..142 A8
Timbers Wlk SL6 ...202 B5
Timberscombe MK4 ..46 D3
Timberwood SL2 ...187 D1
Timbold Dr MK7 ...48 A7
Timor Ct HP13 ....162 D2
Timpson La MK46 ...7 C3
Timpsons Row MK46 ..7 A3
Tindal Rd HP20 ....101 E2
Tingewick Inf Sch MK18 ..51 B6
Tingewick Rd
  Buckingham MK18 ...52 B8
  Radclive MK18 .....51 E7
Tingewick Road Ind Est
  MK18 ....52 B8
Tinkers Dr MK18 ...65 F3
Tinkers La
  Berkhamsted HP23 ..134 A6
  Windsor SL4 ....209 D5
Tinkers Wood Rd HP13 ..161 E1
Tintagel Cl MK6 ...47 A8
Tintagel Ho SL1 ...205 C5
Tinterne Cl SL1 ...205 C3
Tinterne Cl HP21 ..116 C6
Tippet Cl MK7 .....48 D4
Tiree Ho SL2 ......205 B8
Titchmarsh Ct MK6 ..46 E8
Tithe Barn Dr SL6 ..203 E1
Tithe Cl SL6 ......203 C1
Tithe Ct SL3 ......207 A2
Tithe La TW19 ....212 A1
Titmus Rd HP22 ...131 E7
Tiverton Cres
  Aylesbury HP19 ....101 C3
  Milton Keynes MK4 ..45 E1
Tockley Rd SL1 ....197 B2
Todd Cl Aylesbury HP21 ..115 B6
  Holmer Green HP15 ..163 B6
Toddbury Farm Cvn Pk
  LU7 ....91 D8
Tolcarne St MK6 ...35 A1
Toll Bar Cnr HP27 ..138 D7
Tollgate SL1 ......202 A6
Tollgate Cl WD3 ...167 F5
Tolman Ct HP21 ...115 B6
Tom Scott Ho HP5 ..144 B2
Tomlin Rd SL2 ....197 E1
Tompion Rd HP19 ..100 F1
Tompkins Cl
  Aston Clinton HP22 ..117 F4
  Milton Keynes MK5 ..46 B3
Tompkins La OX27 ..71 E2
Toms Hill Cl HP23 ..120 D5
Toms Hill Rd HP23 ..120 D5
Toms Turn HP15 ...162 F5
Tongwell La MK15,MK16 ..22 C2
Tongwell Rdbt MK15 ..35 D8
Tongwell St
  Milton Keynes,Broughton
  MK10 ....36 A3
  Milton Keynes,Northfield
  MK15 ....35 F5
  Milton Keynes,Pineham
  MK15 ....35 E7
  Walnut Tree MK7 ...48 C6
Toot Hill Cl MK5 ...46 A5
Top Angel MK18 ...52 D5
Top Farm Cl HP9 ..175 A1
Top Mdw MK7 .....48 B3
Top Pk SL9 ....188 C5
Top Station Rd NN13 ..38 A8
Top Station Road Ind Est
  NN13 ....38 A8
Topaz Cl SL1 ......205 B5
Topland Rd SL3 ...177 D3
Topping La UB8 ...201 C2
Torbay MK7 ....85 B4
Tornay Ct LU7 ....91 D6
Torquay Spur SL2 ..198 B2
Torre Cl MK3 .....47 A2
Torridge Rd
  Aylesbury HP21 ....115 D4
  Slough SL3 ....212 B8
Torridon Cl MK2 ...58 D4
Torrington Rd HP4 ..135 B4
Tortoiseshell Way HP4 ..134 F6
Torwood HP4 .....134 F4
Totteridge Ave HP13 ..173 D6
Totteridge Common Cotts
  HP13 ....173 F8
Totteridge Dr HP13 ..162 E1

Totteridge Ho HP13 ..173 E8
Totteridge La HP13 ..162 E1
Totteridge Par HP13 ..173 E8
Totteridge Rd HP13 ..173 D7
Totternhoe Knolls Nature Reserve★ LU6 ....93 B8
Totternhoe Lower Sch
  LU6 ....93 B7
Totternhoe Rd
  Dunstable LU6 ......93 E7
  Eaton Bray LU6 ....92 D7
Towan Ave
  Fishermead MK6 ....47 A8
  Milton Keynes MK6 ..35 A1
Towcester Dr NN12 ..18 B3
Towcester Rd
  Buckingham MK18 ...41 E4
  Old Stratford MK19 ..32 B7
Tower Cl
  Berkhamsted HP4 ...135 A4
  Emberton MK16 .....13 C5
  Flackwell Heath HP10 ..185 C7
Tower Cres MK14 ...34 F6
Tower Ct HP27 ....139 B3
Tower Dr MK14 ....34 F7
Tower Hill WD4 ....146 F1
Tower Ho Iver SL0 ..207 E7
  [4] Slough SL1 .....205 E4
Tower Rd HP7 .....165 A4
Tower St HP13 ....162 D2
Towergate SL8 ....201 E7
Toweridge La
  High Wycombe HP12 ..172 C8
  West Wycombe HP14 ..160 F1
Towers Lea HP13 ...173 C7
Towersey Way HP21 ..115 B7
Town Bridge Ct HP5 ..154 B7
Town Cl MK18 ....50 D6
Town End Cres MK16 ..12 B5
Town End Rd HP14 ..159 C8
Town Farm LU7 ...105 A4
Town Farm Barns HP27 ..139 B3
Town Farm Cl OX49 ..157 B8
Town Field La HP8 ..177 C7
Town La Stanwell TW19 ..213 D1
  Wooburn HP10 .....185 D4
Town Sq [8] SL1 ...205 E4
Townfield HP5 ....154 C7
Townfield Rd [5] HP13 ..173 C7
Townlands Hospl RG9 ..191 D2
Townsend
  Haddenham HP17 ...127 A7
  Marsh Gibbon OX27 ..71 E2
  Quainton HP22 .....85 A5
Townsend Cl MK43 ..37 F8
Townsend Cotts
  Great Horwood MK17 ..55 B3
  Middle Claydon MK18 ..74 D8
Townsend Gr MK13 ..34 B8
Townsend La OX27 ..71 E2
Townsend Piece HP19 ..101 C1
Townsend Rd HP5 ..144 C1
Townside
  Edlesborough LU6 ..92 F3
  Haddenham HP17 ...126 F5
Tozer Wlk SL4 ....209 D4
Trafalgar Ave MK3 ..46 F4
Trafford Cl HP10 ...152 A6
Trafford Rd HP16 ..152 A7
Tram Hill HP18 ....96 B2
Tranlands Brigg MK13 ..34 B4
Transcend SL4 ....210 C5
Trapp's Ct SL7 ....154 C6
Trapp's La HP5 ....154 C6
Travell Ct MK13 ...34 B3
Travic Rd SL2 ....197 E2
Travis Ct SL2 .....198 B2
Travis Gr MK3 ....58 A8
Treacher's Cl HP5 ..154 B8
Treadaway Bsns Ctr
  HP10 ....174 C1
Treadaway Hill HP10 ..174 B1
Treadaway Rd HP10 ..174 B1
Trebah Sq HP19 ...114 F8
Treborough MK4 ...46 D2
Tredington Gr MK7 ..48 B4
Treefields MK18 ...52 B6
Treehanger Cl HP23 ..119 B4
Trees Ave HP14 ...162 A6
Trees Rd Bourne End SL8 ..185 B3
  Hughenden Valley HP14 ..162 A6
Treeside Cl UB7 ..208 C7
Treesmill Dr SL3 ...202 C3
Trelawney Ave SL3 ..206 E3
Tremayne Ct MK6 ..47 A8
Trenchard Ave HP22 ..131 D6
Trenchard St TW19 ..115 A8
Trenches La SL3 ..207 A4
Trengothal Ct NN13 ..26 D4
Trent Dr MK16 ....22 D4
Trent Rd
  Milton Keynes MK3 ..46 E1
  Slough SL3 ....212 B8
Trent Villas Est SL3 ..211 B6
Trentishoe Cres MK4 ..46 D3
Tresco Rd HP4 ....134 F5
Tresham Ct MK5 ...46 A7
Tressell The SL6 ..202 D6
Trevelyan Mid Sch SL4 ..210 C3
Trevelyan Way HP4 ..135 D4
Treves Gr HP21 ...115 E6
Trevithick La MK5 ..46 B3
Trevone Cl MK6 ...47 A8
Trevose Cl SL2 ...198 B1
Trewarden Ave SL0 ..200 D3
Triangle Bsns Pk HP22 ..130 D8
Trident Ind Est SL3 ..212 E4

Tring Bsns Ctr HP23 ..118 E4
Tring Ford Rd HP23 ..119 A7
Tring Hill HP23 ....118 C3
Tring Rd Aylesbury HP21 ..116 B7
  Berkhamsted HP4 ...134 D7
  Dunstable LU6 .....93 E7
  Edlesborough LU6 ..106 E8
  Long Marston HP23 ..104 C3
  Wendover HP22 ....131 C5
  Wilstone HP23 .....104 C1
  Wingrave HP22 .....89 C1
Tring Sch HP23 ....119 B4
Tring Sta HP23 ....120 A5
Tring Rd SL7 .....183 D3
Trinity CE Prim Sch
  RG9 ....191 D1
Trinity Cl
  Old Stratford MK19 ..32 B7
  Stanwell TW19 .....213 C1
Trinity Ct Aylesbury HP19 ..101 D1
  Chesham HP5 ......154 C7
  Marlow SL7 ....183 D3
Trinity Ho SL8 ....195 F6
Trinity Pl SL4 .....210 C5
Trinity Rd
  Hazlemere HP15 ...162 F3
  Marlow SL7 ....183 D3
  Milton Keynes MK12 ..33 B7
Trinity St Stephens CE Fst
  Sch SL4 ....210 B6
Tripps Hill Cl HP8 ..177 A7
Trispen Ct MK6 ....47 A8
Trooper Rd HP23 ..120 C5
Trout Cl SL7 ......194 C8
Trout Hollow HP27 ..148 E8
Trout La UB7 .....208 C5
Trout Rd UB7 ....208 D6
Troutbeck MK6 ...47 C8
Troutbeck Cl SL2 ..206 A6
Trubys Gdn MK6 ..47 C8
Trueman Pl MK6 ...46 F8
Truesdale Dr UB9 ..190 C7
Trumper Way Slough SL1 ..204 F5
  Uxbridge UB8 .....201 C4
Trumpton La MK7 ..48 C7
Trunk Furlong MK17 ..49 D6
Truro Cl SL6 ......202 A7
Trust Cotts HP4 ...107 A1
Trustees Way UB9 ..189 F6
Tubwell Rd SL2 ...199 B4
Tucker Cl HP13 ....173 C8
Tuckers Dr HP15 ...163 C7
Tudeley Hale MK7 ..48 B8
Tudor Ct Amersham HP6 ..154 D1
  [5] Leighton Buzzard LU7 ..80 F7
  Maidenhead SL6 ...196 C2
  Piddington HP14 ...160 C1
  [3] Stanwell TW19 ..213 E1
Tudor Dr HP21 ....185 D7
Tudor Gdns
  Milton Keynes MK11 ..32 E4
  Slough SL1 ....204 C8
  Steeple Claydon MK18 ..63 D3
Tudor Mill HP10 ...185 E6
Tudor Orch HP4 ...134 E6
Tudor Pk HP6 ....154 C7
Tudor Rd HP15 ...163 C3
Tudor Way SL4 ...209 E6
Tudors Cl MK18 ...73 B4
Tuffnell Cl MK15 ...35 E7
Tulip Way UB7 ....208 D2
Tulkers Cl HP16 ...151 D5
Tulla Ct MK2 ......58 C4
Tummell Way MK2 ..58 C6
Tunmers Ct SL9 ...177 C2
Tunmers End SL9 ..177 C2
Tunmers Ho SL9 ..177 C2
Tunnel Way LU7 ...105 C2
Tuns La Henley-on-T RG9 ..191 E2
  Slough SL1 ....205 C4
Turks Head Ct SL4 ..210 C7
Turnberry Cl MK3 ..57 D7
Turner Cl HP20 ....101 F3
Turner Rd SL3 ....206 C4
Turner Wlk [12] HP20 ..101 F3
Turner's Mdw HP22 ..117 B6
Turners Dr HP13 ..173 E8
Turners Field HP13 ..161 E3
Turners Mews MK14 ..34 F6
Turners Pl HP15 ...163 C6
Turners Wlk [4] HP20 ..144 C1
Turners Wood Dr HP8 ..177 D4
Turneys Dr MK12 ...33 A6
Turneys Orch WD3 ..167 D4
Turnfields HP18 ...124 A3
Turnfurlong HP21 ..115 F7
Turnfurlong Inf Sch
  HP21 ....116 A6
Turnfurlong Jun Sch
  HP21 ....116 A6
Turnfurlong La HP21 ..116 A6
Turnfurlong Row HP21 ..116 A6
Turnham Way HP19 ..115 B7
Turnip Cl HP18 ....112 B2
Turnmill Ave MK6 ..35 B2
Turnmill Ct MK6 ...35 B2
Turnoak Pk SL4 ...209 E3
Turnpike Ct MK17 ..49 A5
Turnpike End HP21 ..115 F6
Turnpike La UB10 ..201 C4
Turnpike Rd HP12 ..172 C4
Turnpike The HP18 ..109 D5
Turnpike Way HP12 ..172 C4
Turnstone Way HP19 ..101 E3

Turpins Gn SL6 ......202 A5
Turpyn Ct MK6 ....47 D8
Turton Way SL1 ......205 D3
Turvey Cl HP22 ......117 E5
Turvey Lower Sch MK43 ...8 E6
Turvey Mill MK43 ....8 D5
Turvey Rd Astwood MK16 ...15 F5
Turvey MK43 ....3 E2
Turvill End MK5 ....46 B8
Turville Rd HP21 .....116 C6
Turweston Rd NN13 ....26 A1
Tuscans Cl MK18 ......73 B5
Tweed Cl HP4 ....135 B5
Tweed Dr MK3 ....46 D1
Tweed Rd SL3 ....212 B8
Tweedale MK17 ....67 C7
Tweenways HP5 ....144 E4
Twelve Leys HP22 .....89 B3
Twinches La SL1 .....205 B5
Twinflower MK7 ....48 B6
Twist The HP23 ......119 D2
Twitchell La HP22 ....117 E5
Twitchell Rd HP16 ...152 A7
Twitchell's La HP9 ...176 F5
Twitchen La MK4 ......46 D3
Two Dells La HP5 ....145 A4
Two Gates La HP5 ...143 D7
Two Mile Ash Mid Sch
  MK8 ....33 E1
Two Mile Dr SL1 .....204 E4
Twyford CE Sch MK18 ..62 C2
Twyford La MK7 ....48 C5
Twynham Rd SL6 ......202 B7
Tyburn Ave MK6 ....35 B2
Tyle Pl SL4 ....211 A2
Tyler Wlk SL3 ....206 F1
Tylers Cres HP15 ....163 E3
Tylers Gn MK13 ....34 D3
Tylers Green Fst Sch
  HP10 ....174 D8
Tylers Green Mid Sch
  HP10 ....174 B8
Tylers Hill Rd HP5 ...154 F8
Tylers Rd HP15 ......163 B2
Tylsworth Cl HP6 ....154 D1
Tyne Rd HP21 ....115 D4
Tyne Sq MK3 ....46 D1
Tyneham Cl HP21 .....116 B4
Tynemouth Rise **3** MK10 ..36 A1
Tyrell Cl SL1 ....52 C7
Tyrell Gdns SL4 .....209 F4
Tyrells Gdns MK17 ....69 E8
Tyrells Rd MK17 ......69 E8
Tyrill MK14 ....34 C7
Tyson Pl MK6 ....46 E8
Tythe Cl LU7 ....78 E8
Tythe Gdns LU7 ......78 E8
Tythe Mews LU6 ......92 E3
Tyzack Rd HP13 ......162 F1

U

Ufton Court Yd SL8 ...185 B4
Ufton Cl SL8 ....185 B4
Ullswater Cl SL1 ....204 C8
Ullswater Dr LU7 .....80 C7
Ulverscroft MK10 .....36 B2
Ulyett Pl MK6 ....46 E8
Umberville Way SL2 ..197 F2
Underhill Cl SL6 ....202 E6
Underwood Cotts HP7 .164 C2
Underwood Pl MK6 ....46 E8
Underwood Rd HP13 ...173 D8
Union Bldgs UB8 .....201 B2
Union Bsns Pk UB8 ...201 B5
Union Ct **11** MK11 ....135 D4
Union Ind Est HP12 ..172 A7
Union St
  High Wycombe HP11 ..173 A4
  Newport Pagnell MK16 ..22 D5
Univ of Buckingham
  Buckingham MK18 ....52 C7
  Buckingham MK18 ....52 C8
Univ of Buckingham (Verney
  Pk) MK18 ....52 E7
University Way MK43 ..24 D1
Up Cnr HP8 ....177 C8
Up Corner Cl HP8 ...177 B8
Upcroft SL4 ....210 B4
Upland Ave HP5 .....144 B3
Uplands SL7 ....183 D6
Uplands Cl
  Gerrards Cross SL9 ..188 C3
  High Wycombe HP13 ..173 E8
Uplands Ct HP5 .....144 C1
Uplands The SL9 ....188 E2
Upper Abbotts Hill
  HP19 ....115 A7
Upper Ashlyns Rd HP4 .135 B3
Upper Barn Farm HP18 .84 B1
Upper Belmont Rd HP5 .144 B3
Upper Bourne End La
  HP1 ....146 B7
Upper Bray Rd SL6 ..202 F3
Upper Church St HP18 .112 F1
Upper Coombe LU7 ....80 E8
Upper Dr HP9 ....175 D5
Upper Fifth St MK9 ...34 D2
Upper Fourth St MK9 ..34 D2
Upper George St HP5 .144 C1
Upper Gladstone Rd **2**
  HP5 ....144 C1
Upper Green St HP11 .172 E7
Upper Hall Pk HP4 ...135 E2

Upper Hartwell HP17 .114 E5
Upper Hollis HP16 ...151 F7
Upper Hundreds Way
  HP20 ....115 E8
Upper Icknield Way
  Askett HP27 ....139 E7
  Halton HP22 ....117 F2
  Monks Risborough HP27 .139 D6
  Pitstone HP23,LU7 ..105 E1
  Princes Risborough HP27 .139 B2
  Saunderton HP27 ....148 A5
Upper Lees Rd SL2 ...198 B2
Upper Lodge La HP15 .162 F6
Upper Mdw **2** HP5 ......144 B1
Upper Rd UB9 ....189 D4
Upper Riding HP9 ...175 D2
Upper Second St MK9 ..34 D1
Upper St Quainton HP22 ..85 A5
  Tingewick MK18 .....51 B6
Upper Stonehayes MK14 ..34 F8
Upper Third St MK9 ...34 D1
Upper Ventnor Cotts
  SL6 ....195 C8
Upper Way MK17 ......59 C2
Upper Weald MK19 ....45 A8
Upper Wood Cl
  Milton Keynes MK5 ...45 F3
  1 Shenley Brook End MK5 ..46 A3
Upton Cl **H** Henley-on-T RG9 .191 E1
  5 Slough SL1 ....205 F3
Upton Court Rd SL3 ..206 B2
Upton Gr MK5 ....46 C4
Upton Hospl SL1 .....205 F4
Upton House Sch SL4 .210 C5
Upton Lea Par SL2 ...206 B6
Upton Pk SL1 ....205 F3
Upton Rd Dinton HP17 .114 A3
  Slough SL1 ....206 A3
Upton Terr HP17 .....114 A3
Upway SL9 ....177 F2
Uxbridge Coll UB8 ...201 A5
Uxbridge High Sch UB8 .201 D3
Uxbridge Ind Est UB8 .201 B3
Uxbridge Rd
  Iver Heath SL0,SL3 ..200 B2
  Rickmansworth WD3 ..178 F7
  Slough SL1,SL3 .....206 C7
  Uxbridge UB10 ......201 F2
Uxbridge Sta UB8 ...201 D5

V

Vache La
  Chalfont St Giles HP8 ..177 C8
  Milton Keynes MK5 ...45 F6
Vale Cl SL9 ....177 D2
Vale Ct MK43 ....25 D2
Vale Gr SL1 ....205 E3
Vale Ho HP19 ....115 C3
Vale Ind Ctr The HP19 .101 C1
Vale Park Dr HP20 ...115 E8
Vale Rd Aylesbury HP20 .101 E2
  Chesham HP5 ....144 C4
  Windsor SL4 ....209 F6
Vale Ret Pk HP20 ....115 E8
Vale Rise HP5 ....144 C3
Vale The SL9 ....177 D2
Valens Cl MK8 ....45 E7
Valentine Cl MK8 .....45 E7
Valentine Way HP8 ...177 D7
Valerian Cl MK16 .....21 F4
Valley Cl Brackley NN13 ..38 A8
  Whipsnade HP4 .....107 E7
Valley Cres NN13 .....38 A8
Valley Ctr The HP13 .173 C6
Valley End SL3 ......199 C1
Valley Rd
  Berkhamsted HP4 ...134 F6
  Brackley NN13 ......38 A8
  Buckingham MK18 ....52 F8
  Finmere MK18 ....50 D6
  Henley-on-T RG9 ....191 C1
  Hughenden Valley HP14 .162 A5
  Uxbridge UB10 ......201 E3
Valley View HP5 .....144 B2
Valley Way SL9 .....188 D3
Valpy Cl HP23 ....119 D1
Van Der Bilt Ct MK13 ..33 F6
Van Diemens Cl OX39 .147 C7
Vandyke Cl MK17 .....49 B6
Vane Rd OX9 ....126 B1
Vanguard Cl HP12 ...172 D7
Vanguard Ho **5** TW19 ...213 E1
Vansittart Est SL4 ..210 C6
Vansittart Rd
  Bisham SL7 ....194 E7
  Windsor SL4 ....210 B6
Vantage Ct MK16 .....22 F3
Vantage Rd SL1 .....205 B5
Vanwall Bsns Pk SL6 .202 C5
Vanwall Rd SL6 .....202 C4
Varnell Terr RG9 ....181 C2
Vaughan Copse SL4 ..205 D2
Vaughan Gdns SL4 ..204 F2
Vaughan Way SL2 ...197 E1
Vauxhall MK13 ....34 B6
Vellan Ave MK6 ....35 B1
Venables La MK15 ....35 B7
Venetian Ct MK7 .....48 C7
Ventfield Cl OX33 ...108 A5
Venus Hill HP3 .....156 A8
Verbena Cl UB7 .....208 D1
Verdi Cl MK7 ....48 D5
Verdon Ct SL2 ......198 B2
Verdon Dr MK15 .....35 B7
Verity Pl MK6 ....34 F1

Verley Cl MK6 ....47 C8
Vermont Pl MK15 .....22 C1
Vermont Rd SL2 .....197 F1
Verney Ave HP12 ....172 D4
Verney Cl
  Berkhamsted HP4 ...134 F5
  Buckingham MK18 ....41 D1
  Marlow SL7 ....183 D2
  Tring HP23 ....119 C5
Verney Farm Cl MK18 ..74 F8
Verney Rd Slough SL3 ..207 A3
  Winslow MK18 ....65 E4
Verney Wlk HP21 ....115 D6
Vernier Cres MK5 ....45 E5
Vernon Bldg **7** HP11 ...172 F7
Verona Rd HP20 .....208 C7
Verwood Rd HP20 ...101 E2
Veryan Pl MK6 ....35 B1
Vicarage Cl Cookham SL6 .196 B7
  Seer Green HP9 .....176 D3
  Steeple Claydon MK18 ..63 D2
  Wendover HP22 .....131 B5
  Yardley Gobion NN12 ..18 E6
Vicarage Ct
  Hanslope MK19 ......11 B2
  Steeple Claydon MK18 ..63 D3
Vicarage Dr SL6 ....203 C4
Vicarage Flats SL4 ..210 D8
Vicarage Gdns
  Leighton Buzzard LU7 ..80 E6
  Marsworth HP23 ....105 A2
  Milton Keynes MK13 ..34 A4
Vicarage La
  Bovingdon HP3 ......146 B4
  Ivinghoe LU7 ....105 F5
  Piddington OX25 .....95 E6
  Steeple Claydon MK18 ..63 D2
  Wing LU7 ....79 E2
Vicarage Rd
  Aylesbury HP21 ....115 D5
  Henley-on-T RG9 ...191 E1
  Leighton Buzzard LU7 ..80 E6
  Maidenhead SL6 ....202 F8
  Milton Keynes,Bradwell
    MK13 ....34 A4
  Milton Keynes,Fenny Stratford
    MK2 ....58 D4
  Milton Keynes,Stony Stratford
    MK13 ....32 D6
  Pitstone LU7 ....105 D2
  Whaddon MK17 ....56 B8
  Wigginton HP23 ....119 D1
  Winslow MK18 ....65 E4
Vicarage St MK17 .....49 C4
Vicarage Way
  Colnbrook SL3 ......212 D7
  Gerrards Cross SL9 ..188 F5
Vicarage Wlk MK11 ...32 D6
Vickers Ct **9** TW19 ....213 E1
Vickery Cl HP21 ....115 E5
Vickery Way HP21 ...115 E5
Victor Cl SL6 ....202 B8
Victoria CE Fst Sch
  Berkhamsted HP4 ...135 C4
Victoria Cotts SL6 ..195 C8
Victoria Cres SL0 ...208 A6
Victoria Ct
  Henley-on-T RG9 ...191 E1
  High Wycombe HP11 ..172 F8
  4 Marlow SL7 ......183 E2
  Slough SL1 ....205 E5
  21 Windsor SL4 .....210 D6
Victoria Dr SL1,SL2 ..197 F6
Victoria Gdns
  High Wycombe HP11 ..172 F4
  Marlow SL7 ....183 E2
Victoria Ho SL4 .....211 A2
Victoria Rd
  Berkhamsted HP4 ...135 C4
  Chesham HP5 ....144 C1
  Eton Wick SL4 ......204 F1
  Farnham Common SL2 .198 C6
  Leighton Buzzard LU7 ..80 E6
  Marlow SL7 ....183 E2
  Milton Keynes MK2 ...47 E1
  Slough SL2 ....206 B5
  Uxbridge UB8 ......201 C5
Victoria Row MK18 ...52 D8
Victoria St
  Aylesbury HP20 ....115 F8
  High Wycombe HP11 ..172 F7
  Milton Keynes MK12 ..33 D6
  9 Slough SL1 ....205 F4
  Windsor SL4 ....210 D6
Victory Ct MK1 ....47 B2
Victory Rd
  Berkhamsted HP4 ...135 A5
  Steeple Claydon MK18 ..63 D2
  Wendover HP22 .....131 B5
Vienna Gr MK13 ....33 E6
Villa Park (Mobile Home Pk)
  MK43 ....37 F7
Village Ct MK16 ......13 F2
Village Ct LU7 ....80 D6
Village La SL2 ......187 D4
Village Mews HP3 ...146 A4
Village Rd Coleshill HP7 .164 F3
  Denham UB9 ....190 A4
  Dorney SL4 ....204 D4
Village Sh Ctr The **4**
  SL1 ....205 F4
Village Way HP7 ....166 D7
Villier St UB8 ......201 D3
Villiers Bldgs **8** HP20 ..115 D8
Villiers Cl MK18 .....41 E1
Villiers Ct SL4 .....210 A7
Villiers Rd SL2 ....205 D8

Vimy Ct LU7 ....80 F7
Vimy Rd LU7 ....80 F7
Vincent Ave MK8 ....45 F8
Vincent Dr HP19 ....101 F4
Vincent Rd HP19 ....101 A3
Vincents Way HP19 ..161 D6
Vine Cl Hazelmere HP15 .163 A3
  Stanwell TW19 .....213 A2
Vine Ct SL2 ....199 A6
Vine Gr UB10 ....201 F5
Vine La UB10 ....201 F4
Vine Rd SL2 ....198 F6
Vine Row MK43 ....8 E6
Vine St Uxbridge UB8 .201 C4
  Uxbridge UB8 ......201 D4
Vine The HP18 ......124 D3
Vinetrees HP22 .....131 B4
Viney La HP19 ......114 F5
Vineyard Dr SL8 ....185 A5
Vineyards The HP27 .138 A2
Vinlake Ave UB10 ...190 F1
Vintners Mews MK14 ..34 F6
Violet Ave UB8 .....208 F8
Violet Cl HP22 .....149 D6
Violets Cl MK16 .....24 B6
Virage MK6 ....117 F4
Virginia MK6 ....47 A7
Virginia Gdns HP14 .159 F8
Viscount Cl **18** HP20 ...101 F2
Viscount Ct **12** SL4 ....210 C6
Viscount Ind Est SL3 .212 E4
Viscount Way MK2 ...47 C1
Vivien Cl MK6 ....195 F6
Volta Rise MK5 ......46 C4
Vyne Cres MK4 ....33 F1
Vyners Sch UB10 ....201 F6

W

Waborne Rd SL8 ....185 B4
Waddesdon CE Sch HP18 .99 A6
Waddesdon Cl **8** MK8 ...45 F8
Waddesdon Gn HP21 .115 E4
Waddesdon Hill HP18 .99 C3
Waddesdon Manor (NT)★
  HP18 ....98 E5
Waddesdon Manor Flats
  HP18 ....98 E6
Waddesdon Village Prim Sch
  HP18 ....99 A4
Wade Dr SL1 ....205 A5
Wadesmill La MK7 ....48 A4
Wadhurst La MK10 ...36 B1
Wadworth Holme MK10 .35 E3
Wagner Cl MK7 ....48 C6
Waine Cl MK18 ....52 D7
Wainers Croft MK12 ..33 B4
Wainwrights MK18 ...125 D6
Waivers Way HP21 ...116 A5
Wakefield Cl MK14 ...34 F7
Wakefield Cres SL2 .198 F6
Wakelins End MK5 ...46 A3
Wakeman Rd SL8 ...185 A3
Walbank Gr MK5 .....46 A3
Walbrook Ave MK6 ...35 B3
Waldeck Ho SL6 ....203 A7
Waldeck Rd SL6 ....203 A7
Waldens Cl **4** SL8 ....185 A3
Walducks Cl LU7 .....78 E8
Walford Rd UB8 ....201 D3
Walgrave Dr MK13 ...34 B4
Walk House Cl MK43 ..25 B1
Walk The Eton Wick SL4 .205 A1
  Winslow MK18 ....65 F4
Walker Ave MK12 ....33 A6
Walker Ct SL6 ......202 D7
Walker Rd SL6 .....203 A4
Walkers Rd HP27 ...138 D7
Walkham Cl HP13 ...174 B4
Walkhampton Ave MK13 .34 C1
Walkwood End HP9 ..175 C1
Walkwood Rise HP9 .186 C8
Wallace Cl Marlow SL7 .183 F4
  Uxbridge UB10 .....201 E3
Wallace Dr LU6 ......92 F4
Wallace End HP21 ...116 A6
Wallace Mews LU6 ...92 E6
Wallace St MK13 .....33 E7
Wallace Wlk SL4 ....205 F1
Wallbridge Cl HP19 .115 B7
Waller Rd HP9 ......175 D4
Wallinger Dr MK5 ....46 A3
Wallingford Cl MK13 ..34 B5
Wallingford Gdns HP21 .173 B4
Wallingford Rd UB8 .201 B1
Wallington Rd HP5 ..144 B1
Wallis Ct SL1 ......206 A3
Wallmead Gdns MK5 ..46 B7
Walney Pl MK4 ....45 F1
Walnut Cl
  Great Missenden HP16 .152 A7
  Long Crendon HP18 .125 C7
  Newport Pagnell MK16 ..22 A3
  Stoke Mandeville HP22 .116 C2
Walnut Cres HP27 ..138 D7
Walnut Dr
  Maids Moreton MK18 ..41 F4
  Milton Keynes MK2 ...58 E8
  Wendover HP22 .....131 B6
Walnut Gr UB10 ....185 E6
Walnut Lodge SL1 ..205 D4
Walnut Tree Cl
  Bourne End SL8 ....185 B2
  High Wycombe HP12 .172 C8
Walnut Tree Ct HP22 .116 C3
Walnut Tree Ho HP11 .174 B3
Walnut Tree La HP27 .138 D6

Walnut Tree Rdbt MK7 .48 C7
Walnut Way
  Bourne End SL8 ....185 B2
  Hyde Heath HP6 ....153 C4
Walnuts Sch The MK6 ..47 E5
Walpole Rd SL1 .....204 D7
Walsh's Manor MK14 ..34 D7
Walsingham Gate HP11 .173 A4
Walter Rothschild Zoological
  Mus The★ HP23 .....119 A3
Waltham Dr MK10 ....36 A1
Waltham Ho **4** MK3 ....46 F1
Walton Cl HP13 .....162 E1
Walton Court Ctr HP21 .115 C5
Walton Dene HP21 ..115 F7
Walton Dr
  High Wycombe HP13 ..162 E1
  Walton MK7 ....47 F6
Walton End MK7 .....48 C6
Walton Gn HP21 ....115 E7
Walton Gr HP21 ....115 E7
Walton Heath MK3 ...57 D7
Walton High Sch MK7 .48 C6
Walton La SL2 ......197 F3
Walton Park Rdbt MK7 .48 B4
Walton Pl HP22 ....116 F3
Walton Rd
  Aylesbury HP21 ....115 F7
  Caldecotte MK7 .....48 B3
  Milton Keynes MK10 ..36 A2
  Walton MK7 ....48 B6
  Wavendon MK10,MK17 ..48 D7
Walton St HP21 ....115 E7
Walton Terr HP21 ..115 E7
Walton Way HP21 ...116 A7
Wandlebury MK14 ....35 A8
Wandsworth Pl MK13 ..34 D3
Wannions Cl HP5 ...145 A1
Wantage Cl LU7 .....79 E3
Wantage Cres LU7 ..79 E3
Wappenham Rd NN13 ..27 B8
Wapping HP18 ......125 D6
Wapseys La SL2 ....187 F4
Warbler Cl HP18 ....114 F8
Warburg Nature Reserve★
  RG9 ....179 B5
Ward Cl SL0 ....207 F7
Ward Gdns SL1 .....204 E5
Ward Pl HP7 ....165 B7
Ward Rd Brackley NN13 ..38 A5
  Milton Keynes MK1 ...47 E3
Ward Royal **6** SL4 ....210 C6
Ward Royal Par **3** SL4 .210 C6
Wardes Cl HP16 ....151 C5
Wardle Pl MK6 ....46 E8
Wardrobes La HP27 .149 D8
Wardstone End MK4 ..46 B2
Ware Leys Cl OX27 ..71 E3
Wargrave Rd RG9 ...191 F1
Warmington Gdns MK15 .35 B5
Warmstone Cl HP18 ..99 B6
Warmstone La HP18 ..99 B6
Warneford Ave HP22 .131 D5
Warner Cl SL1 .....204 E5
Warners Cl MK17 ....59 D1
Warners Hill SL6 ...195 D6
Warners Rd MK17 ...57 D3
Warren Bank MK6 ...47 E5
Warren Cl
  Buckingham MK18 ....52 E7
  Slough SL3 ....206 E3
  Stone HP17 ....114 B5
Warren Ct
  Farnham Common SL2 .198 C7
  Little Horwood MK17 ..55 E5
Warren Farm Cotts
  MK18 ....50 A7
Warren Field SL0 ...200 C3
Warren Ho HP19 ....101 B1
Warren Par SL2 ....206 C5
Warren Rd
  Ickenham UB10 .....201 F8
  Little Horwood MK17 ..55 F5
  Yardley Gobion NN12 ..18 F6
Warren The
  Chalfont St Peter SL9 ..177 F3
  Chartridge HP5 ....143 E3
  Hazelmere HP15 ...163 A5
Warren Wood Dr HP11 .173 C5
Warren Yd MK12 .....33 A6
Warrendene Rd HP14 .162 A8
Warrender Rd HP5 ..144 E2
Warrington Ave SL1 .205 C7
Warrington Rd MK46 ..7 B7
Warwick Ave
  High Wycombe HP12 .172 B6
  Slough SL2 ....198 C1
Warwick Cl
  Aston Clinton HP22 .117 C5
  Maidenhead SL6 ...202 B4
Warwick Ct
  Beaconsfield HP9 ..175 D3
  Chorleywood WD3 .167 F6
  7 Slough SL1 ......210 C5
Warwick Dr LU7 .....79 E2
Warwick Ho **7** HP13 ...173 F1
Warwick Pl
  Milton Keynes MK3 ...57 F7
  Uxbridge UB8 ......201 C5
Warwick Rd
  Beaconsfield HP9 ..175 D3
  Hanslope MK19 ......11 A3
  Milton Keynes MK3 ...57 F7
  West Drayton UB7 ..208 E5
  Pitstone LU7 ....105 D2
Warwick Row HP20 ..102 A1
Wash Hill HP10 ....185 E3
Wash Hill Lea HP10 .185 E4

Wash Hill Mobile Home Pk HP10 185 E3
Washfield MK4 46 D3
Washingleys MK43 25 C2
Washington Ct SL7 184 A3
Washington Dr
Slough SL1 204 D6
Windsor SL4 209 E4
Washington Row HP7 165 C7
Wastel MK6 47 B5
Watchcroft Dr MK18 41 E2
Watchet Ct MK4 46 D3
Watchet La
Holmer Green HP15 163 B7
Little Kingshill HP16 152 C1
Water Cl MK19 32 B7
Water Eaton Rd MK2,MK3 58 C7
Water End Rd
Beacon's Bottom HP14 159 D3
Beacon's Bottom,Waterend HP14 159 C5
Water Gdns The HP15 162 E2
Water La
Berkhamsted HP4 135 C4
Bovingdon HP3 146 B1
Ford HP17 128 B7
Leighton Buzzard LU7 80 F7
Sherington MK16 13 E1
Speen HP27 150 C4
Water Mdw HP5 154 B7
Water Meadow Way HP22 131 B6
Water Stratford Rd MK18 51 A7
Waterbeach Cl SL1 205 D7
Waterbeach Rd SL1 205 D7
Waterborne Wlk LU7 80 F7
Waterfield WD3 167 C2
Waterford Cl MK3 46 E1
Waterford Ho UB7 208 C3
Waterglades The HP9 175 C6
Waterhall Comb Sch MK2 58 D4
Waterhouse Cl MK16 22 D4
Waterlily [5] HP19 101 E4
Waterloo Ct MK3 46 E2
Waterloo Rd
Leighton Buzzard LU7 80 E6
Uxbridge UB8 201 C4
Waterlow Cl MK16 22 C2
Waterman Ct SL1 204 E5
Watermead HP19 101 E4
Watermead Slopes & Sails★ HP19 101 D4
Watermeadow HP19 101 F3
Watermill Way HP22 116 F2
Waterperry OX33 123 B1
Waterperry Gdns★ OX33 123 B1
Waterperry Mews HP19 114 F8
Waterperry Rd HP18 123 D5
Waters Reach SL6 196 A1
Waterside
Berkhamsted HP4 135 D4
Chesham HP5 154 D6
Edlesborough LU6 92 F4
Milton Keynes MK6 47 C8
Uxbridge UB8 208 C8
Wooburn Green HP10 185 E7
Waterside Comb Sch HP5 154 D6
Waterside Ct HP5 154 C7
Waterside Dr SL3 207 A4
Waterside Lodge SL6 203 C8
Waterside Pk MK12 33 C7
Waterslade Pens HP17 126 F6
Watersmeet Cl MK4 46 D4
Watery La
Beachampton MK19 44 B6
Brackley NN13 38 A7
Marsworth HP23 104 F1
Wooburn Green HP10 185 E8
Watling St Bletchley MK2 47 D1
Bow Brickhill MK17 58 F8
Granby MK6 47 A3
Milton Keynes,Kiln Farm MK8,MK11 33 B2
Milton Keynes,Shenley Lodge MK6 46 C6
Potterspury NN12 18 C3
Watling Terr MK2 47 E1
Watlington Ct HP16 152 A8
Watlington Rd OX49 157 A7
Watlow Gdns MK18 41 E2
Watson Cl MK8 45 D6
Watten Ct MK2 58 E4
Wattleton Rd HP9 175 E1
Watts Cl MK19 11 A3
Watts Gn HP18 112 B2
Wavell Ct MK15 35 B7
Wavell Gdns SL2 197 F2
Wavell Rd
Beaconsfield HP9 176 B1
Maidenhead SL6 202 B6
Wavendon CE Fst Sch MK17 48 E7
Wavendon Fields MK17 48 F6
Wavendon Gate Comb Sch MK7 48 D6
Wavendon House Dr MK17 49 B8
Wavendon Rd MK17 37 C2
Waveney Cl MK16 22 E3
Waverley Croft MK10 36 A1
Waverley Rd SL1 205 C8
Waverley Wlk HP20 101 D2
Waxwing Cl HP19 101 E3
Wayfarers Pk HP4 134 F4
Waylands TW19 211 E1
Wayside
High Wycombe HP13 173 D7
Speen HP27 150 C4
Wayside Ct HP6 154 C1
Wayside Gdns SL9 188 D4
Wayside Mews SL6 202 F8
Wealdstone Pl MK6 35 A2
Weasel La MK3 57 C6
Weatherby LU6 93 E8
Weathercock Cl MK17 49 B5
Weathercock Gdns HP15 163 C7
Weathercock La MK17 49 C4
Weavers End MK19 11 B2
Weavers Hill MK11 33 A4
Weavers Rd HP23 118 E4
Webb Cl Chesham HP5 144 B1
Slough SL3 206 D2
Webber Heath MK7 48 D4
Webbs Home Cl MK10 36 A2
Webbs Mdw HP19 115 A8
Webster Cl
Maidenhead SL6 202 A5
Thame OX9 125 F1
Webster Rd HP21 116 A6
Websters Mdw MK4 46 C1
Wedgewood St HP19 115 A8
Wedgwood Ave MK14 22 A1
Wedgwood Dr HP14 162 A6
Weedon Cl SL9 177 B2
Weedon Hill HP6 153 D4
Weedon La HP6 154 A3
Weedon Rd HP19 101 C2
Weekes Dr SL1 205 B4
Weill Rd HP21 116 A4
Weir La Blackthorn OX25 81 A4
East Claydon MK18 74 E5
Whitchurch HP22 86 F6
Weirside Gdns UB7 208 D5
Welbeck Ave HP21 116 C6
Welbeck Cl MK10 35 F1
Welbeck Rd SL6 202 D5
Welburn Gr MK4 46 B2
Welby Cl SL6 202 A4
Welden SL2 206 C7
Welders La
Chalfont St Giles SL9 177 A3
Seer Green SL9 177 B3
Weldon Rise MK5 46 B8
Welford Way HP18 112 F3
Well End Cotts SL8 184 F5
Well Head Rd LU6 93 C6
Well La LU7 80 A1
Well St MK18 52 D8
Welland Cl SL3 212 B8
Welland Dr MK16 22 E3
Welland Ho MK3 57 E8
Welland Rd HP21 115 C5
Wellbank SL6 196 E1
Wellbrook Mews HP23 119 B4
Wellcroft LU7 105 F5
Wellcroft Rd SL1 205 B5
Weller Cl HP6 154 E2
Weller Ct LU6 93 C7
Weller Rd HP6 154 E2
Welles Rd HP13 173 F7
Wellesbourne Gdns HP13 162 D2
Wellesley Ave SL0 207 F4
Wellesley Ct SL0 207 F4
Wellesley Ho SL4 210 B6
Wellesley Path SL1 206 A4
Wellesley Rd SL1 206 A4
Welley Ave TW19 211 E3
Welley Rd SL3,TW19 211 E3
Wellfield HP15 163 B3
Wellfield Ct MK15 35 D8
Wellfield Rd HP14 171 B8
Wellhayes MK14 34 F8
Wellhouse Rd SL6 195 E2
Wellhouse Way HP14 161 E6
Wellingborough Rd MK46 6 F5
Wellington Ave HP27 139 B4
Wellington Cl SL6 202 B8
Wellington Pl
Aylesbury HP21 115 E4
Milton Keynes MK3 58 B7
Wellington Rd
Aylesbury HP21 115 E4
High Wycombe HP12 172 E4
Maidenhead SL6 202 D7
Uxbridge UB8 201 C4
Wellington St SL1 206 A4
Wells Cl SL4 210 A7
Wellsmead Fst Sch MK3 46 F1
Wellsmead Mid Sch MK3 46 E2
Welsh La MK18 40 C5
Welsummer Gr MK5 46 A3
Welton Rd HP21 116 B7
Wendover CE Jun Sch HP22 131 B6
Wendover House Sch HP22 131 C3
Wendover Hts HP22 131 C6
Wendover Rd
Bourne End SL8 185 A5
Burnham SL1 204 B8
Ellesborough HP17 130 D3
Wendover St HP11 172 F7
Wendover Sta HP22 131 B4
Wendover Way
Aylesbury HP21 115 F6
High Wycombe HP11 173 B6
Wendover Wood Forest Wlks★ HP23 131 F6
Wenlack Cl UB9 190 A1
Wenning La MK4 46 B2
Wentworth Ave SL2 198 A2
Wentworth Cl HP13 173 C8
Wentworth Cres SL6 202 C6
Wentworth Way MK3 57 C7
Wenwell Cl HP22 118 A3
Werner Ct HP21 115 E4
Werner Terr MK18 73 B6
Werth Dr MK17 49 B2
Wescott Way UB8 201 C3
Wesley Cl HP20 102 A2
Wesley Dene [4] HP13 173 B7
Wesley Hill [1] HP5 144 B1
Wessex Ct
[4] Stanwell TW19 213 E1
[11] Windsor SL4 210 C6
Wessex Inf Sch SL6 202 B4
Wessex Jun Sch SL6 202 B4
Wessex Rd SL8 185 B2
Wessex Road Ind Est SL8 185 B2
Wessex Way SL6 202 B4
Wessons Hill SL6 195 C7
West Acres HP7 165 D7
West Ave HP10 163 C1
West Cl SL7 193 D7
West Comm SL9 188 D6
West Common Cl SL9 188 E6
West Common Rd UB8 201 D6
West Cres SL4 209 F6
West Ct Bray SL6 203 C4
High Wycombe HP13 161 D3
West Dales MK13 34 C5
West Dean SL6 202 F8
West Dr HP13 173 D8
West Drayton Park Ave UB7 208 E3
West Drayton Prim Sch UB7 208 E4
West Drayton Sta UB7 208 E5
West Edge OX27 71 E2
West End HP22 116 E2
West End Cl MK18 63 C2
West End Ct SL2 198 F4
West End La SL2 198 E4
West End Pl HP22 116 E2
West End Rd
Cheddington LU7 104 F7
High Wycombe HP11 172 F7
West End St HP11 172 F7
West Farm Way MK46 13 E8
West Furlong MK18 53 A1
West Hill MK17 49 D4
West Hyde La SL9 178 A4
West La Bledlow HP27 138 B1
Emberton MK46 13 E8
Henley-on-T RG9 191 D2
West Leith HP23 118 F1
West Mead SL6 195 F2
West Pas [11] HP23 119 A3
West Point SL1 204 D5
West Rd
Berkhamsted HP4 135 A5
Cranfield MK43 24 D2
Maidenhead SL6 202 E7
West Drayton UB7 208 F3
Woburn Sands MK17 49 B5
West Richardson St [2] HP11 172 F7
West Ridge SL8 185 B4
West Side Rise MK46 6 F4
West Spur Rd UB8 201 D2
West Sq SL0 207 F7
West St Adstock MK18 53 F1
Aylesbury HP19 101 C1
Buckingham MK18 41 C1
Dunstable LU6 93 F7
Henley-on-T RG9 191 D2
Leighton Buzzard LU7 80 F7
Maidenhead SL6 202 F7
Marlow SL7 183 D1
Olney MK46 6 F4
Steeple Claydon MK18 63 D2
West View Chesham HP5 144 D2
Hardwick HP22 87 B3
High Wycombe HP13 173 B8
West Way HP9 174 F1
West Waye HP13 162 C2
West Well Cl MK18 51 A6
West Well La MK18 51 A6
West Wlk MK9 34 E2
West Wycombe Comb Sch HP14 160 F2
West Wycombe Hill Rd HP14 160 F2
West Wycombe Pk★ HP14 160 F1
West Wycombe Rd HP12 161 C1
West Yard Ind Est HP14 160 C8
Westanley Ave HP7 165 D8
Westborne Ct MK13 34 A6
Westborough Ct SL6 202 C6
Westborough Rd SL6 202 C6
Westbourne St [6] HP11 172 F7
Westbrook End MK17 57 C3
Westbrook Hay Prep Sch HP1 146 D7
Westbury Cl MK16 22 B4
Westbury Court Bsns Ctr OX27 71 C4
Westbury Ho [3] HP20 101 D1
Westbury La MK16 22 A5
Westbury Mill NN13 38 F4
Westbury Terr OX27 71 F2
Westcliffe MK8 33 C2
Westcoign Ho SL6 203 B8
Westcott CE Sch HP18 98 A7
Westcott Venture Pk HP18 98 A6
Westcroft Slough SL2 198 B1
Tring HP23 119 A3
Westcroft Rdbt MK4 46 A2
Westcroft Stables★ HP27 150 B3
Westdean La HP5 143 C3
Westdown Gdns LU6 93 F7
Western Ave
Buckingham MK18 41 C1
New Denham UB9 201 D8
Western Dene HP15 163 A5
Western Dr
Hanslope MK19 11 A3
Wooburn Green HP10 185 E5
Western House Inf Sch SL1 204 F6
Western La MK18 65 F3
Western Perimeter Rd TW6 213 B5
Western Perimeter Road Rdbt TW19 213 C2
Western Rd
Great Horwood MK17 55 A3
Milton Keynes,Fenny Stratford MK2 47 D1
Milton Keynes,Wolverton MK12 33 C6
Tring HP23 118 F3
Westfield Aylesbury HP21 115 E3
Hyde Heath HP6 153 C4
Westfield Ave MK19 31 D5
Westfield Bglws SL7 192 F6
Westfield Cotts SL7 192 F5
Westfield Fst Sch HP4 134 F5
Westfield Rd
Beaconsfield HP9 175 C1
Berkhamsted HP4 134 E6
Dunstable LU6 93 F8
Maidenhead SL6 202 B7
Milton Keynes MK2 58 C7
Pitstone LU7 105 C3
Slough SL2 198 B1
Wheatley OX33 122 A1
Westfield Sch SL8 185 A3
Westfield Wlk HP12 172 D6
Westfields
Buckingham MK18 52 C8
Princes Risborough HP27 139 D4
Westgate Cres SL1 204 F6
Westgate Ct HP13 174 A4
Westgate Sch The SL1 205 A5
Westhill MK14 34 D8
Westhorpe Park Cvn Site SL7 184 B3
Westhorpe Rd SL7 183 F3
Westland Cl TW19 213 E1
Westlands Ave SL1 204 C7
Westlands Cl SL1 204 C7
Westlands Rd HP27 149 E5
Westlington La HP17 113 E1
Westlington Lea HP17 113 E2
Westmead
Monks Risborough HP27 139 B5
Windsor SL4 210 B4
Westminster Cl
Brackley NN13 38 A7
High Wycombe HP11 173 B4
Westminster Cres NN13 38 A7
Westminster Dr
Aylesbury HP21 115 F6
Milton Keynes MK3 47 A2
Westmorland Ave HP21 116 B6
Westmorland Ho MK3 46 F2
Westmorland Rd SL6 202 D6
Westmount Ave HP7 165 C8
Weston Ct HP22 117 C5
Weston La OX9 136 F8
Weston Rd
Aston Clinton HP22 117 C5
Lewknor OX49 157 A8
Olney MK46 6 E3
Ravenstone MK46 5 E2
Slough SL1 204 F8
Weston Turville CE Sch HP22 116 E3
Weston Way HP22 116 A2
Westover Ct HP13 161 D1
Westover Rd HP13 161 D2
Westpits MK46 13 E8
Westrick Wlk HP16 151 C5
Westron Gdns HP23 119 B4
Westside La MK16 12 B6
Westwood HP12 172 B3
Westwood Cl
Little Chalfont HP6 166 D8
Milton Keynes MK8 45 F8
Westwood Dr HP6 166 D8
Westwood Gn SL6 195 F6
Westwood Rd SL7 183 C1
Westwood Wlk [6] HP20 101 F2
Wetherby Gdns MK3 57 D6
Wethered Pk SL7 183 D1
Wethered Rd
Burnham SL1 204 B8
Marlow SL7 183 D2
Wexford Ct SL6 203 B7
Wexham Court Prim Sch SL3 206 C8
Wexham Park Hospl SL3 199 C1
Wexham Park La SL3 199 C1
Wexham Pl SL2 199 D6
Wexham Rd SL1,SL2 206 B6
Wexham Sch SL2 206 C8
Wexham St SL3 199 B3
Wexham Woods SL3 206 C8
Wey La HP5 154 B7
Whaddon CE Fst Sch MK17 56 B8
Whaddon Chase HP19 101 D2
Whaddon Hall MK17 45 B2
Whaddon Rd
Milton Keynes,Shenley Brook End MK5 46 A3
Milton Keynes,Westcroft MK4 45 F2
Mursley MK17 56 C3
Nash MK17 44 D2
Newport Pagnell MK16 22 B3
Newton Longville MK17 57 D3
Whaddon Way MK3 46 F2
Whales La OX27 71 E2
Whalley Dr MK3 47 A2
Wharf Cl
Old Stratford MK19 32 B7
Wendover HP22 131 B5
Wharf Ct UB8 201 C1
Wharf La
Berkhamsted HP4 134 C8
Bourne End SL8 185 A3
Old Stratford MK19 32 C7
Wharf Rd HP22 131 B5
Wharf Row HP22 118 B4
Wharf The
Milton Keynes MK2 58 E6
Milton Keynes,Giffard Park MK14 21 E2
Wharf View MK18 41 E1
Wharfe La RG9 191 E2
Wharfside MK2 47 E1
Wharfside Pl MK18 41 E1
Wharton Ho [2] HP20 101 D1
Whatmore Cl TW19 213 A1
Wheat Cl HP21 115 E3
Wheatbutts The SL4 204 F2
Wheatcroft Cl MK6 47 A5
Wheatfield Cl SL6 202 A4
Wheathouse Copse MK17 55 A3
Wheatlands Rd SL3 206 C3
Wheatley Campus (Brookes Univ) OX33 122 C1
Wheatley Cl MK4 46 C2
Wheatley Park Sch OX33 122 B2
Wheatley Way SL9 177 E4
Wheatsheaf Ho HP10 185 E7
Wheatsheaf Par SL4 211 A2
Wheatstone Cl SL3 206 A3
Wheeler Ave HP10 174 C8
Wheeler Cl HP20 116 B8
Wheelers End OX39 147 C6
Wheelers Flats HP10 174 D8
Wheelers La MK13 34 A6
Wheelers Orch SL9 177 E4
Wheelers Pk HP13 173 D7
Wheelers Yd HP16 152 A7
Wheelwright Mews MK14 34 F6
Wheelwright Rd HP27 138 D7
Wheelwrights HP22 116 F2
Wheelwrights Pl SL3 212 C7
Wheelwrights Way MK19 32 C7
Wheelwrights Yd HP22 85 A5
Whelpley Hill Pk HP5 145 D5
Whet Stone Cl MK13 34 B4
Whichcote Gdns HP5 154 D6
Whichert Cl HP9 175 C6
Whichford MK14 22 A1
Whielden Cl HP7 165 B7
Whielden Gate HP7 164 E4
Whielden Gn HP7 165 B7
Whielden Hts HP7 165 A7
Whielden La
Coleshill HP7 164 E5
Winchmore Hill HP7 164 D3
Whielden St HP7 165 B7
Whinchat HP19 101 E3
Whincup Cl HP11 172 F4
Whinneys Rd HP10 174 C3
Whipass Hill HP9 176 A5
Whipsnade Park Homes LU6 93 F1
Whipsnade Rd LU6 93 F6
Whipsnade Tree Cathedral★ LU6 93 F1
Whipsnade Wild Animal Pk★ HP4 107 E8
Whitby Cl MK3 47 A2
Whitby Rd SL1 205 C6
Whitchurch Cl
Maidenhead SL6 195 E3
Westcott HP18 98 B7
Whitchurch Comb Sch HP22 86 E7
Whitchurch Ho [5] SL6 202 F7
Whitchurch La HP22 86 D8
Whitchurch Rd LU7 78 B1
White Alder MK12 33 E5
White Cl
High Wycombe HP13 161 D1
Slough SL1 205 D5
White Cotts MK18 29 D4
White Cres HP22 131 D7
White Hart Cl
Chalfont St Giles HP8 177 A7
Ludgershall HP18 96 B8
White Hart Field HP22 85 B4
White Hart La HP17 127 A5
White Hart Mdw HP9 175 E1
White Hart Rd
[1] Maidenhead SL6 202 F7
Slough SL1 205 D3

White Hart St **9** HP11 .173 A7
White Hermitage SL4 .211 C2
White Hill
  Ashley Green HP4 .145 C7
  Beaconsfield HP9,HP10 .185 F8
  Chesham HP5 .144 D1
  High Wycombe HP13 .162 B2
  Remenham Hill RG9 .192 A2
White Hill Cl
  Chesham HP5 .144 D1
  Marlow Bottom SL7 .183 C6
White Hill La LU7 .105 D3
White Horse Dr MK4 .46 C2
White Horse La HP22 .87 A6
White Horse Rd SL4 .209 D5
White Hos MK18 .50 D6
White House Cl SL9 .177 E3
White Lilies La SL4 .200 D7
White Lion Cl HP7 .166 A8
White Lion Rd HP7 .166 B8
White Lodge Cl SL7 .183 C6
White Paddock SL6 .202 A2
White Rock SL6 .196 B1
White Spire Sch MK3 .46 F1
White View HP20 **14** .101 F3
Whiteacres Dr SL6 .203 B1
Whitebaker Ct MK14 .34 F6
Whitebrook Pk SL6 .196 C4
Whitecross Rd HP17 .126 F5
Whitefield La HP16 .152 A6
Whiteford Rd SL2 .205 E8
Whitegate Ct MK6 .47 B6
Whitehall SL6 .196 B1
Whitehall Ave MK10 .36 D1
Whitehall Cl UB8 .201 C4
Whitehall Inf Sch UB8 .201 C4
Whitehall Jun Sch UB8 .201 C4
Whitehall La TW19 .212 A1
Whitehall Rd UB8 .201 D1
Whitehall St **6** HP20 .101 D1
Whitehaven SL1 .205 F6
Whitehead Way HP21 .115 C4
Whitehill
  Berkhamsted HP4 .135 D5
  Olney MK46 .6 C5
Whitehill Ct HP4 .135 D5
Whitehorse Way MK11 .32 D5
Whitehouse Cl HP10 .174 E1
Whitehouse La HP10 .174 E2
Whitehouse Way
  Iver Heath SL0 .200 D2
  Slough SL1 .205 F6
Whitelands Ave WD3 .167 C5
Whitelands Rd HP12 .172 D7
Whitelands Way HP12 .172 D7
Whiteleaf Way HP27 .139 D5
Whiteley SL4 .209 E2
Whiteley Cres MK3 .57 F6
Whitelock Ho RG9 .191 E3
Whitepit La HP10 .185 D7
Whites Cl MK18 .63 D3
Whites La SL3 .211 B8
Whitethorn Ave UB7 .208 F6
Whitethorn Cl HP22 .130 A8
Whitethorn Pl UB7 .208 F5
Whitethorns MK16 .22 B3
Whitewood Rd HP4 .135 A4
Whitfield Rd HP14 .162 A6
Whitfield Way WD3 .167 F1
Whitley Cl TW19 .213 D1
Whitley Ct HP21 .115 E4
Whitmees Cl MK46 .6 E4
Whitney Rdbt MK4 .45 E2
Whitsun Pasture MK15 .35 B7
Whittaker Rd SL2 .197 E1
Whittenham Cl SL2 .206 A5
Whittle Parkway SL1 .204 D7
Whitton Way MK16 .22 C3
Whitworth La MK5 .46 B7
Whurley Way SL6 .195 E2
Whybrow Gdns HP4 .135 E6
Whyteladyes La SL6 .195 E3
Whytingham Rd HP23 .119 C4
Wick Rd HP23 .133 D8
Wicken Park Rd MK19 .31 B2
Wicken Rd MK18 .30 E1
Wicket The SL1 .205 E3
Wickets The SL6 .202 C7
Wickstead Ave MK8 .45 D6
Widbrook Rd SL6 .196 B3
Widdenton View HP14 .171 C5
Widecroft Rd SL0 .207 E7
Widewater Pl UB9 .190 C6
Widgeon Ho HP11 .173 C6
Widmer End Comb Sch
  HP15 .162 F6
Widmere Field HP16 .151 C5
Widmere La HP16 .183 A6
Widmore Cl HP5 .143 E5
Widnell La OX25 .95 C7
Wigan's La HP14 .148 C6
Wiggington Ho SL4 .210 D7
Wigginton Bottom
  HP23 .133 D8
Wiggles La HP23 .118 F7
Wigmore Ct HP19 .101 A2
Wigmore Rd HP19 .101 A2
Wigwell Gdns MK17 **7** .55 A2
Wilberforce Mews **7**
  SL6 .202 F7
Wildacre Rd MK5 .46 A4
Wilderness The HP4 .135 C4
Wildgreen N SL3 .207 A2
Wildgreen S SL3 .207 A2

Wildwood Ct WD3 .167 F5
Wilford Cl MK15 .35 C2
Wilford Rd SL3 .206 F2
Wilks Croft MK5 .45 F7
Willen Comb Sch MK15 .35 C7
Willen La MK14 .34 F8
Willen Park Ave MK15 .35 B6
Willen Rd
  Milton Keynes MK10 .35 F3
  Newport Pagnell MK16 .22 D3
Willets Rise MK5 .46 A5
Willetts La UB9 .200 F1
Willey Ct MK11 .32 F4
William Bandy Cl LU7 .79 F3
William Burt Cl HP22 .116 F1
William Ellis Cl SL4 .211 A1
William Fiske Ho **4**
  HP4 .135 C4
William Harding Cl
  HP21 .116 A5
William Harding Comb Sch
  HP21 .116 A5
William Hartley Yd SL3 .199 B1
William Hill Dr HP22 .102 C4
William Ho **4** HP13 .173 F5
William Moulder Ct
  HP5 .144 B3
William Penn Sch The
  SL2 .198 D1
William Shakman Ho
  HP8 .177 B8
William Smith Cl MK15 .35 C3
William St
  Berkhamsted HP4 .135 C4
  Slough SL1 .205 F5
  Windsor SL4 .210 D6
William Sutton Ho MK5 .46 A4
Williams Circ MK7 .48 A4
Williams Cl
  Aylesbury HP19 .101 D1
  Hanslope MK19 .10 F3
Williams Way HP27 .138 D6
Willis Rd HP17 .127 A6
Willoners SL2 .205 A8
Willoughby Rd SL3 .207 B3
Willoughby's Wlk HP13 .161 D2
Willow Ave
  High Wycombe HP12 .172 B4
  New Denham UB9 .201 C6
  West Drayton UB7 .208 F6
Willow Bank SL7 .183 D5
Willow Chase
  Chesham HP5 .144 B1
  Hazlemere HP15 .162 E3
Willow Cl
  Chalfont St Peter SL9 .177 E1
  Colnbrook SL3 .212 C7
  Flackwell Heath HP10 .185 C6
  Moulsoe MK16 .36 E8
Willow Cres E UB9 .201 C7
Willow Cres W UB9 .201 C7
Willow Ct
  Aylesbury,Quarrendon
   HP19 .101 A2
  Aylesbury,Walton St HP21 .115 C6
  High Wycombe HP11 .173 E4
  Walter's Ash HP14 .161 C8
Willow Dr
  Buckingham MK18 .52 F7
  Maidenhead SL6 .203 B8
Willow End HP22 .116 F2
Willow Gate HP18 .112 B2
Willow Gr MK19 .32 B6
Willow Herb HP19 .101 E4
Willow Ho LU7 .80 E7
Willow La Amersham HP7 .165 F6
  Milton Keynes MK11 .32 C5
Willow Par SL3 .207 A3
Willow Pk SL2 .199 A5
Willow Pl SL4 .210 C8
Willow Rd
  Aylesbury HP19 .101 D1
  Brackley NN13 .38 A6
  Chinnor OX39 .147 C6
  Great Horwood MK17 .55 A3
  Poyle SL3 .212 E5
  Thame OX9 .125 F1
Willow Rise HP17 .127 A7
Willow Way
  Loudwater HP11 .174 B2
  Milton Keynes MK2 .58 C7
  Princes Risborough HP27 .139 A3
  Wing LU7 .79 E3
Willow Wlk HP15 .163 A3
Willow Wood Cl SL1 .197 B3
Willow Wren MK14 .21 F2
Willowbank Terr **6**
  HP21 .115 F6
Willowbrook Slough SL4 .205 D2
  Wendover HP22 .131 B7
Willowford MK13 .33 D5
Willowmead HP17 .114 F5
Willowmead Cl **10** SL7 .183 F3
Willowmead Gdns SL7 .183 F3
Willowmead Rd **8** SL7 .183 F3
Willowmead Sq **9** SL7 .183 F3
Willows First Sch The
  MK6 .35 A2
Willows Rd SL8 .185 B4
Willows Riverside Pk The
  SL4 .209 C7
Willows The
  Amersham HP6 .154 B4
  4 Bourne End SL8 .185 B3
  Edlesborough LU6 .92 F3
  High Wycombe HP12 .172 E8
  Longwick HP27 .138 E6

Willows The continued
  Windsor SL4 .209 D7
Wilmar Cl UB8 .201 D5
Wilmin Gr MK5 .46 B7
Wilmot Rd SL1 .197 B2
Wilsley Pound MK7 .48 B8
Wilson Ct MK8 .45 E7
Wilton Ave MK3 .58 A8
Wilton Cl UB7 .213 D8
Wilton Cres
  Beaconsfield HP9 .175 E3
  Windsor SL4 .209 D4
Wilton Hollow HP9 .175 F3
Wilton La HP9 .176 E4
Wilton Rd HP9 .175 E3
Wiltshire Ave SL2 .198 C1
Wiltshire Lodge **2** SL6 .202 F6
Wiltshire Rd **2** SL7 .183 F4
Wiltshire Way MK4 .46 A3
Wimbledon Pl MK13 .34 D3
Wimblington Dr MK6 .47 A4
Wimborne Cres MK4 .45 F2
Wimpole Rd UB7 .208 D5
Winbury St SL6 .202 E7
Winbury Sch SL6 .203 B4
Wincanton Hill MK3 .57 C6
Winch Terr SL4 .209 D5
Winchbottom La
  High Wycombe HP10 .173 B1
  Little Marlow SL7,HP10 .184 B7
Winchendon Rd HP18 .112 B2
Winchester Circ MK10 .36 B1
Winchester Cl
  Amersham HP7 .165 E8
  Poyle SL3 .212 E6
Winchester Ct HP11 .174 B3
Winchester Dr SL6 .202 B3
Winchester Ho HP21 .115 F6
Windermere Cl
  Aylesbury HP21 .116 B6
  Chorleywood WD3 .167 D4
Windermere Dr MK2 .58 D5
Windermere Gdns LU7 .80 C7
Windermere Way
  Slough SL1 .204 C7
  West Drayton UB7 .208 E5
Windmill Cl
  Aylesbury HP19 .115 B8
  Buckingham MK18 .41 F1
  Ivinghoe LU7 .105 F5
  Windsor SL4 .210 B5
Windmill Dr HP15 .162 F6
Windmill Hill
  Chipperfield WD4 .156 F7
  Coleshill HP7 .164 F2
  Princes Risborough HP27 .139 B2
Windmill Hill Dr MK3 .57 D7
Windmill Hill Rdbt MK4 .46 C1
Windmill La HP15 .162 F7
Windmill Par HP15 .162 F6
Windmill Rd
  Chalfont St Peter SL9 .177 D3
  Cookham Rise SL6 .195 E6
  Fulmer SL3 .199 D7
  Haddenham HP17 .126 F6
  Slough SL1 .205 D5
  Thame OX9 .126 E1
Windmill St **4** .96 A1
Windmill Way
  Cranfield MK43 .25 C3
  Tring HP23 .118 F4
Windmill Wood HP6 .154 A2
Windrush Ave SL3 .207 B3
Windrush Cl
  Ickenham UB10 .201 F8
  Milton Keynes MK15 .35 A6
Windrush Ct
  Aylesbury HP21 .115 D4
  High Wycombe HP13 .173 F6
Windrush Dr HP13 .173 F6
Windrush Ho SL8 .185 B4
Windrush Way
  Maidenhead SL6 .202 F8
  Maidenhead SL6 .203 A8
Windsor & Eton Central Sta
  SL4 .210 D6
Windsor & Eton Riverside Sta
  SL4 .210 E7
Windsor Ave
  Leighton Buzzard LU7 .80 F7
  Newport Pagnell MK16 .22 C4
Windsor Boys' Sch The
  SL4 .210 B6
Windsor Bsns Ctr The
  SL4 .210 C7
Windsor Castle* SL4 .210 E7
Windsor Cl
  Bovingdon HP3 .146 A3
  Burnham SL1 .197 C1
Windsor Cres HP10 .174 C2
Windsor Ct HP6 .154 D1
Windsor Dr HP13 .162 D1
Windsor End HP9 .186 F8
Windsor Girls' Sch SL4 .210 A4
Windsor Hall SL4 .210 F4
Windsor Hill
  Monks Risborough HP27 .139 C5
  Wooburn Green HP10 .185 F5
Windsor Ho **4** SL1 .205 F3
Windsor La Burnham SL1 .197 C1
  Little Kingshill HP16 .152 C2
Windsor Rd
  Aylesbury HP21 .116 A7
  Chesham HP5 .144 B3
  Datchet SL3 .211 A7
  Gerrards Cross SL9 .188 C3

Windsor Rd continued
  Maidenhead SL6 .203 C2
  Oakley Green SL4 .209 A7
  Pitstone LU7 .105 C3
  Slough SL1 .205 E4
  Wraysbury TW19 .211 E1
Windsor Royal Sta **1**
  SL4 .210 D6
Windsor St
  Milton Keynes MK2 .58 C7
  Milton Keynes,Wolverton
   MK12 .33 C6
  Uxbridge UB8 .201 C5
Winemar Cl MK19 .11 A3
Winfold La MK4 .46 B1
Wing Cl SL7 .183 C1
Wing Rd Cublington LU7 .78 C1
  Leighton Buzzard LU7 .80 D5
  Stewkley LU7 .78 F6
Wingate Ave HP13 .173 E7
Wingate Circ MK7 .48 A4
Wingate Cl HP13 .173 E7
Wingate Wlk MK10 .116 A7
Wingfield Gr MK10 .36 A2
Wingrave CE Comb Sch
  HP22 .89 A3
Wingrave Cross Rds
  HP22 .88 F4
Wingrave Rd
  Aston Abbotts HP22 .88 A4
  Long Marston HP23 .104 D1
  Tring HP23 .119 B5
Winkers Cl SL9 .177 F2
Winkers La SL9 .177 F3
Winkfield La SL4 .209 A1
Winkfield Rd SL4 .209 A1
Winnock Rd UB7 .208 D5
Winsford Hill MK4 .46 E3
Winslow CE Comb Sch
  MK18 .66 A5
Winslow Field MK18 .151 F8
Winslow Gdns HP13 .174 A7
Winslow Rd
  Granborough MK18 .75 D7
  Great Horwood MK17 .54 F1
  Little Horwood MK17 .55 D1
  Nash MK17 .55 C8
  Swanbourne MK17 .66 F3
  Wingrave HP22 .89 B3
Winstanley La MK5 .46 C4
Winston Cl SL6 .202 A8
Winston Gdns HP4 .134 F4
Winston Ho HP11 .174 A4
Winstone Cl HP6 .154 B5
Winter Ct **6** SL7 .183 E2
Winter Hill SL6 .184 C1
Winter Hill Rd SL6 .195 A4
Winterburn MK13 .34 B5
Winters Way HP15 .163 D7
Winterton Dr HP15 .115 E4
Wintoun Path SL2 .197 E1
Winvale SL1 .205 E3
Winwood Slough SL2 .206 C7
  Windsor SL4 .209 F6
Winwood Cl MK19 .31 E5
Winwood Dr HP22 .85 A5
Wise La UB7 .208 D2
Wisewood Rd MK4,MK5 .45 F1
Wishart Gn MK7 .48 E5
Wisley Rd MK13 .34 D3
Wistmans MK4 .46 D4
Witan Ct MK9 .34 D2
Witan Gate MK9 .34 D1
Witchell HP22 .131 B4
Witham Ct MK3 .46 D1
Witham Way HP21 .115 C4
Witheridge La HP9,HP10 .175 B7
Withey Cl SL4 .209 E6
Withington MK13 .34 A5
Withycombe MK4 .46 E3
Withycroft SL3 .206 E7
Witney Cl UB10 .201 F8
Wittington Cotts SL7 .193 D6
Wittmills Oak MK18 .41 E1
Wixon Path HP19 .115 A8
Woad La MK14 .34 E8
Wodehouse Wlk MK16 .22 E3
Wolf La SL4 .209 E4
Wolfscote La MK4 .46 B3
Wolsey Gdns MK13 .34 A4
Wolstan Cl UB9 .190 A1
Wolston Mdw MK10 .35 F3
Wolverton Rd
  Castlethorpe MK19 .20 B5
  Milton Keynes,Giffard Park
   MK16 .21 D2
  Milton Keynes,Stony Stratford
   MK11 .32 E6
  Milton Keynes,Wolverton
   MK12,MK19 .33 E8
  Newport Pagnell MK16 .22 B4
Wolverton Sta MK19 .33 E7
Wooburn Common Rd
  HP10,SL1 .186 A2
Wooburn Grange HP10 .185 D3
Wooburn Green La HP9 186 A8

Wooburn Manor Pk
  HP10 .185 E5
Wooburn Mead HP10 .185 E6
Wooburn Mews HP10 .185 E5
Wooburn Town HP10 .185 D4
Wood Cl SL4 .210 C3
Wood End
  Little Horwood MK17 .55 C8
  Nash MK17 .55 C8
Wood End Cl SL2 .198 E7
Wood End Fst Sch MK14 .34 D8
Wood End La MK16 .23 E1
Wood La
  Aspley Guise MK17 .49 C6
  Iver SL0 .207 C8
  Milton Keynes MK14 .34 E8
  Slough SL1 .205 A4
  South Heath HP16 .152 E8
  Tingewick MK18 .51 B6
  Weston Underwood MK46 .6 A2
Wood Lane Cl
  Flackwell Heath HP10 .173 F1
  Iver Heath SL0 .200 D2
Wood Pond Cl HP9 .176 C4
Wood Rd MK43 .3 F7
Wood St
  Milton Keynes MK13 .33 F7
  Waddesdon HP18 .99 A2
  Woburn Sands MK17 .49 B4
Wood View Cotts HP5 .144 B7
Wood Way HP9 .174 F1
Woodall Cl MK10 .35 E3
Woodbank HP27 .149 C5
Woodbank Ave SL9 .188 D5
Woodbank Dr HP8 .177 D7
Woodbine HP27 .138 E5
Woodbine Cotts SL9 .188 D8
Woodbridge Ho UB8 .201 C5
Woodbury Cl SL8 .185 C3
Woodchester Pk HP9 .175 C6
Woodcock Ave HP14 .161 B8
Woodcote SL6 .202 D6
Woodcote Gn HP13 .161 D2
Woodcote Lawns HP5 .144 A4
Woodcroft Rd HP5 .144 D3
Woodfield HP27 .149 D6
Woodfield Dr SL6 .202 A6
Woodfield Pk HP6 .154 B3
Woodfield Rd HP27 .139 C4
Woodford Cl HP19 .115 B7
Woodford Way SL2 .198 A2
Woodhall Cl UB8 .201 D7
Woodhill Ave SL9 .189 A5
Woodhill Ct
  Amersham HP6 .154 D2
  Gerrards Cross SL9 .188 E4
Woodhouse Ct MK14 .34 D6
Woodhurst Dr UB9 .189 F6
Woodhurst Rd SL6 .196 B1
Woodhurst S SL6 .196 C1
Woodland Ave
  Leighton Buzzard LU7 .70 F2
  Slough SL1 .205 D6
  Windsor SL4 .209 F3
Woodland Cl
  High Wycombe HP12 .172 C6
  Marlow SL7 .183 E4
  Tring HP23 .118 F2
Woodland Glade SL2 .187 D1
Woodland La WD3 .167 D6
Woodland Pl WD3 .167 F5
Woodland Rd WD3 .178 D5
Woodland View
  Chesham HP5 .154 D6
  Milton Keynes MK12 .33 D5
Woodland Way
  Marlow SL7 .183 E4
  Woburn Sands MK17 .49 B4
Woodlands SL6 .188 F5
Woodlands Ave HP4 .135 D3
Woodlands Bsns Pk
  SL6 .202 A2
Woodlands Cl
  Buckingham MK18 .41 E2
  Gerrards Cross SL9 .189 A5
  Holmer Green HP15 .163 C6
Woodlands Cotts **1**
  SL2 .198 C7
Woodlands Cres MK18 .41 D2
Woodlands Dr
  Beaconsfield HP9 .175 C4
  Walter's Ash HP14 .161 C8
Woodlands Farm SL6 .195 C6
Woodlands Glade HP9 .175 C4
Woodlands Hill HP10 .186 E5
Woodlands Park Ave
  SL6 .202 A2
Woodlands Park Prim Sch
  SL6 .202 A1
Woodlands Park Rd
  SL6 .202 A3
Woodlands The
  Amersham HP6 .154 C4
  Tylers Green HP10 .162 F3
Woodlands View HP13 .174 A7
Woodlane Cl HP10 .173 F1
Woodlane Gdns HP10 .174 A1
Woodley Cl HP7 .165 D8
Woodley Headland MK6 .47 C7
Woodley Hill HP5 .154 D5
Woodman Cl LU7 .79 F3
Woodmans Cl MK19 .31 E5
Woodmans Croft HP19 .115 A8
Woodmoor End SL6 .196 B7
Woodpiece Rd OX25 .94 E7
Woodruff Ave MK14 .34 E4
Woodrush Cl MK6 .47 B4
Woods La NN12 .18 E3

Woods Pl [13] Tring HP23 .119 A3
Wendover HP22 ....131 B4
Woodside
 Aspley Guise MK17 ....49 D3
 Eaton Bray LU6 ....92 E6
 Flackwell Heath HP10 ..185 C6
 Milton Keynes MK11 ...32 E6
Woodside Ave
 Amersham HP6 ...154 D3
 Beaconsfield HP9 ...175 C4
 Flackwell Heath HP10 ..185 C7
Woodside Cl
 Amersham HP6 ...154 D1
 Beaconsfield HP9 ...175 C3
 Chalfont St Peter SL9 ..177 E1
 Loudwater HP11 ...174 B2
Woodside Hill SL9 ..177 E1
Woodside Jun Sch HP6 154 E1
Woodside Rd
 Amersham HP6 ...154 D1
 Beaconsfield HP9 ...175 C3
 High Wycombe HP13 ..174 A8
Woodside Way
 Leighton Buzzard LU7 ...80 D6
 Tylers Green HP10 ..174 C8
Woodspring Ct MK10 ...35 F1
Woodstock Ave SL3 ..206 D2
Woodstock Cl
 Aylesbury HP21 ...116 B6
 Maidenhead SL6 ...195 F1
Woodstock Ct MK13 ..34 B7
Woodstock Dr UB10 ..201 F8
Woodview Cl HP12 ..161 B2
Woodview Dr HP16 ..150 C5
Woodville OX39 ...147 C5
Woodville Cres NN12 ..18 E6
Woodward Ho [4] MK2 ..58 C8
Woodward Pl MK8 ..34 A1
Woodway HP27 ...149 D6
Woodways HP17 ...127 A6
Woodwicks WD3 ...178 D5
Woollerton Cres HP22 .131 D5
Woollerton Ct HP27 ..139 B4
Woolmans
 Fullers Slade MK11 ...33 A4
 Milton Keynes MK11 ...33 A4
Woolrich Gdns MK11 ..32 E5
Wooster Rd HP9 ...175 D4

Wootton Dr HP10 ...185 E8
Wootton Gn OX27 ...72 E6
Wootton La HP17 ...113 E1
Wootton Way SL6 ..202 C6
Worcester Cl
 Maidenhead SL6 ...202 D3
 Newport Pagnell MK16 ..22 A3
Worcester Gdns SL1 ..205 D4
Worcester Ho MK3 ...46 F2
Worcester Rd UB8 ..208 D8
Wordsworth Ave MK16 ..22 A4
Wordsworth Dr MK3 ..58 A7
Wordsworth Rd
 High Wycombe HP11 ..173 A5
 Slough SL2 ...197 D1
Wordsworth Way UB7 .208 E2
World's End La HP22 ..130 F8
Worminghall Rd
 Ickford HP18 ...123 F4
 Oakley HP18 ...109 D4
Wormsley Cres HP14 ..158 C4
Wornal Pk HP18 ...123 C8
Worple The TW19 ...211 F1
Worrelle Ave MK10 ..36 A3
Worster Rd SL6 ...195 E6
Worthies The HP7 ..165 B7
Worthington Rd LU6 ..93 F8
Wotton End HP18 ...96 C7
Wotton Path HP21 ..115 E3
Wotton Rd HP18 ...97 E1
Wr Twr Cl UB8 ...201 E7
Wray Ct MK4 ...46 A2
Wraysbury Prim Sch
 TW19 ...211 E1
Wraysbury Sta TW19 ..212 A1
Wren Cl MK18 ...52 F7
Wren Ct SL3 ...207 A3
Wren Dr UB7 ...208 D3
Wren Path HP19 ...114 F8
Wren Rd HP16 ...151 C5
Wren Vale HP13 ...173 A8
Wren Wlk LU6 ...92 E4
Wrens Pk MK10 ...36 B2
Wrensfield SL7 ...183 C2
Wright SL4 ...209 C4
Wright Sq SL4 ...209 C4
Wright Way SL4 ...209 C4
Wright's La HP16 ...151 C5

Wrights Cl HP14 ...171 B5
Wrights Yd HP16 ...152 A7
Wroxton Ct MK4 ...45 F2
Wyatt Cl HP13 ...172 F8
Wyatt Rd SL4 ...209 D4
Wyatt's Covert Cvn Site
 UB9 ...189 F7
Wyatt's Rd WD3 ...167 F5
Wychwood HP16 ...152 B4
Wychwood Gdns HP12 .172 C6
Wychwood Rise HP16 .152 B4
Wyclands Ho HP12 ..161 B2
Wycombe Abbey Sch
 HP11 ...173 A6
Wycombe Cl HP21 ...116 B4
Wycombe End HP9 ..175 E1
Wycombe General Hospl
 HP11 ...173 A6
Wycombe High Sch
 HP11 ...172 F4
Wycombe Ind Mall
 HP11 ...172 F4
Wycombe La HP10 ..185 E2
Wycombe Mus* HP13 .173 B7
Wycombe Rd
 Beacon's Bottom HP14 ..159 D3
 Holmer Green HP15 ..163 B6
 Lacey Green HP14 ...149 B4
 Marlow SL7 ...183 E4
 Marlow Bottom SL7 ..183 E6
 Prestwood HP15 ...151 C5
Wycombe Ret Pk HP11 .173 F4
Wycombe View HP10 .174 A2
Wye Cl Aylesbury HP21 .115 C5
Wye Ct [2] SL8 ...185 A3
Wye Est HP11 ...173 E5
Wye Gdns HP12 ...172 D8
Wye Rd HP10 ...185 D8
Wye Valley Sch The
 SL8 ...185 B4
Wykeham Gate HP17 .126 F5
Wykeham Rise OX39 .147 D6
Wykeham Way HP17 .126 F6
Wykeridge Cl HP5 ...144 B4
Wylands Rd SL3 ...207 A2
Wylie End MK13 ...34 A7
Wymering Rd HP21 ..116 C6

Wymers Cl SL1 ...197 B3
Wymers Wood Rd SL1 .197 A3
Wymondham MK10 ...36 B1
Wynbury Dr HP13 ...162 E1
Wyndale Cl RG9 ...191 E1
Wyndham Ave HP13 ..161 F2
Wyndham Cres SL1 ..197 B3
Wyness Ave MK17 ...59 E5
Wynford Gn HP21 ...115 F6
Wyngates LU7 ...80 E5
Wyngrave Pl HP9 ...175 C5
Wynn Gr HP15 ...163 B3
Wynne-Jones Ctr HP21 .115 F8
Wynnstay Gdns SL7 ..183 E5
Wynnswick Rd HP9 ..176 C5
Wynyard Ct MK6 ...46 E7
Wyre Cl HP17 ...127 A5
Wyvern Fst Sch MK12 ..33 C6
Wyvern Way UB8 ...201 C4

Y

Yalts Brow MK4 ...46 B2
Yardley Ave LU7 ...105 D4
Yardley Gn HP20 ...101 F2
Yardley Gobion CE Prim Sch
 NN12 ...1 A7
Yardley Hastings Prim Sch
 ...1 A7
Yardley Rd
 Cosgrove MK19 ...19 D2
 Olney MK46 ...6 E6
 Potterspury NN12 ...18 F4
Yarmouth Rd SL1 ...205 C6
Yarrow Pl MK14 ...34 E4
Yarrowside HP7 ...166 B7
Ye Meads SL6 ...203 E5
Ye Meads Cotts SL6 ..203 E5
Ye Meads Ho SL6 ...203 E5
Yeates Cl Thame OX9 .125 F1
 Winslow MK18 ...65 F4
Yeats Cl MK16 ...21 F5
Yeomans Cl NN13 ...38 A8
Yeomans Dr MK14 ...22 B1
Yeovil Ent Ctr SL1 ..204 F8
Yeovil Rd SL1 ...204 E8
Yew Ave UB7 ...208 E6

Yew Tree Cl
 Beaconsfield HP9 ...175 F1
 Botley HP5 ...145 A1
 Eaton Bray LU6 ...92 F5
 Maidenhead SL6 ...202 E8
 Newton Longville MK17 ..57 C3
 Stoke Mandeville HP22 .116 A1
Yew Tree Dr
 Bovingdon HP3 ...146 B3
 Hazlemere HP15 ...162 F6
Yew Tree Rd Slough SL1 .206 A3
 Uxbridge UB10 ...201 F4
Yew Wlk HP15 ...163 A3
Yewtree Cl LU7 ...105 E5
Yiewsley Ct UB7 ...208 E5
Yolsum Cl HP17 ...126 E6
Yonder Slade MK18 ...52 D6
York Ave Slough SL1 ..205 C2
 Windsor SL4 ...210 B5
York Cl HP7 ...165 F8
York Ct [3] LU7 ...80 F7
York Ho
 High Wycombe HP13 ..173 F8
 Milton Keynes MK3 ...57 E7
York Pl HP21 ...115 D7
York Rd Henley-on-T RG9 .191 D2
 Maidenhead SL6 ...203 A7
 Marlow SL7 ...183 D2
 Milton Keynes MK11 ...32 D5
 Uxbridge UB8 ...201 D5
 Windsor SL4 ...210 B5
York Way HP12 ...172 E4
Yorke Cl HP22 ...117 E5
Youens Rd HP12 ...172 C5
Young Cl HP21 ...116 A6

Z

Zealand Ave UB7 ...213 E7
Zetland Ct SL6 ...203 B8
Zodiac Bsns Pk UB8 ..208 D7

Addresses

Name and Address	Telephone	Page	Grid reference

Name and Address	Telephone	Page	Grid reference

Any feature in this atlas can be given a unique reference to help you find the same feature on other Ordnance Survey maps of the area, or to help someone else locate you if they do not have a Street Atlas.

The grid squares in this atlas match the Ordnance Survey National Grid and are at 500 metre intervals. The small figures at the bottom and sides of every other grid line are the National Grid kilometre values (**00** to **99** km) and are repeated across the country every 100 km (see left).

To give a unique National Grid reference you need to locate where in the country you are. The country is divided into 100 km squares with each square given a unique two-letter reference. Use the administrative map to determine in which 100 km square a particular page of this atlas falls.

The bold letters and numbers between each grid line (**A** to **F**, **1** to **8**) are for use within a specific Street Atlas only, and when used with the page number, are a convenient way of referencing these grid squares.

Example *The railway bridge over DARLEY GREEN RD in grid square B1*

Step 1: Identify the two-letter reference, in this example the page is in **SP**

Step 2: Identify the 1 km square in which the railway bridge falls. Use the figures in the southwest corner of this square: Eastings **17**, Northings **74**. This gives a unique reference: **SP 17 74**, accurate to 1 km.

Step 3: To give a more precise reference accurate to 100 m you need to estimate how many tenths along and how many tenths up this 1 km square the feature is (to help with this the 1 km square is divided into four 500 m squares). This makes the bridge about **8** tenths along and about **1** tenth up from the southwest corner.

This gives a unique reference: **SP 178 741**, accurate to 100 m.

Eastings (read from left to right along the bottom) come before Northings (read from bottom to top). If you have trouble remembering say to yourself "Along the hall, THEN up the stairs"!

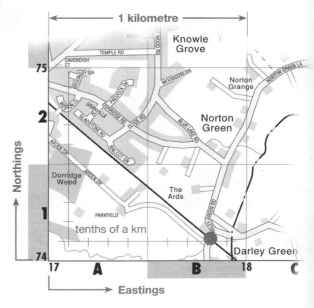

PHILIP'S MAPS

the Gold Standard for serious driving

- ◆ Philip's street atlases cover every county in England and Wales, plus much of Scotland

- ◆ All our atlases use the same style of mapping, with the same colours and symbols, so you can move with confidence from one atlas to the next

- ◆ Widely used by the emergency services, transport companies and local authorities

- ◆ Created from the most up-to-date and detailed information available from Ordnance Survey

- ◆ Based on the National Grid

BEST BUY • BEST BUY •
Auto EXPRESS
• BEST BUY • BEST BUY •

PHILIP'S
STREET ATLAS
London
The definitive Lon
from Britain's national ma
PHILIP'S

PHILIP'S
STREET ATLAS
Devon
Unique comprehensive coverage
BEST BUY
with time-saving through-routes
Includes Lyme Regis, Saltash and Wellington, plus
Exeter and Plymouth city centres at extra-large scale

PHILIP'S
STREET ATLAS
Norfolk
Unique comprehensive coverage
BEST BUY
with time-saving through-routes
Includes Norwich city centre at extra-large scale,
plus town maps of Bury St Edmunds and Lowestoft

PHILIP'S
STREET ATLAS
Cumbria
Unique comprehensive coverage
BEST BUY
Every named street, road and lane
Plus town maps of Dumfries and
Morecambe, with Carlisle city centre
at extra-large scale

PHILIP'S
BRITAIN'S MOST DETAILED ROAD ATLAS
NAVIGATOR Britain
Ultra-large scale mapping
1½ miles to 1 inch
50 fully indexed
town plans
'Extremely clear maps
with the most detail by far'
Auto Express
Recommended by
the Institute of
Advanced Motorists

For national mapping, choose **Philip's Navigator Britain** – the most detailed road atlas available of England, Wales and Scotland. Hailed by Auto Express as 'the ultimate road atlas', this is the only one-volume atlas to show every road and lane in Britain.

Street atlases currently available

England

Bedfordshire	Staffordshire
Berkshire	Suffolk
Birmingham and West Midlands	Surrey
Bristol and Bath	East Sussex
Buckinghamshire	West Sussex
Cambridgeshire	Tyne and Wear
Cheshire	Warwickshire
Cornwall	Birmingham and West Midlands
Cumbria	Wiltshire and Swindon
Derbyshire	Worcestershire
Devon	East Yorkshire Northern Lincolnshire
Dorset	North Yorkshire
County Durham and Teeside	South Yorkshire
Essex	West Yorkshire
North Essex	**Wales**
South Essex	Anglesey, Conwy and Gwynedd
Gloucestershire	Cardiff, Swansea and The Valleys
North Hampshire	Carmarthenshire, Pembrokeshire and Swansea
South Hampshire	Ceredigion and South Gwynedd
Herefordshire Monmouthshire	Denbighshire, Flintshire, Wrexham
Hertfordshire	Herefordshire Monmouthshire
Isle of Wight	Powys
Kent	**Scotland**
East Kent	Aberdeenshire
West Kent	Ayrshire
Lancashire	Edinburgh and East Central Scotland
Leicestershire and Rutland	Fife and Tayside
Lincolnshire	Glasgow and West Central Scotland
London	Inverness and Moray
Greater Manchester	
Merseyside	
Norfolk	
Northamptonshire	
Northumberland	
Nottinghamshire	
Oxfordshire	
Shropshire	
Somerset	

All England and Wales coverage

How to order

Philip's maps and atlases are available from bookshops, motorway services and petrol stations. You can order direct from the publisher by phoning **01903 828503** or online at **www.philips-maps.co.uk**
For bulk orders only, phone 020 7644 6940